MW01050973

THE NORTHERN SHOSHONI

THE NORTHERN SHOSHONI

by

Brigham D. Madsen

CAXTON PRESS

Caldwell, Idaho 83605

2000

First Printing 1980
Second Printing January, 2000

© 1980
The Caxton Printers, Ltd.
Caldwell

All rights reserved. No part of this book may be reproduced in any manner without the express written consent of the publisher, except in the case of brief excerpts in critical reviews and articles. All inquiries should be addressed to: Caxton Press, 312 Main Street, Caldwell, ID 83605.

Library of Congress Cataloging in Publication Data

Madsen, Brigham D.
      The Northern Shoshoni

      Bibliography: p.
      Includes index.
      1. Shoshonean Indians—History. I. Title.
E99.S39M325   970'.004'97   78-53138
ISBN 0-87004-266-1

Lithographed and bound in the United States of America
CAXTON PRESS
Caldwell, Idaho 83605
165705

To the Shoshone-Bannock People

CONTENTS

LIST OF ILLUSTRATIONS

MAPS

PREFACE

Writing a history of the Northern Shoshoni involves an examination of not one, but four, distinct groups of Shoshoni and a related band of Northern Paiute, the Bannock. To increase the complexity, the five groups covered a wide expanse of plains and mountains from the buffalo grounds of Montana and Wyoming to eastern Oregon and northeastern Nevada and from Great Salt Lake on the south to the Flathead country of western Montana on the north. Also, the culture and way of life varied from strong, horse-owning traits among the easternmost group to a more sedentary salmon-fishing and less plains-oriented existence for the bands of western Idaho.

The most northerly of the Northern Shoshoni, the Lemhi Indians, had a distinct and separate history until they chose to settle at Fort Hall in 1907. Their story is told in another volume under the title, *The Lemhi: Sacajawea's People*. The Bannock in the Fort Hall area likewise pursued their own way until the Bannock War of 1878 curtailed their very independent course of action. The Fort Hall Shoshoni soon settled in at the Fort Hall Reservation, whose history became identical with them after 1869. The same was true of the Boise and Bruneau peoples of western Idaho after they moved to Fort Hall in 1869. The last group, composed of the several bands of Northwestern Shoshoni, continued an independent life until the 1880s, when the pressure of white settlement forced nearly all of them to Fort Hall. The only exception was a small group of about 150 people who joined the Mormon Church, settled at Washakie in Malad Valley on the Utah-Idaho border, and remained a separate and distinct band until they became absorbed into the neighboring white population during the years after World War II.

The Introduction by Merle W. Wells describes the culture, home areas, and yearly subsistence movements of the various groups and their interaction with the early fur traders. Chapter I summarizes early governmental attempts to establish some kind of control over the Northern Shoshoni through the superintendencies of Oregon and Washington. De facto supervision actually fell to the superintendent of Indian Affairs for Utah Territory, and the text describes his attempts to deal with the Fort Hall Shoshoni and

Bannock, as well as with his own Northwestern Shoshoni through the periods which included the Bear River Massacre and Doty treaties which followed.

Chapter III is concerned with the relationships between the Boise and Bruneau Shoshoni and the white settlements in that area, as the new Idaho Superintendency took over the responsibility of the Idaho Indians. The establishment of Fort Hall created a center where the Fort Hall Shoshoni, the wandering Bannock, the Boise and Bruneau, and some of the Northwestern Shoshoni could be assembled. The year 1870 becomes a kind of watershed year in the entire story of all the Northern Shoshoni groups.

The next two chapters examine various aspects of the economic and social development of Fort Hall during the years 1870 to 1880. The first decade was particularly significant, as government officials and Indians sought to work out a modus operandi which would satisfy the needs of both. There was much confusion and backing and hauling until the Office of Indian Affairs and the Indian leaders reached a workable agreement, which was under constant pressure for change from the two groups. The Bannock War of 1878 focused the attention of Idaho citizen and government official alike on the continuing problem of the 1870s at Fort Hall — the lack of sufficient rations to subsist the tribesmen while they learned how to farm. The 1870s also saw the difficulties encountered by the Northwestern Shoshoni of Utah in attempting to maintain their home in the northern valleys of that state, and Chapter VI portrays the removal of all but the Washakie group to Fort Hall as the result of a "scare" manufactured by the Gentile people of Corinne.

Northern Shoshoni history from 1880 to the present has been involved chiefly with the various agreements by which the Indians surrendered a large part of the reservation to the government, by legal conflicts with the encroaching white civilization, by the struggle to learn to become ranchers and farmers, by the frustrating battle to secure an irrigation system, by the development of mineral and timber resources, and by the social impact of adjusting to a new way of life through a process of education and missionary activity. The narrative, in Chapters VII through XV, follows a topical approach in examining these items from 1880 to the present. The last chapter emphasizes the increasing importance of maintaining intact the remaining land area of the reservation and an acceptance of a new system of justice. After a hundred years of reservation life the Shoshoni-Bannock are today again gradually gaining control over their homeland and strengthening their cultural heritage.

Because most of the correspondence and printed material used in the research process reflect the sentiments of federal officialdom and white settlers, a serious attempt has been made to include the rare recorded statements made by the various Shoshoni and Bannock leaders, usually in direct quotations, so as to highlight the Indian point of view. It is unfortunate that so few Shoshoni and Bannock speeches and written materials are available. There have been some attempts to record tribal oral history, but they have not so far been very productive.

The appendices list the Treaty of Fort Bridger of 1868 (the basic document defining the relationship of the tribes with the government) and a chronological chart listing the important events in the history of the various groups of Northern Shoshoni. The tables of crop and stock statistics offer some notion of agricultural developments at the reservation. A citation at the end of a paragraph refers to all the material in the paragraph.

The source material for the history of the Northern Shoshoni is scattered from the U.S. National Archives in Washington, D.C. (which is, of course, the main depository) to the regional archives of the federal government at Seattle, Washington, which holds the more recent documents of Fort Hall history. The state historical societies of Idaho, Montana, and Utah contain significant materials on the Northern Shoshoni. Idaho State University at Pocatello has some important correspondence and other papers concerned with the Lemhi Reservation. The Fort Hall Agency files are particularly good for the period of the last forty years. An important document at Fort Hall is the Fort Hall Letter Book covering the years 1870 to 1875. The L.D.S. Department of History in Salt Lake City contains much information concerning the early Utah Superintendency and the history of the Washakie settlement. Finally, the University of Utah Library has an almost complete set of the U.S. congressional documents, which is a veritable gold mine of Indian commissioner's and Indian agents' reports, as well as many other items dealing with the Northern Shoshoni.

An author is indebted to many people by the time a manuscript is completed. The staffs of the above archives were most helpful in guiding me to relevant materials and in making them available. I especially wish to thank Dr. Merle W. Wells, Director of the Idaho State Historical Society, for his reading of the material. Dr. Wells' introduction is based on the careful work of the late Dr. Earl Swanson of Idaho State University and that of Dr. Sven Liljeblad, also of Idaho State University, whose lifetime of service and scholarship in behalf of the Shoshoni-Bannock should be recognized. Finally, I should like to thank Mr. Scott Borg for his efforts in marshaling the evidence and in putting together a rough draft of the material on irrigation at Fort Hall.

Any errors of fact or interpretation are, of course, my responsibility.

Salt Lake City, Utah
July 1976

THE NORTHERN SHOSHONI

INTRODUCTION

Merle W. Wells
Idaho State Historical Society

Climatic Factors

Long before anyone got around to settling the country eventually taken over by the Northern Shoshoni, a series of continental ice sheets expanded southward east of the Rockies across the Great Plains. During the most recent of these glacial sequences, people from Siberia had a chance to move into North America. So much seawater went into formation of vast ice fields that ocean levels declined and coast lines changed. In the process, Bering Strait between Alaska and Siberia disappeared and became a broad land connection which united North America with Asia. Elephants from Asia gradually worked their way over this passage into Alaska, and big-game hunters followed them. Over a period of thousands of years North and South America were settled, as population expanded and people adapted to new conditions. They had to avoid the ice fields as they moved across the continent. Much of the country adjacent to the ice sheet got plenty of moisture, and great interior lakes developed in the basin of places like Utah and Nevada. In the country between the continental ice sheet and these giant pluvial lakes, Asian elephants and some of the people who pursued them found the right kind of conditions in which they could thrive. The environment they needed lasted in that part of the country for several thousand years.

People have lived in the Salmon River mountains and the Snake River Plains — the traditional homeland of the Northern Shoshoni — for the past fourteen thousand years or more. During that time major changes in climate have transformed the region more than once. With changes in climate came changes in population. Big-game hunters adapted for survival in a colder, wetter era inhabited the Snake River Plains 140 centuries ago. Then, as the country got warmer and the continental ice sheet (which never reached the Snake country but came by east of the Rockies) receded, population increased rapidly for a thousand years or more starting about twelve thousand years ago. Around eight thousand years ago the climate gradually got too hot and dry — eventually hotter and drier than any time since. Much of the big game left. Giant sloths and elephants no longer could be found after the lower plains turned into desert. Many of the early elephant hunters followed the game, moving north and east to stay with the cooler, wetter climate to which they had been accustomed. Other people stayed or moved in. Hunting conditions certainly changed. Buffalo and mountain sheep could be found at higher elevations, however, so the region's pioneer big-game economy did not disappear entirely. Still, with movement and modification or replacement of early inhabitants, major cultural changes associated with climatic changes brought new ways of living to the peoples of the Snake River Plains around eight thousand years ago.

Two differing cultural groups, tracing back about eight thousand years, gradually emerged over a thousand years or so in the Salmon River mountains and the Snake River Plains. One group which developed along the southern margin of these plains (among other places) may be regarded as an archaeological expression of the modern Western Shoshoni. Farther north the other group, which may be traced on Birch Creek and identified on the Salmon below Shoup, offers eight thousand years of cultural continuity down to the time of the Northern Shoshoni. In the former, a desert way of life is more evident. In the latter, buffalo and other big-game hunting were more pronounced. These characteristics continued to distinguish Northern from Western Shoshoni down to the days of the fur trade.

The Snake River regional cultures eventually associated with the Northern and Western Shoshoni are identified as Bitterroot to the north and South Hills to the south. New technologies distinguished life in the past eight thousand years from the previous pioneer big-game hunters' economy which had flourished for six thousand years or more. Perhaps these innovations reflected an introduction of bows and arrows. In any case, some of the details of these changes still elude archaeologists who are reconstructing the story of life in the Snake country prior to the eighteenth century. Both regional cultural groups continued to subsist on big game, using buffalo jumps in the Owyhee country as well as in the Salmon River area. During the eight thousand years of regional cultural development, the climate went through a hot, dry era that interfered with occupation of the lower valley, which became an arid desert by 5200 B.C. Gradually another wet phase set in, but by 1450 B.C. this second cycle was completed by another warm, arid sequence. Still another cold, wet climate emerged during a final cycle that extended until around 1850 A.D. In the middle of the nineteenth century — at the end of the fur-trade era and at about the beginning of white settlement — a warming trend yielded the climate which persists to the present time. The two regional cultures continued through these times of environmental change, and Bitterroot culture gradually developed into the Northern Shoshoni way of life.

Tribal Organization

Prior to Spanish exploration and settlement in North America, the Shoshoni of the Snake country lived and travelled in relatively small extended family groups. Combining basin and plateau cultural elements, they gathered seeds, pine nuts, and wild wheat in the tradition of Great Basin residents to the south, and dug camas and bitterroot as did plateau Indians farther northwest. In addition, the Snake country Shoshoni fished for salmon (typical of plateau culture) but engaged in communal rabbit and sage hen drives — as well as antelope drives — characteristic of basin culture. This blend of basin and plateau traits had a firm geographic origin: As an avenue of communication from the Great Plains to the Pacific Northwest, Snake River Valley cut through a whole series of ridges which, running north and south in the basin and range country of the interior west, interrupted travel across the continent. Cultural interchange, fostered by this natural route of travel, continued from prehistoric times down past the years of the fur trade. Through Snake River Valley, Indians from the Great Plains had access to salmon fisheries in the Boise and Salmon Falls regions. In the process of utilizing salmon fisheries in their regular seasonal migratory food-gathering cycle, inhabitants of the Great Plains came in contact with peoples from the northwest plateau country. From this cultural interchange emerged the Northern Shoshoni, with a composite of basin and plateau traits.

In clothing and housing, early-day Shoshoni on the Snake River Plains favored basin over plateau cultural elements. Women had sage-bark dresses, and men wore breechclouts and leggings. Rabbit-skin blankets were used in winter. (In contrast to the Shoshoni and basin peoples, plateau Indians would not descend to chasing rabbits or to using rabbit skins.) Northern Shoshoni of the Snake Plains lived in conical grass huts (devised from beehive-shaped cupolas of the Great Basin) prior to the time they imported teepees from the Great Plains. This change — part of a complex of new cultural influences that came when the Shoshoni acquired horses early in the eighteenth century — came with plains clothing and a plains buffalo-hunting economy adopted by many (but not all) of the people of the Snake Plains.

Horses changed the Shoshoni way of life — at least for those who preferred to shift to a newly developed plains style culture. Buffalo hunting became much easier for mounted bands, although use of the old buffalo jumps in the Challis region continued long after horses gave the Indians greater mobility and a more practical hunting method. Some of the Northern Shoshoni who had horses did not use them for hunting expeditions. But after an equestrian life was adopted by the Great Plains Shoshoni — beginning with the Comanche, a Shoshoni group with close access to Spanish sources of horses in New Mexico, which had been colonized in 1598 — that kind of plains culture spread to the Snake River region. Many, but by no means all, of the old extended family Shoshoni groups at last could organize into bands. Mounted bands could travel in a more extended seasonal hunting, fishing, camas-digging, and food-collecting cycle.

When French trappers came into contact with the Shoshoni in the Great Plains of Wyoming or South Dakota in 1742, the Indians with whom they were travelling fled in terror from the dreaded Snakes, as they called them. (To a number of major Great Plains tribes, the Shoshoni were known as Snakes — presumably because the Shoshoni painted snakes on sticks to frighten their plains enemies. French and later English explorers of the northern plains usually referred to the Shoshoni as Snake Indians, and Snake River was named in 1812 for the Snake Indians who inhabited that region.) In the middle of the eighteenth century the Shoshoni dominated much of the Great Plains, ranging into the Saskatchewan River country which later became Alberta. Then a smallpox epidemic afflicted the northern plains Shoshoni in 1781, and their traditional enemies, the Blackfeet, acquired firearms from French trappers.

By the end of the eighteenth century the once formidable Shoshoni had retired from the Saskatchewan and much of the upper Missouri. Some of the Northern Shoshoni still ventured from Lemhi Valley and Big Hole out to the Three Forks region of the Missouri, and the Eastern Shoshoni still inhabited the Wyoming plains. Farther west, the Northern Shoshoni continued to hold the Snake River Plains. Gradually some

Northern Paiute Indians (related closely to the Shoshoni in language and in basin culture) found their way from northern Nevada and eastern Oregon into the Snake River Plains. After obtaining horses from the Northern Shoshoni at one time or another, individual Northern Paiutes joined the Fort Hall Shoshoni in a mounted, buffalo-hunting band. By the time white explorers and trappers reached the Snake country, these Northern Paiute (known as Bannock Indians) had become well-established travellers with the Fort Hall Shoshoni. Over the years the Bannock gradually merged with the Northern Shoshoni; then, through intermarriage and close association, the Bannock and Fort Hall Shoshoni developed a mutual relationship in social and political affairs.

With the ascendancy of several mounted Northern Shoshoni bands of buffalo hunters (including many of the Boise, Lemhi, Fort Hall, and some other Shoshoni groups of southeastern Idaho), the Indians of the Snake country had an interesting option. Those who preferred to get into a more ambitious seasonal migratory cycle could do so; more conservative exponents of traditional ways retained their old customs. Some of the Mountain Snakes (or Sheepeaters, as they often were called) became the Lemhi band of mounted buffalo hunters; others rejected that innovation. Some of the Boise Shoshoni formed into a mounted buffalo-hunting band, while others found their great salmon fishery resource in the Boise region adequate and did not make the long annual trip to the buffalo country. Across Snake River, the Bruneau Shoshoni concluded that they could get along just as well without using their horses for buffalo hunting and widespread travel. They did not organize into a mounted band but moved in a different migratory cycle into territory farther south. Because of this distinctive route of migration and separate geographical location, they developed their own dialect — Western Shoshoni — in common with other Shoshoni farther into Nevada.

As was the case with the Bannock, individuals and families among the scattered Shoshoni who preferred to go buffalo hunting could join one of the annual expeditions. Band organization, for the Shoshoni who had such an arrangement, remained pretty flexible; individual Indians or families shifted about rather freely. Band leadership had less of the rigidity typical of the Great Plains tribes. Shoshoni leaders generally thought of themselves as all about equal. Except for the white man's need to have Indian chiefs with whom to deal, the Shoshoni avoided any such system. White explorers and trappers identified (and, where necessary, appointed) Indian chiefs for the Shoshoni although the Indians generally

remained somewhat unimpressed by imposition of such a foreign arrangement.

Able to cover large distances once they had horses to ride, the Fort Hall Shoshoni developed an annual migratory cycle of twelve hundred miles or more. Each spring they headed west to Camas Prairie to dig camas bulbs in May or June. Then they continued to Boise River and the Snake for summer salmon fishing. After their return to excellent grazing lands in the Fort Hall bottoms, they finally set out in the fall to chase Montana or Wyoming buffalo herds. They had an option of riding north through Targhee Pass across the Continental Divide to a plains hunting area in Montana between the Musselshell and Yellowstone rivers. Between fall and spring buffalo hunts they would spend the winter on Yellowstone River. Upon returning to Fort Hall in the spring they would prepare for another Camas Prairie trip and another annual migratory cycle. As an alternative to a Yellowstone expedition via Targhee Pass, they could set out for Green River and join the Eastern Shoshoni of Wyoming. In this case they would hunt buffalo in the Crow Country. No matter which way they went, they saw a lot of territory. In their travels they had a sequence in which they arrived at the right place at the right time to subsist upon camas, salmon, buffalo, or whatever was appropriate.

In contrast to these migratory buffalo hunters, the Mountain Snakes — Northern Shoshoni who lived in the Salmon River mountains or in the ranges which extended eastward into the Yellowstone country of Wyoming — had to travel less. Living on the Nez Perce borderland, they had frequent contact with some of the Nez Perce bands. In any event they had essentially a plateau, rather than a desert, culture. As big-game hunters they commanded respect for their unusual ability to pursue mountain sheep. (In later years, they generally were known to the whites as Sheepeaters.) Some of these Sheepeaters — who, like the other Northern Shoshoni, also subsisted on camas, salmon, and other products available in their country — formed a mounted band that hunted buffalo in a seasonal cycle different from the Fort Hall pattern. This band, which in later years attracted a considerable number of Bannock Indians, finally was distinguished as the Lemhi because of their Lemhi Valley base. But a small remnant of culturally conservative Sheepeaters kept up their old mountain life long after the other Shoshoni had settled on reservations.

Because their population was scattered over a vast terrain, with considerable peril to individual survival, the early Shoshoni lived in expanded families. That way a modest-sized group of closely related interdependent people could take care of each other's needs. In each generation only four relationships were recognized: older brother, older sister, younger brother, and younger sister. Cousins were regarded as brothers and sisters, with no distinction between what the whites called cousins and brothers. To state this in another way, if a Shoshoni told a white man that someone was his brother, the white would have no way of knowing whether the Shoshoni meant (in English terms) brother, half-brother, or cousin — unless he asked who the literal parents of each of the Shoshoni brothers were.

In the most notable case of this kind of relationship among the Northern Shoshoni, Sacajawea told Lewis and Clark that Cameahwait, the band leader they met on the Lemhi, was her brother. Whether this meant brother or cousin cannot be determined; for the Shoshoni the difference between brother and cousin did not matter. In their families a man often had two wives who were sisters. Less often two brothers would share the same wife. In that kind of situation the English relationships of brother, half-brother, and cousin began to merge. On that account the Shoshoni saw no point in keeping track of the complexities that arose in their more expansive family relationships. Although monogamy was the most common system of Shoshoni marriage, these other forms were neither excluded nor despised. Shoshoni expanded families, assembled on the basis of siblings who lived together, often developed into these other arrangements (such as a brother with two sisters for wives) when only part of an expanded family survived.

Many of the Shoshoni would have had to go a long way to find a marriage partner who was not a fairly close relative, on account of the sparse, widely dispersed population. Partly because of this, all kinds of complex, multiple relationships developed within families. With frequent loss of one or both parents, children often were cared for by grandparents, if they proved to be the survivors. Shoshoni expanded families included grandparents, parents (often with more than one husband or wife, with the extra partner's brothers or sisters), and children who might be siblings or cousins. With grandparents often responsible for grandchildren, Shoshoni families tended to follow the old ways and to resist change. Cultural conservatism of this kind showed up particularly among the Mountain Shoshoni or Sheepeaters. In any event, these expanded families that formed the basis for Shoshoni society (and for cultural preservation) also provided in the best way possible for individual survival of family members. Any adults who happened to survive looked out for all the children.

Traditional expanded families retained their importance, even for those Shoshoni who formed into mounted bands in order to range more widely over the country. Particularly among the Lemhi, a talented expanded family provided the leadership which brought the band together and preserved it as one generation succeeded another. In the case of the Fort Hall band, a Bannock family often provided leadership essential to preservation of an important mounted group of travelling families. For several generations Peiem and his family led the mounted Boise Shoshoni. When a group of mounted bands decided to travel together around 1810–1820, Peiem's family provided leadership for fifteen hundred or two thousand travelling Shoshoni. In Shoshoni culture, expanded families formed the basic units, as bands were developed among those Shoshoni who organized into bands. For Shoshoni who never adopted a mounted way of life and who never joined into loosely organized bands, expanded families were about the only social unit familiar to them. Eventual Shoshoni adjustment to problems brought by white settlement had to be made in the context of this system of expanded families.

Northern Shoshoni Culture

Shoshoni religious practices featured individual guardian spirits. In contrast to the whites, the Shoshoni had no organized religion, no dogma, and no dependence upon theocratic principles. Shoshoni religious belief provided personal help from nature that awarded individual self-reliance and skill, courage, and wisdom to meet life's problems in an often difficult environment. A Shoshoni child at about the age of twelve was supposed to go out to a butte or mountain to have a major religious experience. With luck the result would be a dream or vision that would provide, from nature, a personal guardian spirit: an animal or plant, the sun or moon, or almost any natural phenomenon that would offer help and protection from then on. They were close to nature, and almost anything might serve this purpose. With the guardian spirit came a personal song. Sometimes in literature dealing with Indians of this kind of religion (and that includes many besides the Shoshoni) this song is misidentified as a death song. Such misinterpretation would arise because in any crisis — sometimes including a fatal one — the guardian spirit's song would be sung to invoke help.

These songs and the guardian spirits associated with them varied in merit or power, but a child fortunate enough to come back after a dream or vision would be equipped with a personal guardian spirit that would serve for a lifetime. Some children, less fortunate in their search for a guardian spirit, would not be favored with an essential dream or vision. In that event a necessary song and guardian spirit could be acquired through purchase. A particularly potent song could be taught to others. Commercial traffic in guardian spirits and songs was not encouraged, but especially powerful songs could be preserved that way for more than one generation. Some Shoshoni, as is the case in white society, were freethinkers who dispensed with guardian spirits and songs. In contrast to the Nez Perce, who almost had to have a guardian spirit, the Shoshoni were more practical and were under less social pressure to have one. However, most of the early Shoshoni adhered to these religious values throughout their lives.

In Shoshoni religion, anyone favoured with an exceptionally potent guardian spirit had an obligation to use a powerful song to help others. An eagle or buffalo, a wolf or a bear, a beaver or a rattlesnake stood high in the scale of guardian spirits. The songs themselves, through their impact upon listeners, had variable power. Anyone with a powerful enough guardian spirit could become a shaman who might help others in need of healing.

Shamanism involved belief, vision, and an art of manipulation. An ordinary person got by somehow with help from his guardian spirit, but, in a crisis, medical help could be obtained through intervention of a shaman. The Shoshoni thus had a system of socialized medicine, and practioners had special privileges appropriate for their important humanitarian contribution to society. Sometimes a shaman, although obligated to offer service in time of need (by singing a spirit's song), also was rewarded in food or clothing if the song produced a cure. A shaman was not supposed to use these powers for personal gain, though no doubt some of them did. Those who did their duty could get into trouble if a song yielded unsatisfactory results. An unsuccessful shaman invited death in the event of failure; the Shoshoni lacked a less drastic system of malpractice insurance. But anyone with an unusually powerful guardian spirit, knowing of this advantage, could go out to accomplish exceptional personal feats. This kind of Shoshoni religious practice with antecedents far in the prehistoric past, continues uninterrupted after close to two centuries of white contact.

Shoshoni culture also was enriched with a tradition of legends to explain the distant past. A variety of complex mythological tales of creation make up an important part of the Shoshoni heritage. Ordinarily these portray two participants: wolf and coyote. Wolf usually starts as creator, while his younger brother, coyote, enters as a trickster responsible for death, disease, and pain. Coyote brings ill to the world, normally through carelessness, laziness, or error. His mistakes confused and disrupted the original perfection of wolf's creation and resulted in a world less good which replaced the perfection of the original world. As an example, in one of these creation stories wolf (who was wise and knew what was needed for an ideal earth) told coyote to lay soil on the original water on which their land was formed. Following wolf's instructions, coyote ran over the area in all four directions placing land on the water as required. But coyote was too lazy to keep running long enough to make territory sufficient for everyone who would need living space. Because of the coyote's lack of industry the earth grew overcrowded. Yet coyote also appears as a culture hero who saved fire for people to use and who introduced technical perfection as a by-product of his lazy ways. In their accounts of creation (there are also stories of destruction of the earth's original people by fire or by flood) the Shoshoni share ancient legends with early peoples of California, among other places. With earlier antecedents in traditional creation accounts of Asian derivation, these explanations — notable for their variety within a general structural framework — continue to form an essential element in Shoshoni tradition.

In Shoshoni cosmology, the earth, while not regarded as spherical, had properties more compatible with modern observation than some popular pre-Columbian European explanations suggested. To the Shoshoni the earth was a round disc which turned back and forth in a reciprocal motion that explained sunrise and sunset. A part of a layer-cake universe composed of three discs, the earth occupied space between a flat lower disc, or underworld. A long lost hole connected the two lower discs or earths. In the remote past an unusually bold explorer had descended through the connecting hole into the underworld. When he returned, he reported that the underworld disc reciprocated opposite to the earth so that during the earth's daytime, the underworld had nighttime, and vice versa. People of the underworld had the same culture as the Shoshoni, and their way of life was reinterpreted as Shoshoni culture changed. When the Shoshoni got horses, for example, inhabitants of the underworld got horses. Although the location of the connecting hole had been forgotten long ago, the Shoshoni had learned what they needed to know about the earth as a central layer in three discs.

Shoshoni astronomy identified constellations in patterns that differed from the Greek and Babylonian system accepted by the whites. For the Shoshoni, the handle of the Big Dipper (along with the connecting star in the dipper) was a rabbit net. The two dipper stars pointing to Polaris were coyote's net. Polaris was recognized as an unmoving star, and Antares, the red star in Scorpio, was known simply as the red star. Most other names differed greatly from European versions:

Orion's belt was three mountain sheep husbands, and Sirius, the dog star in English, was crazy woman chasing.

As with most peoples, astronomical observation provided the Shoshoni with the basis for their calendar. They had twelve lunar months of thirty days each, taking up their year-end slack of five or six days in midwinter with a long month which they called the long month. Like the Greeks they did not bother with weeks, which are of Babylonian origin unrelated to natural phenomena. Shoshoni mathematics, limited greatly by absence of a written notation, were adequate for maintaining a calendar and for meeting most other Shoshoni needs. Operating on a base ten system, they could add, subtract, multiply, and divide. These arithmetic functions were accomplished through linguistic devices, and since they had numbers that went past a thousand (in a system that could be expanded indefinitely) they could handle most problems that they normally encountered. Actually, counting accurately beyond a thousand with no written notation is more of a strain than most Shoshoni (or any other people) care to undergo. When Donald Mackenzie asked their great leader, Peiem, how many Shoshoni people he had, Peiem (on account of limitations imposed by adequacy of Shoshoni census data and capability of Shoshoni mathematics) preferred to dodge the issue. When Mackenzie explained that he needed to provide this information to King George IV, Peiem reflected a moment and replied, "Tell him then that we are as numerous as the stars."[1]

Ceremonial dancing, as well as ancient mythology, has provided the Shoshoni with an important form of religious and social expression. Four indigenous dances come from ancient Shoshoni tradition. A circle dance, performed each spring as a grass dance, had the greatest importance of all of them. Limited to the Northern Shoshoni and the peoples of the Great Basin, this dance did not gain acceptance in plateau culture. Songs with words (as poems) accompanied this native dance, which introduced hunting season or salmon season in forms of a salmon dance. Other variants of this circle dance applied to other seasons, and in ancient times, a fathers' dance appeared as a reinterpretation of the spring dance or grass dance.

Next in importance to the circle dance, a bear dance developed as a back and forth dance in which men and women faced each other in two long lines that advanced and retired. Originally a hunting dance, this ceremony had nothing to do with bears, except possibly to ward them off. Because its antecedents had long since been forgotten, this dance finally was explained as the contribution of a half man-half bear creature whom, in an old legend, taught the dance to an ancient Shoshoni people. Used only by the Shoshoni and the Utes, this dance took two forms: In one, musical accompaniment was provided by a drum; in the other, an upside-down basket, scraped by a rasp stick, produced a fantastic sound to inspire the dancers.

In addition to their circle dance and their bear dance, the early Northern Shoshoni had a rabbit dance and a scalp dance. Unlike the others, the rabbit dance excluded women. Men, who dressed up like rabbits and acted like game, did the rabbit dance by themselves as individual performers. The scalp dance was done primarily by women. Men beat hand drums while women with eagle feathers or beaded costumes danced around a scalp pole. Successful scalp hunting against the Blackfeet or Nez Perce was highly regarded, and scalp-dance songs were composed specifically for the occasion. This ceremony had many variations suited to the particular occasion which evoked the dance.

Sometime before white contact the Northern Shoshoni acquired a plateau spirit dance from the north. Performed in the winter (more recently between Christmas and New Year's) this three-night dance came from the lower Columbia. Featuring songs of guardian spirits, this dance had special religious significance. In addition, four other dances reached the Shoshoni in later years. These included a Northern Paiute reinterpretation of the spring dance as a ghost dance in 1889. With the ghost dance, the Indians were supposed to regain their country from the whites. When that did not quite work out, the ghost dance was abandoned at Fort Hall. But around 1890 the Fort Hall Shoshoni became interested in the traditional plains war dance; a decade later they began to take up the plains sun dance as well. Finally, in more recent times, the plains owl dance — a social dance — gained currency at Fort Hall. These dances are not to be confused with the old traditional ceremonies of the Northern Shoshoni.

Ceremonial games and songs also added variety to the Shoshoni way of life. Prior to white contact they had a gambling game in which one side guessed the hand in which an opposing player held a particular bone. This was known as a stick game, for the tally sticks. Accompanied by songs audible half a mile away, stick games could go on all night and get wild and uncontrollable. Melodies and words for these songs varied with the location of the performers. These ceremonies served as a device to release tension and eventually as a substitute for intertribal warfare. In their songs, the Northern Shoshoni used melodious Great Basin music (complete with words and poems) along with harsh, wordless chants from the Great Plains. This combination of cultural elements from different neighboring peoples came naturally to the

Northern Shoshoni because they occupied a territory geographically adapted for that kind of interchange.

Shoshoni science, aside from astronomy and mathematics, developed primarily in biology. (Prior to white contact, they also had considerable interest in maps and geography, but aside from using place names and making temporary maps in sand, their possibilities for pursuing these matters were restricted by absence of a written language.) They had an organized botanical taxonomy based upon use: seed plants, berry plants, leaf plants, grass and roots. Their four zoological classifications also reflected a hunting and fishing economy: large game, fish, lizards and reptiles, and birds. Naturally their botanical and zoological observation was restricted to the country with which they were familiar yet they inhabited a diverse and varied terrain. In addition to an expansive seasonal migratory cycle, mounted Shoshoni bands set off on long trips. Even the Boise Shoshoni would take off for distant places such as Spanish New Mexico. They also ranged well into Oregon. Contact with other travelling Indians also gave them a broader experience. Even before Lewis and Clark they were aware of great ships that sailed the Pacific Ocean. With broad exposure to diverse peoples and places they were well prepared to take advantage of opportunities for cultural interchange.

In the broad valley of the Snake, two centers of Northern Shoshoni occupation had special importance over a long period of time. (Late in the years of the fur trade each of these had a post of importance: Fort Hall and Fort Boise.) Around later Fort Hall, in the vicinity where the Blackfoot, Ross Fork, the Portneuf, and Bannock Creek meet the Snake, horse-owning Indians had an exceptionally good base of operations — if they didn't mind the mosquitoes too much. Here the Fort Hall Shoshoni and Bannock bands maintained their horse herds in luxury. Further west, in a zone between Camas Prairie and the area where the Boise, Owyhee, Payette, and Weiser flow into the Snake, the Northern Shoshoni had an important trading center active during salmon season long before the Hudson's Bay Company built Fort Boise. Here the Northern Shoshoni met other Indian peoples from a broad western area for a great intertribal fair during salmon-fishing season. Nez Perce and Walla Walla horses, Northern Paiute obsidian arrowheads, Pacific Coast ornamental seashells (brought in by Umatilla and Cayuse intermediaries), and Shoshoni buffalo hides and meat from the eastern plains were bartered there year after year. In addition, Cheyenne and Arapaho bands dragged superior cedar tipi poles from Colorado by the hundreds, and Crows came from Wyoming in search of wives. So did many others; the entire festival formed a grand marriage market as well as horse market and general trade fair. Ordinary horses served as their standard medium of exchange, each valued at ten arrows painted red and green. Nez Perce horses commanded a premium. Two additional northwestern annual intertribal gatherings — at the Mandan villages on the Missouri in North Dakota and at the Cascades and The Dalles of the Columbia in Oregon — served the same purpose. The Northern Shoshoni had an important function as host for one of the few major regional summer festivals.

By the end of the eighteenth century the Northern Shoshoni had entered a cultural golden age. Those who had survived the smallpox epidemic had gained some advantages (principally horses) of remote white contact, unaccompanied by the disadvantages of white settlement in their lands. From contact with Indians of the Great Plains they had acquired some useful and decorative cultural traits that enriched their lives. They began to live in tipis, to switch from basin to plains clothing (including feathered headdress for festive occasions), to jerk meat for preservation in winter, and to use skin containers in place of their old woven baskets. They had organized, in part, into bands, with trusted leaders along the plains model. This whole complex of new living habits, dress, equipment, and political organization helped prepare them for the time when they would have to begin to deal with white explorers and trappers who would promote still more extensive cultural adaption.

Around three or four thousand Northern Shoshoni lived in the Snake country of Idaho and Wyoming late in the eighteenth century, not counting the Comanche — plains Indians who spoke Shoshoni but after 1600 A.D. ranged over a different geographical area. Some of the Northern Shoshoni had drifted into Montana and Utah, and some of those with horses went on expeditions to New Mexico or Oregon. Considering that the Eastern Shoshoni ranged far into Wyoming, that the Comanche held plains territory farther south, and that the Southern Shoshoni lived in California and Nevada around Death Valley, the Shoshoni as a whole covered a lot of territory, even though they had been retrenching for a generation and had pulled back from Alberta and much of the northern plains.

Fur Trade Era

Shortly after Lewis and Clark met a Northern Shoshoni band in Lemhi Valley in 1805, fur hunters began to travel through the domain. John Colter of the Lewis and Clark Expedition returned to Shoshoni country in 1808, exploring

Teton Valley and upper Yellowstone. In 1810 Andrew Henry had to take refuge on Henry's Fork in the upper Snake River Valley after Blackfoot opposition had driven his band of trappers from the forks of the Missouri to the north. Henry's winter post was abandoned the next spring, but that fall an overland trappers' expedition, representing John Jacob Astor's Pacific Fur Company, turned up at Fort Henry on the way to the Pacific Coast. This band of trappers built canoes in order to descend Snake River. However, several trappers decided to stay in the Snake country, so from 1810 the Northern Shoshoni had extended exposure to white ways.

Late in 1813 John Reid of the Pacific Fur Company built a post at the confluence of the Boise and the Snake — right in the middle of the traditional salmon fishery and summer fairgrounds. This intrusion alienated the Bannock, who wiped the establishment out early in 1814. Because the Pacific Fur Company already had failed, Reid's post would have had only a temporary function anyway. He had come, in part, to notify some detached trappers that the operation had been sold out to the North West Company of Montreal. With two unsuccessful temporary posts, the Snake country fur trade had got off to an unpromising start. Still, the Northern Shoshoni had a modest exposure to white ways during these less than spectacular trapping operations from 1810 to 1814.

Even though initial white attempts at fur hunting failed consistently in the Snake country, the setback proved temporary. Donald Mackenzie, who had led the advance party of Overland Astorians through the western part of Snake River Valley, came back to the Pacific Northwest in 1816. By 1818 he got his annual Snake expedition into some extremely rich beaver country in the Boise region. Before the season ended he went out to explore Northern Shoshoni territory as far as Bear River and the Yellowstone. Convinced of the fur wealth of the terrain he held a trappers' rendezvous in Boise Valley in the summer of 1819, along the model used six years later by W. H. Ashley for the Rocky Mountain fur trade. This interesting addition to the regular annual summer Indian festival incurred determined Nez Perce resistance. Mackenzie started to build another permanent post close to the site of John Reid's unfortunate venture six years before, but Nez Perce opposition halted his plan.

Mackenzie still did not give up. That winter he camped with his Snake brigade of trappers and with a large composite Northern Shoshoni band on Little Lost River in a sheltered valley close to the Snake River Plains. There he held a grand peace rally in a largely successful effort to get the Northern Shoshoni and Bannock bands to allow

his fur-trapping enterprise to prevail. Dealing with Peiem, leader of the Boise Shoshoni, and a number of other prominent band leaders, Mackenzie reached an accord with the Indians. His annual Snake expedition, organized originally for the North West Company, continued under auspices of the Hudson's Bay Company until 1832. Travelling through the country in an annual migratory cycle in search of furs and of food for subsistence, Mackenzie's fur brigade operated essentially in Northern Shoshoni fashion. Taken out by Michel Bourdon for the Hudson's Bay Company in 1822, by Finnan MacDonald in 1823, and by Alexander Ross in 1824, this annual Snake expedition resisted the Blackfeet (who were penetrating Northern Shoshoni territory) without upsetting the Northern Shoshoni unduly. Through the fur trade, the Shoshoni were induced to go into a sideline of beaver hunting. In return they obtained useful white articles of trade: beads, blankets, needles, and other implements, along with the guns amd ammunition they needed to resist the Blackfeet.

When Peter Skene Ogden took over the annual Snake expedition late in 1824, a new element had entered the Northern Shoshoni world. Jedediah Smith and six prominent trappers investigating the country for William H. Ashley's St. Louis-based fur-hunting enterprise brought unwelcome competition to the Hudson's Bay Company. Firm Bannock resistance to the St. Louis trappers (whose Indian troubles greatly exceeded the problems encountered by the better-organized British and Canadian operation) led to a fair amount of tension. Yet during these years of competition among white fur hunters, with a substantial resulting impact upon the local Indians, the Northern Shoshoni had their major problem with Blackfoot intrusions into their Snake country.

In order to resist the Blackfeet more successfully, the Boise, Fort Hall, and a number of Northern Shoshoni joined into much larger composite bands. Ogden, in fact, met two such great composite bands on their way from buffalo-hunting grounds to Salmon Falls. One of these he identified as the Lower Snakes, the other as the Plains Snakes. Ogden's Lower Snakes are the Bannock (led by The Horse); his Plains Snakes are Peiem's Northern band and Eastern Shoshoni. Travelling with the latter were the Cache Valley and Malad River Shoshoni, who were south of Snake River but not far from the Green River wintering grounds of the Eastern Shoshoni. Such large Shoshoni composite bands were loosely joined groups of bands which congregated periodically for protection while travelling from one food area to another. They operated under some kind of joint leadership provided perhaps by the leaders of the various bands that made up the composite. These two large composite bands did not include all the Shoshoni. Those without horses and therefore not organized into small local bands, naturally would not join one of the composite groups. Their purpose in assembling into large bands seems to have been to protect their horses from Blackfoot raiders.

During the winter these great seasonal bands broke up into the smaller bands of the kind which Lewis and Clark had found two decades earlier. Ogden was impressed by the order maintained by the two composite bands he met and by their equipment. Their organization, though, did not compare with that of the stable units of the Plains Dakota. When the great menace of Blackfoot raiding ended, large bands no longer were essential. Even after 1850, when the composite bands no longer assembled, Shoshoni organization in smaller bands still was highly flexible, although better organized than before. Treaties and government pressure — and still more, gold miners' pressure — then called for more organization and stronger leadership. There still was much changing in individual membership back and forth from one band to another.

As different companies of trappers entered the Snake country fur trade, the Northern Shoshoni were subjected more and more to alien cultural exposure. As early as 1818 an Iroquois band travelling with Donald Mackenzie joined the Boise Shoshoni for a season and introduced an Iroquois strain into the Northern Shoshoni population.[2] A number of Scotch and French Canadian trappers had Shoshoni wives and families. After mountain men based in St. Louis entered the Snake country with Jedediah Smith in 1824 this kind of population blend increased. Parties of Rocky Mountain fur trappers often spent the winter in Cache Valley, and the Cache Valley Shoshoni suffered particularly from excessive cultural pressures inherent in this kind of contact. Early trappers' rendezvous sessions in Cache Valley and around Bear Lake brought more than white culture to the local Northern Shoshoni, and the 1832 rendezvous in Pierre's Hole turned out to be a high point of the Rocky Mountain fur trade. Indians and whites from a large western area joined in that summer frolic and trade fair. Aside from white trappers, a variety of Indian tribes made long journeys into Northern Shoshoni country to participate. The celebration terminated in a wild battle at Pierre's Hole, mainly between the Nez Perce and Gros Ventre — after an Iroquois with a white trapping party set off the fight.

Bands of fur hunters then set out to trap the more remote areas of the Northern Shoshoni domain. By that time not too many beaver were left to maintain a strong commercial fur trade, partly as a result of Hudson's Bay Company pol-

icy to trap out the Snake country so the Rocky Mountain fur trade would not expand farther into the Pacific Northwest. Still, Captain B. L. E. Bonneville built a winter post in the Lemhi country in 1832, and Nathaniel J. Wyeth founded Fort Hall on Snake River in 1834. Agents for the Hudson's Bay Company retaliated with an early version of Fort Boise late in 1834. So about the time the Rocky Mountain and Snake country fur trade had reached a period of decline, permanent white installations occupied the two main Northern Shoshoni centers of the Snake River Plains: Fort Hall and Fort Boise.

Within two years Nathaniel J. Wyeth had to try to sell out to his rivals, after an unsuccessful attempt to enter a joint fur-trading enterprise with the Hudson's Bay Company. Eventually the British took over management of Fort Hall in 1838, and the Northern Shoshoni remained under British influence at the end of the fur trade. Declining fur prices led almost all the independent mountain men to retire from the fur trade by 1840. With their departure, the Northern Shoshoni had less white contact. Richard Grant, who managed Fort Hall for the Hudson's Bay Company from 1842 to 1852, induced his sons to establish large Shoshoni families, so British influence among the Indians was increased. Yet by 1849, with declining beaver prices, the Northern Shoshoni fur trade practically had ceased. Richard Grant reported that "the Indians have become careless, and still more indolent than they ever were in hunting furs . . . some old ones no doubt might yet be enticed to hunt beaver. . . ."[3] Grant really could not anticipate much in the way of revitalizing his Northern Shoshoni fur business. A temporary price increase in 1850 helped briefly, but the Fort Hall Shoshoni had gone back mainly to big-game hunting for subsistence and for emigrant trade. As might have been expected, the Northern Shoshoni never had seen very much sense in hunting beaver when plenty of deer, elk, antelope, and buffalo were around. Sometimes they tried to divert white trappers into big-game hunting as an obviously more rewarding business that anyone with intelligence would pursue.

In any case, by the end of the fur trade the Northern Shoshoni emerged with an improved way of life that preserved most of their traditional values and provided a few appropriate conveniences and luxuries to give them an easier existence. If their legacy from the fur trade had included nothing more, they would have come out reasonably well off. But the beginning of white migration over emigrant roads to Oregon and California — also a heritage of the fur trade — introduced another, quite different, consequence of their exposure to white culture.

By the later years of the fur trade Blackfoot intrusions into the Snake country no longer offered a serious menace to the Northern Shoshoni. Blackfoot expansion and incursions had resulted from an earlier stage of the Canadian fur trade. By 1836 the Blackfeet had suffered enough through excessive white contact (particularly through white diseases) that they no longer threatened fur hunters in the Snake country, who drove them out after more than a decade of hostilities. Since the Northern Shoshoni no longer had to travel in large composite bands for protection they resumed their earlier way of life and continued their migratory cycles as a number of mounted bands. Those who never had organized into major travelling bands continued their old pattern of existence, no longer molested by fur hunters or hostile Blackfoot parties. The Northern Shoshoni still were a somewhat diverse group. The Boise Shoshoni, the Lemhi, and the Fort Hall Shoshoni and Bannocks continued to travel about the land. The Bruneau Shoshoni, Cache Valley and Bear Lake bands, and the isolated Sheepeaters or Mountain Shoshoni preserved their traditional ways as best they could. Until white settlers came into their midst, they did not have excessive difficulties.

Notes

1. Alexander Ross, *Fur Hunters of the Far West* (Norman: University of Oklahoma Press, 1956), p. 168.

2. A band of Iroquois trappers remained active in the Snake country until 1836, when John Grey led them down the Missouri to settle in a retired trappers' community. One of these mainly Iroquois founders of Kansas City was a Shoshoni (or possibly a Bannock) member of Grey's party.

3. Richard Grant to George Simpson, February 22, 1850, quoted in Louis Seymour Grant, "Fort Hall on the Oregon Trail," (M.A. thesis, University of British Columbia, 1938), p. 92.

CHAPTER I

SHOSHONI HOMELAND

Emigrants on the Oregon Trail

Until the 1840s the beaver trapper reigned supreme in Northern Shoshoni territory and had surprisingly little trouble from the friendly native inhabitants. The Shoshoni and Bannock and other neighboring tribes learned the cultural habits of the white men, came to appreciate firearms and iron utensils, and sampled, for the first time and mostly from the American traders, the awesome delights of firewater. The latter came usually from the Rocky Mountain rendezvous established first in 1825 at Green River in Wyoming, where Shoshoni, Nez Perce, Flathead, and any other Indians who could walk or ride went to trade furs for the white man's accouterments of civilization. As Liljeblad says, "It was a time of prosperity and mutual amity between Indians and whites." The impact made by French-Canadian trappers on the life of the Northern Shoshoni is still noticeable. Family names of unmistakable French origin, Shoshoni folktales with a Gaelic flavor, and a different philosophy toward the policies and behavior of later white neighbors mark these differences.[1]

1840

With their tribal country trapped out by the 1840s, the Shoshoni-Bannock again were left by themselves. With the exception of Hudson's Bay traders at Fort Hall and occasional visits from wandering Americans, they managed their own affairs, used their new-found weapons to protect themselves from the Blackfeet, and had only the summer emigrants to Oregon and California to be concerned about. Even here there was comparative peace; the annual migration of American "pilgrims" went through the Fort Hall area during late summer when the Indians were absent on their annual excursion after buffalo. True, space for wandering was becoming a little more cramped as the whites continued to crowd in, but the arid Snake River Plains and mountains did not offer great inducement to eastern farmers accustomed to greenery and frequent rains.[2]

There was one concern. After a long journey back from Wyoming or Montana, with their heavily laden and jaded ponies anticipating pleasant pastures and good forage, the sight of burned-out campfires, denuded woodlands, and cropped-over pastures left by needy overland travelers caused some apprehension about the destruction of the provender and fuel needed by the Indians for winter survival. George R. Stewart, in his book *The California Trail*, estimates that by 1857 one hundred sixty-five thousand people and a million animals had crossed the continent on their way to California, with twenty-two thousand five hundred people and sixty thousand animals traveling the road in the one year, 1849. Furthermore, the migration to California continued even beyond the completion of the transcontinental railroad in 1869.[3] George W. Fuller gives travel figures to Oregon between 1842 and 1852 as 18,287 people and a possible fifty thousand animals. Again, the Oregon emigration continued late into the nineteenth century.[4] Also, with the discovery of gold in Montana in 1862 the north-south Montana Trail was opened between Salt Lake City and the gold camps in western Montana. Heavy traffic over this route continued until 1880, when the Utah and Northern Railroad was finished as far as the Montana boundary.

1849

With the exception of perhaps 10 percent of the emigrants who went past Great Salt Lake, travel over the Oregon and California trails forged right through the homeland of the Shoshoni and Bannock. Even when Hudspeth's Cutoff became the accepted route, travelers crossed lower Marsh Valley, later the southern portion of the Fort Hall Reservation. Nearly all travelers from Great Salt Lake to Montana passed through the Portneuf-Snake River area of the Northern Shoshoni. A conservative estimate, based on the above figures, shows that at least two hundred forty thousand emigrants with 1.5 million animals traveled through the home country of the Fort Hall Indians, spending at least one night camped out on the Portneuf or Snake rivers and allowing their stock to graze in pastures which for centuries had been the property of the Shoshoni Indians. Without any interference from the aboriginal inhabitants of the area, the white settlers were allowed to proceed across Indian lands and use Indian forage and firewood with no thought of compensation to the owners. Such a proposal would have been looked upon as ridiculous by most Americans, who soon were claiming the entire Western Hemisphere from the aurora borealis on the north to Tierra del Fuego on the south, as one put it. Nevertheless, the Northern

1849

Shoshoni were annually being deprived of tribal assets essential to their livelihood. F. W. Lander, in his comprehensive report of February 18, 1860, referred to a petition signed by sixty emigrants who complained that from Salt Lake City to as far as Bear River they were charged "from twenty-five cents to five cents per head a night for pasturage of their stock." Using these figures as the going rate and adopting an average of fifteen cents per head as a reasonable fee, the Northern Shoshoni might have received $222,750 for the 1,485,000 animals that grazed on their tribal lands during the period of western emigration if they had been compensated as were their white neighbors along the Oregon Trail.[5]

1860

Oregon and Washington Superintendencies

With a homeland located at the crossroads of the West one might suppose that the Northern Shoshoni would have aroused keen interest on the part of the American government in their affairs, but because of twin accidents of history and geography the reverse was true. It was difficult for the Indians to understand that an imaginary line drawn along the forty-second parallel cut them off from any governmental contact with the nearby Mormon settlements in Utah and placed them under the jurisdiction of some far-off representative in a town called Oregon City. Their Wyoming neighbors (the Eastern Shoshoni under Chief Washakie) were looked after, "talked to," and supervised by an agent of the Great Father in Salt Lake City, Utah Territory, but only an occasional visitor came to see the Shoshoni-Bannock during the 1850s and early 1860s.

When Britain and the United States agreed in June 1846 upon the forty-ninth parallel as the boundary between the Oregon Country and Canada, supposedly the American government immediately accepted the responsibility of supervising the Indian inhabitants of the vast area between the forty-second and forty-ninth parallels and the Continental Divide and the Pacific Ocean. But when a bill seeking territorial government for Oregon was introduced into the next session of Congress no action was taken because the provisional government of the area had declared against slavery, which aroused the opposition of some of the southern members. There might have been a long wait for any formal action if the Cayuse Indians had not massacred Dr. Marcus Whitman and his party. This well-publicized incident resulted in a territorial government being proclaimed at Oregon City on March 3, 1849. All at once the Northern Shoshoni were wards of the American government, although that fact was kept secret from them for many years. Fort Hall

1846

1849

was just too far away from Oregon City to allow close supervision of Indians.

Depredations on passing emigrant trains, however, did have a way of focusing governmental attention on the Snake River Indians. In 1851 Governor John P. Gaines of Oregon requested troops "to keep in check all the tribes upon Snake and Upper Columbia, some of whom are of very uncertain temper and well-disposed to theft and insolence. . . ."[6] Superintendent Anson Dart of Oregon Territory already had written the Commissioner of Indian Affairs, "Having no agents or sub-agents to locate in the Rogue River and Snake country, and the improbability of visiting them in person this season will prevent me from having that control over them that is desirable."[7] These two statements are so typical of the correspondence of the Oregon superintendent concerning Indian affairs along the Snake River during the 1850s that it is not necessary to relate further the inability of the far-away Indian officials to supervise the natives of the area properly.

1851

Intermittent attacks on emigrant parties brought intermittent interest in sending agents to deal with the Shoshoni. The Ward Massacre of August 1854, in which nineteen members of a wagon train were killed by Boise Shoshoni, did bring a visit to the Fort Hall area by Special Agent Nathan Olney. He reported that the Snakes numbered three thousand — a tribe composed of fifteen hundred Green River Snakes, twelve hundred Fort Hall Snakes (of whom two hundred were Bannock), and three hundred Too-koo-ree-keys or Sheepeaters.[8]

1854

The Oregon superintendents of Indian Affairs routinely applied for sums varying from $20,000 to $45,000 "for expenses of Negotiating Treaties with all the tribes east of the Blue Mountains, among which are included the Klamath, Shooshoney, Boonack, Snake and Mountain Snake tribes, and for presents and provisions incident to that service."[9] Even if the money were appropriated, which is doubtful, the treaties were not negotiated or the presents given. There was some hope that when Washington Territory was formed in 1853 the hard-pressed Oregon superintendent might have more time to examine affairs in his far eastern district of Fort Hall. His agent's 1857 annual report reveals otherwise. The agent wrote, "Of these Indians ('Sho-Sho-nies or Snakes') but very little is known. . . ."[10]

1853

The opportunity for government representatives to become acquainted with the upper Snake River Indians was lost when the Oregon and Washington superintendencies were reunited into one agency in 1857, which led Superintendent James W. Nesmith to complain:

1857

The duties in either Territory while the offices were distinct afforded ample business for the Superintendents. If any change was originally necessary it was that the country east of the Cascade Mountains should have been erected into a Separate district. My apparent neglect or omissions in the discharge of my official duties can very properly be attributed to an excessive amount of business.[11]

1857

A month later he formally recommended that an eastern superintendency be established, one separate and distinct from an Oregon and Washington district. A special agent, J. Ross Browne, supported his contention by warning that the Mormons were "constantly instigating them [Northern Shoshoni] to acts of aggression. Is it well, then, to suffer this fine country to fall into the hands of a renegade and debased people, from whom nothing but evil can come?"[12] But even the threat of Utah Mormons penetrating into Oregon Territory failed to arouse Washington, D.C. authorities to organize an eastern Indian superintendency.

1858

An occasional government official did warn his supervisors about the consequences of neglecting the Shoshoni and Bannock. Superintendent F. W. Lander of the Fort Kearney, South Pass, and Honey Lake wagon road wrote of the necessity of some kind of compensation to the Indians for the road right-of-way through their country. He pointed out that, although the more warlike Sioux and Cheyenne had been paid annuities for many years, the Northern Shoshoni had never received any substantial presents. His colleague, C. H. Miller, pointed out in a letter of November 1858 that emigrant stock continually destroyed the grass where the Indians usually wintered their horses and that the government should pay the tribes for this use of their lands. In addition, the destruction of the wild game upon which the Indians subsisted was continuing, with no attention being paid by the government to the necessity of providing other food supplies.[13]

1861

To make matters worse, a Washington Superintendency was cut off from that of the state of Oregon to include what is now Idaho. This was in May 1861, and the new superintendent now sat in an office at Olympia, many miles farther away from Fort Hall than Oregon was.[14] With the increase in distance came enlarged ignorance of the tribes along the Snake River. The map which accompanied the Washington superintendent's annual report for 1862 shows a large expanse of nothing, with the word "Unexplored" just south of the Salmon River drainage, the words "Shoshones or Snakes" printed in the area of the plains north of Snake River, and the caption "Mountain

1862

Snakes" placed along the river.[15] There was very little else. In two other reports a local Oregon agent and the Washington superintendent wrote of the Bannock as a "mysterious people, living in rude lodges made of the willow brush," and of the "Snakes" who live "amongst the sagebrush, hiding in the canons, skulking behind the rocks," both tribes of whom "it is presumable that they are mostly within this Territory, as the sphere of their marauding operations commences south of Fort Hall, and extends to the Blue Mountains."[16]

Superintendent C. H. Hale, writing from Olympia, informed his superior that he had been delayed from visiting the tribes east of the Cascades because of lack of funds. He proposed that the appointment of a regular agent there would be the most economical approach in keeping the Indians quiet.[17] Nothing came of the suggestions. Any supervision that the Northern Shoshoni received came not from their legally constituted governmental officials on the Pacific Coast but from a de facto relationship with a southern neighbor, the Indian superintendency at Salt Lake City.

NOTES CHAPTER I
SHOSHONI HOMELAND

1. Liljeblad, *The Idaho Indians in Transition, 1805–1960*, 21.
2. Ibid., 28–29.
3. Stewart, *The California Trail.*
4. Fuller, *A History of the Pacific Northwest,* 190.
5. Madsen, *The Bannock of Idaho*, Chs. II and III; U.S. National Archives, *Letters Received by the Office of Indian Affairs, 1859–1860,* Utah Superintendency, Roll 899.
6. Governor John P. Gaines of Oregon to President Fillmore, Oregon City, Oregon Territory, June 13, 1851, U.S. Congress, *Military and Indian Affairs in Oregon,* Senate, Ex. Doc., I, No. IV, no. 11, 32nd Cong., 1st Sess., Serial No. 611, 144.
7. Anson Dart to C.I.A., Oregon City, Oregon Territory, May 7, 1851, 119, U.S. National Archives, *Records of the Bureau of Indian Affairs, Oregon Superintendency,* Copies of Letters Received and Sent, 1850–1855, No. 3.
8. Nathan Olney to Joel Palmer, Camas Prairie, Oregon Terr., July 30, 1855, U.S. National Archives, *Records of the Bureau of Indian Affairs, Oregon Superintendency,* No. 10, F, Letter Books, 57–59.
9. Joel Palmer to C.I.A., Dayton, Oregon Terr., March 5, 1856, U.S. National Archives, *Letters Received by the Office of Indian Affairs, 1824–81, Oregon Superintendency, 1842–1880,* Microcopy no. 234, Roll 610.
10. A. P. Dennison, U.S. Indian Agent, N.E. District, Oregon Terr., to J. S. Nesmith, Supt. Ind. Affairs, Dalles, Oregon Terr., August 1, 1857, ibid.
11. J. W. Nesmith, Supt. Indian Affairs, O.&W.T., to C.I.A., Salem, Oregon, June 16, 1867, ibid.
12. J. Ross Browne, San Francisco, California, to C.I.A., November 17, 1857, ibid.
13. "Report of the Secretary of the Interior on Pacific Wagon Roads," U.S. Congress, H. of Rep., Ex. Doc. 108, 35th Cong., 2nd Sess., Serial No. 1008, March 1, 1859, 49–73.
14. Simeon Francis to C.I.A., Portland, Oregon, May 18, 1861, U.S. National Archives, *Letters Received by the Office of Indian Affairs, 1824–81, Washington Superintendency, 1861–1862,* Microcopy No. 234, Roll 907.
15. "Map of Wash'n Terry," *Report of Sup't. Indian Affairs,* 1862.
16. "Report of Agent J. M. Kirkpatrick, Powder River, Oregon, July 22, 1862," in *C.I.A. Report for 1862,* 267; "Report of Supt. C. H. Hale, Olympia, Wash. Terr., Oct. 19, 1862," in *C.I.A. Report for 1862,* 399.
17. C. H. Hale To C.I.A., Olympia, W. T., Aug. 13, and Sept. 4, 1862, U.S. National Archives, *Letters Received by the Office of Indian Affairs, 1824–81, Washington Superintendency, 1861–1862,* Microcopy No. 234, Roll 907.

CHAPTER II

UTAH NEIGHBORS

Brigham Young's Indian Policy

The settlement of the Mormons on the shores of Great Salt Lake made them the closest white neighbors of the main group of Northern Shoshoni. The Northwestern Shoshoni bands now began a long relationship with Brigham Young's pioneers, who soon began to build homes and farms in Bear Lake, Cache, Weber, Salt Lake, and Malad valleys — the traditional homeland of the Utah Shoshoni.

Not only were the Northwestern Shoshoni a Utah responsibility, but the proximity of Fort Bridger on the east meant that Chief Washakie's Eastern Shoshoni also looked to the governor of Utah for guidance and help in learning to live with white men and their very different ways. The Fort Hall Indians, too, were drawn to the Mormon capital, hoping for some of the presents which Washakie's group received annually. The Utah superintendent became, like it or not, the informal and occasional government representative of the Northern Shoshoni. It was an uneasy marriage. There never was enough money appropriated even to subsist and clothe the Utah tribes. When Idaho was made a territory in 1863 and assumed responsibility for the Snake River Indians, the Utah agents were not unhappy.

1847 The settlement of Salt Lake Valley and the Mexican Cession placed the Mormons again under the American flag, with the necessity of furnishing them with a government. Because Utah meant Brigham Young, the Mormon prophet was soon installed by his people as governor of the territory and ex-officio superintendent of Indian Affairs. His chief counselor in the church hierarchy was Heber C. Kimball, who proposed that the pioneers should not pay the Indians of Salt Lake Valley for the lands — for, if the Shoshoni were thus compensated, the Utes and other tribes also would demand payment. In Kimball's opinion, the land belonged to "our Father in Heaven and we expect to plow and 1850 plant it."[1] His typical frontier point of view was not shared by Young, who on numerous occasions counselled his people that it was "manifestly more economical, and less expensive to feed and clothe, than to fight them."[2]

Holding steadfastly to this course, even when the Mormon settlers began to become restive under the never-ending Indian demands on their meager food supplies, Brigham Young continued to preach tolerance and forbearance. In a typical statement to the Utah Legislature he argued:

> We exhort you to feed and clothe them so far as lies in your power; never turn them away hungry from your door; teach them the art of husbandry; bear with them in all patience and long suffering, and never consider their lives as an equivalent for petty stealing; remember that it is a part of their existence, practiced by them from generation to generation, and success in which paved the way to renown and influence amongst them. Induce them from those ideas and notions by your superior wisdom and genial influence and intercourse with them. . . . Finally brethren, be just and quiet, firm and mild, patient and benevolent, generous and watchful in all your intercourse with them; learn their language so that you can explain matters to them and pay them the full and just reward for their labor, and treat them in all respects as you would like to be treated.[3]

1852

His philosophy toward the native inhabitants of the American West differed markedly from most western frontiersmen, who considered the Indian a nuisance to be isolated on some unwanted spot of real estate, far removed from whites.

Young was so successful with his policies that when the U.S. government sent an army to gain control of affairs in Utah in the Utah War, 1857 Brigham Young had difficulty in restraining some of the Indian leaders from fighting the Americans in his behalf. For example in 1858 Arrapeen, a Utah chief, met with the Navajo and some of the Northern and Eastern Shoshoni and Bannock and reported to Young that he had lined up sixteen nations. With the Mormons making seventeen nations, Arrapeen was sure the combined force could "wipe out the Americans."[4] Successful in dissuading the warlike chief, Brigham Young earlier had had to counsel Washakie not to fight the Americans for the Mormon people, "for we can take care of ourselves. I am your Brother."[5]

Despite his unorthodox views as a westerner, Brigham Young applied his commonsense approach to Indian affairs and very early divided 1851 Utah Territory into three districts, of which the Second or Uinta Agency was to care for "all of the Snakes or Shoshones within said Territory. . . ."[6] The two groups were the Northwestern and Eastern Shoshoni. But they, like all the other Indians of Utah Territory, had to share in the very modest sums appropriated for them. One of the superintendent's agents reported that the

Shoshoni contrived to be friendly despite the very few presents given to them. He voiced a common complaint of all Indian representatives that "the price of goods is so high here that the appropriation does not serve to go far for the Indians of this Territory are so very numerous."[7] A later superintendent, James Duane Doty, described a pitiful scene among the Western Shoshoni where he "saw their children, lying on their bellies on the margins of the streams, cropping the young grass" and wrote that he hoped to receive the goods overland from the department "in time to clothe their nakedness before the snow falls."[8]

1862

Doty was one of the successors to Brigham Young. The Mormon prophet was relieved of his Indian duties in July 1858 as a result of the Utah War.[9]

Unlike the uninformed Indian superintendent of Oregon and Washington territories, the Utah agents knew a great deal about the Northern Shoshoni and Bannock. As early as 1851 Brigham Young was able to describe quite accurately the habits and life-style of these Indians, explaining that the Fort Hall and Wind River Shoshoni were "the chivalry of the tribe" and were much better off than their western cousins, who had only the "canopy of heaven" for a shelter.[10] Of course the Western Shoshoni did have the advantage of being within the purview of the Utah Superintendency and received both visits and presents from the Salt Lake agents, especially when they threatened the stations of the Overland Mail Company.[11] In September 1853 Agent J. H. Holeman made an extended trip through the Humboldt River area dispensing gifts and food and met a group of Bannock under Te-vu-va-wenah (the long man), who must have wondered why no government officials ever visited the Fort Hall area with presents for the deserving Bannock and Northern Shoshoni.[12] Later, in August 1855, Dr. Garland Hunt visited the Nevada Shoshoni and signed a treaty with them which promised annual supplies and food. Two "Banacks . . . who belong to Oregon Territory" happened along and no doubt returned word to their friends and relatives of the attention paid the Nevada group by the representatives of the Great Father in Washington.[13]

1851

1853

1855

When the white officials failed to visit them in their homeland, the Shoshoni and Bannock took the initiative and traveled to Salt Lake City to talk to Brigham Young as the nearest federal plenipotentiary. On May 24, 1852, the Mormon prophet met in council with "some Snake Indians from Fort Hall." The seven leading Indians present were: Shineck (the Whites Have Married My Girls), Pahro, Yambot (the name of an edible root), Tatober (a name the Americans gave him; he refused to give his own name), Yeshoo, Tur-

gometter (Horse Whipper), and Showetz (Soldier Whipper).[14] Some Bannock met with Superintendent Young in May of 1853[15] and also in September of 1857.[16] The big medicine man of the Bannock, Tim-a-poo, came to Salt Lake City to assure the white leader that the Great Spirit "says it is not good to fight and shed human blood."[17]

1857

1858

Behind the pleasantness was an insistence to the Utah superintendent that the government provide supplies and food as was being done for neighboring tribes. Indian Agent E. A. Bedell reported to Young that a deputation of seven Bannock leaders spent several days in his office because of a raging storm outside and protested that "they have never received any presents from the Great Father," although the Mormon people had been kind to them. Bedell distributed shirts, tobacco, and food.[18] Governor Young, in 1860, asked the Utah Legislature to adopt a memorial to be sent to Washington asking that commissioners be appointed to treat with the wandering tribes of Bannock and Shoshoni who roamed the Oregon area just north of Utah.[19] That same year the military also requested the secretary of the Interior to appoint agents for the "Shoshonee and Bannock Indians."[20] Nothing was done.

1860

Neglect of Fort Hall Indians

Federal troubles with the Mormons in Utah and the continuing emigration across the continent caused apprehension among the western tribes, which in turn engendered tribulations and concern in the Office of Indian Affairs. The commissioner asked F. W. Lander, superintendent in charge of construction for the Fort Kearney, South Pass, and Honey Lake wagon road, to report on conditions among the Indians whose territory was crossed by the new emigrant route. Lander's forty-two page document remains one of the better accounts of Indians affairs in the western Wyoming and southern Idaho region. He wanted to classify some Shoshoni groups as Bannock, but with that exception his description was accurate and knowledgeable. He met Mopeah's band of three hundred Bannock near Salt River where he made his "first payment to them" on July 20, 1859. The evening after the presents were distributed a war party of Bannock arrived at the camp under the leadership of Tash-e-pah, who apparently also received gifts.

Lander believed the Bannock were not "irreclaimably hostile" but acknowledged that their "horse stealing proclivities prevent amicable arrangements with them to become lasting." Mopeah reported that, the year before, the tribe had gone to Fort Bridger to visit the soldiers, prove tribal friendship, and receive presents.

When no supplies were given them, they went away enraged and immediately stole horses on their return journey. Part of the Bannock were considered hostile at that time; Lander sent the presents intended for them to California, where the goods were sold to the credit of the Indian Department.[21]

It was difficult for the Fort Hall Shoshoni to understand why the white government officials of nearby Utah ignored their wants while paying special attention to the needs of their hunting companions and neighbors, the Eastern Shoshoni. The vagueness of artificial boundaries, which placed Washakie's people under Utah jurisdiction while they were assigned to negligent and indifferent agents in Oregon some six hundred miles away, left the Northern Shoshoni bewildered and angered.

1851   Only four years after the settlement of Utah in late 1851, the Salt Lake agent met with the Eastern Shoshoni. He then escorted eighty of their principal men to a grand treaty held at Fort Laramie, where they met with Sioux and Cheyenne and heard much "talk."[22] From this time on there was constant concern in assuring that Chief Washakie's people were well cared for and kept peaceful and content. Extra efforts were made to effect peace between the ever-warring Utes and Eastern Shoshoni. Brigham Young held a grand council with the chiefs of the two tribes at Salt Lake City in August 1852. There was much smoking of the pipe of peace, much conversation, and, of course, many gifts distributed.[23] Although both tribes gave full assurance of everlasting peace and amity, six years later it was necessary for Agent Jacob Forney to hold another full-scale council with the two Indian groups to gain a permanent peace. One suspects that the Indians rather enjoyed these peace sessions which always included an opportunity for oratory and the receipt of fine presents. The Bannock came unin-

1858   vited to the last meeting. That seemed to be the only way for them to share in the excitement and gifts of the councils with Brigham Young.[24]

The Fort Hall Indians were the poor country cousins who were never invited to the party. A typical request of Superintendent Young for Washakie to visit Salt Lake City in 1854 would have been much envied by the Northern Shoshoni if they had heard of it. Chief Washakie and his tribe were invited to come about September 4, "when the moon will be full, to give good light." Their camp would be at Parley's Park where the "grass is good," and beeves would be presented to his people, Young concluded, "I love the Shoshones very much . . . we think a great deal of them."[25] In September 1856 the Utah agency expended $4,596.50 for supplies for the Eastern

Shoshoni, who received the presents "spread upon the green adjacent to Fort Bridger."[26]

By the time F. W. Lander began meeting with the Northern and Eastern Shoshoni in 1859, the   1859 former had learned the art of just happening to show up when supplies were to be issued to their Wyoming friends. Lander ordered $3,321 worth of goods for the Washakie group of three hundred "single half"-lodges, a similar amount for their "friends and visitors," three hundred half-lodges of Western Snakes (the Snake River Shoshoni), and $2,214 worth of supplies for the "Northern Bannack & Sheep Eaters."[27] Formal and annual payments of goods were made only to the Eastern Shoshoni. For the Idaho Indians it was a hit-and-miss affair; they were subsisted if they happened along at the right time.

The government finally decided to negotiate a formal treaty with the Eastern Shoshoni in an attempt to reduce their participation in raids on emigrant trains on the Oregon Trail — or "holy road," as the plains Indians rather sardonically called it. Henry Martin, a special agent, was commissioned in July 1862 to join with Agent Luther   1862 Mann, Jr., in a meeting with the Washakie group. Martin asked for a military escort and for the balance of $5,000 of the original appropriation for extra provisions for the Indians because of their extreme hostility.[28] The mixed bands of Eastern Shoshoni and Bannock already had left for the annual buffalo hunt, so Agent Martin got only as far as Carson Valley from his initial departing point at San Francisco. He wrote that treaty negotiations would have to be postponed until the next year.[29]

Commenting on the failure of the mission, James Duane Doty advised the commissioner of Indian Affairs that it would be unwise to make an agreement with the Eastern Shoshoni without at the same time forming separate pacts with the Bannock and Utes. In fact, he reported that the latter two tribes "say that the Shoshonees receive presents for killing the white men; and conclude that they will be rewarded in like manner if they do the same." Doty, therefore, decided to wait until Congress could make an additional appropriation for treaties with the Bannock and Ute before proceeding with the Eastern Shoshoni. In fact, the Ute had threatened to attack the mail station west of the Salt Lake City, "saying that until they do so they will not receive from the whites what they demand in provisions and clothing."[30]

The Bannock began to impinge on the consciousness of government Indian affairs in one other way. As early as 1855 Chief Washakie was   1855 asking Superintendent Young to select a piece of farming land for him on Green River, "as he can't trust to his own judgment in the selection of farming land." But Bannock who hunted with the

1859

Wind River Indians and were always obviously around, were not considered by Superintendent Young for any farms.[31] Later, in 1859, Agent Jacob Forney recommended that the twelve hundred Indians under Washakie and the five hundred Bannock "who go and live where his [Washakie's] Tribe go and live" should be settled on a large farm in Henry's Fork Valley, about forty miles south of Fort Bridger. The suggestion was not followed by the commissioner of Indian Affairs.[32]

Mormon Occupation of Northwestern Shoshoni Lands

The Northwestern Shoshoni were the only group of Northern Shoshoni whose homeland lay within Utah and who were, therefore, the responsibility of the Salt Lake agents. After the early 1850s the Northwestern bands found their old way of life disrupted, their game disappearing, their lands appropriated by Mormon farmers in the northern valleys of Utah. Eventually they were goaded into becoming participants in the Battle of Bear River in 1863 — a central reason for the five treaties negotiated that year by Superintendent Doty.

1851

When whites first started encroaching on their land the Indians reacted in the old accustomed manner. In July 1851 a party of Northwestern Shoshoni stole several horses. They were pursued into Cache Valley, and one Indian was killed by a party of eighteen "brethren" from Ogden. The expedition was bad news for the Indians because the pursuing men discovered that Cache Valley was one of the best they had seen in Utah "for soil, timber, and water."[33] A more serious incident came as a result of the wanton killing of two Shoshoni women by a group of emigrants from Illinois. The northern Indians then started a series of depredations against all whites, "such as pasturing horses in the grain, robbing the corn fields, abstracting from melon patches, running off cattle and horses, etc., etc." They "massacred" a man at Ogden River and in return were driven away by a detachment of Mormon troops.[34]

1852

The following winter a difficulty was reported between the citizens of Box Elder County and the Snake Indians. The affair was "amiably settled" according to the laconic report.[35] The Shoshoni were also active south of Salt Lake City, where eighty of them engaged a band of Ute Indians and killed three of them.[36] Charges were made that some of the northern bands were raiding the Oregon and California trails north and west of Great Salt Lake. Once Brigham Young wrote far-off Agent John Owen in Bitterroot Valley asking him to investigate.[37] Agent J. H. Holeman then visited the Indians in Box Elder County and

1854

found them in possession of quantities of gold and emigrant property, for which they had very plausible explanations. The Mormon settlers accepted the accounts as true, while Holeman placed little credence in the stories. He distributed presents anyway.[38]

After this early flurry of hostility the Northwestern Shoshoni began to soften under the "easier to feed than fight" policy of Brigham Young. They continually asked for talks, during which they naturally expected and received some presents, "though not so many as desired," and they hung around the villages gleaning wheat from the fields and asking for food.[39] Sometimes they received advice from the Utah superintendent to go to the buffalo country for the winter because most of the game had disappeared and, one suspects, to keep them from drawing on the meager rations of the Mormon settlers.[40] Young occasionally complained to the commissioner of Indian Affairs that the Indians of Cache Valley and neighboring areas had received very "little at the expense of the government although a sore tax upon the people. . . ."[41] At such celebrations as Pioneer Day it became customary for the Mormon farmers to invite the neighboring natives to the usual outdoor picnic. One Deseret News correspondent reported that at Box Elder "a table was also spread for the Sho-shone Indians, and nearly 50 of them partook of the bounties placed before them, much to their satisfaction and delight."[42] To attempt to reduce the drain on his people, the Mormon prophet granted licenses to traders who located in Bear Lake and Malad valleys.[43]

1855

1857

1856

1860

As the northern valleys continued to fill up even more, the condition of the Northwestern bands became quite desperate. The Deseret News hoped the Indians could be taught to farm "instead of hunting, fishing and begging for subsistence" but conceded they had a greater aversion to labor than the Indians in southern Utah. The editor voiced a forlorn hope that the Indian superintendent would not forget the Northwestern bands.[44] On April 1, 1861, Chief Bear Hunter and about twenty of his tribe came into Salt Lake City on foot to ask for presents. The superintendent supplied them quite liberally and dressed the chief in a suit of citizen's clothing.[45]

1861

Perhaps a quotation from a letter by James Duane Doty can best describe the suffering and need of the Indians at this time. Doty was caught by a storm in Cache Valley for four days in the early spring of 1862 and reported:

1862

The Indians have been in great numbers, in a starving and destitute condition. No provision having been made for them, either as to clothing or provisions, by my predecessors. I have been compelled to purchase supplies where they could best be obtained and transport them to the places where the Indians had assembled, and where they were enduring great suffering. . . . The Indians' condition was such — with the prospect that they would rob the mail stations to sustain life.[46]

The superintendent bought supplies of food and doled it out gradually to the starving natives. He advised furnishing them with stock so they could become herdsmen instead of beggars. Two years before, Agent Jacob Forney had recommended a farm for the homeless Indians of the northern valleys, but a decade was to pass before a reservation on the Snake River Plains would allow them the opportunity to become cattlemen and farmers.[47]

Like typical frontiersmen almost everywhere in America, the Mormon pioneers settled on the land with no thought that any agreement should be made or compensation offered to the Northwestern Shoshoni. When Agent Forney considered the situation of these Indians, whom he thought numbered about fifteen hundred under Chief Little Soldier, he found that so much of the arable land in northern Utah had already been occupied that only Cache Valley offered an opportunity for a farm or reservation for them. He even considered establishing a reserve in Salmon River Valley in central Idaho as a home.[48]

1861

He and Brigham Young also engaged in a spirited contest to win the support of these Indians during the Utah War. Little Soldier and his subchief, Ben Simons, assured both the Mormons and the government officials that they wanted no part in the conflict.[49] Their chief concern was getting enough food to stay alive. They informed Agent Forney that they had hunting parties out at the time, that they had killed over a hundred elk during the winter of 1857–1858 and a large amount of smaller game, and that they were then trapping for otter and beaver on Bear River.[50] Simons told Forney that General Albert Sidney Johnston of the U.S. Army in Wyoming had offered the Indians $150 for every Mormon they would bring him and $1,000 for the Mormon guerilla leader, Lot Smith. The Indian chief said they would not get involved in the controversy but that the thousand Northwestern Shoshoni camped on Bear River did expect a visit from an Indian agent that day (April 1858) to distribute $15,000 worth of goods to the tribe.[51] With the threat that the Indians might ally with the Mormons, the government in this instance may have met the commitments that Chiefs Little Soldier and Ben Simons were awaiting, but the record is silent here.

1857

Another Northwestern chief who achieved some prominence in Idaho and Utah history came to the attention of the government agents for the first time. This was "Po-ca-ta-ro," who in 1859 had promised to meet F. W. Lander at City Rocks "when the grass was beginning to dry." Lander discovered that the Indian leader had been captured and put in irons by Major Isaac Lynde's army group on charges of attacking emigrants.

1859

Prior to the arrest the whites had distributed presents to the chief and his leading men. Lander thought Pocatello "a very wild and reckless chief" but still believed him innocent of the charges. The white agent felt that, because of the great influence of Pocatello, the army should not have arrested him on mere suspicion.

After the release of Pocatello, Lander sent him some small presents and then went without an escort to the Indian camp in the mountains, where he was received hospitably and with great courtesy. Lander was much impressed with the young chief and reported that Pocatello was much angered by the "assaults of ignomiy" on his people by the emigrants who had killed Indian women and children indiscriminately and that therefore he could not control the "bad thoughts" of his young men who were determined to avenge the deaths of their relatives by killing whites. Pocatello added that he knew there was a man more powerful than Big-um (meaning Brigham Young) and that when he was sure the White Father would treat him as well as Big-um did he would then be a friend of the Americans. Lander concluded his portrayal of the meeting with Pocatello with an urgent request that money be appropriated for goods and supplies for the Northwestern band.[52] There is no indication in the records that the appeal met with any success.

1860

"Battle" of Bear River

As the emigrant trains continued to roll along the Oregon and California trails, resentment began to build among the Northern Shoshoni and Bannock as they watched their grasslands and game disappear. It became particularly strong when their women, children, and men were shot and killed by the white pioneers as though they were some kind of wild animals to be hunted along the way. Near Fort Hall, and especially west of Raft River and Shoshone Falls, the young men of the tribes began to strike back, raiding the wagon camps and returning with food and booty. By 1859 the correspondence of the commissioner of Indian Affairs reflected the growing menace to travelers, as westerners bombarded his office with appeals for military protection and for agents to go among the southern Idaho tribes to quiet them and get them away from the overland route.

1859

A recital of the many attacks or rumors of attacks on emigrants would be too tedious for the purposes of this narrative.[53] Closer to the point was the effect the rising crescendo of dissatisfaction had on relations between the Northern Shoshoni and the settlers in northern Utah. The several bands of the region watched with apprehension as the Mormon farmers continued to expand their holdings until the Malad, Bear Lake and Cache valleys were entirely filled with the homes, fields, and stock of the newcomers. The Indians became more and more demanding of food from the whites, understanding well the instructions the Saints had received from their prophet. The younger men in the tribes became bolder and began to raid the cattle and horse herds in Cache Valley, which invited follow-up attempts by the armed and exasperated owners of the stock.

1858   By 1858 attacks became so frequent and severe that many of the white families withdrew from the valley. Brigham Young finally instructed Peter Maughan in September of that year that a company of about forty men could return to the valley if they would build a strong fort and maintain a

1859 guard while others harvested the crops.[54] The following spring one group of Indians traveled to Salt Lake City on snowshoes because they had heard there was "to be a fight, and . . . they came to see about it."[55] Concerned officials like D. R. Eckels, chief justice of the Utah Supreme Court, wrote Washington that an agent should be appointed for the Shoshoni and Bannock or a general Indian war could not be avoided. This was in

1860 late 1859.[56] In May 1860 one Cache Valley citizen wrote that the Indians were very hostile and had already stolen $1,500 worth of horses from the

1861 inhabitants so far that year.[57] A settler on the Portneuf River in Idaho informed the Utah superintendent that the soldiers from Camp Floyd, stationed in his area the summer before, had only aroused the contempt of the Indians. He urgently requested that an agent be sent to deal with the warlike bands whose "appetites for blood and plunder appear to be sharpened."[58] The friendly chief, Little Soldier, warned of a general rising of the Shoshoni and Utes and said that the Gosiute bands of the Tooele and Rush valleys were joining in the robberies and demanding not

1862 only food but cooked meals from the frightened settlers.[59]

Indian leaders disposed to be friendly toward the whites came to be in the minority as the starvation of their peoples emboldened the more rash among them. By fall of 1862 the Mormon settlers discovered that when they went in pursuit of a herd of stolen horses it was no longer possible to talk to the Indian raiders and attempt to recover the stock by peaceful means. Instead, "the Indians immediately showed fight," and the white men were forced to withdraw.[60] Superintendent Doty requested that agents be stationed at Soda Springs or Fort Hall and that a military post be established at one of these spots at once.[61] The preceding Congress had made an appropriation for the purpose of negotiating treaties with the Fort Hall and Northwestern bands, and a commission was appointed consisting of Superintendent Doty,

Agent Luther Mann of Fort Bridger, and Special Agent Henry Martin.[62] Because of the lateness of the season, the meetings had to be postponed until the following summer. Doty suggested holding the treaty sessions near Fort Hall, which was the junction of the Oregon and California trails and also on the path to the newly opened gold mines in western Montana.[63]

The increased travel on the Montana Trail further heightened the difficulties between Utah authorities and the Northwestern Indians and led to intervention by the military. The Union government already had issued orders to raise troops in California to protect the western mail routes from Indian attack and, at least some thought, also to keep an eye on the Mormons during the Civil War. In the fall of 1862 Colonel Patrick Edward Connor and his California Volunteers marched into Nevada, where the Salt Lake City *Deseret News* took first notice of them — "The Indians will of course be tremendously scared, and horse-thieves, gamblers, and other pests of community wondrously attracted by the gigantic demonstration."[64] The approximately seven hundred troops had little interest in "freezing to death around sagebrush fires" when there was

L.D.S. Church Archives

General Patrick E. Connor

more honor to be won in fighting the Rebels in Virginia, and they petitioned the government to send them east.[65] The request went unheeded; Connor marched his troops to Salt Lake City, where Governor Stephen S. Harding greeted them with the statement that he was disappointed in their coming to the city and wondered what disposition was to be made of them.[66]

The army's tactics en route should have forewarned the governor. The Deseret News reported that in a number of small engagements with the Nevada Indians from the "nature of the orders . . . given by the Colonel commanding . . . it was but reasonable to suppose that all the natives found had been killed, whether innocent or guilty."[67] The situation in northern Utah was therefore ideal for a group of westerners looking for glory on the battlefield and for conflict with Indians who were considered nuisances at best. The Volunteers first tried to free a white boy held prisoner by the Northern Indians. The colonel sent word to Cache Valley that unless the captives were released he "would wipe every one of them out."[68] The Indians were just as belligerent, leading most citizens of Utah to believe they were eager for a battle with the troops.[69] This attitude was strengthened by the Volunteers' killing of four Indian hostages when some stolen horses were not returned to the white owners.[70]

1863 The stage was set for battle when some miners from Grasshopper Creek in Montana were killed by Indians while traveling through Cache Valley. The Utah chief justice issued a warrant for the arrest of Chiefs Bear Hunter, Sanpitch, and Sagwitch and asked the military to support the U.S. marshall in serving the warrant.[71] Fearing that the Indians might leave their camp and deprive the soldiers of a fight, Connor marched his troops at night. On the early morning of January 29, 1863, the Volunteers attacked the entrenched Indians across the ice-choked Bear River at Battle Creek, just north of Franklin, Idaho. At first the Indians

1863 were successful in driving back the soldiers, but a flanking attack soon turned the engagement into a massacre as the troops pursued the disorganized Indians, killing men, women, and children. According to some accounts the colonel had commanded, "Kill everything — nits make lice."[72]

The ruthlessness of the troops was revealed in the casualty figures: The California Volunteers suffered 22 deaths, while the number of Indians slain varied from the death count of 224 reported officially by Connor, to 255 reported by Superintendent Doty, to 368 recorded by James J. Hill and other Utah citizens who visited the battlefield the next day. The bodies of almost 90 women and children were noted. The troops also destroyed 70 tipis, captured 175 horses, and collected over 1,000 bushels of grain. Many of the articles

gathered from the Indian camp obviously came from emigrant trains.[73] The scalp of Bear Hunter was hung at Camp Douglas when the troops returned to their headquarters,[74] and the Deseret News thought the Volunteers had "done a larger amount of Indian killing than ever fell to the lot of any single expedition of which we have any knowledge."[75] When a Deseret News correspondent visited the site of the battlefield five years later he reported, "The bleached skeletons of scores of noble red men still ornament the grounds" and expressed regret that Pocatello and his "gang" had not also been annihilated in the massacre.[76]

Instead of cowing the Northwestern Shoshoni into submission, as some writers suggested, there is overwhelming evidence that the reverse happened. Mormon authorities reported that the Indians were now so angry with the soldiers that they intended to "steal and kill every white man they could find." The accounts prove they meant to do just that, although the bands were very careful to stay out of newly promoted General Connor's way when he started north to establish a military post, Camp Connor, at Soda Springs.[77] A petition came from Snake River miners asking Connor for protection;[78] another from Bannack City appealed for help;[79] and the Mormon settlers in Cache Valley became desperate as attacks and horse-stealing raids multiplied.[80] Ezra T. Benson wrote one of the Mormon officials asking for permission to strike back at the natives who, he said, "intend having their pay out of the Mormons as they are afraid to tackle the soldiers . . . while they are doing these things they are eating the very flour that has been donated to them by the brethren."[81]

Reports began to circulate in late April that General Connor intended to secure the emigrant routes by establishing his army post near Soda Springs and that Superintendent Doty was to accompany the expedition to establish his headquarters there, although the Idaho country "has not heretofore been included in the Utah Superintendency." Connor returned from his trip on June 3 after leaving a detachment of troops at Camp Connor and warning all Indians he met that they had better be good.[82]

Doty Treaties of 1863

The commissioner of Indian Affairs had already written Superintendent Doty some pious platitudes about the projected meetings with the Shoshoni of Utah, Wyoming, and Idaho. He did end his letter with the very commonsense observation that his office could not know the situation because of the long distance separating Washington, D.C. from Utah and thus would leave to Doty's judgment what must be done to bring peace to the settlements and trails.[83] The Oregon superintendent also wrote at length that he hoped the $20,000 appropriated by Congress in 1862 for negotiating the treaties would accomplish much good.[84] Doty accepted the geographical realities by deciding it would not be possible to bring all the Shoshoni tribes together in one grand council.[85] First he negotiated an oral agreement with Chief Little Soldier, who was then living in the mountains above Provo, Utah.[86] Most of the band was probably composed of "Weber Utes" by this time, although a few Northwestern Shoshoni may still have been with the chief. The *Deseret News* hoped that the treaty with Little Soldier augured well for the other pacts to be negotiated with the numerous Shoshoni.[87]

With help of Agent Luther Mann, Doty started an arduous summer's work of signing treaties with the five main Shoshoni groups. The two men first met with Washakie's tribe at Fort Bridger and signed a treaty on July 2, 1863. Then, with the help of General Connor, Doty gathered together ten Northwestern Shoshoni bands at Box Elder in Utah Territory and concluded the second treaty on July 30, 1863. The superintendent had been afraid Chief Pocatello would not be present and was relieved to have that much-feared warrior show up. In fact, Pocatello's people were so destitute and the chief was so anxious to participate that he had sent word he would give ten horses to prove his sincerity. The nine chiefs who signed the treaty were: Pocatello, Toomontso, Sanpitch, Tasowitz, Yahnoway, Weerahsoop, Pahragoosohd, Tahkwetoonah, and Omrshee. The tenth chief, Sagowitz, had been shot by a white "fiend" while the Indian leader was under arrest by the California Volunteers and was unable to leave his "weekeeup" but agreed to all the provisions.[88]

The treaty with the Northwestern Bands provided for $2,000 worth of provisions and goods at the time of signing. The other articles were the same as adopted for the Eastern Shoshoni: Friendly relations were re-established between the United States and the Shoshoni; routes of travel for emigrants were to be made safe, with permission being granted for the government to establish posts in Indian areas; telegraph, overland stage routes, and railroad rights-of-way could be granted through Indian territory; boundaries of the tribes were defined; and a final amendment provided that the Indians could have no greater title or interest in the lands involved than existed in them at the time they were acquired from Mexico under the terms of that country. In each of the five treaties Doty was able to get only a partial definition of the boundaries of the tribes, the Northwestern Bands agreeing to Raft River on the west and the "Porteneuf" Mountains on the east.

The Utah superintendent negotiated other treaties with the Western Shoshoni at Ruby Valley, Nevada Territory, on October 1, 1863; The Gosiute Shoshoni at Tuilla Valley, Utah Territory, on October 2, 1863; and the mixed bands of Bannock and Shoshoni at Soda Springs, Idaho Territory, on October 14, 1863. The last agreement was accepted by 150 men and their families under the Chiefs Tasokwauberaht (or Grand Coquin), Tahgee, and Matigund. The Fort Hall Shoshoni-Bannock agreed to the same provisions as contained in the treaties with the Eastern Shoshoni and the Northwestern Bands, and, in addition, agreed to keep safe the roads used by whites between Soda Springs and the Beaverhead mines and between Salt Lake City and the Boise River mines. The Indians received $3,000 in presents at the signing. Their boundaries were defined as extending from the lower part of Humboldt River and the Salmon Falls of Snake River to the Wind River Mountains. The amendment concerning claims under original Mexican law was included, although it was unnecessary because the Indians did not claim or occupy any territory south of the forty-second parallel.

Chief Tindooh (Tendoy) sent word that his people — the mixed bands of Shoshoni, Bannock, and Sheepeaters from the Lemhi River area — assented to the treaty and wished to be considered parties to it but that, because of the lateness of the season, they were forced to leave for their fall buffalo hunting in Montana. Doty had met both Tendoy's tribe and the Fort Hall Indians earlier in May and found them friendly and peaceable. The government agreed to pay the combined Shoshoni and Bannock under the four principal treaties $20,000 annually and the Gosiute Shoshoni $1,000 annually for a period of twenty years. The Northwestern Shoshoni were to receive $5,000 each year and the Eastern Shoshoni $10,000.

Using an official map of the General Land Office, Superintendent Doty drew in the boundaries encompassing the limits of territory claimed by the Shoshoni under the five treaties and sent it and the treaties to the commissioner of Indian Affairs for action by Congress. On March 7, 1864, the five treaties were ratified by the Senate, with the amendment concerning interest in the lands under Mexican law which became Article 7 of the treaty with the Eastern Shoshoni and Article 5 of the other treaties. The Western Shoshoni treaty was amended to grant this Nevada tribe $5,000 annually worth of goods for twenty years. In subsequent meetings the Eastern Shoshoni, Northwestern Shoshoni, Western Shoshoni, and Gosiute Shoshoni gave formal approval to the treaties.

1864

The government officials were never able to assemble the mixed bands of Bannock and Shoshoni to obtain their consent to the amendment to the treaty of Soda Springs voted by the Senate. It was an unfortunate occurrence because, as already pointed out, their homeland was not a part of the Mexican cession territory.[89]

Perhaps a quotation from the *Annual Report of the Commissioner of Indian Affairs* for the year 1863 best sums up the condition of all the Shoshoni at the time they signed the above treaties:

> The scarcity of game in these Territories, and the occupation of the most fertile portions thereof by our settlements, have reduced these Indians to a state of extreme destitution, and for several years past they have been almost literally compelled to resort to plunder in order to obtain the necessaries of life. It is not to be expected that a wild and warlike people will tamely submit to the occupation of their country by another race, and to starvation as a consequence thereof.[90]

The Doty treaties did not establish a treaty relationship with the government for the Northern Shoshoni portion of the Shoshoni tribes. As already indicated, the treaty with the Fort Hall and Lemhi group was never ratified, and in later years the government failed to honor the annuity payments to the Northwestern bands.

Of all the Northwestern leaders party to the Treaty of Box Elder, Chief Pocatello contrived to be the main concern of the military and civil authorities. Ben Holladay had established a stage line from Salt Lake City to the new mines in western Montana and complained to General Patrick E. Connor at Camp Douglas about the threatening activities of Pocatello's band along the stage line through Marsh and Portneuf valleys in Idaho. Thereupon the general arrested Pocatello. Connor's rather prompt action brought another letter from Holladay explaining that the allegations against the Indian leader were not as serious as he had supposed, so Connor wrote Utah Indian Superintendent O. H. Irish that he was transferring Pocatello to his care. Irish concluded the incident by releasing the chief with instructions to find the Northwestern bands, who had fled to the mountains with the promise of going to war if General Connor hanged Pocatello as threatened. Irish planned to meet the Indians in council as soon as Pocatello could get them together and wrote, with some asperity, to the commissioner, "If the Military Authorities will allow me to manage these Indians without any further interference, I am satisfied that by a judicious use of the appropriations made I can maintain peace."[91]

The superintendent met the Northwestern bands a couple of weeks later, submitted the amendments to the Box Elder Treaty to them, and distributed $3,000 worth of provisions and goods. He requested that the balance of $2,000 due under the treaty for annuity supplies be sent to him for distribution of food during the winter. He reported that, whereas the tribe had been the most troublesome Indians in the Utah Superintendency in the past, they were now "remarkably well disposed" toward the government and were particulary pleased with the release of Pocatello and the distribution of presents to them.

Irish's only worry was that the Indians belonging to neighboring superintendencies, including Idaho, would cross the unseen borders during the hard winter months seeking to share in the food and subsistence provided for the Utah Indians.[92] This fear was particularly relevant concerning the Fort Hall Indians, who were closely related to the Northwestern Shoshoni and only a few miles away from their wintering grounds. Irish recommended that a reservation be established for the Shoshoni of Utah where they could learn the art of farming, pointing out that wild game was fast disappearing and that "the old hunting grounds are occupied by our people to their exclusion."[93] The only alternatives were either to support the Indians in idleness or allow them to prey upon the emigrant trains. He thought it more economical to found reservations.

As the next autumn approached Superintendent Irish began the annual mental ordeal of all Indian agents, wondering whether the annuity goods would arrive before the winter snows blocked the freight-wagon trains. If not, his only recourse was to obtain food and supplies from the local merchants until the annuity provisions came in. Fortunately the goods were delivered on time, and the governor, in late October 1865, accompanied Superintendent Irish to Box Elder to witness the distribution of presents to the Northwestern Shoshoni, who received them "with much satisfaction."[94] In his annual report Irish enumerated three bands under Chief Pocatello, Black Beard, and Sanpitch and advised that the approximately fifteen hundred Northwestern Shoshoni ranged more in Idaho Territory than in Utah and probably should be the responsibility of the Idaho superintendent. He said, "They suffer frequently from hunger" and indicated that he had had to feed them quite frequently during the past winter. He explained that he had been able to make an arrangement with some of the citizens of the northern counties to employ Black Beard and his band to herd cattle in return for flour and beef. With what few supplies he could furnish the Indians they were able to survive the winter storms.[95]

The following year Pocatello and Black Beard joined with Washakie's people on their annual buffalo hunt, which pleased the Mormon settlers even more than it did the Indian superintendent. One correspondent wrote the *Deseret News* in August that Washakie's band had come into

1864

1865

1866

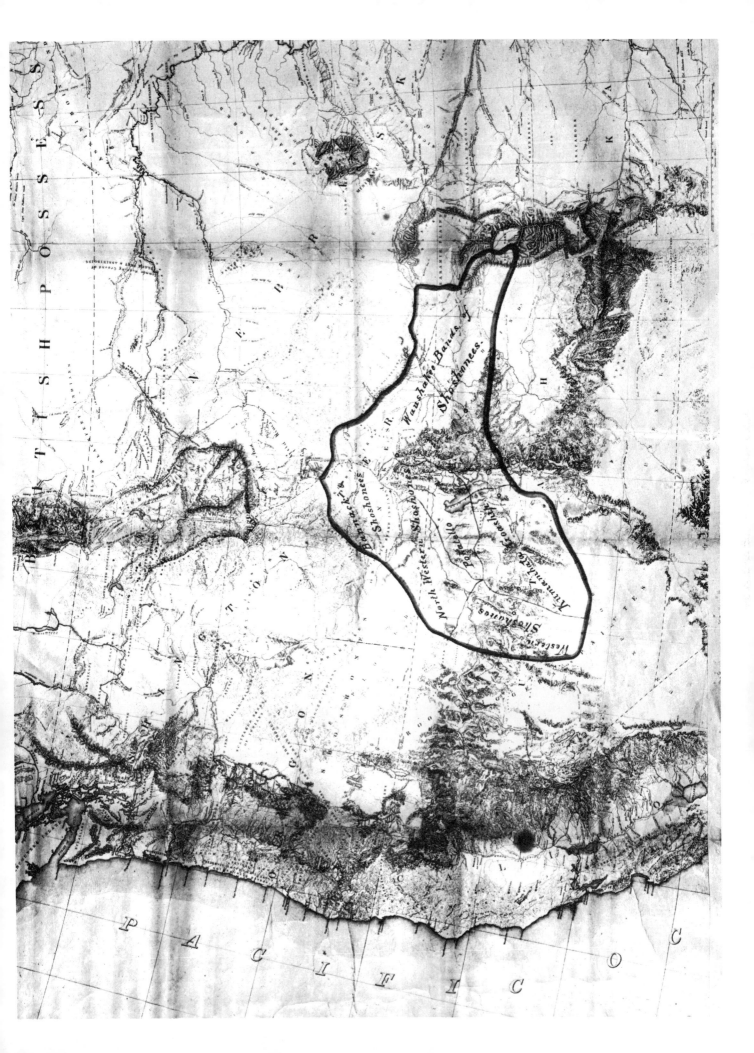

Huntsville, Utah, in the mountains east of Ogden, where the settlers felt constrained to observe the Indian scalp dance in the public square, after which the following donations of food were made to the Indians: four beeves, nine sheep, several sacks of flour, and about seventy-five bushels of potatoes, carrots, beets, turnips, etc. The Indians then departed, which led the writer to conclude, "though their company is very agreeable, our philanthropy is so large that we are willing their presence should benefit other settlements as well as ours."[96] Superintendent Irish explained that the $5,000 annuity was sufficient to clothe them, but he was forced to supplement whatever food the Indians could get from the Mormon people with additional supplies from his meager appropriation.[97] One of the settlers at Clarkston, Cache County, recorded that some of the people were forced to move in to the larger settlement of Smithfield for protection during the winter of 1866. He reported as many as "twenty wigwams pitched at one time in City Creek hollow."[98]

1866

To make matters worse, the Northwestern Shoshoni were forced to share their small annuity of $5,000 with the mixed or "broken band of Bannock and Shoshonees," whom the Utah superintendent, F. H. Head, estimated to number fifteen hundred Shoshoni and a thousand Bannock. The Treaty of Soda Springs stipulated that these Indians were to share in the $10,000 and $5,000 annuities provided, respectively, for the Eastern and Northwestern Shoshoni. The superintendent pointed out the unfairness of the treaty article which, in effect, reduced the annuity for the latter two tribes. When approached with this proposal, Washakie "evidently and sensibly objected to such arrangement." Head did invite a portion of the mixed bands (later identified properly as the Fort Hall Shoshoni and Bannock) to be present and share in the annuities of the Northwestern group. He also found $2,000, with which he provided other supplies to the Fort Hall Indians, and he applied for $5,000 in his next year's budget for their subsistence. The mixed bands very properly came under the Idaho Superintendency, but at this time they were de facto charges of the Utah officials. Salt Lake City was not only closer than Boise, but over the years the Fort Hall Indians had come to look southward for help from the Great Father.[99] The commissioner endorsed the proposal for a $5,000 annuity for the Fort Hall Indians and passed it on to the secretary of the Interior and Congress for action.[100]

1867

By 1868, although there were rumors that Idaho authorities were beginning to take action to find a permanent home for the Fort Hall and Northwestern Shoshoni, Utah Indian officials were still faced with the problem of subsisting all

1868

the latter group and a portion of the former. No Indian agent had yet undertaken the formidable task of trying to make farmers out of the Northwestern Indians, who were willing to be stockmen but not agriculturists. Superintendent Head gave them sixteen cows as breeding stock and was reassured a few months later when he discovered that they had not eaten any of the cattle. The poverty of the tribe was somewhat revealed by the fact that, although there were an estimated eighteen hundred individuals in the several bands, they possessed only one hundred sixty-six horses compared to an Eastern Shoshoni population of two thousand who owned seven hundred horses.[101]

Brigham Young's dictum of "feed rather than fight" the natives was still operative, but some Mormons had doubts. J. C. Wright wrote the Deseret News in September 1868 severely criticizing the wisdom of signing the Treaty of Box Elder with "six or eight little one-horse-power, self-made chiefs — the biggest rowdies, robbers, and rascals in the whole nation." The writer indicated that the Indian practice was to assemble at Brigham City about a month prior to the annuity payment. The five or six hundred Indians then levied a tax on the Mormon settlers by begging and stealing everything in sight. Wright estimated the amount of goods stolen in Box Elder County in 1868 would reach fifteen hundred bushels of wheat, worth $3,000; five hundred bushels of corn, worth $750; $1,000 worth of oats, barley, squash, and potatoes; with another $1,000 for horses and other property taken; and $2,000 for the materials obtained through begging — a total of about $8,000. He concluded that it would be better for the citizens of the county to pay the $5,000 annuity out of their own pockets, which might enable them to continue their peaceful relations with the Indians.[102]

The Utah Agents and the Mormon people tried hard during the years from 1847 to 1863 to care for the wants of the Shoshoni of northern Utah and southeastern Idaho, many of whom had been dispossessed of their lands and staple foods by the white pioneers. The task exceeded the capabilities of the new settlers and government officials. The problem was not helped by the squadrons of emigrants in their covered wagons which traversed the Oregon and California trails through these regions during the period. In desperation the natives struck back at both settlements and wagon parties, until a neglectful government was forced to intervene with some half-hearted treaties which did not provide the means for settling the Northern Shoshoni on lands of their own or for subsisting them while they learned to farm. The gold discoveries in Idaho and Montana had the merit of at least bringing in new territorial governments, dividing the responsibilities in caring for the Indian inhabitants and leaving only the Northwestern branch of the Northern Shoshoni to the care of Utah officials.

NOTES CHAPTER II
UTAH NEIGHBORS

1. Young, *Manuscript History*, Feb. 1850.
2. Young, *Message to the Legislative Assembly of the Territory of Utah*, Fillmore City, Utah Terr., Dec. 11, 1855, 53.
3. Young, *Manuscript History*, May 30, 1852, 53.
4. Ibid., Oct. 31, 1858, 1057.
5. Young, *Indian Affairs, Indian Correspondence*, Nov. 2, 1857.
6. Young, "Proclamation, G.S.L. City, July 21, 1851," U.S. National Archives, *Letters Received by the Office of Indian Affairs, 1849–1855, Utah Superintendency*, Roll 897.
7. F. A. Bedell to Brigham Young, Indian Agency Office, Ty., April 6, 1854, ibid.
8. James Duane Doty to C.I.A., Great Salt Lake City, July 30, 1862, ibid.
9. Young, *Indian Affairs, Miscellaneous Correspondence*, July 9, 1858.
10. Ibid., Aug. 13, 1851.
11. A. J. Center to C.I.A., New York, Nov. 19, 1861, U.S. National Archives, *Letters Received by the Office of Indian Affairs, 1861–1862, Utah Superintendency*, Roll 900.
12. J. H. Holeman to Brigham Young, Great Salt Lake City, Sept. 30, 1853. U.S. National Archives, *Letters Received by the Office of Indian Affairs, 1849–1855, Utah Superintendency*, Roll 897.
13. *Journal History*, Aug. 27, 1855.
14. Young, *Indian Affairs, Miscellaneous Papers*, May 24, 1852.
15. *Journal History*, May 21, 1853.
16. Ibid., Sept. 15, 1857.
17. Young, *Indian Affairs, Indian Correspondence*, 1858.
18. Ibid., April 6, 1854.
19. *Deseret News*, Nov. 14, 1860, 296.
20. John B. Floyd, Secretary of War, to J. Thompson, Secretary of the Interior, Jan. 23, 1860, U.S. National Archives, *Letters Received by the Office Affairs, 1859–1860, Utah Superintendency*, Roll 899.
21. F. W. Lander to C.I.A., Feb. 18, 1860, ibid.
22. J. H. Holeman to Brigham Young, Great Salt Lake City, Nov. 10, 1851, U.S. National Archives, *Letters Received by the Office of Indian Affairs, 1849–1855, Utah Superintendency*, Roll 897.
23. Brigham Young to C.I.A., Great Salt Lake City, Sept. 29, 1852, ibid.
24. Jacob Forney to C.I.A., Fort Bridger, Utah Territory, May 21, 1858, U.S. National Archives, *Letters Received by the Office of Indian Affairs, 1856–58, Utah Superintendency*, Roll 898.
25. Young, *Indian Affairs, Indian Correspondence*, Aug. 15, 1854.
26. Brigham Young to C.I.A., Salt Lake City, Utah, Aug. 30, Sept. 30, 1856, U.S. National Archives, *Letters Received by the Office of Indian Affairs, 1856–1858, Utah Superintendency*, Roll 898.
27. F. W. Lander to C.I.A., Washington, D.C., Feb. 18, March 23, 1859, ibid.
28. Henry Martin to C.I.A., July 19, July 22, Oct. 9, 15, Dec. 9, 1862, U.S. National Archives, *Letters Received by the Office of Indian Affairs, 1861–62, Utah Superintendency*, Roll 900.
29. James Duane Doty to C.I.A., Great Salt Lake City, Aug. 25, 1862, ibid.
30. Jame Duane Doty to C.I.A., Great Salt Lake City, Nov. 26, 1862, ibid.
31. Brigham Young to C.I.A., Great Salt Lake City, June 30, 1855, U.S. National Archives, *Letters Received by the Office of Indian Affairs, 1849–1855, Utah Superintendency*, Roll 897; *Journal History*, June 30, 1855.
32. Jacob Forney to C.I.A., Great Salt Lake City, Feb. 15, 1859, U.S. National Archives, *Letters Received by the Office of Indian Affairs, 1859–1860, Utah Superintendency*, Roll 899.
33. Young, *Manuscript History*, July 10, 1851.
34. *Deseret News* Sept. 21, 1850.
35. Young, *Indian Affairs, Stephen B. Rose Correspondence*, March 31, 1852.
36. Young, *Indian Affairs, Miscellaneous Correspondence*, Sept. 22, 1854.
37. Young, *Indian Affairs, J. H. Holeman Correspondence, 1851–1853*, Nov. 10, 1851.
38. Ibid., March 30, 1853.
39. Young, *Manuscript History*, Sept. 4, 1854; *Journal History*, Aug. 23, 1855.
40. Young, *Indian Affairs, Miscellaneous Correspondence*, Nov. 21, 1854.
41. Brigham Young to James W. Denver, C.I.A., G.S.L. City, Sept. 12, 1857, U.S. National Archives, *Letters Received by the Office of Indian Affairs, 1856–1858, Utah Superintendency*, Roll 898.
42. Young, *Journal History*, July 24, 1856.
43. Young, *Indian Affairs, Miscellaneous Licenses, Permits, etc., 1854–1856*, Jan. 15, 1855; "Affidavit, Great Salt Lake City, Sept. 20, 1860," U.S. National Archives, *Letters Received by the Office of Indian Affairs, 1861–1862, Utah Superintendency*, Roll 900.
44. Young, *Manuscript History*, May 19, 1862.
45. Ibid., April 1, 1861.
46. James Duane Doty to C.I.A., Great Salt Lake City, April 15, 1862, U.S. National Archives, *Letters Received by the Office of Indian Affairs, 1861–1862, Utah Superintendency*, Roll 900.
47. Jacob Forney to C.I.A., Washington, D.C., Feb. 27, 1860, U.S. National Archives, *Letters Received by the Office of Indian Affairs, 1859–1860, Utah Superintendency*, Roll 899.
48. Jacob Forney to C.I.A., Great Salt Lake City, Feb. 15, 1859, ibid.; Jacob Forney to C.I.A., Great Salt Lake City, Jan. 20, 1861, *Letters Received by the Office of Indian Affairs, 1861–62, Utah Superintendency*, Roll 900.
49. Young, *Indian Affairs, Indian Correspondence*, March 10, 22, 1858; Jacob Forney to C.I.A., Camp Scott, Green River County, Utah Territory, Dec. 4, 1857, and March 11, 1858, U.S. National Archives, *Letters Received by the Office of Indian Affairs, 1856–1868, Utah Superintendency*, Roll 898.
50. Jacob Forney to C.I.A., Fort Bridger, April 17, 1858, ibid.
51. Young, *Manuscript History*, April 9, 1858.
52. F. W. Lander to C.I.A., Washington D.C., Feb. 18, 1860, U.S. National Archives, *Letters Received by the Office of Indian Affairs, 1859–1860, Utah Superintendency*, Roll 899.
53. Brigham D. Madsen, "Shoshoni-Bannock Marauders on the Oregon Trail, 1859–1863," *Utah Historical Quarterly*, Vol. 35, No. 1 (Winter 1967), 3–30.
54. Young, *Manuscript History*, Sept. 23, 1858.
55. Ibid., April 2, 1859.
56. D. R. Eckels to Secretary of Interior, Camp Floyd, Utah Territory, Sept. 23, 1859, U.S. National Archives, *Letters Received by the Office of Indian Affairs, 1859–1860, Utah Superintendency*, Roll 899.
57. Young, *Manuscript History*, May 4, 1860.
58. Henri M. Chase to Col. B. Davis, Superintendent of Indian Affairs, Utah Territory, Port Neuf, Snake River Canyon, May 5, 1861, U.S. National Archives, *Letters Received by the Office of Indian Affairs, 1861–1862, Utah Superintendency*, Roll 900.
59. James Duane Doty to C.I.A., Great Salt Lake City, Aug. 13, 1862, ibid.
60. *Deseret News* Oct. 8, 1862.
61. James Duane Doty to C.I.A., Great Salt Lake City, Sept. 16, 1862, U.S. National Archives, *Letters Received by the Office of Indian Affairs, 1861–1862, Utah Superintendency*, Roll 900.
62. William P. Dole, C.I.A., to Caleb B. Smith, Secretary of the Interior, Washington, D.C., Nov. 26, 1862, *Report of C.I.A., 1862*, 32.
63. Jame Duane Doty to C.I.A., Great Salt Lake City, November 26, 1862, U.S. National Archives, *Letters Received by the Office of Indian Affairs, 1861–1862, Utah Superintendency*, Roll 900.
64. *Deseret News*, June 25, 1862.
65. Ibid., Oct. 15, 1862.
66. Ibid., Oct. 22, 1862.
67. Ibid., Nov. 19, 1862.
68. Young, *Manuscript History*, Nov. 25, 1862.
69. *Deseret News*, Dec. 10, 1862.
70. Ibid., Dec. 17, 1862.
71. Ibid., Jan. 28, 1863.
72. Hull, *Autobiography*, 2.
73. There are numerous accounts of the Battle of Bear River. See Rogers, *Soldiers of the Overland*; Tullidge, *History of Salt Lake City; War of the Rebellion*, Series I, Vol. L, Pt. 1; *Deseret News*, Feb. 11, 1863; Daughters of Utah Pioneers, "Testimony of Daniel B. Richards taken from Hill Family Record," 222–225; James Duane Doty to C.I.A., Great Salt Lake City, Feb. 16, 1863, U.S. National Archives, *Letters Received by the Office of Indian Affairs, 1863–1865, Utah Superintendency*, Roll 901; Madsen, *The Bannock of Idaho*, 111-139; Barta, "Battle Creek: The Battle of Bear River," M. A. thesis, Idaho State College, 1962.
74. Young, *Manuscript History*, Feb. 3, 1863.
75. *Deseret News*, Feb. 4, 1863.
76. Ibid., May 20, 1868.
77. Ibid., April 1, May 20, 1863; Young, *Manuscript History*, Feb. 8, 1863.
78. Eight Citizens to Gov. W. H. Wallace of Idaho Terr., Nov. 23, 1863, Idaho State University Archives, Ms. 249.
79. Idaho State University Archives, Ms. 249.
80. Young, *Manuscript History*, April 12, 1863.
81. Ezra T. Benson to Daniel H. Wells, Logan, Utah, May 9, 1863, Utah State Historical Society, Military Records, Ms.
82. *Deseret News*, April 29, May 6, June 3, 1863.
83. William P. Dole to James Duane Doty, Letter Books, C.I.A., Vol. 70, 475.
84. J. W. Huntington to C.I.A., Salem, Oregon, June 1, 1863, U.S. National Archives, *Letters Received by the Office of Indian Affairs, 1863–1865, Utah Superintendency*, Roll 901.
85. James Duane Doty to C.I.A., Utah Territory, June 20, 1863, ibid.
86. James Duane Doty to C.I.A., Great Salt Lake City, July 18, 1863, ibid.
87. *Deseret News*, July 1, 1863.
88. James Duane Doty to C.I.A., Great Salt Lake City, Nov. 10, 1863, U.S. National Archives, *Letters Received by the Office of Indian Affairs, 1863–1865, Utah Superintendency*, Roll 901; Alvin Nichols to James Duane Doty, Brigham City, July 11, 1863, *Utah Superintendency Files*, (field records), Misc. 1862–3–4, Unprinted Record; *Deseret News*, Aug. 5, 1863.
89. Kappler, *Indian Affairs Laws and Treaties*, Vol. II 848-851; U.S. Court of Claims, *The Northwestern Band or Tribe of Shoshoni Indians and the Individual Members Thereof, v. The United States, Plaintiff Indians' Request for Findings of Fact, and Brief*, No. M-107, filed December 29, 1939; James Duane Doty to C.I.A., Great Salt Lake City, Nov. 10, 1863, U.S. National Archives, *Letters Received by the Office of Indian Affairs, 1863–1865, Utah Superintendency*, Roll 901; *Report to the C.I.A.*, Oct. 31, 1863; *Deseret News*, Oct. 14, 1863.
90. *Report of the C.I.A.*, Oct. 31, 1863, 37–38; see balance of this chapter and Chapter VI.
91. O. H. Irish to C.I.A., Great Salt Lake City, Nov. 9, 1864, U.S. National Archives, *Letters Received by the Office of Indian Affairs, 1863–1865, Utah Superintendency*, Roll 901.
92. O. H. Irish to C.I.A., Great Salt Lake City, Nov. 22, Dec. 9, 1864, ibid.
93. *Report of the C.I.A.*, Nov. 15, 1864, 315.
94. *Deseret News*, Nov. 2, 1865; O. H. Irish to C.I.A., Great Salt Lake City Oct. 9, 1865, U.S. National Archives, *Letters Received by the Office of Indian Affairs, 1863–1865, Utah Superintendency*, Roll 901.

95. *Report of the C.I.A., 1865*, 144.
96. *Deseret News*, Aug. 30, 1866.
97. *Report of the C.I.A., 1866*, 123.
98. Heggie, *Story of the Shoshoni Indians in Clarkston*.
99. *Report of the C.I.A., 1867*.

100. F. H. Head to C.I.A., Wash., D.C., Feb. 12, 1868, U.S. National Archives, *Letters Received, Utah*.
101. *Report of the C.I.A., 1868*, 151–153.
102. *Deseret News*, Sept 15, 1868.

CHAPTER III

A RESERVATION AT FORT HALL

Boise and Bruneau Treaties

After many years of looking to Salt Lake City for guidance concerning the wishes of the federal government, the Indians along Snake River were placed under a new government with the creation of Idaho Territory by the Organic Act of March 1863 3, 1863. William H. Wallace, the first governor, arrived at Lewiston, the capital, on July 10, 1863. The commissioner of Indian Affairs already had sent him information that the government had treaties with the Nez Perce, who received an annual appropriation of $26,600; with the Flatheads, who received $20,000; and with the Blackfeet, who were to receive three more payments of $35,000 each. The last two tribes came under Montana Territory with its creation the following year. Wallace was to acquaint himself with the Indian tribes and send an estimate of funds needed for his office as ex-officio superintendent of Indian Affairs. The commissioner hoped it would no longer be necessary for him to receive "such reports of fraud and neglect on the part of the government officials under your charge as appear to have characterized some of those who have heretofore been placed in charge of the interests of the Indians in that country. . . ." It was most important that Governor Wallace first make a tour of the territory to observe the needs of the Indians.[1]

The first governor was in Idaho hardly long enough to turn around before he was named delegate to Congress and left for Washington, D.C. Idaho's next governor was "Caleb Lyon of Lyonsdale," a rather erratic and picturesque character 1864 who assumed office in 1864. The commissioner wrote him a letter almost identical to that sent his predecessor. Lyon was to make a tour, negotiate treaties where necessary, locate possible reservation sites, and send all pertinent information concerning Indian affairs in Idaho because the commissioner had no more recent knowledge than that contained in his annual report of 1862.[2] It seemed as though all facts concerning southern Idaho Indians gained by Utah Indian officials had been lost, and the Office of Indian Affairs had to start over. In 1859 F. W. Lander had designated two Shoshoni groups as Kammas-prairie and Fort Boise Pannacks, the latter being under Chief Po-e-ma-che-oh or Hairy Man.[3] By 1865 Idaho officials were able to

discriminate to the extent of listing one thousand Boise Shoshonees and two thousand Kammas Prairie Shoshonees as the main tribes in southern Idaho.[4]

For residents of the newly named capital at Boise City, Governor Lyon's most important act was the negotiation of a treaty on October 10, 1864, with the Indians along Boise River. It was a grandiloquent affair in which twenty-three leading Indians agreed to give up title to all lands lying thirty miles on each side of Boise River and to all the land drained by the tributaries of that stream "from its mouth it its Source." In return the government agreed to set apart a reservation on the river or at some other place to be designated later. The Indians were to have equal rights with the citizens of the United States to fish the streams. The Shoshoni also agreed to surrender all murderers, horse thieves, and other violators of the law among them to the authorities of the United States.[5] The *Idaho Statesman* was ecstatic and praised the governor for his "prompt and energetic action" in bringing together the 283 Indians under their head chief, "Tam Tomeco." The editor doubted that the tribe would cease its "murder and plunder" but rejoiced that at least a *legal* extinction of their title to the land had been achieved.[6]

The commissioner was not fulsome in his praise and reported that Lyon had made "a kind of preliminary treaty agreement" by which the government on fulfillment of "certain rather loosely defined conditions" would gain a large portion of southwestern Idaho from the Indians. Because the treaty was not in proper condition to be submitted to the Senate, the commissioner said he would ask Governor Lyon to repeat the performance and draw up a proper, legal document. "Caleb of Dale," as some unfriendly newspapers were beginning to call him, also reported to Washington that there was a tribe of Kammas Prairie Indians at Fort Hall who had signed a treaty under the direction of Governor Doty of Utah and who were very desirous of getting a reservation as a permanent home.[7] To bring these Indians under control, the governor, on December 10, 1865, appointed A. G. Turner to be 1865 special agent for all the natives at the headwaters of the Snake River and at the Goose Creek Mountains.[8]

The rush to the Boise gold mines and the rapid growth of the Boise region aroused increased hostility on the part of the Shoshoni along Snake River. The year 1865 witnessed a number of attacks by Indians on whites, followed by retaliation from citizen soldiers or by troops from Fort Boise. In February a detachment from the fort killed ten Indians and took others captive. Another force of men headed for the Owyhee River, where it was reported that the Indians were in possession of 450 sheep and a number of horses and cattle taken from the settlers. About three weeks later a party of settlers searching for Indians came upon two in a camp and shot them down. The *Idaho Statesman* approved and thought something should be done "to wipe out the Indians that infest the Owyhee country."[9]

In other incidents through the summer and fall, two white cattlemen lost eleven oxen to Indian raids; soldiers were dispatched to protect the overland road near Salmon Falls and Rock Creek; two white families were killed on the Owyhee River; in an attack on Rock Creek Stage Station three Indians were killed; and in a late November raid a half dozen Indians attacked and killed a white man and ran off fifteen head of stock. Pressure was mounting among the white settlers to get rid of the Indians in the Boise area by any means, placing them on a reservation if possible or exterminating them if there were no other way.[10]

1865   While some of the Indians along the lower Snake River were harassing the settlers, the Shoshoni and Bannock at Fort Hall were quite peaceful but wondering what had happened to the wonderful promises given them by government officials at the Treaty of Soda Springs. M. A. Carter, recorder and auditor of Oneida County at Soda Springs, wrote two letters in behalf of the Indians asking for the appointment of agents and traders and for the fulfillment of the treaty stipulations. The first letter was addressed to J. M. Ashley, a member of the House of Representatives, pointing out that the Bannock, six hundred in number, were friendly despite "many circumstances which would have aggravated Indians of less kind feelings to open hostility. Namely, the neglect of the Gov't to provide them an agent." He continued that the treaty obligations of 1863 never had been carried out, a circumstance which the Indians could not understand: "They have not received what has been solemnly promised to them."[11] Carter then wrote Governor Lyon that their chief, "Tigee," took his people to Camp Connor to trade their furs. He said Tahgee would have the tribe there next spring in hopes that the governor would meet with them to explain the intentions of the government. If this were not accomplished, Carter

feared the "calamities" which might come to the citizens of the Soda Springs area.[12]

Governor Lyon aroused so much controversy with his defense of the Indians and in quarrels with some of the leading citizens, including James Reynolds, editor of the Boise *Idaho Statesman*, that his chance of earning any tenure in the Idaho position seemed little short of miraculous. In a letter to the secretary of the Interior on February 17, 1866, he attacked Senator James W. Nesmith   1866 of Oregon for his proposal to the people to "kill all Indians wherever they can be found." The governor added that the Idaho settlers were listening to "Bar Room advice" to murder, scalp, and rob Indians and use them for "revolver practice." He included a clipping from the *Owyhee Avalanche* which reported a meeting of citizens who chose twenty-five men to go Indian hunting and offered bounties of $100 for an Indian man's scalp, $50 for a woman's scalp, and $25 for the scalps of children under ten years of age, provided that "each scalp shall have the curl of the head."[13] The *Idaho Statesman* printed a copy of the letter, changing the closing salutation from "with burning indignation" to "with cursing indignation" and concluded that Lyon, "as much a villain as a fool," was already virtually removed from office.[14]

The main controversy between the governor and his constituents revolved around the issue of Indian attacks and settler retaliations, which worsened during 1866. When Captain J. H. Walker and his troops came upon an Indian camp in late February they attacked and killed eighteen Indians, including six women and children. The captain reported that the Indians "fought with desperation asking no quarter" and was quoted by the *Idaho Statesman* as wanting "no better sport" than to set out on another such expedition. Until November, attack and counterattack were the order of the day. The letter-writing war between Lyon and Reynolds continued. The governor charged the editor, "than whom a greater scoundrel never lived," with inciting the massacre of sixteen friendly Indians at Mores Creek, of whom fourteen were women and children. Reynolds had written, "We long to see this vile race exterminated. Every man who kills an Indian is a public benefactor." The editor claimed the whole story was a lie but admitted he had advocated the extermination of all Indians in the area known to be inhabited by hostile bands.

The seesaw conflict continued through the summer and fall. On June 5 an army detachment killed seven Indians; eleven days later some Indians killed a white man, using a shovel; on July 7 two hundred and fifty Indians surrounded thirty-five whites, who finally escaped untouched; on September 4 a military expedition killed thirty

Indians in the Goose Creek Mountains; on November 8 four Indians were slain after stealing grain from Fort Boise; late in November the Indians ran off three hundred head of stock and then killed a white man.[15] Finally, in December, the new governor, David W. Ballard, called for the formation of a militia.[16] The total killed seemed to favor the firepower of the army over "lo," as the newspapers liked to call the Indians.

It was a bloody year, and it left the peaceful Indians afraid to leave camp for their usual hunts and food-gathering activities. Special Agent George C. Hough reported concerning the Bruneau Shoshoni on August 31, 1866:

And from the fact that so many depredations have been committed on the whites by the Py-Utes and outlawed Shoshones . . . teamsters, packers, herders, ranchers, and miners all over the country have become exasperated, and through fear, and in some cases a fear from mere wantonness, shoot Indians at sight. As a consequence the Indians do not roam over the country and hunt and trap so as to supply themselves with clothing and food as they did previous to the settlement of the country by the whites.

As a consequence they are reduced to remaining in considerable parties, and that immediate along the streams, and depending entirely on fishing for a living, and should the salmon be scarce (as there is every prospect they will be), unless the government assist those Indians with clothing, bedding, and provisions, they certainly must freeze and starve to death during the coming winter.[17]

Hough concluded that the Boise Shoshoni and the "Kammas" bands were just as destitute.

The Bruneau band of about three hundred people had received a treaty from Caleb Lyon on April 10, 1866. The document was signed by forty-one of the Indian leaders. Speaking for the tribe, Subchief Always Ready agreed to surrender the land south of Snake River between Goose Creek and the Owyhee River in return for a promise that the fourteen-mile-long Bruneau Valley be reserved for the Indians. Always Ready complained that

our brothers are killed, our women are killed for crimes we did not do. Stop this and we are your friends. We will give you the country where white men now live, but leave us in peace where we are. We do not lie, murder, nor steal. We want to be at peace, for ever at peace.

Chief Biting Bear (more accurately known as Annoyed Bear or Irritated Bear) was even more incisive, "We know there are bad white man as well as bad red men. Cannot the Great Father at Washington make them good." The seven articles of the treaty included a proposed payment of $80,000 for the above cession; a provision that a farmer, a physician, teachers, and other personnel be assigned to the reservation; and the usual admonitions about surrendering individuals accused of breaking the white man's law. Neither the Boise nor Bruneau treaty was ever ratified.[18]

Indian-White Hostilities in Boise Region

Governor Lyon soon abandoned the territory, leaving his acting secretary to take care of Indian affairs in Idaho. The secretary said he did not feel authorized to go beyond merely promising the Indians they would not be molested or disturbed as long as they remained where they were. With citizen scalp-hunters and glory-seeking army units roaming the countryside, the Bruneau did not need that advice.[19] Governor Ballard wrote in July 1866 that, although he had heard of the treaty and it had been sent to the Senate for confirmation, he could find no evidence of it in the Idaho Indian Office and had no idea what the terms were.[20] Major Marshall from Fort Boise also visited the Bruneau shortly after the treaty council and reported that the Indians had no cattle and few horses and were "nearly destitute of everything except what they obtain by fishing."[21] Governor Ballard could testify to the poverty of these people when, on his visit in October, they shared with him all the food they had, "salmon trout fried on a stick."[22]

Government officials, and Indians were by this time all agreed that a reservation should be established as a home for the wandering tribes, albeit the reasons were somewhat different for each group. The *Idaho Statesman* had exhorted Governor Lyon to set apart a reservation between Salmon Falls and the mouth of the Bruneau River extending south to the Nevada line. There were no settlers in the area, there was little inducement for whites to go there, and it would therefore be a *suitable* place for the Indians. The governor was advised to give up his insane idea of planting a reservation in the midst of thick settlements along the Boise River.[23]

By August Governor Ballard was instructing Agent Hough to visit the Bruneau Indians, learn their wishes about a reservation, and examine the area along that river for a possible site. The Commissioner agreed, suggesting that the governor make arrangements to confer with the Indians of southwestern Idaho and locate a proper reservation for them. Word was sent to Washington that the instructions would be carried out at the "earliest convenience."[24] Agent Hough was convinced that the Bruneau area was not suitable and that the reservation should be placed on the Malad, Shoshoni (Snake), or Payette rivers, with the region around Fort Hall being the most practicable and economical site.[25]

When George C. Hough had been appointed special agent at the request of Governor Ballard, the commissioner had written similar letters to the two men explaining that the Washington office was in "a lamentable state of ignorance in regard to Indian affairs in your territory, resulting from the failure of your [Ballard's] predecessor to furnish the current information required."[26] With his trip to Bruneau land behind him, Hough set out to investigate a possible reservation location on Payette River. He found the valley to be about sixty to eighty miles long and well-adapted to farming. He discovered that the Shoshoni claimed the south fork of the Payette and just missed visiting with the seventy-five or hundred Shoshoni Indians who lived in Payette Valley. The agent was told that the band was friendly and probably could be induced to settle on a reserve.[27]

Hough had not had to make a special effort to visit the Boise Shoshoni. They were practically underfoot, since Governor Lyon had brought them to Fort Boise in February to place them under the protection of the military. He reported them to be "in a very destitute condition," subsisting on fish, raiding farmers' fields, taking timber for fish traps and firewood, begging food from the citizens of Boise, and doing menial work around the town in exchange for old clothing and provisions. As with the other tribes, they had been afraid to go hunting for game and roots, and the agent wrote that there would be much suffering among them or even actual starvation during the coming winter unless flour was furnished.[28]

On December 6, Hough wrote the governor describing the pitiful condition of the Bruneau, shivering in the cold, wrapped in threadbare and coarse horse blankets given them in the spring by Governor Lyon. The agent summed up by saying, "Their condition is most deplorable, and from a residence of thirty years among various tribes of Indians, I am constrained to say — these Bruneau Shoshones are the most poverty stricken Indians I ever saw and unless they are fed — must necessarily starve during the present rigorous winter." He asked that food be sent them immediately.[29]

While much attention was paid to the starving and/or hostile Indians near the capital city, the far-off Northern Shoshoni and Bannock at Fort Hall had to continue to shift for themselves. The formation of Idaho Territory had seemingly not changed their isolated and neglected status. They still tried valiantly to interest the Utah superintendent in their welfare. That gentlemen noted in August that his predecessor had given a "small lot of goods" to the mixed bands of Bannock and Shoshoni.[30] The Bannock meanwhile traveled to Fort Bridger hoping to share in the annuity goods of their friends, the Eastern Shoshoni, but Agent Luther Mann did not have any presents for them and learned that the Great Father had not given them any in times past. He finally supplied them with a few articles of food from his own pocket and recommended that in the future they be allowed to share in the annuity goods of Washakie's group.[31]

The neglect of the southern Idaho Indians

came in large part from the constant changes in agents and superintendents due to political demagoguery. The two-year record of incompetence by Caleb Lyon was only an extreme example. One could almost agree with the violence of the *Idaho Statesman* in referring to him as conducting Indian affairs "with an ignorance unparalleled, and a disregard of the rights and wants of the Indians" and an observation that his continued absence from the state during the last months of his tenure was a real blessing.[32]

Governor David W. Ballard was more energetic and wise in his administration as ex-officio superintendent of Indian Affairs, but he was not able to stop the Indian hostilities in southwestern Idaho. During 1867 the *Idaho Statesman* recounted ten major attacks by Indian marauders, most of which involved the stealing of horses and cattle, with only a few killings of white settlers. But in the eyes of most Idahoans of the time, the life of one white was worth more than all the Indians in the territory, and retaliation was swift and terrible. General George Crook took over the task of punishing the Indians and did so quite indiscriminately, killing twenty-five or thirty Indians in one incident early in January. His command then forced the surrender of a small band which was saved from annihilation only by the efforts of the general. In February the troops attacked another Indian camp and charged across open ground "killing everything before them." About sixty Indians were killed in this "battle" and thirty were taken prisoner. A short while later, in another skirmish, the soldiers killed five more Indians. Most of the engagements involved no casualties among the troops.[33]

During the rest of the year Indian malcontents continued the running warfare by driving off stock and attacking parties of two or three whites in widely separated incidents. The *Idaho Statesman* asked for "fighting men . . . who hate the red devils like snakes" to aid the military. While Crook was camped just south of the Idaho border the Indians stole ninety horses from him, converting his command from a cavalry unit into instant infantry. Crook had to recruit more horses from California.[34] By year's end the depredations were still underway, and the general was upset because he was unable to recruit more scouts from among the Boise Shoshoni. Nineteen of the "Boise Pets" had served well in his command during the year.[35] The main result of the intermittent warfare, as far as the southeastern Indians were concerned, was to keep them confined to designated camps where they could be protected from angry whites and to deny them the age-old privilege of gathering the fish and roots necessary for survival.

The Idaho governor reported in March 1867

that he was still feeding the entire group of Boise Shoshoni and fifty of the Bruneau at the camp established for them four miles from Boise City. As his funds were depleted, he was forced to contract some debts or let the Indians starve. Fortunately the winter had been mild, and the Indians had been able to earn extra money by sawing wood for the town's citizens, who overcame their suspicions about the hostile nature of the Shoshoni at least long enough to extract some labor from them.[36] The governor also sent a special agent, E. S. McCandless, to the mouth of Bruneau River to bring the remaining Shoshoni encamped there to Boise to assure their safety. The agent found 47 Bruneau Indians living on Catherine Creek; they had chosen to remain when another 179 had moved to Boise in February.[37]

By May 1 there were 222 Bruneau and 194 Boise Shoshoni in the camp near the Idaho capital and 19 Boise absent as scouts with General Crook, making a total of 435 Indians. McCandless was issuing 200 pounds of flour and 50 pounds of bacon per day as rations to keep them from starving.[38] About a week later the agent was again dispatched to Catherine Creek, where he found two Indian men and brought them into the main camp.[39] Even though spring was at hand, the agency was gloomy about providing subsistence for the combined bands. George C. Hough wrote that their "situation is deplorable in the extreme." It was impossible to send the Bruneau back to Catherine Creek, where they could fish and hunt. Hostile raiding parties were all around, which meant that the danger of being mistaken for "bad" Indians would invite massacre by the enraged citizenry.[40] The superintendent suggested a temporary reservation for the Indians until Washington could decide on a permanent location.[41]

To add to the problem of the Idaho Indian Office, word came that a "party of unselfish patriots (?) at Rocky Bar and vicinity intended to go up and attack the Indians and clean them out." The Indians in question were the followers of Bannock John and his brother Bannock Jim, who were camped just south of Camas Prairie.[42] Lt. Thomas Barker was hurriedly dispatched to bring them into Boise before the whites had a chance to launch an attack.[43] The two Indian leaders, who were married to sisters of the head Bannock Chief, "Tar-gee," had taken their groups of seventy-six men, women, and children to dig for camas roots on the prairie.

Governor Ballard met the Indians in council and attempted to gain as much information as possible about the Fort Hall Bannock. It was the first time an Idaho superintendent of Indian Affairs had had the opportunity to do so. The governor learned that Tahgee was head chief and that Koo-Ser-Gun was second chief of about sixty to a hundred lodges, with a average of from eight to eleven persons per lodge. These rather vague figures meant a range of four hundred and eighty to eight hundred people, with the latter total being more accurate. Bannock John said that Tahgee had had a talk with Utah Governor Doty in 1863, during which the latter agreed that the Bannock should be permitted to continue to hunt buffalo and go into the Boise country whenever they wished. The Bannock leader said his people would be willing to go onto a reservation as long as they could also hunt and fish "at proper times." He would make no commitments because "Targee would want to talk first." The meeting concluded with instructions from Ballard that Bannock John's group should be placed at a camp about twenty miles from Boise and should be given permission to leave for long enough periods to do some hunting and to dig roots because they "could not live on white man's food. . . ."[44]

To assure the proper care of the three bands of Indians near Boise, the commissioner sent Special Agent C. F. Powell to Idaho. His instructions as he took charge on July 1 were to find a suitable place on the Boise River where the Indians could help subsist themselves and where there was good grass for their ponies, of which Bannock John's band had eighty. The restive Bannock were to be moved there at once and the Boise and Bruneau as soon as practicable. All of them would then be deprived of the "pittance" they had been able to earn by doing odd jobs around Boise City, but the superintendent hoped that the available hunting and fishing would reduce the provisions his department would have to furnish.[45] Without waiting to clear the matter with Ballard, Agent Powell allowed seventeen Indians with Bannock John to go to Camas Prairie for roots. The governor thereupon sent him a sharp note pointing out the difficulties he might have created — the Bannock would be absent if word happened to come to move them to a reservation; they might be murdered by hostile whites; or they might become involved with some of the bad Indians who were raiding white ranchers.[46]

In July Powell "pitched the Indian tents" at the forks of the Boise River, thirty miles from the capital, and tried to impress on the Indian mind the necessity of husbanding rations to last a week. Here he admitted failure: "Give him a day's ration and he will try and eat it & waste it at a meal. Supply him for a week and he will endeavor to get rid of it in a day. . . ."[47] The agent's reports were forwarded to the commissioner by Ballard, who reported that the Bannock were growing restless and that he was reluctant not to let them go hunting when he had no assurance he could subsist them if they remained at the camp.[48] The commissioner replied that he was sending a draft for $2,000 for provisions and clothing for the Indians. He approved the request that fresh beef be furnished for food during the winter season, since they would be unable to get wild game.[49] When the contracts for provisions were not yet approved by the department, Governor Ballard refused to issue any more supplies. This caused Powell to predict a general Indian war after his remaining food was issued by December 31.[50] It became a common complaint of the Idaho Indian agents that the Washington office did not realize how slowly wagon freight moved through the mountains and deserts of the West. Powell's estimates for supplies to subsist the Boise and Bruneau Shoshoni were: December, $1,706.83; January, $3,834.33; February, $1,740.50; and March, $1,840.71.[51] Governor Ballard made arrangements to bring another band of Indians from Bruneau River to the established camp, which no doubt increased the cost of the provisions.[52]

Another budget item which began to appear more and more frequently was the provision for medicine and a medical doctor for the Boise and Bruneau, who did not seem as athletic and healthy as the very active Bannock. In May Ballard informed the commissioner that he had employed a physician at $1,200, with the doctor agreeing to furnish all medicines. The Superintendent thought this was cheaper than paying by the visit to the tribes.[53] A month later Dr. C. Wagner gave Ballard a list of the diseases prevalent among the Boise and Bruneau: intermittent fever, twenty cases; remittent fever, five cases; diarrhea, ten cases; dysentery, two cases; phituses palmonates, three cases; rheumatism, five cases; catarrh, fifteen cases; and pneumonia, four cases. The only surgery was to care for a gunshot wound and the bite of a vicious dog.[54] When the tribes were moved to the forks of the Boise River, Powell requested a small supply of drugs and some patent medicines because there would be no physician available.[55] Agent Hough received advice from one doctor who visited the camp at Boise about how to administer certain drugs. The medical care was not very good but was abundantly better than the Indians had received before.[56]

Idaho Territory also suffered a sickness — the constant shuffling of public officials, their tenure in office subject to the whims of politicians in Washington, D.C. Governor Wallace was in office only long enough to be chosen as delegate to Congress. Caleb Lyon, according to the *Idaho Statesman*, had stolen at least $40,000 from the Indian appropriations. In fact Lyon took the "entire undisbursed Idaho Indian fund" of $46,418.40 and kept it, although action was later brought against his bondsmen to recover the

money. Now that David W. Ballard had demonstrated integrity and efficiency in the job, he was summarily dismissed from office because of charges concerning his handling of the "Snake" war. So went the rumors in Boise. The editor of the local newspaper hoped the U.S. Senate would refuse to concur in the suspension of the governor. The Idaho Indians probably suffered most from this constant changing of the guard; just as soon as a capable official began to learn about them, he suddenly disappeared.[57]

With most Boise attention directed toward the problem of the Boise, Bruneau, and Bannock John's tribes, other Indians, farther removed and located mostly in uninhabited regions, did not get the notice of the superintendent's office. The citizens of the city learned in June, much to their surprise, that there was a small band of Indians living near the head of the Weiser River.[58] The commanding officer at Fort Boise informed the governor that he lacked the manpower to send a scouting party to look for them,[59] but he did dispatch a small expedition three months later when word came of depredations on the Weiser. Lt. Thomas Barker found only an abandoned campsite, which he estimated had held seventy-five to eighty Indians. In addition he measured an Indian track which he announced was 17½ inches long. Big Foot, as the *Idaho Statesman* immediately named this phantom, became an instant celebrity, although no white person had yet seen him. Barker returned much chagrined at not being able to bring back a single scalp, but his evaluation that there were about seventy-five Indians on the Weiser proved accurate as the band began to be mentioned more and more frequently over the next decade.[60]

Selection of Fort Hall for Reservation

After twenty years of contact with settlers and government officials, there still remained much ignorance about the Bannock and Fort Hall Shoshoni. In their annual reports for 1867 the agents from Utah, Wyoming, and Idaho gave conflicting reports. F. H. Head of Utah thought there were twenty-five hundred Indians, of which fifteen hundred were Shoshoni and a thousand Bannock who had just spent the past three or four months at Bear Lake and Cache Valley. Head's numbers undoubtedly included some Northwestern Shoshoni. Luther Mann at Fort Bridger had been instructed to enlist Washakie's help in gaining information about these "broken bands of Bannocks and Shoshones" of the Doty Treaty stipulations. He described a large tribe of Bannock numbering one hundred lodges, a few lodges of Shoshoni with them, and a band of Sheepeaters. About fifty lodges of Bannock were on hand at the distribution of supplies to the Eastern Shoshoni the year before. In a long conversation with Mann, Chief Tahgee informed the agent "that his Indians feel very hurt to think that the Great Father had not made them presents, knowing, as they did, that all the Indians by whom they were surrounded were receiving goods every year."

The new white settlements had compelled the Indians to travel long distances in search of buffalo, which subjected them to raids by other tribes and the loss of some of their valuable horses, about sixty having been taken the past winter. Because of the impropriety of sharing the annuities of the Northwestern and Eastern Shoshoni to subsist the Bannock-Fort Hall Shoshoni as stipulated in the Treaty of Box Elder, Superintendent Head proposed awarding $5,000 a year for the Fort Hall group, while Mann thought $10,000 a more just sum, considering the size of the tribe.[61]

There had been earlier interest in a reservation for the Snake River Indians — but from Utah Superintendent James Duane Doty. He wrote the commissioner of Indian Affairs on April 8, 1864, strongly urging that a reserve be set aside at Soda Springs, Idaho. His reasons for the selection of the site were that it was on the route to California, Oregon, and Montana; it was near a military post, Camp Connor; and it was forty miles from the nearest Mormon settlement.[62] Agent Luther Mann wrote from Fort Bridger in the latter part of the same year recommending a reservation for the Shoshoni, who were in "extreme destitution" and needed the protection of the government until they could learn to care for themselves.[63]

The secretary of the Interior issued instructions on September 22, 1865, to the commissioner of Indian Affairs to negotiate a treaty with the "Great Kammas Indians" which would provide a permanent home for them on a reservation at some point on the "Shoshonee River" where there was good fishing.[64] Governor Lyon, who finally received the orders, was also to locate a summer reservation near "Great Kammas Prairie" and obtain a cession for the United States of all other lands claimed by the Indians. The superintendent was to provide the Indians with a farmer, blacksmith, miller, and teacher, plus a gristmill, a sawmill, and agency buildings. In compensation for the land cession, the Shoshoni were to receive agricultural implements, livestock, and other improvements. This early recognition of Indian rights to Camas Prairie was finally made part of the Treaty of Fort Bridger.[65]

Lyon reacted at once by sending an estimate of $72,300 necessary to complete the negotiations for a treaty, including $14,000 for a gristmill, $30,000 for annuity goods, $6,000 for a sawmill, and $10,000 for agency buildings.[66] While the

commissioner was recovering from that shock, Special Agent George C. Hough proposed as possible reservation sites Little Camas Prairie, Big Camas Prairie, and a location encompassing the area from Salmon Falls to Wood River, which he thought would be the "most judicious selection." The southern Indians could be granted a reservation on the Owyhee River. Hough thought it imperative that the reservation be claimed at once by the government before white settlers could start squatting on the only "practicable" areas along Snake River.[67]

Agent Hough seemed to have difficulty making up his mind; the commissioner reported that the agent was meeting with little success in locating a suitable place. In addition to the areas already suggested, Hough now added the Payette and Malad rivers and, finally, the Snake River at Fort Hall, where he thought all the bands of southern Idaho could be concentrated at a saving of money and administration expense. David Ballard was of a more decisive turn and notified the commissioner that, in company with Hough, he had visited along Snake River to the Fort Hall area, which he thought offered the best possibilities for a large reservation for the Shoshoni and Bannock. He described the area chosen:

Commencing on the South bank of Snake River at the Junction of the Port Neuf river with Said Snake river, thence south 25 miles, to the Summit of the mountains dividing the waters of Bear river from those of Snake river — thence easterly along the Summit of said range of mountains 70 miles to a point where Sublette road crosses said divide — thence North about 50 miles to Blackfoot river — thence down said stream to its junction with Snake river — thence down Snake river to the place of beginning.[68]

The governor then posted signs on the main roads warning all white inhabitants as to the boundaries of the proposed reserve.

With almost a chamber-of-commerce flourish he described the luxuriant grasses growing in the important bottomlands along Snake River, the available firewood and the rich timber in the mountains, the mill sites on the Portneuf, the fine fishing, and the abundance of "antelope and deer, sage hens, grouse, ducks and geese, beaver, otter, and musk rats." The winters were fairly mild, with snow rarely falling to a depth of more than one foot and remaining only a short time. Further, Fort Hall was at the crossroads of the California, Oregon, and Montana trails; it would be only a short distance from the transcontinental railroad line; and there was a telegraph line crossing through the reserve from Salt Lake City to Virginia City, Montana. There were already six or eight settlers within the reservation, and fast action would be necessary to forestall other ranchers from taking up homesteads in the area. The governor's final injunction was to establish a military post near Old Fort Hall. He thought the Fort

1864

1865

1866

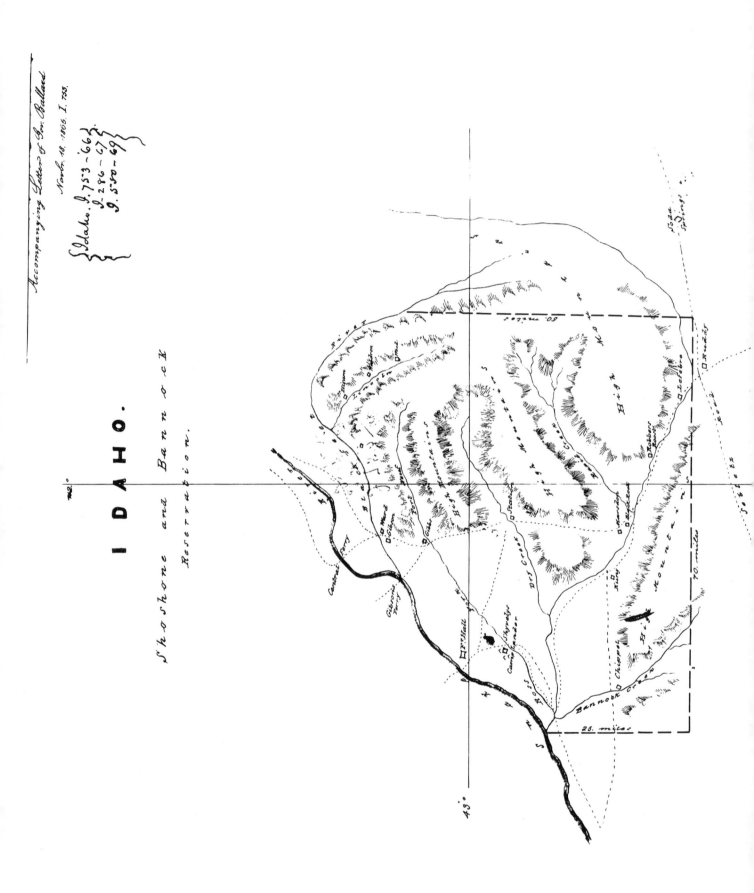

Hall Reservation would accommodate twenty-five hundred Indians.[69]

By March and April of 1867 he was nagging the commissioner to take action. He reported that ranchers in the vicinity of Fort Hall were pestering him to ascertain whether the reservation was to be confirmed. He wanted very much to get the Indians moved in time to harvest a hay and grain crop for winter subsistence.[70] The governmental mill slowly began to grind out the needed orders and legislation as the commissioner explained to the secretary of the Interior that the Boise and Bruneau Shoshoni were not sufficiently organized to negotiate a treaty with the United States and should be moved onto the reservation without any formal document signed by either party. The commissioner was of the opinion that the contemplated reservation was included in the area granted the Eastern Shoshoni by the Treaty of 1863, and that Washakie's consent would have to be obtained. The General Land Office then did its part by approving the reservation boundaries, which its staff computed to contain 1.8 million acres of land. Finally, the secretary of the Interior forwarded the documents to President Andrew Johnson, who issued an executive order on June 14, 1867, setting apart the Fort Hall Indian Reservation.[71]

The formal actions by Washington opened the way for some grassroot operations in Idaho. The General Land Office insisted, despite the belief of the Idaho agents, that no survey had yet been made of the Fort Hall tract.[72] Superintendent Ballard asked for $98,804 worth of facilities, supplies, equipment, and salaries to get the reservation in operation, plus $45,000 for the expense of moving the Indians to Fort Hall and subsisting them for one year.[73] He also granted permission to the Pioneer Mining Company to prospect for gold and silver within the confines of the reservation, although he had reported earlier his belief that the basaltic nature of the area precluded the chance of discovering any precious metals.[74] Perhaps it should be left to the *Idaho Statesman* to conclude the spate of activities concerning the Fort Hall Reservation during the summer and fall

of 1867. The editor opined that the military should continue killing Indians "until the last Indian in the Territories was either on his reservation or enriching the sagebrush with his decaying carcass." With the Fort Hall reserve a fact, if the Indians refused to move there, "they will be killed or put on the reservation by force, and certainly shot if they don't stay there." Furthermore, the editor continued, "The idea that the Indians have any right to the soil is ridiculous. . . . They have no more right to the soil of the Territories of the United States than wolves or coyotes. . . ." Relenting somewhat, he decided that perhaps in the

name of justice and humanity they could be granted enough land for their wants.[75] By August Ballard had still not received any instructions to move the friendly Indians of southern Idaho to Fort Hall.[76]

Many people began to give advice to the superintendent of Indian Affairs in Idaho about the Indian removal to Fort Hall. The *Idaho Statesman* rather plaintively remarked that the citizens of Boise would miss the friendly Boise Shoshoni who had been performing menial chores for them at nominal pay.[77] Charles Powell was worried about certain promises made the year before to the "powerful" and "superior race" of Bannock Indians and the consequences if the promises were not fulfilled. He noted that nearly all the responsibility for the tribes of southern Idaho had fallen to him.[78] B. F. White, a prominent citizen of Malad City, warned Ballard that the Indians were expecting to move to Fort Hall. He said Tahgee had told him the Bannock would soon be arriving at the reservation from a camp on Bear Lake and would expect food and supplies from the government. He continued that Pocatello and his three hundred Indians were in Cache Valley and were planning to appear at the reservation. While the Bannock were friendly, White was of the opinion that Pocatello's group were "very bad Indians" and arrangements had better be made to satisfy their wants.[79] Finally Albert Heed wrote both the commissioner and the secretary of the Interior from Boise City, claiming that not a single one of the territorial governors had discharged his duties toward the Indians and that the only person who showed any competency or concern for the Indians was Charles Powell. He continued that Lyon and Ballard had "no more of the Indian character than a *Chinaman.*" Heed was of the opinion that when such individuals were assigned to the Indian Department they put on "what we term here *Stud horse airs*," and the Indians only made sport of them. He thought Camas Prairie should have been chosen as the location for the reservation.[80]

Agreement with Chief Tahgee and Bannock

By a mere fluke Tahgee, the great head chief of all the Bannock, finally had an opportunity to have a face-to-face talk with the government official who had jurisdiction over his tribe. While the Bannock were on their way to the buffalo country in August 1867, an Indian runner overtook them with the message that Governor Ballard wanted to meet Tahgee at Boise. The chief very wisely mistrusted the message as the runner had "no paper with writing on it," but he decided to seize the opportunity. He asked Telford Kutch, the white owner of a Snake River ferry near Fort Hall, to proceed to Boise to attempt to set up a meeting with the governor.[81]

The council was scheduled and held at Long Tom Creek near Camas Prairie, fifty miles from Boise. Superintendent Ballard gave a long speech explaining he had not been authorized to negotiate but felt it was good to have the meeting. He described the inexorable advance of white civilization in Idaho and the destruction of the game and food roots; he advised Tahgee that the Bannock should agree to go on a reservation and learn to be farmers. The chief responded in a very eloquent plea which allowed the floodgates of years of frustration to spill over as he took his first opportunity to tell a representative of the Great Father what he would like for his people:

> I thought when the white people came to Soda Springs and built houses and put Soldiers in them it was to protect my people, but now they are all gone, and I do not know where to go, nor what to do; the white men have come into my country, and have not asked my consent. Why is this — and why have no persons talked to me before? I have never known what the white people wanted me to do — I have never killed white men who were passing into my Country. What you say now I will never forget. All my people [the Bannocks] will obey me, and be good, but the "Sheep Eaters" are not my people; they may Steal, but I am not responsible for them, I will answer for the Bannocks. The Boises and Bruneaus are poor, they cannot travel far, they have no horses for hunting the Buffalo, but they are good Indians, and are my friends.
>
> The Buffalo do not come so far south now as formerly, so we must go further to the north to hunt them, the white people have scared them away. I am willing to go upon a reservation, but I want the privilege of hunting the Buffalo for a few years. When they are all gone then we hunt no more, perhaps one year, perhaps two or three years, then we stay on the reservation all the time.
>
> I want the reservation large enough for all my people and no white men on it, except the Agent, other officers and employees of the Government. I want the right-of-way for my people to travel when on the way to and from the Buffalo Country, and when going to sell their furs and skins. I want the right to camp and dig roots on Camas prairie, when coming to Boise City to trade. Some of my people have no horses; they could remain at Camas prairie while others went on to Boise.
>
> Our hunting is not so good as it used to be, or my people so numerous. I will go from here to the Buffalo Country; there I will meet all my tribe, and will tell them of this talk, and of the arrangements we may make. I am willing to go onto the reservation as you propose, but when will you want us to go? We could go next Spring.[82]

The governor said he hoped the Bannock could go on a reservation by the next spring but could make no definite promise. The two leaders then signed an agreement, which Ballard recommended be "consummated" by the government. The document provided that the Bannock would move to a reservation before June 1, 1868; the Indians would abide by rules prescribed for such reservation if they were given the assurance that it would be theirs *forever*; the government would provide facilities to teach farming, with the necessary agent, teachers, mechanics, books, etc., to be furnished also; and the Bannock promised to relinquish all claim to their aboriginal lands extend-ing from the forty-second to forty-fifth parallels and from the 113 degree meridian to the Rocky Mountains. The agreement was signed on August 21, 1867, with an addendum of August 23 in which Bannock John agreed to influence as many Sheepeaters as possible to abide by the stipulations.[83]

By June 20, 1868, George Hough was writing about how important it was to put the new reservation in "working order" for the Shoshoni and Bannock,[84] politicians in Washington were recommending people as carpenters, etc., for the employee force at Fort Hall,[85] and as late as August 22 Governor Ballard was asking a private citizen, John P. Gibson at Fort Hall, to reassure Tahgee that the governor was trying desperately to get the necessary appropriation from Washington so the Indians could be settled on the reservation.[86]

Another private citizen, Robert Anderson of Eagle Rock, Idaho, emphasized the mistreatment the Bannock were still receiving and had always received from the government. In a letter to Major W. J. Cullen of Washington, D.C., Anderson said that during the four years he had lived in that portion of Idaho the Bannock had received nothing from the government agents. Although friendly to the whites, Tahgee and his tribe "complain bitterly that they receive no annuities, while the Sioux and other tribes who keep their lands red with the blood of the whites are comfortably provided for." He continued that Tahgee was a bold chief who saw to it that his people were self-reliant — all except a few "poor wretches" without horses who existed on fish in the summertime but as soon as the streams froze over must then beg or barter their "squaws to unprincipled whites for the means to keep body and soul together." During August Tahgee had brought his tribe to Fort Hall, where they had waited forlornly and without results for the government agents to appear as promised. Finally, "disappointed, disheartened, and humiliated," the chief had taken his "mutinous" band to the buffalo country. Anderson thought it would be difficult to gather them together at Fort Hall again. He concluded that the chief had left behind fifty "souls" who must have aid or they would surely perish.[87] By September 1868 there still was no word from Washington, while agents, citizens, and Indians wondered when an appropriation would be forthcoming to get the reservation started.[88]

Treaty of Fort Bridger, 1868

The Bannock were not dependent upon the actions of the Idaho Superintendency alone but continued to hunt with the Eastern Shoshoni, turning up regularly at annuity time hoping to get a share of the supplies issued to Washakie's group. For a number of years the Utah agency had attempted to get a comprehensive treaty signed with the Eastern Shoshoni, and in January 1868 Superintendent F. H. Head sent another appeal to the commissioner for a council to assign the Wind River area as a reservation for the Washakie band. By April he was writing again, expressing thanks for the invitation from the Indian Peace Commission to meet at Fort Bridger to negotiate a treaty with the Eastern Shoshoni and Bannock. He thought June to be the best time; after that the tribes scattered to dig roots and to fish and hunt.[89]

When the Indian Peace Commission met at Laramie, Wyoming, in May 1868, the members decided to send General C. C. Augur to negotiate a treaty with the "Snakes, Bannacks, and other Indians along the line of the Union Pacific R.R. in Utah." The two tribes were notified to meet with General Augur on May 15 at Fort Bridger, which they did. The Indians and the white negotiators waited two weeks until the presents arrived and were distributed. With a good mood thus engendered, the treaty talks got underway on July 3. All of the Eastern Shoshoni and the "larger part" of the Bannock under "Aggie" were present. Augur spoke first, emphasizing the necessity of the tribes' settling down on one reservation where they could learn to farm and thus provide for themselves. The government would furnish farmers and mechanics to teach them to farm, gristmills and sawmills, a physician to care for their ills, and an agent to look after them. The general finally proposed that the two tribes share one reservation under one agent. Washakie responded first. He said he was very happy that the government had finally gotten around to treating with his people and declared he wanted the Wind River country for a reservation. Tahgee replied, "As far away as Virginia City our tribe has roamed. But I want the Porte Neuf country and Kamas plains." When asked whether he would consent to go on one reservation with the Eastern Shoshoni, he answered, "We are friends with the Shoshones and like to hunt with them, but we want a home for ourselves." Further, he insisted he did not want to have to travel to the Shoshoni reservation to get his annuity goods: "We want to receive anything that is for us on our own ground." As indicated earlier in this chapter, Tahgee had already made arrangements with Governor Ballard to go to Fort Hall. Augur replied that he was not sufficiently acquainted with the country to agree to a reservation for the Bannock at that time but would ask the President to send someone to lay out a reservation in the areas the Bannock desired. Until that time the Bannock would be expected to pick up their annuity goods at Fort Bridger. The chiefs gathered the next day and signed the treaty.[90]

Augur included in his report a discussion of the treaty with "the mixed Bands of Bannocks and Shoshones" negotiated by James Duane Doty in 1863 and concluded that, because of its defective nature, "the Bannocks have never received a cent from the Government, except a few casual presents the Superintendent was able to give them from funds of an incidental nature." The Bannock received $4,000 in goods at the time of the signing of the treaty.[91] Luther Mann said they were well-pleased: "Taggie, their chief, is a most reliable and excellent Indian, and to his prudent counsels the moderation and patient endurance of broken faith by this tribe is due."[92] 1869

The Treaty of Fort Bridger has had such importance for the Bannock and Shoshoni of Fort Hall that it is quoted in full in the appendix. Some of the controversial articles included: the misinterpretation of the word "Camas" by the treaty recorder who spelled it "Kansas" Prairie, although the participants were clear about what was meant; the permission to hunt on the unoccupied lands of the United States, which set the stage for future conflict; the agent who was to make his home on the Wind River Reservation but who was, at the same time, to direct and supervise affairs on the Bannock Reservation, an impossible task; and the provision that the Bannock must receive their annuity goods at Fort Bridger. But it was a treaty, and when President Andrew Johnson signed the document on February 24, 1869, the Bannock 1869 had an understanding with the government — a pact with a number of provisions which later came to apply to the other Indian residents of Fort Hall as well.[93]

Removal of Boise and Bruneau to Fort Hall

With the Fort Hall Reservation established and the Bannock under treaty to the government, all that remained to settle the problem of the "strolling" bands of Indians in southern Idaho was to gather them up and move them to the reservation. The continuing conflict in the southwestern part of the territory between Indians and whites merely emphasized the necessity for quick removal of the friendly Indians. While Governor Ballard could compliment the army on its new 1868 policy "to treat as military prisoners, instead of killing all who will lay down their arms," nevertheless the killings and depredations on both sides continued.[94] In March 1868 a white man and a Chinese were killed on the road from Boise to Silver City;[95] in May, two whites were wounded and a stage driver killed by marauding Indians.[96] Finally, as usually happened, the military started out on a planned revenge expedition along the

Owyhee River, where the troops attacked an Indian camp and killed the "entire party, thirty-four in number," including women and children.[97] The Boise Shoshoni scouts brought back several scalps for display.

From this time on the war began to wind down, as news of the terrible vengeance of the soldiers began to spread among the scattered bands of Indians. By August the *Idaho Statesman* declared the conflict at an end.[98] There were still some Indian prisoners held at Fort Boise. Fifty of them escaped on June 16,[99] but by November the commander of the post was trying to give his remaining twenty-six Indian prisoners to the superintendent of Indian Affairs to become that official's responsibility.[100]

1868

Life off a reservation was just too dangerous for Idaho Indians. For example, in March an Indian called Bruneau Jim was killed by a white man, John Brody, while the Indian was attempting to forestall an attempted rape of two Indian women by Brody and two companions. After much publicity Brody was brought to trial on a charge of manslaughter. Two different juries could not reach a verdict, the judge released Brody and his two white companions on their own recognizance, and the three at once left Boise for parts unknown. The commissioner cited the case as evidence of the extreme hostility of the white settlers against all Indians. He asked for a law permitting Indians to testify in such criminal cases.[101]

The risk of moving about in search of food was so great that the friendly Indians remained immobilized and faced winter without the usual store of provisions. Hearing of such a group on the Bruneau River, Governor Ballard dispatched Agent Hough to search for them. The agent found twenty-four Bruneau Shoshoni freezing in weather of 25 degrees below zero. They were absolutely destitute, without food or clothing. They were either old, decrepit, and sick or so young they could not readily travel. The military escort placed them in wagons and brought them into Boise, where they were put under the care of Agent Powell.[102]

News also came of a "band of thieving Snakes" on the headwaters of Weiser River. The commander of Fort Boise immediately sent out a scouting party, and on August 19, 1868, Captain James B. Sinclair reported back at the post with Eagle Eye and his band of forty-one Indians, of which thirteen were men. In addition the captain brought in twenty-one horses and a large quantity of dried roots and salmon, part of which was used as rations by the eighteen soldiers for the last twenty days of the trip. The Indians probably did not appreciate this assault on their winter food supply by their captors, especially a few days later when, in a council with Eagle Eye, Governor Ballard and the army officers satisfied themselves that these Shoshoni were not really hostile and allowed them to return to Weiser Valley.[103] A short while later the governor learned to his chagrin that apparently the same group of Indians had begun committing depredations along the Weiser. He decided it was necessary to dispatch Agent Hough to bring them back if they could be found. Eagle Eye's band continued to cause slight excitement in the area for a number of years before they were finally persuaded to move to a reservation after the turn of the century.[104]

1868

Throughout 1868 the agents at Boise kept sending urgent requests for sufficient funds to subsist the 283 Boise and 300 Bruneau Shoshoni at the camp on Boise River. Charles F. Powell received $3,834.34 for the first quarter of the year and then increased the amount needed to $5,912.33⅓ for the second quarter because fifty-six Boise scouts had returned from military duty with the Fort Boise troops. The agent asked for a special sum of $5,655 in September to buy blankets, shirts, shoes, and cloth for the winter ahead.[105] The Washington office must not have supplied sufficient food because two months later Agent Hough complained that the Indians came to him frequently to say they were hungry. He also had to stop the practice of certain white men who were running footraces with the Indians and winning many of their blankets. A draft for $15,000 finally arrived, out of a total appropriation of $30,000, but it was for establishing the "strolling bands" of Shoshoni and Bannock on the reservation at Fort Hall.[106] Governor Ballard noted to Powell on December 2 that for the two prior months there had been no funds for subsisting the Boise and Bruneau. As a result they had scattered over the countryside searching for food. Ballard made the command decision to use the $15,000 to gather the Indians together again and provide the necessary food and clothing then to move them to Fort Hall as soon as practicable.[107]

The governor also decided to learn what other Indians would and should be settled at Fort Hall, inasmuch as Washington was finally giving the word to move. He therefore sent Special Agent Powell on an Indian-gathering expedition along the Snake River from Boise to Fort Hall. Powell's report of January 14, 1869, gave an accurate description of the scattered bands of Shoshoni in southern Idaho at the time. Near King Hill he met the first of a number of small bands and gave a specially prepared talk; the Great Father had found a permanent home for them and desired that they move there. The Indians objected at first, saying they wished to remain at their ancestral home. After some explanation they reluctantly agreed to meet with Powell in the spring and also agreed to try to persuade other small groups of Indians to go with them.

1869

At Rock Creek Powell met with ten or twelve "Wickaups" of Indians and repeated the message. They had no head man and seemed to be well-provided with food for the winter. While at Rock Creek Powell investigated a report that the Indians there had stolen about sixty head of cattle. He found the cattle had just strayed away. The white owners had been too indolent to search for the stock and instead had demanded that the Indian Department reimburse them for the stolen herd. At Malad City he found a portion of Pocatello's Northwestern band, but their chief was on a buffalo hunt in the Wind River Mountains with Tahgee. The Indians were pleased to learn of the reservation and promised to move to Fort Hall in the spring.[108]

At the reservation he found the weather "comfortably pleasant" after the cold and snow of the highlands through which he had just passed. There were about two hundred fifty Shoshoni and Bannock along the bottoms, existing mostly on beaver meat. The flour he gave them was much appreciated. Among the group was a small detachment of Eastern Shoshoni from Washakie's tribe, who stated they wished to remain and make Fort Hall their home. The agent promised to talk to the Utah superintendent to see if it could be arranged. Powell told the few white settlers not to make any other improvements on their ranches and to warn other whites to stay off the reservation. He described the three houses, a barn, and a shed which J. L. Shirley had built in 1864 and recommended their purchase as residence and storage facilities for the agency employees. For the agency he chose a site about six miles from the Portneuf River on a stream running from the Bannock Mountains. It was a centrally located place, with easy access to all parts of the reservation. He urged that the Indians be moved to Fort Hall not later than April so they could get in some crops of potatoes, vegetables, etc.[109]

Shortly after Powell's trip Governor Ballard received official notification that he should proceed with the removal of the Indians near Boise to Fort Hall.[110] At the same time Ballard wrote General George E. Crook, commanding the Department of the Columbia, to ask that a military post be established at Fort Hall.[111] Agent Powell informed the commissioner that the Boise, the Bruneau, and the small group of Bannock at the camp six miles from Boise City were fairly comfortable and had agreed to move, although reluctantly. He was particularly concerned about an epidemic of measles which was coursing through the camp. He also asked for aid in vaccinating the Indians against smallpox, as both diseases "affect persons of dark skin more fatally than of white." At a Bruneau camp on Catherine Creek he particularly urged that certain white men who were living with Indian women "as a convenience" not be allowed to accompany the women to Fort Hall. As a last measure of preparation he requested that the military return the Boise Shoshoni scouts to Boise by March 5 so they could accompany their band to the reservation.[112]

Superintendent Ballard advertised for bids to deliver 20,000 pounds of flour, 10,000 pounds of bacon, 4,000 pounds of beans, 2,000 pounds of sugar, and some miscellaneous equipment — all of it totalling about 60,000 pounds of freight to be delivered at Fort Hall in March.[113] The purchase of the supplies exhausted all funds appropriated and, in answer to Ballard's appeal, the Indian Office sent another $18,000 to cover the cost of the move and initial settlement on the reservation.[114] Fort Boise agreed to send a military escort for protection.[115]

A few of the Boise and Bruneau were unhappy about leaving their old home, and some sadness was expressed by the governor, who described them as "the best Indians I have ever seen — true to the whites in peace, and good allies in war."[116] Even the editor of the *Idaho Statesman* admitted a few pangs of regret over their departure. He thought they were not really bad Indians, "On the contrary we never knew of a tribe who did less harm." They had been good servants, had fought the hostile Snakes, and had exhibited exemplary conduct about town. In fact, he added, "their absense [sic] will occasion some little inconvenience," but then, seemingly repentent about his unusually kind remarks, he concluded, "The town looks better, however, without them than with them strolling about in their uncouth garb, or no garb at all, as the case may be."[117]

When the whole entourage of freight wagons, soldiers, and Indians pulled out of Boise City on March 13 the editor breathed a sigh of relief that the days of hostility were over. Perhaps, he said, "we may hope for a slow though sure recovery." A few Indians, however, refused to move — the peaceable and friendly Sheepeaters beyond Wood River and Eagle Eye's band on Weiser River. Walter Mason was sent to urge the Weiser band to join the Boise and Bruneau in the move to eastern Idaho, but Eagle Eye was adamant. As long as no one interfered with the fishing, his people could subsist themselves, and he demanded a talk with the Big Chief of the whites. Mason thought that if they were taken to Fort Hall, "they will be retained with great difficulty."[118]

Agent Powell reported that the journey from Boise to Fort Hall took twenty-nine days. He could not keep the Indians together, as they were continually wandering off to fish and hunt. He ended up with fewer Indians at Fort Hall than had started the journey, and he was afraid that some of his charges might turn around and go

1869

1869

1869

back home to Boise.[119] The governor tried to help out by sending his clerk, Captain J. W. Porter, to round up the straying Indians. The captain found about fifty Indians between Boise and Clark's Ferry. All promised to start for Fort Hall by April 15 when Porter explained they were liable to be killed if they continued wandering around without a military escort. He reported his warning had a "salutary effect" on them.[120] The governor announced there were also some "renegade" Bannock, Sheepeaters, and Boise at Big Camas Prairie who would probably not go to the reservation "until some of them are killed."[121]

On arriving at Fort Hall Powell found many Bannock and Shoshoni, although Tahgee and Pocatello, with their main bands, were away on the annual buffalo hunt. The Indians were pleased to see the government finally was in earnest about caring for them.[122] Governor Ballard visited the reservation, and he and Powell started the reservation farmer at the task of getting vegetable gardens and grain fields planted. Ballard also directed Powell to purchase one hundred head of cattle for subsistence for the Indians.[123] With the consent of J. L. Shirley, Powell took over two of his buildings as an initial headquarters.[124]

The six years from 1863 to the opening of Fort Hall Reservation in 1869 had been eventful ones for the Indians of southern Idaho. The pressure of white settlement in the vicinity of Boise drove the Boise and Bruneau Shoshoni close to the capital, where they were protected from determined white settlers and from raids by the military which had been called to arms when a few exasperated and hungry Indians attacked the new white interlopers. At a time when most Idaho citizens were
1866 applauding the suggestion of the *Owyhee Avalanche* that smallpox-infected blankets be distributed among the natives, Governor Caleb Lyon, an avowed friend of the Indians, was unable to get his treaties of amity with the Boise and Bruneau approved and soon was forced out of the territory.[125] His successor finally arranged for a reservation at Fort Hall for the southwestern Idaho Shoshoni. He even made arrangements for the Bannock under Tahgee to settle on the same reserve, although General Augur, at the Fort Bridger Treaty, unknowingly tried to locate the Bannock at Wind River.

Throughout the period the Northern Shoshoni and Bannock suffered want and privation as their hunting areas and homelands were usurped by
1867 white settlers. As Tahgee said, "I do not know where to go, nor what to do." The confusion of Idaho politics, the utter neglect of Indian interests by the national government for many years and the virulent hostility of the whites forced the more sedentary tribes into small and barren enclaves along the western Idaho streams and drove the

more independent Bannock and Fort Hall Shoshoni to the buffalo plains. The Indians of southern Idaho finally had a home, but it would be many years before they would learn enough about farming and stock raising to become self-sufficient. During the period of transition there would be some desperate, starving times.

NOTES CHAPTER III
A RESERVATION AT FORT HALL

1. Wm. P. Dole to W. H. Wallace, Wash., D.C., March 23, 1863, U.S. National Archives, *Records of the Superintendencies and Agencies of the Office of Indian Affairs — Idaho, Register of Letters Received, 1867-70, Letter Received from the Commissioner, 1867-1870,* Microcopy No. 832, Roll No. 1.
2. Charles E. Mix to Caleb Lyon, Wash., D.C., June 22, 1864, ibid.
3. F. W. Lander to C.I.A., Wash., D.C., Feb. 18, 1860, *Utah Superintendency,* Roll 899.
4. *Report of the C.I.A.,* 1865, 589.
5. "Copy of the Treaty with the Boise Shoshoni, Boise City, Oct. 10, 1864," U.S. National Archives, *Letters Received by the Office of Indian Affairs, 1863-1867, Idaho Superintendency,* Roll 337.
6. *Idaho Statesman,* Oct. 11, 13, 1864.
7. *Report of the C.I.A.,* 1865, 30.
8. Caleb Lyon to A. B. Turner, Boise City, Dec. 10, 1865, U.S. National Archives, *Records of the Superintendencies and Agencies of the Office of Indian Affairs — Idaho,* Microcopy No. 832, Roll No. 3.
9. "Affidavit by Charles Owens, Silver City, Idaho, May 6, 1865," ibid.
10. Ibid., May 6, 13, July 13, 15, August 1, Nov. 11, 1865.
11. M. A. Carter to J. M. Ashley, Soda Springs, July 19, 1865, Bureau of Indian Affairs, *Letters Received,* Idaho State University Archives, Ms. 468.
12. M. A. Carter to Caleb Lyon, Soda Springs, Nov. 14, 1865, ibid.
13. Caleb Lyon to James Harlan, Boise City, Feb. 17, 1866, *Idaho Superintendency,* Roll 337; *Idaho Statesman,* May 12, 1866.
14. Ibid., March 1, June 14, 1866; J. H. Walker to Commanding General Department of Columbia, Fort Boise, March 1, 1866, *Idaho Superintendency,* Roll 337; Caleb Lyon to C.I.A., Boise City, March 13, 1866, ibid.
15. *Idaho Statesman,* June 5, 16, July 7, Sept. 4, Nov. 8, 20, 27, Dec. 6, 1866.
16. D. W. Ballard to C.I.A., Boise City, June 16, 1866, *Records of the Superintendencies and Agencies of the Office of Indian Affairs—Idaho.* Microcopy No. 832, Roll No. 3.
17. *Report of the C.I.A.,* 1866, 109.
18. Caleb Lyon to Secretary of the Interior, Jame Harlan, Boise City, April 12, 1866, *Idaho Superintendency,* Roll 337; Wells, "Caleb Lyon's Indian Policy," *Pacific Northwest Quarterly,* October 1970, 193-200; *Caleb Lyon's Bruneau Treaty, 12 April 1866,* Idaho Historical Society, Reference Series, No. 369, August 1968.
19. S. R. Howell to McCandless, Boise City, June 7, 1866, U.S. National Archives, *Records of the Superintendencies and Agencies of the Office of Indian Affairs — Idaho,* Microcopy, No. 832, Roll No. 3.
20. D. W. Ballard to C.I.A., Boise City, July, 1866, ibid.
21. *Idaho Statesman,* April 19, 1866.
22. Ibid., Oct. 30, 1866.
23. Ibid., March 27, 1866.
24. D. W. Ballard to George C. Hough, Boise City, Aug. 17, Nov. 1, 1866, U.S. National Archives, *Letters Sent and Miscellaneous Records, 1863-70, Idaho Superintendency,* Roll 3; C.I.A., to D. W. Ballard, Washington, D.C., Sept. 1, 1866, ibid.
25. *Report of the C.I.A.,* 1866, 189.
26. C.I.A. to D. W. Ballard, Washington, D.C., June 8, 1866, U.S. National Archives, *Register of Letters Received, 1867-70, Letters Received from the Commissioner, 1863-70, Idaho Superintendency,* Roll 1; C.I.A. to George C. Hough, Washington, D.C., June 8, 1866, ibid.
27. D. W. Ballard to George C. Hough, Boise City, Sept. 18, 1866, U.S. National Archives, *Special Agents, 1866-69, Idaho Superintendency,* Roll 2; D. W. Ballard to C.I.A., Boise City, June 23, 1866, U.S. National Archives, *Letters Sent and Miscellaneous Records, 1863-70, Idaho Superintendency,* Roll 3; George C. Hough to D. W. Ballard, Lewiston, Idaho, Oct. 12, 1866, *Idaho Superintendency,* Roll 337; *Idaho Statesman,* Sept. 25, 1866.
28. *Report of the C.I.A.,* 1866, 187; George C. Hough to D. W. Ballard, Boise City, Sept. 22, 1866, U.S. National Archives, *Special Agents, 1866-1869, Idaho Superintendency,* Roll 2; George C. Hough to D. W. Ballard, Boise City, Nov. 30, 1866, ibid.
29. George C. Hough to D. W. Ballard, Boise City, Dec. 6, 1866, ibid.
30. F. H. Head to C.I.A., Utah, Aug. 10, 1866, *Utah Superintendency,* Roll 902.
31. *Report of the C.I.A.,* 1866, 127.
32. *Idaho Statesman,* Feb. 21, March 14, 1867.
33. Ibid., Jan. 1, 29, 31, Feb. 5, 12, 1867.
34. Ibid., March 26, April 16, May 28, June 6, 22, July 20, Oct. 22, 24, Nov. 7, 16, 28, Dec. 16, 19, 24, 28, 1867.
35. George Crook to Geneen, Camp Warner, Oregon, Dec. 16, 1867, U.S. National Archives, *Miscellaneuos Sources, 1863 and 1866-69, Idaho Superintendency,* Roll 2.
36. D. W. Ballard to C.I.A., Boise City, March 18, 1867, U.S. National Archives, *Letters Sent and Miscellaneous Records, 1863-70, Idaho Superintendency,* Roll 3; D. W. Ballard to C.I.A., Boise City, April 1, 1867, ibid.
37. D. W. Ballard to E. S. McCandless, Boise City, April 3, 1867, ibid.; D. W. Bal-

lard to C.I.A., Boise City, April 5, 1867, ibid.; D. W. Ballard to E. S. McCandless, Boise City, April 4, 1867, ibid.

38. McCandless to Ballard, Boise City, May 1, 1867, ibid.

39. Ballard to McCandless, Boise City, May 8, 1867, ibid,; McCandless to Ballard, Boise City, May 15, 1867, ibid.

40. George C. Hough to C.I.A., Washington, D.C., April 25, 1867, *Idaho Superintendency*, Roll 337.

41. Ballard to C.I.A., Boise City, May 7, 1867, U.S. National Archives, *Letters Sent and Miscellaneous Records, 1863–70, Idaho Superintendency*, Roll 3.

42. *Idaho Statesman*, June 29, 1867.

43. "Thomas Barker, Special Orders, Fort Boise, June 18, 1867," U.S. National Archives, *Letter Sent and Miscellaneous Records, 1863–70, Idaho Superintendency*, Roll 3.

44. D. W. Ballard to C.I.A., Boise City, June 30, 1867, ibid.

45. C.I.A., to D. W. Ballard, Washington, D.C., May 30, 1867, ibid.

46. D. W. Ballard to Charles F. Powell, Boise City, July 1, 6, 13, 1867, ibid.

47. Charles F. Powell to David W. Ballard, Indian Camp at Fork of Boise River, July 23, 1867, U.S. National Archives, *Special Agents, 1866–69, Idaho Superintendency*, Roll 2.

48. D. W. Ballard to C.I.A., Boise City, July 31, 1867, U.S. National Archives, *Letters Sent and Miscellaneous Sources, 1863 and 1866–69, Idaho Superintendency*, Roll 3.

49. C.I.A. to Charles F. Powell, Washington, D.C., Oct. 29, 1867, U.S. National Archives, *Letters Received from the Commissioner, 1863–70, Idaho Superintendency*, Roll 1; *Idaho Statesman*, Aug. 27, 1867.

50. C.I.A. to Charles F. Powell, Washington, D.C., Oct. 31, 1867, U.S. National Archives, *Letters Received from the Commissioner, 1863–70, Idaho Superintendency*, Roll 1.

51. Charles F. Powell to C.I.A., Boise City, Nov. 28, 1867, *Idaho Superintendency*, Roll 337.

52. D. W. Ballard to Brvt. Major General W. L. Sullivan, Commanding District of Owyhee, Fort Boise, Dec. 30, 1867, U.S. National Archives, *Letters Sent and Miscellaneous Records, 1863–70, Idaho Superintendency*, Roll 3.

53. D. W. Ballard to C.I.A., Boise City, May 31, July 31, 1867, ibid.

54. C. Wagner to D. W. Ballard, Boise City, June 30, 1867, U.S. National Archives, *Special Agents, 1866–69, Idaho Superintendency*, Roll 2.

55. Charles F. Powell to D. W. Ballard, Indian Camp at Forks of Boise River, July 23, 1867, ibid.

56. George C. Hough to C.I.A., Boise City, Sept. 30, 1867, ibid.

57. *Idaho Statesman*, Sept. 14, 17, 1867; "Territorial Governors of Idaho," *Idaho Yesterdays*, Vol. 7, No. 1 (Spring 1963), 15–16.

58. *Idaho Statesman*, June 27, 1867.

59. Thomas Barker to D. W. Ballard, Fort Boise, July 1, 1867, U.S. National Archives, *Miscellaneous Sources, 1863 and 1866–69, Idaho Superintendency*, Roll 2.

60. *Idaho Statesman*, Oct. 5, 14, 1867.

61. *Report of the C.I.A., 1867*, 178, 188–189.

62. James Duane Doty to C.I.A., Washington, D.C., April 8, 1864, U.S. National Archives, *Bureau of Indian Affairs, Letters Received, Idaho*.

63. *Report of the C.I.A., 1864*, 316.

64. James Harlan to C.I.A., Washington, D.C., Sept. 22, 1865, *Idaho Superintendency*, Roll 337.

65. C.I.A. to Caleb Lyon, Washington, D.C., Sept. 22, 1865, Department of Interior, *Office of Indian Affairs, Court of Claims Case M107*, 238–239.

66. Caleb Lyon to C.I.A., Washington, D.C., Sept. 26, 1865, ibid.

67. George C. Hough to C.I.A., Washington, D.C., Dec. 2, 1865, ibid.

68. D. W. Ballard to C.I.A., Boise City, Nov. 18, 1866, ibid.; *Report of C.I.A., 1866*, 38, 189, 191.

69. D. W. Ballard to C.I.A., Boise City, Nov. 18, 1866, Department of the Interior, *Office of Indians Affairs, Court of Claims Case M107*, 238–239.

70. D. W. Ballard to C.I.A., Boise City, March 18 and April 1, 1867, U.S. National Archives, *Letters Sent and Miscellaneous Records, 1863–70, Idaho Superintendency*, Roll 3.

71. N. G. Taylor to O. H. Browning, Washington, D.C., May 23, 1867; Joseph S. Wilson to W. T. Otto, Washington, D.C., June 6, 1867; W. T. Otto to President Andrew Johnson, Washington, D.C., June 13, 1867; "Executive Order Washington, D.C., June 14, 1867," C.I.A., "Report on Indian Affairs, 1878, Executive Orders Relating to Indian Reserves, Idaho, Coeur d' Alene Reserve and Fort Hall Reserve," 248–250.

72. Commissioner of General Land Office to C.I.A., Wash., D.C., Sept. 6, 1867, *Idaho Superintendency*, Roll 337.

73. D. W. Ballard to C.I.A., Boise City, Aug. 14 and Aug. 19, 1867, U.S. National Archives, *Letters Sent and Miscellaneous Records, 1863–70, Idaho Superintendency*, Roll 3.

74. D. W. Ballard to Whom It May Concern, Boise City, July 9, 1867, ibid.

75. *Idaho Statesman*, July 20, 1867.

76. *Report of the C.I.A., 1867*, 248.

77. *Idaho Statesman*, March 21, 1868.

78. Charles F. Powell to C.I.A., Boise City, April 14, 1868, *Idaho Superintendency*, Roll 338.

79. B. F. White to D. W. Ballard, Malad City, May 8, 1868, U.S. National Archives, *Miscellaneous Sources, 1863 and 1866–69, Idaho Superintendency*, Roll 3.

80. A. Heed to C.I.A. and Secretary of the Interior, Boise City, May 14, 1868, *Idaho Superintendency*, Roll 338.

81. *Idaho Statesman*, Aug. 20, 1867.

82. Ibid., Aug. 29, 1867; D. W. Ballard to C.I.A., Boise City, Aug. 31, 1867, U.S. National Archives, *Letters Sent and Miscellaneous Records, 1863–70, Idaho Superintendency*, Roll 3.

83. Ibid.

84. George C. Hough to C.I.A., Boise City, June 20, 1868, *Idaho Superintendency*, Roll 338.

85. D. E. Williamson to C.I.A., Green Castle, Indiana, Aug. 3, 1868, *Utah Superintendency*, Roll 902.

86. D. W. Ballard to John P. Gibson, Boise City, Aug. 22, 1868, U.S. National Archives, *Letters Sent and Miscellaneous Records, 1863–70, Idaho Superintendency*, Roll 3.

87. R. Anderson to W. J. Cullen, Eagle Rock Bridge, Snake River, Sept. 29, 1868, *Montana Superintendency*, Roll 488.

88. *Report of the C.I.A., 1868*, 200.

89. F. H. Head to C.I.A., Salt Lake City, April 14, 1868, *Utah Superintendency*, Roll 902.

90. C. C. Augur to the President of the Indian Peace Commission, Omaha, Nebraska, Oct. 4, 1868, U.S. National Archives, *Bureau of Indian Affairs, Irregular-sized Papers*.

91. Ibid.

92. *Report of the C.I.A., 1869*, 712–713, 716.

93. "Treaty between the United States of America and the Eastern Band of Shoshonees and the Bannock Tribe of Indians, Proclaimed Feb. 24, 1869," U.S. National Archives, *Bureau of Indian Affairs, Letters Received, Idaho*.

94. D. W. Ballard to C.I.A., Boise City, Feb. 1, 1868, *Idaho Superintendency*, Roll 338.

95. George C. Hough to C.I.A., Boise City, March 19, 1868, *Idaho Superintendency*, Roll 338; *Idaho Statesman*, April 1, 1868.

96. Ibid., May 26, 1868.

97. Ibid., June 4, 1868.

98. Ibid., Aug. 8, 1868.

99. Ibid., June 16, 1868.

100. Ibid., Oct. 20, 1868; D. W. Ballard to Bvt. Lt. Col. George K. Brady, Boise City, Nov. 26, 1868, U.S. National Archives, *Letters Sent and Miscellaneous Records, 1863–70, Idaho Superintendency*, Roll 3.

101. *Report of the C.I.A., 1868*, 200–210; *Idaho Statesman*, March 10, 14, 1868; George C. Hough to C.I.A., Boise City, March 11, 1868,: *Idaho Superintendency*, Roll 338.

102. George C. Hough to D. W. Ballard, Boise City, Jan. 14, 25, 1868, *Idaho Superintendency*, Roll 338; D. W. Ballard to George C. Hough, Boise City, Jan. 10, 1868, U.S. National Archives, *Letters Sent and Miscellaneous Records, 1863–70, Idaho Superintendency*, Roll 3.

103. *Idaho Statesman*, Aug. 25, Sept. 8, 1868.

104. D. W. Ballard to George C. Hough, Boise City, Sept. 12, 1868, U.S. National Archives, *Letters Sent and Miscellaneous Records, 1863–70, Idaho Superintendency*, Roll 3.

105. Charles F. Powell to C.I.A., Boise City, Jan. 2, Feb. 3, 12, Aug. 28, Sept. 7, 1868, *Idaho Superintendency*, Roll 338.

106. George C. Hough to C.I.A., Boise City, Nov. 30, 1868, U.S. National Archives, *Special Agents, 1866–69, Idaho Superintendency*, Roll 2.

107. D. W. Ballard to Charles F. Powell, Boise City, Dec. 2, 1868, U.S. National Archives, *Letters Sent and Miscellaneous Records, 1863–70, Idaho Superintendency*, Roll 3.

108. Charles F. Powell to D. W. Ballard, Boise City, Jan. 14, 1869, Bureau of Indian Affairs, *Letters Received, 1869, Idaho Superintendency*, 76.

109. Ibid.

110. C.I.A. to D. W. Ballard, Wash., D.C., Jan. 26, 1868, U.S. National Archives, *Letters Received from the Commissioner, 1863–70, Idaho Superintendency*, Roll 3.

111. D. W. Ballard to Gen. George E. Crook, Boise City, Jan. 18, 1869, U.S. National Archives, *Letters Sent and Miscellaneous Records, 1863–70, Idaho Superintendency*, Roll 3.

112. Charles F. Powell to C.I.A., Boise City, Feb. 2, 1869, U.S. National Archives, *Special Agents, 1866–69, Idaho Superintendency*, Roll 2.

113. *Idaho Statesman*, Feb. 18, 1869.

114. C.I.A. to D. W. Ballard, Wash., D.C., March 9, 1869, U.S. National Archives, *Letters Received from the Commissioner, 1863–70, Idaho Superintendency*, Roll 1.

115. D. W. Ballard to Col. Elmer Otis, Boise City, Feb. 23, 1869, U.S. National Archives, *Letters Sent and Miscellaneous Records, 1863–70, Idaho Superintendency*, Roll 3.

116. D. W. Ballard to C.I.A., Boise City, March 4, 1869, *Idaho Superintendency*, Roll 338.

117. *Idaho Statesman*, March 9, 1869.

118. Ibid., Feb. 11, March 13, 1869.

119. Charles F. Powell to D. W. Ballard, Fort Hall Reservation, April 26, 1869, U.S. National Archives, *Special Agents, 1866–96, Idaho Superintendency*, Roll 2.

120. D. W. Ballard to C.I.A., Boise City, April 30, 1869, *Idaho Superintendency*, Roll 338; *Idaho Statesman*, Apr. 17, 1869.

121. Ibid., April 29, 1869.

122. Charles F. Powell to D. W. Ballard, Fort Hall Reservation, April 26, 1869, U.S. National Archives, *Special Agents, 1866–69, Idaho Superintendency*, Roll 2.

123. D. W. Ballard to C.I.A., Boise City, April 30, 1869, *Idaho Superintendency*, Roll 338.

124. Charles F. Powell to D. W. Ballard, Fort Hall Reservation, April 26, 1869, U.S. National Archives, *Special Agents, 1866–69, Idaho Superintendency*, Roll 2.

125. *Owyhee Avalanche*, Jan. 20, 1866.

CHAPTER IV

BUFFALO AND GOVERNMENT BEEF

A Reservation Without Rations

1869

Although officials in Washington, D.C., were satisfied that the southern Idaho Indians had finally been located at a permanent site, local Idaho agents and particularly the Bannock and some Shoshoni were not definitely assured and kept up a constant drumfire of questions to the commissioner's office. Charles Powell wrote on June 30, 1869, that Chief Tahgee wanted his people to be assigned to the Fort Hall Reservation, that "promise after promise has been made to them," and that the Bannock wanted to "talk" with some Big Chief who could outline what the government wished the Indians to do.[1] Governor Ballard supported Powell's point of view, writing that the agreement to go to Fort Hall was only "tacit" and lacked the "detailed stipulations" which would allow the Indians a homeland in return for assurances from the government to provide for "their future comfort."[2]

In response, the commissioner recommended that the Fort Hall Reservation be designated as the reserve provided for the Bannock in the Treaty of July 3, 1868.[3] While the Idaho Superintendent was still talking of another treaty with the Bannock and Shoshoni,[4] the commissioner informed him that President Ulysses S. Grant had signed an executive order on July 30, 1869, placing the Bannock at Fort Hall.[5] The commissioner also made it quite clear that in accepting their assignment to the reservation the Bannock were relinquishing "all title, claims, or rights" to any other area in the United States, which meant that the "Kansas" or Camas Prairie was no longer to be part of the homeland of the Bannock and Shoshoni.[6] From this time on the two tribes might visit the Camas grounds "rich in the various roots of which they are exceedingly fond" but would have no further claim to the prairie.[7]

As a final clarification the Idaho superintendent was told by the Office of Indian Affairs that the Shoshoni on the Fort Hall Reservation were to enjoy all the privileges and benefits granted by the Treaty of July 3, 1868, to "their friends," the Bannock.[8] With this promise of "equal rights" to all the Fort Hall Indians, the Fort Bridger Treaty now became the basic agreement between both tribes and the U.S. government.

With treaty rights on the reservation defined, both local and national officials now looked forward to the time when all the Indians of southern Idaho would be settled as peaceful farmers at Fort Hall. In June 1869 the commissioner of Indian Affairs inaugurated the practice of appointing army officers to direct Indian affairs, and Col. De Lancey Floyd-Jones reached Boise June 12 to assume the post of superintendent for Idaho. Lt. W. H. Danilson arrived from the east on July 27 and three days later was at Fort Hall to become agent for the reservation.[9]

Lieutenant Danilson soon met his first problem. Several white families, long established on ranches which had now become part of an Indian reservation, began a long and frustrating attempt to be compensated by the government for their land and improvements. J. S. Kinney asked $2,720 for his holdings; J. P. Gibson requested $7,500 for his ranch and the loss of his business as a ferryman across Snake River; Charles Hygham wanted $1,500 for his property.[10] In rather curt terms the commissioner informed Floyd-Jones that there were no funds available to pay for such improvements.[11] This decision did not end the matter. The three petitioners, soon joined by other white claimants, persisted in their efforts; the cases dragged on over a period of several years.

A more immediate and important task for the new agent was to assist the Indians in learning to become farmers, as outlined by the objectives of the Fort Bridger Treaty. Each head of a family was to receive 320 acres. Each person over eighteen years and not the head of a family was to receive eighty acres. The individual farms were to be assigned permanently and no longer held in common. Each Indian farmer was to receive $100 worth of seeds and agricultural implements the first year and $25 for each of the succeeding three years. Furthermore, the ten most productive farmers were to receive presents of $500 each annually for three years as an incentive to encourage others to participate in agriculture.[12] The plan seemed eminently fair and workable, based as it was on the white experience. Only later did the Shoshoni and Bannock begin to realize that the old communal system of land ownership might better preserve their reservation in the face of constant white encroachment.

1869

With the arrival of the Boise and Bruneau Shoshoni at Fort Hall in April, Charles Powell immediately had his white farmer plow about forty acres of ground. He constructed a small irrigation ditch and planted grain, potatoes, and some vegetables.[13] He tried to interest the Indians in planting some crops of their own, but "they soon tired of work and away they went in pursuit of game and fish."[14]

Superintendent Floyd-Jones cautioned the commissioner that it was impracticable to expect the Indians to give up immediately their lifelong pursuits in exchange for the "domestic habits of the white man."[15] Nevertheless, upon his arrival at Fort Hall Agent Danilson optimistically reported that when Chief Tahgee came to the reservation for a supply of rations, the old Bannock leader said he hoped this would be the last time he would have to take his tribe to Montana to hunt buffalo and that he wanted his people to become farmers and "live more like white folks."[16] At that time Danilson reported the permanent population on the reservation to be eleven hundred — six hundred Bannock and five hundred Shoshoni.[17]

By year's end Superintendent Floyd-Jones announced only "limited success with the farming effort. Of the thirty-five acres planted, only seven produced some potatoes and turnips, the grain crops having been destroyed by drouth and grasshoppers.[18] With the purchase of fifteen yoke of work cattle and three heavy farm wagons, it was hoped that the next year would bring better results.[19]

The meager gains in agriculture were matched by unsuccessful efforts of the Idaho Superintendency to get enough funds from Washington to clothe and subsist the residents of Fort Hall. In reply to Floyd-Jones' request for the $55,000 appropriated by the Forty-first Congress for Fort Hall Reservation, the commissioner sent only $20,625, or "three-fourths of one-half" of the total, explaining that he was retaining one-fourth the amount in case it was needed to settle southwestern Oregon Indians on the Klamath Reservation, as provided in the appropriation act.[20] Undaunted by this disappointment, Agent Danilson then requested the clothing promised the Bannock — and authorized for the Shoshoni by the ruling of the Office of Indian Affairs under Article IX of the Fort Bridger Treaty. He also asked for eleven hundred blankets, to be paid for out of the allowance of "ten dollars per head for each Indian roaming and twenty dollars for each Indian engaged in agriculture." Danilson urged prompt action, especially for the Boise and Bruneau Shoshoni who "are very destitute."[21]

Some time later the commissioner informed Floyd-Jones and Danilson that while

it is true that by the terms of said treaty, the Bannocks are entitled to the clothing for which the Agent estimates; but, as Congress failed to make the necessary appropriations under that treaty, although an estimate was submitted to that body, there are no funds at the disposal of this Department that can be used to purchase the required clothing or any part thereof.[22]

Idaho officials were referred to the letter of July 28 — and the sum of $20,625, which was apparently all the money they were to get for Fort Hall for the fiscal year 1869–1870.

Superintendent Floyd-Jones tried once more, asking that the $30,000 appropriated to settle Shoshoni and Bannock upon the Klamath Reservation be transferred to Fort Hall. In his opinion, no members of the two tribes ever would be located at the Oregon site.[23] With some asperity the commissioner denied the request, instructing Floyd-Jones to "please govern yourself in accordance with the instructions" of the July 28 letter.[24] Two months later the Idaho superintendent again tempted fate and promotion by asking for $5,000 to relieve the "destitute condition" of the Boise and Bruneau Shoshoni. His plea was again denied.[25] The commissioner did authorize $8,000 for the purchase of a saw and grist mill with a shingle machine attached. Danilson traveled to Chicago to make the purchase and arrange for transportation back to Fort Hall.[26]

While grist and sawmills gave promise for the future, lack of funds for clothing and particularly for sufficient rations caused some of the Boise and Bruneau groups to wander back to their old homes in western Idaho, following the traditional migration cycle. As early as June 1869 the *Idaho Statesman* reported Indians on the streets of Boise, wandering around, begging for food, and complaining about the lack of "muck-a-muck on the reservation."[27] When Agent Powell came under attack for permitting the Indians to leave Fort Hall, he defended himself by explaining that he had allowed the Indians to visit Camas Prairie, and they had gone on to Boise. Further, he explained that he refused to keep them in idleness; they wouldn't even fish the stream for food, and in two days they used up rations which were supposed to last for fifteen.[28] The errant Indians were returned to Fort Hall by a detachment of troops from Fort Boise.[29] Another group was back in late November, which led the local editor to remark that the Indians "have no more idea of staying on a reservation than a band of cattle have of remaining in a poor pasture adjoining a corn field surrounded by insufficient fence."[30]

By December the food situation at the reservation was becoming critical. Danilson reported that the number of rations he was forced to distribute had increased by 300 percent since the first of October, with more Indians coming in every day. He estimated that the flour and bacon supplies would not last beyond February 1, 1870. Of the Boise and Bruneau, he wrote:

> Many of them have only such shelters as they can make of grass and bushes, with scarcely rags enough to cover their nakedness. They are without exception the most miserably destitute people imaginable. Requisitions for clothing for this people cannot be filled because Congress failed to make an appropriation for that purpose. Are they "The Wards of the Nation" to perish this Winter? Cannot some provision be made for them? Its heart-rending to visit them in their so-called Camps, this cold weather and see their wretched condition....

"All of the Indians . . . feel they are sadly neglected."[31]

The Bannock, back from the buffalo hunt, had good "Wigwams," some warm clothing, and "a good supply of Ponies." Seeing the plight of the Shoshoni, they must have had an object lesson about what to expect from an uncaring government far away in Washington which rather capriciously disregarded sacred treaty obligations. [32]

To those who knew conditions at the reservation it was not surprising that some of the Indians wandered back to Boise looking for food, which immediately aroused cries from white settlers for the military to force the tribesmen back to Fort Hall. As early as January Agent Powell had begun a ceaseless campaign to get a military post established at Fort Hall, both for the protection of the Indians from unscrupulous whites[33] and, as Superintendent Floyd-Jones put it, "to retain these people on their proper domain" because "moral persuasion" was not sufficient.[34] The *Idaho Statesman* was more blunt: "In order to gain the respect and obedience of the Indian, he must be taught to stand in fear of you like your horse or dog."[35]

By the autumn of 1869 Idaho officials had succeeded in getting the slow-moving government machinery to approve the establishment of a military post at Fort Hall — although there seemed to be some uncertainty, because of "the peculiar geographical position" of the reservation, whether the Department of the Platte or the Department of the Columbia should have jurisdiction over the post. The latter unit of the War Department was finally assigned the responsibility.[36]

In late April 1870 Company C of the Twelfth U.S. Infantry, with ninety privates and noncommissioned officers under the command of Captain J. E. Putnam, reached Fort Hall, coming from Camp Bidwell in northern California.[37]

A site for the post was selected on Lincoln Creek, fifteen miles away from the Indian agency "to prevent the necessary belongings of each, from annoying the other," to use the quaint language of Superintendent Floyd-Jones.[38] But the presence of troops did not affect the results desired by agent and superintendent. For example, when Boise Jim and ten other Boise Shoshoni left the reservation in June 1870, heading for the Boise River, the military commander at Fort Hall refused to aid in returning the Indians. He indicated he had no horses for his men and, furthermore, had no instructions that the troops were to interfere with the Indians in any way.[39] Floyd-Jones asked the commanding general of the Department of the Columbia to correct this "impression that obtains among the troops"[40] but apparently without success, because in late November 1870 the company commander refused a request by the agent to arrest an Indian accused of assaulting some Indian women.[41] Throughout the thirteen years that the military post was maintained at Fort Hall, there continued to be an uneasy association between the local Indian officials and the army troops.

Of much more importance to the Fort Hall agents was their frustrating relationship with the Office of Indian Affairs in Washington and the government's apparent lack of concern about living up to its treaty obligations with the Shoshoni and Bannock. The foregoing detailed description of affairs at Fort Hall during the first year of the reservation shows the pattern which was to occupy the whole decade of the 1870s and lead to an outbreak of violence in the Bannock War of 1878. It will only be necessary to survey in general the happenings of the period until then to realize the government's serious neglect of the Fort Hall Indians.

With the intention of remaking the tribesmen over into exact imitations of white farmers, Congress continuously failed to appropriate the annual funds necessary to complete the transformation. When the Indians, by necessity, were driven back to their old food-hunting habits — digging roots at Camas Prairie and chasing buffalo in Montana — the white citizens and Idaho officials insisted the army return the natives to the reservation, where starvation and the lack of clothing and supplies became the twin spectors of privation.

An example of the gap between fiscal intention and final appropriation on the part of the government occurred in 1870 when the Forty-first Congress was asked for a total of $63,075 to take care of the following items for the Bannock under their treaty of 1868: $10,775 for clothing; $30,000 for articles for roaming Indians and those engaged in farming; $6,800 for the pay of a physician, teacher, and other employees; $500 for prizes for individuals who grew the most valuable crops; and $15,000 for transportation of supplies to the reservation.[42] These sums, of course, did not include any money for the Shoshoni at Fort Hall. The actual amounts finally granted Agent Danilson were $10,125 for the first two quarters of 1870 (of which only $3,125 was for subsistence and $7,000 for the re-establishment of the tribes

Idaho State Historical Society

Shoshoni women and baby on cradleboard.

at Fort Hall[43]) and $6,150 for the third and fourth quarters.[44] Danilson immediately asked for another $1,900 for the operation of the agency, $1,800 to pay for the delivery of 100,000 feet of saw logs, and funds for the fourth quarter — apparently deliberately misreading the commissioner's direction that the $6,150 was for both final quarters of the fiscal year.[45] In reply the commissioner informed Floyd-Jones that, of the $40,000 appropriated for the support of the Shoshoni and Bannock in southern Idaho and southeastern Oregon, only $10,482.88 was left to provide funds for the rest of 1870.[46]

1870   In support of Danilson's plea for more money, Agent J. W. Wham of Fort Bridger in December 1870 asked for the $20,000 due the Bannock under their treaty, reporting that the tribe had been forced to run the risk of destruction in Sioux, Arapaho, and Cheyenne enemy country by hunting buffalo because "the stubborn truth is they must either hunt or starve."[47] Despite the illogic of forcing the Bannock to travel to Fort Bridger for their annuity goods now that Fort Hall was designated as their reservation, the Office of Indian Affairs insisted. Apparently this was easier than revising the bureaucratic system in Washington to accommodate the change.[48]

A final confirmation of the desperate financial straits came when J. N. High relieved Danilson as agent in December and reported that he needed $33,206.19 to support the Fort Hall Indians for the rest of the year. This included $12,412.21 in debts which Danilson had contracted in buying supplies and paying wages, $3,715.88 of this amount being for the third quarter alone.[49] High indicated if he could get the $24,500 which he said was due the Bannock and Shoshoni under the Fort Bridger Treaty, "our trouble ends."[50] The above narrative of moneys asked and only partially delivered was typical of the 1870s.

As late as June 1870 the commissioner was advising Agent Danilson that, since Congress had made no appropriation for supplies, the Indian Office did not know when annuity goods could be issued.[51] As a stop-gap measure the agent was able to get permission to use $355.50 in proceeds from the sale of hay to the local stage company to buy blankets for the Shoshoni at the reservation.[52] When word came that Tahgee would be coming to the reservation by the last of May expecting his annuity goods, Danilson expressed his fears that the disappointment of not receiving them would lead to trouble and the departure of the Bannock to the buffalo plains for another year.[53] A week later, when the chief showed up and found no blankets available, he said *he would not stand it*, which Danilson thought was "strong talk" and might lead to a war unless Floyd-Jones visited the agency at once to help mollify the Bannock.[54] The

three hundred Indians with Tahgee "came in with few Robes, their Ponies jaded and worn out while the Indians themselves were badly off for clothing and blankets."[55] By August Danilson was able to get from Corinne and Salt Lake City only one-fourth the number of blankets required. The commissioner finally authorized a special fund of $3,000 to satisfy the clothing demands of the Bannock, who immediately left for the winter's buffalo hunt.[56] On November 17 the annuity goods finally arrived, several months late, and Danilson kept 156 issues for the Bannock upon their return from the buffalo grounds.[57] In his report to the commissioner, Superintendent Floyd-Jones "regretted" that the article of the Fort Bridger Treaty providing for the distribution of clothing to the Fort Hall Indians each year was "not complied with."[58]

After their fall hunt the Bannock encountered further difficulties. Agent J. W. Wham at Camp Brown, Wyoming Territory, wrote that he had sent a courier after the tribe to bring them into the camp so their presents could be distributed. Wham was certain they would have to be fed — with no food supplies on hand for them. The agent then discovered that an unscrupulous post trader at Fort Ellis, Montana, had lured them there with promises of rifles and revolvers in exchange for their furs and hides. With such confusion reigning about where they were to receive clothing (insufficient for their needs anyway) and with no rations, there should have been no surprise that Tahgee elected to continue the age-old habits of food gathering and that he refused to settle his people permanently at Fort Hall.[59]

Even with the Bannock gone, Agent Danilson reported on November 7 that the cold weather had driven the Shoshoni in from the mountains and that his supply of rations was almost exhausted. He entreated Superintendent Floyd-Jones to furnish sufficient funds so food could be purchased for the hungry Indians before winter snows blocked the roads.[60] A month later he was still writing, "The Agency is destitute of nearly all kinds of winter supplies."[61]

Faced with no assurance of food at Fort Hall, groups of Shoshoni and Bannock wandered away from the reservation to fish for salmon along Snake River, to dig roots at Camas Prairie, or, as in the case of one group of Bannock, to travel to the Umatilla Reservation to trade for horses.[62] Complaints from white settlers and newspaper editors were directed to Danilson, who insisted that only a few families were absent from Fort Hall and that the wandering Indians must not be reservation residents.[63] The editor of the *Idaho Statesman* thought that the "sooner the filthy creatures leave [Boise], the better," and in one outburst attacked easterners who "are not aware that

the tomahawks of most of the tribes in the territories have been baptized in white men's brains."[64] Such animosity on the part of whites left the Shoshoni and Bannock with a Hobson's choice of starving on the reservation or being punished by the military when they left in search of food. The military did not help matters by trying to enlist thirty Bannocks to serve as army scouts, a practice which only encouraged the exciting pursuit of war instead of settling down to become farmers.[65]

More Hunting than Farming

In January Agent Danilson sounded a very pessimistic note about the possibilities of engaging the Indians in agriculture:

> The small amount of funds due the reservation . . . will very much cripple our operations in building and farming in the Spring. It will be impossible to start an Indian farm, and as they have been led to believe . . . that they would be located on little farms of their own in the Spring I fear it will cause a good deal of dissatisfaction.
>
> It seems as though the government has failed in almost every particular in complying with the terms of the treaty made at Fort Bridger in July 1868.
>
> The failure in obtaining clothing for the Indians has caused considerable dissatisfaction and now to fail in giving them seeds, implements, etc. for farming purposes will I fear prove most disastrous to the success of the reservation for the next two or three years.[66]

1870 Despite his doubts and with typical energy and business acumen, Danilson forged ahead and captured the enthusiasm of the Shoshoni, who genuinely wished to learn how to farm. Facing up to the realities of the situation, he was able to convince the Indians that working together on a reservation farm under the direction of a knowledgeable white farmer would be truly advantageous, preparing them for the time when individual farms could be assigned.[67]

In May he reported that the Boise Indians were working "much better than I had reason to expect" with their chief, Captain Jim, directing thirty-three men in the various tasks. A camp of five lodges of Bannock, on the other hand, "positively refused to work" and left for the mountains.[68]

Soon the energetic agent had 125 acres under cultivation and expected to plow another 25. As he said, "The farm is looking fine."[69] He made arrangements to purchase a combined reaping and mowing machine and hay rake.[70]

Then disaster struck. On July 15 the fields were "visited by the grasshoppers." Except for a few potatoes and a portion of the wheat, the crops were destroyed, despite the efforts of the discouraged Indian farmers who burned the grass on the reservation in an attempt to stop the clouds of insects.[71] Nevertheless, Danilson thought the year's experience in farming had prepared his

256 Shoshoni to operate small farms of their own. He doubted that the 520 Bannock assigned to Fort Hall would give up their fondness "for the chase" until circumstances forced a change.[72] Superintendent Floyd-Jones had already made it clear to Danilson that the Fort Hall Reservation was designed as a "permanent home of all the Indians of Eastern and South Eastern Idaho" and not just for the Shoshoni band under Captain Jim Collins and the Bannock tribe under Chief Tahgee.[73]

During the year Lieutenant Danilson also demonstrated his building skills by erecting a saw and shingle mill. By year's end he had 105,000 feet of lumber on hand; had constructed a grist mill, two cottages for employees, carpenter and blacksmith shops; and was bombarding the commissioner for $3,000 to build a barn.[74]

Unfortunately for the Shoshoni and Bannock, Lieutenant Danilson was removed as agent on December 20, despite an unusual and remarkable evaluation by Catholic Father Touissant Mesplie that under Danilson's supervision the Fort Hall Reservation was "one of the best conducted reservations I have yet seen." With twenty years' experience as a missionary in the Pacific Northwest, Father Mesplie was in a position to know, and he said he was "astonished" to learn that "the Agency was yet in its infancy."[75] His plea to the secretary of the Interior that Danilson be retained was unsuccessful; J. N. High took over as agent.[76] At about the same time the Idaho Superintendency was dissolved, and soon the Fort Hall agents were reporting directly to the commissioner in Washington, D.C.[77]

J. N. High had barely settled down at Fort Hall before another change occurred when the agency was transferred from the missionary charge of the Methodist Church to that of the Roman Catholic Church, whose representative, Father Pierre De Smet, recommended that Montgomery P. Berry of Salem, Oregon, be named agent at Fort Hall. Berry's appointment was approved March 27, 1871, and he began his duties on July 1.[78] Their predecessor, W. H. Danilson (now apparently out of the army and addressed as Major Danilson by the *Corinne Reporter*), had begun a ranching operation just north of the reservation. Within four years he would be back as agent at Fort Hall.[79] 1871

The change of agents in 1871 did not alter the pattern of insufficient food, the necessity to leave the reservation on hunting trips, and the discouraging attempts at farming. Chief Tahgee had died during the winter, and without his strong hand the Bannock broke up into smaller groups. One of the larger groups under Otter Beard finally agreed to settle permanently at Fort Hall by September 1 if promised subsistence while they learned to farm.[80] Agent High was able to encourage six Shoshoni to plow "without assistance of whites" and had a number digging ditches to irrigate the farm. He hoped to raise enough produce to feed the Indians during winter,[81] but on July 15 grasshoppers invaded and left "the fields bare."[82] Berry was of the opinion that winter wheat should be sowed in the fall so it would be far enough advanced that the grasshoppers could not destroy it.[83]

Even more disastrous than the insect plagues was the rising indebtedness of the reservation as the paucity of funds forced the agents to contract for supplies and services with no money in the bank. By June 26 High reported a liability of $6,646.93,[84] and soon the lack of a proper congressional appropriation forced the commissioner to issue orders suspending most operations at Fort Hall. Berry inherited the precarious situation and began discharging all the white employees except the chief herder and one or two assistants. With the release of the white farmers the Indians were left alone and still untrained in the art of agriculture.[85]

In late October the Office of Indian Affairs sent Agent Berry $16,020.60 with which to pay an indebtedness which had already risen to $23,097.80 by September 30.[86] Perhaps this was one of the reasons why Berry was officially relieved on December 25 by Johnson N. High, who immediately requested $8,696.33 for the debts contracted during the fourth quarter of 1870, the year before.[87] The constant changing of the guard in Indian agents did not provide the continuity which might have helped improve the financial and subsistence situation at Fort Hall.

All the agents at Forts Hall and Bridger particularly feared the sudden appearance of six hundred aggressive Bannock, who by this time were using the two posts as mere camping places for a couple of months each year to obtain ammunition, clothing, and some food to prepare them for another buffalo hunt. J. N. High wrote in January that he did not know the whereabouts of the Bannock and did not have sufficient appropriation to subsist them if they should suddenly appear.[88] James Irwin at the Wyoming station told the commissioner that he expected the Bannock any day and "I . . . earnestly request you to telegraph telling me what to do."[89] M. P. Berry was of the opinion that the Bannock could have been induced to give up hunting and remain permanently at Fort Hall "had this Agency been prepared to subsist them."[90]

When the tribe came to the reservation in August the Indians were "very much outraged" because they had discovered herds of hogs pastured at Camas Prairie destroying one of their precious food crops.[91] The *Idaho Statesman* carried an article quoting General Edward Canby that he could not furnish any more troops to Idaho Territory to keep the Indians on their reservations and that one of the reasons for their restiveness and bad behavior was the occupation of Camas Prairie by white settlers.[92]

Agent Berry summed up the situation at Fort Hall when he wrote that he was not at all "astonished" at the actions of his predecessors in pushing the Indians off the reservation to hunt and fish. In September 1871 he sent the Shoshoni out to hunt in the area of the Tetons and acknowledged that he would undoubtedly receive some censure from white settlers and officials for his action.[93] He put the problem more succinctly in December, "I have informed the Chief and Headmen, that the young men must hunt, and while I know hunting in this country to be an adsurdity, nevertheless it occasionally leaves more for the indigent."[94] There was not as much concern for the more independent Bannock; Berry knew they would again have to risk attacks from the Blackfeet, Sioux, and other plains tribes in order to get a supply of buffalo meat and robes.

Disappointed in not getting sufficient supplies at Fort Hall so they could abandon their exhausting and unproductive annual hunts, the Bannock turned to the Wind River Reservation, hoping to get some satisfaction for the provisions of their treaty of 1868. Here they encountered increasing hostility from the Sioux, Cheyenne, and Arapaho, who became so bold that the agent at Wind River despaired of keeping his Indians around enough to teach them farming or even to subsist them, and the army could not offer them the needed protection.[95] Agent James Irwin was not particularly enamored of the Bannock, anyway, and usually favored the more pliable Eastern Shoshoni under Washakie. For example, in April of 1872 he arbitrarily took 384 blankets from the Bannock allotment of 1,200 to give to the Shoshoni who, although greater in numbers, had been given only 900 blankets for that year.[96]

Irwin eventually received permission from the secretary of the Interior to convene the Eastern Shoshoni to determine whether they would agree to allow the Bannock to settle permanently at Wind River and thus resolve the constant pulling and hauling of the tribe between that reservation and the one at Fort Hall.[97] After some deliberation in the council meeting the Shoshoni gave their decision:

> Before Tie-gee [Bannock Chief] died the Bannocks had ears. Now they have a great many Chiefs, and they don't hear, any of them, and they will not hear us. They have got no ears. They go off to the Crows and steal horses, and we are afraid they will get us all into trouble. . . . We think it is not best, and do not wish to have the Bannocks as a tribe settled with us.[98]

Irwin added in defense of the Bannock, "They are a superior Indian physically and mentally, to

Bureau of American Ethnology

As early as 1872 (when W. H. Jackson took this picture at Fort Hall Reservation), the Indians were using modern farm machinery.

the Shoshones, and with proper encouragement are capable of making rapid progess." He also indicated that the tribe preferred the Portneuf country, as Tahgee had insisted back in 1868.

The Wyoming agent persisted in trying to get the Bannock permanently settled at Fort Hall, saying that the Eastern Shoshoni were reluctant to begin farming as long as the Bannock were around to "devour their living." He also tried to arrange for the Bannock annuity goods to be redirected to Fort Hall.[99] These actions were so successful that by November 1872 Agent High at Fort Hall was complaining that now that the tribe "was making this their home instead of a temporary camp," he needed additional funds for subsistence and to pay the freight charges to transship the annuity goods from Wind River.[100]

The almost twelve hundred Indians at Fort Hall taxed the ingenuity and efforts of the agent to find enough food for them, despite their first really successful year at farming. By year's end there were 250 acres under cultivation which could have been "2,000 acres instead of what it is if the treaty stipulations had been regarded on the part of the Government." At least J. N. High thought so. He reported a yield of 3,450 bushels of grain and 4,500 bushels of potatoes, com-

mended the "excellent farmhands" from among the Shoshoni, and reiterated that the "vagabond" Bannock could also become good farmers if only the government would provide for them while they learned. High also regretted that the grist mill was not operating because of a lack of lumber to complete it and that 123,780 feet of sawlogs had been rotting in the yard for two years for lack of funds to hire people to convert the logs into usable material.[101]

The improved harvest of 1872 still was not sufficient to provide for the needs of the almost twelve hundred Indians at Fort Hall. Therefore, M. P. Berry inquired at the first of the year for permission to grant permits to the Shoshoni and Bannock to travel to Camas Prairie to get their annual supply of roots. He explained in some detail that, in addition to being an area for food production, the camas prairies of the west were looked upon by all tribes as neutral ground where their people could gather to trade horses, visit, and be immune for a while from the intertribal warfare which usually characterized their nations. He again explained that the Bannock had a legal right to the Camas Prairie under their treaty and under the provision which allowed them to hunt on the unoccupied lands of the United States.

Berry expressed the fear that white occupation of the great Camas Prairie and the practice of feeding hogs there would lead to hostility with the Indians. Already the Fort Hall people had admitted they allowed their dogs to worry to death three or four hogs.[102] When the Shoshoni and Bannock left for the camas grounds in late May the stage was set for the first year of major confrontation with white settlers over possession of Camas Prairie — a tragedy which was re-enacted each succeeding year until about two hundred Bannock warriors went to war with the United States in 1878 to protest the invasion of the prairie by the hog ranchers.[103]

1872

A war scare soon filled the columns of the Idaho newspapers when a dozen or so young Bannock braves attacked a party of three white men on Wood River in June, killing one, wounding another, and stealing several horses belonging to the whites. Governor Thomas W. Bennett of Idaho immediately sent Clitus Barbour to investigate. Barbour reported back that the story of the attack was true, that there were twelve hundred Indians at Camas Prairie composed of Lemhi under Chief Tendoy and a large number of Fort Hall Indians under the nominal leadership of Bannock Jim, and that he had advised them to return to the reservations while the white citizens were sending their wives and children to Boise for safety.[104]

Agent High dispatched S. G. Fisher, post trader at Fort Hall, to investigate. Governor Bennett also met some of the Indians about fifty miles east of Boise and exacted a promise that they would return at once to the reservation, a promise which they broke by continuing on to Weiser River. Understandably the belligerent *Idaho Statesman* editor accused High of sending the Indians away from the reservation "in order to get rid of feeding them" which certainly was true.[105] The *Owyhee Avalanche*, claiming the Indians were peaceful, entered the fray by accusing the *Idaho Statesman* of "wilfully" printing exaggerated reports of the incident.[106]

As the newspaper war continued, the *Idaho Statesman* became more and more bloodthirsty, editorializing that "If they [Indians] attempt another raid through here we will give some of them passes that will do them for all time and ensure their safe transit to their happy hinting [sic] ground."[107] Later, in October, the editor thought that if the Indians left the reservation again "they should be shot down."[108] Agent High, on the other hand, reported that the Bannock and Shoshoni were frightened about the Wood River murder and were moving to Fort Hall as rapidly as possible.[109] He indicated that the killing was done by young men of Pagwite's band under the influence of some medicine men[110] and said he

Bureau of American Ethnology

A Shoshoni cattle herd in the reservation corral also interested Jackson.

Bureau of American Ethnology

Although they had a modern barn for their cattle, Jackson found that the Shoshoni still lived in tipis on their reservation.

was confident of arresting the murderers and charging them with the crime.[111] The whole affair foreshadowed further troubles over Camas Prairie.

During the troubled year, 1872, Fort Hall Reservation experienced a double change of agents. Johnson N. High relieved M. P. Berry on May 25[112] and then requested a leave of absence "for the purpose of meeting a matrimonial engagement" while all the turmoil was taking place at Camas Prairie.[113] High was notified on November 16, rather summarily, "that his services as Special Agent will be dispensed with," and Henry W. Reed of Iowa took his place on January 7, 1873.[114] The Shoshoni and Bannock could hardly keep up with the rapid turnover of officials who were supposed to care for them.

1873

The new agent found the same basic problem faced by his predecessors — not enough food supplies for his wards. By early January 1873 he had only enough beef to last four weeks, with almost fifteen hundred Indians relying on his efforts to obtain food.[115] The annuity goods for the Bannock had been directed again to Wind River. Because of transportation difficulties they finally arrived in April, about eight months late, and were sufficient to meet only half the needs of the

tribe. Reed reported the supplies would have been "of far greater worth to them during the severity of the winter" but "they made the best of the matter" with the meager provisions.[116]

The Indians were anxious to begin farming for themselves. Thirty were regularly employed at the agency, among them several Bannock "a thing unknown until this year."[117] In his annual report of October, Reed described the thirty or so "cheerful" workers and many others who were ready to do almost anything to earn a livelihood. "It seems a sad pity to see hundreds of men and women ready to labor even for the smallest income, and yet have to remain from year to year with nothing to do."[118] Twenty-five lodges of the Bannock, perhaps one hundred and fifty in number, refused to put up with the inactivity and lack of food on the reservation and left for the buffalo country in late fall.[119]

As early as January 1873 Agent Reed had questioned the commissioner concerning the prospects of enough subsistence supplies to keep the Indians at Fort Hall — or, he asked, should he allow them "to scatter out" to Camas Prairie and Boise River as well as the Montana plains.[120] The answer was obvious. By late April many groups were hunting for subsistence at their old haunts, just

Bureau of American Ethnology

While at the Fort Hall Reservation, Jackson also photographed this large family group, which retained their native hair styles but had a mixture of new and traditional clothing.

when news broke of the Modoc War in northern California.

The murders of General Canby and "a Doctor Thomas" by Captain Jack, the Modoc leader, during a peace parley sent a wave of hysteria through the west. The *Idaho Statesman* gave a run-down of the whereabouts of Indian groups: one hundred under Eagle Eye at the head of Weiser River, twelve or so at the mouth of the river, and other small bands on the Owyhee, Malheur, Boise, and Bruneau rivers.[121] Despite protestations from Indian officials that the Indians from Fort Hall and elsewhere were peaceable and friendly, engaged only in food gathering,[122] the frontier news editions were convinced they were "saucy" and were burning fences, turning their horses into green fields, and worst of all, roaming about.[123] Other excited citizens reported a band of thirty Indians from Fort Hall who had commandeered three beeves from a local Malad rancher, a dangerous group of Indians in Payette, and a war dance held near Elko, Nevada.[124]

As rumors spread, the citizens took military preparations into their own hands, organizing a militia company at Boise, some horse guards in Payette Valley, and a company of 120 horse guards at Warren "if all could be found sober at once." Governor T. W. Bennett authorized the distribution of 500 Springfield rifles and considerable ammunition to the various local militia groups.[125] Father Mesplie of the Catholic Mission in Idaho came under vicious attack by the *Idaho Statesman* for issuing "recommend papers" to some of his Indian converts who had been "baptized and are good Indians." The editor proposed "that they be immersed, and the longer they are held under the better." He insisted the "Indian problem" needed to be settled at once and permanently.[126]

Bureau of American Ethnology

Wastawana

1873

Agreement of 1873

Part of the problem between white settlers and Indians at Fort Hall was the undefined boundaries of the reservation. Starting in 1869 the agents had persistently requested that an accurate survey be made, but nothing was accomplished until the summer of 1873 when the outside lines of the reserve were finally and explicitly marked. The surveyor general of Idaho at first recommended that the Fort Hall Reservation be abolished and another location found for the Shoshoni and Bannock. He finally agreed to the survey, with the advice that the reservation should be subdivided. This would satisfy the needs of the Indians for a definite and permanent home and would grant legal possession of farms to about fifty families of white settlers in Marsh Valley on the southern portion of the reserve.[127]

Throughout the summer of 1873, while surveying parties were out and while white citizens were drilling and arming themselves to contain the Indians, negotiations were underway to revise the Fort Bridger Treaty of 1868. In a long letter dated February 15 Idaho Governor Bennett described the necessities of the situation. First, the provision encompassing Camas Prairie as a portion of the Fort Hall Reservation should be abrogated. Second, the right of the Bannock and Shoshoni to hunt on unoccupied lands of the United States needed to be revoked. Third, the "painted savages" must be confined to their reservations and not allowed to roam around, particularly to Camas Prairie where they met annually with other tribes in a "general frolic." To effect these objectives, the governor recommended a special commission to meet with the Shoshoni and Bannock to revise their treaty.[128]

The secretary of the Interior responded by naming General J. P. C. Shanks, a congressman from Indiana, Governor T. W. Bennett, and Agent Henry W. Reed as the three members of the commission.[129] In his charge to Shanks, the secretary directed the general to insist to the Indians that they remain on their reservation and "adopt agricultural and pastoral pursuits" in which they would receive "proper encouragement and assistance."[130] To another delegation of government officials the secretary instructed G. W. Ingalls and J. W. Powell to try to induce the Western Shoshoni of northeastern Nevada and the Gosiute Shoshoni of western Utah to move to the Fort Hall Reservation.[131]

When General Shanks did not appear to meet with the Indians on July 12, as scheduled by the governor, the disappointed Shoshoni and Bannock left for the camas grounds and the salmon fisheries.[132] The delay prompted the secretary of the Interior to broaden his instructions to the commission to include established conferences with the "scattered and wandering tribes" of southern Idaho to persuade them to move to Fort Hall. "In fact the whole subject of our Indian relations in Idaho should be canvassed."[133] Henry Reed agreed and suggested that the main council with the Shoshoni and Bannock be held in mid-August at Camas Prairie, where the nonreservation Indians could participate.[134] Unfortunately, the nomadic natives had already scattered when the commission reached the prairie. The council was postponed until October, when it was held at Fort Hall.[135]

The *Idaho Statesman* was pessimistic about the success of the new agreement in limiting the Indians to roam over the country "on the pretense of fishing and hunting."[136] The editor's doubts increased when he received a report of General Shank's recommendation, which generally outlined a very enlightened program for the Indians. The *Statesman* responded that the general apparently considered the white man's right to be secondary: "The general don't get out of the old fogy notions about the Indian." The editor preferred Governor Bennett's approach that Indians had no real ownership of the soil and should be forced to go to a reservation chosen by the government "without consulting the Indians."[137]

While the provisions concerning the trespass of white cattlemen, freighters, and stagecoach companies is discussed in the chapter dealing with cattle raising, it is important to consider the other recommendations of the commission. The key provision nullified the right of the Bannock and Shoshoni to hunt on the unoccupied lands, which supposedly would confine them to the reservation and eliminate the chance of conflict with white settlers. Supplementary to this was the requirement that the following wandering tribes be required to make Fort Hall their permanent home: Eagle Eye's band from Weiser River, Winnamucca's band near the Central Pacific Railroad, Bannock Johns' band of rovers, John Winnamucca's band of rovers, and Anamon's band in Box Elder County in Utah. The second most important recommendation about which the commission dwelt at length was to move the Lemhi tribe from the Salmon River area to Fort Hall and then to place all the Indians at the reservation under the command of "Tin-a-dore," chief of the Lemhi and "one of the noblest Indians in America." Through his wisdom, business acumen, and impressive leadership, it was hoped the government agents would be able to control affairs at Fort Hall and teach the Indians the arts of civilization.[138]

In conclusion the commission approved the reservation system as the best approach and urged the government as soon as possible to apportion the lands at Fort Hall to heads of families, who could then learn to farm and support themselves: "It would ruin any people to feed and maintain them in idleness at a common crib." Thus, with the characteristic approach of the aggressive Anglo-Saxon philosophy, the commissioners proposed the allotment system which, over the years, proved almost catastrophic to a people steeped in the tradition of communal land ownership. In a final judgment the commissioner regretfully wrote, "The people of Idaho have the general dislike to Indians that is felt to some extent all over the West" a condition which the commissioner thought would be greatly alleviated if the Indians were confined to the reservation and kept apart from white settlers.[139]

Continued Lack of Funds and Food

As federal officials decided the fate of the two tribes and pondered the most effective methods of keeping them locked up at Fort Hall where they could be "civilized," charges were made that the internal administration in that small unit of government was not conducive to the betterment of the Shoshoni and Bannock. The *Idaho*

Statesman reported another "Credit Mobilier" in the Indian Service and cited as an example Fort Hall, where $10,000 worth of improvements were the result of a $100,000 investment. The newspaper blamed the voucher system, which allowed the agent to fill in any amount after getting a blank voucher signed by the employee.[140] Later the paper charged that Agent Reed was wronging the Indians in his distribution of annuity goods and "in various other ways, too numerous to mention."[141] It was true that former agents apparently saw opportunities for profit at the reservation; mention has already been made that W. H. Danilson settled north of the reservation, where he engaged in the profitable business of selling beef cattle to the agency. Former agent Johnson N. High, now of Ross Fork, applied for a license to trade with the Indians. This was denied by Agent Reed, who soon came under attack by High's friends for his action.[142]

Reed also was charged in March of 1874, as a result of an inspection by Thomas K. Cree, with furnishing food for his family and white employees from the sale of hides of the beef cattle slaughtered for the use of the Indians. Further, Reed's daughter was employed as the cook and her husband as the assistant farmer.[143] The agent replied at length to the attack that he was only following the practices set by his predecessors; that the cattle were delivered net weight and therefore the hides had not been paid for out of Indian funds; and that he assumed the commissioner wanted white employees with families to assure a stable and moral atmosphere.[144]

Reed soon became embroiled in another dispute with former Agent High over renewal of the latter's license as post trader. High, stating he wanted only sufficient time to close out his affairs and dispose of his goods so he could return East, claimed that Reed wished to award the tradership either to C. C. Roberts of Salt Lake City or, preferably, to his own son-in-law.[145] Several friends supported High's request, and he and Reed finally agreed on a sale to anyone whom the agent might designate, in return for a new license to allow time for High to sell his goods. One other stipulation required High to get rid of his partner, S. G. Fisher, who apparently had earned the intense dislike of Reed.[146]

At this juncture the Shoshoni and Bannock became active participants in the dispute. Fisher convened them in council, secured an interpreter, and supervised the drafting of a letter from the Indians to Governor Bennett, listing many grievances against Reed and asking for his removal. Among the accusations were that Reed's only concern was for the members of his own family — who were paid well for doing little work and were fed the best foods "while our women and children

are hungry for flour and meat. For three weeks our children have been crying for food; in that time he has given us nothing. There is flour — hundreds of sacks — and beef cattle at the agency. Why should we suffer?" A second charge was that the agent would not allow them to travel to Camas Prairie and to the Umatilla Reservation — but the next paragraph attacked Reed for not keeping the Indians at Fort Hall where the chiefs could control them. A third indictment was that Reed sold lumber, hogs, hay, and beef hides and pocketed the money. In a final denunciation the Indians protested that Reed allowed his son-in-law and other white men to debauch Indian women. The letter closed with these words:

> We want you to speak loud so they can hear you in Washington.
>
> We are not mad. We are very tired of talking. . . . If you lose our words like the men who have been here before, we are afraid our people will all scatter so only the wind can find them. . . . Our Agent has no ears, no eyes, no heart. . . . We want an Agent who always speaks the truth; who will not let us suffer; who will not wrong us, and will make this our home and be our father.

The missive was signed by Chiefs Captain Jim and Pocatello John and by Headmen Gibson Jack, Jack Ballard, and Cash [Cache] Valley Tom.[147]

Reaction to the Indian request was immediate. The *Idaho Statesman* called for Reed's removal;[148] Reed revoked the trading license for High;[149] and the latter again appealed to the commissioner, accusing the agent of attempting to get High to connive to break the law.[150] In his defense to Washington, Reed listed his reasons for revoking the license: High and Fisher kept their store open on the Sabbath; they allowed profane and obscene language to be used in the store; and, what was worse, one of the partners (Fisher no doubt) made "dirty, false and profane remarks about the Agent" before the Indians.[151] Evidently the Washington office now made the decision that Reed's usefulness at Fort Hall had come to an end. On October 8, 1874, the secretary of the Interior formally accepted the resignation of Henry W. Reed. James Wright of the Crow Agency was transferred to Fort Hall, taking over as agent officially on December 24.[152]

As one considers the charges and recriminations a hundred years later, Fisher certainly had every incentive to get rid of Reed, but he was very circumspect in the way he handled the writing of the Indian letter to Governor Bennett. High apparently wanted only to escape back to Ohio with as much of his investment intact as possible. Reed was quite probably guilty of peculation and was certainly culpable of being a grasping man of poor judgment, whose concern for the Indians was apparently minimal.[153] As for the Shoshoni and Bannock, they suffered most of all; any improvement in their condition was severely hampered by the year-long quarrel over who should have the opportunity to extract profits from them.

While the internal troubles at Fort Hall escalated, the impoverished Indians continued their usual peregrinations after food and encountered the resultant white opposition to their nomadic wanderings. Governor T. W. Bennett wrote a long letter to the commissioner complaining that Eagle Eye's band on the Weiser River was striking terror among the settlers, that there were a number of straggling bands along the Snake and Bruneau rivers, and that the Lemhi under Tendoy were uncared for. He recommended, first, that all these Indians be placed on either the Fort Hall, Lapwai, or Umatilla reservations, by force if necessary; second, that the Indians should never be permitted to leave except in small groups and with special passes; and third, that a special agent be assigned at Boise to deal with any Indians who might illegally appear in that area.[154]

The Eagle Eye band was considered to be the worst threat, as petitions came in to the governor asking that the Indians be sent to Fort Hall.[155] While waiting for action from the commissioner in Washington, the governor requisitioned ninety Springfield rifles and the same number of Colt revolvers, to be distributed to the militia companies.[156] In September Agent Reed reported that the Lemhi and Weiser still refused to move to the reservation, partly because of lack of funds to effect the move.[157]

The governor and Idaho Delegate John Hailey worked hard to get a congressional appropriation of $20,000 to finance the roundup of all the scattered Indians to be placed on reservations. The amount was scaled down to $10,000 and finally voted, but in late October the commissioner informed Bennett that the sum was not to be used for the purpose intended. Instead, it was to be divided among the various Idaho agents because the amount was "barely sufficient, with the strictest economy to meet necessary contingent expenses of the Fort Hall, Fort Lemhi and Nez Perce Agencies."[158]

1874   The panic of 1873 had worsened the usual precarious financial condition of the Office of Indian Affairs. The Fort Hall Agency especially felt the bite of the congressional wolf at the door. In August Reed still was waiting for funds to pay deficiencies already accumulated, including a debt owed the beef contractor and back wages owed various Indian employees.[159] A month later he still was "embarassed"[160] and finally had to get the consent of the Bannock to use the clothing fund for debts contracted the previous fiscal year.[161] When Wright took over in December he listed $9,705.25 in overdue accounts, for which he asked a special appropriation.[162]

Apparently one of the main reasons for the indebtedness was Reed's practice of ordering sufficient food supplies whether funds were available or not. As a result he was able to report in March 1874 that he had heard "scarcely" a complaint from the Indians about rations.[163] When Wright examined the agency in November, prior to taking official charge, he found only enough funds to provide beef to January 1, which meant he would not be able to keep the Indians on the reservation and that "they will be compelled to rove and live as they can by stealing or begging."[164] On December 30 he was still imploring the Indian Office for subsistence funds to feed the 1,462 Indians at Fort Hall. He concluded, "The credit of the Peace Policy of the Government is at stake. If these people can be subsisted here they are willing to stay, and do what they can in order to support themselves."[165] As for the annuity goods, he reported, "These people are anxious to adopt citizens' dress." He asked the Indian Office to be guided in its selection of clothing for the Indians in light of this change.[166]

The lack of comprehension on the part of Washington officials about the situation at Fort Hall was dramatically illustrated during the summer of 1874. Agent Reed was notified that rations would be issued to all able-bodied male Indians only if they performed some kind of service equal in value to the food they received. Reed patiently explained that if the instructions were followed many of the Indians would immediately leave the reservation to return to their hunting habits. He pleaded for a suspension of the orders so he could continue to subsist the Indians while they learned to farm.[167] Constant reports indicated that the Shoshoni and some Bannock were anxious to begin farming, and, with no crickets or grasshoppers during the growing season, the agency farm was quite successful in 1874.[168] In his annual report Agent Reed indicated the enthusiasm with which Indians anticipated operating farms of their own and said he regretted the lack of funds which prohibited him from furnishing enough white farmers to teach the arts of agriculture.[169] It was ironic that the commissioner, in his final report, could say, "The results of efforts to induce civilization upon this reservation have not so far satisfactorily corresponded with expenditures as at most other points." Furthermore, he said, there was insufficient information "by which the Office can account for these small results."[170] Perhaps he failed to notice Reed's note to the effect that the Agreement of 1873 with the Shoshoni and Bannock had not been ratified. They were now not sure what their obligations were or what privileges, if any, they had as wards of the government.[171]

The first five years of reservation life had been

anything but promising. The rapid turnover of agents, governmental neglect in appropriating the funds called for under the Treaty of Fort Bridger, and the unsuccessful attempts at farming (made worse by the lack of implements and seeds and by the annual attacks of grasshoppers) forced the more independent Shoshoni and Bannock to continue their traditional migrations in search of food, with the concomitant requests from white settlers that the military return the Indians to their reservation. Changing the habits of centuries would have been difficult enough with all the financial assistance and moral support the government could have supplied. Without these crucial aids the Shoshoni and Bannock wandered in despair, trying to keep from starving while an apathetic Washington made desultory attempts to care for them

The Agreement of 1873, if it had been ratified, would have solved some of the problems of trespass and could have brought in additional revenue from white users of reservation lands. Again, the Indians were to learn that agreements sacred to them were apparently of inconsequential concern to the Great Father.

NOTES CHAPTER IV
BUFFALO AND GOVERNMENT BEEF

1. Charles F. Powell to C.I.A., June 30, 1869, *Idaho Superintendency*, Roll 338.
2. D. W. Ballard to C.I.A., July 15, 1869, ibid.
3. C.I.A., to Sec. of Interior, July 23, 1869, *Idaho Superintendency*, Microcopy No. 832, Roll 1.
4. De L. Floyd-Jones to W. H. Danilson, Aug. 7, 1869, *Idaho Superintendency*, Microcopy 832, Roll 3.
5. C.I.A., to De Lancy Floyd-Jones, Aug. 24, 1869, *Idaho Superintendency*, *Field Papers*, Exhibit No. 214, Indian Claims Commission, Docket Nos. 326, 366, 367; Kappler, *Indian Affairs: Laws and Treaties*, Vol. 1, 839.
6. Ibid.
7. De L. Floyd-Jones to C.I.A., Aug. 26, 1869, *Idaho Superintendency*, Microcopy 832, Roll 3.
8. De L. Floyd-Jones to C.I.A., Sept. 2, 1869, *Idaho Superintendency*, Roll 338; Acting C.I.A. to De Lancy Floyd-Jones, Sept. 13, 1869, *Idaho Superintendency*, Microcopy 832, Roll 1; C.I.A., to De Lancy F. Jones, Sept. 11, 1869, ibid.
9. *Idaho Statesman*, June 5, July 13, 27, 1869; W. H. Danilson to De L. Floyd-Jones, July 30, 1869, *Idaho Superintendency*, Microcopy 832, Roll 2.
10. J. C. Kinney to Charles F. Powell, April 13, 1869, ibid.; W. H. Danilson, Sept. 1, 1869, *Idaho Superintendency*, Roll 339; Charles Hygham to W. H. Danilson, Sept. 18, 1869, *Idaho Superintendency*, Roll 339.
11. Acting C.I.A., to De L. Floyd-Jones, Sept. 14, 1869, *Idaho Superintendency*, Microcopy 832, Roll 1.
12. "Treaty with Shoshonees and Bannacks, July 3, 1868," *Statutes at Large*, No. 15, 673–678.
13. Charles F. Powell to D. W. Ballard, April 26, 1869, *Idaho Superintendency*, Microcopy 832, Roll 2; Charles F. Powell to D. W. Ballard, May 30, 1869, ibid.
14. Charles F. Powell to D. W. Ballard, June 30, 1869, ibid.
15. De. L. Floyd-Jones to C.I.A., Aug. 26, 1869, *Idaho Superintendency*, Microcopy 832, Roll 3.
16. W. H. Danilson to Floyd-Jones, Aug. 30, 1869, *Idaho Superintendency*, Microcopy 832, Roll 2.
17. W. H. Danilson to Floyd-Jones, Aug. 1869, ibid.
18. Floyd-Jones to C.I.A., Sept. 25, 1869, *Idaho Superintendency*, Microcopy 832, Roll 3.
19. W. H. Danilson to Floyd-Jones, Nov. 15, 1869, *Idaho Superintendency*, Microcopy 832, Roll 2.
20. C.I.A., to Floyd-Jones, July 28, 1869, *Idaho Superintendency*, Microcopy 832, Roll 1.
21. W. H. Danilson to Floyd-Jones, Sept. 13, 1869, *Idaho Superintendency*, Roll 338; W. H. Danilson to Floyd-Jones, Aug. 30, 1869, *Idaho Superintendency*, Microcopy 832, Roll 2.
22. C.I.A. to Floyd-Jones, Oct. 4, 1869, *Idaho Superintendency*, Microcopy 832, Roll 1.
23. Floyd-Jones to C.I.A., Oct. 5, 1869, *Idaho Superintendency*, Microcopy 832, Roll 3.
24. C.I.A. to Floyd-Jones, Oct. 16, 1869, *Idaho Superintendency*, Microcopy 832, Roll 1.
25. C.I.A. to Floyd-Jones, Dec. 28, 1869, ibid.
26. Floyd-Jones to Danilson, Sept. 22, 1869, *Idaho Superintendency*, Microcopy 832, Roll 3.
27. *Idaho Statesman*, June 26, July 15, 1869.
28. Ibid., Aug. 3, 1869.
29. Floyd-Jones to Col. J. B. Sinclair, Sept. 24, 1869, *Idaho Superintendency*, Microcopy 832, Roll 3; Floyd-Jones to C.I.A., Sept. 25, 1869, ibid.; Floyd-Jones to Col. J. B. Sinclair, Sept. 28, 1869, ibid.
30. *Idaho Statesman*, Nov. 27, 1869.
31. W. H. Danilson to Floyd-Jones, Dec. 3, 1869, *Idaho Superintendency*, Microcopy 832, Roll 2.
32. Ibid.
33. D. W. Ballard to General George E. Crook, Jan. 18, 1869, *Idaho Superintendency*, Microcopy 832, Roll 3; Charles F. Powell to D. W. Ballard, May 30, 1869, *Idaho Superintendency*, Microcopy 832, Roll 2; E. D. Townsend to Secretary of Interior, July 29, 1869, *Idaho Superintendency*, Roll 338; Secretary of Interior to C.I.A., July 30, 1869, ibid.; C.I.A. to Floyd-Jones, Aug. 3, 1869, *Idaho Superintendency*, Microcopy 832, Roll 1.
34. Floyd-Jones to C.I.A., October, 1869, *Idaho Superintendency*, Microcopy 832, Roll 3; Floyd-Jones to Capt. Nickerson, Oct. 2, 1869, ibid.
35. *Idaho Statesman*, June 19, 1869.
36. E. D. Townsend to General P. H. Sheridan, Nov. 2, 1869, *Idaho Superintendency*, Roll 338; E. D. Townsend to General George H. Thomas, Dec. 2, 1869, ibid.
37. *Utah Reporter*, April 28, 1870.
38. Floyd-Jones to E. H. Sudington, May 17, 1870, *Idaho Superintendency*, Microcopy 832, Roll 3.
39. W. H. Danilson to Floyd-Jones, June 2, 1870, *Fort Hall Letter Book*, 41.
40. Floyd-Jones to General George Crook, June 28, 1870, ibid.
41. Lt. George Wilson to W. H. Danilson, Nov. 30, 1870, *Record Group 393*.
42. *Statutes at Large*, Vol. XVI, 352.
43. Floyd-Jones to W. H. Danilson, Feb. 3, 1870, *Idaho Superintendency*, Microcopy 832, Roll 3.
44. Acting C.I.A. to Floyd-Jones, Oct. 11, 1870, *Idaho Superintendency*, Microcopy 832, Roll 1.
45. W. H. Danilson to C.I.A., Nov. 23, 1870, *Idaho Superintendency*, Roll 339.
46. C.I.A. to Floyd-Jones, Nov. 30, 1870, *Idaho Superintendency*, Microcopy 832, Roll 1.
47. J. W. Wham to C.I.A., Dec. 1, 1870, *Wyoming Superintendency*, Roll 953.
48. Acting C.I.A. to W. H. Danilson, June 18, 1870, *Idaho Superintendency*, Microcopy 832, Roll 1.
49. J. N. High to C.I.A., Dec. 21, 1870, *Idaho Superintendency*, Roll 339.
50. J. N. High to C.I.A., Dec. 30, 1870, ibid.
51. C.I.A. to W. H. Danilson, June 18, 1870, *Idaho Superintendency*, Microcopy 832, Roll 1.
52. C.I.A. to Floyd-Jones, April 2, 1870, ibid.; W. H. Danilson to Floyd-Jones, March 5, 1870, *Fort Hall Letter Book*, 31.
53. W. H. Danilson to C.I.A., May 24, 1870, *Fort Hall Letter Book*, 346.
54. W. H. Danilson to Floyd-Jones, June 2, 1870, ibid., 40.
55. W. H. Danilson to Floyd-Jones, July 9, 1870, ibid., 44.
56. W. H. Danilson to Floyd-Jones, Aug. 26, 1870, ibid., 48–49.
57. W. H. Danilson to C.I.A., Dec. 3, 1870, ibid., 60.
58. Floyd-Jones to C.I.A., Sept, 10, 1870, *C.I.A. Annual Report*, 647.
59. J. W. Wham to C.I.A., Nov. 30, 1870, *Wyoming Superintendency*, Roll 953; J. W. Wham to C.I.A., Dec. 10, 1870, ibid.; J. W. Wham to C.I.A., Dec. 19, 1870, ibid.
60. W. H. Danilson to Floyd-Jones, Nov. 7, 1870, *Fort Hall Letter Book*, 56–57.
61. W. H. Danilson to C.I.A., Dec. 3, 1870, ibid., 61.
62. *Idaho Statesman*, March 10, June 25, 1870.
63. W. H. Danilson to Floyd-Jones, March 17, 1870, *Fort Hall Letter Book*, 33–34.
64. *Idaho Statesman*, April 16, June 25, 1870
65. D. S. Gordon to George D. Ruggles, April 19, 1870, *Wyoming Superintendency*, Roll 953; J. A. Campbell to General C. C. Augur, April 30, 1870, ibid.
66. W. H. Danilson to Floyd-Jones, Jan. 10, 1870, *Fort Hall Letter Book*, 24–26.
67. W. H. Danilson to Floyd-Jones, March 5, 1870, ibid., 31–32; W. H. Danilson to Floyd-Jones, April 6, 1870, ibid., 35; W. H. Danilson to Floyd-Jones, April 9, 1820, ibid., 37.
68. W. H. Danilson to Floyd-Jones, May 2, 1870, ibid., 38–39.
69. W. H. Danilson to Floyd-Jones, June 2, 1870, ibid., 41–42; W. H. Danilson to Floyd-Jones, July 9, 1870, ibid., 44–45.
70. C.I.A. to Floyd-Jones, April 27, 1870, *Idaho Superintendency*, Microcopy 832, Roll 1.
71. W. H. Danilson to Floyd-Jones, Aug. 9, 1870, *Fort Hall Letter Book*, 46–47; *Helena Herald*, Aug. 2, 1870.
72. W. H. Danilson to Frances A. Walker, Sept. 1, 1870, U.S. National Archives, Bureau of Indian Affairs, *Field Papers, Idaho Superintendency*.
73. Floyd-Jones to W. H. Danilson, May 28, 1870, ibid.
74. *C.I.A. Annual Report, 1870*, 562–653.
75. T. Mesplie to Secretary of Interior, Nov. 22, 1870, *Idaho Superintendency*, Roll 339.
76. J. N. High to C.I.A., Dec. 20, 1870, ibid.; Lt. Danilson was removed as the result of Congressional passage of a bill on July 15, 1870 forbidding military personnel to hold civil office.
77. C.I.A. to Floyd-Jones, Nov. 3, 1870, *Idaho Superintendency*, Microcopy 832, Roll 1.
78. Secretary of Interior to C.I.A., March 24, 27, 1871, *Idaho Superintendency*, Roll 339.
79. M. P. Berry to C.I.A., July 31, 1871, ibid.; *Corinne Reporter*, May 24, 1871.
80. J. W. Wham to C.I.A., May 26, 1871, *Wyoming Superintendency*, Roll 953; M. P. Berry to C.I.A., July 8, Aug. 10, 1871, *Idaho Superintendency*, Roll 339.
81. J. N. High to C.I.A., May 5, 1871, *Fort Hall Letter Book*, 69.
82. M. P. Berry to C.I.A., Aug. 8, 1871, ibid., 75.
83. M. P. Berry to C.I.A., July 8, 1871, *Idaho Superintendency*, Roll 339.
84. J. N. High to C.I.A., June 26, 1871, ibid.
85. M. P. Berry to C.I.A., Sept. 2, 1871, ibid.

86. M. P. Berry to Acting C.I.A., Oct. 25, 1871, ibid.
87. J. N. High to C.I.A., Dec. 22, 1871, *Fort Hall Letter Book*, 367.
88. J. N. High to C.I.A., Jan. 3, 1871, ibid., 64–65.
89. James Irwin to C.I.A., Sept. 1, 1871, *Wyoming Superintendency*, Roll 953.
90. M. P. Berry to C.I.A., Sept. 1, 1871, *Fort Hall Letter Book*, 78.
91. M. P. Berry to C.I.A., Sept. 4, 1871,: ibid., 89–90.
92. *Idaho Statesman*, Aug. 29, 1871.
93. M. P. Berry to C.I.A., Sept. 1, 1871, *Fort Hall Letter Book*, 87.
94. M. P. Berry to C.I.A., Dec. 1, 1871, ibid., 97.
95. James Irwin to Commanding General, Department of the Platte, Apr. 3, 1872, *Wyoming Superintendency*, Roll 954; James Irwin to C.I.A., May 1, 1872, ibid,; James Irwin to C.I.A., May 24, 1872, ibid.
96. James Irwin to C.I.A., April 27, 1872, ibid.
97. Sec. of Interior to C.I.A., March 2, 1872, ibid.
98. James Irwin to C.I.A., May 24, 1872, ibid.; Felix R. Brunot to C.I.A., Oct. 26, 1872, ibid.; James Irwin to C.I.A., May 31, 1872, ibid.
99. James Irwin to C.I.A., Aug. 26, Oct. 3, Oct. 24, 1872, ibid.
100. James Irwin to C.I.A., Nov., 4, 1872, ibid.
101. *C.I.A. Annual Report, 1872*, 656–657.
102. M. P. Berry to C.I.A., Jan. 1, 1872, *Fort Hall Letter Book*, 102–103.
103. M. P. Berry to C.I.A., May 25, 1872, ibid., 111.
104. M. P. Berry to C.I.A., July 1, 1872, ibid., 112–113; *Corinne Reporter*, June 18, 1872; *Idaho Statesman*, June 18, 25, July 2, 9, 1872.
105. Ibid., July 11, 16, 20, 27, 1872.
106. Ibid., Aug. 1, 1872.
107. Ibid., Aug. 17, 1872.
108. Ibid., Oct. 17, 1872.
109. J. N. High to C.I.A., Sept. 5, 1872, *Fort Hall Letter Book*, 117.
110. J. N. High to C.I.A., Sept. 11, 1872, ibid., 127.
111. J. N. High to C.I.A., Oct. 1, 1872, ibid., 128.
112. M. P. Berry to C.I.A., May 25, 1872, *Idaho Superintendency*, Roll 340.
113. J. N. High to C.I.A., June 1, 1872, ibid.
114. Sec. of Interior to C.I.A., Nov. 16, 1872, ibid.; *Corinne Reporter*, Dec. 20, 1872, H. W. Reed to C.I.A., Jan. 7, 1873, *Idaho Superintendency*, Roll 341.
115. H. W. Reed to C.I.A., Jan. 4, 1873, *Fort Hall Letter Book*, 137.
116. H. W. Reed to C.I.A., March, April 29, 1873, ibid., 148, 150.
117. H. W. Reed to C.I.A., May 31, June 30, 1873, ibid., 154, 156.
118. H. W. Reed to C.I.A., Oct. 8, 1873, *C.I.A. Annual Report, 1873*, 615.
119. H. W. Reed to C.I.A., Dec. 16, 1873, *Idaho Superintendency*, Roll 341.
120. H. W. Reed to C.I.A., Jan. 12, 1873, *Fort Hall Letter Book*, 139.
121. *Idaho Statesman*, April 26, 29, May 3, 1873.
122. G. W. Ingalls to C.I.A., May 2, 1873, *Idaho Superintendency*, Roll 341.
123. *Idaho Statesmen*, May 3, 1873.
124. Ibid., May 22, 29, 1873.
125. Ibid., May 15, 20, 24, June 14, 1873.
126. Ibid., Sept. 16, 1873.
127. S. F. Carter to Commissioner General Land Office, Jan. 4, 1873, *Idaho Superintendency*, Roll 341; D. S. Thompson to H. W. Corbett, Jan. 23, 1873, ibid.; C.I.A., to Secretary of Interior, Feb. 11, 1873, ibid.; S. F. Carter to Commissioner General Land Office, April 29, 1873, ibid.; Bureau of Land Management, Boise, Idaho, *Field Notes of the Survey of the Exterior Boundaries of Ft. Hall Indian Reservation in the Territory of Idaho*, by John B. David, April 5, 1873; *Idaho Statesman*, Nov. 22, 1873.
128. T. W. Bennett to Secretary of the Interior, Feb. 15, 1873, *Idaho Superintendency*, Roll 341.
129. Secretary of Interior to C.I.A., March 26, 1873, ibid.
130. C.I.A. to J. P. C. Shanks, April 11, 1873, ibid.
131. Secretary of Interior to G. W. Ingalls, April 22, 1873, U.S. National Archives, Bureau of Indian Affairs, *Letters Received, Nevada*.
132. T. W. Bennett to C.I.A., May 6, 1873, *Idaho Superintendency*, Roll 341; *Idaho Statesman*, May 24, 1873; H. W. Reed to C.I.A., July 28, 1873, *Fort Hall Letter Book*, 159.
133. C.I.A. to J. P. C. Shanks, July 1, 1873, *Idaho Superintendency*, Roll 341.
134. H. W. Reed to C.I.A., July 19, 1873, ibid.
135. *Idaho Statesman*, Aug. 23, Oct. 23, 1873.
136. Ibid., Oct. 23, 1873.
137. Ibid., Oct. 25, 1873.
138. John P. C. Shanks, T. W. Bennett, Henry W. Reed to C.I.A., Nov. 17, 1873, *Idaho Superintendency*, Roll 342.
139. John P. C. Shanks, T. W. Bennett, Henry W. Reed to C.I.A., Nov. 17, 1873, *C.I.A. Annual Report, 1873*, 525–527.
140. *Idaho Statesman*, Feb. 13, 1873.
141. Ibid., June 21, 1873.
142. J. C. Donaldson to C.I.A., Aug. 25, 1873, *Idaho Superintendency*, Roll 341.
143. Thomas K. Cree to C.I.A., March 6, 1874, *Idaho Superintendency*, Roll 342
144. H. W. Reed to C.I.A., April 6, 1874, ibid.
145. J. N. High to C.I.A., July 18, 1874, ibid.; Abel M. Corey to Assist. Sec. of Interior, July 25 1874, ibid.; E. J. Davis, B. F. White, and W. F. C. Jones to C.I.A., Sept 3, 1874, ibid.; C. C. Roberts to High and Fisher, Aug. 2, 1874, ibid.
146. "Agreement between H. W. Reed and J. N. High, Ross Fork, Idaho, Aug. 10, 1874," ibid.
147. *Idaho Statesman*, Aug. 29, 1874.
148. Ibid.
149. H. W. Reed to High and Fisher, Sept. 2, 1874, *Idaho Superintendency*, Roll 342.
150. J. N. High to C.I.A., Sept. 5, 1874, ibid.
151. H. W. Reed to C.I.A., Sept. 7, 1874, ibid.
152. Acting Sec. of Interior to C.I.A., Oct. 8, 1874, ibid.; James Wright to C.I.A., Nov. 21, 1874, ibid.; James Wright to C.I.A., Dec. 24, 1874, ibid.; *New Northwest*, Nov. 21, 1874.
153. Shoshoni and Bannock, and S. G. Fisher to C.I.A., Aug. 30, 1874, U.S. National Archives, Bureau of Indian Affairs, *Letters Received, Idaho*.
154. T. W. Bennett to C.I.A., April 13, July 11, 1874, *Idaho Superintendency*, Roll 342.
155. Citizens of Weiser Valley to T. W. Bennett, Sept. 13, 1874, Idaho State Historical Society, Ms.
156. T. W. Bennett to Chief of Ordnance, July 13, 1874, ibid.
157. *C.I.A. Annual Report, 1874*, 592–593.
158. *Idaho Statesman*, Oct. 20, 1874.
159. H. W. Reed to C.I.A., Aug. 29, 1874, *Idaho Superintendency*, Roll 342.
160. H. W. Reed to C.I.A., Sept. 19, 1874, ibid.
161. Acting Sec. of Interior to C.I.A., Oct. 10, 1874, ibid.
162. James Wright to C.I.A., Dec. 26, 1874, *Fort Hall Letter Book*, 201.
163. H. W. Reed to C.I.A., March 1, 1874, ibid., 171.
164. James Wright to C.I.A., Nov. 21, 1874, *Idaho Superintendency*, Roll 342.
165. James Wright to C.I.A., Dec. 30, 1874, *Fort Hall Letter Book*, 207–208.
166. James Wright to C.I.A., Dec. 31, 1874, *Idaho Superintendency*, Roll 343.
167. H. W. Reed to C.I.A., July 30, 1874, *Idaho Superintendency*, Roll 342.
168. H. W. Reed to C.I.A., March 1, 1874, Fort Hall Letter Book, 173.
169. *C.I.A. Annual Report, 1874*, 592.
170. Ibid., 83.
171. Ibid., 592.

CHAPTER V

CAMAS PRAIRIE WAR

A Starving Time

1875   While the Agreement of 1873 languished in the halls of Congress, the Shoshoni and Bannock and their agent fell back on the provisions of the Fort Bridger Treaty. James Wright wrote the commissioner on January 20, 1875, inquiring whether the government intended to live up to Article VI of the 1868 Treaty to place each Indian family on a 320-acre farm. Wright reported, "Everyday I am asked by Some of them, if Washington has *talked* to me about farming." He thought it would be possible to establish three settlements of Indian farmers.[1]

James Wright also asked whether an appropriation were to be made to fulfill Article X calling for the employment of a physician, teacher, carpenter, miller, engineer, farmer, and blacksmith. The sum approved for 1875 was only $3,000, or $428.57 each, an amount insufficient to employ even a common laborer. He listed the minimum needs of the reservation for the professional and trained help provided for under Article X: a physician, $1,400; for the other six employees, $1,000 each for a total of $6,000; for the support of a school, $2,000; an assistant farmer, $720; for two white men to teach the Indians how to work, $1,200; a second blacksmith, $1,000; for employment of Indian labor, $4,000; for the construction of a shoe and harness shop, $2,000 — a grand total of $18,320. This sum would be in addition to the amount necessary to furnish the clothing and subsistence for the Indians at Fort Hall.[2] There was little expectation at the agency that the $18,320 would be funded.

Unfortunately for Wright and the regular Indian residents on the reservation, many of the Bannock, for the first time since the settlement at Fort Hall, decided to forego their annual hunt in the Yellowstone country and settled down for the winter at the agency. As a result beef supplies were exhausted by January 1, and more destitute Indians were coming in all the time, due to their lack of success in hunting. Wright first reduced the ration to one pound of beef each per day and then cut it to three pounds per week. He indicated that if other newcomers showed up he would have to stop the issue altogether. He fixed April 1 as the date beyond which all he could do would be to "hold the public property and keep it from going to waste." As soon as the weather broke, he intended to send all the Indians who could travel to Camas Prairie and the buffalo country, despite the probability that they might "annoy the inhabitants."[3]

When no word of relief came from Washington, Wright announced that he could not keep the farm and the school in operation and therefore intended to rent out the farm to whites and discharge the head farmer as well as the Indian employees.[4] In another letter of the same date he wrote:

> We have flour enough on hand to issue to them untill April 1st. We can also let them have potatoes occasionally. We have beef for one more issue. Now what will be done with these people . . . . They cannot get out to hunt, there are no roots to be had, fishing time will not have come. If Congress would only appropriate means to subsist them untill Spring comes. They *can* make out to live during the Summer. It will be impossible however for them to farm unless they have subsistence furnished them by the Government.[5]

In desperation he finally purchased $898.12 worth of beef, incurring the debt in direct disobedience to the commissioner's orders because it was "an act of mercy."[6] The Washington Office of Indian Affairs was not unaware of conditions at Fort hall; whatever other qualities he may have lacked Agent Wright was an inveterate and prodigious letter writer.

His protestations of want and neglect at Fort Hall were not the product of weakness or overwhelming concern for his charges. This fact was supported by Captain John L. Viven, commander of the Fort Hall military post, who characterized Wright as a "more energetic business man than his predecessor" whose "only recourse" was to send the Indians off to hunt, discharge all the employees except the interpreter, and then try to safeguard the public property by himself as everything came to a standstill. The captain warned his superior that the Indians were still dissatisfied 1875 that the Agreement of 1873 had not been ratified and, with the refusal of the government to feed them might take to the warpath. Finally, he regretted that the Indians were not furnished with the necessary food and farming implements. The year before, he had noticed among them a decided enthusiasm and desire to engage in farming.[7]

At about the same time former agent Reed was

posting his final report, in which he wrote that the future of farming operations for the Indians looked "dark." He thought the business of cattle raising was better suited to the habits of the Indians and to the climate and soil at Fort Hall.[8] But Wright persevered and asked for an 1876 appropriation to pay for five miles of fence to enclose 960 acres of land, plus $11,000 for the wages of the necessary mechanics and for farm equipment.[9] The commissioner's response was to question the necessity of discharging all the employees and renting the farm. Wright very patiently explained again, "Having no means to furnish subsistence to them, nor to furnish them harness or wagons, very few can do anything at farming."[10] Finally recognizing the seriousness of the situation the commissioner sent a draft for $4,000 with which to operate the farm until July 1, a sum Wright thought inadequate for the purpose.[11]

The lack of food worsened. By April 1 the agent had stopped issuing any beef at all, "want of means" being the reason. By this time he was able to issue only a little flour, potatoes, and coffee.[12] Some of the Indians had already asked for his removal because he had been unable to furnish them with beef.[13] Finally the only Indians to whom he was able to grant any substantial rations were the seven families who were farming and those who worked for the agency by the month. He was of the opinion that he could get fifty Indians to work if he only had the means to subsist them.[14]

After just a few months as agent, and probably to his relief, he submitted his resignation because of a neuralgia condition. This was in May.[15] In one of his last letters he summed up his frustrations, "If these people could be aided, they would soon be self-supporting. But with the limited means at the disposal of the Dept. it is not to be expected that any great degree of advancement will be made."[16] Fortunately for the Shoshoni and Bannock, the very practical and down-to-earth W. H. Danilson was reappointed as agent and took over on July 1, 1875.[17]

The Office of Indian Affairs noted an abrupt decrease in correspondence from Fort Hall. The new agent spent more time in the field and less at the desk, although he did write informative monthly reports. In his first such effort he noted the small appropriation for the agency and urged those Indians who were not working to go to the mountains for a hunt so there would be a larger amount of subsistence left for the coming winter. He calculated that with the annual funds at his disposal he could furnish each Indian one meal per day for only two days each week; there was no alternative but to risk white hostility. Danilson was wise enough to secure the support of the Indians, who "fell in with the idea at once."[18]

After four years away from the agency he thought the Indians had learned a great deal about farming and that "quite a number" were now capable of cultivating small tracts by themselves. In one respect the Shoshoni and Bannock had "retrograded." They had learned to steal; they appropriated to their own use anything they found lying around the agency.[19]

Danilson explained to the commissioner the realities of the situation at Fort Hall. First of all, as a result of the lack of beef during the past winter, the Bannock had become thoroughly disgusted with conditions at the reservation; it would be difficult to keep them at home in the future. Secondly, to feed the fifteen hundred Indians gathered at Fort Hall would require 547,500 ¹⁸⁷⁵ pounds of flour and the same net weight of beef. The appropriation for the next fiscal year provided only 125,000 pounds of flour and a similar amount of beef. Finally, some little help could be expected from the production of crops on the 234-acre farm. The 1875 yield included 1,800 bushels of wheat, 800 bushels of oats, 150 bushels of barley, 2,000 bushels of potatoes, 1,000 heads of cabbage, and 100 tons of hay. All these crops were produced by Indian labor. Also five Indian families, including Tyhee, the reservation chief, had cultivated 42 acres of land. Danilson expected that another fifteen families would be ready for independent farming during 1876 if seeds and tools could be furnished.[20]

In a personal letter to the commissioner, which, one suspects, involved the subtle and deliberate assistance of Danilson, the five leading Indians at the reservation requested help in establishing individual farms and houses for the tribes and indicated that with most of the Indians returning from Camas Prairie and the Yellowstone region, "We don't know how all are to be fed — our beef and flour will not last all winter. What are we going to do?" The letter was signed by Tyhee, Bannock chief; Goodyer, Bannock headman; and three Shoshoni headmen — Gibson Jack, Pocatellah John, and Anamin.[21]

Neighboring white ranchers found themselves involuntarily engaged in these subsistence activities with the Indians. Stanton G. Fisher, for example, included many diary notations about feeding the residents of Fort Hall: "A red image of God & his lady here for dinner," "a Bannock came here this afternoon got his hash & litt out North," and "Gibson Jack took supper here."[22] The scarcity of food supplies, however, did not deter Danilson from requesting and getting permission to exempt the "roaming" Indians from the section of the Act of March 3, 1875, which required that they must work for any provisions they received.[23]

The physical aspects of the agency were almost as distressing to Danilson as the lack of food.

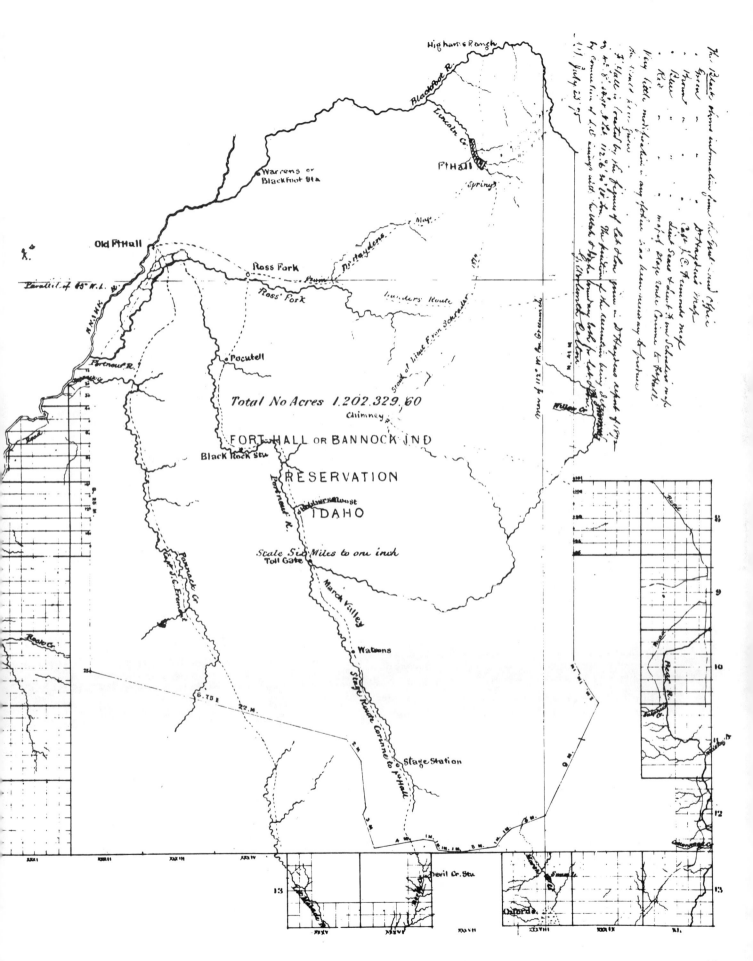

1875 After six years of effort he noted that the corrals were "worthless"; the miller's house and the gristmill were still unfinished; the flour house was without a floor; and there was no hospital or home for the aged and infirm. He was certain that with $3,000 and Indian labor he could renovate the present buildings and build some new ones.[24] He reminded the Indian Office that the Indians had not received "a pound of Subsistence stores" as part of their annuities in 1875. The agency was out of "*all* kinds of hardware."[25]

1876 The persistent problem was food. In a comprehensive analysis of his situation, Danilson wrote in late January 1876 that during the previous fall he had been of the opinion that there were sufficient supplies to carry the agency through the winter. When the resident population continued at twelve hundred he was forced to reduce the allotment of food to half-rations of flour, potatoes, and beef. The Indians were so "beef hungry" that the issue really only made "one square meal" per week. The flour and potatoes lasted about five days, so every Thursday and Friday he was "beset with hungry Indians begging for bread." Danilson's plan was to increase the beef ration to one pound per day to each person, which would subsist the Indians until April 1. He would need an additional 75,000 pounds of beef and 35,000 pounds of flour to carry them through to June 30. He asked for a telegraphic response to his request "for the Indians are half famished."[26]

When no relief came from Washington by April 20 the agent reported that he had been forced to stop all issues of beef and flour except to some three hundred Indians who were the families of workers or aged and infirm. Over one thousand were thus

thrown upon their own resources and are obligated to get their living as best they can; they believe its my fault, that I could get Flour for them if I would. They come to the Office with tears in their eyes begging most piteously for food for their children to eat. Would to God that those who hold the destiny of these people in their hands could be here to see for themselves, their necessities.[27]

These were rather bold words to the Commissioner. In his annual report written in August Danilson softened somewhat his description of the suffering and added, "they behaved most admirably under their misfortune, and left the agency with sad and sorrowful hurts."[28]

Exasperated with the inaction of the Office of Indian Affairs, Danilson proceeded to order flour in June, acknowledging that his course of action was not "exactly regular."[29] A month later he bought another ten thousand pounds without any authorized fund. In a scribbled note on the back of his letter is this statement by the commissioner, "What right had this Agent to buy flour without instructions from this office." Next to it is another

handwritten note instructing Danilson that his purchase was approved but not to buy any other supplies without first getting authorization.[30]

The anguished cries from the starving Indians created some apprehension at the military post fifteen miles away, where Captain Augustus H. Bainbridge noted the dissatisfaction which he said was caused by Agent Danilson receiving only one-fourth of the appropriation due his reservation. The captain said he had heard of a few. depredations but not in the vicinity of the post.[31] His command at the time consisted of a company of fifty-three men.[32] The Indian agent thought the military presence had an influence in supporting his authority on the reservation but had no effect in helping to introduce morality or civilization to the Indians.[33]

A flurry of Indian movements around Boise stirred up the citizens there for a brief period in late August 1876. It caused several petitions to be circulated to the governor, who asked General O. O. Howard of the Department of the Columbia to reinforce Fort Boise with two full companies of troops because the force of twenty-eight men there, "and infantry at that," was insufficient to quell the rebellious natives. The fifty or so Weiser Indians, plus some groups from the Owyhee country, were turning their horses into grainfields, telling the white owners "in good English to go to hell," and abusing other white farmers with such "arrogant and brutal expressions" as "How is **1876** Custer?"[34] The disturbance was only a preliminary to the next three years of war, which would involve most of the tribes of Idaho.

The fears at Boise did not reach Fort Hall. Danilson reported a most "tranquil" year, free of "contention and strife." Despite the starving time of the previous eight months, the Indians were peaceably disposed by September and proud of their achievements in farming. Twenty-four families had cultivated 120 acres of farmland, raising 500 bushels of potatoes and 2,000 bushels of wheat, worth $3,000. Said the agent, "They are thoroughly in earnest in this matter." He had furnished them with $800 for seeds and tools and was pleased at how rapidly they broke their ponies to harness, "I wish the enemies of the present policy could see these Indians at work and the golden fields of grain grown by their labor." He reduced the agency farm to one hundred acres for better management, got out fifteen hundred feet of sawlogs, built a corral, and did a "vast amount" of other work.[35] He asked for permission to use the Bannock "beneficial fund" to pay $1,000 for the Indian labor necessary to achieve the progress reported.[36] One gets the notion that Agent Danilson knew how to extract the most from his Indian charges and had the knack of instilling enthusiasm for the projects which would bring security. The spectre of famine no doubt also contributed to the burst of energy that year.

The increase in Indian farming was even more dramatic for 1877, when seventy families cultivated 240 acres, breaking up new land, digging irrigation ditches, and building corrals and fences. A devastating attack of grasshoppers almost wiped out their efforts, but despite the disheartening results they expressed their determination to continue operations the following year and asked for wagons, harnesses and other equipment. Danilson reduced the agency farm so he could encourage and aid the Indian agriculturists. He also built a wagon shed and another corral and began to erect a water sawmill near a stand of timber in the mountains.[37]

Even the subsistence problem was somewhat ameliorated when about four hundred and fifty Bannock, thoroughly weary of the humiliation and suffering caused by the lack of rations the year before, left to "take their chances in the buffalo country." A mild winter allowed the remaining Indians to supplement their food supplies by hunting in the nearby mountains.[38] Danilson had to reassure the commissioner about the practice of allowing the Indians to buy small amounts of ammunition from the post trader for hunting purposes — a procedure which later came under fire when the Nez Perce War scare hit Fort Hall.[39]

Danilson suffered a personal attack during the year when Idaho Delegate to Congress S. S. Fenn held up the agent's confirmation in the Senate by charging that he had squandered the appropriation for Fort Hall; that the Indians under his care were still "worthless, wandering vagabonds" and "pampered . . . pets"; that the number of Indians had decreased since Danilson took over; that he had done nothing to teach them the arts of agriculture; and the various Indians had visited Boise to complain to the governor about these conditions.[40] Danilson claimed that Fenn's accusations were politically motivated, since he had worked actively to defeat Fenn at the last election.[41]

Caught in the middle of the political infighting, the secretary of the Interior appointed Danilson as farmer-in-charge of the reservation and instructed him to transfer the agency property to himself as the farmer while his nomination for agent was settled by the Senate.[42] A number of people now came forward in support of Danilson. The head farmer during 1875–1876, O. F. Parmeter, testified to the agent's effectiveness;[43] five nearby ranchers attested to Danilson's competency and answered Delegate Fenn's charges one by one;[44] Johnson N. High, former agent, wrote that Danilson had accomplished more in a little over one year than all the other agents "combined including myself,";[45] and Captain Bainbridge of the Fort Hall military post considered him to be

"an exemplary Christian, an honest man, and an excellent Indian Agent."[46] There were others, including a letter from the Reverend J. M. Jameson.[47]

The struggle was still going on in December 1877, when Danilson asked for back pay for nine months. The Office of Indian Affairs continued to support him, expecting that Senate approval would finally be achieved.[48]

Nez Perce War Excitement

Throughout the year's contest to make him agent, both Danilson and the Shoshoni and Bannock met a more serious situation. Their neighbors, the Nez Perce, finally refused to move to the Lapwai Reservation by the imposed deadline of June 14, 1877, and instead went to war. Three of their young men killed whites on the day preceding the ultimatum. The first battle of White Bird Canyon on June 17, in which thirty-four soldiers were killed, emphasized the grave consequences which the war would undoubtedly have for white citizen and peaceful Indian alike.[49]

Danilson assured a concerned Office of Indian Affairs that the Indians at Fort Hall were peaceful and would not join the warring Nez Perce and that those still roaming around southern Idaho would move to the reservation of their own accord and take up farming as soon as Washington gave him an appropriation large enough to subsist them. He thought $17,000 would be sufficient to bring in the wandering bands, who by this time had excited the fears of the white residents of the territory.[50]

The military officers soon joined the ranks of those concerned with whether the Shoshoni and Bannock would remain friendly, now that the intriguing opportunity of displaying valor in battle was possible. Captain Bainbridge at the Fort Hall military post asked the agent to inform him as to the "whereabouts, and authority for being absent from their Agency" of all the Indians who might be at large in southern Idaho.[51] Danilson replied that he had 510 Indians engaged in agriculture and 100 coming and going, for a total of 610 on the reservation. There were 700 at "Kansas Prairie" and the Goose Creek Mountains, 50 near the settlements in Cache Valley, and 150 in the mountains south of Virginia City, Montana. He assured the captain that all were peaceably disposed.[52]

Sensing the responsibilities of his position, Idaho Governor Mason Brayman decided to reassure himself and his constituents about the Fort Hall Indians by sending two representatives, Thomas E. Logan and I. N. Coston, to Big Camas Prairie to have a "peace talk" with Captain Jim and other Indian leaders.[53] At the same time the governor talked "by telegraph" with Chief Winnemucca of the Northern Paiute of Nevada and the Owyhee country to see whether he intended to remain friendly.[54] It was well known that the Bannock were constant visitors to members of the Northern Paiute tribes, and there were fears that the two might bolster each other's courage and enter the exciting war started by the Nez Perce.

The Logan-Coston mission was successful in learning that the Shoshoni and Bannock had been visited by Nez Perce but the invitation to join in the fight against the soldiers had been rejected by the peacefully disposed Fort Hall tribes. The two agents were then able to persuade the leaders to travel to Boise to have a talk with the governor, and the *Idaho Statesman* reported the council in some detail. James Dempsey, an Irishman long friendly with the Indians, acted as interpreter.

The governor first learned that there was no single head chief of the Fort Hall Indians but several chiefs of equal authority: Captain Jim of three hundred Boise Indians; Major Jim of seven hundred Bannock (representing Tetoba in the absence of Tendoy, who was sick in camp at Camas Prairie); Major George of the Bannock at Fort Hall, a brother of Captain Jim; and Bannock John, who lived at Salmon Falls on Snake River.[55]

1877

After reiterating their peaceful disposition, Major Jim asked the question, "I wish you to tell me who owns this country." When the governor did not respond, the chief answered his own question:

> Your people make farms and fence up all the country; the Indians make their farm too, which is the Great Camas Prairie, where our women dig roots to feed them and the children. The white men drive too many hogs and cattle upon the prairie, which eat up the roots of the Camas and destroy the plant . . . . When the Camas is destroyed our children will suffer from hunger . . . Donaldson the Agent at Fort Hall, is always angry with us, and treats us roughly. He . . . sells the good horses from the Reservation and puts poor Indian ponies in their place. . . . We do not like Fort Hall. It is too cold. Nothing will grow there. We wish to have the Great Camas Prairie put with the Fort Hall Reservation, so that we can live there in summer and dig Camas. We never sold, or gave away Camas Prairie. We had nothing to do with any treaty which would take it away from us . . . .
> There are three Reservations for the Bannocks and Shoshones: The Wasakee Reservation, on Wind River, the Fort Hall Reservation, and the Lemhi Reservation. . . . *A dog with three homes has no home at all.* We would like to have one Reservation rather than three.[56]

Agent Danilson felt called upon to answer the charges by "Major Bannock Jim," who, he said, could have no knowledge of conditions at Fort Hall because he did not live there and had not even visited during the two years Danilson had been agent. As for James Dempsey, he was "a meddlesome, mischiefmaking squaw man despised wherever known," working in the interests of Delegate S. S. Fenn, who was trying to have Danilson removed.[57]

Governor Brayman's reactions to the council and to the Nez Perce War were incorporated in a statement to the secretary of War. He indicated that among the Indian leaders he had met, at least four had served as scouts for the U.S. Army; Captain Jim under General George Crook; Major Jim; Major George; and Buffalo Horn, "a young Bannock brave" who had served in the recent Sioux War under General Nelson A. Miles and had won distinction by killing a Sioux chief on Wolf Mountain the previous January. Brayman said all were inclined to be friendly but had grievances about dishonest agents and the "appropriation of their root-producing prairies by the encroaching whites," the latter being one of the causes of the Nez Perce outbreak. Finally, the governor outlined the measures he had taken to outfit certain militia companies in Boise and in Weiser Valley, where Eagle Eye's band of seventy Indians was causing some apprehension, although they seemed too frightened of the Nez Perce to cause any trouble among the white citizens.[58]

Captain Bainbridge continued to take precautions at Fort Hall. He warned J. C. Anderson at Eagle Rock to be on the alert for suspicious movements by any large body of wandering Indians, and he met with the headmen on the reservation to ascertain their state of mind about the northern war.[59] The captain had every right to be somewhat nervous; Captain Jim had told the residents of Boise that he and his band would never consent to be settled at Fort Hall.[60] In addition, the reservation population began to swell as the Nez Perce War drove the hunting Indians back to Fort Hall. Danilson asked for an increase of 75 percent in the supply of beef and flour, and there was concern that the lack of food might foment trouble and dissatisfaction among the concentrated group at the agency.[61]

The excitement and unsettled conditions at Fort Hall engendered by the Nez Perce conflict were somewhat assuaged when the military enlisted fifty Bannock scouts, including Buffalo Horn, to help General O. O. Howard round up Chief Joseph's warriors.[62] Danilson thought the scouts "would do good service" and that their employment would be beneficial to the agency. Later there might have been some doubts. Under the old law of physics that a body in motion tends to remain in motion, the Bannock found it difficult to leave their well-loved pursuit of war to settle back to the placid life of standing in a ration line at the reservation.[63]

The enlistment was for one month, and Stanton G. Fisher, employed as chief of scouts, led his crew on a 150-mile journey to join General Howard at Sand Hills on the Montana Stage Road.[64] Earlier the scouts had traveled to Boise where they held a war dance, during which Buffalo Horn especially delighted the assembled white residents of the city.[65] The four sergeants appointed from among the fifty scouts were Pagwite, Jerry Ballard, Good Year, and Bronco Jim.[66] The enlistment ended September 17, 1877, when the Bannock returned to the reservation to find war fever gripping those who had stayed home.[67]

Troops Move to Fort Hall

The *Idaho Statesman* on August 9 graphically described a "great tournament and sham battle on horseback," which the warrior element at Fort Hall held in anticipation of fighting Joseph's Nez Perce band which was expected to show up at any minute.[68] What the editor did not know was that the day before a young Bannock brave, "dressed in war habiliments," had armed himself with a Winchester repeating rifle and a revolver and started toward the agency building. He shot the first white man he encountered, a teamster driving an ox team. Continuing on towards the agency, the Bannock shot another white freighter, as Indians desperately tried to stop him from shedding more blood. He escaped but those in pursuit kept after him hoping to capture him and place him in jail for trial. The two white men, Robert Boyd and Orson James, were seriously wounded but were expected to recover.

Danilson immediately called a general council meeting of all the Indians and was able to calm them. He discovered that a "tramp" had spread the rumor that soldiers were being sent to fight the Indians at Fort Hall. The chiefs and headmen assured the agent there would be no further disturbance and that the would-be murderer would be caught and turned over to the proper authorities. Danilson still thought the situation was critical.[69]

Washington officialdom moved cautiously to be prepared for any further trouble. A company of infantry was dispatched to Fort Hall from Camp Douglas, Utah, in late August to reinforce the detachment already at the military post on the reservation.[70] Captain Bainbridge expressed his concern over Indians from Fort Hall harassing the ranchers along the Montana Trail, and he took careful action to stop the sale of arms and ammunition to the Indians by store owners along 1877 the route.[71] The commissioner of Indian Affairs did his part by taking Danilson to task for issuing passes to Indian parties which allowed them to hunt away from the reservation. The agent predictably answered that 150,000 pounds of beef and 125,000 pounds of flour were inadequate and concluded, "Please figure for yourself and see how long this will feed 1400 or 1500 Indians."[72] His only recourse was to issue passes and get them away from the reservation for as long as possible.

The sequel to the shooting of the two teamsters now occurred. The attacker was captured and placed in jail at Malad, Idaho, to await trial. In retaliation his friend, a Bannock named Tambiago, shot and killed a white man, Alex Rhoden, near the post trader's store at the agency. Captain Bainbridge called a council meeting of the headmen, who promised to seek out the murderer and turn him over to the military. Buffalo Horn and about fifty other Indians started in pursuit. The captain was of the opinion that, while the Shoshoni were friendly, the Bannock were troublesome and would have to be punished.[73]

General Philip Sheridan was notified that an outbreak might occur at any moment, so he ordered an additional one hundred soldiers to be sent to Fort Hall.[74] The Bannock moved their camp seven miles away from the agency, began purchasing ammunition, and started preparing for war, although Danilson thought the cold weather might dampen their enthusiasm.[75] In other dispatches Sheridan confirmed the sending of the one hundred soldiers but thought the agent was "stampeded" and hoped that he and Bainbridge would be able "to make it last," as the Indians promised to deliver up Tambiago "alive or dead."[76]

Captain Bainbridge listed his reasons for believing that a Bannock war was imminent: first, the fact that the Indians were not really serious about capturing Tambiago; second, the vow that the Bannock would kill another white man if Tambiago were arrested; third, the threatening manner displayed by the Bannock since the murder; fourth, the fears expressed by Agent Danilson, who knew the Indians very well. The captain recommended that his military post be moved to within five miles of the agency, which would allow for prompt measures when trouble arose.[77]

When Colonel John O. Smith arrived with reinforcements and took command, he supported the captain's evaluation of the situation. He recommended strong measures to bring the Bannock to terms: pay the Shoshoni scouts but withhold the pay of the Bannock; stop issuing rations to the Bannock; and warn them the soldiers would attack immediately if they did not live up to their treaty obligations. After waving the big stick the colonel then added he thought it inadvisable to "stir them up" until he was supplied with more troops, transportation, and supplies in case the Bannock should "get off."[78]

General George Crook issued the necessary orders, and three companies of cavalry were sent to 1878 Fort Hall to disarm and dismount the Bannock. There was by this time a general belief that the tribesmen were merely waiting for warm weather and grass for their ponies before going on the warpath.[79] Danilson questioned the wisdom of disarming the Indians, which would only exasperate them further. He thought plans should be formulated to remove them entirely from the reservation. By this time the murderer of Rhoden had been captured by the military about sixty miles north of the agency.[80]

When the cavalry arrived Colonel Smith ordered the Bannock to surrender their weapons and horses. Joseph Skelton, a white settler on Pocatello Creek, described the incident, "They [cavalry] Serrounded the Bannock Camp at 2 a Clock the next morning [January 16] the Soalders told them to come out and Sho the Blod of their mothers But they would not Sho them Selves they made a rush and tore down their lodges and they disarmd them and taken their horses from them and them marcht them up to the Agency."[81] The soldiers captured thirty-two very old rifles, no revolvers, and three hundred ponies. Forewarned, the fifty-five Bannock braves had hidden their best weapons. Danilson reported that the cavalry was scheduled to return to Fort D. A. Russell, having accomplished the mission. He asked either that the Bannock be taken with the mounted soldiers or that other troops be stationed at Fort Hall to keep the Indians in subjection.[82]

In reporting the affair, the *Idaho Statesmen* warned that the Bannock should not be allowed to visit Camas Prairie the next summer unless a military guard went along.[83] Apparently the Shoshoni were so alarmed by the turn of events that about fifty of them moved to Marsh Valley to escape involvement, while the greater number moved near the agency for safety. Several white citizens near the reservation reported the threatening attitude of the Bannock and took measures to protect their families and property.[84]

The increasingly dangerous situation led the Office of Indian Affairs to request that the military post at Fort Hall be moved closer to the agency. In reply, General of the Army William T. Sherman insisted that the agency should be moved to the vicinity of the fort: "Mahomet should go to the mountain for protection & safety." He was just a little exasperated with an Indian agent who one day complained about soldiers corrupting the Indians and the next day asked that the troops be moved back to protect "his person against the Indians."[85] Needless to say, neither post was moved.

The main irritant resulting from the raid on the Bannock camp was the herd of three hundred captured horses in the military corral at the fort. Danilson thought they should be sold and the proceeds used to buy stock cattle for the Bannock.[86] Captain Bainbridge attempted to get rid of a portion of the ponies by inviting Shoshoni, who claimed some of them, to come and identify their horses and take them away.[87]

Another concern was the need for more supplies, after the decision was made to keep the Bannock and Shoshoni on the reservation. The agent reported his food supplies would last only until April 6. He said he would require 70,000 pounds of flour and 180,000 pounds of beef to subsist the Indians until June 30. As he pointed out, when the reservation was first established appropriations were designed for eleven hundred Indians and the Bannock were nearly always absent during the winter. Now there were over fifteen hundred Indians at Fort Hall. Danilson would be unable to encourage the Shoshoni to farm without sufficient rations to feed them. In addition, the Shoshoni were afraid the Bannock would steal and destroy their crops. This was another reason for removing the Bannock, who were a "barrier to agricultural pursuits."[88]

With all his troubles, Danilson did receive some good news on February 26 when his nomination as agent was finally approved by the Senate.[89] Three months later he was reminding the commissioner that he had not been paid for fourteen months.[90] Apparently his pay soon reached him, as did his official appointment, the latter on July 23, 1878.[91]

The inevitable disenchantment between the agent and the military erupted when W. B. Royall, an inspector general, reported to his superiors that the reason the Bannock were liable to break out at any moment was that Danilson had earned their hostility and had lost control of them.[92] General Sherman was more blunt — the agent was "unduly scared" and troops were needed to "protect him." The general added the entirely gratuitous remark that he had been told that Danilson was a cattle raiser with six hundred head of stock grazing on the reservation.[93]

Another commander, Captain Bainbridge, was having his own problems in controlling Tambiago and the prisoner's father and two brothers, all incarcerated at the Fort Hall military post.[94] The captain was treating them in true army fashion, forcing them into soldier's clothing and cutting their long hair so they resembled "prize fighters." The father, protesting the latter indignity, seized a soldier's rifle and had to be subdued by force.[95] While the court at the county seat, Malad, was preparing to try the murderer, Bainbridge kept asking that the other three prisoners be sent to Fort Leavenworth — or any place but his post.[96]

After the three companies of cavalry were withdrawn, the three infantry companies from Camp Douglas were retained until orders came in early March to return them to their Utah post. Danilson immediately wired the Office of Indian Affairs that the employees and adjacent white citizens on the reservation would leave and he would be forced to abandon the agency.[97] The troops started marching anyway but after one day's journey away from Fort Hall were ordered back, much to their disgruntlement.[98] The *New Northwest* was of the opinion that, despite the presence of troops at the fort, the Bannock would commence a war some distance from the reservation as soon as the grass was green.[99]

In an attempt to pacify the Bannock who had lost their horses, Danilson now reversed his position about selling the ponies and recommended, with military approval, that the animals be returned. He pointed out that the loss of only three hundred ponies would not cripple the Indians for purposes of war, the Bannock would become increasingly angry over the loss, those among them who wanted to farm would be unable to do so, and the expense of selling the horses would be greater than the return.[100] General Crook also advised, without success, the return of the weapons, which were quite inferior and used only for hunting small game.[101]

Crook was convinced by this time that the whole proceeding in disarming and dismounting the Bannock had been a mistake. With the return of the horses he now ordered the companies of infantry back to Camp Douglas, leaving only one officer and twenty-two men to ensure the safety of the agency.[102] Danilson was beside himself and demanded that at least one company of troops be retained, saying the "Military prefers the Luxuries of Salt Lake."[103]

Others as well as the agent were disturbed at the withdrawal of the troops. Governor Brayman wrote that from his experiences as a soldier in the Civil War he always made allowances for exaggeration, but in this instance he agreed with Danilson that there would be "further disturbances early in the Spring."[104] As for the Idaho Statesman, the reaction was as expected — the Bannock were not to be trusted while five of their number were held "in captivity."[105] There were many other protestations of fear from citizens who, at least in this instance, were good prophets.

From all the troubles with the Bannock, one basic fact emerged on which white settlers, Indian officials and military could agree: There was an insufficient supply of rations and annuity goods for the increased Indian population at Fort Hall. As early as March 22 Danilson was warning that he had only twelve days' supply of flour and beef and that "prompt action" was necessary.[106] A month later he wired that there were fourteen hundred Indians at the agency: "They must be fed send instructions immediately."[107] Two days later he sent this message, "One hundred and twenty families farming they must have rations or abandon work."[108] General Crook advised issuing the same rations as those granted the Sioux because "the present allowance is entirely inadequate." His superior, General Sheridan, wrote that the Fort Hall reserve was surrounded by white settlements, hunting was no longer possible, and "it would be inhuman to hold them [Indians] on reservations and starve them."[109] Captain F. E. Trotter, in command of the troops at Ross Fork,

pointed out that the Indians at Fort Hall were being issued for a week's supply five pounds of beef and four pounds of flour "and nothing else." This meant that during the last three days of the week they had nothing to eat. Trotter said the Shoshoni and Bannock knew that the Crow and Sioux received twice that amount and naturally concluded, "When we fight him, the Great Father gives us plenty, when we do as he tells us and are good Indians, we get little or nothing."[110]

Agent Danilson expostulated further that it was "perfectly absurd" to expect the Indians to stay on the reservation and starve, and he particularly regretted seeing eight hundred farming Indians denied rations so they were forced to abandon their crops. Hearing nothing from the commissioner, Danilson began issuing passes for hunting forays.[111]

1878

The Bannock Go to War

As early as May 1, 1878, both Captain Bainbridge and some of the newspapers were reporting that the Bannock were friendly and that there was no danger of an outbreak.[112] However, within two weeks Governor Brayman was notified that a hundred members of the tribe at Silver City were trying to persuade the Paiutes to go to war.[113]

The editor of the Statesman recorded a friendly visit of Buffalo Horn to Boise on May 18 and thought he was "as well disposed as ever,"[114] but three days later the newspaper noted a rumor that the Indians gathered at Big Camas Prairie were planning depredations at the same time the trial of Tambiago was proceeding at Malad City. The editor saw a connection between the two.[115] Several citizens on the Malad River in Alturas County petitioned the governor for arms and wrote that "things look blue."[116] Finally the Statesman, reported that seventeen lodges of Indians at Glenn's Ferry appeared sullen and refused to answer questions and that another group of twenty armed braves at Camas Prairie were seen sitting on their horses around a beef just butchered by some Indian women. When eight or ten white stockmen approached the circle of silent Indians, the hostility was so obvious that, without a word, the ranchers left to drive their horses and cattle off the prairie as fast as they could.[117]

On May 22 Buffalo Horn told four of the white stockmen that the prairie was his country and warned them to remove their cattle at once. Eight days later the son of Bannock John — a wild man who had been drinking and had lost all his property during a gambling spree — in desperation persuaded another young brave to accompany him, and the two went to the camp of some white herders and critically wounded two of them. When the news reached Buffalo Horn he told the other Bannock that, inasmuch as Captain Bain-

Bureau of American Ethnology

Buffalo Horn (on horse at far left) accompanied this Indian group that W. H. Jackson photographed on either his 1872 or 1878 trip to Fort Hall Reservation.

1878

bridge had said he would hold the whole tribe responsible for any killings, they might as well go to war at once and obtain all the horses and supplies they could. A portion of the Bannock on Camas Prairie declared for peace and left for the reservation. Buffalo Horn eventually led about two hundred warriors south and west in the direction of their friends, the Northern Paiute bands, in hopes of gaining some recruits.[118]

General O. O. Howard, in command of the Department of the Columbia, had the task of defeating and capturing the warring Bannock. He endeavored to determine the cause of the outbreak and was informed by Idaho Governor Brayman that Camas Prairie had been assigned to the Bannock under the Treaty of 1868. The governor explained the clerical error which had resulted in the reference to "Kansas Prairie" and described in some detail the camas root and its function as "their only sure and abundant supply of vegetable food." He noted that, for the Bannock and Shoshoni Camas Prairie was their "garden," which was being destroyed by herds of hogs digging up the roots.

After his detailed description the governor further explained that the government had failed to follow through with the treaty stipulation to as-

sign the prairie as part of the reservation for the Bannock. He requested immediate action either to do so or to compensate the Indians in some other way and allow the white settlers to take over the camas grounds.[119] Obviously the many letters and dispatches to Washington over the previous decade had never gotten past the clerks in the Office of Indians Affairs, or, if they had, the responsible officials had been unable to secure the attention of Congress to this detail of an insignificant treaty providing for another Indian tribe in the Far West. Now all at once the perspective had changed, as white lives were threatened.

The Bannock War has importance in the story of the Northern Shoshoni mainly to emphasize that the grievances of the Indians at Fort Hall could force part of their number to take such desperate measures. From the first of June until the last engagement at Dry Fork in Wyoming on September 12 the war consisted of the U.S. Army chasing the Bannock warriors and their allies, the Northern Paiute under Chief Egan, from the southeastern corner of Idaho, across that territory, and into Wyoming and Montana. Buffalo Horn and Chief Egan were killed, in different engagements. After that their demoralized followers tried to escape the vengeance of the soldiers as best they could.[120]

With the outbreak of war, the peaceful Shoshoni and Bannock hurried to the shelter of the reservation. Captain Jim started to Fort Hall with thirty lodges. He lost all but twelve on the way, the remainder going to Salmon River on a fishing expedition. To subsist the unexpected surge of Indians into the reservation Danilson requested an additional $3,000 for more food supplies.[121] When the Office of Indian Affairs took its usual lengthy time in getting assurances the provisions were needed, the friendly Bannock at the agency left for the mountains to the northeast to hunt for small game. The agent reported he had "scarcely enough" supplies to feed the Indians engaged in farming.[122]

Danilson decided to play it safe; he asked for additional troops at Fort Hall, indicating that one officer and twenty-five men could not handle any serious situation which might arise.[123] Captain Bainbridge, thinking the agent was "stampeded" again, nevertheless supported the request, and two companies of cavalry were dispatched to the agency on June 13.[124]

As the Bannock War progessed and more and more national attention was focused on it, General George Crook, commanding the Department of the Platte, visited Fort Hall to ascertain for himself the causes of the outbreak and to reassure frightened citizens that the military was on the alert. He found the Indians peaceably disposed and engaged in farming. He recommended that the military post be relocated on the new Utah and Northern Railroad, which was fast approaching and which would extend through the reservation.[125]

Of more interest was an interview with the general after his visit to Fort Hall. A reporter of the *Omaha Herald* asked Crook why the Bannock had gone to war. The general replied, "*Hunger. Nothing but hunger.*" He explained that the Indians would not submit to starvation, that there was "scarcely a jackrabbit left" on their reservation, and that the government had failed to live up to the various treaty obligations. The truth was, he said, "We have swindled them from the days of William Penn until now." He pointed out that the Indians had to be subsisted while they learned how to farm: "It cannot be expected that they will stay on reservations where there is no possible way to get food, and see their wives and children starve and die around them. We have taken their lands, deprived them of every means of living. . . ." Perhaps the most significant statement came from the reporter, "It is strange that this state of affairs has never become public." In some frustration General Crook replied that he had expressed these sentiments in his official correspondence for years with no results.[126]

In a letter of September 23 General Crook reiterated his feelings about the Shoshoni and Bannock but in terms much more blunt, "Our Indian policy has resolved itself into a question of warpath or starvation; and, being merely human, many of them will choose the former alternative

U.S. Geological Survey

Fort Hall military post shortly after 1870.

where death shall at least be glorious."[127] The editor of the *Idaho Statesman* could hardly restrain himself in attacking these sentiments of one of the outstanding frontier generals. He settled for calling Crook a "tender-hearted Indian fighter" but concluded that "It was not the want of food which started them [Bannock] upon the warpath, but their savage thirst for blood, which had not been restrained and prevented by proper discipline and Governmental supervision."[128]

1878   Captain Augustus Bainbridge gave his final evaluation of the war by pointing out that each Indian, as late as December 1878, was still receiving only five pounds of beef and four pounds of flour every week and yet was denied the privilege of leaving the reservation to hunt. "You can draw your own inferences as to the natural consequences of such starvation rations and such orders."[129]

In his final report for the year the commissioner of Indian Affairs summed up the reasons, as he saw them, for the almost two years of Bannock violence at Fort Hall: insufficient appropriations for food and supplies while the tribesmen learned to farm; the disappearance of game from the usual hunting ranges; the excitement of the Nez Perce War; and a "chronic dislike" for the Shoshoni, whose peaceable dispositions and favors from the agent only exacerbated Bannock feelings.[130]

Finally Secretary of the Interior Carl Schurz made some positive recommendations about avoiding further Indian troubles: Appropriations from Congress must be liberal enough and delivered promptly enough to support the Indians; the Indian Service should have contingency funds to meet emergencies; and citizens of the western territories must be willing to grant farm and pasture lands to the Indians and not then attempt to take from them "by force or trickery, every acre of ground that is good for anything." He thought the Bannock outbreak was caused by inadequate food (the ration being equal to "less than four and one-half cents per head per day") and the arrest and subsequent hanging of Tambiago for the murder of Alex Rhoden.[131]

All the reasons cited above certainly played a part in the decision of the Bannock to go to war, but it must be remembered that the conflict started on Camas Prairie, which had not been reserved for the tribe as promised in the Treaty of Fort Bridger. Their "garden," the chief supplier of their annual food, was being destroyed; at the same time there were no rations for them at Fort Hall. In desperation they followed age-old instincts and struck what they well knew would be a futile but perhaps an attention-getting blow at white power. As General Crook put it, while the Bannock and Shoshoni had long been friends of the whites and starved because of it, "the Sioux —

so lately our bitter enemies — have twice the amount of supplies provided them."[132] Time would tell whether the same magic would work for the Indians at Fort Hall.

Perhaps the troubled year of 1878 should end with the brighter panorama painted by Danilson. There was an increase of 55 families in the number engaged in agriculture, making a total of 125 who cultivated 400 acres of land which produced 6,000 bushels of wheat, 5,500 bushels of potatoes, and 20 tons of hay. The agency had a herd of 350 cattle which furnished the reservation with 121,448 pounds of beef. The sawmill produced 80,000 feet of lumber, and the agent had plans to refurbish the old buildings and to erect some new ones.[133] Danilson seemed indefatigable in his efforts to make a going concern out of the Fort Hall Reservation.

With two years of trouble and conflict behind him, the agent hoped to be able to turn his full attention to the task of creating farms out of the sagebrush wilderness at Fort Hall. When he took over the agency the second time in 1875 there were four Indian farmers. By the end of 1879,   1879 150 families were engaged in agriculture on 530 acres of land. During the year they produced 6,200 bushels of wheat, 8,100 bushels of potatoes, 50 tons of hay, and other cereal and vegetable crops worth a total of $11,662. The individual farms were located at Bannock Creek, 147 acres; Portneuf, 32 acres; Pocotellah, 5 acres; Emigrant Rock, 122 acres; and at the agency, 224 acres.[134] Danilson made plans to build extra granaries at three of the sites, using Indian labor and teams without any expense to the government except wages of one carpenter.[135] He also purchased a new thresher which could be moved to the various farm acres.[136] To encourage other Indians to start farms he announced that a cow would be given to each family "as a reward for their industry." Again this was at little expense to the government because animals would come from the agency herd.[137] When Governor Brayman visited Fort Hall he was much impressed with the "rapid progress" he witnessed.[138] The only impediment in transforming most of the reservation into on oasis on the barren Snake River Plains seemed to be lack of a large-scale irrigation system to provide the necessary water for the crops.[139]

Danilson was hopeful that at least 250 families would be able to provide their own flour during the coming winter, which would reduce the drain on the food supplies furnished by the government.[140] The population on the reservation had been reduced by 205 as a result of the Bannock War, but there were still 888 Shoshoni and 331 Bannock to be subsisted.[141] By late October the same dismal report came from the agency that the Indians had already been reduced to half rations. Because of the strict orders that none could leave to go on a buffalo hunt or for any other reason, the commissioner was asked to increase the beef and flour rations by a least 25 percent.[142]

The close confinement of the Shoshoni and Bannock on their reservation was deemed the only wise course, in light of the extreme hostility of Idaho citizens as a result of the Nez Perce and Bannock wars. The military commander at Fort Hall required the commanding officer at Ross Fork to make a weekly report of "the condition and temper of the Indians";[143] Governor Brayman warned the Indians to "refrain from visiting white settlements unprotected" because of the "bitter feeling" against them.[144] The *Idaho Statesman* editor vented his hatred by suggesting that Alaska be made a kind of Botany Bay for all hostile and discontented Indians.[145] Even better, "To shoot them down would be an act of justice to the human family."[146] Both military authorities and Indian officials continued their warnings throughout the year against straying from the reservation, and the scare which came from the insignificant Sheepeater War of 1879 intensified the efforts.[147] The results were gratifying, at least to Idaho settlers, when one of them could report in late September that there was not a single Indian to be seen at Big Camas Prairie.[148] Only occasional passes were given to Indians who wished to leave Fort Hall on important errands.[149]

As for the Bannocks taken prisoner during the war, the military at first advised that they should not be returned to Fort Hall for at least two years but very soon turned them back to the agency for safekeeping and the expense of subsistence.[150] Forty-six prisoners were confined at Fort Hall in late 1878;[151] fifty-seven were delivered there from Fort Brown in July of 1879;[152] and forty-three arrived in October from Fort Ellis, twenty others having escaped during the trip "on account of insufficient force to guard them properly."[153] Agent Danilson reported that the prisoners had shown "a spirit of subordination that is most remarkable."[154] Obviously the days of war were over, and the Indians could now only hope that their reservation could be made a comfortable, safe, and productive place to live.

That objective seemed to be in sight with the active and practical-minded Danilson in charge, but his penchant for being involved in many activities soon cost him the agent's post. A letter to the *Salt Lake Tribune* started the process toward dismissal. The writer accused Danilson of neglecting his reservation duties to supervise a sawmill which he owned on the Snake River about twenty-five miles above Eagle Rock.[155] Soon the vultures gathered. George P. Taggart applied for the agent's position because he understood Danilson was about to resign under pressure.[156] The receiver of the Land Office at Oxford, Idaho, accused Danilson, along with others, of cutting timber illegally on public lands.[157]

In reponse to the allegations the commissioner of Indian Affairs sent Inspector John McNeil to investigate. He reported:

1879

I found everything in excellent condition at the Agency — Business well conducted, property well cared for — Indians working with great increase of acreage, and growing interest and pride in their farms. . . .
I . . . regard him as an exceptionally good Agent, and a man of much superior qualifications to what can be generally had for the wages he received.

The problem seemed to be that Danilson, despite his obvious integrity and industry, was not content with his poor salary and was successfully operating not only the sawmill, which was producing as much as 1.5 million feet of lumber a year, but also a cattle ranch with five hundred head of stock. He was careful to get leaves of absence from the Indian Service at appropriate times to care for his private business. McNeil thought that, except for a certain independence and lack of obedience to some bureaucratic orders from Washington, Danilson was an outstanding agent and should "be retained with advantage to the service."[158] But the opposition was too persistent, and Danilson was too independent. He was requested to resign and did so on September 3, 1879.[159]

Somewhat bitter over being "kicked out like a dog !!!" after his rewarding efforts, he nevertheless, and with characteristic energy, made plans to phase out his sawmill and began to consider operating a hardware store at the junction of the Oregon Road.[160] Mrs. Danilson, described by the Reverend J. W. Reid as a "veteran laborer among the aborigines," traveled to Washington, D.C. to protest to the commissioner of Indian Affairs about her husband's dismissal, but to no avail.[161]

The loss of Danilson was a sharp blow to the prospects of advancement by the Shoshoni and Bannock. John A. Wright was appointed as temporary agent.[162] He was soon replaced by J. M. Haworth, who complained against the administrative decision which placed him in charge of both the Fort Hall and Lemhi reservations and who soon decided it would be better to leave the Indian Service than to try to direct the affairs of two reserves two hundred miles apart.[163] Within another week Haworth recommended that Wright be named agent at Fort Hall. He also pointed out, significantly, that a school had been conducted for only a few months during Danilson's tour of duty.[164]

1879

From this time on the agents who came and went with monotonous regularity seemed to be more interested in "civilizing" the Indians by imposing a white-oriented educational system than in trying to improve their material needs. Indian interest in farming began to lag as enforced acculturation became the order of the day and as the agents and the government failed to provide the necessary irrigation system so that farming operations could be expanded in the interests of all the Indian residents of Fort Hall.

The build-up of tension and frustration during the nine years of reservation life with the resultant explosion at Camas Prairie was, perhaps, only the natural consequence of attempting to force a proud and independent race within the confines of a small and unproductive area whose resources lay untapped due to the failure of the government to furnish funds for developing the dry acres. Watching families and friends starve while white ranchers despoiled tribal camas grounds, Buffalo Horn threw all restraint to the winds. In an act of desperation he and his followers struck out in what they must have known would lead to inevitable destruction.

The chief bright note in the late 1870s was the energetic and commonsense Danilson, who might have accomplished even more if the Nez Perce and Bannock wars had not interrupted his activities. The gains he made came without significant help from Washington and often in direct opposition to orders from the Office of Indian Affairs. The first decade of reservation life did little more than accustom the Indians to staying in one settled place, away from the camas prairies and buffalo plains which had served them so well in the past.

NOTES CHAPTER V
CAMAS PRAIRIE WAR

1. James Wright to C.I.A., Jan. 20, 1875, *Fort Hall Letter Book*, 221.
2. James Wright to C.I.A., Jan. 21, 1875, ibid., 222–224.
3. *C.I.A. Annual Report, 1875*, 760; James Wright to C.I.A., Jan. 28, 30, 1875, *Fort Hall Letter Book*, 226–230.
4. James Wright to C.I.A., Feb. 6, 1875, ibid., 233.
5. Ibid., 235.
6. James Wright to C.I.A., Feb. 15, 1875, ibid., 237.
7. John L. Viven to General, Department of California, Feb. 18, 1875, *Idaho Superintendency*, Roll 343.
8. H. W. Reed to C.I.A., Feb. 20, 1875, ibid., 242–243.
9. James Wright to C.I.A., Feb. 4, 1875, *Idaho Superintendency*, Roll 343.
10. James Wright to C.I.A., March 13, 1875, *Fort Hall Letter Book*, 251–252.
11. James Wright to C.I.A., March 25, 1875, ibid., 258.
12. James Wright to C.I.A., April 1, 1875, ibid., 260.
13. James Wright to C.I.A., Feb. 27, 1875, ibid., 245–246.
14. James Wright to C.I.A., April 30, 1875, ibid., 266.
15. James Wright to C.I.A., May 4, 1875, ibid., 271.
16. James Wright to C.I.A., June 1, 1875, ibid., 278.
17. W. H. Danilson to C.I.A., July 14, 1875, ibid., 286.
18. W. H. Danilson to C.I.A., July 31, 1875, ibid., 290–291.
19. Ibid.
20. *C.I.A. Annual Report, 1875*, 760–761.
21. Danilson to C.I.A., Sept. 15, 1875, *Idaho Superintendency*, Roll 343.
22. Stanton G. Fisher, *Diary, 1875*, Idaho State Historical Society, Ms. 106.
23. Danilson to C.I.A., Nov. 30, 1875, *Idaho Superintendency*, Roll 343; C.I.A. to Danilson, Dec. 29, 1875, ibid.
24. *C.I.A. Annual Report, 1875*, 761; Danilson to C.I.A., Nov. 1, 1875, *Fort Hall Letter Book*, 313–314.
25. Danilson to C.I.A., Nov. 2, 1875, *Idaho Superintendency*, Roll 343.
26. W. H. Danilson to C.I.A., Jan. 24, 1876, *Idaho Superintendency*, Roll 344.
27. W. H. Danilson to C.I.A., April 20, 1876, ibid.
28. *C.I.A. Annual Report, 1876*, 446–447.
29. W. H. Danilson to C.I.A., June 2, 1876, *Idaho Superintendency*, Roll 344.
30. W. H. Danilson to C.I.A., July 3, 1876, ibid.
31. A. H. Bainbridge to Dept. of Platte, July 5, 1876, Fort Hall, *Record Group 393*.
32. U.S. Congress, *Report of the Secretary of War*, Vol. I, House, Exec. Doc. 1, Part 2, 44th Cong., 2d Sess., Serial No. 1742, 48.
33. W. H. Danilson to C.I.A., Sept. 3, 1875, *Fort Hall Letter Book*, 304–305.
34. *Idaho Statesman*, Aug. 19, Sept. 7, 1876.
35. *C.I.A. Annual Report, 1876*, 447.
36. W. H. Danilson to C.I.A., Feb. 8, Sept. 7, 1876, *Idaho Superintendency*, Roll 344.
37. *C.I.A. Annual Report, 1877*, 474–475.
38. Ibid.
39. W. H. Danilson to C.I.A., Jan. 17, 1877, *Idaho Superintendency*, Roll 345; Acting C.I.A. to Board of Indian Commissioners, Feb. 2, 1877, ibid.
40. S. S. Fenn to C.I.A., March 19, 1877, ibid.
41. W. H. Danilson to C.I.A., April 2, 1877, ibid.
42. Secretary of Interior to C.I.A., May 11, 1877, ibid.
43. O. F. Parmeter Deposition, June 18, 1877, ibid.
44. "Affidavit of Fred S. Stevens, W. N. Shilling, S. G. Fisher, A. T. Stout, and Joseph Warren, July 6, 1877," ibid.
45. Johnson N. High to C.I.A., July 8, 1877, ibid.
46. Captain A. H. Bainbridge to C.I.A., July 16, 1877, ibid.
47. W. H. Danilson to C.I.A., July 20, 1877, ibid.
48. W. H. Danilson to C.I.A., Dec. 11, 1877, ibid.
49. Beal and Wells, *History of Idaho*, 456–459.
50. W. H. Danilson to C.I.A., June 16, 1877, *Idaho Superintendency*, Roll 345.
51. Captain A. H. Bainbridge to W. H. Danilson, June 20, 1877, Fort Hall, *Record Group 393*, 101–102.
52. W. H. Danilson to A. H. Bainbridge, June 21, 1877, *Idaho Superintendency*, Roll 346.
53. *Idaho Statesman*, June 21, 1877; T. E. Logan and I. N. Coston to Governor M. Brayman, June 22, 1877, Idaho State Historical Society, Ms.
54. *Idaho Statesman*, June 23, 1877.
55. Ibid., June 26, 1877.
56. Ibid.
57. W. H. Danilson to Governor Brayman, June 30, 1877, Idaho State Historical Society, Ms.
58. Governor M. Brayman to Secretary of War, June [probably July] 2, 1877, *Idaho Superintendency*, Roll 346; *Idaho Statesman*, June 26, 1877.
59. A. H. Bainbridge to J. C. Anderson, July 10, 1877, Fort Hall, *Record Group 393*, 110–111; A. H. Bainbridge to Dept. of the Platte, July 10, 1877, ibid., 111–112.
60. *Idaho Statesman*, Aug. 30, 1877.
61. W. H. Danilson to C.I.A., Aug. 7, 1877, *Idaho Superintendency*, Roll 345.
62. A. H. Bainbridge to Dept. of the Platte, July 10, 1877, Fort Hall, *Record Group 393*, 112; P. H. Sheridan to E. D. Townsend, Aug. 18, 1877, *Idaho Superintendency*, Roll 346; A. H. Bainbridge to Dept. of Platte, Aug. 22, 26, 1877, Fort Hall, *Record Group 393*, 122–125.
63. W. H. Danilson to C.I.A., Aug. 13, 1877, *Idaho Superintendency*, Roll 345.
64. "A. H. Bainbridge, Special Orders, Aug. 18, 1877," Idaho State Historical Society, Ms. 106; Stanton G. Fisher, *Diary*, Idaho State Historical Society, Ms. 106.
65. *Idaho Statesman*, July 12, 1877.
66. "A. H. Bainbridge, Special Orders, Aug. 19, 1877," Idaho State Historical Society Ms. 106.
67. Stanton G. Fisher, *Diary*, Idaho State Historical Society, Ms. 106.
68. *Idaho Statesman*, Aug. 9, 1877.
69. W. H. Danilson to C.I.A., Aug., 9, 1877, *Idaho Superintendency*, Roll 345, *C.I.A. Annual Report, 1877*, 475.
70. *Idaho Statesman*, Aug. 21, 1877.
71. A. H. Bainbridge to W. H. Danilson, and Circular, Sept. 8, 1877, Fort Hall, *Record Group 393*, 132–134.
72. W. H. Danilson to C.I.A., Nov. 7, 1877, *Idaho Superintendency*, Roll 345.
73. A. H. Bainbridge to Dept. of the Platte, Nov. 26, 1877, ibid.; *Idaho Statesman*, Dec. 1, 1877.
74. P. H. Sheridan to Thomas M. Vincent, Nov. 27, 1877, *Idaho Superintendency*, Roll 346; George Crook to P. H. Sheridan, Nov. 28, 1877, ibid.
75. W. H. Danilson to C.I.A., Nov. 29, 1877, ibid.
76. P. H. Sherdian to Thomas M. Vincent, Nov. 29, 1877, ibid.; P. H. Sheridan to E. D. Townsend, Dec. 4, 1877, ibid.
77. A. H. Bainbridge to Dept. of the Platte, Dec. 6, 1877, Fort Hall, *Record Group 393*, 164–166.
78. John O. Smith to Dept. of the Platte, Dec. 25, 1877, *Idaho Superintendency*, Roll 348.
79. George Crook to P. H. Sheridan, Jan. 3, 1878, ibid.
80. W. H. Danilson to C.I.A., Jan. 13, 1878, *Idaho Superintendency*, Roll 347.
81. Joseph Skelton to Colonel George A. Shoup, Jan. 21, 1878, Idaho State University Archives, Ms. 585.
82. W. H. Danilson to C.I.A., Jan. 16, 1878, *Idaho Superintendency*, Roll 347.
83. *Idaho Statesman*, Jan. 17, 1878.
84. Ibid., Jan. 22, 25, 1878.
85. Wm. T. Sherman to Secretary of War, Jan. 21, 1878, *Idaho Superintendency*, Roll 348; Secretary of War to Secretary of Interior, ibid.
86. W. H. Danilson to C.I.A., Jan. 26, 1878, *Idaho Superintendency*, Roll 347.
87. A. H. Bainbridge to Major M. Bryant, Feb. 4, 1878, Fort Hall, *Record Group 393*, 177.
88. W. H. Danilson to C.I.A., Jan. 28, 1878, *Idaho Superintendency*, Roll 347.
89. W. H. Danilson to C.I.A., Feb. 26, 1878, ibid.
90. W. H. Danilson to C.I.A., May 9, 1878, ibid.
91. W. H. Danilson to C.I.A., July 23, 1878, ibid.
92. W. B. Royall to Dept. of the Platte, March 19, 1878, *Idaho Superintendency*, Roll 349.
93. W. T. Sherman to Sec. of War, April 3, 1878, *Idaho Superintendency*, Roll 348.
94. Sec. of War to Sec. of Interior, April 4, 1878, ibid.
95. *New Northwest*, March 8, 1878.
96. A. H. Bainbridge to Dept. of Platte, March 9, 1878, Fort Hall. *Record Group 393*, 191; George Crook to E. D. Townsend, April 25, 1878, *Idaho Superintendency*, Roll 349.
97. W. H. Danilson to C.I.A., March 2, 4, 1878, *Idaho Superintendency*, Roll 347.

98. *New Northwest*, March 15, 1878.
99. Sec. of War to Sec. of Interior, March 19, 1878, *Idaho Superintendency*, Roll 348.
100. W. H. Danilson to C.I.A., March 2, 1878, *Idaho Superintendency*, Roll 347.
101. George Crook to P. H. Sheridan, April 2, 1878, *Idaho Superintendency*, Roll 348.
102. George Crook to Dept. of Platte, April 3, 1878, ibid.; *C.I.A. Annual Report, 1878*, 447.
103. W. H. Danilson to C.I.A., April 4, 1878, *Idaho Superintendency*, Roll 347.
104. M. Brayman to Irwin McDowell, March 7, 1878, *Idaho Superintendency*, Roll 348.
105. *Idaho Statesman*, April 4, 1878.
106. W. H. Danilson to C.I.A., March 22, 26, 1878, *Idaho Superintendency*, Roll 347.
107. W. H. Danilson to C.I.A., April 3, 1878, ibid.
108. W. H. Danilson to C.I.A., April 5, 1878, ibid.
109. George Crook to Phillip H. Sheridan, April 2, 1878, *Idaho Superintendency*, Roll 349; Philip H. Sheridan to Division of Missouri, April 4, 1878, ibid.
110. F. E. Trotter to Dept. of Platte, April 6, 1878, *Idaho Superintendency*, Roll 348.
111. W. H. Danilson to F. E. Trotter, April 1, 1878, ibid.
112. A. H. Bainbridge to Dept. of Platte, April 30, 1878, Fort Hall, *Record Group 393*, 21; *New Northwest*, May 3, 1878.
113. *Idaho Statesman*, May 14, 1878.
114. Ibid., May 18, 1878.
115. Ibid., May 21, 1878.
116. R. Justice to Governor Brayman, May 21, 1878, Idaho State Historical Society, Ms.
117. *Idaho Statesman*, May 23, 1878.
118. Ibid., June 1, 13, 1878; General McDowell to Adjutant General, U.S.A., June 12, 1878, *Idaho Superintendency*, Roll 349.
119. M. Brayman to O. O. Howard, June 13, 1878, ibid.
120. See Brimlow, *The Bannock Indian War of 1878*; and Madsen, *The Bannock of Idaho*, Chapter 8.
121. W. H. Danilson to C.I.A., June 7, 1878, *Idaho Superintendency*, Roll 347; Sec. of War to Sec. of Interior, June 21, 1878, *Idaho Superintendency*, Roll 349.
122. *Idaho Statesman*, June 11, 1878; W. H. Danilson to C.I.A., June 10, 1878, *Idaho Superintendency*, Roll 347.
123. W. H. Danilson to C.I.A., June 6, 1878, ibid.
124. A. H. Bainbridge to Dept. of the Platte, June 2, 1878, Fort Hall, *Record Group 393*, 218; Sec. of War to Sec. of Interior, June 13, 1878, *Idaho Superintendency*, Roll 349.
125. George Crook to Division of the Missouri, July 27, 1878, Montana State Historical Society, *Letters, 1875–1888*, No. 4.
126. Geo. L. Miller to Carl Schurtz, July 29, 1878, *Idaho Superintendency*, Roll 348.
127. George Crook to Division of the Columbia, Sept. 23, 1878, Montana State Historical Society, *Letters, 1875–1888, No. 4*.
128. *Idaho Statesman*, Dec. 3, 1878.
129. A. H. Bainbridge to Dept. of the Platte, Dec. 13, 1878, *Idaho Superintendency*, Roll 351.
130. *C.I.A. Annual Report, 1878*, 446–447.
131. *Idaho Statesman*, Dec. 1878.
132. George Crook to Division of the Missouri, Sept. 23, 1878, Montana State Historical Society, *Letters, 1875–1888*, No. 4.
133. *C.I.A. Annual Report, 1878*, 545–547.
134. U.S. Congress, *Report of the Governor of Idaho*, House, Exec. Doc., 46th Cong., 2d Sess., Vol. 10, 422–423; *C.I.A. Annual Report, 1879*, 52–53.
135. W. H. Danilson to C.I.A., July 24, 1879, *Idaho Superintendency*, Roll 350.
136. *C.I.A. Annual Report, 1879*, 52–53.
137. W. H. Danilson to C.I.A., Aug. 13, 1879, *Idaho Superintendency*, Roll 350.
138. U.S. Congress, *Report of the Governor of Idaho*, House, Exec. Doc., 46th Cong., 2d Sess., Vol. 10, 422–423.
139. *C.I.A. Annual Report, 1879*, 52–53.
140. W. H. Danilson to C.I.A., Feb. 14, 1879, *Idaho Superintendency*, Roll 350.
141. *C.I.A. Annual Report, 1879*, 52–53.
142. *New Northwest*, March 21, 1879; J. M. Haworth to C.I.A., Oct. 23, 1879, *Idaho Superintendency*, Roll 350.
143. Joseph Hall to William A. Kimball, Jan. 9, 1879, Fort Hall, *Record Group 393*, 278.
144. U.S. Congress, *Report of the Governor of Idaho*, House, Exec. Doc., 46th Cong., 2d Sess., Vol. 10, 422.
145. *Idaho Statesman*, March 25, 1879.
146. Ibid., Sept. 30, 1879.
147. A. H. Bainbridge to W. H. Danilson, Aug. 19, 1879, Fort Hall, *Record Group 393*, 95; John A. Wright to C.I.A., Sept. 19, 1879, *Idaho Superintendency*, Roll 351.
148. *Idaho Statesman*, Sept. 25, 1879.
149. W. H. Danilson to C.I.A., July 18, 1879, *Idaho Superintendency*, Roll 350.
150. Sec. of War to Sec. of Interior, Nov. 6, 1878, *Idaho Superintendency*, Roll 347; P. H. Sheridan to E. D. Townsend, Feb. 14, 1879, *Idaho Superintendency*, Roll 351.
151. W. H. Danilson to C.I.A., April 1, 1879, *Idaho Superintendency*, Roll 350.
152. W. H. Danilson to C.I.A., July 1, 1879, ibid.
153. John A. Wright to C.I.A., Oct. 3, 1879, *Idaho Superintendency*, Roll 351; A. H. Bainbridge to Commanding Officer, Fort Ellis, Montana, Oct. 4, 1879, Fort Hall, *Record Group 393*, 55.
154. *C.I.A. Annual Report, 1879*, 158.
155. W. H. Danilson to C.I.A., April 30, 1879, *Idaho Superintendency*, Roll 350.
156. Geo. P. Taggart to J. D. Cameron, June 10, 1879, ibid.
157. T. F. Singiser to Commissioner, General Land Office, June 30, 1879, ibid.
158. John McNeil to C.I.A., Aug. 15, 1879, ibid.
159. John McNeil to C.I.A., Sept. 4, 1879, ibid.
160. W. H. Danilson to Fred J. Kiesel, Sept. 17, 1879, ibid.
161. J. W. Reid to C.I.A., Nov. 5, 1879, *Idaho Superintendency*, Roll 351.
162. John McNeil to John A. Wright, Sept. 4, 1869, ibid.; Acting Sec. of Interior to C.I.A., Sept. 11, 1879, *Idaho Superintendency*, Roll 350.
163. J. M. Haworth to C.I.A., Oct. 9, 1879, ibid.
164. J. M. Haworth to C.I.A., Oct. 17, 1879, ibid.

CHAPTER VI

WANDERERS ALONG THE BORDER

Mormon Aid for Northwestern Bands

While the Shoshoni and Bannock at Fort Hall spent the decade of the 1870s attempting to get enough subsistence so they could develop individual farms, their relatives, the Northwestern Shoshoni, found themselves frozen out of their aboriginal homelands by the productive and hard-working Mormon farmers in the valleys of northern Utah. The 1863 treaty of Box Elder had assured the ten wandering bands of an annuity of $5,000 to provide clothing and rations, but the government seldom funded the amount, which was insufficient anyway to provide for twelve hundred Indians. The fact that there was no reservation or designated location at which the Indians could be furnished rations or cared for made it easier for government officials to ignore them. Also, because they roamed along the border of Utah and Idaho territories they became a "lost tribe," claimed by neither governmental unit.

The Utah Indian officials were forced to recognize them when they hung around the Cache Valley settlements and especially near Brigham City and Corinne, begging for food, putting their horses into cultivated fields for pasture, and annoying the settlers. The *Corinne Reporter* carried frequent articles about groups of Northwestern Shoshoni, usually referred to by the editor as "Mr. Lo and family," who manifested signs of "biting hunger" as they searched for scraps of food or begged at the homes of the town's residents.[1] The *Deseret News* also commented occasionally; in June 1869 an article noted that Chief Pocatello and his band had paid a "begging visit" to the Bear Lake settlements. The editor thought Pocatello had "a reputation for honesty . . . almost as great as that of a Congressman" and that the "definition of the word Po-ca-tello, in English, literally rendered means 'give-us-another-sack-of-flour-and-two-beeves.' "[2] Apparently the old dictum of Brigham Young that it was easier to feed than fight the Indians had fallen from grace as the settlers were swamped by the destitute Shoshoni.

Chief Pocatello was at least ecumenical in his demands for food, for he also frequently visited Fort Hall. Charles F. Powell wrote that the chief showed up at the reservation with two hundred of his people, asking for presents. The agent supplied a small amount of bacon and flour and listened as Pocatello pleaded, "Come and 'talk' with us so that we may know what you wish with us."[3]

Superintendent of Indian Affairs for Utah J. E. Tourtellotte echoed these sentiments to his superiors as he asked for the modest sum of $1,500 to fulfill the treaty with the Northwestern bands.[4] He wrote further that, even though these Indians were "less inclined to agriculture," it would be impossible to find any suitable areas "unoccupied by whites" for the Shoshoni because of the great expense of furnishing irrigation systems.[5]

In the annual reports for 1869 both Tourtellotte and the Indian commissioner asked that the Northwestern Shoshoni be settled on a reservation "where they may have available land, without continued danger of being crowded off by approaching whites, and where, with reasonable assistance from the government, they may be encouraged to become self-supporting."[6] The petitions were ignored. The mostly pedestrian bands, who possessed only 170 horses, spent their time searching for food as they attempted to get permission to buy ammunition at Corinne so they could hunt small game in the hills and mountains north of Great Salt Lake.[7]

During the summer months the Indians usually stayed clear of the settlements, but when the starving time of winter came they could be found clustered along lower Bear River, where handouts from the citizens of Corinne, Brigham City, Ogden, and the smaller villages could be begged or bartered for a little work.[8] The Mormon people suffered mostly in silence the drain on their foodstuffs, but the Gentile population at Corinne was vociferous in loathing the poverty-stricken natives. A typical blast came from the editor of the *Corinne Reporter* in July 1870. He decried the custom of allowing Indians to ride freight cars along the Union Pacific and Central Pacific lines. "The idea of pestilent odors being swept from their filthy bodies through the crowded cars is not a pleasant reflection for travelers."[9]

In the fall of that year, Agent William H. Danilson from Fort Hall and Colonel J. E. Tourtellotte, superintendent of Indian Affairs for Utah, accompanied by Utah Governor Vernon H. Vaughan, met about three hundred of the Northwestern Shoshoni near Corinne to distribute a portion of the annuity goods called for under the Treaty

Idaho State Historical Society

Bronco Jim's residence at Fort Hall.

of Box Elder. It was significant that the agents from both Idaho and Utah participated, a sure recognition that these Indians belonged either to both superintendencies or perhaps to none. The *Reporter* described the affair with typical flourishes. He noted that ten chiefs were present, including Pocatello, and that such items as red shirts, blankets, fishhooks, pans, pots, traps, hatchets, butcher knives, and combs were given out. The editor thought that some "ten thousand dollars worth of the people's property" were thus dispersed to the "filthy vagrants,"[10] but the sum was probably the $1,039 accounted for to the commissioner by Tourtellotte on December 6, 1870.[11] Earlier, in July, Danilson had already had to issue rations and clothing to one hundred of the Northwestern Shoshoni who had come in to the reservation from "Bear River Valley, Utah." The small bands hovered between Fort-Hall and the Brigham City area, picking up whatever supplies they could from both places.[12]

In an attempt to discover what should be done with the wandering groups, Superintendent Floyd-Jones of Idaho met with several of the Indian leaders at Fort Hall. He listened to Bruneau Jim, Captain John of the Boise Indians, Captain Jim of the Fort Hall Shoshoni, and Pocatello of the Northwestern segment. The first three indi-

cated their desire to live at Fort Hall. Pocatello answered, "Me stop in Mormon home, me come to Fort Hall to see you. You talk, me go to Mormon home and tell Indians. All my Indians in Mormon home and in Buffalo country. Me no want to stop here. Me stop on Deep Creek. My agent at Box Center [Elder?] give me blanket, clothing, and so forth. He gives me oxen, plow, powder, and so forth. . . ." This was a pretty accurate description of the movements and wishes of the Northwestern Shoshoni. Captain Jim supported Pocatello's statement by saying, "he no stop here."[13]

1870

The Mormon peace policy of feeding the Shoshoni of northern Utah sometimes was interrupted by spurts of hostility from rumors started by Mormon-haters. In July 1870 L. L. Pohnanteer, a citizen of Rich County, Utah, reported a meeting he held with Chief Sagwitch and about two thousand Shoshoni and Ute Indians who demanded to know, "What the hell does all this talk mean?" Apparently someone had spread the word that Brigham Young was on his way to Rich County with an army to "use us up," as one of the Indians leaders put it. The tribes were reassured by Pohnanteer and agreed to "stick to the Mormons."[14]

The Cache Valley Saints also paid their share of

annuities and food to keep the Indians tranquil. Peter Maughan reported to the *Salt Lake Herald* that the settlers were expecting a visit from some Bannock after having fed a Shoshoni group "for days." He continued, "The good people of the Territory are paying out hundreds of thousands to 'Poor Lo' in free will offerings" because of the policy laid down by Brigham Young and "that humanity and justice command us to show them kindness."[15]

In his annual report of 1870 Superintendent Tourellotte again repeated his plea that the roaming bands of Northwestern Shoshoni be settled on a reservation where government employees could open a farm for them and teach them the arts of agriculture. He said the twelve hundred Indians had a good supply of horses and owned a few cows, cultivated no land at all, but just "rove among the mountains and valleys."[16]

Keeping account of where these wandering bands were located from time to time is a difficult task as one refers to the scanty records of that day, but at least that portion which inhabited the 1871 lower Bear River Valley had excellent news coverage as the *Corinne Reporter* included spot announcements of Indian activities, sometimes daily. During 1871 the editor noted Indians attending baseball games, searching in the alleys for "thawed swill and other luxuries," travelling around in "majestic tatters," holding funerals for departed loved ones, "sawing wood for palefaces," buying liquor from unscrupulous whites, selling furs and swapping horses, patronizing local fruit stands, playing cards on the sidewalks, and being too numerous "in town these days for the general good."[17]

In June the editor described a large assemblage of Indians, recently returned from the Wind River buffalo country and gathered on the banks of Bear River about two miles from Corinne. The "Grand Pow-Wow" was an entirely Indian affair but probably would "concoct some new mode of inducing Uncle Sam to *pot-latch* a new installment of guns, ammunition, etc., for their use."[18]

The Indian presence could also lead to depredations, as the bolder of the hungry natives attempted to get provisions by force. In one incident cited by the *Reporter* some Shoshoni broke into a citizen's house, stole all the food, and broke up the furniture for a campfire.[19] During a second raid on a Corinne judge's home, the official hit one of the intruders over the head with a shovel.[20] Another citizen reported that Pocatello and his followers had forcibly taken a horse from a man. Agent M. P. Berry, reporting the affair to the commissioner, said the chief was a "terror to the settlers" and asked that he and his band be returned by the military to Fort Hall.[21] Berry finally travelled to Corinne to investigate the troubles. He found two lodges of Pocatello's people

and ordered them to return to Fort Hall, but he did not disturb another two hundred fifty Indians who had never been on the reservation.[22]

In his annual report Agent Berry mentioned that about one hundred Northwestern Shoshoni from Cache Valley had settled on the reservation during 1871 and that he expected them to take kindly to the labor of farming after observing what their white neighbors had accomplished with agriculture.[23] There were still about forty lodges scattered between Corinne and Salt Lake City who had no home, lived "on the offal of slaughter houses" and as "general scavengers." The Mormon bishop at Brigham City occasionally gave them wheat and flour from the local storehouse.[24]

Other Mormon officials, especially at Franklin, Idaho, in northern Cache Valley, faced serious consequences as the result of the constant drain on their resources to feed neighboring Indians. Mayor L. H. Hatch wrote to Utah Agent J. J. Critchlow begging for relief. Apparently some of the Indians contracted smallpox and had to be supported from the city treasury to keep them away from the white inhabitants, some of whom caught the disease anyway. From the beginning of the settlement, said the mayor, the citizens had been forced to feed "quite a number of half starved Indians who are continuously in our midst" and had spent thousands of dollars, preferring to feed them rather than fight them. Hatch asked that the government assume its rightful responsibility and not leave the care of the Indians to a "poor frontier people."[25]

Special Agency for Utah Shoshoni

The constant barrage from Utah and Idaho Indian officials finally moved the commissioner to appoint the Reverend Dr. George W. Dodge of South Bend, Indiana, as special agent for the Western, Northwestern, and Gosiute tribes. The decision to establish a special agency was a good one for the Northwestern bands, but the choice of Dodge to fill the position was unfortunate, to say the least. He turned out to be all heart and no head, as far as the Office of Indian Affairs was concerned.[26]

Agent Dodge began 1872 by writing the commissioner that he had met fifty Northwestern Shoshoni who were destitute and that there were others who belonged at Fort Hall and should not be expecting rations from his small stock. He also met some "suffering" Indians at Ogden, Utah, and bought a few provisions for them.[27] To these first Indians he issued half-rations of flour and two rations of beef per week.[28]

By February he had begun to discover just how many Indians were dependent upon him for subsistence and how poor they were. He sent in an estimate asking for $125,000, a sum much larger

1872

than the previous year's appropriation. He also intended to locate a reservation for the three groups of Indians under his charge.[29] The *Corinne Reporter* thought he was being too benevolent when he served four pounds of beef to each of four hundred Shoshoni who "take to the raw beef like coyotes in the tailrace of a butcher shop." The editorial was entitled "Stuffing Savages."[30]

While the people of Corinne were not treated to as many comments from their friendly editor in 1872 concerning the Northwestern Shoshoni, there were occasional references to drunken Indians being permitted to loiter in the city[31] or mounted Indians in large numbers: "Keep a close eye on the bloody dogs."[32] By September, a number of Indian women were gleaning in the grainfields adjacent to the town.[33]

The commissioner back in Washington wondered what kind of representative he had sent to care for the needs of the scattered Shoshoni. In March he ordered the new agent to cancel all contracts to supply provisions for the Shoshoni, and he disapproved the rental of a building in Salt Lake City as an office. Dodge complied but remonstrated, "It is the most painful step I have ever been called upon to take in a business line. How Indians are to live without food I know not. If they *can*, they have different stomachs . . . generally from mine." He continued that he had restrained his emotions, knowing that he had done as conscience would direct in ordering the supplies for Indians, who had "*nothing* to subsist upon." He also reported that the Indians were suffering from a smallpox epiemic and that the Mormons were "tampering" with the Indians by withholding food so as to embarrass the government. What horrified him even more was the practice of the Indian women selling themselves to white men in exchange for food. When questioned by Dodge they replied, "White man no give it any other way." He said his cheeks burned "with shame" at the necessity for such a course and hoped that his government would be "*generous*" if it were not "*Christian*." The final blow was the disallowance of any clerical help, even though the Indians under his charge were scattered over six hundred miles from Echo Canyon to Virginia City, Nevada.[34]

In his April report Dodge explained that he was not asking for any seeds for the Northwestern Shoshoni because none farmed and that he had more trouble with their gambling, begging, and selling away their annuities than any other Indians under his charge. He found them to be "very poor" and promised to try to send them on a hunting expedition. He disapproved their habit of using tobacco but asked for $200 to purchase some because they "*will have it*."[35] The agent attacked the Mormons again for always harping

than the government was not taking care of the "Descendants of Joseph." He asked the commissioner not to pay the bill of Ben Hampton at Bear River Crossing for feeding some Indians, even though he acknowledged that Hampton had probably done so. To him it was a bad precedent, and he felt that other Mormons would then surely present bills.[36]

The Reverend Dodge's anti-Mormon bias came into full flower in a twenty-four-page letter of July 24 in which he described the "mysterious movement" of thousands of Indians into Utah or adjacent territories, including six thousand Sioux and Cheyenne to Camas Prairie, Idaho, and Chief Pocatello to northern Utah. A Paiute prophet from Nevada was stirring up the Indians of the West, and Brigham Young and the Mormons were aiding and abetting the coming insurrection by preaching that the government agents were not providing for the wants of the Indians. The Mormons were further teaching that a "white prophet" would soon appear to confirm that the Indians were descendants of Manasseh and were to be under the supervision of the Mormons. Further, although he had given strict orders to the Mormon authorities not to feed the Indians, so as to try to stop the influx into Utah Territory, the Latter-day Saints refused to obey his instructions. To ensure that the commissioner would take him seriously, Dodge said his fears were supported fully by Colonel Henry A. Morrow of Camp Douglas.[37] By October the agent was being more explicit — the Mormon leader was urging the Indians to commit depredations and was telling his followers to aid the natives "all we can."[38]

A twenty-nine-page report by Dodge in August did not indicate that the Indians were playing any favorites. He reported that about six thousand were camped near Logan in Cache Valley, levying "contributions on the settlers for subsistence, claiming it as their due for rentage" of their land. At the conclusion of his letter, Dodge's remark that he was "scarcely able physically to make this report" leads a reader of his verbose correspondence to wonder why he did not resort to fewer and more succinct statements.[39] His yearly report was more to the point. He told of the difficulties in reaching all his wards and said his "heart has had to ache during the year" because he was forced to say that the appropriation was insufficient. He was able to give blankets to only one out of ten Indians. He concluded that the yearly amount of money should have been $100,000 instead of one-fifth or one-fourth that amount.[40]

The dispute between the Utah and Idaho superintendents about who should care for the Northwestern Shoshoni continued as Agent Berry at Fort Hall analyzed the status of Pocatello's band. He indicated that Pocatello would not claim to be chief, giving the agent the names of three

1872

other individuals who acted in that capacity. Berry was not impressed. Pocatello was really the "business man" of the tribe but had learned through hard experience that there were liabilities as well as honors connected with such a leadership role. Berry asked that a decision be made as to where the band should be located and recommended the Fort Hall Reservation if sufficient funds were appropriated for them each year.[41] Dodge thought the Northwestern group was ready to commence farming either at Fort Hall or in Indian territory if the necessary support could be given them.[42]

1872

The agent was never able to follow through on his wish to place the Indians under his charge on reservations. On December 11 he acknowledged orders discontinuing the special agency and hoped that his year's stewardship had been efficient and acceptable. Otherwise, he urged an official examination of his conduct of affairs.[43] Ten days later he wrote that he feared the reason for the abrupt cancellation of the agency was due to his "supposed excess of instructions" in describing his administration of affairs. The appointment of Colonel Henry A. Morrow to fill another position which took over virtually the same responsibilities led Dodge to believe that he was being dismissed for dereliction of duty. He requested an explanation, which no doubt was not given.[44] His evaluation of the reason for his dismissal seems, at this point in time, to be quite accurate.

1873

The Powell-Ingalls Commission

With the disappearance of George Dodge from the scene, the Northwestern Shoshoni lost a special pleader for their cause, and the bands continued the old habit of hanging around the Utah settlements to scrounge and beg for food. The people of Corinne, especially, found their presence to be distasteful. The editor of the local paper rejoiced when a Utah-Northern train ran over an Indian and decapitated him: "Hurrah for the Utah Northern, the guillotine of the savage."[45] There were reports of Indians breaking into houses in search of food, of Indians shoplifting in the local stores or visiting local ranchers and demanding a beef or two in return for leaving the premises.[46] The *Corinne Reporter* editor was particularly upset when the encampment of Shoshoni on Bear River near the town held a war dance in honor of the Modoc Indians' victory in a battle with whites. "They ought to be skinned alive for their insolence," he said.[47] From the point of view of the Indians, there seemed to be no other recourse than to beg, steal, or demand food, — whichever course would promise the most success.

The constant presence of the Shoshoni around the northern Utah settlements, the failure of the Dodge Special Agency to locate reservations for the widely scattered bands, and the constant pres-

sure of feeding the Indians faced by the Mormon farmers and others — all these factors, plus the responsibility felt by Washington officials, finally led to the appointment of a special commission to investigate the condition of the Northwestern, Western, and Gosiute Shoshoni and recommend what should be done for them. The two commissioners, John Wesley Powell and G. W. Ingalls, arrived in Salt Lake City in May 1873 to begin their arduous task of visiting the Indians and deciding on reservations for them.[48]

After some initial meetings the two commissioners were of the opinion that the Sanpits, Seigwitz, and Pocatilla bands would not consent to go to Fort Hall but would agree to a reservation site about seventy-five miles southwest of Fort Hall, probably in the Raft River area.[49] A month later the commission decided on a different course and recommended that the Northwestern Shoshoni be assembled at Fort Hall to receive their annuities and be informed that they were to settle at Fort Hall.[50] Washington approved the final decision, as well as the request of Powell and Ingalls that food and supplies should no longer be given to Colonel Morrow to distribute to the Indians at Salt Lake City but should be placed under the charge of the commissioners, who would decide when and where the supplies would be given out.[51] The latter change was made because the Utah superintendent of Indian Affairs had made a practice of sending the annuities to Mormon

L.D.S. Church Archives

Part of Pocatello's Band.

bishops for distribution, with the resultant belief on the part of the natives that the Mormon Church was their benefactor. Also, the Indians had found it very convenient to barter their gifts away to unscrupulous white citizens in the large towns. At remote reservations such trade would be more difficult, and the allotment of goods at the reservations would accustom the Indians to living there permanently.[52]

1873

The commission met with Northwestern Shoshoni groups in Cache Valley, at Ogden, and at Corinne, where in November annuity goods were distributed to about three hundred men, women, and children under Chiefs "San Pits" and "Suiquits." The goods given out included 240 shirts, 356 blankets, 12 suits of clothes to chiefs and subchiefs, 800 yards of blue drill, 850 yards of bedticking for dresses, 500 yards of red flannel, and a number of hardware items. Newspaper reporters on the scene indicated that this Northwestern band was to be placed on a reservation in Nevada, inasmuch as northern Utah was "settled up," which left no "stamping ground" for the Indians.[53] The report was wrong. Not only had the special commission decided on Fort Hall as the home for the Northwestern Shoshoni but when another commission (J. P. C. Shanks, T. W. Bennett, and H. W. Reed) met with the Corinne group of Shoshoni in Salt Lake City in November 1873 these three officials were able to persuade the Indians to accept Fort Hall as their home.[54]

In their final report Powell and Ingalls indicated they had no reliable information about the number of Northwestern Shoshoni but felt that the Fort Hall Reservation was large enough to hold a sizeable group. Furthermore, according to the commissioner's interpretation of the Treaty of Box Elder on July 13, 1863 (which referred to Article 2 of the Fort Bridger Treaty of July 2, 1863) the Northwestern bands were entitled to settle at Wind River Reservation but would probably prefer Fort Hall, where large numbers of them were already located. Chief Pocatello had already settled at Fort Hall, Sanpits and Saigwits were prepared to go there, and Taviwunshea had taken his small band to Wind River. A delegation from the Sanpits and Saigwits contingents traveled to Fort Hall; picked out two sites, one just south of the Agency and another on Bannock Creek; and promised they would return in the spring prepared to begin life as farmers, with the expectation that the government would provide them with subsistence and the necessary seeds and tools. Each family was to get a cow, and the government would also undertake to build proper irrigation systems.[55]

1874

But the promises of last year were easy to forget, as the three hundred or so Northwest Shoshoni of the Sanpits clans returned to their old haunts near the mouth of Bear River, conveniently located halfway between the Mormon town of Brigham City and the Gentile village of Corinne. The newspaper of the latter place again carried short items of complaint about drunken and begging Indians hanging around the business district, sawing wood for town residents, or just generally annoying the citizens.[56] The editor asked why Agent G. W. Ingalls was not caring for his charges.[57]

The Mormons, on the other hand, were still doing their best to follow the admonition of their prophet to feed the Indians. In Cache Valley, Mayor L. H. Hatch of Franklin, Idaho, with the help of L. B. Huntington, a Mormon Indian agent, was trying to encourage the "broken band" of Shoshoni of his neighborhood to go to work for the adjacent farmers. The headman, Tsi-Gwitch, "meaning to catch or grab," agreed to talk to his young men. About twenty of the group had become "taxpayers" and indicated a desire to take up homesteads. At the conclusion of the council, directed by Mayor Hatch, a Mormon brother led the assembled Indians and whites in a rendition of the hymn "O Stop and Tell Me, Red Man."[58]

Corinne Indian "Scare"

At Brigham City, Mormon Bishop Alvin Nichols was also doing his duty by the Indians, distributing beef and other supplies "on a liberal scale" to the encampment of Shoshoni at Bear River. This was in November 1874.[59] The band left on a short hunting expedition to the Promontory Summit region but was back by December looking for more food.[60]

There were more than two hundred Indians in camp, with more coming each day. This aroused much apprehension on the part of the people of Corinne, whose newspaper editor attacked Mormon and Indian with nice impartiality. He thought the two would unite in any difficulty which might take place with the Gentiles, that the chief of the encampment was a Mormon bishop, and that the citizens of Corinne deserved some government protection from these "Latter-day pets" who said they would not go to Fort Hall.[61]

1874

George W. Hill, a Mormon with a missionary concern for the Shoshoni, wrote the commissioner of Indian Affairs on December 14, 1874, inquiring whether any annuity goods were to be issued by the government to the Bear River band. The Indians had reported to him that they had not received any rations for two years, with the exception of twenty-five sacks of flour and a few blankets given them by Agent Ingalls during the previous September and some other articles to a camp of twenty-five lodges the year before. Hill wrote that they were a "continued expense" to him and that they were suffering and should be placed on a reservation "in their own country." They were

Utah State Historical Society

Corinne, Utah, 1870

receiving almost none of the $5,000 annuity promised them under the Treaty of Box Elder. The Mormon leader wished to know whether the Indian Department would reimburse him if he fed them during the winter.[62]

George W. Hill had been "called privately" in April 1873 to serve as a missionary to the Indians, or Lamanites as the Mormons called them, of northern Utah. In a first meeting with the group at Corinne, Hill baptized 101 Indians into the Latter-day Saints Church. This was on May 1, 1874. Three weeks later he was at Franklin, Idaho, where he helped Mayor Hatch organize that band and establish a farm — which was abandoned in the fall as an unsatisfactory location. In April 1875 Hill was given the specific assignment to establish a mission among the Indians at Brigham City and Corinne. He gathered the natives at a spot between the Malad and Bear Rivers and put in about one hundred and forty acres of wheat, corn, and potatoes, "the Indians taking hold of their work well." In the latter part of May he moved the camp to a spot lower on Bear River due to the bad water at the Malad. Within a few more weeks large numbers of Indians began to gather at the camp "from abroad." Hill started a series of evangelical meetings which resulted in 574 baptisms by August 12.[63]

The agent at Fort Hall became concerned as he saw many of his wards leaving to join the encampment on Bear River. He reported to the commissioner that, as the result of a visit to Corinne, he had discovered several hundred Indians from the Wind River Agency as well as those from his reservation. He said that many baptisms were being performed and that Indians were being "taken through the 'Endowment House' (whatever that is or means) and then called 'The Lords Battle Axes.'" He asked that a special agent, independent of Mormon authority and supported by the military, be sent to return the Indians to their respective reservations. [64] A few weeks later Agent Wright again warned the commissioner that the Mormons had sent Indian representatives to Fort Hall and Wind River to recruit for their flock. He said this was endangering the discipline of both reservations and would surely result in trouble. The Indians, he said, "go away in the night," deny they had done so, and "when pressed get mad."[65] He regretted, because of insufficient rations, to have to allow the Indians to leave the reservation when many of them immediately left for Utah "to get washed & greased and enrolling themselves in the cause of the Mormons." Wright accused the Mormon missionaries of teaching that the Indians were chosen

1875

of the Lord to establish God's kingdom on earth and that they should hate the government.[66]

With Indian officials so worried, it is perhaps understandable that the people of Corinne, led by their news editor, began to evince a stronger case of the jitters than ever before, as they witnessed a larger and larger influx of Indians into the camp a few miles from town. Articles earlier in the year had already built up apprehension,[67] and by July 9 the *Daily Mail* was reporting that the valley was "swarming" with Indians who were being assured by the Mormon authorities that the land they were farming belonged to them as a reservation. The editor demanded that the Shoshoni be returned to their proper reservations.[68]

1875

As a background for the scare which developed in Corinne, it should be noted that the *Daily Mail* prominently played up the trial being held at Beaver, Utah, for John D. Lee, accused as the Mormon leader in the infamous Mountain Meadows Massacre — in which, it was reported, a group of Missouri emigrants had been killed by a combined force of Indians and Mormons.[69] Secondly, because of the results of the panic of 1873 and a downturn in business, the freight trade of Corinne was in the thrall of "hard times," the genesis of a charge later made by Utah residents that the scare was gotten up to bring in free-spending soldiers to help spark the economy of the town.[70]

On August 9 the following headlines appeared in the *Corinne Mail*, "Mormons Meddling with the Indians! Mountain Meadows to be Repeated!!" By this time according to the newspaper, there were over one thousand Indians encamped ten miles north of the town and preparing to attack.[71] The next day the editor explained the reason. Brigham Young, afraid of the countervailing influence of the Gentile town, had earlier come to the banks of Bear River, and raising his arms "in the name of God pronounced a curse on the town and said it should pass away." Obviously Corinne had not disappeared, so the Mormons had gathered the Indians to ensure the success of the prophecy.[72]

On August 11, the *Mail*, pronounced a "Night of Terror!!!" during which a body of fifty armed citizens had been able to frighten away an attacking army of Indians. Even the editor acknowledged that some of the town's citizens had said that frightening white women and children unnecessarily in this way was an "outrage." Placing all his fears before him, and resolute in the defense of his home amd hearth and those of his neighbors, he defiantly called for reinforcements to save the citizens from a bloodbath at the hands of the murderous Indians to the north.[73]

1875

By evening of August 12 three companies of troops were in Corinne to protect the people. General George Crook had been notified that other troopers should be dispatched at once, the governor of Utah arrived to take personal charge, and a deputation of military officers and citizens visited the Indian encampment to learn that another five hundred Indians supposedly were on their way as reinforcements for the projected attack. The military commander warned the Indians to disperse and return to their reservations at once or he would use troops to move them. The discouraged and frightened Indians began to leave at once, and George Hill started for Ogden.[74]

When it became obvious that the Indians had intended nothing more than to tend their crops and hold their annual summer visit with their friends and relatives, the troops were recalled and the excitement subsided. A newspaper war now ensued between the *Corinne Mail* on the one hand and the *Ogden Junction* and the *Deseret News* on the other, with even the *Omaha Herald* and *Sacramento Union* getting involved. Perhaps the *Junction* had the better of the discussion in commenting that the disturbance was a "ruse on the part of certain bankrupt Corinneites to galvanize their town into life."[75] The *Deseret News* thought the whole affair "another attempt of a certain class of 'Mormon' haters to make political capital against the 'Mormons.'" The *Sacramento Union* headed its article, "The Corinne Farce."[76]

The constant appeals from certain people in Corinne prompted General Philip Sheridan to make a personal inspection at Corinne on August 21. As a result he ordered a company of troops to be stationed at the town until the Indian question was settled.[77] The troops were recalled on September 23.[78]

As was too often the case in such scares as the one manufactured at Corinne, the Indians were the victims. When the military commander ordered the Shoshoni to disperse and return to their reservations the tribesmen were just completing the second day of their harvest, having cut twenty-five acres of wheat and two acres of peas. Everything else from the 140 acres of crops was lost, as the thoroughly frightened Indians poured into Fort Hall for protection. This led Agent Danilson to write, "The question naturally arises how are they all to be fed this winter. The present allowance will not do it."[79] Agent J. J Critchlow of the Utah Superintendency, as a result of his investigation of the Corinne scare, wrote that the farm, started under the supervision of George Hill, had been created to teach the Indians to "settle down and become good citizens of the government and obey its laws."[80] The twenty lodges of about one hundred and twenty Indians from Fort Hall returned to their reservation from the farm at Bear River "disgusted with the whole proceeding" and having "lost faith in the Mormons," according to Agent Danilson.[81] The *Deseret News* was quite exp-

1875

licit, "These shameful Indian scares are actual robberies — they rob the Indians of their hard earned crops and of the right to dwell in peace."[82] Perhaps the most telling and perplexed cry came from Chief Sagwitch Timbimboo, the survivor of the Massacre of Bear River, who said in some anguish, "What have I stolen? Who have I killed?"[83]

Except for a few isolated families, the expulsion from the Corinne area marked the end of large groups of Northwestern Shoshoni gathering annually at the mouth of Bear River. Most found a home a Fort Hall from then on. The remainder, almost three hundred, remained faithful converts to Mormonism and began to prosper as the church helped them learn the arts of civilization.

1876　With proper missionary zeal, and undeterred by the disaster of 1875, George W. Hill at once established another farm, this one located between the Bear and Malad rivers, just south and west of Hampton's Bear River Crossing (present Collinston). The area encompassed about nine thousand acres of land, enclosed on the north by a fence a mile in length from stream to stream and on the south by another fence one and one-quarter miles long. With the help of other Mormon missionaries Hill constructed a dam containing five hundred loads of rock, and started a canal sixteen miles in length, of which three miles 1876　were completed during 1876. By midsummer Hill had eighty acres of wheat ready for harvest, which the Indians accomplished with their own reaper. Another eighty acres of spring wheat had been planted, plus several acres of vegetables. Aided by the Mormons, fourteen Indian families applied for homesteads on about seventy-five acres of the land and started getting out logs to build houses. When they applied for homestead patents, the Indians abandoned their tribal allegiance and agreed to give up any rights to government annuities. The Mormon *Journal History* said a more "orderly, prayerful, and preserving colony of men and women would be hard to find." A few of the Indian families stayed at the farm, but most went to winter at Promontory, where there was fuel and feed.[84]

1877　The revival of missionary effort among the small group of Northwestern Shoshoni on Bear River sparked more anti-Mormon charges in 1877, with demands that the Indians be forced to move to the Fort Hall Reservation. The first attack came in August, when an Ogden resident, Ephraim Young, wrote the secretary of the Interior that George W. Hill had gathered four or five hundred Indians on "public land" and that the Indians were "well armed and their horses in first-class order."[85] Asked by Secretary Carl Schurz to investigate, the U.S. district attorney for Utah reported that the Indians were members of the Mormon Church, had "passed through the Endowment Home," were completely under the

control of Mormon authorities, and therefore had become "at once disloyal." He said the settlers were apprehensive and that not only should the Indians be placed on a reservation but Hill should be prosecuted for "illegally tampering with the Indians."[86]

Governor George W. Emery supported the contention of the district attorney concerning Indian annoyances, claiming that "The Mormon people who have to suffer, complain bitterly about these things as well as the Gentiles. . . ." He pointed out that twenty-seven Indians had filed on home- 1877 steads, that there was no way to prevent them from doing so, and that they should be moved to Fort Hall. Emery included clippings from the *Salt Lake Tribune* which listed thirty entries for homesteads. He was of the opinion that these land entries would eventually go to the Mormon Church and that the Indians were being used merely as dupes to get the land for the church. The governor advised the Interior Department to force the Indians to the reservation, which they visited often to get annuity supplies anyway.[87]

Finally, Utah Indian Agent J. J. Critchlow was dispatched to visit the farm and give a first-hand report. He discovered that the settlement had begun in 1876 with about one hundred and twenty-five Indians, that there were never more than about three hundred at the Bear River site, and certainly not the fifteen hundred Indians the people of Corinne claimed were living at Hampton's Crossing. Critchlow saw no immediate danger, although he was of the opinion that if the Indians could be persuaded to move to Fort Hall it might be better for all concerned.[88] The agent was convinced that the Indians had never made Fort Hall their home but had always resided along the Bear River. The district attorney urged that a military force be employed if the government were truly in earnest about moving the Indians to a reservation.[89]

W. H. Danilson of Fort Hall was now asked his opinion, as the result of a visit to the farm. He found three Mormon missionaries, hard at work, and forty Indian families, twenty-four of whom had taken lands under the Homestead Act. There were two hundred acres sown to wheat and eight small houses. In his council with the Indians he found a few who expressed a desire to move to Fort Hall, but most were content to remain under Mormon tutelage, having always lived in Utah. Danilson wrote that they did not belong to his agency but recommended that the two hundred forty "Bear River Indians" be sent to Fort Hall with the understanding that the Office of Indian Affairs would supply him enough funds to subsist them.[90] 1877

A group of apostate Mormons residing on Sublette Creek, twelve miles from Raft River, raised a note of concern in a letter to the Idaho governor about the Northwestern Shoshoni. "The Indians is aloud two leve thare reservation and come Out here and burn the grase and timber and stele cattle and horses." The writer asked for arms for protection, saying, "The people of Corinth in Utah have just receved armes and they live rite on the Ral rode and ten times more Safer than us."[91]

Washakie Settlement

1878 To put such fears to rest one way or the other, Utah Agent Critchlow visited the Bear River settlement again and found Isaac Zundell in charge, George W. Hill having been assigned to an Indian mission at Bear Lake. Critchlow found "several Indians actually at work" in the fields and recommended that the group be allowed to remain under the care of Mormon authorities, which would relieve the government of the necessity of caring for them. He did not agree with those Gentiles who "believe that everything Mormons do must necessarily be evil." With gifts of farm implements and other supplies from the government, which he advised, he thought the Indians "worthy of it and even of homesteads and citizenship." From this time on the government followed his advice almost literally, allowing the Mormon Church to care for the "Washakie" settlement of over two hundred (as it was now called in honor of Chief Washakie) with very little help or hindrance from the Office of Indian Affairs.[92]

1880 Mormon leaders were convinced that the location on the banks of Bear River did not offer enough land for the size of the Indian community and that it was too far removed from the fuel afforded in the mountains. On April 15, 1880, they purchased for $6,180 a tract of 1,700 acres at the site presently known as Washakie, Utah, in the southern end of Malad Valley. The Indians were moved and farming operations begun at the new mission station. Eventually the Mormon Church increased the size of the land holdings to 18,000 acres and undertook a long-range program of making its Indian members at that place self-sustaining members of society.[93]

1882 The progress of the Washakie colony can be followed from occasional news stories in the *Deseret News*, which took special interest in the development of the Indian brethren living in Malad Valley. Two years after the initial settlement the newspaper's correspondents reported that a school had been built; a schoolmaster, James J. Chandler, appointed; and thirty-five students enrolled. There were the usual battles with crickets and drouth. The water problem was solved by digging a fourteen-mile canal carrying water from the town of Samaria to Indian farms. About one hundred "Snake" Indians were each cultivating eighty-acre farms, building houses, raising stock, and trapping and fishing. Mormon missionaries

with carpenter skills were "called" to instruct their red brethren in the art of building. Moroni Ward, who by this time had labored in the Shoshoni vineyard for four years, described his converts as a "sober, moral community." In 1882 the Indians raised 1,600 bushels of grain on irrigated lands and 1,800 bushels on dry farms. The reporter said the Indians were much pleased with their prospects and appreciated the efforts of the missionaries who had "reclaimed them from a nomadic life."[94] 1883

By 1883 there were four full-time Mormon elders engaged in working with the Indians at Washakie — Bishop Isaac E. D. Zundell; his two counselors, Alexander Hunsaker and Moroni Ward; and the teacher, James Chandler. Sunday services were regularly attended by the devout Indians, with an Indian choir providing the hymns. Final proof was being made in support of twelve homestead claims, under such names as Was-pitch, Gavits-Ova, Ashinbo Pitsy, and Que-di-gidge. A few of the families lived in houses (some constructed of brick from the Indian brick kilns) but most people still preferred the comfortable tepees. There was a cooperative store, 150 acres of irrigated land, 450 acres of dry farm, and 1,500 head of sheep. Unused to the new life, many of the Indian children died. In one year, 1882, there were fifteen deaths from measles, thirteen from whooping cough, and five from other diseases. But the Indians continued in their faith — Washakie Ward contributed $8,000 toward the erection of the Mormon Temple in Logan, Utah.[95]

All was not perfect in the little Zion. The missionaries met a lot of frustrations in their attempt 1883 to make the Indians into carbon copies of themselves. In one incident, one of the Mormon elders was directing a group of Shoshoni farmers in stacking grain. The work was not progressing fast enough, so he shouted in the Indian language, "Stand over there." Unfortunately he used the wrong word and actually said, "Sit over there." His willing charges proceeded to obey with much amusement. Another story was reported in the *Utah Journal* about Brother Tope, a Washakie Indian, who was asked if he was a Mormon. He replied, "Yes . . . me heap good Mormon." Whereupon the storekeeper with whom he was talking answered, "You are not a Mormon at all; you've apostatized. Why, only the other day I heard you say that you no like Co-op; Indian United Order farm at Malad no good." In further disgruntlement Tope had said he put seventeen horses into the order and could only get seven back. Also he had complained that all the grain was locked up in the granary, for which he had no key. When confronted by the charges Tope replied that he had told the Mormon authorities that these stories of his complaints were all lies, "Me talk two ways; that's all right, me two kinds of friends."[96]

1886   A *Deseret News* report of 1886 listed about two hundred and fifty Indians living at Washakie. They produced enough grain on 235 acres of irrigated land for their own consumption and devoted the rest of their efforts to caring for 1,500 sheep and herding another 2,000 sheep on shares. They still owned a large herd of horses but had no cattle except one milk cow per family. They owned their property in common, stayed on their farms the year around, and were a temperate and industrious people, according to the correspondent.[97]

1887   The passage of the Dawes Act in 1887 established allotments in severalty on the Indian reservations of the United States. This brought at least one request from a Washakie Indian for an allotment on Bannock Creek at Fort Hall, where his father had a home. It was an indication that some of the Northwestern Shoshoni at Washakie were attracted to Fort Hall. Certainly over the years, as the population declined at the Mormon settlement, some of the Indians who left went to Fort Hall.[98]

1889   Agent S. G. Fisher at the reservation tried to induce one Indian to remain at Washakie. This was an individual named Per Dash, who abandoned his homestead entry on the pretext that there was no irrigation water for it. Upon investigation Fisher discovered that the Indian had been asked to surrender the land to a white man, under orders from the Mormon bishop. Having "more confidence in the Mormon Church than he had in the Government," Per Dash released his homestead, whereupon Agent Fisher "gave it up" in some disgust.[99]

1893   Reports of the devout and highly moral conduct of the Washakie Mormon Indians usually made up most of the *Deseret News* accounts, so it is difficult to get a picture of daily life at the settlement. The news correspondents only incidentally mentioned such mundane matters as (in 1893) that most of the Indians lived in houses by this time, used stoves and furniture, and wore "citizen's" dress. Moroni Ward was now the bishop.[100]

1898   One non-Mormon who passed by the settlement in 1898 did leave an interesting description of a neat little village, fenced fields, modern farm machinery, good wagons and teams, and Indians at work on their farms. He thought someone should be rewarded for the "large amount of faith, perseverance, and much hard labor in bringing this remnant of the children of the forest to such a state of independence and civilization."[101] Moroni Ward was probably delighted with this accolade to his contribution and

1902 no doubt was even more pleased when his son George was made bishop of Washakie in 1902.[102]

The Office of Indian Affairs was strangely silent about the little Indian colony at Washakie during all the years after 1878 but began to pick up an interest by 1912. One special Indian agent 1912 reported that year that George M. Ward was still in charge. The agent had not been able to visit the settlement but had talked to several members, two of whom reported a good school supported by county and state funds, 3,120 acres under cultivation in one township, and 1,366 acres in a second township, the latter having been leased for $2,700 in 1911. The Indian farmers raised grain and owned their own "thrashing" machine. They were intelligent and well-dressed, and the agent did not consider "it necessary to visit this band as yet." After some of the other little groups he had visited at Skull Valley, Deep Creek, and Indianola, the appearance of the Washakie Indians he met convinced him that, by comparsion, they were indeed well off.[103]

Another indication of Washington interest by the 1920s and 1930s was an annual census taken of the Washakie group. From 1921 to 1932 the population remained fairly constant at about 123 Indians; it increased to approximately 133 during the 1930s. The difference between these figures and the almost three hundred who originally joined the Mormon Church and settled at Washakie probably resulted from removals to Fort Hall, deaths from a new and unfamiliar sedentary life, or a merging into the white culture.[104]

The one contant in the life of the Washakie Indians was the devotion to their progress demon- 1923 strated by the Mormon Church. As the L.D.S. *Journal History* put it on April 26, 1923, "These Indians are under the jurisdiction of the Fort [Hall] Indian Agency, but little government aid has been given them." George M. Ward was still bishop but had the help of two Indian counselors. Moroni Timbimboo and Quegembitch. The colony was self-supporting, and the Indians were strict in devotion to their religion, keeping the Sabbath Day holy, adjuring the use of tobacco and strong drink, attending prayers regularly, and contributing a tithe to their church. So said the church reporter, adding, "Temple marriages are becoming more common."[105] The Mormon 1926 Church authorities of Malad Stake financed short-term missions for counselors Moroni Timbimboo and Henry Woonsook in 1935 so they 1935 could preach their religion to the Indians on the Fort Peck Reservation in Montana. In January 1939 the Salt Lake Mormon authorities an- 1939 nounced "the beginning of a new era for these Indians" with the ordination of Moroni Timbimboo as the first Indian bishop in the history of the church. His counselors were also Indian — Nephi Perdash and Jim John Neaman. At the same time church officials dedicated a new chapel at

Idaho State Historical Society

William Otagary, Washakie, Utah

1945 Washakie. Six years later, however, a white man was named bishop, and his successors were all white men.

World War II brought more employment opportunity to the Washakie Indians, and the congregation began to disperse to nearby towns for defense work. By 1960 Salt Lake authorities dis-
1960 organized the Washakie Ward and made it an independent branch. This in turn was discontinued
1966 in January 1966, with the remaining few members being transferred to the L.D.S. ward in Portage, Utah. This action ended the formal Mormon Church support of a religion organization at Washakie, as nearly all the Indians had left the old settlement.[106]

During the years from the 1920s to the dissolution of the Mormon ward at Washakie, the Fort Hall agent, under prodding from his superiors at Washington, began to exercise more interest and involvement in the affairs of his "subagency," one hundred miles south of Fort Hall. A typical incident, which forced him to pay attention to his
1922 wards at Washakie, occurred in 1922 when two of the Indians wrote the commissioner that they "are get trouble about on the deers." Evidently Willie Ottogary and George P. Sam had been caught hunting deer out of season and claimed a right to hunt wherever and whenever they wished under the stipulations of the 1868 Treaty of Fort Bridger. As they expressed it, "Because is our

game, and not his [white man's] game . . . you give this right permitt to our Chief Teorne at Fort Hall some years ago." After an investigation by Superintendent William Donner from Fort Hall, the commissioner instructed the two hunters to obey the game regulations of the state of Utah.[107]

A year later Donner was protesting the assig-
1924 ment of $750 of Fort Hall tribal funds to pay school tuition at Washakie as "this little band of Indians have no interest in the Fort Hall reservation . . . [and] have no tribal rights in the Fort Hall Reservation."[108] Nevertheless, in his budget estimates for 1924 and 1925 he asked for $400
1925 for each year for "Support and Civilization of Indians, Utah," the money to be used for traveling expenses to Washakie and for food and medical assistance to ten or twelve very old people who were "unable to get out and beg and rustle for themselves in some way."[109]

In 1933 Superintendent F. A. Gross gave a re-
1933 port of an inspection he made of Washakie and informed the commissioner: "This is really a wonderful little school. . . . The influence of the church on these Indians has been very good." He said there was a need for a home-demonstration worker because, while the government had done a great deal for Indian men, "the women have been left behind."[110] Gross also deplored the lack of a tribal organization at Washakie but indicated he would attempt to hold a council and have three men elected who could deal with the government on tribal matters.[111]

School problems came to occupy much of the small percentage of time which the Fort Hall Superintendent could devote to Washakie. A spe-
1938 cial inspector in 1938 visited the school and found thirty-five students being taught in a one-room structure by two teachers. He recommended that F. A. Gross meet with Box Elder School District officials to see whether they could finance a project to provide a second schoolroom. The Washakie school was apparently entirely funded from state and federal appropriations; Box Elder County officials arguing that, inasmuch as the Indians were wards of the government, the county had no responsibility. In an additional criticism the inspector noted, "The Mormon Church has consistently failed to preserve proper order in this community, and the general moral tone of the Indian inhabitants is at a very low level." This state of affairs was the result of a long-held belief on the part of the Mormon authorities that the local courts did not have jurisdiction over the Indians. Bishop Joseph Perry, the L.D.S. incumbent at Washakie, confirmed the fact and indicated that only recently had the courts begun to take a responsibility. Two convictions had been procured, one for the theft of a horse and the other for a statutory offense. Both the bishop and the

Utah State Historical Society

Washakie Day School, Washakie Reservation, Utah

inspector thought conditions would now improve.[112]

1939   With the help of the Mormon Church the Box Elder School District agreed to build a one-room addition to the Washakie School and to furnish a new school bus to transport students to class. Samuel H. Thompson, supervisor of Indian education, was much impressed with the progress of the students and paid tribute to Mormon efforts: "Without the strong support of the L.D.S. Church which owns 1800 acres of land around the Washakie School, it would be difficult to have very much of a school program." He discovered there were twelve Indian children enrolled in Bear River High School, a school of 726 students, and that, with one exception of a temporary nature, every school-age child was attending the Washakie grammar school.[113] The 1945 school census listed thirty-four students enrolled, while other Indian children from the Washakie group were attending schools at Bear River, Garland, Tremonton, and Honeyville — an indication that World War II had tended to disperse the Washakie people. In fact, in 1952 the Fort Hall Agency declared the school to be excess and no longer needed. For $1,750 the building and property were sold back to the L.D.S. Church, which had originally deeded the property to the United States in 1925 "for the sum of $1.00 and desire to promote public welfare."[114] The L.D.S. Church had accomplished its purpose of

1945

1952

integrating the Indians into the general society, although later some of the Indians regretted their absolute separation from any tribal identity.

Aboriginal Land Claims Case

The dissolution of the Washakie settlement did not mean the end of governmental interest in these Indians. A legal action started in the 1920s was destined to proceed slowly through federal channels until a final disposition in 1972. This was a claim for compensation for aboriginal lands as outlined in the Treaty of Box Elder of 1863 with the Northwestern Shoshoni. White friends of the Washakie band introduced legislation into Congress to achieve permission for the Court of Claims to hear the arguments of the Northwestern Shoshoni that they should be paid for lands claimed under the Box Elder Treaty. The House Committee on Indian Affairs recommended on March 23, 1928, that the Court of Claims be granted jurisdiction in the case, on the grounds that while the Western Shoshoni and Eastern Shoshoni were granted treaties of settlement for land claims, the Northwestern group had been neglected. By Executive Order of May 10, 1877, 521 acres had been set aside for them at Carlin Farms in northern Nevada, but upon their refusal to accept this very small tract President Hayes had withdrawn the order on January 16, 1879.[115]

1928

102   THE NORTHERN SHOSHONI

Utah State Historical Society

Roderick Korns with Washakie Reservation Shoshoni

1931 In 1931, three years after the initial House action, hearings were scheduled at Ogden, Salt Lake City, and Pocatello to allow attorneys to examine witnesses and gather information. By this time the case had been expanded to include the much larger area claimed by the other Shoshoni at Fort Hall and Wind River reservations and the regions once occupied by the Western Shoshoni and the Gosiute — a total claim to compensation for about seventy-three million acres of valuable aboriginal lands: thirty-eight million acres for the Fort Hall, Wind River, and Northwestern bands; five million for the Lemhi; six million for the Gosiute; and twenty-four million for the Western Shoshoni.

In addition the Northwestern band contended that, although promised a $5,000 annuity for twenty years at the Treaty of Box Elder, only $2,000 had ever been paid them. This claim also became part of the general suit. Indian leaders from Fort Hall, Tooele County in Utah, McDermitt and Owyhee in Nevada, and from Brigham City testified before the commission. George Paharagasam of the Washakie settlement described the Massacre of Bear River in 1863 and threats from General P. E. Connor and others that "they [Northwestern Shoshoni] would be exterminated if they did not give up their lands and move." Elderly white residents of Brigham City and elsewhere testified that prior to the treaty of 1863 a fierce battle had taken place between the Ute and Shoshoni which had established the boundary between the two tribes to be Weber Canyon, from which area the Shoshoni could claim all the land northward to the Snake River plains. After the hearings ended, the Indians and their attorneys began the long, time-consuming, and laborious process of pressing Washington for a resolution of their claim.[116]

1934 While the mills of government were slowly grinding out the grain and chaff of the aboriginal land-claims case, Superintendent F. A. Gross called the attention of the Office of Indian Affairs to the need of providing sufficient farming land to the Washakie Shoshoni so they could become self-sufficient and not dependent on the largesse of the Mormon Church. He rehearsed the history of the group. The forty original homesteads filed on by the Indians had now shrunk to eleven allotments, and "some of the allotments were acquired by white men through fraud or other irregular means." He hoped title to the eleven could be cleared, and he exhibited a smidgen of resentment against L.D.S. authorities at Washakie who said their only trouble from the Indians came from disgruntled individuals who traveled to Fort Hall looking for food and sympathy. The U.S. attorney general already had filed suit against the L.D.S. Church, Box Elder County, Oregon Short Line Railroad Company, and thirteen other firms, plus a number of individual whites, to determine

Indian ownership of the remaining eleven homesteads. The specific charges were that the defendants had deprived the Indians of their lands and water rights and should restore same to the wards of the government.[117]

After the usual delays and slow processes the 1939 Tenth Circuit Court of Appeals decreed that six of the tracts, entered under the Act of 1884 which protected the Indians' rights to the land for twenty-five years, should be returned to the Indians but that the other five, entered under the Act of 1881 which protected the land for only five years, should be retained by the present white owners. By 1961 only five of the six Indians pa- 1961 tents were still being held in trust for individual Indians by the government.[118]

Five homestead entries did not care for the needs of the Washakie, and there were other efforts to provide sufficient land for farming pur- poses. In a comprehensive report in 1935 J. E. 1935 White, supervisor of Subsistence Homesteads, summarized the situation of the Washakie Indians. There were twenty-seven Indian families at the settlement. Among them they owned only about five hundred acres, having lost approximately sixteen hundred acres which "white people took from them for nontax payment." In addition the L.D.S. Church owned 1,870 acres, which the church had purchased so the Indians could always have a home and a place to raise food. The church also owned enough shares in irrigation water, controlled by the Samaria Irrigation Company, to water 450 acres of land. Indian Agent White recommended that the government furnish the Indians sufficient stock and farming equipment so they could become self-sufficient. He also advised that conditions were excellent for the establishment of subsistence homesteads under the National Industrial Recovery Act, granting each Indian family an irrigated farm of about twenty acres. He thought turkey production would be a profitable venture for the Indians.[119]

After much correspondence (including a request from Chief Enos S. Pubigee, chairman of the Northwestern Shoshoni group at Washakie, asking that each Indian be alloted 160 acres of farming and grazing land) the commissioner wrote that there was not sufficient money to buy the 6,400 acres needed to establish the Indians on their own farms. The U.S. Supreme Court decision declaring the NIRA unconstitutional dealt the final blow to these high hopes. Again it was left to L.D.S. Church officials to try to help the Indians, which they did with a carefully planned development project. This included the new chapel mentioned above, completed in 1939. The commissioner of Indian Affairs became "intensely interested" in the L.D.S. Church project and asked numerous detailed questions about its operation. The program served the Washakie residents very well until their dispersal into the general population of northern Utah.[120]

1939   While the above efforts were underway to provide the Indians with land, the attorneys for the Northwestern Shoshoni were finally able to file, on December 29, 1939, their *Request for Findings of Fact and Brief* in the U.S. Court of Claims. The printed document was 452 pages in length and described in detail the history of the bands and the neglect of the government toward them.[121] About twenty-eight years later, on
1966   November 7, 1966, Frank L. Timbimboo, grandson of the Chief Sagwitch who had participated in the Massacre of Bear River, was called upon to testify before the Indian Claims Commission. He described how, after the disaster at Bear River in 1863, his people were

. . . leary of the white man. So they didn't quite trust them to live on a reservation. So they proceeded on their own and traveled around. They did try to settle at Crinn [Corinne], Utah, but they also left there because information was received that soldiers were going to engage them in a battle again. After this, the white settlers, the pioneers, became friendly with them, and then they eventually settled at the Washakie Settlement.

Timbimboo concluded, "We never had any help from the United States government like they do on the reservations." At this time there were 178 people on the Washakie Subagency rolls.[122]

1971   The report, finally filed on October 11, 1971, as a result of the aboriginal land claims case, gave a detailed picture of the 205 individuals who then comprised the Northwestern Band of Shoshoni, or, more accurately, the Washakie remnant of that tribe. The remaining members had long since settled at Fort Hall. Only two families still resided at Washakie, farming 560 acres of the original homesteaded lands. About one-half the remainder lived in the cities of northern Utah, 65 or one-third lived on the Fort Hall Reservation, and the remaining 37 resided in other western states and Florida. Northwestern Shoshoni owned about 9 percent of the Fort Hall Reservation lands, or 44,454 acres, in 266 separate tracts. Of the 64 households interviewed, nearly all the able-bodied adults were gainfully employed. Ten percent were in college or were college graduates, and about 50 percent had graduated from high school. Of the 64 families, 46 percent owned their own homes. The final approval bestowed by the very precise government report noted:

This comparatively small group of Northwestern or Washakie Band of Shoshoni Indians is generally well integrated, well educated, and relatively independent through employment in fairly good jobs. The 30 percent who live on Fort Hall Reservation are reservation-oriented and depend upon the Bureau of Indian Affairs for various services, but the other 70 percent have had very little attention from the Bureau and have assumed their role in society on the same basis as their non-Indian neighbors.

It would appear that there are few major problems among the Northwestern Band of Shoshoni Indians.[123]

1972   Of the $15,700,000 judgment in the consolidated claims case against the government for the original thirty-eight million acres of land of three Shoshoni groups, $500,000 was awarded to the Shoshoni-Bannock tribes of Fort Hall Reservation as compensation for reservation claims; $1,375,000 plus earned interest, less an $181,732 offset, was granted to the Northwestern bands; and the balance was divided between the Shoshoni-Bannock tribes and the Shoshoni tribe of Wind River according to an agreement between them of May 1965. The Northwestern Shoshoni were to receive their share on a per capita basis.[124]

With the apportionment of the land claims case, the history of the Washakie Northwestern Shoshoni, as a tribal entity, came to an end. The
1975   aged Moroni Timbimboo died in 1975. His son, Frank Timbimboo, lives at Brigham City, where he is employed at the Intermountain Indian School. This grandson of Chief Sagwitch has expressed a longing for a small parcel of ground near Washakie — eighty acres or so — which would always belong to the tribe and would represent a kind of shrine to which his people could return occasionally to renew their identity with a culture almost forgotten.[125]

The hit-and-miss concern for the Northwestern Shoshoni displayed by the Office of Indian Affairs during the 1870s and well into the twentieth century came as a result of several factors. Chief among them, was the perennial lack of funds generally endemic to the Indian Service. The relationship of the Mormon Church and settlers to the dispossessed Indian bands of northern Utah also reinforced the apathy of Washington officials toward the Northwestern Shoshoni. After the Saints of Utah had taken over Indian lands and agreed to feed the hungry natives, why should the government intrude upon such a nice and inexpensive way of taking care of these Indians? Further, the Fort Hall Reservation was close at hand and ready to receive the border wanderers any time they chose to move.

The 1875 Corinne "scare" convinced most of the Northwestern groups they had better leave their homeland for the safety of Fort Hall, even though they did so reluctantly. The few who chose to stay under the tutelage of the Mormon Church settled at Washakie, Utah, and for all practical purposes no longer became the responsibility of the Fort Hall agents and superintendents. Their integration into white society by the end of World War II ended their separate existence as a Northwestern band.

Perhaps the Washakie group's chief contibution to Northern Shoshoni history came from the court case which they initiated to gain compensation for their lost aboriginal lands. All the rest of the Northern Shoshoni, including the Eastern

Shoshoni at Wind River, eventually benefitted from that first entry into legal battle with the United States. The Mormon effort had demonstrated that, with patience and much help, an Indian group could learn to "live like white men," although there were some regrets, finally, for the loss of a culture.

NOTES CHAPTER VI
WANDERERS ALONG THE BORDER

1. *Corinne Reporter*, Oct. 23, 1869.
2. *Deseret News*, June 2, 1869.
3. Charles F. Powell to C.I.A., June 30, 1869, *Idaho Superintendency*, Microcopy 832, Roll 2.
4. J. E. Tourtellotte to C.I.A., July 9, 1869, *Utah Superintendency*, Roll 902.
5. J. E. Tourtellotte to C.I.A., December 3, 1869, Bureau of Indian Affairs, *Letters Received, Utah.*
6. *C.I.A. Annual Report 1869*, 670–672.
7. Frederick A. Sanger to C.I.A., December 29, 1869, *Utah Superintendency*, Roll 902.
8. *Corinne Reporter*, April 28, November 9, 1870.
9. Ibid., July 30, 1870.
10. Ibid., November 11, 16, 17, 1870.
11. J. E. Tourtellott to C.I.A., December 6, 1870, *Utah Superintendency*, Roll 903.
12. W. H. Danilson to C.I.A., July 9, 1870, *Fort Hall Letter Book*, 44.
13. "Report of De. L. Floyd-Jones, 1870," *Idaho Superintendency*, Microcopy 832, Roll 2.
14. "Report of L. L. Pohnanteer, June 18, 1870," L.D.S. Church, Department of History, *Indian Affairs, Misc. Papers 1866–1873*, Folder 60.
15. *Salt Lake Herald*, July 3, 1870.
16. *C.I.A. Annual Report, 1870*, 605.
17. *Corinne Reporter*, January 6, February 8, March 22, 27, April 6, June 24, July 1, 26, 29, 30, August 5, 1871.
18. Ibid., June 16, 17, 1871.
19. Ibid., February 14, 1871.
20. Ibid., February 15, 1871.
21. M. P. Berry to C.I.A., July 10, 1871, *Idaho Superintendency*, Roll 339.
22. M. P. Berry to C.I.A., October 13, 1871, *Fort Hall Letter Book*, 91–93.
23. *C.I.A. Annual Report, 1871*, 956.
24. M. P. Berry to C.I.A., November 24, 1871, *Idaho Superintendency*, Roll 339.
25. L. H. Hatch to J. J. Critchlow, February 10, 1871, *Utah Superintendency*, Roll 903.
26. Sec. of Interior to C.I.A., Oct. 7, 1871, ibid.
27. G. W. Dodge to C.I.A., Jan. 6, 1872, *Utah Superintendency*, Roll 903.
28. G. W. Dodge to C.I.A., Jan. 26, 1872, ibid.
29. G. W. Dodge to C.I.A., February 2, 1872, ibid.
30. *Corinne Reporter*, February 3, 1872.
31. Ibid., Feb. 21, 1872.
32. Ibid., August 22, 1872.
33. Ibid., September 18, 1872.
34. G. W. Dodge to C.I.A., March 18, 1872, *Utah Superintendency*, Roll 903.
35. G. W. Dodge to C.I.A., April 20, 1872, ibid.
36. G. W. Dodge to C.I.A., April 26, 1872, ibid.
37. G. W. Dodge to C.I.A., July 24, 1872, ibid.
38. G. W. Dodge to C.I.A., October 28, 1872, ibid.
39. G. W. Dodge to C.I.A., August 16, 1872, ibid.
40. *C.I.A. Annual Report, 1872*, 678.
41. M. P. Berry to C.I.A., Dec. 5, 1872, *Fort Hall Letter Book*, 133–134.
42. G. W. Dodge to C.I.A., Dec. 7, 1872, *Utah Superintendency*, Roll 903.
43. G. W. Dodge to C.I.A., Dec. 11, 1872, ibid.
44. G. W. Dodge to C.I.A., Dec. 21, 1872, *Utah Superintendency*, Roll 904.
45. *Corinne Reporter*, March 20, April 5, 18, 29, 1873.
46. Ibid., April 4, 14, 16, 1873; *Idaho Statesman*, May 29, 1873.
47. Ibid., April 30, 1873.
48. *C.I.A. Annual Report, 1873*, 409.
49. C. W. Ingalls to C.I.A., June 13, 1873, *Utah Superintendency*, Roll 904.
50. J. W. Powell to C.I.A., June 18, 1873, ibid.; C.I.A. to J. W. Powell, June 25, 1873, ibid.; Henry A. Morrow to C.I.A., Jan. 30, 1873, ibid.
51. J. W. Powell and G. W. Ingalls to C.I.A., ibid.
52. J. W. Powell to C.I.A., Nov. 4, 9, 1873, ibid.; G. W. Ingalls to C.I.A., July 20, 1873, ibid.; *Corinne Reporter*, Nov. 8, 1873; *Deseret News*, Nov. 10, 1873.
53. Ibid.
54. J. P. C. Shanks, T. W. Bennett, H. W. Reed to C.I.A., Nov. 17, 1873, *Idaho Superintendency*, Roll 342.
55. *C.I.A. Annual Report, 1873*, 409–527.
56. *Corinne Reporter*, Sept. 7, 15, 22, Oct. 1, 2, 5, 1874.
57. Ibid., Sept. 12, Oct. 6, 1874.
58. *Journal History*, L.D.S. Department of History, Aug. 9, 1874.
59. Ibid., Nov. 12, 1874.
60. *Corinne Mail*, Dec. 7, 1874.
61. Ibid., Dec. 7, 10, 14, 15, 21, 1874.
62. G. W. Hill to C.I.A., Dec. 14, 1874, *Utah Superintendency*, Roll 904.
63. Charles E. Dibble, "The Mormon Mission to the Shoshoni Indians," *Utah Humanities Review*, July 1947, 284–285; Laurence G. Coates, "A History of Indian Education by the Mormons, 1830–1900," Ph.D. dissertation, Ball State University, 1969, 304–306; Lars C. Christensen, *Journal*, 1–3.

64. James Wright to C.I.A., June 10, 1875, *Idaho Superintendency*, Roll 343.
65. James Wright to C.I.A., June 30, 1875, *Fort Hall Letter Book*, 283–284.
66. James Wright to C.I.A., July 31, 1875, ibid., 289–291.
67. *Corinne Mail*, Jan. 6, 8, April 15, May 4, 1875.
68. Ibid., July 9, 19, 1875.
69. Ibid., July 23, Aug. 11, 1875.
70. Ibid., July 30, 1875.
71. Ibid., Aug. 9, 1875.
72. Ibid., Aug. 10, 1875.
73. Ibid., Aug. 11, 1875.
74. Ibid., Aug. 12, 1875.
75. Ibid., Aug. 14, 16, 1875; Dibble, "The Mormon Mission . . . ," 286–287; *Ogden Junction*, Aug. 14, 1875; Coates, "A History of Indian Education . . . ," 306.
76. *Deseret News*, Aug. 18, 1875.
77. *Corinne Mail*, Aug. 23, 25, 1875.
78. Ibid., Sept. 23, 1875.
79. W. H. Danilson to C.I.A., Oct. 4, 1875, *Fort Hall Letter Book*, 309.
80. Coates, "A History of Indian Education . . . ," 306.
81. *C.I.A. Annual Report, 1875*, 760.
82. *Deseret News*, Sept. 22, 1875.
83. Colin H. Sweeten, Jr., *Washakie* (Malad, Idaho: Unpublished article in author's possession, 1973); *Deseret News*, Sept. 22, 1875.
84. Ibid., July 17, Dec. 18, 1876; *Journal History*, Sept. 29, 1876, L.D.S. Church, Department of History.
85. Ephraim Young to Sec. of Interior, Aug. 9, 1877, *Utah Superintendency*, Roll 905.
86. Sumner Howard to Charles Devers, Sept. 11, 1877, ibid.; see also E. C. Watkins to C.I.A., Oct. 16, 1875, *Record Group No. 75*, 2–4.
87. George W. Emery to Sec. of Interior, Oct. 2, 1877, ibid.
88. J. J. Critchlow to C.I.A., Oct. 4, Oct. 26, 1877, ibid.
89. Sumner Howard to Charles Devers, Nov. 10, 1877, ibid.
90. W. H. Danilson to C.I.A., Nov. 22, 1877, *Idaho Superintendency*, Roll 345.
91. Jerome B. Kimpton to Governor, Idaho Territory, Nov. 26, 1877, Idaho State University Archives, Ms.
92. J. J. Critchlow to C.I.A., May 8, 1878, *Utah Superintendency*, Roll 905.
93. Sweeten, *Washakie*, 9.
94. *Deseret News*, June 10, 27, Oct. 20, 1882.
95. Ibid., Feb. 9, June 18, Nov. 27, 1883.
96. *Journal History*, Sept. 26, Nov. 27, 1883.
97. *Deseret News*, April 22, 1885.
98. Frank W. Warner to C.I.A., Feb. 22, 1887, *Record Group No. 75*.
99. S. G. Fisher to C.I.A., Oct. 22, Nov. 11, 1889, ibid.
100. *Deseret News*, Feb. 11, 1893.
101. Ibid., May 26, 1898.
102. *Journal History*, April 15, Dec. 24, 1902.
103. Lorenzo D. Creel to Sec. Of Interior, Jan. 3, 1912, U.S. Congress, H. of Rep., 62d Cong., 2d Sess., Doc. No. 389, Vol. 139, *Indians of Skull Valley and Deep Creek, Utah* (Wash., 1912), 5–6.
104. *Indian Census Rolls, 1885–1940*, U.S. National Archives, Fort Hall Reservation, Roll 144.
105. *Journal History*, April 26, 1923; *Deseret News*, April 10, 1926.
106. Ibid., Feb. 18, 1939; *Journal History*, Oct. 14, 1934, June 29, 1935, Jan. 22, 1939, March 11, 1945, Feb. 10, 1947, Jan. 14, 1957, Nov. 20, 1960, Jan. 2, 1966.
107. C.I.A. to Willie Ottogary, Feb. 19, 1923, *Record Group No. 75*.
108. William Donner to C.I.A., April 12, 1924, ibid.
109. William Donner to C.I.A., Fort Hall, Nov. 20, 1924, April 23, 1925, ibid.
110. F. A. Gross to C.I.A., May 22, 1933, *Fort Hall Agency Records*.
111. F. A. Gross to C.I.A., Aug. 6, 1933, *Record Group No. 75*.
112. School Inspector to F. A. Gross, Nov. 8, 1938, *Fort Hall Agency Records*.
113. Samuel H. Thompson to C.I.A., April 15, 1939, ibid.
114. *School Census, Washakie, Utah*, June 23, 1945, ibid.; Carl W. Beck to Eberhart Zundell, April 28, 1947, ibid.; Earl Wooldridge to E. Morgan Pryse, Jan. 4, 1952, ibid.; Harold E. Zimmer to E. Morgan Pryse, Dec. 5, 1952, ibid.
115. *Court of Claims to Hear Claim of Northwestern Band of Shoshoni Indians*, U.S. Congress, H. of Rep., 70th Cong., 1st Sess., Report No. 1030, Vol. 2, Report No. 1579, Vol. 4 (Wash., 1928).
116. *Journal History*, June 30, 1931; *Ogden Standard Examiner*, June 28, 29, 30, July 1, 2, 1931; *Salt Lake Tribune*, July 2, Oct. 16, 1931; *Pocatello Tribune*, July 5, 7, 1931.
117. F. A. Gross to C.I.A., Aug. 18, 1934, *Record Group No. 75*.
118. "U.S. of America vs. L.D.S. Church, et al., U.S. District Court, Jan. 17, 1935," ibid.; U.S. Circuit Court of Appeals, Tenth Circuit, No. 1686, January term, 1939," U.S. of America vs. L.D.S. Church et al., Jan. 11, 1939;" Charles S. Spencer to Robert O. Davis, Aug. 11, 1961, *Fort Hall Agency Records*.
119. J. E. White to A. C. Cooley, Jan. 14, 1935, *Record Group No. 75*.
120. Henry Tootiwara to C.I.A., July 12, 1835, ibid.; A. C. Cooley to M. O. Ashton, June 13, 1931, *Fort Hall Agency Files*.
121. U.S. Court of Claims, No. M-107, *The Northwestern Band or Tribe of Shoshoni Indians and Individual Members Thereof, Plantiff*, v. *The United States, Defendant.* Plaintiff Indians' Request for Findings of Fact, and Brief (filed Dec. 29, 1939).
122. Indians Claims Cmmission, Docket No. 326-D-G, 326-H, 366, 367, Nov. 9, 1967 (Wash., D.C.), 53–72.
123. *Providing for the Apportionment of Funds in Payment of a Judgment in favor of the Shoshoni Tribe in Consolidated Dockets Numbered 326-D, 326-E, 326-F, 326-G, 326-H, 366, and 367*, U.S. Senate, 92d Cong., 1st Sess., Calendar No. 392, Report No. 92-393, Oct. 11, 1971 (Wash., D.C.), 14–19; *Providing for the Apportionment, etc.*, U.S. House of Rep., 92d Cong., 1st Sess.; Peport No. 92-701, Dec. 1, 1972 (Wash., D.C.), 3, 9–15.
124. Ibid.
125. Interview with Colin Sweeten, Jr., Malad, Idaho, June 28, 1974.

CHAPTER VII

NEGOTIATING WITH WASHINGTON

Reservation Boundaries Redrawn

While the few remaining members of the old Washakie settlement long for a few acres as a shrine, the main tribes at Fort Hall are still engaged in a desperate struggle to retain the few acres left to them. For years they have watched the boundaries of their reservation recede before the advance of land-hungry whites, spreading out "like stains of racoon grease on a new blanket," as Chief Black Hawk of the Sauk and Fox tribes once put it. To the Shoshoni and Bannock it seemed they lost more rights and more land every time they signed a treaty or agreement with the government. From the unratified Treaty of Soda Springs in 1863 to the Pocatello Cession of 418,000 acres in 1900, the Indians watched their homeland disappear — first, by the outright loss of Big Camas Prairie, contrary to the guarantee of the Treaty of Fort Bridger in 1868, and finally from an original reservation of 1,800,000 acres in 1869 to one of about 520,000 acres by 1932.[1]

1866   When Governor D. W. Ballard first visited the Fort Hall area in 1866 he outlined the exterior boundaries of the reservation as follows:

Commencing on the South bank of Snake River at the junction of the Port Neuf river with said Snake river, thence south 25 miles, to the Summit of the mountains dividing the waters of Bear river from those of Snake river — thence easterly along the summit of said range of mountains 70 miles to a point where Sublette road Crosses said divide — thence North about 50 miles to Blackfoot river — thence down said Stream to its junction with Snake river — thence down Snake river to the place of beginning.
All of which will be readily seen by the enclosed map.[2]

The "enclosed map" referred to, drawn by hand on cloth-backed paper, may still be seen as Map No. 747 in the U.S. National Archives map collection.[3] The U.S. General Land Office faithfully reproduced the exterior boundaries of Fort Hall Reservation, as shown by the Ballard map, in all the official Idaho maps up to 1873.[4]

1873   In that year, as the result of constant requests from Indian officials, the Fort Hall agents, and the late Governor D. P. Thompson of Idaho, a contract was finally made by L. F. Cartee, surveyor general of Idaho, with John B. David to survey the exterior boundaries of the reservation.[5] David commenced his work on June 18 and completed the survey July 23, 1873.[6]

David took care of the ambiguity in the Ballard instructions, which had directed that the southern line should proceed from the summit of the range dividing the waters of Bear River from those of the Snake (actually the head of Bannock Creek) "easterly along the summit of said range of mountains 70 miles to a point where Sublette road crosses said divide. . . ." The original Ballard map showed a line running directly east from the head of Bannock Creek, but in doing so the line did not follow the main divide. David explained his position in the matter, "Believing it to be the meaning of my instructions to follow said divide, rather than an Easterly direction, I did so."[7] In the process he moved the southern boundary south, in a triangular shape, to include all the Marsh Valley area. He then fixed the southeastern corner of the reservation at a point only forty miles, rather than the original seventy miles, due east from the southwestern corner.

David's decision had grave consequences. Not only did he cut off from the reservation an area thirty by fifty miles in extent along its eastern border, but he also enclosed along Marsh Creek a large settlement of white farmers. Most of the settlers had built homes and commenced farming before the reservation was designated by Governor Ballard in 1866. Furthermore, the settlers had been assured by the governor that their farms were located outside the boundaries of the reservation.[8]

From 1873 until the Pocatello Cession of 1900 the southern boundary as drawn by Surveyor David remained firm, despite all protestations, petitions, and constant agitation from agents, Idaho officials, and settlers alike. The 1873 commission of Shanks, Bennett, and Reed was the first to remonstrate, pointing out that fifty-two families "nearly all of whom are quiet, well-behaved people" were improperly included in the reservation. The fifth article of the proposed treaty drawn up by the commission would have redrawn the southern line of the reservation approximately along that marked by the original Ballard map near the southern bend of Portneuf River at the present town of McCammon, Idaho.[9]

There were numerous plans concocted to correct the mistake perpetrated by John David. Governor D. P. Thompson in 1876 explained that an agreement had been made with the Shoshoni and Bannock to cede the Marsh Creek Valley to the

1873

1876

Map of the Exterior Lines of the Fort Hall Indian Reservation.

government in exchange for a section of country north of the Blackfoot River.[10] When nothing came of this plan, Agent Danilson proposed that, because of the troubles he was having with Marsh Valley settlers who continued to cut hay and farm on Indian lands, the government should redraw the southern boundary in a straight line due east from the southwest corner of the reservation, which would place Marsh Creek basin outside his jurisdiction and relieve him of a number of problems of trespass.[11]

1879   The disputed section of reservation property even became embroiled in Idaho politics when the territorial legislature debated whether to count the votes of the Marsh Valley citizens who resided on Indian land and were therefore on federal and not territorial property.[12] To try to settle the matter once and for all the legislature dispatched a memorial to Delegate S. S. Fenn in Washington, "Praying for a change of the Southern boundary of the Fort Hall Indian Reservation." The memorial was duly printed, but action was postponed as usual.[13]

1878   The fears nurtured by the Bannock War of 1878 prompted the white settlers along Marsh Creek to forewarn the government of their contemplated actions should any Indians become "trespassers" on their property and attempt to "roam through this section of Country." The petition, forwarded to the commissioner of Indian Affairs on December 4, 1878, announced that after proper notice if any Indians were found within the boundaries of the white settlement *"it shall be the duty of all Concerned in this meeting to kill the same if possible."*[14]

1879   With the blunt threat from Marsh Creek and continued pressure from the legislature at Boise, S. S. Fenn, by now "Late Delegate from Idaho Territory," did his best to resolve the boundary difficulty. He put together a remarkable document which reviewed the entire history of the establishment and survey of the reservation and included a copy of the legislative memorial listing four reasons why a new boundary line should be run: The reservation was too large for the number of Indians settled there, the southern area of the reserve was not used by the Indians, the region to be dedicated was rich in minerals, and white settlers had built homes and farms on Marsh Creek before the reservation was set aside. The legislative proposal would have marked the southern boundary from Snake River at its confluence with the Portneuf, up the Portneuf to the mouth of Pocatello Creek, thence up that creek to its source, then east to the original boundary — a line which would have cut the reservation in half. Fenn thought the legislature was asking for much too large a reduction and recommended that the original Ballard line be made the southern boundary. No action resulted from his suggestion.[15]

Cession Agreement of 1881

The dispute over whether Marsh Valley should be included in the reservation continued for many years, but it was not the only instance of intrusion and trespass on Indian land. After completion of the transcontinental railroad which bypassed Salt Lake City, Brigham Young directed his followers in constructing the Utah Central Railroad connecting the City of the Saints with Ogden. The success of this cooperative effort soon led to a demand for a narrow-gauge line linking Cache Valley with Salt Lake City. The result was the organization of the Utah Northern Company, which broke ground to start the road on August 26, 1871, at Brigham City. By April 30, 1874, the little railroad was at Franklin, Idaho. After a period of inactivity due to the financial panic of 1873, the road was taken over in 1877 by the Union Pacific and reorganized under the name of Utah and Northern.[16]

1878   Revitalized by the financial strength and operating know-how of the Union Pacific Company, construction began northward from Franklin in 1878. By June the road had reached Oneida, just west of present-day Arimo on Marsh Creek and on reservation property.[17]

Agent W. H. Danilson immediately notified the Office of Indian Affairs and asked for advice about the evident trespass on Shoshoni and Bannock lands. In his series of telegrams he warned that whiskey shops had been established, that plans were fixed to move the terminus to Black Rock right in the center of the reservation, and that the railroad company was cutting timber for ties.[18]

While Washington officials hesitated, President Sidney Dillon of the Union Pacific traveled to the nation's capital to obtain permission to cross the reservation and to quiet the fears of the agent and his wards, who by this time were holding a war dance near Pocatello Creek to indicate their displeasure. The Indian Office advised Dillon to negotiate with the Indians to get their consent. This seemed a necessary move, especially when the rail lines reached the agency at Ross Fork on November 26, 1878.[19]

Danilson now asked whether he should use military force to stop construction, a maneuver which was effectively countermanded when the War Department decreed that the railroad was a military necessity to ensure the safety of the citizens of Idaho and Montana.[20]

W. N. Shilling, a resident of Fort Hall with a six-months expense account from the Union Pacific and a promise of a contract to supply ties for the road, traveled to Washington, D.C., where he was granted authority to negotiate with the Indians to secure a right-of-way.[21] Danilson met with the Shoshoni and Bannock, who agreed to yield a right-of-way in return for 500 head of stock cattle.[22] By this time the commissioner was wondering whether the Fort Hall Reservation was a reservation:

1879

> A railroad has been constructed across it. White settlers go upon and occupy it. At the Territorial election of 1878, polls were opened, a large number of votes, including those of some one hundred and fifty native Indians, received and counted. Upon a contest in the general assembly of a seat claimed upon returns including these Indian votes, it was gravely decided upon investigation and report of committees that no such reservation had been legally established.[23]

The *Idaho World* agreed, "It would be to her [Idaho's] interest to . . . get the Fort Hall Reservation blotted out."[24]

1880

To further complicate matters the Idaho Supreme Court, in the case of Utah and Northern Railroad Company v. Willard Crawford, District Attorney for Oneida County, made the decision that U.S. courts did not have jurisdiction over persons residing within the boundaries of the Fort Hall Reservation. The *Idaho Statesman* was worried that railroad employees and other whites could now break the law with impunity.[25]

The Marsh Creek settlers continued their entreaties that the southern portion of the reservation be cut off. Another petition signed by 130 settlers was addressed to the President of the United States on October 8, 1880.[26] Leading the signers was H. O. Harkness, who was attacked along with the Indian agent because he was being given special consideration in that the new line would exclude his lands, although they lay north of the Marsh Creek settlement.[27] In two letters of

1881

support for the petition, one citizen said that if the tract were not set apart the fifty or so families would have to "get up & get," while the second writer proposed drawing the line through Black Rock station, some six miles or so above the confluence of Marsh Creek with the Portneuf.[28]

The agitation of these settlers, plus the concern of the Office of Indian Affairs for the situation of the Lemhi Indians on a reservation too small for their needs, finally resulted in a visit of seven chiefs and headmen of the Lemhi and Shoshoni and Bannock tribes to Washington, D.C. The commissioner and his aides hoped, first, to impress the Indians with the power and grandeur of the government, and, second, to accomplish the desired objectives of the department: to move the Lemhi to Fort Hall and to extract a cession of the March Creek basin from the Shoshoni and Bannock. An agreement was reached on May 14, 1880, and signed by Ten Doy, Tissi dimit, Grouse Pete, Jack Gibson, Ti Hee, Captain Jim, and Jack Ten Doy.[29]

The agreement included the following provisions: The Lemhi agreed to surrender their tiny reservation and move to Fort Hall, there to take up lands in severalty; the Shoshoni and Bannock

Bureau of American Ethnology

Taihi

Bureau of American Ethnology

Grouse Pete

agreed to accept the Lemhi and to cede the southern portion of their reservation, about 325 thousand acres; the Lemhi were to receive $4,000 a year for twenty years and the Shoshoni and Bannock $6,000 a year for twenty years; allotments in severalty were to be made on the basis of 160 acres of farmland and another 160 acres of grazing land to each head of a family, with 80 acres each of farming and grazing land to individuals under eighteen years of age; and the government bound itself to survey the reservation and to issue patents to the allotees as soon as necessary legislation was passed permitting the action.[30] To insure proper assent to the agreement, a council was held at the reservation on November 14, 1881, which secured the signatures of 250 adult male Indians to the pact signed in Washington the year before by their chiefs and headmen.[31]

The commissioner continued to urge congressional approval, writing in late 1881, "The Indians cannot understand the delay, and are impatient to have the agreements carried into effect."[32] A complicating factor was the final refusal of Tendoy and his Lemhi people to move to Fort Hall. Even though this portion of the agreement

1881 was now inoperative, the Commissioner recommended the ratification of the portion ceding the southern section of the Fort Hall Reservation.[33] Agent E. A. Stone was particularly impatient, believing that if the $120,000 promised the Fort Hall Indians could be paid in six installments instead of twenty, the sixth year "will see these Indians feed and clothe themselves."[34]

Two Railroad Rights-of-Way

While negotiations were being carried on to take care of the Marsh Creek problem, a parallel movement was underway by the Utah and Northern Railroad Company to obtain an east-west right-of-way through the reservation for what would become the Oregon Short Line Railway, another subsidiary of the Union Pacific — even though a final settlement had not been made with the Indians for the first crossing. On July 8, 1881, U.S. Assistant Attorney General Joseph K. McCammon held a council with the Shoshoni and Bannock, during which every adult male Indian present agreed to cede a right-of-way of 772 acres, including depots, siding, water tanks, etc., for $6,000, or about $7.77 per acre. The cession would give the railroad a strip of land one hundred feet in width, except at Pocatello station where an area two hundred feet wide was deeded. McCammon said he had consulted with army officers and other knowledgeable men, all of whom thought the terms fair and reasonable. He indicated that among other concerns of the Indians was a particularly urgent request that the Office

of Indian Affairs do somethig about "certain squatters along the Portneuf River."

During the council meeting the Bannock leaders at first refused to agree because "the Shoshoni have done all the talking." Finding an opportunity to speak, the Bannocks were quoted as remonstrating that "The whites have settled down there and they don't like it." At the time there were apparently about two hundred whites residing unlawfully on the reservation. McCammon reassured the Indians and promised they could ride on the trains free of charge whenever they chose.[35]

The *Blackfoot Register* was pleased that "the ignoramous who formerly held the position" of 1881 agent was "out of the way" so the agreement could be negotiated.[36] The cession of this second railroad right-of-way reminded the more thoughtful Indians that their location at the junction of the old Oregon, California, and Montana trails could have certain liabilities.   1882

Of the two agreements before Congress, the one pertaining to the railroad right-of-way proceeded rather swiftly past the congressional logjam no doubt with the expert help of the strong Union Pacific lobby. The cession act seemed to get nowhere. With only a nonvoting territorial delegate working for the bill, it did not require much prescience to predict at least a long delay and probably no action at all. Delegate George Ainslie felt the need to respond to his constituents at home, who were reporting a large immigration to reservation lands as a result of the two rail lines.[37] He proposed sponsoring a new bill which would double the cession of land, moving the southern boundary of the reservation north of Pocatello station. Eventually the line was drawn there many years later, as the result of political effort on the part of the citizens of the new town of Pocatello.[38]

Agent A. L. Cook made a strong plea in August 1884 1884 for a new treaty which would move the southern line far enough north to accommodate all the white settlers in the ceded area. The proposed cession would add only 100 thousand acres to that included by the unratified agreement, leaving 800 thousand acres in the reduced reservation. Washington seemed unconcerned about this parcel of ground lying in scantily populated southeastern Idaho Territory.[39]

Notice was taken of the Utah and Northern Railroad which, the commissioner found to his surprise, had been operating for several years through Fort Hall Reservation without any compensation to the Indians. The matter came to his attention in 1884 when the Union Pacific filed a map asking for definite location of its right-of-way and eight stations at various points on the reservation.[40]

A complete history of the case was finally submitted to Congress in December 1885, pointing 1885 out that the railroad was using 2,126 acres of land unlawfully, much to the embarrassment of the Office of Indian Affairs and to the injury of the Indians. Under acts of Congress March 3, 1873, and June 20, 1878, the Utah and Northern was granted the right to build its road through the "public lands" of the United States, which did not include lands on Indian reservations. Therefore the Office of Indian Affairs withheld approval until a council meeting could be held to get the consent of the Shoshoni and Bannock. As already noted, Agent Danilson had been able to get the approval of the Indians on October 23, 1878, in return for 500 head of stock cattle. As the commissioner then put it, "For some unexplained reason the matter appears to have here rested," and the cattle were not delivered by the railroad. Congress had ratified the agreement concerning the east-west right-of-way, and the Union Pacific paid the $6,000 required under the contract. Now the matter of seven years' occupancy of the south-north right-of-way had to be settled, with proper compensation made to the Indians.[41]

The Utah and Northern received some more bad news. The Idaho Territorial Supreme Court, in the case of Utah and Northern Railway Company v. Fisher, County Assessor, held on February 16, 1884, that the railroad and its property were subject to taxation, "notwithstanding its location and situation upon the Fort Hall Indian reservation."[42] Gradually Idaho officials were defining the legal responsibilities and limits imposed by the creation of the reservation.

The power of government also began to affect the Mormon settlers in Marsh Valley. Some of them became discouraged and left, believing they would never be able to secure legal title to their farms. Agent A. L. Cook reported in November 1885 that he had removed several new families who had tried to settle in the Marsh Creek area and that the town of Arimo, near the former railroad depot of Oneida, now contained only three dwelling houses.[43]

1885
The trespass situation at Pocatello station, however, was much more serious. The agent had received over one hundred applications to build at Pocatello during the previous two years and had had to tear down one house and burn another to halt the "concerted movement." Other structures were being erected on reservation land outside the railroad right-of-way by both citizens and the Utah and Northern. As the junction for the railroads north to Montana and west to Oregon, Pocatello was handling more than seven hundred and fifty tons of freight each day. Cook asked for instructions on what course of action he should take.[44]

Rumors began to fly that the Union Pacific had plans to move its shops from Eagle Rock, where they had been located since 1881, to Pocatello.

This would immediately place another 250 employees with their families on the forty acres of land granted to the railroad. It did not take a wizard to prophesy what was going to happen. No wonder, said those in the know, that the Union Pacific was preparing to ask the government for another two thousand acres to accommodate growth at Pocatello station.[45]

Soon letters began to pour into Washington to the office of Idaho Delegate John Hailey and to certain federal officials, asking that J. W. Keeney be allowed to maintain his barn and corrals on reservation property just next to his hotel built on adjacent railroad property at Pocatello; that Fred J. Kiesel be permitted to continue his warehouse, which was built by "an unfortunate blunder" on Indian land at Pocatello; and that others also be granted a stay of execution of sixty days until the Union Pacific could negotiate another grant of about two thousand acres at the station. James W. Savage, writing from Omaha, was more direct: "As you and I and every one who has been at Pocatello know . . . [it is] a barren waste utterly valueless to Indians or anyone else — except to hold a few buildings up." The secretary of the Interior granted the sixty-day moratorium and instructed the Office of Indian Affairs to take no further action to remove trespassers during that period.[46]

1886

In May 1886 the Union Pacific made a formal request for an additional 1,600 acres at "Pocatillo," as further protestations and appeals came to Washington.[47] The new agent at Ross Fork, Peter Gallagher, asked for instructions about trespassers.[48] He was accused of allowing J. W. Keeney to keep his barn on reservation property while he harassed other interlopers.[49] Forty-one residents at Pocatello petitioned the secretary of the Interior, explaining that the railroad company had used up all the land at the station for shops, forcing the employees onto reservation property, where their families had been living in tents. With winter approaching, they asked for approval to build houses. They were willing to pay rent or whatever price would be asked: "This land which we now occupy is of no use whatever to the Indian, he can not utalize [sic] for any purpose under the sun."[50] Responding to the pressure, the commissioner of Indian Affairs in September 1886 recommended that the bill before Congress to compensate the Shoshoni and Bannock for the Utah and Northern right-of-way be amended to allow for negotiations with the Indians to sell another 1,600 acres at Pocatello to the Union Pacific.[51]

1887

Crowding at the new town was becoming critical. Agent Gallagher wrote for instructions about the problem;[52] two citizens complained to the secretary of the Interior about J. W. Keeney at the Pacific Hotel selling whiskey to the Indians;[53] the deputy marshal for Idaho, W. S. Hopson, warned that the Indian agent and the railroad superintendent were looking the other way as squatters built shanties on reservation property, which in turn encouraged others to "make a brake [sic] for Pocatello";[54] and Delegate Fred T. Dubois inquired, innocently, when the commissioner of Indian Affairs was going to take some favorable action for the "peaceful and industrious people" who were trespassing only "in a slight degree" on the Indian reserve.[55]

Agent Gallagher, no man to shirk his duty, continued to press his superiors — not only about the newcomers flocking to Pocatello but also to serve warning on the white farmers in Marsh Valley that the Office of Indian Affairs had suspended eviction notices two different times — from December 11, 1885 to the adjournment of Congress and from August 7, 1886, to March 4, 1887. He now notified the settlers that they must leave their farms and homes by March 30, 1887.[56] An urgent telegram was sent by the frightened families to both the secretary of the Interior and the commissioner of Indian Affairs, pleading for a delay until the 1880 treaty could be ratified by Congress.[57] In reply, and for a third time, the commissioner's office suspended the order "asking for all the facts in the case," a request which fully recognized the power of voting constituents as opposed to nonvoting and nonarticulate Indians.[58]

Within two weeks the secretary of the Interior received a formal petition from ninety-seven citizens residing in the Marsh Creek area, sixty-two of whom had settled there prior to July 30, 1869. Each signed an affidavit to that effect, and the petition listed the same reasons in support of the cession under the Treaty of 1880 as had been advanced each year since that time. A stronger case was made this time by claiming that "peaceable possession" for over eighteen years meant a tacit recognition of the legal rights to their property, worth now about $138,700.[59]

Sale of Pocatello Station – Agreement of 1888

Having dispensed a temporary mercy to the Marsh Creek farmers, the secretary of the Interior now directed the commissioner of Indian Affairs to send a representative to meet with the Shoshoni and Bannock to negotiate a sale of 1,600 acres at Pocatello station, or so much land "as the public welfare demands." The area was to be laid off into lots and sold to the highest bidders at public auction. In the interim the agent at Fort Hall was to stop any further encroachments and summarily remove all trespassers and any buildings they should erect.[60] Gallagher subsequently reported that there were sixty buildings, mostly houses, resting illegally on reservation property adjacent to Pocatello station. About fifteen of

Bureau of American Ethnology

Tisidimit

them were business establishments, including one to house the courtroom of Justice of the Peace A. W. Fisher.

Meanwhile, Special Indian Agent William Parsons, sent by the Office of Indian Affairs on a routine inspection of Fort Hall operations, reported the lack of space to accommodate houses for the thousand to fifteen hundred inhabitants of Pocatello. Parsons saw advantages in encouraging the growth of the town as a market for Indian produce and as an incentive for the Indians to learn to labor. He recommended that one square mile of reservation property at Pocatello be sold to encourage expansion of the settlement.[61]

Everything looked favorable to Washington officials. Inspector Robert S. Gardner was instructed on May 16, 1887, to meet with the Shoshoni and Bannock to conclude an agreement for the sale of the required Pocatello land. At the council, held on May 27, the Bannock were represented by Ty-Hee, Pag White, Race Horse, and Ke-O, the Shoshoni by Gibson Jack, Captain Jim, and Captain Joe. After the usual long speech by the government representative, Gibson Jack began the conference by saying the Bannock had the best right to speak first because they had a better claim to the reservation than the Shoshoni. Pag White then volunteered, "We cannot allow it; what is the reason the white man keeps coming up

1887

1887

close on the land all the time?" Big Joe thought that already there was too little land for their needs and not enough water. Captain Ke-O said he did not want to sell because "this is a small mountain and there is not much land or ground to hunt upon." Race horse joined in, "I do not know the reason Washington wants my little land . . . God gives us this land." An old man, Padzee, protested that the white man was building fences and crowding him out: "You want to dig me out and pretty soon I fall into the ground." Gibson Jack then spoke at length for the Shoshoni, concluding, "It is hard for me to part with any of my land, how is it that you want me to do so?"[62]

1887   Inspector Gardner, with the effective help of Agent Gallagher, did his best to reassure the Indians that the agreement, if signed, would be ratified and the proceeds of the sale of lots paid to the tribes. The decision to sell finally came as the result of a short speech from Chief Tyhee, who had been silent up to this time:

> I do not like the way they have been talking here, one, one way, and one another, they do not agree and it does not suit me. When they held a council here the other day, two weeks ago, I thought I was doing what was right for the good of the Indians, I thought they needed money. Now, I want you all to come to one understanding and agree to sell Pocatello. . . . The money that we get for this piece of land will not be for our benefit, it will be for the rising generation.[63]

The other leaders immediately acquiesced, with only Gibson Jack demanding and getting one other stipulation — the right of all Indians to ride on the freight trains.

The 311 Indians who signed the document on May 27 agreed to sell 1,840 acres at Pocatello, to be subdivided into lots and sold at auction to the highest bidders. They were to receive $8 an acre for a 200-foot right-of-way (plus grounds for water and other purposes) from the Union Pacific for the original crossing of the reservation by the Utah and Northern Railway.[64] A matter of some concern which was not settled was the source of a water supply for the new town. Gallagher thought it could only come from the Portneuf River, a prospect which boded ill for the parched lands of the reservation, where the future depended on a plentiful water supply.[65]

1888   According to Delegate Dubois the railroad company had already taken possession of some springs on reservation property without any legal right and had built a pipeline to Pocatello station.[66] Gallagher agreed but thought the main source of water for Pocatello would still have to be the Portneuf River.[67] To protect Indian rights in this water supply the Interior Department amended the 1887 agreement to allow "access to and use by the citizens of the town in common with the Indians of the water from any river, creek, stream, or spring flowing through the reservation lands in the vicinity of the townsite." In-

stead of protection, the change merely offered more opportunity for Pocatello residents to get control of adjoining water sources held in common with the Indians.[68]

While the cession agreement of 1880 still languished in the halls of Congress, the new agreement of 1887 granting the Union Pacific more land at Pocatello did not encounter the same apathy. It passed both houses within a short period but was pocket-vetoed by the President, who thought he sensed some speculation at the expense of the Indians. The *Idaho Statesman* saw the action as only a temporary setback until the time "when the Fort Hall reservation shall be opened up" for white settlement.[69]

The editor of the *Statesman* could view the situation with equanimity but not so the tribesmen on the reservation. They met with Agent Gallagher and demanded that their leaders be allowed to go to Washington as they had in 1881 to "see the Great Father, shake hands and feel good" and incidentally perhaps get their two treaties ratified and "catch" the money owed them. The agent feared that the "obstreperous" Bannock who "care less about work and love fight more" might get some of the "heap fight" knocked out of them by seeing at first hand the power of the government.[70] The trip might reassure the Indians, who were dissatisfied about the promises which apparently were only "made to be broken by the General Government."[71] After having had "to face the music of a pow wow and not getting 'paper from Washington,' " Gallagher was able to get the Office of Indian Affairs to approve the trip to the national capital by Chief Tyhee and other leading men in May 1888.[72] Gallagher used the opportunity to request the use of the $6,000 granted the Indians under the Agreement of 1882, money still being held in trust for them by the Treasury Department.[73]

With the Indians somewhat mollified, the agent could now turn his attention to the increasing threat of white trespass on the reservation. First, 1888 the Marsh Creek settlers were openly defying him, were refusing to pay grazing "taxes," and were "behaving very badly." He asked how he should proceed to get them to pay.[74] At Pocatello the agent was forced to order his Indian police to tear down a shoe shop built contrary to departmental orders, and the "denizens" of Pocatello became quite exercised over the spectacle of "an Indian arresting a white man." Gallagher expected further trouble from other would-be businessmen or women opening stores on reservation property next to the town.[75] Mrs. S. E. Hollbrook announced that she intended to start a "millinery and ladies' furnishing goods establishment."[76]

While awaiting the ratification of the 1887 agreement, which would improve the situation at the railroad station, both Agent Gallagher and the

Bureau of American Ethnology

Yan Maow [Big Nose]

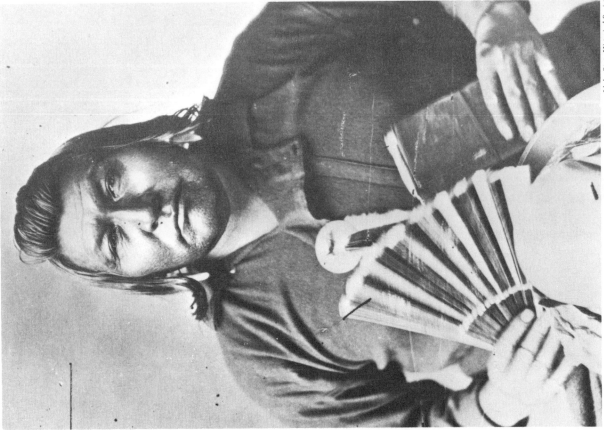

Idaho State Historical Society

Captain Jim

commissioner attempted to get the old cession agreement of 1880 back on the congressional track again. Gallagher suggested that, due to the lapse of time, the initial payments to the Lemhi and the Shoshoni and Bannock should be raised from $4,000 to $8,000 for the former tribe and from $6,000 to $12,000 for the Fort Hall Indians.[77] The commissioner thought the section granting H. O. Harkness title to his property and improvements was improper, that Harkness was an intruder and should be removed with the same "rigor" as if he were a poor man.[78]

But the Agreement of 1880 was an orphan compared to the care and nourishment which the Union Pacific lobby and friends heaped on the Agreement of 1887, despite the presidential veto. Gallagher suggested several amendments and appealed for as much money for the Indians as could be obtained from the sale of the townsite lots: "God only knows they need it."[79] When news reached Boise that both houses of Congress had passed the revised bill, the *Idaho Statesman* announced that the citizens of Pocatello held a "grand jubilee" in honor of the event.[80]

1888   The bill was approved by the President on September 1, 1888, with the principal provisions intact as outlined earlier.[81] The wondrous event brought more headaches to the agent as settlers abandoned all restraint and began to scramble for the best sites.[82] Soon there were almost a thousand buildings under construction, including the Western Saloon which sponsored gambling.[83] Gallagher warned that the Indians might take matters into their own hands because the white man "makes fence, builds house & no pay."[84] The *Pocatello Reporter* led the attack on Gallagher for his attempts to stop the trespassing until the lots could be sold at public auction: "Gallagher I, Czar of all the Bannacks and Shoshones, Prince Regent of Ross Fork and the broad domain appertaining thereto. . . ."[85] It was a losing cause for the agent; even the less aggressive citizens attempted to get around the law by suggesting that Article 5 of the agreement meant that all persons who made improvements prior to the eventual survey and not prior to the signing of the act would have first rights to purchase their property.[86]

The Department of Justice soon rectified this latter erroneous and grasping-at-straws attempt on the part of the sooners to gain advantage from the sale of the Pocatello townsite.[87] Gallagher was authorized to post public notices warning trespassers to leave.[88] When the proclamation had no effect he posted a new one which announced that all improvements would be seized and forfeited to the Indians.[89] The second warning still made little impression. Soon a shooting gallery, a saloon, and other buildings began to rise. Gallagher thought he had a "second Oklahoma" in the making and

1889

was having difficulty convincing the Indians that all will "come out right in the end."[90]

The trespassers soon received some quasi-legal support for their actions when Judge C. H. Berry of the Third District Court of Idaho held that the land enclosed in the Pocatello townsite was no longer Indian country since the passage of the act affirming the sale of the land by the Indians.[91] Immediately even timid settlers who had held back began to move onto the surveyed lots and erect houses. Two more saloons were "running full blast," and there were other establishments. The commissioner of Indian Affairs wired that the Pocatello townsite was still "subject to the Indian intercourse laws," but few heeded the edict.[92]

By October 1, 1889, the survey of the lots was still underway. The commissioner had chosen two representatives and the Indians another to appraise the lots; the Utah and Northern had paid $7,621.04 for the north-south right-of-way at the rate of $8 an acre. The additional 149.94 acres to be obtained at the townsite also would compensate the Indians $8 an acre, plus the proceeds of the public auction sale of the lots.[93] Both Agent Gallagher and Walter P. Ramsey, the Indian representative in the appraisal, were of the opinion that if prompt action had been taken by Congress the Indians might have realized much more from the lots; Gallagher said $250,000 was a possible total. The agent believed one-half that amount was now irrevocably lost to the Shoshoni and Bannock.[94]

The slowness with which Congress had moved to approve the Pocatello townsite bill was lightning compared to its action on the old 1880 agreement for removal of the Lemhi to Fort Hall and cession of the southern portion of the reservation. On February 23, 1889, Congress finally ratified the measure which ceded approximately 297 thousand acres of reservation land in the Marsh Creek area for a consideration of $120,000. Again the Lemhi refused to leave their Salmon River haunts, and this part of the agreement was abrogated.[95] A further complication came from the settlers of Marsh Valley, who indicated that, through an error in drawing the bill, about thirty families occupying a section six by five miles wide west of Marsh Creek were not included in the cession. They asked that the act be amended and concluded, "Your petitioners will ever pray. . . ." If experience meant anything, it would take more than prayers.[96]

The disgruntled Indians at Fort Hall had to experience their share of waiting for the survey, appraisal, and sale of the land they had agreed to cede to the railroad. By October 1891 the Office of Indian Affairs was able to report proceeds of $13,182.72 for the sale of lots within the 150 acres granted to the Utah and Northern at Pocatello and about $115,000 for the lots from the general

1891

Idaho State Historical Society

Pocatello John (not the original Pocatello) and Major Peter Gallagher.

cession at the town.[97] Agent S. G. Fisher complained that the growing metropolis of three thousand citizens was having a "demoralizing" effect on the Indians, too many of whom were getting in the habit of begging at kitchen doors or visiting the slaughter pens to pick up discarded offal.[98]

Pocatello Cession Agreement of 1900

1893   The citizens of Pocatello now started on a deliberate and long-range program to free the city of its isolation in the center of an Indian reservation and to open up the entire area to white settlement. The fact that the project would dispossess the Indians of their homeland was of little consequence. The more energetic of the Shoshoni and Bannock would receive allotments of farms under the Dawes Act, passed in 1887. This would still leave much fertile land for more enterprising white farmers. The *Pocatello Tribune* announced the program:

Not the least of the elements which promise future greatness to the town of Pocatello is the Fort Hall reservation adjacent to the city. It comprises something over a million acres of land, more than half of which is the finest of agricultural land. This reservation is at present held by about 500 Bannock and 900 Shoshoni Indians, but the day is not far distant when all this land must be thrown open to settlement. In the mountainous districts of the reservation are rich mineral prospects that will be worked just as soon as the red men have relinquished their title.[99]

With variations on this theme the *Tribune* trumpeted the above objectives from 1893 until they were mostly achieved by 1902.

To carry out the provisions of the Dawes Act to grant allotments in severalty to the Fort Hall Indians, an appropriation of $12,000 was made in 1889 to survey the reservation — a project not started until January 21, 1892.[100] The newly formed Chamber of Commerce of Pocatello, fully in accord with the *Tribune's* aims, now sent former agent Peter Gallagher to Boise to check on the completed survey. The chamber concluded that the survey was a "fake from beginning to end," apparently because it did not meet the purposes of Pocatello.[101]

Plans were laid to ensure that Republicans and Democrats would forget their political differences and work in nonpartisan fashion to reduce the reservation and free the lands.[102] Senator George L. Shoup wrote from Washington that he had assurances that the Interior Department "will expedite the allotment of lands to the Indians as rapidly as possible, and will enter into a treaty with the Indians for the residue of the reservation." Senator Shoup warned that considerable time would elapse before such a treaty could be negotiated and ratified so the valuable Indian lands could be thrown open to settlement. He was a good prophet; it took the indefatigable citizens of Pocatello nine years to accomplish their aim.[103]

1894   As the *Pocatello Tribune* expressed it in early 1894, "The life of the city depends upon the opening of the reservation and the prosperity of every enterprise within its border."[104] The survey was not going fast enough; another survey had to be made; politics were intervening — to the impatient citizens everything seemed to be stalling the allotment of land to the Indians so the balance of the reservation could be thrown open.[105]

During the city election some supporters of the Democratic party spread the word that if Edward Steen were elected mayor he would have the reservation opened in a year.[106] Scoffing at such preposterous claims the *Tribune*, a Republican organ, next denounced claims by some Democrats that their candidate for governor, if elected, would surely free Indian lands for settlement.[107]

A frightening rumor gained currency that a Salt Lake City mining firm was attempting to get a monopoly for the development of all mineral deposits on the reservation. The Indian Agent at Fort Hall was supposed to be in collusion with the company. In a paroxysm of anxiety the *Idaho Herald* helped the scare along with several columns in a number of issues devoted to attacks on the purported grab. The *Herald* also dismissed the concern that a few people were voicing about protecting Indian rights to the land. It quoted from the *Montpelier Republic*, which represented a small village lying on the eastern edge of the reservation: "The silly twaddle about this land belonging to the noble red man and that we have no right to rob him of what was given him by the creator, and a great deal more of like nonsense, should cease . . . that the place where painted savages held weird revelries would spring up colleges and sanctuaries of peace."[108]

A new agent, J. T. Van Orsdale, attempted to defend the Indian rights which the Montpelier paper denied. He took action to remove the thirty families of white settlers along Marsh Creek who, unfortunately for them, had not been included in the 1889 act confirming the earlier cession agreement of 1880.[109] Van Orsdale removed one settler by force. The others were preparing to leave when Fred T. Dubois came to their aid and asked that an inspector be sent by the Indian Office to arrange for purchase of these lands from the Shoshoni and Bannock. The Office of Indian Affairs responded with alacrity.[110]

Another group of trespassing settlers along Garden Creek also had a visit from an Indian inspector, who asked them to swear to the value of the improvements they had made on their farms. The move was looked on with suspicion because several years earlier the settlers had paid an amount equivalent to the value of their improvements into a fund to send a representative to Washington "to get them cut off the reservation." They feared this was a scheme to get more money from them.[111]

In support of the wishes of these citizens, as well as the residents of Pocatello, the Idaho State Legislature addressed a memorial to the President on February 4, 1895, indicating that the Indians at Fort Hall were "ripe for a trial of the severalty system" which would, of course, throw open the rest of the reservation to white settlement.[112] Agent Thomas B. Teter supported the move, recommending that 370 thousand acres of the southern portion of the reserve be sold and the proceeds used to build an irrigation system for Indian farmers. The cession would only displace twenty-five Indian families, Teter said, and would confirm title to lands held by white settlers on Marsh Creek, who were cultivating about ten thousand acres of farmland.[113]

The *Pocatello Tribune*, in a comprehensive end-of-the-year report on December 25, 1895, summarized the history of Pocatello and Fort Hall, beginning with the statement, "The crowding of a pushing and enterprising population into the narrow limits of the railroad right-of-way at once resulted in agitation for more room." The editor explained how, during the public auction, no one had been allowed to bid on those city lots containing improvements — which explains Agent Gallagher's earlier contention that the Indians lost about $125,000 in revenue as a result. The article also explained the necessity for the canal being planned to run along the bench east of Pocatello. Not only was the canal necessary before the Indians could receive allotment, but also the city would benefit from the water. Finally, the editor painted an exciting and colorful picture of the great "mineral prospects" and the "vast deposits of copper, silver, and gold" awaiting the eager prospectors when the reservation was finally opened.[114] Agent Teter agreed with the need for the canal but condemned "the shortsighted policy, gross neglect, or worse, which allowed the white settlers to file upon water in the streams on and adjacent to the reservation."[115]

Early in 1896 Senator Dubois was successful in getting $15,000 added to the Fort Hall appropriation to establish a three-member commissioner to

1895

1896

Idaho State Historical Society

Rabbit Tail

Idaho State Historical Society

Young Shoshoni men adapted white technology for traditional costume styles at Fort Hall.

meet with the Shoshoni and Bannock to achieve all the wonderful prospects outlined by the *Tribune*,[116] although Agent Teter warned that if the commissioner did not get to Fort Hall before the Indians began to earn money from work on the canal it would be "extremely difficult to coerce them into entering into a treaty."[117] His choice of a verb was quite revealing. The plan was to negotiate a cession at the Ross Fork line, which would free Pocatello from being surrounded by Indian lands.[118]

By September 12, 1896, Commissioners John B. Goodwin and C. G. Hoyt were at Fort Hall. They were soon joined by Benjamin F. Barge.[119] To their surprise the commissioners found that "The attitude of these Indians is peculiar, and we do not expect to find a like condition on any other Reservation." The attitude was not only peculiar but actually hostile. The three commissioners explained the causes: First, the Bannock were quite aggressive and used their influence over the Shoshoni to stymie any progress in the negotiations; second, the tribes were very angry over the refusal to allow Indians to hunt any longer on unoccupied lands of the United States, this action stemming from recent troubles in the Jackson Hole area of Wyoming; third, the year before, Agent Teter had imprisoned some of the Indian leaders as a result of a disagreement; fourth, the irrigation canal had not been completed on time, and many of the 1895 crops had been lost; fifth, the Indians had been "swindled" in a cattle deal which saw yearlings and dry cows being delivered to them instead of three-years-olds and cows with calves; and finally, "they complain that they have been so often deceived by the whites that they don't know what to believe, and they wish to be assured personally by the Great Father that the Commission sent by him to negotiate with them will treat them fairly and assure them that everything promised in the new agreement will be carried out, and their interests protected."[120]

The commissioner's appeal to send a delegation of six chiefs to Washington to get the President's support was denied. Senator Dubois tried to obtain a reversal of the ruling, believing the Indians would continue to refuse negotiations without reassurances from the Great Father. He continued to press for further meetings with the Indians,[121] while the commissioners decided to suspend the talks at Fort Hall and travel to other reservations — where, they hoped, more friendly receptions awaited them.

1896

1897

Senator Dubois was successful in arranging for a visit to Washington of the determined Shoshoni and Bannock. The group of six included Jim Ballard, Kanacka Johnson, Bob Smith, Frank Randall, and Tom and Pete Pocatello. Agent Teter wrote the commissioner that, with the exception of the two Pocatellos, the delegation represented the "hunting, uncivilized, and nonprogressive element" who had offered nothing but annoyance and trouble to the agents over the year — espe-

cially Kanacka Johnson who was "one of the meanest Indians on the reservation."[122] The Indian leaders responded by demanding the discharge of Teter before they would consent to an agreement. They further said that, although they had on five different occasions asked for a new agent, the Office of Indian Affairs had not responded. According to them the chief clerk at the agency was involved in some kind of fraud, and they also had been cheated out of a herd of cattle.[123] The commissioner immediately sent an inspector to investigate, at the same time firing Agent Teter.[124]

With Teter out of the way and the Indians having satisfied themselves by talking to President Grover Cleveland, the commissioners met again with the tribes in April 1897, and a tentative agreement was reached to cede a portion of the reservation.[125] In June the commissioners returned to inspect the new boundary line and to try to conclude the negotiations.[126] While they were away the *Pocatello Tribune* engaged in a newspaper war with certain cattlemen it charged were trying to stop any cession of Indian lands which would interfere with their grazing privileges.[127]

In September the Shoshoni and Bannock finally came to terms and agreed to sell 150 thousand acres at the southern end of the reservation at $4 an acre, for a total of over $600,000. The *Tribune*

Bureau of American Ethnology

Frank Randall

Bureau of American Ethnology

Pokotel Tom

was astonished at the high price: "This is the best deal we have ever heard of anyone making with the U.S. government." The Indians were to receive $150,000 three months after ratification of the agreement and $100,000 annually for four years. The line was to run about six miles north of Pocatello.[128]

A week later the agreement came to an abrupt end when the government refused to pay what was considered by Washington to be an exorbitant sum. The Indians reduced their price to $3, the Commissioner insisted on a larger cession, and the meeting ended in an impasse. It was rumored in Pocatello that a visiting delegation of Nez Perce had advised their friends at Fort Hall that they had recently sold some land at $3 an acre but could have gotten $5 for it. The Shoshoni and Bannock had apparently accepted the advice.[129]

1898   After a cooling-off period, Commissioner C. G. Hoyt was back at Fort Hall in February 1898 and was able to get an agreement which was submitted to the Office of Indian Affairs on February 5. Two hundred and fifty of the male adult Indians agreed to the following provisions: The Indians were to cede approximately 418,500 acres (of which about 50,000 acres were arable and the rest mountainous) to the government, with the southern boundary of the main reservation seven miles north of Pocatello; they were to receive $600,000 for the lands surrendered, or about $1.25 per acre (of which $75,000 was to be expended in

building a school plant), with the balance in pro rata shares to be granted each Indian on the basis of $50,000 a year; Indians now residing on the ceded portion were to have the option of remaining or of accepting an allotment at Fort Hall, with their improvements being sold at auction for their benefit; the Shoshoni and Bannock were to continue to have the right to cut timber for their own use, to pasture livestock, and to hunt and fish on the ceded land; the main traveled roads from McCammon to Blackfoot and from McCammon to American Falls were declared public highways; and water from streams on the ceded portion was reserved for irrigation purposes for the Indians who chose to remain there.[130] Agent Irwin regretted that the Indians would not agree to reserve another $75,000 for completion of their irrigation system. In a final bit of advice he wrote that the agreement should be ratified as it was, and promptly, for "Indians are very suspicious: they have agreed once, and it would be almost useless to ask them to agree again to some different treaty."[131]

The latter was important; after the Senate passed the bill ratifying the agreement, the House raised some objections to the terms. The representatives thought the price for timber and stone land should be increased to at least $2.50 an acre and the lands lying under the new Idaho canal should be worth no less than $10 an acre. Also, the congressmen wanted to strike the free home-

Bureau of American Ethnology

Pokotel Pete

stead provision. While members debated, adjournment time came. The bill was lost for the session, to the great disappointment of the citizens of Pocatello.[132]

1899   In January 1899 Idaho Senator George Shoup used the tactic of adding the Fort Hall bill as an amendment to the Indian Appropriation Act, a maneuver that the House killed by striking the amendment after two months of parliamentary in-fighting. The *Pocatello Tribune* followed the congressional activity with almost daily articles, using such titles as "That Bill of Ours."[133] The bill was postponed again, and the Indians became quite "impatient" over the delay.[134]

By the time the Fort Hall bill was taken up again by Congress in December 1899 the Shoshoni and Bannock were becoming as restive as their white neighbors at Pocatello.[135] A special Indian agent at Fort Hall inquired for his wards about the status of the legislation, noting that the Indians "have an idea that the bill carries more

1900   land than the treaty called for."[136] The Fort Hall residents were reassured but, as the *Pocatello Tribune* reported, "Pocatello people were considerably cast down Tuesday evening when they read that Congressman Chickering had inconsiderately thrown himself out of a fifth story window and killed himself. . . ." — inconsiderate because the incident postponed further action on their very important bill.[137]

The long wait finally ended for both Indian and white when the House of Representatives approved on June 5, 1900, legislation ratifying the agreement negotiated two years earlier. The President signed the measure the next day.[138] Amendments for carrying out the provisions of the agreement were mostly concerned with the disposal of the ceded lands: First, Congress decided to grant $100,000 in a first pro-rata payment to the Indians; second, the sum of $1,000 was appropriated for a survey of the reservation so allotments could be made; third, the ceded lands would be opened by a proclamation of the President and would be "subject to disposal under the homestead, townsite, stone and timber, and mining laws of the United States" except for the sixteenth and thirty-sixth sections, which would be reserved for common-school purposes; fourth, all lands lying under the Idaho Canal which were susceptible of irrigation would be sold at the rate of $10 an acre; fifth, all agricultural lands not under the canal would be sold at $2.50 an acre and grazing lands at $1.25 an acre; sixth, all the lands within five miles of the boundary line of Pocatello would be sold at public auction and at not less than $10 an acre; and seventh, any mineral lands within the five-mile limit would be disposed of under the mineral laws of the United States, except that the price would "be fixed at ten dollars per acre instead of the price fixed by the said mineral laws."[139]

Idaho State Historical Society

Shoshoni camp near Fort Hall Agency.

Idaho State Historical Society

Plains Indian clothing styles were common at Fort Hall late in the nineteenth century.

"The Day of the Run"

Immediately upon receipt of the long-awaited news, impatient sooners among the five thousand people living at Pocatello went onto reservation lands and began staking mining claims — as many as a hundred in the first three days. The Indian agent called out his entire force of Indian police, who pulled up the stakes and notices as fast as they were placed. Prominent citizens at Pocatello argued in all solemnity that the police were committing a crime in doing so, although Agent Caldwell announced that the ceded lands were still part of the reservation until the President issued a proclamation opening the area. The pull

of supposed riches in gold, silver, and copper was too strong for the excited miners. Other free enterprisers were digging irrigation ditches, fencing and ploughing farms, and driving large herds of cattle onto pasture lands within reservation boundaries. The secretary of the Interior wired Caldwell to post notices that unless the trespassers left the reservation at once troops would be called in to remove them by force.[140] The magic word, "troops," cleared the ceded lands in a hurry — except for the cattlemen, who now agreed to pay the customary fifty cents per head grazing fee.[141]

In September an inspector arrived to determine how many of the 242 Indians (61 families) living on the ceded portion of the reservation would choose to remain and how many would elect to take allotments on the reduced reservation. About two-thirds of the families decided to move.[142] The General Land Office also hired Oscar Sonnenkalb to survey the new boundary line separating the ceded lands.[143]

To the Shoshoni and Bannock the most important event in the entire cession process was the distribution of the first $100,000 on September 6, when the approximately fourteen hundred Indians each received $71.68. The *Pocatello Tribune* made much of the manner in which the money was spent, recording, for example, that one Indian bought a buggy which cost $130. Presumably the merchants of Pocatello were not unhappy with the sudden influx of cash.[144] There would be eight more annual disbursements of $50,000 each and a final one of $25,000. In 1901 each of the 1,435 Indians at Fort Hall received $34.50 and at the same time received a vaccination for smallpox, which caused some objections from Jim Ballard and others.[145]

1901

The entire year 1901 was taken up with the completion of three necessary operations before the ceded lands could be thrown open for settlement. On the ceded lands, allotments amounting to 7,177.17 acres were made to ninety individuals, while the total appraised value of the twenty-three families electing to move to the diminished reservation was $5,851.50.[146] Agent Caldwell inquired whether the Indians choosing to remain outside the reservation would continue to receive rations and enjoy the same benefits as those who had never lived on the ceded portion.[147]

The second problem was to get a proper survey completed. The *Pocatello Tribune* pursued the matter with vigor, reporting almost every move made by the survey crews. Lastly, it was necessary to classify the lands into agricultural, grazing, and timber categories. All three of the above objectives had been accomplished by year's end, and citizens and Indians awaited the President's proclamation.[148]

A ruling by the Attorney General's Office that only lands actually in possession and occupancy of an Indian family could be allotted (and then only up to 320 acres) necessitated a revision of the allotments by Agent Caldwell. Another four months elapsed before he could report 79 allotments instead of 90. Sales of improvements at Blackfoot had returned $9,270 to the Indian owners by October 1902.[149]

With Indian ownership of property of the ceded lands settled, the way was open for the proclamation which President Theodore Roosevelt signed on May 7, 1902. More than 400 thousand acres of land were to be opened to settlement on June 17, 1902, at 12 o'clock noon at the Blackfoot Land Office. The lands within the five-mile limit of Pocatello would be sold at public auction at the same land office starting July 17, 1902.[150]

The *Pocatello Tribune* congratulated itself on having brought about the great event.[151] Earlier the newspaper explained that an Oklahoma-type lottery system could not be used in opening the new lands because of the unique situation calling for a public auction of the five-mile limit acreage and the necessity of selling the irrigated lands at $10 an acre.[152]

The absolute assurance in the minds of Pocatello residents and others about the rich mineral deposits on the cession lands permeated conversation and newspaper column alike.[153] Senator Dubois was the only person of prominence to risk public displeasure and ridicule by insisting there were no rich mines on the five-mile lands.[154] Most stories were like the account of the two miners arrested and forced off their reservation claim on May 23 by Indian police. The mine they were working was, of course, "quite rich."[155]

To keep optimistic intruders off reservation property, Agent Caldwell doubled his police force to sixty-five, although it was evident that even this number could not keep the "sagebrush sooners" away from all that gold, silver, and copper.[156] The land office also had to give a stiff warning to sheep owners who had massed their herds on the cession boundaries and were prepared to move onto the new lands on opening day.[157]

As June 17 approached the *Tribune* outlined the rules: An individual must start from any point outside the reservation, proceed to the desired land to set stakes, and then race for the land office in Blackfoot where filing would be done on a first-come-first-served basis. People were warned that the railroad right-of-way was not considered part of the exterior boundary of the reservation. Agent Caldwell announced that all sooners arrested would be locked in jail until opening day was over. Payment for the five-mile limit lands would be by cash and did not require filing, only an offer of the highest bid.[158] Agent Caldwell assured everyone that at noon on June 17 he would withdraw his police, and "the miners can go out and find whatever there is to find and dig all they want to dig to find it."[159]

The Oregon Short Line received so many requests for special trains that its management finally announced one train would leave McCammon on the southern boundary at 1:30 P.M., allowing an hour and a half for lands to be posted. It would stop for two mintues each at Inkom and Pocatello and arrive at Blackfoot at 3:00 P.M.[160] There were probably two thousand strangers camped around Pocatello, with another four thousand gathered at the borders of the reserva-

Eugene O. Leonard Collection

Shoshoni camp near city of Pocatello.

Eugene O. Leonard Collection

"The Day of the Run" Pocatello, Idaho, June 17, 1902.

tion. The *Tribune* gave notice to its readers that there would be no issue on June 17; reason — the staff would be participating in the rush.[161]

At noon on June 17 the "great shop whistle" at the railroad yards blasted forth, the spectators on the Red Butte south of the town cheered, and the rush was on.[162] Ray Stannard Baker, a reporter for *The Century Magazine*, was on hand to write a classic description of a land rush. Starting with a description of how Pocatello, like a camel, had gotten its head into the reservation tent, he then computed how much the Shoshoni and Bannock had lost in the Pocatello cession of land. The government had paid $1.45 an acre for 418,000 acres and received in return $600,000 for 60 thousand acres at $10, $250,000 for 100 thousand acres at $2.50, and $322,000 for 258,000 acres at $1.25 — for a total of $1,720,000. The cost was $600,000, leaving a net profit to the government of $572,000, which he said should have gone to the Indians.[163]

Apparently Baker caught the train later at Pocatello and was in the crowd that watched as riders, who had taken off their shoes and were sitting their horses bareback, prepared to race against men in buggies and on bicycles. The most interesting spectacle was probably Will Hillman; he had arranged a relay of fifteen horses between McCammon and Blackfoot, believing he could beat the train to the land office by at least twenty minutes. He had tied red and green ribbons on his hat and around his knees to lend a dramatic air to his entry. As the train pulled into Blackfoot

seventeen minutes ahead of schedule, it passed Hillman just in sight of town. The rail passengers, some precariously riding the brake beams, cheered Hillman but gave him a last place in line and a lemon to suck to assuage his thirst and disappointment.[164]

Men jumped from the moving train, some landing on their heads and having to visit the doctor before being able to get to the land office, where they found a long line ahead of them. Among those to lose their lands were two Marsh Creek settlers, Meyers Cohen and 83-year-old Mrs. Marley, who had been on their improved farms for over twenty years. They and others immediately filed suit to recover their lands. Some bitterness was evident.[165] Caldwell noted that within a few minutes after noon men were in line before the land office, and many believed that the best lands had gone to the unscrupulous sooners.[166] But there were no shootings, and Baker reported one old-timer saying, "This ain't like the old rushes. It sure ain't."[167]

The sale of the five-mile limit lands did not return the sales profits which Pocatello optimists had predicted. Of the 1,505 forty-acre tracts, only 69 were sold, for $42,337.80. By the end of the year Pocatello boosters were supporting legislation to sell the remainder of the land at $1.25 an acre. Some feared the acreage would not attract buyers even at this low price.[168]

For the Shoshoni and Bannock, the loss of a large part of their reservation was the unfortunate but probably inevitable consequence of living

1902

at the western crossroads of Fort Hall, which had led directly to the railroad junction and the growth of a city in their midst. At long last, perhaps, they would be left undisturbed on the few remaining acres. Certainly they could no longer roam free to hunt the mountains as in the olden days.

The thirty-year process of reducing the Fort Hall Reservation to less than one-third its original size proceeded inexorably under pressure from white settlers, who paid little attention to Indian rights or needs. While the Marsh Valley farmers found great difficulty in obtaining legal title to their farms, the residents of the new town of Pocatello, with the aid of the powerful Union Pacific Railroad, faced only the traditional lethargy of congressional action in accomplishing a cession of the southern portion of the reservation. The railroad was finally forced to compensate the tribes for the two rights-of-way, although in retrospect the settlement seems quite inadequate.

With a burgeoning city — complete with railroad shops, merchants, and workers located in the very center of Indian lands — it was only a matter of time (and Idaho state pressure applied in Washington) until the Shoshoni and Bannock would be forced to relinquish the lands surrounding Pocatello. The President's proclamation opening the ceded portion, which loosed a horde of land-hungry settlers and miners, marked the end of attempts to reduce the reservation further but inaugurated the more subtle and equally dangerous process of alienating parcels of Indian land within the boundaries of the reserve. That encroachment continues today.

NOTES CHAPTER VII
NEGOTIATING WITH WASHINGTON

1. "Survey of Conditions of the Indians in the United States," U.S. Congress, 72d Cong., 1st Sess., Part 27, Wyoming, Idaho and Utah, Sept. 12, 13, 14, 1932 (Washington, D.C., 1934), 14639.
2. D. W. Ballard to C.I.A., Nov. 18, 1866, *Idaho Superintendency*, Roll 337.
3. "Map Accompanying Letter of Governor Ballard, Nov. 18, 1866," U.S. National Archives, Map No. 747.
4. "Maps of Public Survey in Idaho, 1869, 1970," U.S. National Archives, U.S. General Land Office, Idaho Maps No. 1 and 2.
5. L. F. Cartee to Commissioner, General Land Office, Jan. 4, Apr. 29, May 14, 1873, *Idaho Superintendency*, Roll 341; D. P. Thompson to H. W. Corbett, Jan. 23, 1873, ibid.; Commissioner of General Land Office to Sec. of Interior, Feb. 11, 1873, ibid.
6. John B. David, *Field Notes of the Survey of the Exterior Boundaries of Ft. Hall Indian Reservation in the Territory of Idaho*, under contract dated April 5, 1873, Agricultural Surveys, Idaho Territory, No. 78, Bureau of Land Management Office, Boise, Idaho, Dec. 14, 1873, 155–245.
7. "S. S. Fenn, late Delegate from Idaho to President of U.S., March 18, 1879, Extract from field notes of survey Fort Hall Indian Reservation, Idaho Terry," *Idaho Superintendency*, Roll 351.
8. Ibid.; "Map No. 784, Fort Hall Indian Reservation, Aug. 26, 1873," U.S. National Archives Collection; "Bannack and Other Indians in Southern Idaho," U.S. Cong., House, 43d Cong., 1st Sess., Ex. Doc. No. 129, Vol. 10 (Wash., D.C., 1874), 3–4; E. C. Watkins to C.I.A., Oct. 16, 1875, U. S. National Archives, *Record Group No. 75*, 6–7.
9. Ibid., "Bannock and Other Indians . . . ," U.S. Cong., House, 43d Cong., 1st Sess., Exec. Doc. No. 129, Vol. 10 (Washington, D.C., 1874), 3–4.
10. *Idaho Statesman*, Jan. 15, 1876.
11. W. H. Danilson to C.I.A., Feb. 24, 1876, *Idaho Superintendency*, Roll 344; W. H. Danilson to C.I.A., May 1, 1879, *Idaho Superintendency*, Roll 350.
12. *Idaho Satesman*, Jan. 21, 1879.
13. Ibid., Jan. 23, Feb. 17, 1877.
14. Charles Parker to W. H. Danilson, Dec. 4, 1878, and forwarded to C.I.A., Dec. 11, 1878, *Idaho Superintendency*, Roll 348.
15. S. S. Fenn to President of U.S., Mar. 18, 1879, *Idaho Superintendency*, Roll 351.
16. Beal, *Intermountain Railroads*, 1–59.
17. *C.I.A. Annual Report, 1878*, 547.
18. W. H. Danilson to C.I.A., Sept. 22, 26, Oct. 2, 1878, *Idaho Superintendency*, Roll 347.
19. Beal, *Intermountain Railroads*, 59–60.
20. Ibid., 60.
21. Ibid.
22. W. H. Danilson to C.I.A., Oct. 23, 1878, *Idaho Superintendency*, Roll 347.
23. *C.I.A. Annual Report, 1879*, 424.
24. Beal, *Intermountain Railroads*, 62.
25. Supreme Court Idaho Territory, Utah & Northern Railroad Company vs. Willard Crawford, District Attorney, Idaho State Historical Society, Drawer 9; *Idaho Statesman*, Feb. 14, 1880.
26. "Petition to President of U.S. from Citizens of Marsh Creek, Oct. 8, 1880," *Idaho Superintendency*, Roll 352.
27. W. C. Hawkins to C.I.A., Sept. 17, 1880, ibid.
28. August Duddenhausen to Geo. Ainslie, and S. W. Phelan to Geo. Ainslie, Feb. 2, 1881, U.S. National Archives, *Records, Office of Indian Affairs*.
29. *C.I.A. Annual Report, 1880*, 105–106; E. A. Stone to C.I.A., Oct. 4, 1881, U.S. National Archives, *Records, Office of Indian Affairs*.
30. Ibid.
31. E. A. Stone to C.I.A., Nov. 14, 1881, ibid.
32. *C.I.A. Annual Report, 1881*, 50–51.
33. *C.I.A. Annual Report, 1880*, 105–106.
34. E. A. Stone to C.I.A., Oct. 4, 1881, U.S. National Archives, *Records, Office of Indian Affairs*.
35. E. A. Stone to C.I.A., July 7, 1881, ibid.; Joseph K. McCammon to C.I.A., August 16, 1881, ibid.; Joseph K. McCammon to C.I.A., Aug. 25, 1881, ibid.; *Agreement of 1881, Correspondence*, Utah State Historical Society; "Message from President of U.S.," "U.S. Congress, Senate, Exec. Doc., 48th Cong., 1st Sess. (Wash., 1884), 5.
36. *Blackfoot Register*, July 9, 1881.
37. Ibid., July 1, 1882.
38. George Ainslie to Sec. of Interior, Aug. 5, 1882, U.S. National Archives, *Records, Office of Indian Affairs; Blackfoot Register*, Aug. 26, 1882.
39. C.I.A. Annual Report, 1884, 107–108.
40. C.I.A. Annual Report, 1885.
41. "Utah and Northern Railroad," U.S. Congress, Senate, 49th Cong.,1st Sess., Exec. Doc. No. 20, Vol. 1, Serial No. 2333 (Washington, D.C., 1886), 1–7; see footnote No. 22.
42. "Utah Etc. Ry. Co. v. Fisher, Feb. 16, 1884," *Reports of Cases Argued and Determined in the Supreme Court of Territory of Idaho*, Vol. 2 (Bancroft-Whitney Company, 1930), 52–58.
43. A. L. Cook to C.I.A., Nov. 10, 1885, U.S. National Archives, *Case No. 99*.
44. Ibid.
45. W. H. B. Crow to Sec. of Interior, Nov. 21, 1885, U.S. National Archives, *Case No. 99*.
46. Packet of letters, dated from Nov. 16 to Dec. 11, 1885, ibid.; E. D. Bannister to C.I.A., Oct. 3, 1855, U.S. National Archives, *Record Group No. 48*.
47. Shellabarger & Wilson to Sec. of Interior, May 24, 1886, U.S. National Archives, *Case No. 99*.
48. P. Gallagher to C.I.A., June 1, 1886, ibid.
49. R. J. McCarty to C.I.A., Sept. 23, 1886, ibid.
50. Petition of Forty One Residents of Pocatello to Sec. of Interior, Oct. 14, 1886, ibid.; Geo. B. Pearsons to C.I.A., Jan. 1, 1887, U.S. National Archives, *Record Group No. 48*.
51. *C.I.A. Annual Report, 1886*, 108–109.
52. P. Gallagher to C.I.A., Jan. 18, 1887, U.S. National Archives, *Case No. 99*.
53. William Burns and Thomas Brown to Sec. of Interior, Feb. 15, 1887, U.S. National Archives, *Records, Office of Indian Affairs*.
54. W. S. Hopson to C.I.A., Feb. 24, 1887, ibid.
55. Fred T. Dubois to C.I.A., March 15, 1887, ibid.
56. P. Gallagher to C.I.A., March 28, 1887, U.S. National Archives, *Case No. 72*.
57. John M. Evans to Sec. of Interior and C.I.A., March 23, 1887, ibid.
58. P. Gallagher to C.I.A., March 28, 1887, ibid.
59. Petition of Ninety-Seven Citizens to Sec. of Interior, April 2, 1887, U.S. National Archives, *Records, Office of Indian Affairs*.
60. Sec. of Interior to C.I.A., April 7, 1887, U.S. National Archives, *Case No. 99*; P. Gallagher to C.I.A., May 20, 1887, ibid.; A. W. Fisher to Arthur P. Gorman, March 10, 1887, ibid.
61. William Parsons to C.I.A., April 16, 1887, U.S. National Archives, *Records, Office of Indian Affairs*.
62. Sec. of Interior to C.I.A., June 8, 1887, U.S. National Archives, *Case No. 99*; R. S. Gardner to C.I.A., May 13, 1887, U.S. National Achives, *Record Group No. 48*.
63. Sec. of Interior to C.I.A., June 8, 1887, U.S. National Archives, *Case No. 99*.
64. Ibid.; see footnote No. 22.
65. P. Gallagher to C.I.A., Nov. 7, 1887, ibid.
66. Fred T. Dubois to Sec. of Interior, Jan. 16, 1888, ibid.
67. P. Gallagher to C.I.A., Jan. 23, 1888, ibid.
68. Sec. of Interior to President, Feb. 4, 1888, U.S. Congress, House, 50th Cong., 1st Sess. Exec. Doc. No. 140, Serial No. 2558 (Wash., D.C., 1889), 3.
69. *Idaho Statesman*, Jan. 19, 1888.
70. P. Gallagher to C.I.A., Feb. 7, 1888, U.S. National Archives, *Case No. 99*.
71. P. Gallagher to C.I.A., Feb. 27, 1888, ibid.
72. P. Gallagher to H. E. Hindmarsh, March 25, 1888," ibid.; "P. Gallagher to C.I.A., May 4, 1888, ibid.
73. P. Gallagher to C.I.A., May 18, 1888, ibid.; P. Gallagher to C.I.A., May 21, 1888, U.S. National Archives, *Case No. 72*.

74. P. Gallagher to C.I.A., April 7, 1888, ibid.
75. P. Gallagher to C.I.A., April 10, 1888, U.S. National Archives, *Case No. 99.*
76. P. Gallagher to C.I.A., April 24, 1888, U.S. National Archives, *Records, Office of Indian Affairs.*
77. P. Gallagher to C.I.A., May 21, 1888, U.S. National Archives, *Case No. 72.*
78. C.I.A. to Sec. of Interior, Feb. 23, 1888, U.S. Congress, House, 50th Cong., 1st Sess., Report No. 2754, Serial No. 2605 (Wash., D.C., 1888), 3.
79. P. Gallagher to C.I.A., May 21, 1888, U.S. National Archives, *Records, Office of Indian Affairs.*
80. *Idaho Statesman,* July 12, 1888.
81. *C.I.A. Annual Report, 1888,* XLVIII; 25 Stat. 452, 1 Kappler 292; see footnote No. 64.
82. P. Gallagher to C.I.A., Sept. 8, 1888, U.S. National Archives, *Records, Office of Indian Affairs.*
83. Frank W. Beane to Commissioner, United States Land Office, Nov. 26, 1888, ibid.
84. P. Gallagher to C.I.A., Nov. 17, 1888, ibid.
85. P. Gallagher to C.I.A., Sept. 9, 1888, ibid.
86. Fred T. Dubois to Commissioner, General Land Office, Dec. 5, 1888, ibid.
87. A. H. Garland to Sec. of Interior, Jan. 4, 1888, ibid.
88. Sec. of Interior to P. Gallagher, Jan. 21, 1888, U.S. National Archives, *Case No. 99.*
89. P. Gallagher to C.I.A., Feb. 5, 1889, ibid.
90. P. Gallagher to C.I.A., June 3, 1889, ibid.
91. Walter P. Ramsey to C.I.A., Aug. 20, 1889, U.S. National Archives, *Records, Office of Indian Affairs.*
92. W. S. Hopson, Deputy Marshal, to C.I.A., Aug. 24, 1889, U.S. National Archives, *Case No. 99.*
93. *C.I.A. Annual Report, 1889,* 19, 38.
94. Ibid., 174–175; Walter P. Ramsey to C.I.A., Aug. 20, 1889, U.S. National Archives, *Records, Office of Indian Affairs.*
95. *C.I.A. Annual Report, 1889,* 78.
96. Henry Crump, et al. to Sec. of Interior, April 10, 1889, U.S. National Archives, *Records, Office of Indian Affairs.*
97. *C.I.A. Annual Report, 1891,* 97–100.
98. Ibid., 230.
99. *Pocatello Tribune,* Feb. 17, 1893.
100. Ibid., Nov. 24, 1893.
101. Ibid., Jan. 6, 13, 20, Feb. 10, 24, March 3, 17, 1893.
102. Ibid., April 3, 1893.
103. Ibid., Oct. 27, 1893.
104. Ibid., June 8, 1894.
105. Ibid., March 30, June 16, June 30, 1894.
106. Ibid., March 31, April 3, 4, 1894.
107. Ibid., Oct. 13, 1894.
108. *Idaho Herald,* Jan. 26, Feb. 9, 16, 1894.
109. J. T. Van Orsdale to C.I.A., April 22, May 8, June 20, 1894, U.S. National Archives, *Records, Office of Indian Affairs.*
110. Sec. of Interior to C.I.A., Oct. 1, 1894, ibid.
111. *Pocatello Tribune,* Dec. 1, 1894.
112. "Joint Memorial of Legislature of State of Idaho to President, Feb. 4, 1895," U.S. National Archives, *Records, Office of Indian Affairs.*
113. Thomas B. Teter to C.I.A., Jan. 8, 1896, ibid.
114. *Pocatello Tribune,* Dec. 25, 1895.
115. *C.I.A. Annual Report, 1895,* 143.
116. *Pocatello Tribune,* Feb. 22, March 23, April 25, June 13, 1896.
117. Thomas B. Teter to C.I.A., March 6, 1896, U.S. National Archives, *Records, Office of Indian Affairs.*
118. *Pocatello Tribune,* April 25, 1896.
119. Ibid., Sept. 12, 1896.
120. Goodwin, Barge and Hoyt to C.I.A., Oct. 24, 1896, U.S. National Archives, *Records, Office of Indian Affairs;* John B. Goodwin to C.I.A., Nov. 10, 1896, ibid.; *Pocatello Tribune,* Dec. 26, 1896.
121. Fred T. Dubois to C.I.A., Nov. 16, 1896, U.S. National Archives, *Records, Office of Indian Affairs.*

122. Thomas B. Teter to C.I.A., Jan. 8, 1897, ibid.
123. *Pocatello Tribune,* Jan. 23, 1897.
124. Ibid., Feb. 27, 1897.
125. Ibid., March 12, 14, April 15, 1897.
126. Ibid., June 5, 1897.
127. Ibid., June 30, July 4, 1897.
128. Ibid., Sept. 11, 15, 1897.
129. Ibid., Sept. 22, 1897.
130. "Agreement with Crow, Flathead, and Other Indians, etc., March 3, 1898," U.S. Congress, Senate, 55th Cong. 2d Sess., Miscellaneous Document No. 169, Vol. 11 (Wash., D.C., 1899), 1–16; *Pocatello Tribune,* Feb. 2, 1898.
131. *C.I.A. Annual Report, 1898,* 143; F. G. Irwin, Jr., to C.I.A., Feb. 7, 1898, U.S. National Archives, *Records, Office of Indian Affairs.*
132. *Pocatello Tribune,* Feb. 19, March 12, June 11, 15, July 9, 13, Aug. 3, 1898; "Ratification of Agreement with Indians of Fort Hall Reservation, June 4, 1898," U.S. Congress, House, 55th Cong., 2d Sess., Report No. 1507, Vol. 6 (Wash., D.C., 1898), 1–4.
133. *Pocatello Tribune,* Jan. 7, 21, Feb. 8, 11, 15, 18, 22, March 1, 1899.
134. *C.I.A. Annual Report, 1899,* 183.
135. *Pocatello Tribune,* Dec. 20, 1899.
136. Elisha B. Reynolds to C.I.A., Feb. 10, 1900, U.S. National Archives, *Records, Office of Indian Affairs.*
137. *Pocatello Tribune,* Feb. 17, 1900.
138. Ibid., June 6, 1900.
139. "Copy of Act to Ratify Agreement with Ft. Hall, Kiowa, and Comanche Indians, June 20, 1900," U.S. National Archives, *Records, Office of Indian Affairs.*
140. *Pocatello Tribune,* Feb. 24, June 9, 13, 27, 1900.
141. A. F. Caldwell to C.I.A., July 6, 1900, U.S. National Archives, *Records, Office of Indian Affairs.*
142. *Pocatello Tribune,* June 27, Sept. 8, 1900.
143. Ibid., Oct. 27, 1900.
144. Ibid., Aug. 11, 29, Sept. 8, 12, 1900.
145. Ibid., Oct. 1, 1901.
146. *Annual Report of Secretary of the Interior, 1901,* LIII.
147. A. F. Caldwell to C.I.A., March 11, 1901, U.S. National Archives, *Records, Office of Indian Affairs.*
148. *Pocatello Tribune,* March 12, May 7, June 15, Oct. 29, Dec. 10, 1901.
149. *C.I.A. Annual Report, 1902,* 121.
150. *Pocatello Tribune,* May 7, 1902.
151. Ibid., May 8, 1902.
152. Ibid., April 5, 1902.
153. Ibid., May 12, 1902.
154. Ibid., May 14, 1902.
155. Ibid., May 23, 1902.
156. Ibid., June 6, 1902.
157. Commissioner of Public Land Office to H. V. A. Ferguson, June 6, 1902, U.S. National Archives, *Records, Office of Indian Affairs.*
158. *Pocatello Tribune,* May 24, June 7, 8, 1902.
159. Ibid., June 12, 1902.
160. Ibid., June 14, 1902.
161. Ibid., June 16, 1902.
162. *Deseret News,* June 17, 1902; *Pocatello Tribune,* June 17, 1902.
163. Baker, "The Day of the Run," *The Century Magazine,* Vol. LXVI (Sept., 1903), 644–646.
164. Ibid., 647–653; *Pocatello Tribune,* June 18, 20, 1902.
165. *Deseret News,* June 18, 1902; Baker, "The Day of the Run," 655.
166. A. F. Caldwell to C.I.A., June 19, 1902, U.S. National Archives, *Records, Office of Indian Affairs.*
167. Baker, "The Day of the Run," 655.
168. *Pocatello Tribune,* July 8, 21, Dec. 12, 1902; "Ceded Lands on Fort Hall Indian Reservation," U.S. Congress, Senate, 57th Cong. 2d Sess., Report No. 2213, Vol. 1 (Wash., D.C., 1903), 2.

CHAPTER VIII

HOME ON THE RESERVATION

Culpable Agents and Roaming Indians

The long and uncertain period of negotiation with the government over land cessions coincided with the twenty-year period during which the Shoshoni and Bannock were attempting to change from centuries of traditional roaming after food to a more settled and probably less exciting way of life. The transformation was difficult and made more so by agents who too often lacked the administrative skills and cultural understandings necessary to convert hunters into farmers.

1880   With the departure of W. H. Danilson as agent by 1880, John A. Wright took over. He encountered opposition almost at once. For some reason the nearby *Blackfoot Register* took a strong dislike to him, sprinkling its columns almost daily with attacks on him. He was "sanctimonious," a "liar," "mean," and "ignorant." Most of the epithets were included under such titles as "Wright's Wrongs."[1] The Indians accused him of starving them and having no concern for their welfare. As noted before, most agents were caught in this trap of insufficient appropriations for rations, with consequent disgruntlement on the part of the tribesmen.[2]

1881   The newspaper charges against Wright took on more substance when a letter from eight agency employees to the Office of Indian Affairs requested an investigation of his administration. One of the signers was Fred T. Dubois, later to become U.S. Senator from Idaho. The list of accusations compiled by the employees did not indicate a person of sterling qualities: First, Wright was dishonest; second, he had neglected his duties "to the pecuniary loss of the Government and Indians"; third, he had no reputation for integrity or "moral honor"; and last, his mismanagement had reduced the rations to one-quarter of the necessary beef and one-half the flour required to subsist the Indians. The employees concluded, "He is unfit for the position . . . and is a detriment to the service."[3]

The final *coup de grace* came within a few days, when all the prominent Indian leaders descended on the agent and complained that their children were crying for food, the gristmill had been shut down all winter, he did not teach them to farm, and they "could get no satisfaction out of him about anything."[4] Wright responded by resigning.

He was then accused by the *Register* of throwing open the warehouse doors and allowing the Indians to take anything they wanted — all to embarrass his successor and throw things into turmoil.[5] A final note was printed by the newspaper, which accused Wright of trying to get even with Dubois by charging him with being a drunkard in order to stop his confirmation as U.S. marshal of Idaho.[6]

Before his final departure in May 1881 Wright was confronted with a problem which seemed almost endemic to agents at the Fort Hall Reservation — the marked difference between the "turbulent and rebellious . . . idle and improvident" Bannock and the "quiet and peaceful" Shoshoni.[7] Some agents were more discerning and remarked on the independent and intelligent nature of the Bannock, but to most Indian officials at Fort Hall it seemed that the Bannock were usually at the root of any trouble that occurred. Certainly the citizens of Idaho took for granted that the Bannock were involved in any Indian disturbances in the Snake River area.

1881   In April 1881 a Bannock named Dave Moose received written permission from Wright to visit Red Rock, Montana, to bring his wife home. Instead, in the company of three other Bannock from Fort Hall, Moose traveled to the Yellowstone River, where the four men stole twenty horses from a camp of Blackfoot Indians. While they were escaping with the horses, a squaw man, James Walters, shot and killed Moose, accusing him of stealing a horse belonging to himself. The three returning Bannock denied the charges and claimed their only exploit was getting away with twenty horses belonging to their traditional enemies. The Bannock at the reservation became "considerably agitated" over the killing of one of their number and threatened retaliation. The incident demonstrated the difficulty of changing age-old cultural habits among a proud and independent people.[8]

By September E. A. Stone, the replacement for Wright, was receiving reports of marauding Bannock in Bruneau Valley, which he denounced as untrue.[9] He did report the arrival at Fort Hall of about ten Bannock from Wind River who had been driven from the Wyoming reservation by Chief Washakie. Another twelve Bannock also came in, refusing to tell where they came from. A final group of twenty Western Shoshoni arrived from Duck Valley Reservation — claiming a right at Fort Hall, where many of their relatives lived and where there was "better land than they had."[10]

1882 A year later another thirty Shoshoni from Duck Valley appeared at Fort Hall asking for haven, also claiming relatives on the reservation.[11] Special Agent Arden Smith, sent to investigate the movement of Shoshoni from the Idaho-Nevada reservation to Fort Hall, recommended they be allowed to remain for the winter but be told they must return to Duck Valley the next spring. His advice was the same for nineteen Shoshoni who had recently come from Wind River.[12]

The annual scare that Bannock warriors were about to swoop down upon helpless settlers, or upon friendly Shoshoni, came in May 1882 when the agent for the Northern Paiutes in Nevada telegraphed the Office of Indian Affairs that the Bannock were talking "bad about going out" and that the Western Shoshoni at Duck Valley were frightened.[13] The next rumor placed the doughty Bannock in the Goose Creek Mountains on their way to the Nevada reservation.[14] The military was aroused to investigate. Major George B. Sanford said in his report that he was told the Bannock intended to lead a general uprising the next spring among all the tribes in the Pacific Northwest north of the Central Pacific Railroad. According to Sanford's evaluations the Western Shoshoni were a "timid people," who were afraid of being killed by the Bannock if they refused to "go out" with the Fort Hall tribe. The Duck Valley Indians were so fearful that they had stopped farming altogether. The major thereupon sent Captain C. C. C. Carr to attend a council of the Western Shoshoni at Elko, Nevada, on October 2. Carr's conclusion was that there would be no general war started by the Bannock and that both they and the Western Shoshoni were quite peaceful.[15] Surely the word Bannock could conjure up scenes of indescribable ferocity and terror. The Bannock might have been pleased to know that so much power and influence were attributed to them.

The description which Agent A. L. Cook gave of the Bannock and Shoshoni in September 1882 did not correspond to the fearsome picture portrayed by some newspaper editors. Cook reported nine hundred of the Fort Hall Indians engaged in agriculture, four hundred in hunting and fishing, and three hundred "lazy vagabonds," who did nothing but complain and beg for food. He found many of the Indians entirely dependent on the Office of Indian Affairs, refusing to work and answering his advice to take up farming with, "No, Washington give Indian all; you no ask him for it." After he reduced their rations, a number began to invest in farm equipment. They bought three mowing machines, six hay rakes, and two lumber wagons.[16]

Cook took over the agency after a short tour of duty of only a few months by E. A. Stone. With the above point of view, it was little wonder that the Indians reciprocated by opposing their fourth agent in three years. The attack started when the agency physician, Dr. Jesse K. Dubois, a brother of Fred T., listed Cook's shortcomings: He was a liar and a hypocrite, was incapable of performing his duties as agent, was under the influence of irresponsible persons, used government property for his own benefit, allowed other individuals to use government property for their personal use, and secretly bribed some of the Indians "for reasons unknown."[17] 1882

Following the initial letter, Cook was charged by three other people. The matron of the school said he was a disgrace and that he had hired a Mormon woman of "disreputable character" as cook.[18] The Union Pacific agent at Blackfoot testified that most of the Fort Hall employees had been forced to quit because of Cook's "untruthfulness and underhanded treatment" of them — all except Stephen Moe (the agency farmer and a bad character) who was "virtually running" the agency.[19] The new physician, W. D. Monnet, supported the latter allegation.[20]

Special Agent Arden R. Smith was sent to investigate the affairs of the agency. He allowed Agent 1883 Cook to see his report, to which Cook added an explanation. The charges, said Cook, were so vague and general that they would not be admitted into a court of law; the employees complained because he had discharged them although he had the endorsement of the Washington office and it was "in the interests of harmony necessary to a successful administration"; and the whole incident was the work of discharged Dr. Dubois, his brother, and the post trader, W. N. Shilling.[21]

There followed a petition signed by some of the leading Indians. The most serious charges were that the agent had not kept their "bellies full" or given them farming tools. In Cook's explanation, the only Indians who did not receive rations were a few who had actually received a supply of food and then came back for more with the excuse that they had not been in the ration line due to their inability to catch their horses. As for the refusal to issue farming tools, Cook said some of the Indian farmers had received plows the year before and now had come in with the report that the implements were worn out. He refused to issue more plows to these improvident few, telling them a plow should last eight or ten years. The other accusations were of a similar nature.[22] The *Blackfoot Register* took up the hue and cry of the "havoc by his notorious mismanagement."[23]

Reading the conflicting testimony a century later leads to the conclusion that Cook was probably right in his assessment that the Dubois brothers, and particularly Shilling, had instigated the Indian petition and had urged certain whites to complain to the commissioner of Indian Affairs. It is noteworthy that the Washington office, after a thorough investigation, kept Cook as agent for another three years. Truly, the life of an agent was not a bed of roses. It also was significant how relatively easy it was for the three white men to channel the dissatisfaction of the Soshoni and Bannock over reduced rations and inadequate support for farming into a petition for the removal of Cook. In his annual report, Cook again spoke of the Shoshoni as being "industrious, good-natured and quiet" while the Bannock were "restless and roving, and much more difficult to control."[24]

When the grass turned green in the spring of 1883 the Indians began to move about the countryside as usual, causing some white ranchers on the west bank of the Snake River to contemplate moving their families into Blackfoot for safety. Apparently Indians were visiting homes asking for food and in one instance "would accept nothing but pie." Several Indians went to a stock camp kept by a white freighter on the reservation bottomlands and said threateningly, "Why don't you pay us money for the mules to eat grass here?"[25] The *Salt Lake Herald*, located some two hundred miles from Fort Hall, pooh-poohed the idea of an Indian outbreak.[26]

Other reports in May spoke of the possibility of Bannock raiders in the Bruneau Valley. This time the *Idaho Statesman* ridiculed the fears of the Owyhee citizens.[27] *The Wood River News-Miner* also deprecated any possibility of an outbreak.[28] Perhaps Shoshoni Major George best expressed the feelings of the Fort Hall Indians when he spoke to a *News-Miner* reporter about the rumor that "bad Indian want to fight white man." George said that was not right: "Bannock and Shoshoni no want to fight white man. You make um proper talk."[29]

1883   A disturbance did occur in September when a party of white men tracked a stolen horse to Little Camas Prairie, where about eighty Bannock and Shoshoni were digging camas roots. In the confrontation that followed, a white man struck an Indian, who retaliated. The result was two whites wounded, one Indian killed, and three others wounded.[30] Apparently in another altercation, four more Indians were killed during the year at Big Camas Prairie.[31] The worst incident involved a white rancher living about fifty miles north of Eagle Rock who shot and killed an Indian merely on suspicion that the tribesman had stolen a horse. As the result of an investigation, Agent Cook discovered the Indian had nothing to do with the stealing. The Shoshoni and Bannock

were quite incensed about the killing, and the rancher was arrested to be held for a hearing.[32]

Despite such incidents, which played on the fears of the white settlers of southwestern Idaho, the War Department went ahead with its plans to close the Fort Hall military post. It was finally abandoned in early July.[33] General O. O. Howard agreed with the decision. With a railroad running past Fort Hall Agency it would be only a matter of hours until troops could be transported from Fort Douglas at Salt Lake City to any trouble spot on or near the reservation.[34] The citizens of Idaho were not as convinced as the general, but they were forced to accept the decision.

In another consolidation move the Office of Indian Affairs attempted again without success to induce the Lemhi to move to Fort Hall and also to close out the Duck Valley Reservation by moving its 286 Western Shoshoni to Fort Hall. Very strenuous efforts were made by Special Agent 1884 Cyrus Beede early in 1884 to achieve the latter goal, but without results.[35] He secured the assent of the Shoshoni and Bannock to accept their "brothers" from Duck Valley only after promising that the supply of rations at Fort Hall would not be reduced by distributing the same amount to a greater number of Indians. At the same time he gave the Fort Hall residents "no encouragement, of perpetual continuance, of even the limited amount they now receive."[36]

The Western Shoshoni refused to give up their reservation; it had become their home. Their agent supported the stand they took. Above all they feared being on the same reservation with the Bannock. As Agent Beede explained, the Western Shoshoni held the Bannock in "very poor repute" and believed them to be thieves.[37] Agent John S. Mayhugh of Duck Valley volunteered the information that his Western Shoshoni would be "contaminated" by the Bannock, who were "badly deceased [sic] of a private nature."[38] Captain Sam, head chief at Duck Valley, was apparently afraid of the Bannock due to an old argument with them. The chief was also opposed to a reservation crossed by two railroads, which introduced whiskey sellers who would get his young men drunk and in trouble.[39] Beede recommended instructing the Western Shoshoni that their rations would be given out only at Fort Hall and nowhere else — all to no avail, as the Nevada Indians refused to move.[40]

The deliberate decision by Washington to curtail and finally to eliminate the distribution of rations at Fort Hall in an attempt to force the Indians to support themselves by farming led to much suffering. Special Agent Beede, in his visit to Fort Hall, found the Shoshoni and Bannock "really suffering for want of necessary food." They received only two pounds of beef and one and three-quarter pounds of flour per week instead of the regular Indian Department appropriation of ten and a half pounds of beef and three and a half pounds of flour. He said, "They cannot put in their crops on empty stomachs" and recommended a substantial increase in the appropriation for rations. His plea went unheeded.[41]

Understandably, both Beede and Agent Cook were able to report an increase in the number of Indians engaged in farming. Beede estimated that three-fourths of the Shoshoni were farmers but only one-fourth of the Bannock. In 1884 Indian farmers on 593 acres at Fort Hall raised 18,650 bushels of produce, including 3,000 bushels of wheat, 8,000 bushels of oats, 5,000 bushels of potatoes, and 1,000 tons of hay.[42]

The urgent need for a "flouring mill" had already been mentioned by Beede,[43] but two of the Indian leaders undertook to write personal letters to the Indian Department and to the President of the United States asking for a gristmill. Gibson Jack explained that during the previous year the Indians "lost lots of wheat . . . on account of not having any." The chief of the Shoshoni also castigated Agent Cook because "he Never gos any where to see the Indians or sends any one to instruct them."[44] In a second letter Shoshoni Jim supported Gibson Jack's assertions.[45] In his 1885 report the commissioner explained the above lack of instruction in farming. He devoted a large por-

1885

tion of his comments to the need for "additional farmers" at the various reservations and specifically mentioned Fort Hall.[46]

The subject of the differences between the Shoshoni and Bannock appeared again in 1885. Agent Cook expostulated on the Bannock's stubborn refusal to work, while accepting their share of the diminishing amount of rations allowed the Fort Hall Indians. Cook had a difficult time explaining to the Shoshoni farmers why they had to work hard while the "improvident" Bannock received equal rations for doing nothing. He still cautioned that it was better to feed the Bannock than not to provide food, which would surely be "disastrous" and lead to the Bannock killing cattle "to sustain themselves."[47]

The agent's fears were well illustrated in June 1885 when he sent his Indian police to arrest two Bannock accused of stealing horses from Wind River Agency. The two thieves killed one of the policemen and were, in turn, shot to death by a posse of 150 of their own tribesmen, under the direction of Chief Tyhee.[48] Cook became quite alarmed over the critical situation and for a time spoke of the need for calling in troops.[49] As a result of the incident five of the Bannock threatened to shoot some whites, but Cook believed the excitement would die down. Chief Tyhee demanded presents for himself and posse members for saving the agency from destruction.

Utah State Historical Society

"Ration Day" at Fort Hall Agency.

Cook advised that Tyhee's efforts to prevent an outbreak should be recognized; in the interim he presented gifts of sugar and coffee to the Tyhee group to "quiet them."[50]

1886 A. L. Cook left such problems to a new agent by resigning in March 1886 to open a trading store at Pocatello. The official post trader, the firm of Campbell & Walker, immediately objected on the grounds that their company was the only one to be licensed to trade with the Indians.[51] The transformation from agent to trader seemed to be a logical step for many of the Fort Hall agents. Or the reverse might be true — as when trader S. G. Fisher, long-time friend of the Shoshoni and Bannock, was named agent in 1888 and served in that position for four years.[52]

Part-Time Farmers, Occasional Hunters

Peter Gallagher took over the Fort Hall Agency from Cook and for the next three years swamped the Washington office with verbose and chatty letters. Nevertheless, he did a fairly creditable job as agent. A major concern during his first year was a matter which would occupy the attention of the agency for a decade until a court decision would settle it — the right of the Shoshoni and Bannock to hunt on the unoccupied lands of the United States as outlined in the 1868 Treaty of Fort Bridger. The first major incident involving this privilege occurred in May 1886 when some white ranchers living in Beaver Canyon on the Idaho-Montana border just west of Yellowstone Park protested the practice of the Lemhi and Fort Hall Indians who burned the grass to drive game to waiting hunters.[53] After a long investigation and an even longer report Gallagher concluded that, although a few Indians were hunting in the area, many of the fires were probably started by careless white campers. The Bannock, who were naturally blamed by the ranchers for the fires, denied having committed any depredations in the area. Gallagher explained, "They get credit for a great deal more crime than they are entitled to." In fact, he said, "The Indians in endeavoring to procure meat for winter use are interfering with some white men who make their living chiefly by hunting and trapping." The agent insisted on the right of the Indians to hunt on the unoccupied lands because a "strict confinement to the reservation" would retard rather than aid their advancement.[54]

After five months on the job Agent Gallagher reported in 1886 that "farming operations, like many other things, might be written as a burlesque on civilization." He found that part of the problem was insufficient ration supplies, which provided only one-fourth of the amount required "to sustain life." The Indians subsisted themselves by acquiring another fourth of their food from

hunting and fishing, while the remainder came as the result of toil on their farms. Gallagher proclaimed the hard doctrine, "By the sweat of thy face shalt thou eat bread" and declared the end of the "go-easy" times.[55]

In a long year-end report he recommended moving the agency headquarters to Pocatello Creek as a more central location and drew a sad picture of the "rotted down" and "propped up" buildings. He concluded,

> I would beg of you that something be done for these unfortunates, for be assured if matters & things go unchanged much of the progress in the future will be in keeping with results attained in the past, & then we can make up our minds to have these Fort Hall Indians on our hands for generations to come, & that too at a pretty heavy cost.[56]

1887

Gallagher again requested more white farmers to help instruct the Indians in agriculture. He described the locations of the fifteen hundred Shoshoni and Bannock under his care — three hundred at Bannock Creek, two hundred at Portneuf, two hundred near Blackfoot, three hundred at upper Ross Fork, five hundred at lower Ross Fork and near the agency. The farming activities of all these Indians were being supervised by one employee. "Well, I forbear comment" was Gallagher's conclusion.[57]

Although he had further trouble with the Bannock, three of whom he had to jail for stealing horses from the Wyoming Arapaho, he explained that horse stealing had always been a favorite pastime of the Bannock, and certainly the Shoshoni also, but that he had hopes of getting the "obstreperous Bannocks" to settle down to farming. He thought he had no right to complain because during the previous year the Bannock, with no help or direction at all, had sowed and reaped four hundred bushels of wheat, "and among these some of the hardest cases among them."[58] Gallagher seemed to be a practical, fair-minded man, of whom Special Indian Agent William Parsons could say, "Agent Gallagher seemed to be a very competent and faithful officer" who had the goodwill and confidence of the Indians and who maintained excellent discipline on the reservation.[59]

The agent was not held in that kind of high regard by James S. Campbell of the post trading firm of Campbell & Walker, mentioned earlier. Campbell accused Gallagher of supporting the rival trading company of S. G. Fisher. In denouncing Gallagher as a "dam'd rascal" he also called the Commissioner of Indian Affairs "a dam'd old crank, and a son of a b——."[60] The commissioner thought the language "not lacking in expression" but heeded the advice of investigator William Parsons that Campbell be dropped from the firm or the company's license be revoked.[61] Both the commissioner and the agent had a petition from the Indians asking for

Campbell's removal because he did not give them good prices, spoke "with two tongues," and used obscene language "even to cursing his own children," which horrified the Indians.[62]

The Shoshoni and Bannock supported Peter Gallagher in the controversy over the post trader and seemed to like and respect the agent. He reciprocated their feelings. He was an enthusiastic supporter of their efforts to become farmers and reported significant gains for them. From 1885 to 1888 the number of acres under cultivation at Fort Hall increased from 773 to 1,130, the number of mowing machines and rakes from 25 to 71, and the number of tons of hay cut from 825 to 2,500. As Gallagher expressed it, "What hath God wrought!" in just three short years.[63]

1888

He discounted the many rumors during 1888 that the Bannock were going on the warpath again:

The Bannocks have given themselves some little notoriety, for a small band, by their love of "heap fight"; but whilst given to deeds of boldness and daring in the past, and as much as going to war more than once, and furthermore put down by my predecessors as an obstreperous and ungovernable kind of human beings — far different from the Shoshones in this respect, and which I think too true — still I must say of them, since my assuming charge they have given me comparatively but little trouble.[64]

Gallagher replied to a letter of complaint from the superintendent of Yellowstone Park that Fort Hall Indians had annoyed park visitors for the past two summers. The agent defended his Indians, saying he did not believe they were "guilty as charged," although they may have hunted outside the boundaries of the park.[65]

Responding to two petitions from ranchers on big Lost River that during the preceding year Indians from Lemhi and Fort Hall did "Kill Maim and Runn off" stock from the various ranges, Gallagher first asked for specifics and then reported that the Fort Hall Indians "deny in toto" the charges made against them by the Custer County settlers.[66]

A final and rather ludicrous scare occurred in the Owyhee area when the settlers became frightened at the sight of two hundred Indians hunting in the region. They hastily moved their families to safety and called for troops; supposedly the Bannock from Fort Hall were preparing for another war. Even the *Idaho Statesman* ridiculed the sending of troops reporting, "It will be a picnic for the boys" and "The Brave Soldiers Sleep on their Arms." When the troops returned the paper announced, "An Advance guard came in [to Boise] early in the morning to see if it were safe for the rest." There was even a rumor that six people had been killed by Indians at Fort Hall.[67] Throughout all the rumors and complaints Agent Gallagher promised to do his best to keep the Indians on the reservation.

The following year additional concern about Shoshoni and Bannock roaming through Yellowstone Park was addressed to the Department of the Interior by the Boone & Crocket Club of New York City. The distinguished members, in a meeting held at the Knickerbocker Club, resolved that the Fort Hall Indians should not be allowed within twenty-five miles of the park to stop their destruction of forests and game. The memorial was signed by Theodore Roosevelt as president of the club and included, among other intrepid frontiersmen, the names of Rutherford Stuyvesant, Phillip Schuyler, Carl Schurz, and George Bird Grinnell.[68]

1889

Of more importance to the Shoshoni and Bannock was the melancholy news that Peter Gallagher was being replaced as agent. A new Republican administration in Washington now had the pleasant duty of dispensing patronage, and Indian agencies were particularly vulnerable to the spoils system. In his last report Gallagher struck a final blow for his Indians by explaining that a large part of the crop had been lost due to low water conditions for irrigation. He not only asked for an improved system but concluded with an appeal, "If the tribes, as a whole, had but enough last year to sustain life, how are they to get along this year with but the same amount of bread and meat contributed by the Government to their support, which at best is not more than a fourth of what is needed to live."[69] Through a stroke of luck (and the support of such powerful friends as General O. O. Howard) Stanton G. Fisher, longtime friend and neighbor of the Fort Hall Indians, took over as Gallagher's replacement on July 29, 1889. As one of his friends said, if Fisher should ever be at fault as agent, it would be because he would look "too much from the Indian standpoint."[70] To the Shoshoni and Bannock this was a very desirable fault.

Although he was as valiant as Gallagher in his efforts for the betterment of the tribes, Stanton Fisher was, from his point of view, realistic about the Indians among whom he had lived for so long. In a "plain facts" and not a "rose-colored" first annual report in 1890 he wrote that the advancement of the Shoshoni and Bannock over the past eight years had been "almost imperceptible."

1890

All they want is enough to eat, with as little exertion on their part as possible. Half rations with no work is preferred to a full stomach that requires manual labor to fill. They are entirely devoid of gratitude, chronic growlers, never satisfied with what is being done for them, shiftless, careless, wasteful, and extravagant, taking no need for the morrow, and what is worse for the long winter before them.[71]

The balance of the report indicated more progress and hope for Indian improvement than his pessimistic conclusion portrayed. He concluded that the main reason for lack of interest in farming on the part of his wards was the absence of a good irrigation system to provide water for the crops, as not "one in ten" who was willing to till the soil had any water supply.

With such conditions at home it was perhaps understandable that the Shoshoni and Bannock resorted to their old habits and went hunting and visiting, showing up at other reservations to visit friends and ask for rations. Their friends also came to see them. For example, Little Wolf and ten other Arapaho asked for passes to visit Fort Hall for a period of sixty days and, of course, expected to stand in the ration line each week.[72]

The movement of small groups of Shoshoni and Bannock brought the usual complaints from settlers during 1890. There was a petition from settlers in Malheur County, Oregon, asking that the Bannock in their neighbornood be returned to Fort Hall;[73] a citizen of Butte, Montana, asked that Fort Hall Indians be kept away from his slaughterhouse;[74] Yellowstone Park officials complained of Indians from the Idaho agency killing game south of the park;[75] and some miners from Cariboo, Idaho, charged the Indians with starting forest fires and destroying timber needed for mining purposes.[76] Fisher answered the last accusation by saying he was sure the fires were started by white campers, some of whom did so deliberately to get the Indians "driven back to their reservation."[77]

1891

Stanton Fisher hoped to be able to settle the Indians on farms to avoid the annual wanderings off the reservation. He thought that "with water in sight" and despite "the efforts of the old 'beefeaters' " he could get the younger Indians started as farmers. He hoped to be able to make a more favorable report in this respect in 1893.[78]

1892

Having survived an attack on his administration by six disgruntled Indians (whose interview with a local newspaper was entitled "A rotten Indian Agency") he was pleased when other Indian leaders called a special council to defend him with such comforting reassurances as "He is firm as the pine tree. . . . His character is like the eagle, above reproach."[79] Nevertheless he resigned early in 1893 to pursue some mining interests. He was succeeded on July 1, 1893, by Captain J. T. Van Orsdale.[80]

1893

Fisher would have been pleased with his successor's report that "considerable advancement" had been made by the Indians in agriculture, with about 130 families engaged.[81] While commending advances in farming, a special inspector, John Lane, was not as charitable in describing the condition of the agency buildings, reporting they were dilapidated and "in truth nearly uninhabitable," while the slaughterhouse was "in a miserable condition."[82]

1894

Like agents before him, Van Orsdale had to spend too much time with foreign affairs, while his domestic policies suffered. In September 1894 he was forced to take time off from his agency duties to travel to Silver City in southwestern Idaho to investigate reports that Bannock were committing depredations in the area. He found a large group of Western Shoshoni and three lodges of Bannock engaged in hunting wild game.[83] After ordering the Bannock back to Fort Hall, he returned to face a more serious affair with Wyoming officials, who were becoming quite angry over the so-called slaughter of game in the Jackson Hole and Yellowstone Park area.

Governor John E. Osborne of Wyoming had written a sharp letter to the commissioner of Indian Affairs the previous December demanding that Indians from Fort Hall, Lemhi, Wind River, and Crow reservations never be allowed to leave their agencies.[84] The commissioner responded by sending a circular to all Indian agents warning them not to allow their Indians to kill wild game merely for the hides, allowing the carcasses to go unused. This, he said, was a violation of treaty rights granted the Indians. Furthermore, Indians who received passes for visits to friends and then violated the permits by going on hunting expeditions would be prohibited from leaving their reservation again and would also be liable to arrest and punishment by state officials for violating the game laws of the various states.[85]

When a report was circulated in April 1894 that Fort Hall Indians were seen killing game in Yellowstone Park, Van Orsdale denied that any of his wards were involved.[86] He did have to investigate a more serious charge leveled by petitions from three different groups of citizens in Wyoming that Indians from Fort Hall had "wantonly" killed at least twenty and perhaps more elk "for the hides alone." The petitions were sent to the members of Congress for Wyoming.[87] Van Orsdale replied that the Shoshoni and Bannock had a treaty right to hunt on unoccupied lands of the United States and therefore state laws "cannot reach them." He said Fort Hall Indians hunted mostly in the Cariboo and Snake River mountains, which were in Idaho. In conclusion, he explained that "Eastern and foreign" hunters annually hunted in Jackson Hole for the "pleasure of killing," during which they kept only horns of the animals. He pointed out that certain local guides were involved in that business, which was more reprehensible than any hunting done by Indians.[88]

Troubles with Agent Teter

In order to understand the developing situation about Indian hunting in the Jackson Hole area which led to legal and court action, it will be helpful first to review the relationship between the Shoshoni and Bannock and Van Orsdale's successor, Thomas B. Teter, who became agent, early in 1895. From the beginning of his two-year ad-

1895

ministration Teter displayed a penchant for losing friends and alienating people. Anonymous Indian letter writers started the attack in February 1895 by accusing Teter of "Heap cheatin indian take him indian land for whiteman heap steel indian money for water for whiteman. . . . All indian say Teters no good no like him."[89]

In April 209 Fort Hall Indians petitioned Governor William J. McConnell, listing such grievances as insufficient rations, Teter's fear of the Indians (demonstrated by his carrying a pistol when he visited them), and his greater concern for the white citizens of Pocatello than the Indians, particular in getting a canal built across the reservation to the town.[90]

Significantly, both the *Idaho Herald* and the *Pocatello Tribune* came to Teter's defense, claiming he had done more than any previous agent to open the reservation to white settlement and to get a canal built to Pocatello. A counter petition was circulated in the town, representing nine-tenths of the taxpayers of Bannock County, asking that Teter be retained at Fort Hall. The newspaper attacked Mr. and Mrs. A. W. Fisher, residents of Pocatello — especially Mrs. Fisher, who as a long-time friend of the Indians was purportedly the instigator of the Indian petition to the governor in hopes that her husband would be named agent to replace Teters.[91] The commissioner settled this controversy by announcing that Teter was "a very efficient and trustworthy officer" and that, should a vacancy occur, under no circumstances would A. W. Fisher be appointed to fill the position.[92]

Agent Teter then sued the Fishers on charges of inciting the Indians and disturbing the peace of the United States by telling them that if Mr. Fisher were agent they wouldn't have to send their children to school, there would be no canal built across their land to Pocatello, and they would be properly fed. The charges were dismissed for lack of evidence.[93] In final defense of himself Teter wrote the commissioner denouncing certain Agency employees who had attacked him. He concluded his letter with, "It would reflect more credit upon them and their positions, if their wives would not have so many gentlemen friends, and some would kiss their husbands good by, instead of disreputable young men of Pocatello and perhaps other places good by."[94]

After a summer of relative peace and quiet, the personnel war started again when the Shoshoni and Bannock, in a deliberate provocation of their agent, met in council and solemnly proclaimed Mrs. Mary Wise Fisher as "Bee-ah" or "Mother of the Bannock and Shoshoni Indians," a signal honor which granted her certain privileges of visitation as a "field matron."[95] A month earlier Teter had posted an official notice in the

Bureau of American Ethnology

Jim Ballard

Pocatello post office warning all the Fishers to stay off the reservation.[96]

Hard on the heels of the action naming Mrs. Fisher "Bee-ah" came other accusations directed at Teters. Isaac M. Yandell indicted the agent for driving a herd of cattle over his land thus destroying a crop worth $500, for stealing $70 from him, and for "sleeping with one of the white women employees" at the boarding school.[97] The last charge was substantiated during an investigation by the supervisor of Indian Schools, who reported that Mrs. Fannie Perkins, matron at the school, was called Teter's "white squaw" by the Indians.[98]

Teter defended Mrs. Perkins as an "excellent matron . . . active, industrious, and energetic."[99]

In a second and longer petition the Shoshoni and Bannock again asked for Teter's discharge, listing the following deficiencies and indictments: The agent was afraid of the Indians; he lied to them, promising seed if they would plow as much land as they could; he looked out for the interests of the whites instead of the Indians; he used Indian money to build a canal on Indian land for the use of whites; with the money allocated for purchase of cattle he bought cows which had no teeth and were so old they could hardly stand; he allowed white men to use Indian land and appropriate water and timber; he would not allow the Indian fathers and mothers to visit their sick children in school; the agent hired a farmer to instruct them, but the man could not even harness a horse; the Indians wanted A. W. Fisher to be their agent; and finally, "us Indians are poorer now than we were ten years ago when there was farmers then there is nothing but Sagebrush now."[100] Despite the Indian protest, the *Blackfoot News* insisted that the commissioner was "pleased with the management" at Fort Hall.[101]

1896

Some of the Bannock were not pleased, and in January 1896 Jim Ballard and about twenty other Bannock dragged Teter out of his office and prepared a rope to hang him. The Indian police, in true Hollywood fashion, showed up just in time to rescue him. They arrested Ballard and six other assailants. The next day the police, with true impartiality, arrested A. W. Fisher, who was caught traveling on the Fort Hall bottoms.[102] Jim Ballard swore in court that Mrs. Fisher had urged the Indians to remove Teter by force, which was the direct cause of their attack on the agent. Thereupon Mrs. Fisher was arrested and cited to appear before a federal grand jury, where the charges were dropped.[103] The *Pocatello Tribune* later reported that Ballard and five of his cohorts were to be tried at the agency "by a jury of their copper colored peers and a redskin judge as well."[104] The main complaint against the agent by Ballard was Teter's support of the construction of the canal, which the Indians looked upon as a fraud.

1897

As already mentioned, when a delegation of Shoshoni and Bannock went to Washington in January 1897 to consider approval of the Pocatello cession, they insisted they would not agree until Teter was removed as their agent. A. W. Fisher had wangled an invitation as one of the party, and Teter was sure that Fisher's intention was "to get my scalp."[105]

While the Indians were in Washington the Reverend A. H. Lyons, pastor of the Baptist Church of Pocatello and a resident there for nine years, was writing the commissioner recommending Teter's dismissal because "he and his associates are the biggest set of rascals that have adminis-

tered the office of the reservation and the inspectors and officials are chips from the same block." The reverend also could not recommend A. W. Fisher, whom he had come to know while the latter was a justice of the peace and involved in "crooked work while in office." He asked for a western man who was honest and truly concerned for the interests of the Indians.[106]

The commissioner answered the various accusations by sending Inspector J. George Wright to make a through investigation of the Fort Hall Agency. In a ten-page report Wright listed the following charges against Teter and his chief clerk, Ravenel McBeth: Teter had been promised $6,000 by the citizens of Pocatello provided he could get the reservation opened to settlement by July 1, 1895; in two councils held, the Indians bitterly complained about the agent's domineering and autocratic methods with them; clerk McBeth, who practically ran the agency, had his accounts in "a most unsatisfactory condition"; Teter dealt with a Pocatello lumber merchant whose prices were twice as high as most other dealers, who were given no opportunity to bid on lumber for the reservation; inferior lumber or no lumber at all had been delivered to the agency, and payments were made for the materials; coal was ordered and paid for, although the mill for which it was intended had not been in operation for a year; there had been peculation in beef herds; McBeth had demanded and received a bribe of $100 from a cattleman who sold forty bulls to the agency; and finally, Inspector Wright reported, "I have lost all confidence in both McBeth and Agent Teter, and in my opinion they should both be removed."[107] Teter was discharged February 24, 1897, and Lieutenant Francis C. Irwin, Jr., was named acting Indian agent at Fort Hall.[108]

The "Jackson Hole War"

The above narrative of the internal troubles at Fort Hall during Teter's administration may help explain the additional anger and frustration of the Shoshoni and Bannock when an incident occurred in Jackson Hole, Wyoming, in July 1895 which started a series of events leading to loss of their cherished right to hunt on the unoccupied public lands of the United States — as proclaimed by Article 4 of the Fort Bridger Treaty of 1868. On July 17 Governor W. A. Richards of Wyoming telegraphed the Office of Indian Affairs that nine Indians had been arrested at Marysvale, Wyoming, in Jackson Hole on July 15, that one had been killed in an escape attempt, and that troops were needed at once to protect the lives of the settlers. While there were many law-abiding citizens in the Jackson Hole Country there were also outlaws, many of whom made a living by guiding hunting parties and who were determined to keep the Indians from interfering with their lucrative business. As the result of a preconceived plan, twenty-seven of these settlers captured and disarmed a hunting party of nine Indians with their families and supplies. After a whole day's march (and apparently upon a prearranged signal) the white men began to load cartridges into the empty chambers of their guns. Thinking they were to be killed, the Indians made a break for the woods. During the melee one Indian was killed and another seriously wounded. Two children were lost; one was never found.[109]

Troops were dispatched at once to the scene of trouble, while opponents and proponents took to the pen in discussing the incident. Easterners first established that a group of Princeton University students were safe and then began to attack Constable William Manning and his group for brutally murdering the Indian. Messages poured in to the Office of Indian Affairs from the Attorney General's Office, the U.S. Board of Indian Commissioners, the American Sunday School Union, the president of Oberlin College, and others, all denouncing the outrage upon innocent Indians who were pursuing their treaty rights to hunt for a winter's supply of meat.[110]

1895 Idaho newspapers ridiculed the "war," gotten up for the selfish benefit of about twenty-five big-game guides and their determined supporters. The "war" was taken up with gusto by the eastern press, which had not had the pleasure of covering an Indian outbreak for some years. Wyoming officials were just as vehement in denouncing the bloodthirsty redskins and demanding their removal once and for all back to the reservation. The frightened Indians had scurried back to the shelter of Fort Hall but once there had begun to breathe defiance and talk of deputizing three of their number to avenge the death of their comrade.[111]

General J. J. Coppinger, in charge of troop movements, denounced the unwarranted shooting of defenseless Indians,[112] while Agent Teter demanded that Governor Richards be held as an accessory to the act of murder.[113] All soldiers were soon returned to their posts, including the ones sent to Fort Hall during the height of the excitement. Perhaps J. M. Ingersoll, writing from Laramie, Wyoming, best summarized the incident:

For years past the Indian Department has pretended to hold the Indians on a Reservation that is barren and unproductive for want of irrigation, without doing anything to improve it, thereby compelling the Indian to roam miles away from his reservation in search of something to eat . . . . However, it is now evident to all that the Indians former hunting grounds and the game are about all gone from him forever, even if the courts should decide that he has the right to hunt. Starvation will still slap him in the face, so really there is nothing left for the poor Indian to do but to fight, steal or beg until his reservation is improved and made productive, so that he can live at home in peace and plenty.[114]

To quiet the Shoshoni and Bannock and keep them from going out on other hunting parties to get a winter's supply of meat, the commissioner increased the amount of rations at Fort Hall and authorized eight Bannock to go to the scene of the trouble in Jackson Hole to recover the equipment left behind by the Indians who were involved in the "massacre." The equipment included twenty saddles, twenty blankets, one horse, nine packs of meat, and nine tepees.[115]

The commissioner, the agent, and the Justice Department all called for the arrest and trial of Manning and the others for their crime but were convinced that "there are no officials in Jackson Hole — county, State, or national — who would hold any of Mannings posse for trial," including Governor Richards, who had assured the settlers he would back them in driving the Indians out of Wyoming and keeping them out.[116]

During his investigation Teter reported that the settlers evinced bitter feelings towards him, refused to give him information, and threatened to hang him. The agent seemed to figure prominently in threats of lynching, both on the reservation and in Wyoming. He also learned that Constable Manning had said, "We knew very well when we started in on this thing that we would bring matters to a head. We knew someone was going to be killed, perhaps some on both sides, and we decided the sooner it was done the better, so we could get the matter before the courts."[117]

In September 1895 the commissioner attempted to resolve the question of Shoshoni and Bannock treaty rights to hunt on the unoccupied lands by proposing to Governor Richards that a test case be arranged, under which an Indian would be arrested for violating the hunting laws of Wyoming and then be tried in circuit court. The governor agreed. Inspector McCormick of the Office of Indian Affairs thereupon took Race Horse, a Bannock, and one other Indian from Fort Hall to Evanston, Wyoming, on October 3 to have them ready to appear before Judge Riner.[118] Agent Teter had been very careful "to keep them in ignorance, owing to the bad effect it would have upon the Indians on the reservation"[119] Two days later Teter held a council with the Indians to explain the purpose of the test case and found them willing to abide by the decision of the court.

The case was tried before Judge Riner, who on November 21, 1895, directed that the laws of Wyoming were "invalid against the treaty rights of the Indians" and affirmed the right of the Shoshoni and Bannock to continue to hunt on the unoccupied lands. The decision was immediately appealed to the U.S. Supreme Court, which on May 25, 1896, reversed the judgment of the circuit court. By this time Agent Teter had already told the Indians the good news of the Riner decision, so he now had the difficult task of trying to 1896 explain to them the later Supreme Court ruling which meant that their carefree hunting days were over.[120] General J. J. Coppinger thought it unjust that their highly prized privilege acquired by treaty was "legally terminated without their assent."[121]

Judge Riner then demanded that Race Horse be turned over to the state sheriff to stand trial and be punished for having broken Wyoming state law. The attorney general patiently explained that Race Horse was involved in a test case and should in no way be punished, but Judge Riner wanted to ensure that the Fort Hall Indians understood the meaning of the Supreme Court decision and thought a trial was the only way the Indians would understand what had taken place.[122] An appeal was made to Governor Richards, who also was adamant and, in fact, even refused a bond of $500 for Race Horse to ensure his appearance at Court in Evanston on September 7. Agency clerk McBeth was forced to furnish the bond out of his own pocket.[123]

When Judge Jesse Knight of the Third Judicial District of Wyoming prepared to try Race Horse on September 7 and then immediately release him without punishment, the Indian was nowhere to be found. Apparently he had gone on a hunting expedition with other Bannock and Shoshoni to the Jackson Hole Country. Governor Richards demanded that they be returned to Fort Hall at once. Agent Teter journeyed to Jackson Hole, where he found five Shoshoni families hunting. He returned them to the reservation.[124] Teter's Indian police found twenty-five Bannock hunters at Jackson Hole who refused to return to the reservation; white settlers were encouraging them to stay and hunt so they could purchase the elk hides. Teter dispatched the police after the wanderers and said he would call for troops if the Indians did not return.[125] Teter did not go after the Bannock himself because he "did not intend to get shot in the back by some of the outlaws of the Hole." Finally a Wyoming constable arrested four of the Bannock party and placed them in jail in Evanston.[126] Race Horse eventually appeared before Judge Knight, received the proper message to carry back to his people, and was then released.

The decision of nine men sitting on the Supreme Court in far-away Washington would not deter the Fort Hall Indians from their traditional annual hunting forays. Realizing this, Agent Irwin in May 1897 wrote William Manning in Marysvale, Wyoming, suggesting that the constable arrest the first Bannock who slipped away unnoticed from the reservation and showed up in Jackson Hole to do a little elk hunting. In return Manning suggested disarming the Shoshoni and Bannock to prevent any hunting by them anywhere. After the usual referrals to various officials, Agent Irwin effectively stopped the proposal

by explaining that the Indians could replace their weapons very easily in the nearby towns of Pocatello and Blackfoot.[127]

As a final aftermath of the "Jackson Hole War" the Governor of Idaho telegraphed the Office of Indian Affairs on June 28, 1897, that three hundred dangerous Bannock were at Camas Prairie threatening the settlers. Other telegrams flew back and forth, troops were alerted, and city newspapers asked for "at least two hundred words Indian trouble." Agent Irwin's investigation revealed about forty Shoshoni from the Lemhi Reservation and Bliss, Idaho, with a few from Fort Hall, peacefully digging camas root, chasing ground squirrels, and engaging in their annual Grass Dance. The origin of the scare was apparently one rancher who wanted the Indians removed because his frightened wife had left home; he was lonely and wanted her to return.[128]

The *Pocatello Tribune's* account was headlined "Tis Love Not War" and explained that the Grass Dance was a traditional occasion when the "dusky brave wooes the timid Indian maiden and bears her away to her lodge."[129] Local businessmen in Hailey, Idaho, were disappointed that the Indians would not be able to participate in the horse races — but the order forcing the Indians back to Fort Hall before the camas harvest was complete was a more serious matter for the tribesmen. There might well be another starving time at Fort Hall the following winter.

Confined to the Reservation

Some nonreservation Indians accustomed to digging camas at the prairie and living apart from Indian Office supervision were skeptical about life at Fort Hall. Senator George L. Shoup forwarded a letter to the commissioner of Indian Affairs in February 1898 recommending that an inspector be sent to try to induce a band of Shoshoni on the North Fork of Payette River and a second group of "Weiser" Indians now living near Bliss, Idaho, to move to Fort Hall where they could be rescued from their "destitute" condition.[130] When the agent from the reservation visited the Weisers at Camas Prairie, Old Tom and Captain Jack, the headmen, were emphatic about not going to a reservation, chiefly because there was no hunting and the rations issued were sufficient for only two days a week. As they expressed it, "two days eat, five days no eat." They finally agreed to move to Fort Hall if the government would promise them rations for seven days a week plus $100 and a new wagon apiece, which the agent could not do. He reported, "I find they have a great many horses, and by hunting, fishing, and root digging live pretty well."[131] Additional support for their wish to remain near Bliss came from the white settlers there, who asked that the Indians be allowed to

Idaho State Historical Society

Uncle Tom

a class the residents on this reserve are naturally as worthless & shiftless a lot of human beings as are to be found anywhere in the North West." McConnell did speak highly of Agent Irwin, who was just completing his tour of duty.[136]

Acquainted with conditions in the Pocatello area, C. A. Warner showed much promise during his first year as agent. His unfortunate death late in 1899 brought a special agent, Elisha B. Reynolds, to serve in an acting capacity until March 5, 1900, when A. F. Caldwell, postmaster at Pocatello, was offered the post.[137] Major Caldwell, a veteran of the Civil War and long-time resident of Pocatello, was a most fortunate choice for the Shoshoni and Bannock.[138] He served as agent for ten years, during which he gained the respect and good wishes of both the Indians and the citizens of Pocatello — an unusual feat. His administration marked not only the start of a new century but also the beginning of a final transformation at Fort Hall of a nomadic group of hunters into a sedentary, industrious people who faced the realities of reservation boundaries which were no longer imaginary.

Caldwell's first annual report reflected this vision when he announced that he was listing the Shoshoni and Bannock as a combined tribe of

1899
1900

Idaho State Historical Society

stay as long as no other tribesmen were permitted to come into the area.[132]

By this time, June 7, 1898, F. G. Irwin had left the agency at Fort Hall; C. A. Warner, a native of Pocatello and a lawyer, had been appointed to replace him. Warner reported that none of the Indians had visited Jackson Hole during the year.[133] Perhaps one way in which he attempted to keep the Bannock leaders content was by building houses for them. At least independent Jim Ballard received a new house from the agent.[134]

Warner was quite restrained in his first evaluation of the two tribes under his care, commenting that the Bannock "prefer to remember their warrior fathers, and think it disgraceful to work," while the Shoshoni were "quiet" and industrious individuals. Both were "temperate and moral people."[135] His remarks were in sharp contrast to Inspector W. J. McConnell, who reported that "as

A. F. Caldwell, Superintendent at Fort Hall, with three Shoshoni Women.

HOME ON THE RESERVATION   139

1,395 individuals because they were so intermarried that it was almost impossible to distinguish them. In his conclusion he essayed an overly optimistic note by writing, "Many of these Indians are now self-supporting, and . . . if all governmental aid were withdrawn, they would continue to live, and live well, too."[139] He was to discover a few obstacles on the high road to success, most of them having to do with getting water for crops.

One of the noteworthy events of Caldwell's term at Fort Hall was the final removal of the Lemhi from their small reservation near Salmon City. After more than thirty years of effort the Office of Indian Affairs finally succeeded in getting the tribe to move to the larger reservation during the spring of 1907. They were well-accepted by their friends and relatives at Fort Hall and soon settled in to learn the arts of agriculture. Another narrative recites their hundred-year history under the guidance of the memorable Chief Tendoy, who didn't live to make the final journey to the Snake River reservation.

The twenty-five year period after 1880 was one of frustration and trouble with agents. Some were incompetent or not sympathetic to tribal culture; others tried hard as good administrators to meld the Shoshoni and Bannock into a different civilization but found the lack of funds and white hostility and encroachment very serious impediments. Bannock independence and occasional recalcitrance tended to alienate most of the agents to a display of favoritism toward the more peaceful and sedentary Shoshoni. When the Fort Hall post was closed in 1883, agency officials showed some apprehension about the loss of a military presence to overcome the Bannock.

Much of the period was taken up with complaints from white citizens about the Fort Hall Indians roaming about off the reservation and hunting in areas which were coming to be looked upon as white preserves. The troubles in Jackson Hole resulted in the Supreme Court decision which ended hunting on the unoccupied lands of the United States. This rather abruptly ended most permits to leave Fort Hall, and the Shoshoni and Bannock became truly reservation Indians.

An accompanying process was the attempt by Washington officials to move the Duck Valley and

Idaho State Historical Society

Summer tipi made of interwoven rushes and willows.

Lemhi residents to Fort Hall. The Western Shoshoni were successful in retaining their reservation, but the Lemhi finally capitulated and moved to Snake River, where Indian officials hoped to consolidate the Northern Shoshoni and Bannock into an economic and self-sufficient people by making individual farmers and stockmen out of them.

With the Lemhi tribe settled at Fort Hall, the reservation could now enter the twentieth century with its complement of Shoshoni and Bannock practically complete. All that remained was to establish the conditions which would make for successful farming and stock raising. To be able to describe the development of Fort Hall today, it is first necessary to trace the establishment of grazing and stock growing on the reservation, the construction of an irrigation system, and the growth of industry. The first was easier and less complicated to get underway, so a review of the history of the Shoshoni and Bannock as cattle raisers will be next in order.

NOTES CHAPTER VIII
HOME ON THE RESERVATION

1. *Blackfoot Register*, January 1, 1881.
2. Ibid., Feb. 19, 1881.
3. John R. Richards and Seven Others to C.I.A., March 1, 1881, U.S. National Archives, *Records, Office of Indian Affairs*.
4. *Blackfoot Register*, March 12, 1881.
5. Ibid., April 9, 1881.
6. Ibid., July 15, 1882.
7. *C.I.A. Annual Report, 1882*, 121.
8. John A. Wright to C.I.A., April 11, 18, 1881, U.S. National Archives, *Records, Office of Indian Affairs*.
9. E. A. Stone to C.I.A., Aug. 9, 17, 1881, ibid.
10. E. A. Stone to C.I.A., Sept. 20, 1881, ibid.
11. A. L. Cook to John S. Mayhugh, Oct. 9, 1882, ibid.
12. Arden Smith to C.I.A., Nov. 30, 1882, ibid.
13. Smith to C.I.A., May 9, 1882, ibid.; *Idaho Statesman*, May 16, 1882.
14. Ibid., May 20, 1882.
15. George B. Sanford to Dept. of California, Sept. 29, 1882, U.S. National Archives, *Records, Office of Indian Affairs*.
16. *C.I.A. Annual Report, 1882*, 109–10.
17. Jesse K. Dubois to C.I.A., April 4, 1882, U.S. National Archives, *Records, Office of Indian Affairs*.
18. Ada Fant to C.I.A., April 1, 1882, ibid.
19. W. C. Borland to C.I.A., Sept. 21, 1882, ibid.
20. W. D. Monnet to C.I.A., Oct. 6, 1882, ibid.
21. A. L. Cook to C.I.A., Jan. 16, 1883, ibid.
22. A. L. Cook to C.I.A., April 9, 1883, ibid.
23. *Blackfoot Register*, Dec. 2, 1883.
24. *C.I.A. Annual Report, 1883*, 111.
25. *Blackfoot Register*, March 10, 1883.
26. *Salt Lake Herald*, March 14, 1883.
27. *Idaho Statesman*, May 1, 1883.
28. *Wood River News-Miner*, July 11, 1883.
29. Ibid., June 2, 1882.
30. Ibid., July 18, 1883; *Wood River Times*, Sept. 10, 1883; T. F. Singiser to Sec. of Interior, July 22, 1883, U.S. National Archives, *Records, Office of Indian Affairs*.
31. *Wood River Times*, Sept. 10, 1883.
32. *Idaho Statesman*, Oct. 2, 1883; *Blackfoot Register*, Oct. 6, 1883.
33. *Wood River News-Miner*, May 4, 1883; *Blackfoot Register*, May 5, July 7, 1883.
34. *Report of Secretary of War*, U.S. Congress, House, 48th Cong., 1st Sess., Exec. Doc. 1, Part 2, Vol. 1, Serial No. 2182 (Wash., D.C., 1883), 125.
35. Cyrus Beede to C.I.A., Jan. 26, 1884, U.S. National Archives, *Records, Office of Indian Affairs*.
36. Cyrus Beede to C.I.A., Jan. 28, 1884, ibid.
37. Cyrus Beede to C.I.A., Feb. 25, 1884, ibid.
38. John S. Mayhugh to Rep. George W. Cassidy, Feb. 26, 1884, ibid.
39. Cyrus Beede to C.I.A., March 3, 1886, ibid.
40. Cyrus Beede to C.I.A., Feb. 6, 1884, ibid.
41. Cyrus Beede to C.I.A., March 13, 1884, ibid.
42. Ibid.; *C.I.A. Annual Report, 1884*, 108; *Idaho Statesman*, May 6, 1884.
43. Cyrus Beede to C.I.A., March 13, 1884, U.S. National Archives, *Records, Office of Indian Affairs*.
44. Gibson Jack to Indian Department, July 8, 1884, ibid.
45. Shoshonee Jim to President of United States, July 9, 1884, ibid.
46. *C.I.A. Annual Report, 1885*, 26.
47. Ibid., 290–292.
48. Ibid., 292; A. L. Cook to C.I.A., June 25, 1885, U.S. National Archives, *Records, Office of Indian Affairs*.
49. A. L. Cook to C.I.A., June 21, 22, 1885, ibid.
50. A. L. Cook to C.I.A., June 25, 1885, ibid.
51. Campbell and Walker to Sec. of Interior, June 28, 1886, ibid.; E. D. Bannister to C.I.A., Oct. 13, 1885, U.S. National Archives, *Record Group No. 48*.
52. George L. Shoup to S. G. Fisher, June 13, 1886, Idaho State Historical Sociey, Ms. 106.
53. G. W. Rea to U.S. Land Commissioner, June 2, 1886, U.S. National Archives, *Records, Office of Indian Affairs*.
54. Series of Letters, G. W. Rea, P. Gallagher and others, May 16 to Sept. 22, 1886, ibid.
55. *C.I.A., Annual Report, 1886*, 325–326.
56. P. Gallagher to C.I.A., Dec. 2, 1886, U.S. National Archives, *Records, Office of Indian Affairs*.
57. *C.I.A. Annual Report, 1887*, 150.
58. P. Gallagher to C.I.A., Feb. 23, 1887, U.S. National Archives, *Records, Office of Indian Affairs*.
59. William Parsons to C.I.A., April 16, 1887, ibid.; R. S. Gardner to U.S. National Archives, May 13, 1887, U.S. National Archives, *Record Group No. 48*.
60. Series of Letters Pertaining to James S. Campbell, March 1, 1887, *Records, Office of Indian Affairs*.
61. William Parsons to C.I.A., April 16, 1887, ibid.
62. Series of Letters Pertaining to James S. Campbell, March 1, 1887, ibid.
63. *C.I.A. Annual Report, 1888*, 80.
64. Ibid., 83.
65. Moses Harris to Sec. of Interior, May 4, 1888, U.S. National Archives, *Records, Office of Indian Affairs*; P. Gallagher to C.I.A., June 16, 1888, ibid.
66. P. Gallagher to J. R. Pence, March 21, 1888, ibid.; J. R. Pence to P. Gallagher, April 4, 1888, ibid.; Joseph S. Kelton and 94 Others to Fred T. Dubois, May 17, 1888, ibid.; P. Gallagher to C.I.A., June 16, 1888, ibid.
67. Governor E. A. Stevenson to Sec. of Interior, June 20, 1888, U.S. National Archives, *Interior Dept. Territorial Papers, Idaho, 1864–1890*, Roll 2; *Idaho Statesman*, June 16, 19, 20, 21, 23, 26, 29, 1888.
68. George Bird Grinnell to Sec. of Interior, April 12, 1889, U.S. National Archives, *Records, Office of Indian Affairs*.
69. *C.I.A. Annual Report, 1887*, 174–180; Frank C. Armstrong to C.I.A., May 6, 1889, U.S. National Archives, *Record Group No. 48*; Bannock Jim et al to C.I.A., Oct. 24, 1889, U.S. National Archives, ibid.
70. Guy Howard to C.I.A., Oct. 5, 1889, Gen. O. O. Howard to S. G. Fisher, Oct. 1889, Idaho Historical Society, Ms. 106.
71. *C.I.A. Annual Report, 1890*, 76–78.
72. John Fisher to C.I.A., March 15, 1890, U.S. National Archives, *Records, Office of Indian Affairs*.
73. Petition from D. D. Munger and others to Sec. of Interior, April 29, 1890, ibid.
74. Fred Brown to Indian Department, June 3, 1890, ibid.
75. S. G. Fisher to C.I.A., Sept. 3, 1890, ibid.
76. W. S. Dalliba to Sec. of Interior, Sept. 13, 1890, ibid.
77. S. G. Fisher to C.I.A., Sept. 29, 1890, ibid.
78. *C.I.A. Annual Report, 1891*, 230.
79. Newspaper Clippings Concerning S. G. Fisher, Idaho State Historical Society, 1892, Ms. 106; Pat Lorgy et al to Pres. Grover Cleveland, April 11, 1893, U.S. National Archives, *Record Group No. 48*.
80. *C.I.A. Annual Report, 1893*, 135.
81. Ibid.
82. John Lane to C.I.A., Aug. 23, 1893, U.S. National Archives, *Records, Office of Indian Affairs*.
83. J. T. Van Orsdale to C.I.A., Sept. 3, 4, 1894, ibid.; *Pocatello Tribune*, Sept. 1, 1894.
84. John E. Osborne to C.I.A., Dec. 5, 1893, U.S. National Archives, *Records, Office of Indian Affairs*.
85. *C.I.A. Annual Report, 1894*, 66–67.
86. J. T. Van Orsdale to C.I.A., April 22, 1894, U.S. National Archives, *Records, Office of Indian Affairs*.
87. John C. Hamen to H. A. Cofeen, April 13, 1894, ibid.
88. J. T. Van Orsdale to C.I.A., April 26, 1894, ibid.
89. Anonymous letter to Sec. of Interior, Feb. 1895, ibid.
90. *Idaho Statesman*, Apr. 11, 1895; *Pocatello Tribune*, April 20, 1895.
91. *Idaho Herald*, April 12, 1895; *Pocatello Tribune*, April 20, 1895.
92. *Journal History*, L.D.S. Department of History, quotes Idaho Falls newspaper, April 26, 1895.
93. *Pocatello Tribune*, May 4, 1895.
94. T. B. Teters to C.I.A., July 1, 1895, U.S. National Archives, *Records, Office of Indian Affairs*.
95. A. W. Fisher to C.I.A., Nov. 2, 1895, ibid.; *Pocatello Tribune*, Oct. 19, 1895.
96. Ibid., Sept. 26, 1895.
97. Isaac M. Yandell to C.I.A., Oct. 25, 1895, U.S. National Archives, *Records, Office of Indian Affairs*.
98. A. H. Heinemann to Superintendent of Indian Schools, Oct. 26, 31, 1895, ibid.
99. T. B. Teter to C.I.A., Oct. 29, 1895, ibid.
100. Capt. Daniel T. Wells to Sec. of Interior, Oct. 28, 1895, ibid.
101. *Blackfoot News*, Dec. 21, 1895.
102. *Pocatello Tribune*, Jan. 18, 1896.
103. Ibid., Feb. 1, 1896.
104. Ibid., March 7, 1896.
105. Ibid., Jan. 23, 1897, T. B. Teter to C.I.A., Jan. 8, 1897, U.S. National Archives, *Records, Office of Indian Affairs*; see Ch. VIII, footnotes 22–24.

106. A. H. Lyons to C.I.A., Jan. 18, 1897, ibid.
107. J. Geo. Wright to Sec. of Interior, Feb. 10, 1897, ibid.
108. *Pocatello Tribune*, Feb. 27, 1897.
109. *C.I.A. Annual Report, 1895*, 60–80.
110. Ibid., Mary E. Garrett to C.I.A., July 22, 1895, U.S. National Archives, *Records, Office of Indian Affairs*; Philip G. Garrett to Sec. of War, July 30, 1895, ibid.; Addison P. Foster to C.I.A., Aug. 8, 1895, ibid.; W. G. Ballantine to C.I.A., Aug. 8, 1895, ibid.
111. *Pocatello Tribune*, July 27, Aug. 10, Dec. 14, 1895; *Deseret News*, Aug. 1, 1895.
112. "Report of Brig. Gen. J. J. Coppinger, Aug. 28, 1895," U.S. Congress, House, 54th Cong., 1st Sess., Doc. No. 2, Vol. 1 (Wash., D.C., 1895), 163.
113. T. B. Teter to C.I.A., Sept. 3, 1895, U.S. National Archives, *Records, Office of Indian Affairs*.
114. J. M. Ingersoll to Sec. of Interior, Oct. 10, 1895, ibid.
115. *C.I.A. Annual Report, 1895*, 60–80.
116. Ibid.
117. Ibid.
118. *C.I.A. Annual Report, 1896*, 56–70.
119. T. B. Teter to C.I.A., Oct. 10, 1895, U.S. National Archives, *Records, Office of Indian Affairs*.
120. *C.I.A. Annual Report, 1896*, 56–70.
121. "Report of Brig. Gen. J. J. Coppinger, Aug. 31, 1896, U.S. Congress, House, 54th Cong., 2d Sess., Doc. No. 2, Vol. 1 (Wash. D.C., 1896), 171.
122. *C.I.A. Annual Report, 1896*, 56–70.
123. T. B. Teter to C.I.A., July 27, 1896, U.S. National Archives, *Records, Office of Indian Affairs*.
124. Jesse Knight to C.I.A., Sept. 10, 16, 28, 1896, ibid.; T. B. Teter to C.I.A., Aug. 31, 1896, ibid.; T. B. Teter to C.I.A., Sept. 10, 1896, ibid.
125. T. B. Teter to C.I.A., Sept. 13, 17, 1896, ibid.
126. *Pocatello Tribune*, Sept. 19, 1896.
127. F. G. Irwin, Jr., to C.I.A., June 24, 1897, U.S. National Archives, *Records, Office of Indian Affairs*.
128. *C.I.A. Annual Report, 1897*, 68–71.
129. *Pocatello Tribune*, July 3, 14, 1897.
130. R. S. Browne to George L. Shoup, Jan. 31, 1898, U.S. National Archives, *Records, Office of Indian Affairs*.
131. C. A. Warner to C.I.A., June 27, 1898, ibid.
132. Petition from J. L. Baxter and others to Indian Agent, Ross Fork, Idaho July 6, 1898, ibid.
133. *C.I.A. Annual Report, 1898*, 141–143; *Pocatello Tribune*, May 4, 1898.
134. C. A. Warner to C.I.A., Nov. 12, 1898, U.S. National Archives, *Records, Office of Indian Affairs*.
135. *C.I.A. Annual Report, 1898*, 141–143.
136. W. J. McConnell to Sec. of Interior, April 12, 1898, U.S. National Archives, *Records, Office of Indian Affairs*.
137. *C.I.A. Annual Report, 1899*, 180–183; *Pocatello Tribune*, Dec. 13, 1899, March 21, 1900.
138. Ibid.; Arthur M. Tinker to Sec. of Int., Aug. 31, 1803, *Record Group 48*.
139. *C.I.A. Annual Report, 1900*, 215–217.

CHAPTER IX

RAISING CATTLE AT FORT HALL

Stage and Freight Lines on the Reserve

1847   With the establishment of the Mormons in Great Salt Lake Valley in 1847, there soon developed a trade between Salt Lake City and Fort Hall which was then in Oregon Territory. For the first three years Fort Hall helped supply Mormon
1851 settlers, but by 1851 the flow of goods was reversed as Brigham Young's people profited from the travel of the forty-niners and also as the Saints of Utah became fairly self-sufficient.[1]

During the 1850s this main route north to Fort Hall turned off from the mud-hut village of Malad to cross the Bannock range of mountains, descended along Bannock Creek, then continued in a northeasterly direction across Portneuf River to Fort Hall. From the head of Bannock Creek the road coursed through the Shoshoni-Bannock homeland.[2]

The intermittent but steady flow of wagons
1862 along this trail became a flood after the discovery of gold in July 1862 at Grasshopper Creek, soon to be Bannack City, Montana Territory. Eager gold miners, traveling by wagons, horseback, or "shank's mare," were soon followed by ox trains loaded with freight and seventeen-passenger Concord coaches swamped with as many as thirty-two pilgrims. The stagecoach business looked so promising that Ben Holladay projected a branch of his Overland Stage Company to Montana in early 1864 and changed the route from along Bannock Creek to a road following the Portneuf River from the bend north to Fort Hall. From the Malad Divide the new route still went through Shoshoni-Bannock lands. Furthermore,
1866 the Oneida Wagon Road Company was chartered by the Idaho Territorial Legislature on January 5, 1866, and tolls were exacted from all travelers over the Montana Trail as far as the Idaho-Montana boundary. The Indians received no compensation for the portion of the route which went through their lands.[3]

From 1862 until the narrow-gauge Utah and Northern Railroad reached Blackfoot, Idaho Territory, on December 27, 1878, wagon traffic from Salt Lake City (and later from Corinne) was constant and heavy, as the Montana Trail came to be the principal artery for the shipment of goods and passengers to isolated towns in western Montana. With the exception of a few weeks during the Bannock War of 1878, the Shoshoni-Bannock remained peaceful throughout this period, although several stagecoach companies and immigrants and freighters by the thousands grazed their stock along the road, cut timber for buildings and firewood, and in other ways disturbed the tranquility of the Indian inhabitants without any thought of recompense.

With the establishment of Fort Hall Indian 1869
Reservation by 1869, the United States government agreed to protect its Indian wards from the encroachments of travelers. It failed to do so — as indicated by the correspondence and reports of the agents, the commander of the Fort Hall military post, and private citizens. A typical case was that of the Oneida Wagon Road Company whose owner, William Murphy, with a charter from the Idaho Legislature, a tollgate on the reservation, and a six-gun strapped on his hip, defied the agent and the U.S. government — which he boldly said "had no right to interfere with him."[4] His company charged a freighter $8.00 toll for a wagon loaded with 4,500 pounds (an average load). The editor of the *Helena Herald* estimated that the firm made a profit of $15,000 or $20,000 per annum for travel on its "Port Neuf Canyon road." The *Corinne Reporter* spoke of the "enormous tolls" Murphy accumulated. Using the proposed figure of one-fourth of the toll to be paid the Indians, as outlined in the unratified Agree- 1873 ment of 1873, the Shoshoni-Bannock should have received a just compensation for the travel across their lands. Of course such a proposal would have been greeted with derision by Murphy and his customers alike during the 1870s.[5] One observant traveler, R. C. Knox, counted 862 wagons on the road in the summer of 1878. Usually freighters 1878 made three trips a year to Montana from the railroad depot at Corinne. There was, therefore, a very heavy south-north freight traffic across the reservation.[6] 1870

The toll road company also maintained a tollgate station at the bend of the Portnuef River (near present-day McCammon), collecting fares from passing vehicles. Freight stations or campsites were maintained on the reservation at Birch Creek, Marsh Creek, Harkness Station, Robber's Roost, Pocatello, and Ross Fork. These were more informal and less imposing establishments, but nevertheless they did exist and did take advantage of the resources of Indian lands.[7]

Stagecoach travel also demanded rest stops and stations for the weary travelers through the deserts of Idaho. There were swing stations about every ten or twelve miles where brief stops were made to change horses, and home stations at fifty-mile intervals where passengers could get meals. On the Fort Hall Reservation these were located at Marsh Valley, fourteen miles to Carpenter's (a home station), twelve miles to Robber's Roost, and thirteen miles to Ross Fork (a home station). As many as two coaches a day traveled the road during the summer months, but only three coaches a week tried to battle the snows between Utah and Montana in winter. Nevertheless, the annual stage travel through Fort Hall was heavy.[8] Both freighters and stage companies pastured their stock on reservation lands, with little thought of paying the Indians for the privilege.[9]

1871   The Gilmer and Salisbury Stage Company refused to pay the Indians for hay cut on the reservation for their horses, although hay was selling for $2.50 a ton. The company did pay the agent $355.50 for hay obtained from Indian fields during the first year of the reservation, but a controversy developed in 1871. Agent J. N. High informed stage company officials in rather plain language that, since they had refused to pay their last year's bill for hay, he would "pay no attention to your wants this season." There followed a letter from the Post Office Department in Washington introducing Mr. Salisbury to the commissioner of Indian Affairs for a personal interview on the matter. The firm also wrote a letter of complaint to the secretary of the Interior, who directed the commissioner to instruct his agent to use more courteous language in the future and to allow the stage lines as a mail carrier "to take such hay as may be necessary for the public service as heretofore" if there were no serious objections from the Indian Department. There apparently were none, as the commissioner read the strongly worded reprimand from his superior. Gilmer and Salisbury, therefore, continued their practice of cutting hay and paying the Indians nothing for it.[10]

Trespass by White Cattlemen

Much more serious from the Indian's point of view was the continual practice of white stockmen in grazing their herds on the rich bottomlands of the reservation. Agent Danilson wrote on March 21, 1870, that several whites had ranches on the reservation when it was set apart for the Indians and "as these persons all own Stock and claim the privilege of letting them run on the reservation, cutting hay, wood etc.," it had become a "constant annoyance."[11] A new agent, M. P. Berry, registered a similar complaint in July 1871 that the

settler's stock "eat out the grass of the reservation, without being any source of income to it." Somewhat in desperation he advertised that teamsters and herders desiring winter range for cattle should apply to the agent at Fort Hall.[12]

Private citizens verified statements of the agents covering stock trespass on the reservation. B. F. White of Malad wrote a Washington official that certain cattlemen living near the southern reservation line continually grazed their stock on the reservation and refused to pay any taxes to the county or fees to the Indians. He continued, "They have thus far been enabled to stand us off on it and bid fair to continue to do so." He also informed the official that there were other parties who pastured their cattle on the reservation "for a consideration which they pay the Agent." He had been told by reliable men that there were presently four thousand head of stock on the reservation belonging to outsiders with the approval of the agent "and why it is so seems very strange."[13] One of these cattlemen could have been George   1873 Buterbaugh of Corinne. The *Reporter* of that town commented:

1872

His herds occupy a great portion of the fine pasture lands on Bannock Creek and Snake River, and are in excellent condition. Among the increase in stock this year Mr. B. numbers nine hundred calves, an item that gives an idea of what a successful cattle business may amount to in a short time. It is about the most direct road to fortune that we know of, and no one deserves more prosperity than Mr. Buterbaugh and his associates.[14]

Including, one would suppose, the poor Indians at Fort Hall.

The seriousness of stock grazing and other trespass violations on the reservation was recognized officially in 1873 when the three commissioners — John P. C. Shanks, T. W. Bennett, and Henry W. Reed — met with the Shoshoni and Bannock to negotiate an agreement which included the following articles:

Article 2 – It is agreed further that no public highway shall pass through or continue in said reservation without the consent of the Secretary of the Interior; that the Secretary of the Interior shall regulate the rates and amounts of tolls to be charged on that portion of any toll-road or bridge situated in or running through or into said reservation, and not less than one-fourth of such toll shall be paid over and expended under the order of the Secretary of the Interior to aid such Indians in the pursuits of agriculture.

Article 3 – No person whomsoever other than the Indians entitled to homes on the Fort Hall reservation shall be permitted to pasture, herd, or keep on said reservation any cattle, horses, sheep, mules, or other stock whatever, except the stock necessary for the management of the agency, and such as the government and officers of the military need; nor shall any hay or grass be cut on or removed from said reservation other than for the use or benefit of said Indians, agency, or military.

Article 4 – It is, however, further agreed that the agent may, by agreement in writing, sell grass, hay, or pasture on said reservation, but without detriment to the Indians. Said written agreement, and an itemized statement of the proceeds of such sales and expenditures thereof, which shall be for the benefit of said Indians, shall be reported to the Indian Depart ment. . . .

Article 7 – It is hereby especially agreed that no white person shall be permitted to reside on or remain upon said reservation other than those under the employ and pay of the United States. . . .[15]

The official report accompanying the agreement, which was never ratified, spelled out in even more detail the losses being suffered by the Fort Hall Indians. The commissioner attacked the owners of the toll road through the reservation, "If a road through the reservation is to bring tolls they should sustain it and not be taken by men who trespass on it, cut hay & wood and have pastures and tolls, and building materials without any benefit to the reservation or cost to them." In commenting on the necessity for the third article, federal officials noted that a number of people lived adjacent to the reservation for the "purpose of pasturing their stock on it. Large amounts of stock have been pastured on the reservation by various persons without any reward whatever." They pointed out that the stage company grazed its horses at the six stations on the reservation without any compensation to the Indians. Licensed traders followed the same practice — as did the toll-road company.

The fourth article was inserted to stop private citizens, the stage company and the toll-road company from cutting and removing hay from the reservation. The commissioner regretted not including a section in the agreement which would have prohibited the "cutting and use of building material and firewood," because timber was scarce along the road right-of-way. The traders were in partnership with the stockmen, and the two interests fought tenaciously any attempt to curtail their free use of Indian property.[10]

1874   In August 1874 Agent Reed came under attack by the chiefs and headmen. In a letter to the Idaho governor they accused the agent of gross misconduct and outright fraud. Among other things they charged him with selling "hundreds of dollars worth of hay and lumber" and asked what he had done with the money.[17] The inference was that he was allied with stockmen and freighters, who commonly wintered their stock on the bot- 1875 tomlands. Alex Toponce, a long-time freighter on the Montana Trail, and H. O. Harkness, owner of the toll road, applied for grazing contracts to legitimatize their ranching operation, perhaps fearing that the government might deny them all access to the rich pastures of the reservation. The commissioner rejected both proposals as being "inadequate for the privilege it grants." Instead, he instructed the agent to advertise for bids to lease unused portions of the reservation to stockmen. Agent Danilson protested that this would place the lands under the control of unscrupulous ranchers. Danilson knew whereof he spoke, being

a stockman himself and having lived near the reservation for several years. He advised Washington to allow the outsiders to pasture their stock on Fort Hall lands at a fixed price of so much per head per year and later arrived at 30 cents per head for cattle, 50 cents per head for horses, and $2 a ton for hay, as reasonable figures. The commissioner accepted Danilson's advice and rejected any lease.[18]

There was only one other matter to be straigh- 1876 tened out: H. O. Harkness refused to pay for the hay and pasturage he harvested from reservation lands. Danilson explained that other parties were now paying the fees but were waiting to see how Harkness's defiance of the law would be handled. The agent asked the commissioner to support him in the controversy, otherwise no one would pay. The commissioner did so, although Harkness immediately went over his head in an appeal to the Department of the Interior. He cited the following reasons for asking for exemption: The hay just went to waste anyway, the hayfields in question were forty miles from the agency, he had cut hay on these lands long before there was a reservation and certainly since 1870, and, lastly, Mormon settlers on the southern edge of the reservation were removing fifteen hundred tons of hay a year without paying for it. The secretary of the Interior responded by ordering Agent Danilson "to remove the said Harkness from said Fort Hall Reservation." Harkness reformed, paid the fees and his back bills, and was reinstated as a trader to the Indians.[19] Agent Wright had already confirmed the charge by Harkness that there were trespassers on the southern portion of the reservation. He wrote, "There are several freighters on the south part of the reservation with Cattle and mules. Also some Citizens herd Cattle on the Reservation."[20]

Further evidence of stock trespass on the reservation came from the Fort Hall military post 1877 commander at Lincoln Creek, who wrote the agent that as long as white owners were allowed to cross the Blackfoot River with their herds onto Fort Hall property it was impossible for him to keep them off the post grazing reserve. The day before, his soldiers had rounded up a thousand cattle belonging to almost a dozen owners and had driven them north across the river. Captain Augustus H. Bainbridge suggested that he and the agent, as government officials, should cooperate in keeping trespassers off reservation lands. The agent's reply was that a Mr. Dunn had *tried* to keep his cattle off Indian lands, which brought a 1878 rather testy response from the captain. The next year Bainbridge took the bull by the horns, so to speak, and published an order that all trespassing cattle would be impounded and a charge of 50 cents a head levied for each day the animals remained in impound. The army officer apparently did not get the cooperation he wished from Agent Danilson to keep stock off military and reservation property.[21]

The number of cattle for which grazing fees were paid by white owners in February 1878 amounted to 1,758 animals, with an agency herd of 350. For the third quarter of that year the agent reported receipts of $168 for hay sold to the stage company and $155 for pasturage from two large freighting companies. Two years later 1880 Agent John A. Wright listed income for 1880 as follows: $1,477.83 for pasturage at 30 cents per head per year and $435.50 for sale of hay at $2.50 per ton.[22]

The military at Fort Hall continued to have 1881 problems with cattlemen who allowed their stock to graze in Lincoln Valley. Captain Bainbridge wrote the Walker & Willis Company of Eagle Rock, Idaho, that he had been "trifled with" long enough and if they did not remove their cattle which were in "great number . . . in this valley and on the hills," he would have his troops round them up and turn them over to the Indian agent.[23]

The army was also called upon to settle a dispute between the Indians and some cowboys who were driving a large herd of cattle across the reservation. The Shoshoni and Bannock claimed the cowboys had rounded up Indian cattle with their herd, so three hundred Indians had "made an attack on the cattle." The affair ended peacefully but indicated the problem of mixing "citizen cattle" with stock owned by the Indians.[24]

Sometimes the agent could take advantage of citizen's cattle when his supplies of beef ran out. In one incident Agent John Wright killed seven head of cattle pastured on the reservation and reported, "Some of the cattle may belong to parties having a grazing privilege." His opinion, however, was that the herd was made up of steers which were grazing on the reservation without permission.[25]

Wright was not held in high esteem by the Indians, and they demanded his removal. One of the charges against him was that he allowed "our Reservation . . . [to be] over-run by cattle belonging to white men, against our wishes."[26] Three months later, and perhaps because of this accusation, Wright reported that suits had been filed at Malad, Idaho, against fourteen people as the result of his charges that they were pasturing cattle and cutting hay on the reservation without permission. Six of the stockmen were accused of grazing 4,800 head of stock on Fort Hall lands; no figures were given for the cattle owned by the remaining eight white owners. Wright concluded that, despite the evidence, no indictments were returned because "a number of the members of the Grand Jury were of the Mormon faith."[27]

Wright's replacement as agent, E. A. Stone,

asked the commissioner whether he should continue granting permits to cattle herders at 30 cents per head for summer pasturage and a similar sum for winter grazing. Too many of the cattlemen paid no attention to such niceties, and Captain M. Tuft again complained against two of the worst offenders, Ruben Dunn and the Messlin Brothers. The Indians were particularly incensed because, under their agreement of May 14, 1880, to cede the southern portion of the reservation to the United States, the government had promised to ratify the agreement and pay for the cession. When action was not taken and white settlers continued to pour into Marsh Valley, the Shoshoni and Bannock demanded that they and their herds of cattle be driven off. There were about 175 people living at the village of Oneida on reser- 1882 vation property and "their live stock increasing even more rapidly than themselves. . . ."[28] Some people, hearing of the cession agreement, began writing in asking for information about settling at Pocatello on the reservation. One gentleman who inquired about the prospects of grazing "a little stock" on the reservation was told that he could settle at Pocatello but could not graze cattle.[29]

The Indian Department finally launched a full-scale investigation into the activities of the largest cattle company, which for years had pastured its stock on reservation lands. The agent had charged Rand, Briggs and Company $900 for pasturing three thousand head of cattle at 30 cents per head. The inspector who investigated explained that this particular company and many others had ranches on the border of the reservation. This made it easy to drive a large portion of their herds across the boundary before the spring round-up, when the number of cattle was estimated so fees could be assessed. One witness testified that instead of three thousand the firm had pastured close to ten thousand, scattered over a distance of forty miles on the reservation. Furthermore, most of the cattlemem moved their herds onto Fort Hall land without the consent or knowledge of the agent. The inspector concluded that there were no fences to confine the animals, that they "were running anywhere in this country," and that it was impossible to get any exact count or to be sure which cattlemen should pay a fee for grazing rights.[30] Special Agent Cyrus 1884 Beede, in another report, summed up the situation quite succinctly, "Some of the owners of this stock willingly pay the amount charged, but I apprehend some difficulty in making other collections as well as obtaining correctly the numbers of there several herds." He estimated that up to five thousand head of cattle were pastured on the reservation by outsiders who should have paid 30 cents per head for cattle and 50 cents per head for horses for the privilege of grazing there.[31]

By 1886 the fee had been raised to 50 cents per 1886

head for cattle, and after some difficulty the agent was able to get H. O. Harkness to pay $150 owed for pasturage of his cattle. Charles Aldous complained that he was forced to pay the pasturage tax while others went free. Agent Gallagher replied that the reason the cattleman was upset was that he had apparently escaped the tax earlier but was finally among those being charged. The agent listed the rise in receipts for grazing from 1881 to 1886 as follows:

For Winter of 1881-82, 8 persons or firms, 1237.80
For Winter of 1882-83, 23 persons or firms, 1418.70
For Winter of 1883-84, 24 persons or firms, 1672.10
For Winter of 1884-85, 29 persons or firms, 1687.50
For Winter of 1885-86, 49 persons or firms, 2632.70

Gallagher finished his letter, "I don't think I have gotten all [the cattlemen] . . . also, it may be that Mr. A. like a good many others, will be found out as reporting the number of head far below what he really had on the reserve."[32]

1887   Peter Gallagher and the other agents had been forcing cattlemen who grazed stock on the reservation to buy Indian hay. The ranchers protested having to pay the 50 cents a head tax in addition to the purchase of hay. The agent requested permission to eliminate the tax because the Indians had put up two thousand tons of hay and needed buyers. At $5 a ton, Gallagher did not want to lose the rancher customers, especially when the value of Indian hay had increased from $4,120 in 1885 to $11,170 in 1887.[33]

1890   An interesting footnote to the evasive tactics practiced by stockmen in failing to pay the grazing fee was a complaint from the Rand Company about the agent allowing other cattlemen to come onto the reservation when "our cattle fully exhaust the winter pasturage & hay, & in spite of that suffered very heavy losses last winter."[34] It was testimony to the richness of the grass cover on the Fort Hall bottoms which attracted all ranchers close enough to avail themselves of the bounteous forage.

1894   The cession of the southern portion of the reservation eliminated many of the problems of settlers grazing their stock on Indian lands, but the failure of the government to use some of the money from the sale to purchase cattle for the Shoshoni and Bannock led to a demand on their part that all cattle belonging to white ranchers be kept off the Fort Hall reserve. In a petition signed by thirty-eight chiefs and leading men, the Indians asked the commissioner to release enough of their funds held in the U.S. Treasury to purchase four thousand head of cows and calves. Following this action the agent asked permission to place in the Blackfoot and Pocatello papers a notification to all white stock owners that they would no longer be permitted pasturage on the reservation. Further, crossing fees of 1 cent per head for sheep and 2-½ cents per head for cattle

and horses would be charged for all herds driven across Fort Hall lands, with the additional stipulation that each crossing must be completed within three days.[35]

The cattlemen fought back by aiding the Indians in their attack on Agent Teter who was defended by the *Idaho Journal*. The editor said two or three disgruntled cattlemen "who cannot rob the Indians of hay and grass by reason of the vigilance of Agent Teter" were agitating for his removal, even though the agent was trying to persuade the tribes to relax their prohibition and allow white stockmen to graze their lands for 40 cents a head.[36] The Indians refused to listen to the agent's argument and, instead, complained that he had never held a general council with them to hear their objections to the excessive number of white men pasturing their cattle at Fort Hall.[37]   1896

As indicated earlier, white stockmen also used their influence to forestall another cession of the reservation, which led the editor of the *Pocatello Tribune* in 1897 to near apoplexy as he fulminated against them with a blunt warning, "It would not be healthy for any of these cattlemen even to show up about town just now." With Pocatello landlocked and surrounded by reservation lands, it was essential that the Indians surrender some acreage. Most Pocatello residents agreed with the *Tribune* about the selfish motives of ranchers who wished to continue their long-held practice of nurturing their cattle on reservation grasses, preferably for nothing.[38]   1897

When the agreement was finally concluded and the citizens of Pocatello were assured of taking over a large part of the reservation, most stockmen with cattle on the ceded portion refused to pay the 50 cents per head fee; others, who earlier had not put their herds on the reservation, now drove them on. The secretary of the Interior was forced to intercede. He issued orders to remove the trespassing stock "forthwith" but to hold enough to pay grazing charges. As the *Blackfoot News* had said a little earlier, "Indians for the reservation and the reservation for the Indians."[39]   1900

The Shoshoni and Bannock were determined that after the transfer of property had been made they would allow "no outside stock whatever to range or graze upon the reduced reservation." The decision was made formal by action of a council held at Fort Hall on February 2, 1901.   1901
One of the reasons given was that Indian cattle owners now had enough stock to "eat all the hay and grass" grown on the reservation. By 1903 Indian police were driving all outside stock across the line or impounding the cattle until white owners could pay the necessary dues and recover their herds. Some white men retaliated by moving Indian stock off the reservation. While the agent was kept busy trying to stop this practice, he also   1903

had to determine how to collect the $1 a head fee for trespassing cattle placed on Fort Hall lands by unscrupulous whites. Superintendent A. F. Caldwell finally wrote the commissioner for advice about how to stop the latter practice, apparently acknowledging that it had gotten out of hand.[40]

Allotments and Grazing Leases

By this time Fort Hall Indians were beginning to realize some profits from their labor of raising hay and horses and cattle for sale. Their proceeds from hay alone in 1897 brought them $8,000 in cash, which the *Pocatello Tribune* announced was being spent at the city's gambling tables. Three years later some of the Indians sold four hundred ponies at $3.00 to $3.75 per head. In another three years, the commissioner could point with pride at $16,000 worth of hay sold, several carloads of horses sold at $5 per head, and gross beef valued at $13,000 disposed of to the government as rations to old and sick Indians.[41]

There was significance, therefore, in a report prepared by Special Agent Elisha B. Reynolds which described the luxuriant grazing lands of the Snake River bottoms, the uplands well suited for the growing of alfalfa, and the mountainous areas for summer pasture. He proposed that $100,000 of the cession money be used to purchase cows, calves, and blooded bulls. When his recommendation was not adopted he blamed "the cattlemen who look with longing eye upon the reservation as a range for their own cattle." Reynolds also was of the opinion that renting Fort Hall lands to white stock owners was the principal reason for the backwardness of some of the Indians, who chose to sell their hay to nearby white cattlemen. The sight and acceptance of instant cash sometimes left the Indians' own cattle "to rustle and starve."

The continuing problem of white trespassers on the reservation finally brought further action from the Indians, who decided to put their cattle into one common herd and hire herders who were paid for their services by charging each cattle owner 5 cents per head per month. In addition the herders served as cattle detectives, collecting fees from unscrupulous cattle and sheepmen who allowed their herds to stray over the boundary of the reservation. The agent asked permission to allow the herders to keep whatever they collected so as to motivate them to greater efforts in stopping trespass.[42]

1907 As if troubles with white cattlemen were not enough, Forest Service officials ordered Shoshoni and Bannock off forest reserves when they traveled there to graze their herds and secure wood for fuel. After much correspondence the commissioner of Indian Affairs was able to establish the fact that under the act of June 6, 1900, ceding the Pocatello lands to the government, an express provision was inserted which guaranteed the Indians the right to pasture their stock on public lands of the ceded portion of the reservation. The laws and regulations governing national forests did not, therefore, apply to lands formerly a part of the Fort Hall Reservation.[43]

Even more important to the Indians was the inauguration of the allotment program, which came to Fort Hall later than to many of the Indian reservations throughout the United States. Under a number of acts, resolutions, etc., but chiefly by an act of Congress on March 3, 1911, allotments 1911 of land were to be made as follows: "To each head of a family whose consort is dead, forty acres of irrigable land and three hundred and twenty acres of grazing land, and to each other Indian belonging on the reservation or having rights thereon, twenty acres of irrigable land and one hundred and sixty acres of grazing land." An additional section allowed the secretary of the Interior to make allotments "within the Fort Hall Bottoms" grazing reserve to those Indians "who have occupied and erected valuable improvements on tracts therein." A schedule was established describing allotments numbered from 1A to 70A and from 80 to 1832; Agent William B. Sams supervised the distribution, The schedule covered 338,909.95 acres, with 37,939.15 acres being irrigable and 300,970.80 acres grazing land. There also was established a special Tribal Grazing Reserve of 36,263.07 acres. From that time on, leases of allotments were allowed to be made to Indian and non-Indian alike by the owners of the allotments.[44]

Immediately after establishment of allotments in severalty, the promoters of an irrigation project came forward to ask the Shoshoni and Bannock to sell much of their important bottomland. The proposed project included damming the Snake River at American Falls, which would create an artificial lake that would cover the bottoms. The *Pocatello Tribune* was confident the Indians would sell the Portneuf bottoms (which were "held in common by the tribes for grazing purposes") at a price of $50 per acre. The editor continued that the agent was educating the Indians to raise alfalfa on their irrigated land for winter feed so the bottoms would no longer be needed for winter pasturage.[45] The editor's wishes were no doubt father to his thoughts, because the Fort Hall Indians were not enthusiastic about giving up their sacred bottomlands. 1912

At a hearing held April 26, 1912, at Fort Hall, Pat L. Tyhee, a leading spokesman for the Indians, was quite firm about the necessity of retaining the bottoms:

He states that the majority of the Indians are depending upon that part of the land that we own down there. The majority of them have cattle and horses — some of them own 3, 4, 5 or 600 head of cattle alone, and they depend upon the

Idaho State Historical Society

Pat Tyhee, son of Bannock Chief Tahgee.

land for hay, and they move there in the winter time and feed their cattle there, and that is why they are depending upon that part of the land mostly, and they don't wish to give it up at all. They wish to hold that land for their own use. And there are lots of woods there, and we don't have to make any shelter for the cattle at all. They go under the willows there; and there is good shelter for the horses also. There is lots of hay during winter right along. Oh, I could not tell you how many thousands of tons come from that place there — wild hay.

His speech had the flavor of Old Testament scripture in its simplicity and earnestness as he condemned the white stockmen who continued to trespass on the reservation:

Cattlemen have been holding their cattle upon our reservation for a good many years. Ever since the Government has given us that reservation; there have been cattlemen on there until right up to this time . . . in the bottom there. They have been wintering their cattle there right along; every winter; every year; in summer also. . . . This is along the Snake River. They have herded their cattle also in Chesterfield — that's on our reservation. They have herded their cattle there, but we don't want any more of that. Just forbid the cattlemen to graze their cattle on any part of our reservation.

On account of that it is a very small portion of our reservation that is left now, and we wish to keep it for our own use and benefit. A little land is left there on the reservation today, and we haven't got much left to spare.[46]

1918   Six years later an inspection report indicated that conditions had not improved. The inspecting official found "many strays" at the time of the roundup, and when word got around that a government official was investigating conditions at

Fort Hall, the cattle and sheepmen immediately drove their stock off the reservation to safer havens. The commissioner reprimanded the Fort Hall agent for allowing cattle and sheep to trespass. He added insult to these charges by informing the agent that he had allowed the Indians "to sell more hay than they should, thus causing their stock to suffer."[47]

After the allotments were made, an individual Indian could realize some cash by leasing a grazing area, the average annual price for 160 acres being $24 during the 1917–18 period.[48] The agent protested the addition of a $5 tax for processing the grazing lease in 1921, believing that   1921 the white cattlemen and sheepmen would refuse to buy any leases and leave some of the Indians without any income at all.[49]

Some allotees also added to their income by the sale of crossing permits. A typical case was an Indian, Modiss, who in 1917 granted a permit for $10 to Austen Brothers to trail sheep across his property.[50] The tribes made a little money by selling crossing permits along the various roads through the reservation, the 1915 rates being 1-¼ cents per head per day for the Pole Line Trail, 1 cent per head per day on the Michaud Trail, 1-¼ cents per head per day along Bannock Creek Trail, 1-¼ cents per head per day for Bannock Creek-Rattle Snake Trail, and 5 cents per head for cattle on the Lincoln Creek Trail.[51]

To encourage stock raising among the Indians the commissioner modified departmental regulations by allowing individuals with fewer than 100 head of cattle to cut hay for their herds free of charge. All owning more than 100 head would pay $1 per ton for the amount necessary to feed all animals in excess of 100. With such incentives the Indian cattle increased to 6,000 head by 1922. The cattle were pastured in a community herd at a cost of $2 per head for each Indian owner. The number of Indian cattle had increased gradually over the years from six in 1874 to 4,500 in 1905 to the above figure by 1922. The horse herd at Fort Hall had also gone up from 3,000 in 1876 to 6,000 in 1905. Hay production showed a remarkable increase in the early years from 10 tons in 1872, to 8,000 tons in 1905.[52]

With so many cattle on the reservation, the temptation for rustlers was great. The superin-   1923 tendent reported in 1923 an annual loss of 8 percent of the Indian herd annually to cattle thieves. The Indian cattlemen organized themselves into the Fort Hall Indian Stockmen's Association in 1922 to deal with the problem. The commissioner came to their aid the following year by allowing $750 to be expended from the IMPL (Indian Moneys, Proceeds of Labor) fund for the employment of stock detectives to break up the rustler gang.[53]

The unceasing pressure of white stockmen to   1924

use Fort Hall pasturage included rather frequent appeals to Idaho's congressional delegation to protect their rights against the "excessive" grazing and crossing charges imposed by the Indian Department. For example, R. P. Stewart objected to paying the fee of 50 cents per head per day to drive sixty-seven head of cattle across the reservation. Apparently he assumed (for his own purpose) that the total of $10.05 he paid also took care of the return trip, and he refused to pay the second amount.

As the superindent pointed out, the Indians didn't want cattle or sheep owned by whites to cross the reservation at all, but the white owners chose to do so because it saved them two or three days getting to and from the summer range. At first the superintendent charged a flat fee of so much per head for crossing, but he soon discovered that the cattle and sheepmen would put their animals on reservation lands and leave them there until Indian officials had to push them off. Fort Hall officials had been forced to raise the rates high enough to ensure that stockmen would cross the reservation as quickly as possible. The commissioner said the high rates were necessary because of the "continued trespassing on the part of white persons living in the immediate 1925 vicinity."[54] The superintendent had enough trouble trying to control the cattle, sheep, and horses of the white lessees, most of whom leased the 20-acre allotments for an average fee in 1925 of $75 to $100, farmed a portion, and used the rest as pasture for their stock.[55]

Indian Stockmen's Associations

The obvious answer to the problems of white stockmen using reservation lands was to organize and encourage the tribesmen to engage in the cattle business so there would be no lands left for whites to fight over. In 1922, as noted above, the Indians organized the Fort Hall Stockmen's Association whose objectives included: to encourage raising a better breed of stock, to sell or remove all ponies weighing less than 700 pounds, to keep Indian and white herds within their respective boundaries, and to protect the range. Any Fort Hall Indian owning five or more head of cattle was eligible to join but lost his membership if he ceased to own any stock. Also, if a member with eight head of stock or less did not show an increase in his herd for a period of three years, he would be liable to expulsion. The association was 1928 so successful that in 1928 the superintendent helped organize the Bannock Creek Stockmen's Association for the cattlemen in that area, so far removed from the agency.[56]

1929 The various superintendents did all in their power to help make the two associations successful. The organizations were not required to pay grazing fees for the tribal land included in their range, and in many other ways the Indian cattlemen were helped. By 1929 the Fort Hall groups used 67,576 acres of allotted lands and 6,500 acres of tribal lands and paid allottees 12½ cents per acre for the tracts held within the association's grazing area.[57]

A comprehensive report by the Forest Service 1930 in 1930 gave a good picture of grazing and livestock conditions at Fort Hall. Open range areas approximated 400,000 acres, divided as follows: tribal grazing reserve winter pasture, 9,000 acres; tribal timber reserve, 45,000 acres; unallotted grazing lands, 85,000 acres; allotted grazing lands, 240,000 acres; and alienated lands, 21,000 acres. Individual Indians owned livestock as indicated: 3,140 cows and heifers valued at $157,000; 43 bulls at $8,145; 1,067 steers at $53,350; 1,888 sheep at $18,880; and 1,378 horses at $13,730.

The Bannock Creek Association ran about a thousand head of cattle, mostly on tribal range at the head of Bannock Creek. The Fort Hall Association operated with 4,000 head. They wintered the cattle without charge on the bottoms but paid 12-½ cents per acre for spring and summer range in the eastern section of the reservation. Of the 107,085 acres used by the Indians, only 800 acres were used for sheep; the entire 257,234 acres under white lease were used for sheep. The grazing leases and permits accommodated 5,500 head of Indian cattle and 84,000 sheep, most of the latter being owned by white men. Grazing leases and trespass and crossing fees brought an annual income to the Indians of $45,000. The Fort Hall organization had 134 members, with eight of the members owning 100 or more cattle; the Bannock Creek Association had twenty-nine members, the largest owner having 148 head of cattle. The tribesman who had moved onto Fort Hall Reservation in 1870 would indeed have been amazed sixty years later to see their grandsons and great-grandsons running cattle ranches and concerned with such things as debits and credits.[58]

As the Shoshoni and Bannock struggled to 1927 make a success of their ranching and farming operations they watched with dismay as they saw white stockmen being permitted to run thousands of head of sheep on Indian lands, virtually destroying thousands of acres of pasturage. As the grass cover disappeared from the mountain slopes, the Indian farmer saw his irrigation ditches go dry and his crops burn up as the slopes were no longer able to retain moisture for summer runoff. Superintendent Stephen Janus reported on April 6, 1927, that "the deterioration, and in some instances, the complete destruction, of the farming of the Indians in this district, is common knowledge." The situation was especially severe on the Mt. Putnam watershed:

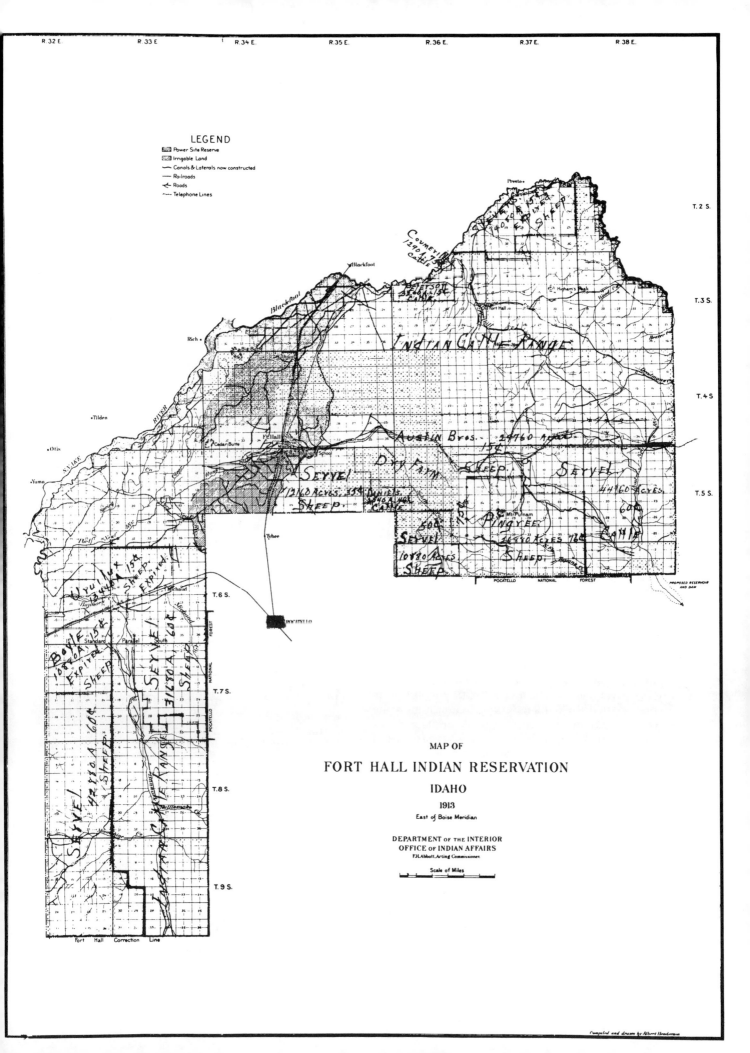

LEGEND
Power Site Reserve
Irrigable Land
Canals & Laterals now constructed
Railroads
Roads
Telephone Lines

MAP OF

FORT HALL INDIAN RESERVATION

IDAHO

1913

East of Boise Meridian

DEPARTMENT OF THE INTERIOR
OFFICE OF INDIAN AFFAIRS
F.H.Abbott, Acting Commissioner.

Scale of Miles

The water supply, wholly derived from the Mt. Putnam watershed, has been steadily diminishing for the past ten years and with such increased rapidity in the past five years, that many farms have been entirely abandoned, and all have been seriously damaged and reduced in area.

Superintendent William Donner had therefore discontinued issuing grazing permits, and he counseled that no others be issued for several years. When he left, and after only one year's rest, the area was opened to sheepmen again. There was no time limit, and the white owners kept their flocks in the mountains until winter snows drove them out. Janus continued, "No count of the sheep going on was made, and I am convinced that the number allowed was exceeded. So the permits were carelessly drawn and do not protect the interests of the Indian's range alone, even if there were no question of the destruction of the Indian farmer's water supply." The grazing receipts amounted to $6,000 while "the damage to the Indian's farming operations is incalculable." He thought the damage exceeded the rentals by ten times.

His letter and accompanying petition from Indian farmers finally led the commissioner to send instructions to cancel the leases for the Mt. Putnam area. The order came too late for perhaps thousands of acres of denuded soil.[59] A little later, 1929 when the white-run Eastern Idaho Grazing Association complained to Idaho congressmen about raising the trespass tax on sheep from ½ cent per head per day to 1 cent per head on the Fort Hall Reservation, Stephen Janus commented, "The sheepmen will go to any extent to acquire range on the Reservation." He used as his argument the bid of one white sheepowner of 51 cents per acre on a certain tract.[60]

1932 Despite the protests of superintendent and Indian alike (and the sympathetic endorsement of the commissioner) in 1932, a year after the latter's order, at least two grazing leases were issued to pasture 2,000 sheep on the Mt. Putnam units — so the overgrazing continued.[61] The forest supervisor warned the Indian Service that although the acceptable figure was ¾ to ³/₅ acres per sheep per month, the Eastern Idaho Grazing Association was reducing the surface allowance as shown in the following table:

Year	Total No. of Sheep on Units	Excess Over Maximum as Authorized by Leases and Permits
1929	15,150	5,062
1930	18,050	7,962
1931	20,700	10,612

As the forest official put it, "The last figure of 20,700 is over twice the authorized capacity and cuts the surface acre allowance down to ⅜ to ³/₁₀ acres per head per month." He said that for many years the U.S. Forest Service had maintained their range "by allowing not *less than 1 surface acre per head per month for sheep*" and unless this standard was observed "there can be but one result — a gradual deterioration and consequential lowering of carrying capacity and damage by erosion: the final result a lower rental on lease value and diminished financial returns to the individual Indian owners."[62] As for the outcry from white sheepmen concerning exorbitant fees for grazing, he pointed out that some Indian reservations in the nation charged as high as 75 cents per head per season compared to the Fort Hall charges of 45 cents.[63]

Two years later, in 1934, forest officials were still condemning the practice of placing too many 1934 sheep on the Fort Hall ranges. Over the period of the last fifty years, sagebrush had gradually taken over foothill lands which were originally covered with grass, a "definite indication of overgrazing." The foresters advised a 25 percent reduction in the number of sheep permitted on the foothills and lower ranges. When one of the range supervisors took a group of tribal leaders on a guided inspection tour of Fort Hall grazing lands, Willie George, the tribal council secretary, exclaimed, "If we were to tell the tribe what we have seen today, they would not believe us."[64] The Forest Service called the action of the Indian Department in allowing the Eastern Idaho Grazing Association to overstock the ranges "as little short of absolute trespass. . . . The fact that these violations have not been stopped in the past is no justification for permitting them to continue in the future."[65]

The Forest Service's deliberate and apparently planned attack on these overgrazing proclivities of the Fort Hall Agency finally brought results; by 1938 1938 it was announced that reservation lands were not overstocked but were carrying their proper capacity. The foresters found that the percentage of grass going to seed was very high on the units reserved for spring sheep range.[66] In extensive hearings held at Fort Hall by the Senate Committee on Indian Affairs on September 12, 1932 13, and 14, 1932, Senator John Thomas of Idaho asked Ralph Dixey, president of the Fort Hall Indian Stockmen's Association, how many cattle the Indians could handle on the reservation. Dixey answered that they could easily handle 10,000 head, compared to the 4,500 head they were presently herding, and that the Indians would prefer to stop leasing to white sheepmen and use the ranges for increased Indian herds.[67]

By 1933 it was also becoming evident to the Of- 1933 fice of Indian Affairs that certain lands owned by whites within Indian grazing areas gave easy access for trespass on adjacent tribal lands. The superintendent learned, in two typical instances, that 100 head of stock were found to have wintered on Indian pastures and 137 head were rounded up on the Mt. Putnam unit. He recommended the purchase of two tracts in particular to stop the long-time practice of white owners who trailed their cattle back and forth from their own lands to other areas off the reservation without paying crossing fees. In other correspondence the superintendent suggested a planned system for buying out white owners in these isolated areas so the tribesmen could control their ranges.[68]

1934 To vary the monotony conerning the evils visited by grasping white stockmen on the Indian, it may be refreshing to learn that there were others who tried to take advantage of the Fort Hall people. In a series of letters in 1934 the superintendent related to the commissioner the injustice rendered some Indians whose cattle were killed by trains crossing through reservation lands when the animals wandered onto a crossing or were struck while grazing within the limits of the Fort Hall townsite. Oregon Short Line Railroad officials merely ignored the claims submitted for damage, despite the superintendent's reference to the Agreement of September 1, 1888, which expressly made the railroad liable for Indian stock killed by trains.[69]

One of the continuing concerns of the superintendent at Fort Hall was to assist the struggling Bannock Creek Stockman's Association to become self-supporting. One of the extension agents expressed the feelings of the Indians who lived along Bannock Creek:

1935

The Bannock Creek Indians feel now that they have been very much neglected when compared with the Indians in the Fort Hall District. They point out that their irrigation water has been largely taken away from them by the whites, and that the Indian Service has given them practically no assistance in building an irrigation system to enable them to make the most efficient use of the little water that they now have. There is a feeling on their part that because they are somewhat isolated from the rest of the reservation, that their needs are overlooked. When one visits the Indians of the Fort Hall District and sees the development that has taken place in this district, and then visits the Bannock Creek District, he is impressed with the marked difference between the two divisions of the reservation. There can be no question but what the Indians living in the Fort Hall division are much more favorably situated and economically speaking have far better opportunities than the Bannock Creek Indians.

Realizing the truth of this observation, the Fort Hall Business Council granted their Bannock Creek neighbors the use of funds paid in as trespass fees, although these were actually tribal funds belonging to all the Indians. As further aid the council also leased two areas of tribal lands to the Bannock Creek association for a period of three years at $1 per contract. At the time, the Bannock Creek organization had forty-five members, was herding 600 head of cattle, had control of 37,275 acres of tribal and allotted land, and was taking in about $17,000 in receipts each year.[70]

By 1935 the superintendent could report that the Fort Hall Stockmen's Association was running 6,450 head of cattle and the Bannock Creek

group had 709 head. The total of the two had decreased slightly to 6,700 cattle by 1969, and there were 2,177 Indian-owned sheep. The 398,000 acres of grazing land reported in 1932 had likewise shown a drop to 328,140 acres in 1969 as more lands had come under cultivation. The Indians had not reached their goal of 10,000 head of cattle — nor had they eliminated the white sheepmen, who were still pasturing 52,000 sheep on Fort Hall lands in 1969.[71]

1969

From wandering tribesmen to successful farmers and ranchmen, the Shoshoni and Bannock now completed the circle of their transformation by starting a buffalo herd, which today ranges on the Snake River bottoms as other buffalo did a hundred and forty years ago. Perhaps it is not so far after all from hunting buffalo to herding buffalo.[72]

1974

The care of livestock was a comparatively easy transition for the Fort Hall Indians, accustomed as they were to the use of horses in hunting game. But the art of planting and nurturing seeds, of hoeing and tilling, of diverting water into ditches, and of harvesting crops — all these tasks were new and were accompanied by back-breaking effort. A particular concern was learning about irrigation practices and about the large-scale projects required to irrigate crops on the dry lands of the reservation. As many of the agents continually pointed out, the allotment of lands in severalty was impossible until water could be provided for the soil. The struggle of the Indians to achieve an effective irrigation system at Fort Hall has been a heartbreaking and frustrating experience.

NOTES CHAPTER IX
RAISING CATTLE AT FORT HALL

1. *Journal History*, L.D.S. Department of History, Dec. 7, 1847; "Utah Early Records," Bancroft Library, Ms. 328.
2. Stansbury, *Exploration and Survey of the Valley of the Great Salt Lake of Utah*, 88–93; *Deseret News*, June 10, 1857; Extracts from Journal of L. W. Shurtliff, *Utah Historical Quarterly*, V (Jan. 1932), 517–530.
3. *Union Vedette*, March 15, 22, April 25, 1864; Frederick, *Ben Holladay, The Stagecoach King*, 144–146; Wells and Wells, "The Oneida Toll Road Controversy, 1864–1880," *Oregon Historical Quarterly*, LVIII (June 1957), 113–116.
4. *Fort Hall Letter Book, 1870–1875*, 338–339.
5. *New Northwest*, Aug. 6, 1869; *Helena Herald*, May 27, 1875; *Corinne Reporter*, April 14, 1870.
6. *Helena Independent*, May 31, 1878; *Helena Herald*, Aug. 1, Nov. 21, Dec. 27, 1878; *Ogden Freeman*, Aug. 30, Sept. 3, 1878; *Idaho Statesman*, Nov. 7, 1878.
7. *New Northwest*, April 8, 1870; Daughters of Utah Pioneers, Box Elder County Chapter, *History of Box Elder County*, 34.
8. Union Pacific Railroad, *The Direct Route to Colo., Ida., Utah, Mont., Nev., and Calif.*, Horan & Leonard, Chicago, 1868; Letterbook in possession of Charles Bovey, Fairweather Hotel, Virginia City, Montana, Stein to Holladay, Oct. 8, 1864.
9. Gilmer and Salisbury, *Letterbook, April 6, 1881–May 5, 1882*, University of Utah Library, Ms. 35, 88; John A. Wright to C.I.A., Sept. 15, 1880, U.S. National Archives, *Idaho Superintendency*, Roll 353.
10. C.I.A. to De L. Floyd-Jones, April 2, 1870, U.S. National Archives, *Idaho Superintendency*, Roll 1; J. N. High to Gilmer & Salisbury, April 15, 1871; Giles A. Smith to C.I.A., April 25, 1871; Gilmer & Salisbury to Secretary of Interior, April 28, 1871; Secretary of Interior to C.I.A., April 29, 1871, U.S. National Archives, *Idaho Superintendency*, Roll 339, *Fort Hall Letter Book*, 337–378.
11. Ibid., 338–339.
12. M. P. Berry to C.I.A., July 8, 1871, U.S. National Archives, *Idaho Superintendency*, Roll 339; Notice by M. P. Berry, Sept., 1871, ibid.

13. B. F. White to S. A. Merritt, Dec. 23, 1872, U.S. National Archives, *Idaho Superintendency*, Roll 341.
14. *Corinne Reporter*, July 19, 1873.
15. U.S. Congress, House of Rep., *Bannock and Other Indians in Southern Idaho*, Ex. Doc. 129, 43rd Cong., 1st Sess., Serial No. 1608 (Wash., D.C., 1873), 4–5.
16. Ibid.
17. Captain Jim and Five other Chiefs to T. W. Bennett, Aug. 30, 1874, U.S. National Archives, Bureau of Indian Affairs, *Letter Received, Idaho; Idaho Statesman*, Aug. 29, 1874.
18. *Corinne Mail*, Feb. 16, 1875; James Wright to C.I.A., March 16, 1875, U.S. National Archives, *Idaho Superintendency*, Roll 343; James Wright to C.I.A., June 2, 1875, ibid.; James Wright to C.I.A., June 28, 1875, ibid.; Secretary of Interior to C.I.A., July 1, 1875, ibid.; Secretary of Interior to C.I.A., Sept. 1, 1875, ibid.; W. H. Danilson to C.I.A., July 28, 1875, ibid.; H. O. Harkness to C.I.A., Aug. 13, 1875, ibid.; W. H. Danilson to C.I.A., Sept. 10, 1875, ibid.; C.I.A., to W. H. Danilson, July 20, 1875, U.S. National Archives, *Idaho Superintendency*, Roll 344; C.I.A., to W. H. Danilson, Sept. 3, 1875, ibid.; W. H. Danilson to C.I.A., Dec. 29, 1875, ibid.
19. C.I.A., to W. H. Danilson, Jan. 12, 1876, ibid.; H. O. Harkness to Secretary of Interior, Jan. 24, 1876, ibid.; W. H. Danilson to C.I.A., Feb. 24, 1876, ibid.' Secretary of Interior to C.I.A., June 12, 1876, ibid.; W. H. Danilson to C.I.A., July 18, 1876, ibid.
20. *Fort Hall Letter Book*, 247–248.
21. Augustus H. Bainbridge to W. H. Danilson, Fort Hall Military Records, *Fort Hall Record Group 393*; Bainbridge to Danilson, April 24, 1877, ibid.; Circular by Bainbridge, Nov. 8, 1878, ibid.
22. W. H. Danilson to C.I.A., Feb. 19, 1878, U.S. National Archives, *Idaho Superintendency*, Roll 347; W. H. Danilson to C.I.A., Oct. 31, 1878, ibid.; John A. Wright to C.I.A., Sept. 15, 1880, U.S. National Archives, *Idaho Superintendency*, Roll 353.
23. A. H. Bainbridge to Walker & Willis, Feb. 24, 1881, U.S. National Archives, Military Records, *Fort Hall Record Group 393*, 181; Bainbridge to Walker & Willis, April 2, 1881, ibid., 188–189.
24. "Military Orders, Fort Hall, May 19, 1881," ibid., 197–198; *Blackfoot Register*, May 28, 31, 1881.
25. John A. Wright to C.I.A., Jan. 22, 1881, U.S. National Archives, *Record Group No. 75*.
26. "Petition to C.I.A., March 2, 1881." ibid.
27. John A. Wright to C.I.A., June 23, 1881, ibid.; J. M. Haworth to Sec. of Interior, Aug. 16, 1880, U.S. National Archives, *Record Group No. 48*.
28. E. A. Stone to C.I.A., Aug. 4, 1881, ibid. E. A. Stone to C.I.A., Oct. 4, 1881, *Record Group No 75*; M. Tuft to Stephen Baker, Aug. 23, 1881, *Fort Hall Record Group 393*, 214–215.
29. H. D. Johnson to G. M. Chilcott, July 4, 1882, *Record Group No. 75*; H. D. Johnson to Geo. M. Chilcott, April 7, 1882, ibid.
30. Arden R. Smith to C.I.A., Nov. 25, 1882, ibid.
31. Cyrus Beede to C.I.A., March 13, 1884, ibid.; E. D. Bannister to C.I.A., Oct. 3, 1885, U.S. National Archives, *Record Group No. 48*.
32. A. L. Cook to C.I.A., Feb. 5, 1886, *Record Group No. 75*; P. Gallagher May 24, 1886, ibid.; Inspector Benedict to Sec. of Interior, Nov. 17, 1883, U.S. National Archives, *Record Group No. 48*, 1–11.
33. P. Gallagher to C.I.A., Sept. 29, 1887, *Record Group No. 75*; P. Gallagher to C.I.A., Aug. 17, 1887, ibid.; P. Gallagher to C.I.A., May 18, 1888, ibid.
34. S. T. Emmons to Belt, July 26, 1890, ibid.
35. J. T. Van Orsdale to C.I.A., Feb. 10, 1894, ibid.; J. T. Van Orsdale, Petition to C.I.A., Feb. 10, 1894, ibid.; J. T. Van Orsdale to C.I.A., March 11, 1894, ibid.
36. *Idaho Journal*, April 13, 1896.
37. J. Geo. Wright to Secretary of Interior, Feb. 10, 1896, *Record Group No. 75*.
38. *Pocatello Tribune*, June 30, July 4, 10, 1897; see Ch. VII, footnote 127.
39. Secretary of Interior to C.I.A., June 22, 1900, *Record Group No. 75*; C.I.A., to H. V. A. Ferguson, June 6, 1902, ibid.; *Pocatello Tribune*, April 6, 1898.

40. A. F. Caldwell to C.I.A., July 6, 1900, *Record Group No. 75*; A. F. Caldwell to C.I.A., June 8, 1901, ibid.; A. F. Caldwell to C.I.A., May 31, 1905, ibid.; A. F. Caldwell to C.I.A., Dec. 19, 1905, ibid.; *Pocatello Tribune*, May 13, Oct. 17, 1903; Arthur M. Tinker to Sec. of Int., Aug. 31, 1903, U.S. National Archives, *Record Group No. 48*.
41. *Pocatello Tribune*, Dec. 1, 1897, May 2, 1900; *C I A. Annual Report, 1904*, 60.
42. Elisha B. Reynolds to C.I.A., March 24, 1900, *Record Group No. 75*; A. F. Caldwell to C.I.A., Sept. 12, 1900, ibid.; A. F. Caldwell to C.I.A., Sept. 25, 1906, ibid.
43. A. F. Caldwell to C.I.A., Oct. 12, 1907, ibid.
44. Fort Hall Allotment Schedule 14A, Portland Area B.I.A. Office, *Original Book of Names & Areas*; C.I.A., to Secretary of Interior, Oct. 28, 1914, Portland Area B.I.A. Office.
45. *Pocatello Tribune*, Aug. 1, 1911.
46. "Report of Hearing Held April 26, 1912, Regarding Fort Hall Matters," *Record Group No. 75*.
47. C.I.A., to H. H. Miller, Feb. 21, 1918, ibid.
48. "Farming and Grazing Lease, for Nanna Chedehap, Fort Hall, Feb. 26, 1917," ibid.
49. William Donner to C.I.A., April 7, 1921, ibid.
50. "Farming and Grazing Lease, for Mo-diss, Fort Hall, May 11, 1917," ibid.
51. Fort Hall Superintendent to Bruce, Crossing Permits, Fort Hall, May 15, 1915, ibid.
52. C.I.A. to William Donner, July 7, 1921, ibid.; "F. E. Brandon Report to C.I.A., July 25, 1922," ibid.
53. Ibid.; C.I.A. to William Donner, Sept. 20, 1923, ibid.
54. C.I.A. to Burton L. French, Jan. 24, 1924, ibid.
55. "Farming and Grazing Leases, Fort Hall, April 2, 1925," ibid.
56. "Constitution and Bylaws of Ft. Hall Indian Stockmen's Association, 1921," *Fort Hall Agency Records*; Stephen Janus to C.I.A., Feb. 29, 1928, *Record Group No. 75*.
57. Elisha B. Reynolds to C.I.A., March 24, 1900, *Record Group No. 75*; C.I.A., to Fred A. Gross, Jan 22, 1930, ibid.
58. Percy E. Melis to C.I.A., Feb. 11, 1931, ibid.; F. C. Campbell to A. C. Cooley, April 20, 1931, *Fort Hall Agency Records*.
59. Stephen Janus to C.I.A., April 6, 1927, *Record Group No. 75*; Petition from Ross Fork Creek Farmers, March 28, 1927, ibid.; C.I.A., to Stephen Janus, April 21, 1927, ibid.
60. Stephen Janus to C.I.A., May 6, 1929, ibid.
61. C.I.A. to F. A. Gross, Feb. 23, 1932, ibid.; C.I.A. to F. A. Gross, March 8, 1932, ibid.
62. W. R. Shoemaker, *Report on Grazing at Fort Hall*, March 10, 1932, Fort Hall Agency Records.
63. W. R. Shoemaker to F. A. Gross, May 13, 1932, *Record Group No. 75*.
64. Richard B. Millin to F. A. Gross, Oct. 20, 1934, ibid.
65. Forest Service to C.I.A., May 24, 1932, *Fort Hall Agency Records*.
66. Richard B. Millin to F. A. Gross, *Grazing Progress Report, 1934–1938*, Fort Hall, ibid.
67. Hearings before a Subcommittee on Indian Affairs, United States Senate, *Survey of Conditions of the Indians in the United States, Part 27, Wyoming, Idaho and Utah*, Sept. 12, 13 and 14, 1932.
68. F. A. Gross to C.I.A., Feb. 12, 1934, *Fort Hall Agency Records*; F. A. Gross to C.I.A., Feb. 10, 1933, *Record Group No. 75*.
69. F. A. Gross to C.I.A., June 29, 1934, *Fort Hall Agency Records*.
70. A. C. Cooley to C.I.A., March 31, 1935, ibid.; "Resolution of Fort Hall Tribal Business Council, March 1, 1935," ibid.; Lee Muck to C.I.A., Jan 9, 1933, ibid.
71. F. A. Gross to Richard B. Millin, Feb. 12, 20, 1935, ibid.; F. A. Gross, Report Prepared for Lynn J. Frazier, Fort Hall, August 1932, ibid.; "Overall Economic Development Program for Fort Hall Reservation, Fort Hall Business Council, April 11, 1969," ibid.
72. "Fort Hall Business Council Meetings, June 20, 28, 1974," ibid.

Chapter X

WATER ON THE LAND

Early Attempts at Irrigation

Irrigation was a problem at Fort Hall almost
from the beginning. Nearly all the crops had to be
irrigated, and a dam at Ross Fork Creek was con-
1869 structed in 1869 to facilitate getting water to the
land. In time the meager water supply at Ross
Fork was overextended. When Indians took up
acreage of their own, they were forced to locate
on ready water sources at Bannock Creek, the
Portneuf River, the Blackfoot River, and Lincoln
Creek. This led to a wide dispersal of the Indian
farmers and made it difficult for the single agency
farmer to superintend their efforts and give them
instruction. One result was that crops often failed.
Another was that the Indians fell into slipshod
farming practices. Both factors compounded the
difficulty of inducing other Indians to become
farmers. Another problem was that the Indians
were not furnished sufficient seed and implements. Moreover, the water supplies in some of
the areas frequently tended to run low, resulting
in destruction of the crops and discouragement to
1895 the Indians. A good example came in 1895.[1] The
Bannock were still adverse to becoming farmers
with only twenty-five families doing any farming.
These families were located on Ross Fork Creek,
and that year, as many times previously, the crop
was destroyed when the creek ran dry. As a result
Agent Teter's efforts to get more Indians to farm
were rendered futile.

Thus, even at places where there was a water
supply the source was often uncertain, frequently
leading to wasted farm efforts that further served
to inhibit the Indians from becoming farmers.
Within a short time free-flow water, readily and
dependably available, reached a vanishing point.
If cultivated acreages were to be increased with a
greater number of Indians farming, new means to
secure water were necessary.

1874 Major John W. Powell pointed out in his 1874
testimony before the House Committee on Indian
Affairs that water rights were valuable and expensive and that land was of value only when supplied with water.[2] The Indian agents echoed his
sentiment year after year in their annual reports.
1872 In 1872 Agent Berry even suggested the construction of a twenty-two-mile canal from the
Portneuf.[3] Government officials thus had long-
standing knowledge that development of Fort
Hall lands would require substantial amounts of
water. It became more and more apparent by the
end of the 1870s that water could be provided
only by elaborate irrigation systems, constructed
either by the government or by private concerns
having concessions and encouragement from the
government.[4] Either way, it was obvious that the
government must become involved. The Indian
Office, however, seemed indisposed to do so until
the late 1880s. As late as 1889 Agent Gallagher 1889
complained of "difficulty attending in bringing to
the full knowledge of the Government light
enough" to convince officials of the need to appropriate money for irrigation.[5] 1890

Two factors help explain why around 1890, the
government began to pursue irrigation. First, the
original project proposals were designed to benefit whites as well as Indians and to help develop
the entire region.[6] Water was needed for the new
town of Pocatello, and the lands that would become available for settlement after the hoped-for
land cession would also need water to be of value.
Irrigation projects were therefore actively pursued by politically vigorous white people in Idaho;
their representative, Fred T. Dubois, pushed their
interests determinedly. Second, irrigation was also
tied to the plan for allotments in severalty and so
again partly designed for the benefit of white
people. Allotments were intended to serve as a 1887
means for acculturating the Indian, turning him
into a "well-regulated and well-to-do farmer"[7] and
to give each Indian his own parcel so the remainder of the tribal land could be opened to
settlement.[8] Indians could not take up lands in
severalty without water for their allotments, and
water could be obtained only through an extensive irrigation system. Irrigation planning was
partially undertaken to expedite the allotment
process and the opening of the reservation.[9]

An effort to investigate the possibility of irrigation ditches for the reservation was begun in the 1886
fall of 1886, when the commissioner asked for a
report and estimate from Agent Gallagher covering irrigation needs.[10] Gallagher asked for $500
to have an engineer make a survey and an estimate of necessary funds. The request was approved in 1887.[11] Gallagher, however, wanted 1887
minute details on how to proceed,[12] and the survey was delayed. The project was not undertaken
until 1889. Known as the Foote survey, it pro- 1889

vided for a canal to run from Idaho Falls southeast across the Blackfoot and Portneuf rivers to American Falls. The canal would have been huge — 38 feet wide at the bottom, 62 feet at the top and 8 feet deep. It would have provided 1,500 cubic feet per second to irrigate 300,000 acres of land and would have cost, according to Foote, $238,000. The government was thinking monumentally. Such a canal would have covered the present Fort Hall project and Michaud Flats lands, together with large nonreservation areas.[13]

The government had finally begun to turn its attention to the irrigation needs of Fort Hall. Prior to the survey in 1888, $3,000 was spent to build ditches on the reservation. But in many ways the government's attention was harmfully dilatory and hesitant. Irrigation water had been needed years before. As Agent S. G. Fisher asserted in 1890, the water condition was such that he could not give five acres of irrigated land to each Indian who wanted to farm.[14] How could the Indians be expected to become farmers if there were too little irrigated land and if dry seasons were already destroying crops on the irrigated land? According to Agent Teter in 1895, if the Indians had been provided water ten years earlier they could have become self-supporting.[15] The continued delays, frustrations, and disappointments with farming led to a less than enthusiastic response about Indian Office policies.

The government was equally short-sighted in the matter of water rights. When the Pocatello townsite was set off, the Utah and Northern Railroad had already taken control of some springs and a little stream near the town on reservation land.[16] Dubois wrote the secretary of the Interior in opposition to allowing the railroad a water reserve right to the springs. He declared that railroad officials had appropriated the water illegally and intended to use it to monopolize the town water supply and thus control the town.[17] Even though the water belonged to the Indians and had been used illegally by the railroad, the government went ahead and conveyed to the Utah and Northern 36.45 acres for a water reserve,[18] with the concurrence of Agent Gallagher.[19] He approved largely in the belief that the conveyance would not hurt Pocatello's water supply since that would have to come mainly from the Portneuf. In fact, Gallagher went out of his way in 1887 to advise the government that a water supply from the Portneuf would have to be guaranteed to Pocatello.[20] It is to be regretted that he did not also take an early interest in protecting the Indians' water rights.

The government should either have defined Indian water rights by statute or else have secured them through purchase. By hesitating, the Indian Office allowed white men to file claims upon almost all the water adjoining the reservation. In

1890

1895

1888

1889 Governor George Shoup wrote the secretary of the Interior that speculators were trying to secure all the water rights in Idaho and that 527 claims had already been filed in Bingham County, immediately north of the reservation.[21] He stated that this threatened to "retard" government irrigation policy and asked for executive action. Apparently nothing was done, and the government continued to allow state jurisdiction over water rights.[22]

Meanwhile whites continued appropriating water rights on the Snake and Blackfoot rivers. What could happen was amply demonstrated in 1888 when ditches and dams high on the Blackfoot River left the lower stretches of the stream dry for Indians and whites in the vicinity of the town of Blackfoot after the Indians had planted a large crop.[23] The status of Indian rights was so unclear that when the north-side users took the matter to court the government did not join the suit. The Indians claimed that since the reservation boundary extended to the midpoint of the river they were entitled to half the water. Because the Indians were not able to join the suit, and because the government did not press the matter, the Indian claim was never heard. The case was tried in state court under state laws, resulting in the Steven's Decree on August 1, 1891. The decision determined water rights of parties involved in the suit according to the state law of "beneficial use." Thus the rights of white users were defined and the application of state law was asserted. Indian water rights were not defined, but the implication was that all water rights must be purchased according to state law and beneficial use then made of the water. Instead of pursuing the case the government apparently conceded by purchasing 500 miner's inches from Blackfoot River at a cost of $1,500 in 1892. In effect the government agreed that state law was to govern water rights for the Fort Hall Reservation.[24]

To complicate matters further, the diversion dams, bridges, and flumes located upstream were partly constructed on reservation land. Agent Gallagher asked the commissioner for an opinion so it could be determined whether treaties, laws, and equity had determined Indian privileges or whether they must still be defined. In any event, he declared, their rights needed to be marked out at once.[25] The government had delayed in the past and continued to tarry, thus throwing reservation water rights into turmoil for several decades.

1889

1888

1891

1888

The First Irrigation System

Another governmental mistake in judgment was the decision to allow a private concern, the Idaho Canal Company, to construct an irrigation system on the Fort Hall Reservation. Private in-

1900

terests had already appropriated most of the water rights.[26] By not building the system itself, the government opened the door to delay, increased costs, and an irrigation debacle. In 1895 Agent Teter deprecated the whole sorry mess, writing that there was

1895

> a positive injustice being done them [the Indians] in delaying the furnishing of water on the reservation a single day. . . . I can not too strongly condemn the short-sighted policy, the gross neglect, or worse, which allowed the settlers to file upon the water in streams on or adjacent to the reservation, thereby preventing the Indians from obtaining water, save for personal uses, and putting them to an expense of thousands of dollars to obtain water on the reservation for irrigation.[27]

1900

Largely due to the complications with water rights and to the correlative fact that the irrigation system would have to be constructed and maintained on land outside the reservation,[28] the government too easily acquiesced in allowing private interests to handle the problem. The company given the contract, the Idaho Canal Company, dominated the irrigation picture during the 1890s. The whole episode is a story in itself.

1890

In early 1890 Joseph A. Clark wrote Agent Fisher asking that the Idaho Canal Company be considered in furnishing irrigation water to the reservation at any point on the Blackfoot River.[29] The recently formed company, not yet incorporated, was building a twenty-five-mile canal south from the Snake River and sought to provide water for $5 per miner's inch. The reservation would be a lucrative customer and would provide a substantial income to the firm, so Clark wrote two weeks later offering a reduced rate of $4 per miner's inch.[30] He stated that this reduced rate was possible only because of the volume involved, 10 to 20 thousand miner's inches. But the next day Clark reconsidered. Although $4 was the "rock-bottom" price, he offered to sell water at $3 per inch, provided 10 to 20 thousand inches were bought.[31] As it turned out the company sold the reservation 500 inches of water in 1892 for the low cost of $3 per inch.[32]

The early dealings amounted to little, except perhaps to initiate a dialogue between the company and the government. The company incorporated on September 16, 1890, and promptly set about obtaining a water contract for the reservation. The new president of the company, L. E. Hall, wrote the commissioner requesting permission to build a canal twenty-three miles from the Blackfoot River to Pocatello.[33] The canal was to be primarily for the town, and — by terms of the Agreement of May 27, 1887, with the Fort Hall Indians — town residents were granted the right to use reservation water in the vicinity for their water supply. Hall felt that the agreement authorized his company to be granted a right-of-way, and of course Pocatello residents favored the canal. The canal would provide water to the

1890

reservation, if desired, and would be twenty to twenty-five feet wide at the bottom and three to five feet deep. Hall said that it could be constructed next season if a contract were let at once.

The proposal impressed the commissioner, who asked the attorney general whether such a right-of-way to a private company was in accord with the 1887 Agreement. The Attorney General's Office issued an opinion on February 10, 1891, holding that the provision for water for Pocatello was a personal one applying only to Pocatello residents and was not assignable to private companies. Therefore, a right-of-way for the Idaho Canal Company was not legal.[34] The commissioner of Indian Affairs then asked for legislative authorization to grant a right-of-way for irrigation to private companies.[35] Congress did so on March 3, 1891, and on July 3 Hall was informed that a right-of-way would be granted his company. The plan was to locate the Indians along the canal so they could obtain irrigation water, as well as to provide Pocatello with water.[36] The right-of-way was granted in the summer of 1891, and the company was authorized to commence its work on the reservation.[37] The firm began work but soon ran into the first of numerous snags that were to plague its operations. On September 6, 1891, Agent Fisher notified the commissioner that the company had informed him that, due to poor cost estimates, the canal would take much longer than originally supposed.[38]

1891

1892

Needing water the next season for Indian farmers located on the Blackfoot River, the government contracted with the Idaho Canal Company for 500 inches of water at $3 an inch for 1892.[39] Rather than rushing ahead with the agreed plan the government launched a reappraisal, during which reports and surveys were made and various irrigation alternatives advanced. The first such report by Special Agent Leonard in June 1892 advised that a general irrigation system was indeed necessary. He informed Indian officials that water rights in the Blackfoot River had all been appropriated and that Snake River water rights were nearly all appropriated. He recommended that funds from the Pocatello land sale be invested to pay for an irrigation system.[40] In August 1892 Agent Fisher echoed the recommendation that the $200,000 in the land-sale fund be used but added that the government should own and operate the system.[41] In October the commissioner instructed Fisher to make his own report, with an estimate for a surveyor if one were needed. Fisher asked for $200 for a surveyor. The authorization was delayed, so Fisher submitted a nontechnical report on January 30, 1893.[42] He recommended that a contract be let for the construction of a 16-mile, 20,000-inch capacity canal from the Snake River to the terminus of the Idaho Canal Company ditch on the Blackfoot

1893

River. The government also would purchase the Idaho Canal Company canal extension on the reservation and extend it to Pocatello, using Indian laborers paid from Indian funds; would enlarge the Pocatello Water Campany canal on the Portneuf and extend it northwest to irrigate 30,000 acres; and would then build a reservoir ten miles up Bannock Creek to irrigate the farms there. The estimated cost for the entire project was $100,000. Fisher concluded portentously by stating that, since the Indians could irrigate only nine-tenths of the irrigable lands, the balance ought to be leased to whites.

On February 8, 1893, Fisher reiterated his opposition to Hall's plan for water to be bought under contract on a perennial basis, emphasizing that the Indians would be better off with the government owning and operating the system.[43] Apparently the report got nowhere, and matters were allowed to drift until August. In the meantime the Office of Indian Affairs contracted with the Idaho Canal Company for 1,000 inches of water for $2,500.[44] The amount was soon increased, due to additional Indians settling along the Blackfoot River. At the same time the Pocatello Chamber of Commerce joined the call to use Indian monies to finance the irrigation system,[45] giving the proposal an added and selfish boost.

In August a surveyor was employed and Special Agent John Lane submitted his report.[46] Lane merely echoed Fisher's belief that it would be better for the Indians if the government owned and operated any irrigation system. He also reported that the Pocatello Water Company was taking water from Gibson Jack Creek and not replacing it with water from the Portneuf as had been agreed.

With two alternate options before the government to build the canals itself or contract with private interests, the opportunistic Hall submitted proposals in November 1894 to cover either one.[47] His company would deliver 300 second-feet to the Blackfoot River for $45,000 and $3,000 annually for maintenance, the firm would furnish a perpetual water right to 300 second-feet in a canal built to Pocatello, with reservoirs on the Blackfoot and Ross Fork Creek for $90,000, with a maintenance cost of $12.50 per each second-foot for the canal on the reservation. As the various reports were not completed, no action was taken.

In December 1893 the new agent, Captain J. T. Van Orsdale, notified the government that a canal from the Snake River with a capacity of 600 second-feet including four or five laterals, would cost $145,000.[48] This investigation was assisted by the surveyor and was received as the official report. The estimated cost, however, proved to be too high for government irrigation funds to finance,[49] and alternatives were considered.

Still with no provisions for steady irrigation water, the reservation needed 1,500 inches, which Van Orsdale contracted for at $3,250.[50] For three years in a row the government paid for water from the Snake River for farms on the Blackfoot River. Washington officials apparently preferred to pay this sum rather than pursue Indian water rights in the Blackfoot River, which the Indians in 1894 were still asserting but without government assistance.[51]

In order to finance the irrigation of the reservation a bill was introduced by Senator Dubois in 1894 to use Indian funds.[52] The bill was included in the Indian Appropriation Act and passed on August 15, 1894. It directed the Secretary of the Interior to contract for the construction of an irrigation system and the acquisition of a water supply by using Indian funds.[53]

Superintendent Walter H. Graves was dispatched to Fort Hall in November 1894 to investigate ways to provide the reservation with water.[54] The Idaho Canal Company already had six miles of canal built on the reservation, together with its short-line canal from the Snake River near Basalt to the Blackfoot River. The other prospective bidder, J. J. Cusick and a Mr. Mower, did not get their proposal to Graves in time, but he portrayed a mildly unfavorable picture of their work.[55] The Idaho Canal Company had a clear advantage unless the government decided to undertake the effort on its own, which Hall began lobbying against at once.[56]

His efforts culminated in a letter on May 20, 1895, in which he discussed in depth the report of Superintendent Graves issued on April 27, 1895.[57] The letter constituted a forceful argument for letting a private company handle irrigation for the reservation, Pocatello, and the proposed land cession, and for allowing his firm to be the one that undertook the project. A few days later both he and Graves conferred with the secretary of the Interior in Washington, at which time Hall advanced his company's interest in person. He was instructed to prepare formal proposals for the delivery of 300 second-feet above and 300 second-feet below Ross Fork on the basis of a perpetual water right. He was also asked for a proposal for sale of the company's short-line canal, with all appurtenances, including the ditch already under construction on the reservation.[58]

Hall submitted his proposal on May 24, 1895.[59] The Idaho Canal Company would supply 300 second-feet in perpetuity to lands above Ross Fork for $90,000 and an annual maintenance fee of around $20. The land below Ross Fork would receive water at $7 per acre for a perpetual water right and a maintenance cost not to exceed 75 cents per acre annually. The company finally of-

1894

1895

fered to sell its short-line canal, together with the construction work already completed on the reservation, for $50,000. On June 1 Graves reported that the Idaho Canal Company proposal was the best one received. On June 19 he drafted a contract, with the recommendation that the Idaho Canal Company proposal be accepted.[60] On July 1 the secretary of the Interior authorized the commissioner of Indian Affairs to notify Hall that a contract would be awarded when suitable maps were prepared, with company approval of the provisions.[61] Two days later the company was granted permission to commence construction.[62] On July 10 the secretary of the Interior approved the contract, which was executed by the company on July 30.[63]

There were serious troubles. Agent Teter and Inspector McCormick were suspicious that the contract was being railroaded, and the swiftness of the proceedings aggravated the feeling. Their apprehension increased when it became clear that Cusick and Mower's proposal was the low bid and had received scant consideration.[64] The two men were not even notified of a public hearing held on the matter. A cry of protest arose, and a countereffort by supporters of the Idaho Canal Company led to all kinds of charges and invectives.[65] In the meantime Cusick offered a new proposal — 300 second-feet for $9,000 a year.[66]

The increasing clamor and the new proposals led the secretary of the Interior to reject all bids and to direct that the construction of a canal system by the government be investigated.[67] Agent Teter and State Engineer F. J. Mills looked into the water-rights matter and reported that nearly all the water in the Snake River had been appropriated by independent parties, thus precluding the government's obtaining water on its own.[68]. Teter recommended that private interests be used to deliver water to Blackfoot River and that the canals on the reservation be built by the Indians with government supervision.[69]

Similar proposals had been well argued in the past, but the government again decided to rely on private companies. The secretary of the Interior authorized new bids on November 15, 1895.[70] If the government had gone ahead with Teter's proposal much delay and frustration could have been avoided, with a resultant reduction in expenditure. As it was, advertisements were placed announcing new bids for the construction of the proposed irrigation system.

Newspaper advertisements of bids began November 27, 1895, and bids were received until December 26. Prospective bidders thus had about one month in which to make their proposals. A couple of years earlier Agent Fisher had stated that a proper bid would require at least twelve month's preparation. The Idaho Canal Company had had a year in which to provide charts and maps and was ready in December to demonstrate the superiority of its proposal.[71] Other companies were not allowed sufficient time and could only submit preliminary bids unaccompanied by the required maps.[72] Consequently the Idaho Canal Company had a dominant position in the bidding. It appeared to many that the matter had already been decided and that the new bidding was merely to give the appearance of form.[73] The construction price proposals of the different bidders were: J. J. Cusick, $74,500; Frank Murphy, $65,000; J. A. Murphy, $69,000; George Winter, $60,000; and the Idaho Canal Company, $90,000.[74]

The Idaho Canal Company was the only bidder on the list of water appropriators and was the only one to comply completely with bidding specifications. Although its bid was the most expensive, the secretary of the Interior signed the contract executed by the company on January 25, 1896.[75] Construction began immediately.[76]

Failure of Idaho Canal Company

The contract bound the company to build a canal from the Blackfoot to Ross Fork Creek "by the highest practicable route;" to deliver 300 second-feet in perpetuity through that canal for $90,000 and an annual maintenance charge of $15 per cubic foot ($4,500); to transport the water from the Snake River via the short-line canal and across the Blackfoot River by means of a flume; to extend the canal from Ross Fork to the Portneuf River; and to deliver 300 second-feet in perpetuity, as soon as demand existed, to the lands below Ross Fork for $5 per acre and an annual maintenance fee of 75 cents per acre.[77]

One hundred cubic feet were to be delivered to a point within four miles of the Blackfoot River by June 1, 1896. Another 100 cubic feet were to be delivered to points near Ross Fork Creek by the beginning of the 1897 irrigation season, and the final 100 cubic feet were to be delivered within a year after that.[78] The company was also required to give preference to the employment of Indians. Indians were thus paid from their own funds to work on the project.

Problems arose immediately. The company could not provide the required 100 cubic feet through the high-line canal by June 1 and asked, through Agent Teter, to be allowed to provide it for the present season only through the low-line canal they had already constructed.[79] The proposal was refused, but new difficulties came in its wake. The engineer employed by Teter restudied the contract provisions and decided that several changes would facilitate water delivery and save money.[80] Teter supported the proposals, as did Inspector John Lane, but the secretary of the Interior decided to adhere to the current contract.[81]

Matters were shaken, however, by Inspector McCormick, who was sent to report on whether the water delivered on June 1 met the terms of the contract. The company had indeed delivered the water as required, but had deviated from the contract. Instead of crossing the Blackfoot with a flume and building a canal parallel to the river down to the delivery point at the head of the main lateral, the company dumped the water into the Blackfoot River and then used its old canal to convey the water out of the river to the delivery point.[82] The canal company denied deviating from the contract,[83] but this was a mere subterfuge. Consequently McCormick and A. P. Davis of the Geological Survey were instructed to look into the matter and report.[84]

McCormick recommended following the lines of surveyor Mitchell so the 600 second-feet would be delivered at the Blackfoot River, dumped there, and conveyed by the river's channel to the point where the Foote survey crossed the Blackfoot.[85] At that point a dam would be constructed to hold 400 second-feet to be diverted toward Ross Fork and Pocatello. The other 200 second-feet would continue down the channel of the river to the point where water was being diverted into the old canal; a second dam would be built there. The new proposal was introduced because the canal which was to run parallel to the Blackfoot River along a divide was considered impractical. The soil was too sandy and the height too great.

In conformity with McCormick's recommendation, the secretary of the Interior directed that a new contract be prepared. It was signed by the company on October 2, 1896, and by the secretary of the Interior on October 22.[86] The new agreement embodied McCormick's proposals, made the company liable for all land damages resulting from the change, and provided that the old canal, four miles long, be conveyed to the Indians. The old canal was granted to the Indians on October 12 for $4,000.[87]

At the same time a charge was levelled by J. M. Ingersoll that might help explain the generous treatment afforded the Idaho Canal Company.[88] According to Ingersoll, several of the stockholders were close friends of Commissioner Browning, and one stockholder, Charles W. Spaulding of Chicago, was the brother-in-law of the commissioner. L. E. Hall worked very closely with Spaulding and spent considerable time in Chicago during the crucial months of 1895. On the other hand, the accusation of collusion might merely have been the tail end of the furor over the charges and countercharges made the year before.

In any event, by the winter of 1896 the Idaho Canal Company had a new contract and set to work on the irrigation canal. Agent F. G. Irwin

1897

reported on July 20, 1897, that work was coming along but that the company was not maintaining the old canal properly, as required in the new contract. This necessitated spending $550 to get water to the Indians at the end of the canal.[89] He recommended the company be billed for the extra cost. Also during 1897 Agent Irwin, using primarily Indian labor, spent $16,929 to build a 4-¾-mile lateral and several ditches.[90] The past problems had created more discontent with the Indians, but with work underway the commissioner too sanguinely averred that the hostility had disappeared.[91] In the fall of 1897 the two diversion dams were completed as required.[92]

Then disaster struck the Idaho Canal Company. Several liens to the amount of $13,944 were filed against the firm, one of its sureties went bankrupt, and the officers of the company were changed.[93] Problems continued to mount, and on March 29, 1898, the company was placed in the hands of a receiver. The firm did no work in 1898, and the government began preparing legal steps to protect the interests of the Indians. In 1899 the affairs of the company were still in the hands of a receiver, but a court order of June 19, 1899, authorized the receiver to contract for completion of the canal.[94] The canal from the Blackfoot to Ross Fork Creek was completed on December 12, 1898. Inspector Graves was sent to report whether the contract had been fulfilled. Graves notified the department on January 26, 1900, that the canal was not constructed according to contract and that final payment of $22,500 should be withheld.[95] Each time water was run into the canal to test it, the water broke through the banks and "washed out unsightly gorges along the side of the mountain and deposited sand over the land below in such quantities as to ruin it for any purpose except as a sand bank."[96] The canal had been built by piling the surrounding material, mostly sand, rather than by actually digging a channel. The Indians lost their crops due to lack of water and became quite discouraged.[97] According to Inspector Graves:

1898

1899

1900

These Indians are so impressed with the idea that this irrigation undertaking is a deception and a fraud and pregnant with so much trouble and disaster for them when they attempt to farm and depend upon the ditch for their supply of water that they will not talk about it nor listen with patience to any explanations concerning the matter. It will take a long time to overcome the prejudice that they have acquired against this company and its ditch system.

If it were possible for the Department to foreclose the business in some manner and acquire the right and contract of this canal from the head of it at Snake River down to the end, and eliminate the Idaho Canal Company altogether from the affairs of the reservation, it would be better for all concerned and would place the Government in position to advance and improve the condition of these Indians in some effective way.[98]

The government notified the receiver on July

27, 1900, that the work must be completed and the defects remedied. Surety holders on the bond were also notified that they would be held personally liable for any default.[99] Some repairs were undertaken, and the government began to consider ways to eliminate the Idaho Canal Company from the irrigation affairs of the reservation. The company was taken over by James H. Brady and operated by him after 1900. Problems with ditch failures continued, as did the company's financial difficulties.[100] The troubles with the Idaho Canal Company and its main canal had proven so vexatious to the Indians that when sufficient water 1903 finally was supplied in 1903 Agent Caldwell could not persuade Indians to take up farming under it for fear the water would fail.[101] Affairs continued in an unsatisfactory manner until the government decided to buy out the Idaho Canal Company's 1908 system, which it finally did in 1908.

NOTES CHAPTER X
WATER ON THE LAND

1. *C I A. Annual Report, 1895*, 142.
2. Statement of Major J. W. Powell, U.S. Congress, House, 43d Cong., 1st Sess., Misc. Doc. No. 86 (Wash., D.C., 1874), 3.
3. *C I A. Annual Report, 1872.*
4. Ibid., *1879*, 65; ibid., *1880*, 77, 549; ibid., *1885*, 290; ibid., *1886*, 326; ibid., *1887*, 151; ibid., *1888*, 80; ibid., *1889*, 175–176, 178; ibid., *1890*, 76; ibid., *1891*, 229.
5. Ibid., *1889*, 175–176; Frank C. Armstrong to C.I.A., May 6, 1889, U.S. National Archives, *Record Group No. 48.*
6. *C I A. Annual Report, 1886*, 176; ibid., *1891*, 76; ibid., *1892*, 52.
7. Ibid., *1887*, 157.
8. Ibid., *1883*, 112; ibid., *1880*, 79.
9. Ibid., *1887*, 150; ibid., *1888*, 80; ibid., *1889*, 176; ibid., *1890*, 76; ibid., *1891*, 230; ibid., *1892*, 68; P. Gallagher to C.I.A., March 29, 1887, U.S. National Archives, *Record Group No. 75.*
10. P. Gallagher to C.I.A., Nov. 11, 1886, ibid.
11. P. Gallagher to C.I.A., July 2, Aug. 15, Oct. 12, 1887, ibid.; *C I A. Annual Report, 1887*, 150.
12. P. Gallagher to C.I.A., Oct. 12, 1887, U.S. National Archives, *Record Group No. 75.*
13. *C I A. Annual Report, 1889*, 176.
14. Fisher to C.I.A., Feb. 3, 1890, U.S. National Archives, *Record Group No. 75.*
15. *C I A. Annual Report, 1895*, 142–143.
16. Fred T. Dubois to Sec. of Interior, Jan. 16, 1888, U.S. National Archives, *Special Case No. 99.*
17. Ibid.
18. Sec. of Interior to the President, Jan. 12, 1888, U.S. National Archives, *Record Group No. 75*; Sec. of the Interior to C.I.A., March 2, 1889, ibid.
19. P. Gallagher to C.I.A., Jan. 23, 1888, ibid.
20. P. Gallagher to C.I.A., Nov. 7, 1887, ibid.
21. Gov. George L. Shoup to Sec. of Interior, July 28, 1889, ibid.
22. "Fort Hall Project Report, 1938," 6, *Fort Hall Agency Records.*
23. P. Gallagher to C.I.A., July 28, 1888, U.S. National Archives, *Record Group No. 75.*
24. "Water Supplies and Water Use," *Fort Hall Agency Records*, 1940, 2–3; Peterson, *Futures: A Comprehensive Plan for the Shoshone-Bannock Tribes — Fort Hall Indian Reservation*, 'Water Supplies and Water Use," *Fort Hall Agency Records*, 6–7; *C I A. Annual Report, 1892*, 233.
25. Gallagher to C.I.A., July 28, 1888, U.S. National Archives, *Record Group No. 75.*
26. *C I A. Annual Report, 1900*, 69.
27. Ibid., *1895*, 143.
28. Ibid., *1900*, 69.
29. Joseph A. Clark to Fisher, Jan. 8, 1890, U.S. National Archives, *Record Group No. 75.*
30. Clark to Fisher, Jan. 23, 1890, ibid.
31. Clark to Fisher, Jan. 24, 1890, ibid.
32. *C I A. Annual Report, 1892*, 233.
33. L. E. Hall to C.I.A., Dec. 26, 1890, U.S. National Archives, *Record Group No. 75.*
34. G. H. Shields to George Chandler, Feb. 10, 1891, ibid.; R. S. Gardner to C.I.A., March 17, 1891, U.S. National Archives, *Record Group No. 48.*
35. "Office of Indian Affairs Memorandum, Feb. 12, 1891," *Record Group No. 75.*
36. *C I A. Annual Report, 1891*, 52; ibid., *1900*, 62.
37. Ibid., *1891*, 229; ibid., *1892*, 233; ibid., *1900*, 62; ibid., *1896*, 31.
38. Ibid., *1900*, 62.
39. Ibid., *1892*, 233.
40. Ibid., *1900*, 62.
41. Ibid., *1892*, 234.
42. Fisher to C.I.A., Jan. 30, 1893, U.S. National Archives, *Record Group No. 75.*
43. Fisher to C.I.A., Feb. 8, 1893, ibid.
44. Sec. of Interior to C.I.A., May 1, 1893, ibid.
45. *Pocatello Tribune*, May 12, 1893.
46. *C I A. Annual Report, 1900*, 62; John Lowe to C.I.A., Aug. 23, 1893, U.S. National Archives, *Record Group No. 75.*
47. Hall to Capt. J. T. Van Orsdale, Nov. 28, 1893, ibid.
48. *C I A. Annual Report, 1900*, 63.
49. Ibid.
50. Van Orsdale to C.I.A., Jan. 27, 1894, U.S. National Archives, *Record Group No. 75.*
51. Van Orsdale to C.I.A., Jan. 11, 1894, ibid.; C. C. Duncan to Sec. of Int., Jan. 22, 1894, U.S. National Archives, *Record Group No. 48.*
52. *C I A. Annual Report, 1900*, 63.
53. Ibid.; *U.S. Statutes at Large*, Vol. XXVIII, 305.
54. *C I A. Annual Report, 1900*, 63.
55. Ibid.
56. *Pocatello Tribune*, Jan. 19, 1895; Hall to Walter H. Graves, March 28, 1895, U.S. National Archives, *Record Group No. 75.*
57. Hall to C.I.A., May 20, 1895, ibid.
58. *C I A. Annual Report, 1900*, 63.
59. Hall to C.I.A., May 24, 1895, U.S. National Archives, *Record Group No. 75.*
60. *C I A. Annual Report, 1900*, 63.
61. Sec. of Interior to C.I.A., July 1, 1895, U.S. National Archives, *Record Group No. 75*
62. C.I.A. to Hall, July 3, 1895, ibid.
63. *C I A. Annual Report, 1900*, 63–64.
64. Teter to C.I.A., April 7, 1895, U.S. National Archives, *Record Group No. 75*, Teter to Sec. of Interior, June 1, 1895, ibid.; Warren and Sutton to Emerson and McCaffrey, June 17, 1895, ibid.; E. P. Blickensderfer to Sec. of Interior, June 22, 1895, ibid.; Contract Form of J. J. Cusick, 1895, ibid.; *Pocatello Tribune*, July 20, Aug. 17, 1895.
65. Ibid., July 18, 20, Aug. 3, 17, Sept. 28, Oct. 5, 12, 26, 1895; A. M. Lyons to C.I.A., July 18, 1895, U.S. National Archives, *Record Group No. 75*; Petition to C.I.A., July 23, 1895, ibid.; C. W. Spaulding to C.I.A., Oct. 9, 1895, ibid.
66. John J. Cusick to Sec. of Interior, Sept. 26, 1895, ibid.
67. Sec. of Interior to C.I.A., Oct. 3, 1895, ibid.; *Pocatello Tribune*, Sept. 28, Oct. 12, 26, 1895; *C I A. Annual Report, 1900*, 64.
68. Ibid.
69. Ibid.
70. Ibid.
71. "Contract Proposal of Idaho Canal Company, Dec. 1895," U.S. National Archives, *Record Group No. 75.*
72. J. A. Murray to C.I.A., Dec. 26, 1895, ibid.
73. Ibid.; *Salt Lake Tribune*, Jan. 5, 1896; *Journal History*, Dec. 26, 1895, L.D.S. Department of History.
74. Ibid.; *C I A. Annual Report, 1900*, 65–66.
75. Ibid.
76. *Pocatello Tribune*, Feb. 22, 1896.
77. *C I A. Annual Report, 1900*, 30–31.
78. Ibid.
79. Teter to C.I.A., March 30, 1896, U.S. National Archives, *Record Group No. 75*; F. W. Smith to C.I.A., April 1, 1896, ibid.
80. H. B. Mitchell to Teter, May 15, 1896, ibid.
81. Sec. of Interior to C.I.A., June 25, 1896, ibid.; *C I A. Annual Report, 1900*, 66–67.
82. Ibid., *1900*, 68.
83. F. W. Smith to McCormick, July 7, 1896, U.S. National Archives, *Record Group No. 75.*
84. *C I A. Annual Report, 1900*, 67–68.
85. McCormick to C.I.A., Aug. 13, 1896, U.S. National Archives, *Record Group No. 75.*
86. "Contract of Idaho Canal Company, Oct. 2, 1896," ibid.; *C I A. Annual Report, 1897*, 30; ibid., *1900*, 69.
87. Ibid., *1897*, 31.
88. Francis E. Leupp to C.I.A., Nov. 19, 1896, U.S. National Archives, *Record Group No. 75.*
89. *C I A. Annual Report, 1897*, 31–32.
90. Ibid., *1897*, 128; *Pocatello Tribune*, Nov. 10, 1897.
91. *C I A. Annual Report, 1897*, 32.
92. Ibid., *1898*, 47.
93. Ibid.
94. Ibid., *1899*, 50, 181.
95. Ibid., *1900*, 60.
96. Ibid., *1900*, 61.
97. Ibid., *1900*, 215; ibid., *1901*, 206.
98. Ibid., *1900*, 61.
99. Ibid.
100. Ibid., *1901*, 26; ibid., *1902*, 182.
101. Ibid., *1903*, 154.

CHAPTER XI

DITCHES AND DAMS

Fort Hall Project

Problems with farming and irrigation continued on into the twentieth century. Irrigation facilities were still insufficient, the Indians had deep-seated prejudices against both farming and irrigation, and crop production did not improve materially for twenty years. Moreover, the water rights of the Indians were still undefined, and whites were taking advantages of the situation by stealing the water of the Indians in such places as Bannock Creek.

Some effort was made to improve irrigation facilities on the reservation during the years 1900 to 1905. The Idaho Canal Company was bought by J. H. Brady, one of its shareholders, who 1903 agreed to complete the work. Consequently in 1903 the work, as far as the canal extension to Ross Fork and the ability to deliver 300 second-feet were concerned, was completed.[1] New contracts for water delivery were let, and Brady was able to provide the needed water for the next few years. The agent further utilized nearly $31,000 of Indian money to pay for canal and ditch construction.[2]

It soon became obvious that irrigation at Fort Hall must be vastly extended and improved. If the Lemhi were to be removed and allotments made, there simply must be more water. At the time there was only enough irrigable land to provide each Indian with an acre or two. Since it was obvious that farming (either by the Indians or by lessees) would have to be practiced rather intensively on the fine soil of the reservation, water rights would have to be secured and the water put to beneficial use to safeguard those rights for the future.

Consequently, what has become known as the 1906 Fort Hall Project was undertaken. On June 21, 1906, Congress appropriated funds to make surveys and prepare plans for an irrigation and storage system for Fort Hall. A group of surveyors was dispatched to the reservation in late 1906. One of the primary objectives was to check out the Blackfoot marsh area (segregated by the sec-retary of the Interior in 1898 for possible reser-1907 voir use) for its suitability as a dam and reservoir site. The surveyor's reports concurred in four major recommendations: (1) Construction of the Blackfoot reservoir; (2) enlargement and exten-

sion of the Idaho Canal; (3) construction of several miles of laterals and ditches, at least enough to be able to carry the 300 second-feet contracted for with the Idaho Canal Company, and (4) extension of the government (or old or North) canal by eight miles, together with sufficient laterals to irrigate 10,000 acres. Engineer John J. Granville originally estimated that the total cost would be $320,000, but in his final report of January 31, 1907, he revised that estimate to $420,919.25[3]

With uncharacteristic speed Congress passed an enabling act for the project on March 1, 1907, appropriating $350,000 for its construction.[4] Work on the laterals and ditches began shortly thereafter. The dam was completed in January 1911,[5] and the rest of the work was finished in 1912.[6] The project was somewhat of a boondoggle and proved to be poorly planned. The work took three years longer and cost nearly twice as much as had been estimated. One problem was that Congress appropriated the funds on the basis of Granville's original estimate of $320,000, rather than his final estimate of $420,000. Even the higher estimate "was totally inadequate for doing the work proposed, and resulted apparently from insufficient preliminary surveys and studies, and a consequent failure to comprehend the magnitude of the work involved."[7] Chief Engineer W. H. Code realized this in August 1907 when he told the secretary of the Interior that the cost might go as high as $600,000 and that in any event additional appropriations would be needed to carry on the work.[8] Even this third estimate proved too low, and Congress appropriated additional sums each succeeding year up through 1911 to complete the project — $100,000 in 1908; $125,000 in 1909; $125,000 in 1910, and $85,000 in 1911. By the time it was completed in 1912 the system had cost $750,000.[9]

Another problem concerned the price of water 1911 rights for whites. Since Indian money had been expended on irrigation prior to the project, it was believed that present construction costs should be borne by white settlers on the ceded area whose lands would benefit from the system. Again relying on Granville's preliminary report, which estimated 60,000 irrigable acres on the ceded tract, Congress authorized the secretary of the Interior to sell water rights to whites for $6 an acre. This was expected to net $360,000.[10] There were actually 12,000 acres in the ceded area, which would have provided the government with a return of only $72,000. The $6 fee was not fixed, however, since the 1907 act also stipulated that the cost of construction should be repaid through the sale of water rights. If the whites were to return the money on the basis of the $420,000 estimate they would have to pay about $45 an acre; if on the basis of the final cost, $62.50 an acre. On other irrigation projects in Idaho at the time, the cost per acre for water rights ranged from $20 to $65, so the $6 was incredibly low while the higher fees were perhaps only a bit steep.[11] The actual expenditure for the Fort Hall Project was about $18 to $20 an acre, including Indian lands. This price would have been the most equitable one to charge white settlers, with the government picking up the balance.

The whites, however, refused to settle for equity. The settlers on the ceded portion formed the Pocatello Water Users' Association. Together with ex-Senator Dubois they put on a strong lobby to keep the $6 per acre fee. Their efforts proved successful, and in the act of April 4, 1910, the fee was fixed at $6. For his efforts to secure the best interests of the white settlers, Dubois was promised $1 per acre from each settler, much of which he was paid.[12]

A final problem with the project was that the construction was poorly administered. The funds provided were still insufficient "for completing the project as originally contemplated and planned, with the result that much of the proposed work had to be either curtailed or entirely abandoned."[13] Moreover, "the canals, laterals, and structures then built, were of necessity made of woefully inadaquate size and capacity."[14] They were also made of cheap materials in many instances. In the rush to complete the project, timber often was used instead of concrete. Many of the structures were not even intended to be enduring. This was largely explained by the desire of the engineers and the commissioner to get the work done in order to secure the beneficial use of water right, but it made the Fort Hall Project incomplete and inadequately constructed. In the long run the hasty construction compounded the money problem and led to innumerable delays.

1908   The situation with the Fort Hall Project, however, was not one-sidedly glum. The work had accomplished many important things, and it laid the foundation for large-scale irrigation of reservation lands. One of the most prudent accomplishments of the irrigation work was the purchase in 1908 of the Idaho Canal Company and all its rights.[15] This action was suggested by Engineer Code in 1907. He advocated using the requirement for 300 second-feet to be delivered beyond Ross Fork as a coercive measure.[16] Code's re-

commendation was not followed, but when the canal needed repairs in 1908 the government used the requirement for leverage in getting Brady to sell out for $90,000.[17]

1907   The government also acted wisely in purchasing from Barzilla Clark in 1907 the right to divert the waters of Gray's Lake into the Blackfoot River drainage, together with a partly constructed canal connecting the two.[18] The 1907 act provided the Indians with water rights without their having to purchase them anew. It further freed them from operation and maintainance costs, except when the land had been leased for three years.

Finally, important steps were taken to secure water rights for the reservation. With the purchase of the Idaho Canal Company, the government acquired undisputed right to 300 second-feet of Snake River water, and by a court decree 1911 (Rexburg Decree: Rexberg Irrigation Company v. Teton Irrigation Company, District Court of Sixth Judicial District, State of Idaho, 1911) the other 300 second-feet of Snake River water claimed by the Idaho Canal Company were granted to the project. With the purchase of lands for the Blackfoot Reservoir, the government acquired 123.6 second-feet of Blackfoot River water. In addition, the government filed for 280 second-feet of Blackfoot River water above the other rights already decreed, for which a certificate was issued on July 9, 1915. Less certain and subject to future court claims were the 29.8 second-feet of Blackfoot River water available to July 1 of each year. This water was part of the Steven's Decree of 1891 and was secured by the government through its acquisition of lands for the Blackfoot Reservoir. Rights to the waters of Gray's Lake were 1907 filed for on June 12, 1907, amounting to 140 second-feet — an action which would later have to be repeated. Lastly, the dispute over Bannock Creek waters, whose headwaters were now off the reservation since the land cession, was solved in court on April 9, 1907, when the Indians were awarded primary rights for 16.75 second-feet, while the whites received junior rights to 19.6 second-feet.[19]

All the above rights were acquired under law, and most were required to be put to beneficial use by September 1916. The action was part of the reason for the rush to complete the project. In 1915 the deadline for filing proof of beneficial 1922 use was extended to September 1922. On September 14, 1944, proof was filed for 34,040.68 acres, including 831 acres of the Little Indian area along the Blackfoot River, however the state government withheld license for several years thereafter.[20]

It was unfortunate that the government filed for water rights under state law and abided by 1907 state regulations. In 1907 the U.S. Supreme Court ruled in the famous Winters Case that the very act of creating by treaty an Indian reserve also granted to the Indians the right to as much water as they ever needed from bodies of water running through or bordering their reservations.[21] By employing the Winters ruling the government could have secured for the benefit of the Fort Hall Indians as much water from the Snake and Blackfoot rivers as they could ever use. The 1907 enabling act stipulated that state laws be followed, but the government neglected to make any attempt either to challenge the meaning of the act or to secure legislation allowing the Fort Hall Project to be excluded from state control. Thus, by continuing to act according to state law, the federal government defaulted on its responsibility to the Indians and contributed to the subsequent confusion over water rights in the Blackfoot River and other bodies of water.

1911   With enough water available for about 20,000 acres of Indian land and 12,000 acres of white land, the government was able to go ahead with allotments in severalty, which were authorized in the 1910 act that provided $100,000 more for the irrigation work. Allotments totaling 28,000 irrigable acres were distributed beginning in 1911 and continuing up to 1913.[22] Here was another reason for speeding the work.

Besides making allotments the government was now able to lease Indian lands to white farmers. 1923 The superintendent administered the leases, which were for the most part improvement leases lasting five years. The government had a kind of conflict of interest underway; if Indian lands were leased for more than three years they were subject to maintenance fees, which could amount to thousands of dollars a year toward reimbursement for construction of the project.[23] Once leasing got underway it kept growing until most of the reservation farm lands were leased, which is true even today. For several years the leases were improvement leases requiring no fee, and for a while they did not require the lessees to pay for irrigation maintenance.[24] When leases were let for the money the price was not very high, only $3 an acre annually in 1924 and $5 an acre in 1926.[25]

The attitude of the government toward leasing was well expressed in a report by the Senate 1930 Committee on Indian Affairs in 1930. Since the Indians were not making full use of their irrigable lands, and because of "the desirability of the Government to economize operational expense and reduce congressional appropriations, it is advisable to make exceptionally favorable terms to lessees, who should be encouraged to do more ex-

Idaho State Historical Society

Early irrigation on Fort Hall Reservation.

tensive land improvement work, for which some credit should be given him on lease payments asked by the Indian owners."[26] This point of view was all the more remarkable when the committee admitted, immediately prior to the above passage, that the Indians could not use their lands because the government would not provide them adequate assistance: "It is apparent that the Indians are not making full utilization of all of their irrigable lands, and under present conditions — lack of homes, domestic water supply, financial assistance for seed and implement, and lack of agricultural knowledge and experience, and inadequate technical advice and assistance, probably will not be able to do so."[27] Instead of helping the Indians farm their own lands, the government advocated leasing the lands to make them productive — and under very good terms for the lessees.

The situation was not so bad during the 1920s and 1930s, when the agricultural depression kept farm prices low. Average crop values per acre for lessees during this time were around $30 to $40. Some lessees lost money on their leases, especially during the first years of farming virgin land. Even then the Indians ended up being cheated because the lessees were notorious for poor conservation practices and took little care of the soil.[28]

After the depression the situation for the Indians worsened. Dry-land leases were executed for 75 cents an acre, for example, and today the situation is scandalous. According to the computations of Jack G. Peterson, the average potato lease today yields a net income (after subtracting production costs) to the lessee of $1,185 per acre, and costs him only $15 per acre for the lease.[29]

Thus a huge amount of money from potato crops grown on the reservation is being kept from the Indians, and unconscionably so. Furthermore, a policy that was originally designed, in part, to get reservation lands prepared for Indians to take them over has become so twisted and misused that its practical application merely perpetuates cheating the Fort Hall Indians and deprives them of much of the advantage of the Fort Hall Project.

1912　When it was finally completed in 1912 the irrigation system immediately ran into difficulties. Blackfoot Dam proved inadequate, springing leaks in 1914. The system as a whole proved too small to provide the necessary water to all the lands under the project. Several laterals and ditches, and even the main canal, experienced washouts.[30] It was obvious that the system would

1922　have to be overhauled. By July 1922, the end of the original construction period, $847,291.14 (exclusive of $370,000 operation and maintenance costs) had been expended to construct an irrigation project that was far from complete.[31]

Congress was reluctant to appropriate additional funds without accurate estimates, and a new engineering report was commissioned in 1917. No

action was taken; a new estimate for completing the project was made by Henry W. Dietz in 1921. The recommendations included repairing Blackfoot Dam, enlarging and relocating part of the Idaho Canal, building a diversion dam on the Blackfoot River, and enlarging the water distribution system. Acting upon the report, Congress authorized the rehabilitation work on May 24, 1922, making $300,000 immediately available and setting a ceiling of $760,000 on the whole reconstruction project.[32]

1927　Extensive work began immediately and was not completed until October 1927. Blackfoot Dam was repaired and raised; the China Hat Dike on the Blackfoot Reservoir was constructed; the Idaho Canal was increased in capacity from 300 second-feet to 840 second-feet in the segment between the Snake River and the Blackfoot River; the capacity of the main canal was increased from 350 second-feet to 1,200 second-feet; 18.5 miles of the main canal were rebuilt on a higher location; about 170 miles of canal, laterals, and ditches were either enlarged or newly built; several thousand irrigation structures such as headgates and pipelines were built or rebuilt;[33] and, finally, 26,000 acre-feet of Gray's Lake water were diverted through Clark's Cut to Blackfoot Reservoir by means of two diversion dams. One hundred fifty second-feet of Gray's Lake water had again been filed for by the government in 1919, together with a storage permit for 100,000 acre feet and diversion permits for 85 second-feet of tributary streams.[34]

1928　The rehabilitation work reached a total of $772,815.46, bringing the total cost of the Fort Hall Project by 1928, exclusive of operation and maintenance costs, to approximately $1,650,000. The government exercised more concern for Indian rights by requiring construction cost repayment contracts from the white settlers amounting to $15 an acre. The government also attempted to charge the Indians the same reimbursement cost, but the proposal conflicted with the 1907 statute and was disallowed. The rehabilitation work increased the irrigable area from 30,000 acres to about 51,000, 38,000 of which were Indian.[35]

1926　The project was originally meant to embrace 60,000 acres, and in 1926 C. A. Engle reminded the commissioner of the earlier estimates. The area left unirrigated was the Ross Fork or Gibson division of about 9,600 acres of rather sandy soil. It had not yet been irrigated because it was felt to be too unproductive. Engle informed the commissioner that it was among the most fertile land in the project. He asked that $151,000 be appropriated to bring the acreage under the Fort Hall Project, since there was available a surplus of 50,000 acre-feet of irrigation water. This would be exactly enough to water the Gibson unit.[36] Consequently Congress appropriated $145,000 on

1929 March 7, 1928, for that purpose. The work was completed in 1929, with the final cost reaching $171,464.07.[37]

The Fort Hall Project now encompassed 60,000 acres and had about 300,000 acre-feet of water.[38] In addition there were several minor units operated by the Indians themselves. These were generally the areas first farmed by the farmers along the streams of the reservation. They included Bannock Creek, 3,724 acres; Lincoln Creek, 1,480 acres; Ross Fork Creek, 2,000 acres; and the Little Indian Unit, which was later incorporated into the 1948 Fort Hall Project, 1,262 acres. In 1948 all the units were incorporated into the Fort Hall Project for administration.[39] The Gibson Unit was excluded because it was found that the soil was indeed too sandy.[40]

The Fort Hall Project was far from complete, however. The drouth of the 1930s demonstrated 1934 that the system would not always produce 300,000 acre-feet of water.[41] A report in 1934 estimated that the project would deliver only a sure 250,000 acre-feet each year. The system would have to increase its storage capacity and improve its distribution facilities to prevent water loss. Subse-1937 quently an equalizing reservoir was constructed in 1936-1937 at the junction of the Blackfoot River and the Idaho Canal in order better to control water distribution and to prevent the large water loss that occurred there.[42]

Other improvements were also undertaken over the next several years, primary among which were continued repairs on the main canal, which lost 15,000 acre-feet annually. Equally important were efforts to enlarge the Blackfoot River channel and to undertake flood-control measures. Although 60,000 acres came under the Fort Hall system, for several years only about half this area received water, due to the inability of the Blackfoot River to carry more water without substantial damage to adjoining lands. During the 1930s several damage claims necessitated further modifications of the project, among which was the equalizing reser-1954 voir. All these factors delayed completion of the Fort Hall Project for several years. Not until 1954 was the system officially completed, with all the 60,000 acres being furnished water. A final 1952 appropriation of $13,875 was made in 1952 to complete the project.[43]

Michaud Flats Project

1931 By an act of February 4, 1931, Congress authorized the development of an irrigation system for 30,000 acres on the Michaud Flats west of Pocatello.[44] Irrigation for the area, under consideration as far back as the Foote Survey and the various engineers' reports in the 1890s, was not included in the Fort Hall Project and eventually assumed an individuality of its own. Believing that

it was a prudent move for future development, Congress on May 9, 1924, authorized the use of 1924 $100,000 of Indian funds (derived from the sale of bottomland covered by the American Falls Reservoir) to enlarge and relocate the main canal as part of the rehabilitation project authorized in 1922. The purpose was to be able to convey enough water to Michaud Flats in the future to irrigate the entire area.[45] A few years later in 1928 1928, Congress furnished $25,000 for surveys and investigations to determine the feasibility and cost of irrigating the Michaud tract.[46] The ensuing reports mistakenly estimated that 424,000 acre feet of water were available annually and asserted that enough water was already available to irrigate all reservation lands in the Michaud Flats (21,912 acres).[47]

The engineers planned to use the available water supply to irrigate Indian lands and to purchase 40,900 acre-feet of water for white-owned lands. The estimated total cost was $2,469,816.23, the per-acre cost for Indian lands being about 25 percent lower than for white lands. Relying on this information, Congress 1931 passed the 1931 authorization act and provided $2.5 million for the work.[48] Repayment contracts were required from the landowners before the money was made available, and, due to the reluctance on the part of landowners to make the contracts, the project was delayed. It soon became evident that the water supply was not nearly as large as estimated, and the work was indefinitely postponed.[49]

Proposals were bandied about for several years thereafter, but no definite action was taken until 1954 the 1950s. By act of August 31, 1954, the Michaud Project was reauthorized, based upon a Bureau of Reclamation report in October 1953 and a Bureau of Indian Affairs report in April 1954. The act appropriated $5.5 million to irrigate 11,035 acres adjacent to the reservation under the authority of the Bureau of Reclamation and $5.5 million to irrigate the 21,000 acres on the reservation under authority of the Bureau of Indian Affairs.[50] The cost-benefit ratio for the project was 2.39 to 1 for nonreservation lands and 5.0 to 1 for reservation lands, making the project quite desirable from this standpoint.[51]

The water supply for the project was finally solved by securing 83,900 acre-feet from Palisades Reservoir, 44,700 acre-feet from the American Falls Reservoir, and 22,000 acre-feet from groundwater in the project area. This supply of water was obtained by the government's waiving all rights to waters flowing through lands covered by the American Falls Reservoir in the Fort Hall bottoms.[52] Even then there were additional delays. Congress considered going ahead with the irrigation of the nonreservation areas of the project and postponing work on the reservation area. Although the work was finally started in 1957 it is still not completed.[53]

Besides the delay, there was one further problem associated with the Michaud Project. The $100,000 of Indian money spent in 1924 for canal capacity for the Michaud area was not put to very good use; the additional capacity lay unused for over thirty years. The Indians agitated for a return of the money, and it is not clear whether they were ever reimbursed for the money, whether they were reimbursed for interest lost on the money while the canal was lying unused, or whether they were given concessions for the loss in the 1954 act.[54]

American Falls Reservoir

Beyond the projects designed to irrigate reservation lands, there was another irrigation system intimately associated with the reservation — the American Falls Reservoir or Minidoka Project. The original proposals for the American Falls Reservoir were advanced by private interests around 1908-1909, about the same time as the beginning 1910 of the Fort Hall Project. The Minidoka Project was a massive undertaking, the intention being to dam the Snake River to such an extent that the reservoir waters would extend nearly to Pocatello and Blackfoot.[55]

1913 These initial efforts failed in 1913, not to be revived until the 1920s.[56] When the project was reactivated, the government proceeded with unaccustomed energy, passing an authorizing act on 1921 March 4, 1921, and preparing engineering studies.[57] The Dyer, Dietz, and Banks report provided for a reservoir with a 1.5 million-acre-feet capacity and a five-foot headboard for wave action. As planned, the reservoir would cover about forty-four thousand acres of Indian bottomland appraised at $755,000.[58] The Indians had objected to the original proposals and many remained adamantly opposed to the new ones.

Their protests could not stop the project, but in time, after the commissioner and the secretary of the Interior approved construction of the project in cooperation with private interests, the proposal was changed. Instead of forty-four thousand acres, the bottomland to be submerged was reduced to twenty-eight thousand an appraisal of $700,000 in value. Legislation to secure the bottomland for the project came with the act of May 1924 9, 1924.[59] By its terms the Indians were granted an easement to use the lands for grazing, hunting, fishing, wood gathering, and other activities that did not interfere with the use of the land for reservoir purposes. In exchange for their lands the Indians were paid $700,000. One seventh of that amount was to be used for enlargement of the main canal for irrigation of the Michaud lands. The remainder of the money, $600,000,

was deposited in the Treasury to bear interest at an annual rate of 4 percent. Construction of the project began in 1925 and was completed in the 1927 spring of 1927, when the government assumed responsibility for its operation.[60]

Although the Indians received $700,000 for the acreage to be under water, they very much opposed the flooding of their bottomlands. The lands were rather special to them, both economically for hay and grazing, and for sentimental and religious reasons. Moreover, the Indians were consulted only desultorily about the land cession, and the feeling that they were cheated still rankles. No provision or payments were made for the loss of streams flowing through the bottoms or for the groundwater. In the 1954 authorization of the Michaud Project, all claims to this water were waived in exchange for water rights in American Falls Reservoir and Palisades Reservoir. The means by which the transfer was made remains questionable, and the trade-off was an inequitable one of 2,000 second-feet for 500 second-feet. Finally, the reservoir expanded beyond the allowed capacity, covering additional Indian lands. Over the years the waters of the reservoir have eroded and damaged surrounding reservation areas.[61]

Theft of Water by Whites

Closely associated with water rights and irrigation was the perennial problem of whites stealing Indian water. The problem began in the late 1880s and goes on even today. The basic cause was the complex and convoluted status of reservation water rights. By complying with Idaho state laws in regard to water rights, the government guaranteed both legal and illegal challenges to its priority claims. Had the government invoked the Winters Doctrine early in the twentieth century its claims would have been simple and authoritative and would have guaranteed Fort Hall Indians the right to as much water as they required for the irrigation of their lands. It would also have saved a great deal of time and expense involved in completing irrigation facilities for the reservation. There would have been, for example, sufficient water for the Michaud Project in 1930 when it was first proposed, and the Indians would never have had to trade off their rights to the submerged waters of the Fort Hall bottoms in order to obtain a supply for the Michaud Flats.[62]

The stealing of Indian water occurred primarily in four areas. First, after the land cessions placed the headwaters of Bannock Creek and its chief tributary, Rattlesnake Creek, off the reservation, whites began to divert the flow before it reached the reservation. A court case in 1907 tentatively 1901– settled matters, but shortly thereafter the diver- 1940 sion started again and continued intermittently for the next thirty to forty years. On some occa-

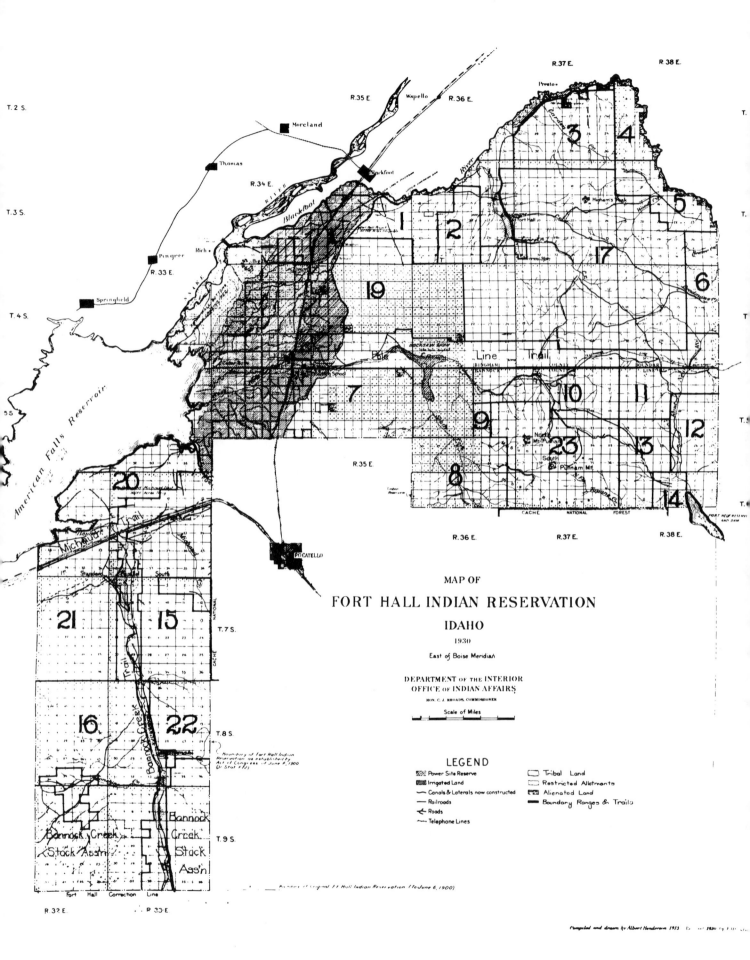

MAP OF

FORT HALL INDIAN RESERVATION

IDAHO

1930

East of Boise Meridian

DEPARTMENT OF THE INTERIOR
OFFICE OF INDIAN AFFAIRS
HON. C. J. RHOADS, COMMISSIONER

Scale of Miles

LEGEND

Power Site Reserve | Tribal Land
Irrigated Land | Restricted Allotments
Canals & Laterals now constructed | Alienated Land
Railroads | Boundary Ranges & Trails
Roads
Telephone Lines

sions the Indians on Bannock Creek were left without any irrigation water, and their crops dried up. Repeated proposals were made for a small dam or two that would make the water supply more consistent, but no action was taken.[63]

1900–1937

Second, on lands belonging to Indians owning allotments on the ceded portion of the reservation, water was frequently diverted from the Portneuf River and its many tributaries by the town of Pocatello, by white farmers, and by the Portneuf-Marsh Valley Irrigation Company. In 1929 Superintendent Stephen Janus reported that the thefts had forced several Indians to abandon their lands or starve. With obvious anger he informed the commissioner that "this has been endlessly reported to your office and has been the subject of endless correspondence but nothing has been done. None of these water thieves have been prosecuted. And apparently, they never will be."[64]

1935–1939

Third, water was taken from the Blackfoot River above reservation diversion points by the north-side water users. Such thefts were particularly common during the drouth years of the 1930s. Sometimes white users diverted the water high enough on the Blackfoot to deprive even the Little Indian Unit of its supply. The situation led to an effort to seek a court settlement by securing an injunction and then utilizing the Winters Doctrine, but the government equivocated for several years and ultimately abandoned the effort.[65]

Finally, whites included in the Fort Hall Project made a habit of using more water than assigned them. Ditch riders were hired to stop the practice, which continued for several years anyway.[66]

1930–1938

Farming at Fort Hall began with reasonable prospects for success. There was goodwill on the part of both the Indians and the early agents. The Indians were willing to abandon the chase and become farmers, though perhaps with some hesitation. What was needed was good faith on the part of the government, but promises and commitments were not kept. During the 1870s Congress pursued an inconsistent and callous course, seldom appropriating enough money to keep the Indians from starving — to say nothing of sufficient funds to take up farming. The supply situation improved during the 1880s, but farm policy became so much a part of the broad effort to subvert Indian culture that it proved counterproductive.

Other problems, such as inadequate implements and instructions, acted to compound the reluctance of the Indians to farm, especially the Bannock. Still some advancement was made by a few Indians such as Captain Jim, and by 1890 large-scale irrigation was necessary if additional acreages were to be cultivated and allotments made. The Idaho Canal Company fiasco served mostly to multiply delays and costs, thereby acting to jaundice many of the Indians to both farming

and irrigation. Subsequent irrigation efforts were carried out in similar slipshod ways and were attended by delays, cost overruns, and frustration, which were increased by the absurd manner in which water rights were secured. Even today the irrigation systems for the reservation are not complete, and the water-rights situation remains confused and uncertain. Moreover, at times — as in the case of land leasing — the Indians were subjected to fraud and loss of rights and money. While some aspects of farming, irrigation, and Indian-government relations have changed over the past hundred years, in the last analysis two factors have remained unchanged: first, the mixed motives of the government; and second, the neglect and indifference of the government to provide adequately for its wards, the Shoshoni and Bannock.

NOTES CHAPTER XI
DITCHES AND DAMS

1. *Pocatello Tribune*, Feb. 9, 1903; W. H. Code to Sec. of Interior, Dec. 7, 1903, U.S. National Archives, *Record Group No. 75*.
2. *C.I.A. Annual Reports, 1900-1907*.
3. John J. Granville to C.I.A., Jan. 31, 1907, *Record Group No. 75*; W. H. Code to Sec. of Interior, Feb. 1, 1907, ibid.; W. B. Hill to W. H. Code, Jan. 20, 1907, ibid.
4. *Pocatello Tribune*, March 5, 1907.
5. *C.I.A. Annual Report, 1908*, 16.
6. John J. Granville to C.I.A., June 10, 1912, U.S. National Archives, *Record Group No. 75*.
7. C. A. Engle to C.I.A., Dec. 6, 1926, *Fort Hall Agency Records*.
8. W. H. Code to Sec. of Interior, Aug. 8, 1907, U.S. National Archives, *Record Group No. 75*.
9. *Survey of Conditions of the Indians in the United States*, "Hearing Before a Subcommittee of the Committee on Indian Affairs," U.S. Congress, Senate, 71st Cong., 2d Sess., Pursuant to Senate Resolution 79, and Senate Resolution 308, Part 6, Jan. 21, 1930, 2473–2474.
10. U.S. Statutes at Large, Vol. XXXVI, Part I, March 1909 to March 1911, 274; "Irrigation Lands on the Fort Hall Indian Reservation," U.S. Congress, Senate, 59th Cong., 2d Sess., Doc. No. 230, Jan. 21, 1911, 197.
11. Evan W. Estep to C.I.A., March 23, 1911, U.S. National Archives, *Record Group No. 75*.
12. *Pocatello Tribune*, Feb. 24, April 13, 1911; Evan W. Estep to C.I.A., Mar. 23, 1911, U.S. National Archives, *Record Group No. 75*.
13. Engle to C.I.A., Dec. 6, 1926, U.S. National Archives, ibid.
14. Ibid.
15. J. H. Brady to C.I.A., April 8, 1908, ibid.; Granville to C.I.A., April 10, 1908, ibid.; C.I.A. to Granville, April 25, 1908, ibid.; Brady to C.I.A., May 4, 1908, ibid.; *C.I.A. Annual Report, 1908*, 55.
16. Code to Sec. of Interior, Aug. 8, 1907, U.S. National Archives, *Record Group No. 75*.
17. J. H. Brady to C.I.A., April 8, 1908, U.S. National Archives, *Record Group No. 75*.
18. Code to Sec. of Interior, Aug. 8, 1907, ibid.
19. Summary of water rights given in *Survey of Conditions . . . etc.*, Senate Hearings, Jan. 21, 1930, 2467, 2482–2483; also see *United States Indian Irrigation Service*, "Annual Report," 1923, *Fort Hall Agency Records*, 17–20, 38–39.
20. Ibid., 19.
21. *Winters v. United States (1908)*, The Supreme Court Reporter, Vol. 28, October Term, 1907 (St. Paul: West Publishing Co., 1908), 207–218.
22. *Survey of Conditions . . . etc.*, Senate Hearings, Jan. 21, 1930, 2466–2467.
23. *United States Indian Irrigation Service*, "Annual Report," 1923, 59–61.
24. *Survey of Conditions . . . etc.*, Senate Hearings, Jan. 21, 1930, 2496–2497.
25. Ibid., 2487.
26. Ibid., 2472.
27. Ibid., 2471.
28. Ibid., 2487; Untitled report, 1929, *Fort Hall Agency Records*, 7; Engle and Burdick, *United States Indian Irrigation Service*, "Annual Report," 1923, 60–61.
29. Peterson, *Futures: A Comprehensive Plan for the Shoshone-Bannock Tribes*, Fort Hall Indian Reservation, June 28, 1974, "Agriculture," 2; Mr. Peterson is the President of Jack G. Peterson and Associates, Inc., located at Boise, Idaho. His firm was hired in 1974 to produce a long-range plan for the development of the Fort Hall Reservation; his report titled 'Futures," not only includes some excellent information on Shoshone-Bannock operations but also reveals a deep sympathy for the tribes.
30. *Survey of Conditions . . . etc.*, Senate Hearings, Jan. 21, 1930, 2477.
31. Untitled report, 1929, *Fort Hall Agency Records*, 5.
32. *Survey of Condition . . . etc.*, Senate Hearings, Jan. 21, 1930, 2477.

33. Ibid., 2478.
34. Engle and Burdick, "Annual Report," 1923, 18–19.
35. Ibid., 8; Margold to Sec. of Int., Sept. 24, 1936, *Fort Hall Agency Files*; Untitled report, 1929, *Fort Hall Agency Records*, 5.
36. Engle to C.I.A., Dec. 6, 1926, U.S. National Archives, *Record Group No. 75*.
37. Ibid.
38. Engle to C.I.A., Dec. 6, 1926, U.S. National Archives, *Record Group No. 75*.
39. Peterson, *Futures*, "Water," 9; Henderson, *Planning Report for Michaud Unit of Fort Hall Project, Dec. 1955*, U.S. Dept. of Interior, Bureau of Indian Affairs, Portland Area, 7.
40. Ibid., 6.
41. Ibid., 8.
42. "Annual Report," *1936*, Fort Hall Agency Records, 14.
43. Henderson, *Planning Report . . . , Dec. 1955*, 5–7.
44. U.S. Congress, House, *Congressional Record, Jan. 28, 1931*, 3488–3524.
45. Henderson, *Planning Report . . . , Dec. 1955*, 7.
46. *U.S. Statutes at Large*, Vol. XLV, Part I, Dec. 1927 to March 1929, 377.
47. "Fort Hall Project," 1939, *Fort Hall Agency Records*, 6; U.S. Congress, House, *Congressional Record, Jan. 28, 1931*, 3490.
48. Ibid., 3495.
49. "Fort Hall Project," 1939, *Fort Hall Agency Records*, 4.
50. U.S. Statutes at Large, Act of August 31, 1954, 68 Stat. 1026, 235–237.
51. Henderson, *Planning Report . . . , Dec. 1955*, 9.
52. U.S. Statutes at Large, Act of August 31, 1954, 68 Stat. 1026, 235–237.
53. Peterson, *Futures*, "Water," 9.
54. "Reimbursement of Funds Appropriated to the Fort Hall Irrigation Project," *Office Memorandum, Nov. 19, 1953, Fort Hall Agency Records*, 1–3.
55. *Pocatello Tribune*, Feb. 14, Sept. 15, Nov. 16, 1910, April 2, 25, May 5, 9, Aug. 1, 1911; R. W. Dixie, Phillip Lavatta, Jacob Browning to C.I.A., Feb. 12, 1910, U.S. National Archives, *Record Group No. 75*.
56. *Pocatello Tribune*, March 10, July 12, 1913.
57. A. P. Davis to Sec. of Interior, Dec. 18, 1920, *Fort Hall Agency Records*; C.I.A. to Secretary of the Interior, Dec. 31, 1920, ibid.; "Appraisal Report on Fort Hall Indian Reservation Lands to be Affected by American Falls Reservoir, Dec. 31, 1921," ibid.; Dyer, Dietz, Banks, "Report of Board of Appraisers, Dec. 30, 1922," ibid.; *Minidoka Irrigation Project, Idaho, March 6, 1924*, "Hearing Before a Subcommittee of the Committee on Indian Affairs," U.S. Congress, House 68th Cong., 1st Sess., Report No. 6864, Vol. 342, Part 1, March 6-13, 1924, 2–4.
58. Ibid., 58; D. W. Davis to Sec. of Interior, Aug. 31, 1923, *Fort Hall Agency Records*.
59. "Public Law, No. 116, 68th Congress, May 9, 1924."
60. *Salt Lake Tribune*, April 17, 1927.
61. C.I.A. to Dan C. Foster, Jan. 16, 1961, *Records, Bureau of Indian Affairs*, Regional Director, Boise, Idaho, to C.I.A., Sept. 16, 1960, *Fort Hall Agency Records*; "Appraisal Report: Past, Present and Future Damages on Fort Hall Indian Lands Along American Falls Reservoir, Minidoka Project, Idaho, Feb. 20, 1959," ibid.; Peterson, *Futures*, "Water," 11.
62. *Survey of Conditions . . . etc.*, Senate Hearings, Jan. 21, 1930, 2496–2497.
63. Caldwell to C.I.A., March 11, 1901, U.S. National Archives, *Record Group No. 75*; Arthur M. Tinker to Sec. of Int., Aug. 31, 1903, U.S. National Archives, *Record Group No. 48*; Petition of Indians on Bannock Creek, 1910, *Fort Hall Agency Records*; C.I.A. to F. A. Gross, Jan. 23, 1930, ibid.; C.I.A. to James, March 4, 1929, ibid.; Gross to C.I.A., Feb. 12, 1934, ibid.; Gross to C. B. Ross, May 19, 1934, ibid.; Bannock Creek Indians to Bert Shay and Julius Ballard, July 7, 1940, ibid.; *Pocatello Tribune*, April 28, May 7, Oct. 4, 1904; *Survey of Conditions of the Indians in the United States*, U.S. Congress, House, 72d Cong., 1st Sess., Part 27, 14732.
64. A. W. Fisher to A. F. Caldwell, May 21, 1900, U.S. National Archives, *Record Group No. 75*; Caldwell to C.I.A., June 19, 1902, ibid.; Caldwell to C.I.A., Jan. 15, 1903, ibid.; M. A. Richards to C.I.A., Jan. 15, 1905, ibid.; Evan W. Estep to Just and Philbrick, Nov. 3, 1911, ibid.; Gross to C.I.A., Nov. 17, 1937, ibid.; Minutes of Fort Hall Business Council, Nov. 16, 1937, ibid.; Stephen Janus to C.I.A., Dec. 1, 1929, ibid.; Estep to C.I.A., Feb. 26, 1912, *Fort Hall Agency Records*; Affidavit of Tom Gibson, Aug. 7, 1914, ibid.; Gross to C.I.A., July 23, 1932, ibid.; Olaf H. Wahl to H. E. Bruce, July 16, 1932, ibid.; Bruce to Mary L. Hunt, July 16, 1932, ibid.; Mans H. Coffin to Wahl, July 17, 1935, ibid.; "Report of Hearing . . . Regarding Fort Hall Matters, Apr. 26, 1912," *Records, Office of Indian Affairs*; "Case of C. S. Skeem *et al.* v. U.S. and Thurman J. Hofhine, May 2, 1921," ibid.; "Case of U.S. *et al.* v. Julia Hibner, *et al.* July 14, 1914," ibid.; C.I.A. to C. A. Engle, Dec. 7, 1929, ibid.; Geraint Humphreys to C.I.A., Dec. 20, 1929, ibid.; *Pocatello Tribune*, July 11, 1911; April 26, May 2, 1912; *Salt Lake Telegram*, May 2, 1921.
65. Kenneth R. L. Simmons to Nathan R. Margold, Nov. 16, 1935, *Fort Hall Agency Records*; Sec. of Interior to Att. General, Jan. 17, 1936, ibid.; C.I.A. to Humphreys, Feb. 14, 1936, ibid.; Oscar L. Chapman to Att. General, Jan. 5, 1937, ibid.; Gross to Wayne C. Williams, March 20, 1939, ibid.; Wayne C. Williams to Gross, March 22, 1939, ibid.; Gross to E. C. Fortier, March 25, 1939, ibid.; "Preliminary Draft of Articles of Complaint Against Northside Users of Blackfoot River Water, titled U.S. v. The Riverton Ditch Co., *et al.*, 1939," *Record, Office of Indian Affairs*.
66. C.I.A. to Humphreys, Feb. 12, 1930, *Fort Hall Agency Records*; Gross to O. W. Davidson, May 17, 1933, ibid.; Gross to C.I.A., Dec. 23, 1934, ibid.; M. A. Ireland to Gross, May 29, 1936, ibid.; Gross to C. D. Thompson, June 4, 1936, ibid.; Charles E. Lovatta to Sec. of Interior, Oct. 3, 1938, ibid.; *Survey of Conditions of the Indians in the United States*, U.S. Congress, House, 72d Cong., 1st Sess., Part 27, 14677.

CHAPTER XII

FROM GOLD TO PHOSPHATES

Illegal Removal of Timber

In the matter of industrial development on the Fort Hall Reservation, the government has likewise been hesitant and dilatory, although many white men have seen the potential in natural resources and over the past hundred years have attempted to harvest the profits which they have seen on every hand. The story of the discovery and exploitation of the natural resources at Fort Hall involved the struggle of agent and Indian alike to conserve whatever assets the land possessed until the Shoshoni and Bannock were prepared to develop them.

The first and most obvious natural wealth on the Indian lands was the luxuriant stand of
1869   timber, which Agent Danilson described in 1869 as "inexhaustible, with thousands of trees, that for twenty feet, will square from ten to eighteen inches, there are also many larger ones."[1] Enterprising and free-wheeling whites were not long in moving up their circular saws to attack this easily exploited and profitable business.

There were undoubtedly timber depredations throughout the history of the Fort Hall Reservation — especially during the early years when the settlers were illegally using land belonging to the Indians (in Marsh Valley particularly) and when the Utah and Northern Railroad was constructing a line across the reservation. However, the only real documentation for timber claims was
1878   in 1878, when there were instances of both settlers and the railroads cutting timber in large quantities on reservation land.

Beginning in September of 1878 there was an open acknowledgment by Jay Gould of the Union Pacific that the railroad was using timber and had done so for the entire time of railroad construction on the reservation.[2] In his letter to the Justice Department, Gould claimed that the railroad had authority to cut the trees under congressional acts relating to the construction of railroads on public lands, and he justified the railroad's actions by adding that a railway would facilitate management of the Indians. In the meantime illegal tree cutters were being arrested, until the U.S. attorney advised local officials to suspend arrests until the rights of the Utah and Northern Railroad were determined. Gould personally thanked the attorney general, but the matter was shortly

reopened by Norman Buck, U.S. attorney for Idaho, who was of the opinion that the UNRR right to use public lands and the materials thereon for railroad construction had absolutely nothing to do with cutting timber on the reservation. He quickly informed the attorney general of his point of view and continued prosecution of the allegedly guilty parties.

In October Attorney General Devens told Buck that he had every right to prosecute Gould's men who were cutting timber on the reservation; Devens informed Gould of this fact in a letter dated October 5. Two men, Hyrum Smith and John F. Merrill, were found guilty of cutting timber and fined rather heavily — the first $1,800 and nine months in prison; the latter $4,000 and three months' imprisonment. The attorney general then informed Gould that if the reservation lands were indemnified for the amount of the timber illegally cut the two convicted men could have their sentences remitted. Gould agreed to do so.

To determine the amount of indemnification, Buck prepared a long report on the depredations. The report indicated that three mills were using lumber at least in part from the reservation, that each mill had a potential of cutting 15,000 feet per day, and that if they were allowed to operate for a year they could destroy all the timber in the area. In any case, Buck's actual charges blamed Smith for cutting 15,000 trees and Merrill for cutting 7,000 trees. The jury found that the values of the timber were $3,836.44 for Merrill and $600 for Smith. Buck indicated that Smith and Merrill were only two of many culprits. Devens then referred the entire matter to the secretary of the Interior, with the recommendation that Gould should pay only for the timber cut by Smith and Merrill.[3]

In November 1878 a letter from W. E. Hollister indicated that the depredations had not ceased and requested that Secretary of the Interior Carl Schurz take some action. It was clear from this source and from the *Idaho Statesman* that there may have been timber cut by settlers and entrepeneurs from northern Utah with mills in Brigham City. In the opinion of the *Statesman*, however, the Indians had forfeited their rights to have the reservation at all. And it was apparent that it may have been the feeling generally among whites that the reservation land was public land

and open to timber exploitation. The *Statesman* wrote:

> If the timber on the reservation is needed for the construction of the railroad it should be used for that purpose regardless of any fancied rights of these Indians, who have so recently shown themselves to be nothing better than fiends in human shape. The country needs this road but has no earthly use for Indians, except to get them out of the way by the speediest method possible.[4]

No better indication of attitudes about Indian property among whites could be found, though any further evidence of actual amounts of timber cut are lacking.

Early Mining Efforts

Interest in the possibility of minerals in the Fort Hall area did not surface until prospectors from the played-out diggings in California and Nevada began to look eastward toward the Rocky Mountains. The discovery of gold and silver in central Idaho and western Montana in the early 1860s drew miners by the thousands. After the initial rush there was the usual search for the precious metals in adjoining areas, with a flurry of excitement now and then when some optimistic miner would report discovery of the mother lode. Prospectors coursed the Snake River and its tributaries during the 1860s but found no great deposits of mineral wealth in the mountains bordering that stream. This was particularly true of the Fort Hall region, which had been easily accessible to sourdoughs from the time of the early trappers to the period of the overland travelers.

Prospectors showed little interest in the country surrounding Fort Hall until establishment of the reservation made the lands off limits to them. Then the lure of unknown riches on the reserve became a powerful magnet which attracted much speculation and excitement among miners who had exhausted most other possibilities on the public lands of Idaho. As the Indian agents at Fort Hall began to use their police to keep prospectors off the reservation, the ebullient gold-seekers became more and more convinced that there must be untold treasure awaiting the lucky man who would get permission to search for it. Or better still: Reduce the reservation to just a few acres for the benefit of the Indians and throw open the remainder to the eager miners, who would then exploit the riches for the glory of God and country and the enrichment of themselves.

Even the agents at Fort Hall were convinced that wealth lay just beyond the hills surrounding the agency; more time was spent prospecting than the agents cared to reveal in their reports to Washington. On July 8, 1871, M. P. Berry did disclose to the commissioner, "It also becomes my duty to inform you that I have commenced prospecting a belt of mountains on this Reserve for

lime-stone or crude lime."[5] Any other metals of a more precious kind which he might have found would not have been unwelcome.

The territorial legislature in far-off Boise was enamoured by mining possibilities at Fort Hall. When it sent a memorial to the President in 1879 asking that a portion of the reservation be added to the territory, one of the arguments used was that "the Territory to be set-off is mountainous and is believed to be rich in mines of the precious metals; Miners have been driven off and not allowed to prospect thereon."[6] "Believed to be rich in mines of the precious metals" — these were magical words which had stirred men's imaginations from the time of Cortez and Coronado to the discoveries of Comstock and Cowan. Fort Hall was to have a small taste of such excitement.

Occasional complaints appeared in the local frontier newspapers about the restrictions against mining on the reservation. The *Blackfoot Register* on June 23, 1882, recorded one from its correspondent of Portneuf Canyon, who announced the discovery there of some iron and lead ore which, he said, would produce $73 per ton, "but as long as the present monotony continues in the shape of an Indian reservation this wealth can not be used to any advantage." He thought the reservation should be reduced to ten square miles and the remainder thrown open to settlement.[7] A second would-be miner wrote directly to the secretary of the Interior in 1887 requesting the opening of Snake River bottomlands to miners, who could then, by the use of rockers, exploit the "flour gold" of the lands along the river. He estimated that fifty miners could be gainfully employed for two years with daily takes of from $2 to $5 each.[8] All such requests were denied.

There was one mineral resource that the Office of Indian Affairs was willing to exploit for the benefit of neighboring white settlers. When the president of the board of directors of the Idaho Insane Asylum at Blackfoot asked permission to remove forty cords of rock from the reservation for construction of a new building, the secretary of the Interior instructed the commissioner to grant permission "if the Indians will consent to the same."[9] The citizens of Blackfoot then asked approval to take loose rock from reservation lands for building purposes, arguing that they would be doing the Indians a favor as well as themselves. Agent Fisher favored the request.[10]

Other petitions began to flood the agents as soon as the news spread that the asylum had been granted the right to purchase building stone. Agent Teter recommended that he be allowed to sell stone to anyone at 20 cents per perch, giving the Indians the employment of hauling the material to the customers. In this instance the U.S. Attorney General advised the Interior Department to disallow the request because there was no au-

1862

1871

1879

1882

1887

1889

1895

thorization under law for the sale of building stone from Indian reservations. Five years later, in 1900, another agent wrote for permission, saying that the necessity of asking the Interior Department for approval entailed "no little annoyance and delay." He also was of the opinion that the sale of rock would benefit both Indians and whites.[11]

1894 A much more grandiose scheme for developing all the mineral resources of the reservation came in 1894 with an application from a Salt Lake City firm, The Pacific Prospecting, Developing, and Mining Company, to mine and reduce "all mineral and precious ore found on said Reservation," for which the company would pay either 5 percent of the cash value of all ores mined or 55 cents per ton gross weight. The Indians could decide which option they wanted, and the company offered to give a bond in any amount set by the Interior Department. The proposal launched a four-month controversy, during which the *Pocatello Tribune* took the stance that such a contract was a monopoly which would deny private citizens the right to prospect and mine reservation lands and would also delay opening much of the Indian lands to white settlement. Agent J. T. Van Orsdale supported the move, expressing umbrage with the short-sightedness of the people of Pocatello, a town that was "practically dead" anyway. He indicated that it would be necessary first to get the consent of the Indians, who had already turned down a similar request and, said he, "The people of Pocatello need not fear being aroused from their present delightful state of repose for two or three years at least."[12]

In a second council called by Van Orsdale the Indians revised their earlier negative decision and voted to approve a ten-year lease to the Pacific Prospecting, Developing and Mining Company — with the qualification that it would not be an exclusive lease and that the Indians could make similar leases to others. The Department of the Interior disapproved the proposal because it would tend to create a monopoly and would delay the opening of Indian lands to public settlement. The businessmen of Pocatello also reversed themselves and petitioned the secretary of the Interior to grant the lease. A second newspaper, the *Pocatello Herald*, now entered the lists, opposing the "iniquitous nature and gigantic proportions of the scheme" and adding that there were at least two thousand men in Pocatello and vicinity "watching with almost bated breath" for the opening of the Indian lands to settlement. The petition from Pocatello and the letter of rejection from the Department of the Interior apparently passed in the mails.[13] In one more try, Van Orsdale and company officials sent another communication to Washington attempting to meet the objections of the department — but to no avail. The editor of

the *Pocatello Tribune* and other citizens of the town were more interested in instructions from the Department of the Interior to proceed with surveys which would allow a possible agreement for cession of the southern portion of the reservation.[14]

The *Pocatello Tribune* continued to warble the siren song of "rich mineral deposits," specimens of ore from locations "within an hour's walk of the city," "several copper claims of richest promise," "some galena ore" so rich that it almost created a "stampede in Pocatello," and hills that "are rich in copper, gold and silver." The only impediments to securing this immense wealth were the Shoshoni and Bannock who were "extremely jealous of their rights." The Indian police routinely arrested every man who showed up on the reservation carrying a pick and shovel. In one 1893 instance in 1893 a determined group of men from Pocatello discovered a copper ledge on Belle Marsh Creek, put a force of men to work to uncover the vein, and persisted after being warned twice and until they were threatened with arrest. Other indefatigable miners wrote their senators in Congress beseeching help so they could take out claims on the reservation.[15]

After a long, agonizing wait and many disappointments, the people of Pocatello finally had 1902 their way; the Indians capitulated and signed away the southern portion of their reservation. As recorded earlier, events then proceeded methodically to the glorious day when the ceded portion of the reserve was opened to settlement and to mining claims — at noon, June 17, 1902.

It is only necessary here to record briefly the jostling and grasping after the supposedly rich veins of ore on the soon-to-be-opened Indian lands. Two years before the President's proclamation setting the exact time of opening, the *Pocatello Tribune* had reported hundreds of men out on the reservation staking claims as fast as they could put down the wooden pegs while "Agent Caldwell . . . turned out his entire force of Indian police and is patrolling the mountains in every direction and all stakes and notices are pulled up as fast as put down."[16] But eager miners and settlers were not to be denied after a fifteen-year wait, and they completely overwhelmed the understaffed Indian agent. Washington officials came to Caldwell's aid by notifying him that he *must* keep all interlopers off the reservation. They offered to furnish him with troops if necessary. Notices of these instructions finally resulted in all but the most courageous or foolhardy claim-stakers leaving Indian lands.[17] Then came a wait of two years before the proclamation was finally announced.

The official pronouncement overcame the timidity of the would-be miners who, after a hiatus of two years, once again began to test the effectiveness of Caldwell's Indian police. The agent sent his police to take care of the mounting pressure of determined sooners, and eighteen of them were rounded up and ejected from reservation lands. As soon as the police turned their backs, most of the miners went right back to their diggings. To avoid trouble among themselves and to forestall claim jumpers, about three hundred miners from camps all over the West met in Pocatello on June 14 to organize a mining district and to establish rules and regulations which would guarantee all an equal opportunity to stake a claim.[18]

Perhaps it is just as well to bring to a close this account of mineral wealth sought but not found. Within a few days after the opening of the reservation, the *Pocatello Tribune* was announcing "Asbestos Ledge is Uncovered," "Big Showing on Copper Belt," "Free Gold Lots of it." Finally came genuine proof that this was a real frontier mining area: "E. M. Fritz and J. S. Donaldson Shot to Death." The double murder occurred about a hundred yards from the Lost Horse claim on Pocatello Creek.[19] For a year or two after the big rush the Pocatello paper spasmodically reported new strikes or great profit being made from rich mines, but by this time some were remembering what Senator Dubois had said about the absence of minerals near Pocatello.

Prospecting in the Twentieth Century

From "The Day of the Run" through the next half century occasional prospectors (attracted by the forbidden, and therefore surely wealthy, areas) sought permission from reservation officials to search once again for the supposed hidden treasure. In 1930 Henry and Joseph Fernandzey applied for a lease of 240 acres for "mining purposes." At the same time George J. M. Goingah, representing the Diamaceous Development Company, sought a lease.[20] The minutes of the Fort Hall Business Council for August 10, 1948, recorded a request by Murray Baum to prospect on the reservation for eighteen months, with the understanding that copies of any assays would be mailed to the council.[21] Three years later the Food Machinery and Chemical Corporation was granted permission to prospect for phosphate ores for a one-year period, after agreeing to eight carefully drawn stipulations, including the promise to hire Indian labor.[22] In 1956, spurred probably by the uranium boom, the business council adopted a very aggressive stance by opening the reservation to prospecting — uranium and oil and gas being the chief products mentioned in the plan of operation.[23] These instances were typical of the requests presented to the Indians for the right to search for minerals on the reservation.

An early interest in coal sparked some enthusiasm that the fuel needs of the Indians could

be met on their own reservation. Agent Caldwell asked for instructions in 1905 as to whether a discovery of a coal outcropping by some of the Indians meant they would have to pay royalties to the other Shoshoni and Bannock.[24] The worry was needless as evident by the withdrawal of the Bannock Creek Mining Company twenty years later from certain leases on that stream "as they failed to locate coal."[25] Another Indian prospector in 1930 reported discovery of a vein of coal — probably the same coal mine which tribal leaders requested be developed when they listed the important needs of the Shoshoni and Bannock in 1936.[26]

All these efforts to mine coal came to naught — as the optimistic explorers could have discovered by reading the 1920 *Bulletin 713* of the U.S. Geological Survey. G. R. Mansfield had made an exhaustive study of the geography, geology, and mineral resources of the Fort Hall Reservation in 1913. He recorded then that, in his opinion, the Bannock Creek deposits were "too shaly to be of value for coal."[27]

Mansfield also described the placer deposits of fine gold found in the gravel of the Fort Hall bottoms. He estimated these areas averaged less than one cent to the yard in gold but thought the "skim-bar" gravels along the river would contain from 65 cents to $4 a yard in gold. Rockers were used most of the time to extract the fine flakes, but at least in one instance horse-drawn scrapers were used to carry the gravel to a sluice box.[28] An earlier 1908 report gave evidence that miners working on a private ranch "may have gotten over on the Reservation at times." In fact, said the official of the Indian Service, a rancher named Driscol had been doing some placer mining "and it is not to be wondered that he would prospect on the Reservation," inasmuch as his property adjoined the Indian lands.[29]

There were continual requests from more law-abiding miners for permission to recover gold from the bottoms. One of the more interesting was from a 67-year old Civil War veteran who claimed he had lost his lifetime earnings during the Panic of 1893 and must therefore make a living any way possible. He wrote:

Served 3 years and 7 months, re-enlisted in the field, was discharged an account of disability, gunshot wound received at battle of Wilderness. I was barefoot at 2nd battle of Bull Run, South Mountain and Antietam, and marched between these battles without shoes, and I don't remember of missing roll call once. I have been in on the frontier of Montana and Idaho since 1868. I get $12 pension. I am sober, don't think I have drank 3 gallons of liquor in my whole life. If you can will you kindly give me a permit to placer mine along Snake River on Fort Hall Indian reservation.[30]

After much correspondence the Washington office refused the old veteran's plea on the grounds that the Indians opposed granting such permits and in fear that, as had occurred on at least one other reservation, the sluice boxes would be used as irrigation ditches to water crops on valuable agricultural lands. In 1912 two other applicants were also told that Indian permission must be received before any approvals could be issued for placer mining.[31]

1912

Although less exciting than searching for the yellow metal, a reservation rock quarry near Blackfoot continued to offer commercial possibilities for building stone. One young Indian leader proposed to a visiting Washington official that the tribe sell the stone to Blackfoot residents, who would be glad to buy as many as 500 cords at $4 per cord. The official thought the estimate over-optimistic, but he did listen to Indian complaints about whites taking fine building stone from a spot near the mouth of Blackfoot River. The Indians pointed out four houses in Blackfoot which they claimed were built of reservation stone.[32]

1908

From the early 1900s until 1936 intermittent efforts were made to locate profitable ores on the reservation. On March 25, 1936, the secretary of the Interior issued an order closing unallotted Indian lands "to exploration, location, and lease for the mining of metalliferous and nonmetalliferous minerals other than oil and gas." The regulation affected the efforts of developers who wished to lease lands on Bannock Creek for the mining of diatomaceous earth — particularly F. M. Bistline of Pocatello, who claimed he had entered his application prior to issuance of the Department of the Interior order. The congressional delegation of Idaho became involved in attempts to help Bistline acquire a lease.

1936

The flurry of activity prompted the Office of Indian Affairs to ask for an investigation of the mining of diatomaceous earth and what sales possibilities there would be for the Fort Hall Indians. The Geological Survey reported that the substance was a volcanic ash found in deposits in the foothills east of Bannock Creek. It was being used as a building insulator and sold at Idaho Falls for $10 a ton. The investigator estimated there was a local market of a hundred tons a year, with a net profit of $6 a ton if the Indians wished to develop the deposit. The Fort Hall Business Council discussed the possibility of developing the mine as a tribal venture but finally voted to suspend action because of the uncertainty of the market and the low price for the material.[33]

Development of Phosphate Deposits

1913

Diatomite, stone, coal or placer gold — none of these metals offered the Shoshoni and Bannock as much possibility for profit as an early but unheralded discovery of phosphate on the reservation. G. R. Manfield's careful report listed deposits of 738,526,700 long tons just waiting to be developed. This was about 13.5 percent of the known deposits in the entire western field of the United States (5,464,082,000 tons). On July 1, 1918, 4,080 acres of phosphate public lands were withdrawn from entry on the Fort Hall Reservation. Most of these lands were located in an area east of the agency.[34] The lack of a rail line to the phosphate areas, plus the lack of commercial interest during the early 1900s, precluded any development. A comprehensive March 1944 report on the Fort Hall Reservation included this observation:

1918

1944

> There are no mineral deposits being worked at the present time and there evidently will be no income to the Indians from this source in the future, except the large phosphate deposits in the eastern part of the reservation. These deposits extend outside the reservation and it is doubtful that they will be commercialized any time in the near future; however, they do remain a potential resource.[35]

By 1947 the resource was being developed through a contract with the Simplot Fertilizer Company, which was granted a right to stockpile its phosphate ore behind the San Diego warehouse near the Union Pacific Railroad tracks at the agency. A tract of land on the railroad right-of-way was also approved for loading facilities for the company.[36] Minor troubles with Simplot included insurance claims for cows killed as a result of the mining operations, but on the whole both Indians and company seemed satisfied with the development.[37] To reduce the cost of trucking the phosphate to the railroad's main line at Fort Hall Station, the Union Pacific built a twenty-two mile branch leading to the Simplot Gay Mine.

1947

1948

Complaints were filed by individual Indians that just compensation had not been paid for damages to allotted farmlands as a result of the railroad right-of-way. Eva Yandell Phippeny charged that, in the case of Edward Queep, the railroad ran right through the middle of his property, but he received only $30 in damages. She cited other examples.

Edward J. Sorrell criticized the initial contract granting a lease of ten square miles to Simplot, claiming there had not been proper payment for the two years of operation, during which the company had shipped a half-million tons of phosphate. In addition Mr. Sorrell said the Union Pacific Railroad had never paid any money for the "invasion" of Indian lands. Ms. Phippeny also objected to the use of $100,000 of tribal money to purchase an interest in the Gay Mine for the tribe. She added that rumors were circulating that the tribe's silver and copper mine on Mt. Putman was to be opened for operation, and she wondered what would be the final disposition of the oil wells which had been drilled on Fort Hall bottomlands by Standard Oil Company and then capped. This was while F. A. Gross was superintendent.[38] The

1949 Indian commissioner answered at least part of the accusations by explaining that the Union Pacific Railroad had paid out $60,606 to sixty allotments and $1,820.50 to nine tracts of tribal land for the twenty-two mile right-of-way, which had been approved by the Fort Hall Business Council on April 13, 1948.[39]

A constant source of friction between Indians and the Simplot Company was the payment of royalties. Reassurances were just as constant by the Fort Hall superintendent that proper audits were being made and that the Indians were getting their proper payments out of the mining operation.

1952 A 1952 report disclosed that income from the extraction of phosphate on the reservation amounted to $17,146.93 in royalties and $2,806.28 in rentals for the tribe, plus $34,914.51 in royalties and $1,789 in rentals for individuals, for a yearly total of $45.656.72.[40]

1954 A council meeting of September 14, 1954, requested that an additional audit be furnished for the period from June 1, 1951, to the close of the 1952 season to ensure that the tribe was receiving its proper royalties.[41]

1960 By 1960 the Westvaco Corporation was also involved in mining phosphates on the reservation, and the council had a prolonged discussion over whether it should allow the Food Machinery and Chemical Corporation to drill test wells for water for a beneficiation plant near the Gay Mine. Opponents argued that the Fort Hall water supply would be injured; proponents dismissed the objection as being not based on fact and pointed out the Indians would lose over a million dollars in royalties if the reduction works were not built. Supporters also said that Department of the Interior charges that Simplot owed the Indians an additional $152,000 in royalties for operations over the past several years would be pursued by the department — a matter which had nothing to do with the question of allowing wells to be drilled.[42]

A resolution of the problems between Simplot and the Shoshoni and Bannock was attempted in a council meeting attended by J. R. Simplot on

1963 August 12, 1963. Points discussed included water for the beneficiation plant, introduction of liquor and firearms by the company (contrary to agreements), the building of roads on reservation lands by Simplot, and a renegotiation of royalty agreements with both Simplot and the Food and Machinery Corporation. Simplot stressed the $1.5 million in royalties his company had already paid the Indians and the $35 million invested by FMC in their phosphate plant. Two other major grievances on the part of the Indians were the fact that Simplot was not unionized and their constant fear that the water supply in the phosphate area would be damaged and thus affect the irrigation and culinary water so essential to the lives of the Shoshoni and Bannock.[43]

At a later meeting in 1963 the Indians asked three things of the Simplot Company: a request that Simplot provide from $10,000 to $15,000 for a scholarship program for the Indians, an insistence that at least 50 percent of the Simplot employees be Indians, and an agreement that the Indians have the right to negotiate directly with the company for increased royalties.[44]

1972 In July 1972 production at the Simplot plant was so high that the company was having difficulty hiring twenty nine Indian workers. There was a question about whether Simplot should be allowed to move the road to the plant. There was also a request that the firm provide the figures for its anticipated yearly income so the tribe could better prepare a budget. The initial twenty-five-year contract ended in 1972, which meant that the tribe from then on would receive 100 percent of the royalties from the phosphate operation instead of 51 percent as agreed for the first twenty-five-year period.[45] One thing was certain — the exploitation of reservation mineral resources had changed remarkably from the days of gold and building stone. The tribe and the phosphate mining corporations were now involved in big business, with its attendant profits and problems.

Rights-of-Way through the Reservation

A development at Fort Hall concomitant to the production of minerals was the necessity to allow roads and telegraph and telephone lines through the reservation. The location of the Fort Hall Reservation astride the junction of the Oregon Trail and the road to Montana brought many problems of right-of-way trespass to officials of the Office of Indian Affairs. As noted earlier, the original north-south route through the reservation had been operated as a toll road prior to the establishment of the area as a home for the Shoshoni and Bannock. On May 6, 1872, the 1872 House of Representatives had printed Bill No. 2663, "Granting a right of way to H. O. Harkness through an Indian reservation in Idaho Territory." The bill was never enacted to set aside a legal right-of-way through the reservation.[46]

The next serious effort to legalize a way through the Fort Hall area was that of the Union Pacific Railroad to protect the right-of-way of its subsidiary, the Utah and Northern Railroad, a matter discussed in some detail in an earlier chapter.[47]

After the settlement of Indian claims for the construction of the Utah and Northern and the Oregon Short Line railroads, other companies sought rights-of-way for telephone and power lines — while Idaho citizens began to clamor for automobile highways to accommodate Henry Ford's new invention.

1898 Agent C. A. Warner, on September 14, 1898, wrote the commissioner of Indian Affairs that on the way back to the agency after inspecting the Idaho Canal dams on the Blackfoot River "we discovered poles with wire on them along and about 100 feet from the U.&N.R.R. Company's tracks, extending a distance of about four miles north of Pocatello." The discovery was made simultaneously by the Indians, who wrote a letter of protest to Washington. Upon further investigation the agent learned that the Rocky Mountain Bell Telephone Company was completing a line from the southern end of the reservation near McCammon to Pocatello, a distance of twenty-four miles, following a wagon road "erroneously supposed by the telephone company to be a public highway." The line continued north from Pocatello to Blackfoot within the right-of-way of the Utah and Northern. The southern section of twenty-four miles was therefore constructed on Indian lands, as no public highway across the reservation had ever been recognized in any of the agreements or treaties with the Shoshoni and Bannock. Later the government assessed damages of $5 per mile against the telephone company for the twenty-four miles of line on Indian lands, a sum which certainly does not seem exorbitant.[48]

1903 The Indians were soon faced with requests to build power lines. The first came from the American Falls Power, Light and Water Company, Ltd., which asked for permission in 1903. Agent Caldwell wrote that he had never received notification that the firm had been granted proper permission.[49] That same year approval was granted a company to construct a line from Pocatello to Blackfoot, which the commissioner thought would be of advantage to the agency and 1940 school.[50] In 1940 the Indians were asked to approve a power line from Grace, Idaho, across the reservation to Anaconda, Montana. One reason given was that the Utah Power and Light Company was "working in conjunction with the National Defense Program."[51] The Office of Indian Affairs seemingly was very careful in protecting Fort Hall interests in the construction of power lines.

The advent of the automobile riveted the attention of Indian and white alike to the need for improved roads, as more and more people began to invest their installment dollars in cars. As early as 1903 1903 the commissioner reported that the Fort Hall Indians had built ten miles of road and repaired fifty, for which they were paid $3,194.99 that year. He also noted that the county commissioners had accepted the main roads across the reservation from Pocatello to Blackfoot and to American Falls and had pledged to maintain 1905 them.[52] Two years later U.S. Senator W. B.

Heyburn applied to the secretary of the Interior for authority for public highways through the reservation, but the matter was not sufficiently clarified as far as the Indians were concerned.[53]

On May 8, 1909, Agent Caldwell reported that 1909 leaders of the tribe wished to travel to Washington to present certain grievances to the President, among which was "the question of railroads across the reservation, the construction of bridges and public highways." Washington officials advised Caldwell that the Indian Office had approved certain regulations for use of the road which had been established across the reservation by the act of March 3, 1901. According to the order of January 9, 1909, the regulations were to be printed on cloth and posted along the highway.[54] The Pocatello Commercial Club then petitioned the county commission to issue orders to homesteaders (who were building fences across the two main-traveled roads from McCammon to Pocatello and thence to Blackfoot and American Falls) to cease and desist so the roads could become thoroughfares again.[55]

Pocatello citizens became increasingly interested in good roads and pushed for construction of a bridge across the Snake River to carry traffic to Tilden on the west bank. As the Tilden bridge neared completion in 1909 Senator William E. Borah was able to secure a right-of-way for the road across the reservation from Pocatello to the bridge. Strict regulations were issued by Agent Caldwell that no camping would be permitted along the road, also that sheep and cattle drovers must first get approval for their drives and then pay "not to exceed" $2 a day for the right to move their stock over the road.[56]

By 1910 there was so much automobile travel 1910 over the Yellowstone Highway from Pocatello to Blackfoot that the residents of the two towns began to agitate for improvement of the six-mile stretch of sandy road between Fort Hall and Blackfoot. The newspaper at Blackfoot recounted the adventures of two gentlemen from Pocatello who "made an excellent run until they struck the sand and then trouble began and in the words of Mr. Davis, it was 20 feet deep and several miles wide." The car's gears were stripped, and the two men were forced to walk to Blackfoot. Both Idaho senators requested that the secretary of the Interior do something to solve the problem. The Bannock County Good Roads Association got into the act; Agent Caldwell was asked for a report on the condition of the road. Senator Heyburn was then informed that the Indian Office could find no money with which to make improvements.[57]

Enterprising autoists in Pocatello next subscribed money to hire Indians to pack the stretch of sand with sagebrush. Lacking the interest of the Gate City boosters, the Indians refused to complete the work. Efforts then were made to interest the Idaho Legislature to appropriate $30,000, while warnings were posted that only the most powerful cars should try to negotiate the bad stretch and that rear tires should be deflated before attempting the crossing. When a state senator introduced the bill in the Idaho Legislature calling for money to "macadamize" the six-mile portion of road, he explained that automobile journals of the United States described "this patch of shifting sand as the worst road in the entire world." An appropriation of $20,000 was made, with the understanding that the balance of $10,000 would be raised among private citizens in the area. The Office of Indian Affairs gave permission to macadamize the road, and after the usual delays the project was completed by the summer of 1912. The following year legislation was introduced in Boise to reimburse the generous citizens who had given money. This time the Indians benefited from the desire of the auto-using public to improve a reservation highway.[58]

1913

In 1913 the Pocatello Commercial Club began a drive to build another road to tap the grainfields in Arbon Valley, which lay at the head of Bannock Creek. It was again necessary to get permission from the Office of Indian Affairs, since the proposed road would cross a portion of the reservation. Eleven years later, in 1924, a request was made by Pocatello residents for assistance from the Department of the Interior to help construct a hard-surfaced road on Bannock Creek. The request was turned down, with the explanation that the highway would serve only about forty Indian families living along the creek and that 95 percent of the traffic was by white people. The road was eventually built, and the Indians again benefited.[59]

1940

A final note about the north-south highway through the reservation is probably in order. In 1940 officials of the Indian Department discovered to their dismay that there were no deeds granting the right-of-way through the reservation. Records revealed that the right-of-way "was obtained in the usual manner by withdrawal, the approval being dated June 4, 1924." This was important because of the decision that former owners or successors in interest of the lands granted for the highway still owned the water rights to those lands. At Fort Hall water was more important than roads.[60]

The development of natural resources on the reservation over the past century has revealed little of interest or worth to the Shoshoni and Bannock, except for the recent exploration of phosphates and the even more important application of water to the land from irrigation and sprinkling systems. The "inexhaustible" supplies of timber soon disappeared; the "flour" gold was soon panned out; the "gold rush" of 1902 revealed no important mineral deposits; there was

no coal of any value; building stone soon lost out in competition with brick and other materials. Only the phosphates, a material which would have excited derision from the forty-niners, proved to be of great value to the Indians at Fort Hall.

Past profits and future income from the Gay Mine and other phosphate deposits hold promise that the mineral may help the Shoshoni and Bannock develop the agricultural possibilities held in rich lava soil and sufficient water. With proper education and training, the residents of Fort Hall may yet make the "little land" remaining to them a truly productive and valuable garden of plenty.

NOTES CHAPTER XII
FROM GOLD TO PHOSPHATES

1. W. H. Danilson to De L. Floyd-Jones, Sept. 17, 1869, *Idaho Superintendency*, Microcopy 832, Roll 2.
2. Jay Gould to Justice Department, September 26, 1878, *Idaho Superintendency*, Roll 347.
3. Ibid., and other letters from Gould, Buck and Nevens dated Sept. 25 to Oct. 21, 1878.
4. *Idaho Statesman*, Oct. 10, 1878.
5. M. P. Berry to C.I.A., July 8, 1871, *Idaho Superintendency*, Roll 339.
6. S. S. Fenn to the President, March 18, 1879, *Idaho Superintendency*, Roll 351.
7. *Blackfoot Register*, July 1, 1882.
8. Frank Campbell to Sec. of Interior, Feb. 11, 1887, *Record Group No. 75*.
9. J. N. Coston to Sec. of Interior, May 18, 1889, ibid.; Sec. of Interior to C.I.A., June 3, 1889, ibid.
10. S. G. Fisher to C.I.A., Dec. 31, 1890, ibid.; Citizens of Blackfoot to C.I.A., Dec. 29, 1890, ibid.
11. Thomas B. Teter to C.I.A., July 14, 1895, ibid.; Ass't. Attorney General to Sec. of Interior, Sept. 9, 1895, ibid.; Sec. of Interior to C.I.A., Sept. 10, 1895, ibid.; Elisha B. Reynolds to C.I.A., Feb. 2, 1900, ibid.
12. L. A. West to J. T. Van Orsdale, Jan. 20, 1894, *Record Group No. 75*; J. T. Van Orsdale to C.I.A., April 5, 1894, ibid.; *Idaho Herald*, Jan. 26, 1894; *Pocatello Tribune*, Feb. 9, 16, 1894.
13. J. T. Van Orsdale to C.I.A., Mar. 17, 1894, *Record Group No. 75*; Sec. of Interior to C.I.A., April 2, 1894, ibid.; *Pocatello Tribune*, March 23, April 1, 1894.
14. Ibid., April 27, 1894; J. T. Van Orsdale to C.I.A., April 26, 1894, *Record Group No. 75*.
15. James Stout to Geo. L. Shoup, Jan. 17, 1898, ibid.; *Pocatello Tribune*, Feb. 17, June 16, 1893, Dec. 25, 1895.
16. Ibid., June 9, 1900; see Ch. VII, notes 153–155.
17. Ibid., June 27, 1900.
18. Ibid., June 6, 10, 14, 1902.
19. Ibid., June 20, 23, 26, 27, July 1, 11, 14, August 11, 1902.
20. Minutes of Fort Hall Business Council, Nov. 25, 1930, *Fort Hall Agency Records*.
21. Ibid., Aug. 10, 1948.
22. Ibid., July 2, 1951.
23. Ibid., March 22, 1956.
24. A. F. Caldwell to C.I.A., Aug. 16, 1905, *Record Group No. 75*.
25. William Donner to C.I.A., Feb. 11, 1925, ibid.
26. C.I.A. to Roy L. Black, April 29, 1930, ibid.; "Report to C.I.A., May 13, 1908," *Fort Hall Agency Records*, 16; Peter Jim and four others to C.I.A., June 1, 1936, ibid.
27. Mansfield, *Geography, Geology, and Mineral Resources of the Fort Hall Indian Reservation, Idaho*, 114.
28. Ibid., 115–116.
29. "Report to C.I.A., May 13, 1908," *Fort Hall Agency Records*, 16–17.
30. Samuel E. Elwell to Sec. of Interior, March 9, 1909, *Record Group No. 75*.
31. Samuel E. Elwell to C.I.A., May 5, 1909.; Sec. of Interior to Samuel E. Elwell, May 10, 1909, ibid.; Sec. of Interior to A. F. Caldwell, May 10, 1909, ibid.; A. F. Caldwell to C.I.A., May 26, 1909, ibid.; Sec. of Interior to Samuel E. Elwell, June 8, 1909, ibid.; C.I.A. to Evan W. Estep, March 12, 1912, ibid.; C.I.A. to William E. Borah, May 23, 1912, ibid.
32. *Fort Allotment Schedule, 14A*, Oct. 28, 1914 (Portland Area B.I.A. Office); "Report to C.I.A., May 13, 1908," *Fort Hall Agency Records*, 1416.
33. "Sec. of Interior, Order of Interior Department, March 25, 1936," *Record Group No. 75*; F. A. Gross to C.I.A., May 2, 1936, ibid.; C.I.A. to F. A. Gross, May 22, 1936, ibid.; C.I.A. to Stewart, June 9, 1936, ibid.; D. Worth Clark to C.I.A., June 19, 1936, ibid.; C.I.A. to U.S. Geological Survey, June 29, 1936, ibid.; C.I.A. to D. Worth Clark, June 29, 1936, ibid.; U.S. Geological Survey to C.I.A., Aug. 3, 1936, ibid.; "Geo. G. Bywater Report, U.S. Geological Survey, Salt Lake City, July 27, 1936," ibid.; C.I.A. to F. A. Gross, Aug. 24, 1936, ibid.; F. A. Gross to C.I.A., Nov. 6, 1936, ibid.
34. Mansfield, *Geography etc. of Fort Hall Indian Reservation*, 105–108.
35. "Fort Hall Agency — March, 1944, Program, Fort Hall Reservation, Idaho," *Fort Hall Agency Records*, 13.
36. Minutes of Fort Hall Business Council, May 13, 1947, *Fort Hall Agency Records*.
37. L. P. Towle to Simplot Fertilizer Co., Oct. 25, 1948, ibid.

38. L. P. Towle to C.I.A., Nov. 1, 1948, ibid.; Edw. J. Sorrell to Sheridan Downey, Sept. 9, 1948, ibid.; Eva Yardell Phippeny to Edw. J. Sorrell, June 2, Aug. 24, 1948, ibid.; Edw. J. Sorrell to Sheridan Downey, June 28, 1948, ibid.
39. C.I.A. to John Sanborn, May 16, 1949, ibid.
40. E. Morgan Pryse to C.I.A., May 12, 1949, ibid.; Earl Woolridge to E. Morgan Pryse, Sept. 10, 1952, ibid.
41. Fort Hall Business Council, Minutes, Sept. 14, 1954, ibid.
42. Association for the Advancement of the Fort Hall People, Minutes, Sept. 28, 1960, ibid.
43. Fort Hall Business Council, Minutes, Aug. 12, 1963, ibid.
44. Council to O. E. Pethier of Simplot Co., Dec. 24, 1963, ibid.
45. Fort Hall Business Council, Minutes, July 11, 1972, ibid.
46. John P. C. Shanks to C.I.A., Dec. 20, 1872, *Idaho Superintendency*, Roll 340.
47. *C I A. Annual Report, 1884*, 23–24; see ch. VII, notes 35–59.
48. Thirty-five Shoshoni and Bannock Chiefs and Headmen to C.I.A., Sept. 14, 1898, ibid.; C. A. Warren to C.I.A., Sept. 14, 17, 1898, ibid.; *Pocatello Tribune*, Sept. 24, 1898; C.I.A. to A. F. Duclos, July 28, 1905, Idaho State University Archives, Ms. 329.

49. A. F. Caldwell to C.I.A., March 2, 1903, *Record Group No. 75.*
50. *C I A. Annual Report, 1903*, 155.
51. F. A. Gross to C.I.A., Aug. 23, 1940, ibid.
52. *C I A. Annual Report, 1903*, 154.
53. *Pocatello Tribune*, Feb. 27, 1905.
54. A. F. Caldwell to C.I.A., Feb. 6, 1909, *Record Group No. 75.*
55. *Pocatello Tribune*, Aug. 10, 1909.
56. Ibid., Jan. 12, 15, May 19, 1909.
57. Ibid., April 30, May 2, June 27, 1910.
58. Ibid., July 6, Dec. 30, 1910; Jan 27, 31, Feb. 17, 20, March 28, April 10, May 1, 15, 23, July 15, Nov. 14, 1911; March 22, June 20, 1912; March 5, 1913.
59. Ibid., June 26, Aug. 22, 1913; William Donner to C.I.A., May 22, 1924, *Record Group No. 75.*
60. Allan F. Hinton, Report on Highway Right-of-Way, Jan. 29, 1940," *Fort Hall Agency Records;* B. S. Varian to A. A. Walker, Feb. 27, 1940, ibid.

CHAPTER XIII

SCHOOLS AND THE OLD WAYS

A Decade of Educational Failure

Even more important than water and land, at least to some of the agents and surely to the Office of Indian Affairs, was the necessity to "civilize" the Shoshoni and Bannock by introducing them (especially the children) to the three Rs and the beneficent influences of learning the English language and the white man's ways. Nearly all Americans of the nineteenth century saw the absolute necessity for education if the Indians were ever to "improve" and "progress." The type of education was obvious — it was to be the kind which had already raised the standard of living for the American people to among the highest in the world and would make the nation a great power among other countries. If the little red schoolhouse and McGuffey's Readers could achieve these miracles they certainly could raise an uneducated people to higher levels. The attempt of the Indian Department to effect such a transformation among the Shoshoni and Bannock has importance, although the story reflects a frustrating, and in many ways an unsuccessful, experience for Indian officialdom.

1868   By the Treaty of Fort Bridger in 1868 the government bound itself under Articles 3 and 7 to provide a school building for the reservation and a teacher "competent to teach the elementary branches of an English education" for every thirty children who chose to attend school. The Indian parents, in turn, pledged to "compel" their children between the ages of six and sixteen years to enroll in the reservation school.

It would be four years before a negligent Congress appropriated enough money to initiate the educational program outlined in the Fort Bridger Treaty. Agent Danilson reported an August 30, 1869, that the Indians "manifest a great interest in having their children sent to school and educated" but indicated that it was impossible due to the lack of a building.[1] The following year Danil-
1870   son was so enthusiastically engaged in setting up mills and starting the Indians in farming operations that he did not even mention the need for a
1871   school.[2] Agent High, in 1871, reiterated the necessity for a boarding school. He said that teachers could be supplied by the "denomination to whom this reservation has been assigned" and regretted the lack of a school "owing to the insuf-

ficiency of appropriations" by Congress.[3] Agent Berry announced in August 1871 that the Reverend Father Toussaint Mesplie had arrived to organize a school. He then requested $94.44 a month for Mesplie's salary, and, finally, reported that he had had to let the Reverend depart and abandon plans for a school because there were no
1872   "proper facilities."[4] By September 5, 1872, Agent High was expostulating that the Indians were anxious to have a school but, through no fault of theirs, there were no houses for the teacher or the school.[5] The inattention of the government to the educational advancement of the Shoshoni and Bannock children during the years 1869-1873 did not augur well for succeeding years; the Indians became disgruntled and soon came to oppose some aspects of the school program.

A new agent, Henry W. Reed, was perhaps more oriented to the necessity of education. He finally gathered together enough material to start
1873   construction of a school building in late 1873. He hoped to be able to induce a few students to attend when the structure was completed.[6] His
1874   hopes were justified; on September 9, 1874, he could proudly announce, "Our school is now in a fair way to be commenced." The new schoolroom was twenty by twenty-two feet in size, and Reed hired Peter O. Mathews, "an educated Indian," as teacher. The agent hoped to attract some students in the "experiment" of education at Fort Hall.[7]

By November 1874 James Wright was reporting the school a success, but he requested the employment of a cook and a matron to take care of the children, who would be boarding with the agent. He also asked for construction of additional sleeping quarters for the students so the school could become "permanent." Wright indicated that some of "these Children of the Prairie" were orphans who were forced to sleep in haystacks for want of a home.[8] There were fourteen students enrolled. Wright concluded his inspection report with the plea, "These Indians are litterally Knocking at the door of civilization. Shall we say 'Stay out.' Give us the means and we will warrant success!"[9]

The philosophy of education propounded by Indian officials for schools such as the tiny one at Fort Hall was well expressed by Commissioners J.
1873   W. Powell and G. W. Ingalls in their famous report of December 18, 1873, for the Shoshoni,

Ute, and Paiute tribes. Under recommendation number eight, they suggested:

It is unnecessary to mention the power which schools would have over the rising generation of Indians. Next to teaching them to work, the most important thing is to teach them the English language. Into their own language there is woven so much mythology and sorcery that a new one is needed in order to aid them in advancing beyond their baneful superstitions; and the ideas and thoughts of civilized life cannot be communicated to them in their own tongues.[10]

This point of view, with few exceptions, continued to dominate Washington thinking until near the present, when a new concern for the recognition of an Indian cultural heritage and bilingual education has come into being. But for the nineteenth century and well into the twentieth, the Shoshoni and Bannock were to be made into carbon copies of their white neighbors.

1875   As indicated in an earlier chapter, Agent James Wright was forced, by extreme budgetary cuts, to dismiss nearly all the agency employees in 1875, retaining only a small staff to secure public property on the reservation. He was so determined to keep the token school in operation that he warned the commissioner he intended to rent out the agency farm and maintain the school. There would not be sufficient rations to feed the majority of the Indians, and he expected to give what little food supplies remained to families who would keep their sons in school.[11]

As one way around the financial squeeze he began the practice (continued by his successor, Danilson) of using for school maintenance the money obtained from grazing fees paid by white ranchers and from a contract with H. O. Harkness, who had agreed to pay $500 a year for permission to continue the operation of his toll road through the Fort Hall area.[12] Wright thought the application of these limited funds for education might help convince the Indians of the importance of schools "if they feel that they cost them something."[13]

Wright met one unexpected problem. A white man, J. M. Fisher, accused the teacher, Peter Mathews, of having intercourse with Indian women and paying them out of reservation supplies of annuity goods. Mathews denied the charge and challenged his main accuser, Chief Pagwhite, that if the chief did not keep his mouth shut, "he would measure arms with him." Both Wright and Danilson supported Mathews' innocence, but the school was hurt. From an average attendance of twenty the number dropped to six, as Indian parents tended to believe the charges.[14]

The affair occurred at an unpropitious time. Danilson had plans to hire a woman teacher, pay her salary out of fees from pasturage, and open a girl's department. He went ahead anyway and employed Mrs. S. E. Danilson, who taught the girls singing and also helped make "outfit[s] of clothing and bedding" for them.[15]

The twenty or so boy students did not have the best of accommodations. They had to sleep in the loft above the 20-by-22-foot schoolhouse, and the arrangements for boarding were quite inadequate. In his final report Henry W. Reed said he doubted that "any Indian school is doing better than this for the time taught and the means to operate it with." He was of the opinion that there would be plenty of scholars if only the government could provide them "with any degree of comfort."[16] Certainly schooling for only twenty scholars did not fulfill the promises of the Fort Bridger Treaty; there were about fifteen hundred Indians living at Fort Hall, with many more children between the ages of six and sixteen who should have been offered an education.

The little boarding school reopened on December 1, 1875, under a new teacher, the Reverend J. M. Jameson, D.D., but a lack of funds 1876 forced its closure on March 28, 1876. There had been twenty-five students enrolled, of whom five were girls. Danilson deplored the closing of the school, particularly when the "scholar's progress in writing and arithmetic was the astonishment of all visitors."[17]

There was no school during the rest of that 1877 year or throughout 1877. Danilson submitted plans and specifications for two dormitory buildings, one for boys and the other for girls. His plans were to move the present school building, place it between the two new structures, and remodel it. With three hundred school-age children — one hundred of them the children of farming Indians — he was sanguine that a permanent boarding school could be started.[18] The structures 1878 were not built; all funds had to be used to subsist the great number of Indians who congregated at Fort Hall during the Bannock War.[19]

In late December, no doubt embarrassed by the attention focused on the Fort Hall Reservation by the Bannock troubles, the Office of Indian Affairs pushed Danilson into starting a day school. At a cost of $30 for wallpaper for the old building, and with a few primers, slates, and pencils, the agent 1879 gathered eight children together and started the school on January 8, 1879. Attendance finally rose to twenty-two. As Danilson said, while a day school was better than no school at all, "children who live at home, and are surrounded by the influences of camp life, must necessarily make slow progress in learning to speak the English language, and in adopting the habits and customs of civilized life."[20]

The commissioner of Indian Affairs finally awoke from his lethargy and inquired of John A. Wright in September of 1879 what accommodations the agency had for a boarding school — apparently he had not read the letters and reports of the past several years. Wright replied that two log structures could be fitted up as dormitories and the old school remodeled to accommodate one hundred students. The building could be readied for occupancy within thirty days.[21]

When Special Indian Agent J. M. Haworth arrived a month later to take charge of the agency, he first rather unfairly criticed Danilson's failure to provide a school and then approved Wright's idea to renovate the old buildings.[22] Haworth proceeded immediately with the repairs and attempted to get the Methodist Episcopal Church in Salt Lake City to furnish a teacher, since it had the responsibility of looking after the religious and educational advancement of the Fort Hall Indians. After a month's delay he concluded that the church's inattention to affairs at his agency precluded any help from that quarter. He also was very firm that a teacher could not be hired for a salary of $600 a year and asked for an appropriation of $840. By year's end he was prepared to start a boarding school if the necessary funds were provided.[23]

The various agents were unanimous in one feeling: encouraging the Indian fathers and mothers to overcome their superstitions and fear about placing their children in a boarding school would have to be a gradual and careful process. Haworth explained the long-held custom of the Shoshoni and Bannock in moving to the Snake River bottoms to spend the winters. With camps twelve miles or so from the agency it would be practically impossible to get Indian children to a day school — hence the need for a boarding school.[24]

A more subtle reason was the necessity of separating the students from what was held to be the debilitating and retrograding influence of the "blanket" Indians and camp life. There was a constant stream of directives from Washington instructing agents at all reservations to stop the iniquitous practices which supported the superstitions and age-old customs of the various tribes. For example, the commissioner issued an order in 1879 prohibiting the sale of beads and paint to the Indians. The trader at Fort Hall, W. N. Shilling, asked permission to continue to sell beads and "Chinese Vermillion," since the Shoshoni and Bannock "consider it an indispensable article" and would persist in buying the items at stores in nearby Blackfoot. This was just another episode in the long struggle between the Indians and Washington officials and agents who were determined to eradicate nearly every vestige of tribal culture and replace it with the civilization practiced by whites.[25]

Establishment of a Boarding School

The boarding school, begun in February 1880, proceeded in the same desultory fashion as had the previous day schools. John Wright started with three children and "by persistent effort" increased the number to twenty-seven, of whom two-thirds were Bannock; the Shoshoni were more opposed to the school. Convinced that the process of education was "the very foundation of the civilization" of the two tribes at Fort Hall, Agent Wright exerted every effort to make the school a success.[26] When eight of the chiefs and headmen traveled to Washington, D.C., Wright arranged for the delegation to visit the Indian boarding school at Carlisle, Pennsylvania, hoping to impress the leaders with what could be accomplished on their reservation.[27] By July he was forced to give the scholars a vacation because of the "scarcity of clothing and other articles" necessary to keep the school in operation.[28]

The two agents who succeeded Wright, E. A. Stone in 1881 and A. L. Cook in 1882, gave very pessimistic reports about the lack of progress with the school. Stone was particularly emphatic, noting that despite an outlay of $1,700 per year, "the fact still remains that not one single Indian on the reservation can read a word." He strongly recommended the construction of a good school building and stressed that the children must be kept away from their parents if the school were to be anything but a "perfect farce, and continual source of annoyance to all concerned."[29] Cook was more succinct but just as critical. The school had several disadvantages, including a poor building and the opposition of most of the Indians.[30]

Agent Stone struck out against the practice of polygamy among the Shoshoni and Bannock, a way of life which he thought they had learned from "their brother polygamists, the Mormons." This impediment to the proper civilizing of the Indians was also mentioned by the commissioner, who asked for legislation barring polygamy among the Indians of the United States.[31]

Another custom which stood in the way of advancing education was the Indian habit of gambling. This came under attack from Agent Cook and especially from Special Investigator Cyrus Beede, who spent one page of a seventeen-page report denouncing the customs which left many of the Indians destitute. He considered "heroic measures" necessary to break up the iniquitous habit and recommended confiscating every item offered for gambling purposes, to be used for the benefit of the tribes as a whole.[32]

Another special agent, Arden R. Smith, threw up his hands in disgust at trying to reform and educate the Shoshoni and Bannock. He thought the entire Indian problem "insolvable" and the white officials "almost powerless to change" conditions. In a final outburst he said, "Humanitarianism can only wait and wonder while ignorance sneers at results," and he concluded, "They are children in their simplicity, but are not to be measured by any cunning system or rule, by which any children or men were ever measured yet." It was his opinion that the Indians were doomed to disappear as a race. He thought the whites should get along with them "as well as we can" until the final Indian had gone to the great hunting ground in the sky.[33] His views represented the thinking of many white Americans in the late 1880s.

In the opinion of many Indian officials local residents did not help matters by their constant requests for the Shoshoni and Bannock to participate in the Fourth of July parades or in other ways exhibit their strange and exotic customs to the curious and awe-struck citizenry. A typical example was the giant barbecue and celebration held at Pocatello in November 1884. The neighboring Fort Hall Indians not only feasted with their white neighbors but also conducted a war dance and then engaged in a sham battle, to the delight of the onlookers. The evening ended with a display of fireworks.[34] To some, such displays to the applause of a crowd only strengthened Indian determination to retain their tribal culture and customs.

The 1882-1883 school year opened on a disappointing note when the new teacher failed to show up. The school finally opened its doors to twenty scholars in December. There was better news when word came that with the closing of the Fort Hall Military Post the buildings and property were to be turned over to the Indian Department for use as an industrial school. The disadvantage, which eventually led to abandonment of the site for a school, was its location on Lincoln Creek — eighteen miles from the agency and almost twice that distance from the Indian wintering grounds along the Snake River bottoms.[35]

With the establishment of the new industrial school, the old boarding school was closed. Soon a

note of optimism crept into the reports of the agents about the chances of a successful educational operation at Lincoln Creek. In 1884 enrollment rose to thirty-eight students, an eight-acre garden plot was cultivated by the boys, and the girls learned household work and sewing. The chief obstacle seemed to be the influence of the Shoshoni medicine men, who taught that the school was "bad medicine, that those who attended it would die." Agent Cook was partially able to overcome this negative doctrine by persuading one of the medicine men to send his children to the school.[36]

Cook reported even greater results in 1885. Forty-seven pupils were in attendance, taught and cared for by a staff of four — two teachers, a matron, and a combination cook and laundress. The school was in operation for nine and a half months.[37]

Those acquainted with the meager educational results at Fort Hall during the seventeen years since the reservation had been established could look with some hope at what was happening; others exuded pessimism. When Shoshonee Jim returned to Fort Hall after an absence of twenty-one years spent in Wisconsin (where apparently conditions for Indians were much better) he complained in a letter to the President that as far as a school was concerned "we have none."[38]

Special Agent Beede did his best to spark a "revival" and some "conversions" to the cause of education by holding a special council in which he pointed out the advantages of schooling. He warned the chiefs and headmen that the recognition of their positions by the government would depend on the number of students they were able to persuade to go to school. He also requested that the commissioner draft a special letter to the Shoshoni and Bannock on the importance of education, to be read to them by their agent.[39]

The lack of support on the part of the government for schools at Fort Hall was emphasized when the new office of Indian school superintendent, created by Congress in 1882,[40] reported the

Fiscal Year	No. children of school age	No. children provided for	No. children unprovided for	Amount for teachers supplies, etc.
1871	90		90	$ 2,100
1872	90		90	2,100
1873	160		160	3,500
1874	160	10	150	3,500
1875	140	5	135	3,500
1876	140	15	125	3,800
1877	130		130	2,800
1878	150		150	3,500
1879	130	10	120	2,800
1880	130	15	115	2,800
1881	153	15	138	3,500
1882	100	15	85	2,100
1883	100	20	80	2,100
1884	100	20	80	2,100
				$39,200[41]

amounts "which should have been appropriated to fulfill provisions of Article 7 of Treaty of July 3, 1868, with the Bannock Indians":

This table was damning in its indictment of the government for its lack of concern about the Indians at Fort Hall and for the disregard of treaty obligations.

In an attempt to improve conditions at the industrial school on Lincoln Creek the Office of Indian Affairs took the responsibility for the school out of the hands of the agent and placed a superintendent in charge. Agent Gallagher opposed the move for two reasons: the school was eighteen miles away from the agency, and the Indians would not recognize the authority of the superintendent. They respected only the father and the Great Father — the agent and the President.[42]

1886

Agent Gallagher may have been correct. Whatever the reasons, the change was not successful, as a special investigation revealed. During his visit in April 1887, the inspector found the following disturbing conditions: buildings in disrepair; dead cattle in the springs which supplied the drinking water; two broken plows and one shovel as implements to work the school farm; the twenty-four girl and fourteen boy students locked in their rooms at night which, to say the least, presented a hazard in case of fire; and a superintendent who was "trifling or stupid . . . sluggish . . . illiterate."[43]

1887

Another special agent, John B. Riley, thought the investigator had been too harsh in his judgment. He pointed out that both Agent Gallagher and a former teacher, now living in Blackfoot, were working diligently to force Superintendent J. D. Everest to resign — which Riley thought he should do under the circumstances.[44] Finally Everest answered the charges by describing conditions when he took over the school: 250 panes of glass missing from the windows; the children filthy and with no discipline at all; only two buggy horses, who were so old and decrepit they laid down in the road on one trip to Blackfoot forcing Everest to walk the rest of the way; and not enough bedding to keep the children warm. He had decided not to try to increase enrollment until conditions were improved but had built up attendance from thirty-eight to seventy-five students. In reading the various reports one must make the judgment that Everest did a better job under very trying conditions than the first inspector indicated — but he did resign.[45]

1888

Nevertheless, the situation was deplorable and was made worse by the fact that there had been eight different superintendents at the school in two years. Agent Gallagher was placed in charge again and given strict orders to increase the enrollment, by force if necessary.[46] The commissioner expressed the philosophy rather bluntly:

The Indians must conform to "the white man's ways," peaceably if they will, forcibly if they must. They must adjust themselves to their environment, and conform their mode of living substantially to our civilization. This civilization may not be the best possible, but it is the best the Indians can get. They can not escape it, and must either conform to it or be crushed by it.[47]

1889

He must also have supported Gallagher's pleas for a larger appropriation for education at Fort Hall; in 1889, the last year of Gallagher's service the agent received funds to build a new domitory. From that time on the physical facilities and the number and caliber of school employees began to improve.[48]

The census report of 1890 indicated that most of the few young Indian men and women who had attended school at Fort Hall during the previous fifteen years had gone back to camp life and were now "degraded and worthless."[49] but Superintendent John Y. Williams gave a much more favorable report in the following year. The average attendance had risen to eighty-six; the buildings were in better repair; the school farm had grown to six hundred acres; there were a harness shop, a carpenter shop, and a sewing room; "moral and religious exercises" were held each evening; and the employees had donated enough money to hire a minister, at $5 per meeting, to hold church services each Sunday.[50]

1890

Enrolling Reluctant Students

The Office of Indian Affairs insisted that every Indian child of school age (now determined to be between the ages of five and eighteen years) must attend school. This uncompromising stand found an able and energetic supporter in the person of Agent S. G. Fisher. When he took over the agency in 1890 he inaugurated active measures to increase school enrollment to one hundred pupils. He became incensed at the "so called Medicine Men," who were teaching that all white men would die soon while all the dead Indians would be resurrected. He requested that they be arrested and removed from the reservation and that two companies of troops be brought in to cow the Bannock into submission.[51] His suggestions were not followed; the Bannock, as well as many of the Shoshoni, continued their determined opposition to the school.

In addition to the preachings of tribal prophets the Indians found other cogent reasons for keeping their children out of school. In 1891 an epidemic of scarlet fever swept through the student body, killing ten of the Indian youngsters and the four-year-old daughter of the superintendent.[52] As Fisher explained, "Unfortunately for the school, the death rate of the children who have heretofore attended school had been far in excess of those who have been permit-

1891

ted to live in tents with their parents." He cited, as an example of the superstitious beliefs of the people, an incident in which one of the most intelligent of the Indian women attributed the deaths of many of the students to the practice of burning the children's hair after cutting it. She asked that neither the hair nor the old clothing belonging to the children be burned.[53]

1892   In reponse to a very strong directive of the commissioner sent on January 16, 1892, Agent Fisher followed the instructions "to the letter" by going in person to force children into school — after his Indian police refused to enforce the edict. In one encounter Fisher was attacked and was saved only through the efforts of a half-breed policeman: "As it was my clothes were torn, and it became necessary for me to choke a so-called chief into subjection." The determined agent did place the children of that particular family in school. One Indian threatened to kill him. All the Indian police resigned rather than face the enraged parents. Only two Shoshoni chiefs withstood the jeers and taunts of the Bannock and some Shoshoni in support of the educational policy handed down from Washington.

As a last resort Fisher called for troops.[54] Instead, the Office of Indian Affairs dispatched a special agent to investigate. J. A. Leonard reported back in support of Fisher, explaining he had met with only insolence and that "religious fanaticism," together with paint and charms, were in full control. He cited the curious coincidence that after the medicine men predicted spring floods "unprecedented rains" had occurred, convincing the Indians to hold to their foolish superstitions. Leonard also asked that troops be sent.[55] The President flatly refused to order soldiers to Fort Hall. After a second urgent request from the commissioner and the secretary of the Interior, the latter reported back, "The President thinks the application of a military force to Indian children to compel them to attend school is not what good judgment requires."[56] The commissioner was told to strengthen the police force at the reservation.

Despite Indian opposition (much of which was furthered by the so-called "messiah craze" coursing through most of the western reservations) the superintendent of Indian schools was able to make a very optimistic report as the result of a visit to Fort Hall in December 1892. He found the buildings in excellent repair, with four classrooms in use; seventeen hundred acres devoted to a school farm and eighty acres under cultivation; a dairy herd of nine milk cows; sixteen employees; and eighty-seven students out of a resident population of 186 of school age. The one depressing discovery was that "there is a larger number of diseased children on this reservation than in many other tribes" due to the "loose and syphilitic"

adult generation. Superintendent Dorchester was critical of Fisher's use of force and thought it had had a "bad effect." He recommended a more positive approach: games, more trades, the organization of a band, and a Christmas party for the children and their parents.[57]

An ironic footnote to the educational troubles at Fort Hall came in a directive from the commissioner's office in August 1892 that all Indian schools were to hold an appropriate celebration in honor of Columbus Day in "line with the practices and exercises of the public schools of this country." Furthermore, the "interest and enthusiasm of the children" were to be "thoroughly aroused." No doubt many of the Shoshoni and Bannock wished Columbus had discovered some other country.[58]

A new superintendent in 1893 dutifully re-   1893 corded that the school was serving seventy-eight students at a cost of $287 each and had sufficient culinary water to care for three hundred pupils and irrigation water for six hundred acres. He ended with "It is a shame that the school has not an average attendance of 150 instead of 78." Special Indian Agent John Lane was more explicit about Indian reluctance to place their children in school.[59] He was of the opinion that securing fifteen Indian boys and five girls from the Fort Shaw area might leaven the lump of resistance at Fort Hall. His very cool reception at the reservation led him to report the nonprogressiveness, the superstitions, and the "pure cussedness" of the Shoshoni and Bannock, especially the latter. The Indians told him that a child's death at the school was caused by "too much book in the head." When he went to visit families in their tepees, instead of asking him to be seated "they will all big, little, old and young wrap themselves up in their blankets, head and body and lay there like a dead person and give no sign of your presence." The silent insubordination of the tribesmen seemed to get to most of the officials of the Indian Service, and Lane was no different. He recommended that troops be brought in.[60]

When Captain Van Orsdale took over the   1894 agency in 1894 he asked exactly what his authority was to deal with the educational recalcitrance of the Indians. He said if it were left to his decision he believed in "reasonably coercive measures."[61] In a special report he stated that the "very expensive plaything" which the school had become should be ended. He recommended closing the industrial school on Lincoln Creek and moving the school to the agency, which would end the duplication of services and eliminate the cost of transporting supplies the additional eighteen miles. Further, he said, the Indians favored the move, and the sale of the old facilities would raise enough money to build new structures. Eventually the department saw the wisdom of his proposal.[62]

Despite opposition the school was gaining more scholars, more staff, and a larger budget, which led to more optimistic reports from the various superintendents and to greater interest on the part of curious residents from Pocatello and Blackfoot. The *Pocatello Advance* reported at length the commencement exercise held on June 27, 1895, and listed the program, which gave some insight into the operation of the school and the type of curriculum. The sewing teacher and two Indian girl assistants had completed 127 dresses, 25 sunbonnets, and 105 large aprons for the girls, and 81 Sunday suits for the boys. The teacher of harness-making worked with his students in repairing harnesses for the Indian farmers. As the interested spectators watched, the students marched into their dining hall in perfect order and said grace in union. At the sound of the first gong they seated themselves; at the second, plates and coffee were placed in position; and at the third, the meal began. Later the program included the following numbers:

Recitation — Visions of the War .... Susie Yupe
Recitation — Connubial Coolness .... A. Parker
Milk Pan Drill .... Twelve Girls
Song — Hunter's Chorus .... 8 Girls, 9 Boys
Recitation — How Girls Fish .... Mary Martin
Recitation — Olden Times .... Jeanette Pocatello

There were many more numbers, and white citizens and the 250 Indian guests enjoyed the festivities.[63]

By the time of this commencement program the school had been transferred back to the responsibility of the agent. The new one was Thomas B. Teter, who received from the secretary of the Interior the accolade of being a "practical, energetic, determined business agent. . . ." The cause of this unaccustomed praise was Teter's feat in increasing the number of scholars from 65 to 156 by untiring visits to Indian camps and on many occasions "personally hauling Indian children out of their father's tepees."[64] The nearby *Idaho Herald* also supported Teter, especially because he stood up to the Bannock leader, Jim Ballard, in the school controversy.[65] Teter's success in filling the schoolrooms probably explained the Indian Office support for so long when most of the Indians and many whites were advocating his discharge, as explained in an earlier chapter.

But signs of discontent with Teter's tactics began to appear. Isaac M. Yandell, long-time white friend of the Shoshoni and Bannock, wrote the commissioner of Indian Affairs that he gave Teter credit for good intentions in forcing the Indian children to school but thought that hell was paved with good intentions and "the man has neither Education, Experience or Brains." Yandell warned there would be blood spilled if Teter did not act with greater moderation.[66] The supervisor of Indian schools defended the school

superintendent against charges made by Teter and advised separation of the school from control of the agent.[67] As indicated before, Teter was finally removed, while the Indian Office debated again whether to play tennis with the school — lobbing its destiny back and forth from agent to superintendent.

The long controversy over whether Indian children would be forced to attend school finally reached a climax during F. G. Irwin's administration as agent. Although Thomas Teter had been able to raise the enrollment to 145 students by July 1896 (with a staff of 21 and a budget of $23,312.28 to take care of them),[68] a year later Irwin faced a crisis. The Indian police, in their annual roundup of school children, gathered in a 14-year-old bride of only a few months. The husband objected to losing his wife to the school and, with the aid of some friends, rescued her from the police. The young Indians then got out of hand by attacking the police, "bruising their noses, taking their arms away from them," and in general treating them with contempt and ridicule. The old Indian women, most of whom had always opposed the school, now conspired with the young men in claiming that almost every young girl on the reservation was married, and they helped take them away from the police. Lieutenant Irwin, a military man not averse to the use of force when necessary, called for a troop of cavalry from Fort Boise. The soldiers soon restored order and increased the enrollment at the school to 207, an unheard-of number. The *Idaho Statesman* and the *Pocatello Tribune* applauded the action. The Indians wisely subsided, after which the troops were withdrawn.[69]

A comprehensive report in January 1898 by the supervisor of Indian schools gave a good picture of the status of the Fort Hall school after almost thirty years of effort to make it a success. Charles D. Rakestraw commended the moral and religious training and the general deportment of the students, the excellent relationship existing between school superintendent and agent (and the latter's commendable efforts in placing children in the school), and the abolition of corporal punishment, which he thought had in the past only increased parental resistance. He cited the necessity to jacket the stoves so the buildings would not catch on fire and mentioned the need to employ a band instructor. He recommended that the Lincoln Creek site be abandoned and a new school built at the agency.

The supervisor noted that in addition to 185 students in attendance at Fort Hall there were eight pupils in the mission school at the agency, two in the public school at Ross Fork, twelve in the industrial school at Carlisle, Pennsylvania, three at Haskell Institute, fourteen excused for illness, two "Ran away to other Agencies," and

1895

1896

1897

1898

nine enrolled in the Pocatello public schools. He visited the latter nine students at Pocatello for one day and was surprised that "their school room work averages well with the white children." On the whole the report ended on a very optimistic tone and indicated a successful school program.[70]

As noted earlier, other agents had advised moving the school to the agency and Lieutenant Irwin was no exception. With Rakestraw's recommendation, the Office of Indian Affairs finally capitulated and asked Irwin to recommend a new site. 1897 He chose a spot two miles east of the agency headquarters and two and a half miles from the railroad station. A major consideration in the prospective removal was the hope that the new location would be healthier and would reduce the anxiety of parents about the health of their children.[71]

The Process of Acculturation

1898 While the younger generation was undergoing haircuts and adopting the raiment of civilization, the older people ("as worthless and shiftless" as ever, according to Inspector McConnell) continued in their old customs and habits.[72] One, John Johnson, traveled to Boise to appeal to the

Idaho State Historical Society
Shoshoni boys learning native dances.

governor to arrange things so he could return to his two wives at Fort Hall without running the risk of being jailed by an Indian judge on the charge of polygamy. The governor complied.[73] The *Pocatello Tribune* noted that a number of Indians were gathered in town, gambling away $8,000 in profits from the sale of their yearly crop of hay.[74] 1897

In August 1897, at the annual Sun Dance celebration held at the bottoms, the Shoshoni and Bannock entertained a number of visitors from the Lemhi, Lapwai, Duck Valley, Wind River, and Uintah reservations.[75] Governor Heber W. Wells of Utah wrote asking that forty Indians from Fort Hall be permitted to participate in the Utah July 1896 Fourth celebration, at the splendid salary of $1.50 a day each plus expenses.[76] And when the Shoshoni and Bannock announced a grand feast in honor of their Indian visitors, five railroad coaches filled with Pocatello residents traveled out to witness the "big eat." The Indians withdrew in silent dignity, while the disappointed white spectators returned to their civilized homes at Pocatello, having missed the opportunity to watch Indians at the table.[77]

The process of acculturation, of forcefully converting the Shoshoni and Bannock into replicas of white Americans, was extended beyond the schoolroom to the older residents of Fort Hall. In 1901 May 1901 Agent A. F. Caldwell announced that the Indian Department had generously provided a number of new farm wagons for those interested in farming, but no Indian would receive one until he agreed to a haircut. Jim Ballard made an emotional speech against the order but to no avail. As the Indians lined up, two barbers spent an entire day cutting the long braids of Indian farmers, who reluctantly submitted to the "civilizing" ordeal in order to get some wheels.[78]

The relentless rounding up of Indian children continued each fall, with the added precaution of having the agency physician examine the prospects so as to get only those "in the best possible physical conditions."[79] Once deposited at the school, some of the students made attempts to escape back to camp life but were often captured and forced to return.[80] Sometimes the culture shock was too great; an occasional student would commit suicide by eating wild parsnip. Two took this drastic step in one week during early 1901.[81]

The agent and school superintendent continued to call for a new school building to be situated near the agency, usually citing the unsanitary conditions at Lincoln Creek, the lack of a bathhouse, the deteriorating structures, and the dearth of sufficient air space in the crowded dormitories.[82] Their appeal was answered when the Pocatello Cession Agreement earmarked $75,000 of the $600,000 allowed for the sale of Indian lands for the construction of a schoolhouse at the agency.[83] The citizens of Pocatello began lobbying to get the structure placed close to town,[84] while Agent Caldwell wondered why fourteen months had elapsed since the passage of the Cession Act of June 6, 1900, with no site yet selected. The Indians were uneasy over the delay, and Caldwell found it difficult to explain the reason to them — "especially as I do not fully understand it myself."[85] The $75,000 was to be used to build a schoolhouse, two dormitories, a kitchen and mess hall, a laundry room, and a warehouse.[86]

1902   Two years went by with no new schoolhouse. The Shoshoni and Bannock objected to sending their children to the old school, accepting with some bitterness that the government had broken faith with them again.[87] After still another year with no new building, Superintendent Locke

1903 wrote in July 1903, "Too long delay makes the heart sick."[88] The cumbersome bureaucracy of

1904 Washington finally produced, in the fall of 1904, a school plant located a mile south of Agency headquarters. The complex included a school building, a dormitory, a mess hall, employees' quarters, a laundry, a boiler, and a pump house.[89]

Superintendent Locke moved in. At the same time he asked for additional buildings; the facilities provided for only 150 students when there were at least 200 children of school age on the reservation.[90] Furthermore, the anticipated removal of the Lemhi to Fort Hall in 1907 would bring in another 65 pupils. The Indian Department responded with unprecedented speed, and a hospital and a new dormitory capable of housing another 150 students were added by late 1907 at a cost of $25,000.[91]

1907

1903

While the Indians waited impatiently for the new school plant they had the opportunity to hear their Big Chief, President Theodore Roosevelt, who stopped off in Pocatello on May 28, 1903, to give a speech filled with typical Rooseveltian flourishes. As the visiting delegation of Indians from Fort Hall sat stoically on horseback in the crowd in front of him, the President rang the changes on the American holy belief in education: "The only outcome of the Indian question [in] this country is gradually to develop the Indian into a property owning, law abiding, hard working, educated citizen; in other words, to train him to drive the path that we are all trying to drive."[92]

If the President had asked Major Caldwell, the agent might have been embarrassed to have to report that the Indian fathers and mothers were as stubborn as ever about keeping their children

Idaho State Historical Society

A Fort Hall picnic about the turn of the century.

Idaho State Historical Society

These pictures of Pat Tyhee were taken the same day, before and after he cut his hair and put on white man's clothes to show he was a Christian.

1902 out of school. The *Pocatello Tribune* described the registration of children for the fall term of 1902:

> The agency officials and the reservation police go out with a wagon, run down the youngsters and haul them to school. . . . Their parents hide them in the sage brush, in the willows, under piles of dirty skins and when they are found the squaws fight like old cats to prevent their being taken away. Sometimes the braves join in the fight. . . . After the youngsters are taken and loaded into the wagons they are hauled off squealing like young pigs while the squaws set up a howl besides which the yelping of a pack of coyotes is musical.[93]

1903 The roundup usually took about three weeks. Apparently the agent had to meet a quota, because the following year, with only 130 pupils in hand, Caldwell continued the chase until he had captured 175 students.[94]

1904 The importance of education in the minds of Washington officials was emphasized anew in 1904 when the Indian Office did away with the position of agent and placed the reservations under bonded superintendents of schools, with the former superintendents being named assistants.[95] From this time on superintendents were in charge at Fort Hall.

Destroying the cultural habits and customs of the Indian and supplanting them with white man's ways went on with a vengeance. The "short hair" edict from Washington which had prompted Caldwell in his unique distribution of farm wagons brought some ridicule to the commissioner. He nevertheless stuck to his guns and continued to insist, as well, that no rations were to be given to able-bodied nonworking Indians. The double combination of withholding rations and "a short confinement in the guardhouse at hard labor" was to be used to enforce the wearing of short hair and the prohibition of the old dances, which were "simply subterfuges to cover degrading acts and to disguise immoral purposes."[96]

1906 The Shoshoni and Bannock, together with their white neighbors in Pocatello, were chastened in 1906 for planning a Sun Dance in town at the time of the July Fourth celebration. Superintendent Caldwell announced that the dance was "absolutely prohibited." Yet the Indians were permitted to hold a "Big Medicine Dance" on the bottoms which attracted a lot of visitors from Pocatello. The tribesmen also participated in the town parade, dressed in war paint, beads, and all the old paraphernalia. "Barbarous" customs seemed to acquire approbation on the white man's Independence Day.[97]

1907 Pocatello residents also liked Superintendent Caldwell's "solution of the servant girl problem," which consisted of placing five girl students from Fort Hall in private homes. Caldwell thought the work and contact with white families would add to the education of the girls. He did caution that "an Indian maiden is different from a white girl . . . they demand different treatment — the utmost kindness and forbearance."[98]

A Shift to Day Schools

1908 The Fort Hall School seemed to be prospering. By 1908 two different reports commented favorably that the majority of the Shoshoni and Bannock knew enough English to transact ordinary business, the new school plant was in excellent condition, the new school farm of 320 acres was productive,[99] and, as Inspector Charles L. Davis expressed it, "the school is kept well . . . and is a great influence for the upbuilding of the tribe. It would improve matters could there be more life and spirit, but further than that no criticism is offered."[100] At the time there were two hundred children enrolled.

Utah State Historical Society

Fort Hall Indian dancers

Inspector Davis had some incisive comments about the two tribes:

> They are not an agreeable people to deal with, exceedingly suspicious and faultfinding, and their moods and temper are exceedingly uncertain . . . they are very liable to do rash things, and that more care is needed in their management than with other tribes. They require rather firm discipline, and desire it . . . many members express themselves as favoring army officers for their agents . . . army officers are strict in their discipline. The fact is the Indians quarrel among themselves, and unless a stronger will or authority steps in and settles their quarrels they live unhapily together. As a people they are given to ill humor, factional strife, much fault finding, and often work themselves into a state of unrest over very small matters.

At the same time he acknowledged that he found "more evidence of thrift and energy on this reservation than among many tribes supposed to be far in advance in point of civilization."[101]

In fact, his long report of over one hundred typed pages of conditions at Fort Hall left an impression of much hope for the educational and industrial future of the two tribes. He recommended that Superintendent A. F. Caldwell be asked to resign, not because he had been a poor official but because changed conditions demanded an individual with management experience who could meet the needs of a twentieth century industrial society.[102] Major Caldwell finally complied and left in October 1910.[103]

1910

Without going into a detailed account of events at the Fort Hall Reservation and school during the next decade, the inspection reports began to reveal less and less optimism about improvements in the lives of the Indians. In sharp criticism to the superintendent, the Indian Office noted that little was being done to enroll children in the school, that there were many runaways who were not returned to the classroom, and that "attributable to some cause unknown . . . there seems to be a hatred by the Indians on the reservation against school." The commissioner asked the cause be ascertained and that the school facilities be put in proper shape.[104]

1918

Three years later, in 1921, the supervisor of Indian education reported to the commissioner that the Fort Hall school had deteriorated "in every respect," and that a once very successful institution was now "a miserable failure" due mostly to the petty bickering of the employees. Of the eighty-two students enrolled there was an average attendance of only 20 percent. A large number of the Indians could not read, write, or speak English. The supervisor wrote that he opposed discontinuing the school. He recommended, instead that it be placed under an efficient and vigorous management capable of restoring a viable institution.[105] A year later the superintendent also strongly advised against combining the school farm with the agency farm. He asked how he could then train Indian boys to be farmers. The

1921

1922

superintendent thought the Fort Hall Indians were not yet ready to enter a system of public schools and that the boarding school should be maintained.[106]

Indian leaders at Fort Hall became more and more involved in doing their own inspections of various aspects of reservation life, including the school. In 1923 six of them visited the school and suggested, among other things, that the sleeping quarters were too small and stuffy and that the children should be given twenty-five minutes in which to eat their lunch instead of the twenty minutes allowed. They noted that the school boys often came home in dirty clothes and with dirty ears. To the last charge, the superintendent replied the boys were large enough to wash their own ears.[107]

1923

The superintendent also had cause to complain. The per capita amount of $165 to $175 for his students would not permit him to feed and clothe them properly or provide the instruction he would like. At the same time a congressional committee was hearing that the average cost per student in the nation's Indian boarding schools was $225 — while instruction in white schools cost between $400 and $500 per student. This may have been a significant reason for the deterioration of the Fort Hall school.[108]

During the fifteen-year period up to 1925 the educational efforts of agency officials to reduce gambling and eradicate the frequent dances seem also to have been ineffectual. Inspector Charles Davis thought gambling was the greatest evil common to the tribes.[109] Ten years later, in 1918, the commissioner demanded that the Indian police be charged with stopping the practice.[110] In another six years U.S. Commissioner Theodore Turner at Pocatello asked the Federal Bureau of Investigation to propose federal legislation under which the Fort Hall Indians would be prosecuted for gambling away cattle and other governmental property given to them. The FBI declined to do so.[111]

1918

1924

As for the dances, a distinction should be made between the Sun Dance, a religious observance, and nearly all the other dances, which were "of a vicious or immoral character," according to one Indian official — although it must be said that when the Sun Dance was prohibited, the Indians very ingeniously insinuated certain aspects of the religious dance into many of the other so-called recreational or physical skill dances. The Office of Indian Affairs therefore began to prohibit even the "shorn style" of Sun Dance. Under the chapter dealing with religion it will be necessary to examine the struggle between Indians and whites about the religious implications of prohibiting the Sun Dance.[112] Perhaps it is enough to say here that even in attempting to curb the less important recreational dances the Indian Department

1912 seemed to be losing ground, despite a strict order issued in 1912 which peremptorily stopped dances which kept "alive certain barbaric impulses."[113]

Supposedly it was quite fitting and proper that sixty members of the Pocatello Elks Club, in a reverse display of pseudoacculturation, should don face paint, feathers, and blankets to travel to Twin Falls where a brother lodge was being installed. And perhaps it was all right for the local baseball club to adopt the name Pocatello Indians, which allowed sports writers to use such picturesque Indian language as "Big Chief Spit-in-his-Mit" or "Chief Work-the-Corners."[114]

1922 Superintendent William Donner finally exploded in wrath against all the little towns for a hundred miles around (even as far as the capital city at Boise) which lured Indians away from their farms to spend from June to October providing a spectacle at fairs and exhibitions for the gaping tourists. The various town committees were not interested in inviting the Fort Hall school band or the Indian athletic teams. They wanted "the old-timers . . . with their paint and feathers to camp on the grounds, eat in the filth, and take part in the parade." He considered such affairs a disgrace to the Indians, and he asked for help in finding a solution.[115]

Most Indian officials thought the answer to Donner's cry for help was to improve the educational system at Fort Hall so that even the old Indians might be won over to an acceptance of "civilization." In 1928 the boarding school concept was still the preferred method of teaching Shoshoni and Bannock children. An inspector that year could proudly report that, while three years earlier there had been ninety-nine elopements from school, there were only twenty-three this year, a definite sign that conditions at the school were much improved.[116] A gym was badly needed, but otherwise the school plant was in good condition. The 340-acre school farm was operating efficiently, and the facilities could easily have accommodated 200 students.[117]

1932 The quite famous *Survey of Conditions of the Indians in the United States*, completed by the U.S. Senate in 1932, noted that there were ninety-three Fort Hall Indian children attending public schools, and that parents were encouraged to send their children to these schools "as much as possible." The committee advised that the boarding school would have to continue for several more years but eventually should be phased out.[118]

1935 This event took place much earlier than expected. The Office of Indian Affairs announced the closing of the school in 1935 and the opening of three day schools on the reservation — at Ross Fork, Lincoln Creek, and Bannock Creek. However the usual delays occurred, and the three

schools did not open until the fall of 1938. At the time the boarding school closed the commissioner was able to report that, of the 494 school-age children, 85 percent attended some school. He added that six hundred of the Shoshoni and Bannock on the reservation could speak and write English, twelve hundred could speak English fluently, and six hundred could not read or write the language.[119] 1938

From the opening of the three day schools in 1938, the Ross Fork unit was quite successful. The Lincoln Creek school started with only eighteen students and dwindled down to twelve; it was closed in 1944. The more isolated Bannock Creek 1944 school was still in operation in 1946, but, because 1946 the parents were not willing to eradicate lice and the itch from among their children, the youngsters were not accepted into the junior high and high school of the American Falls district. The chief inadequacy at the three schools was the absence of an industrial arts program.[120]

Idaho's School Districts Take Over

In 1946 the Idaho Legislature enacted a law al- 1946 lowing reorganization of the state's school districts, and soon the reservation area was made part of the existing districts of Pocatello, Blackfoot, and American Falls.[121] At the time there were 536 school-age children at Fort Hall, of whom 43 were enrolled in the day schools, 59 attended the two public schools on the reservation, and 51 took their schooling at nonreservation boarding schools.[122]

As early as 1939 there was some sentiment to reopen the old boarding school as a trachoma school or, more preferably, a vocational school. The idea reappeared every few years up to 1949. 1949 Today, surprisingly, many Indian parents favor sending their children to the "contemptible" far-off boarding schools provided for Indian youth by the government. The recent decision to maintain the Intermountain Indian School at Brigham City, Utah, received the strong endorsement of the Shoshoni and Bannock Indians. The reason seems to be that boarding schools permit the children to escape the cultural isolation of the reservation.[123] Even some white neighbors of the Indians at Fort Hall recommended a return to government schools, away from the slums of "Eastside Pocatello."[124] Others condemned the government for "trying to dodge its responsibility" by expecting the State of Idaho and the public school districts to assume the burden of Indian education at Fort Hall.[125]

In the aftermath of World War II came public recognition of the long-held feelings of discrimination by some whites against the Indian people at Fort Hall. An early report in 1944 noted the 1944 discrimination shown by white children toward their fellow Indian classmates at the Blackfoot public school during lunch periods. The writer, from the Indian Service, expanded on the theme by pointing out how difficult it was for an Indian to be served at restaurants in Pocatello and Blackfoot. One of the reasons for this discrimination was the wide publicity given by Indian officials at Fort Hall to the prevalence of veneral disease among the Indians.[126]

1952 Education continued to be a difficult process at Fort Hall, but there were some hopeful signs. A Bureau of Indian Affairs report in 1952 cited the following educational levels for the reservation population: 3 college graduates, 50 high school graduates, and 200 who had finished the eighth grade. But there were also 700 Indians unable to read and write and 200 adults who could not speak English. The 1960 census reported 17 college graduates, 241 high school graduates, 212 who had completed the eighth grade, and only 69, or 10.7 percent, who had had no formal 1967 education.[127] A 1967 study placed the average grade level for adults at close to eight, so the drop-out rate after the eighth grade was very high.[128]

The general inadequacy of government efforts to prepare Shoshoni and Bannock children for space-age living (while at the same time allowing the Fort Hall people to nurture and maintain their highly involved culture and tradition) has its roots in the failures of the past. The evident disinterest of the Methodist Episcopal Church in meeting its educational obligations at Fort Hall, the constant migrations of the Indians searching for food on and off the reservation during the late 1800s, the resistance of Indian parents to schooling for their children, and the lack of proper facilities until the completion of the boarding schools in 1904 all contributed to a situation which found only 252 of the 1,500 Indians on the reservation able to read and write at the time the new boarding school opened.[129]

Today there are Indian children whose entry into the public schools at the age of six finds them with no knowledge of English or Shoshoni but able to understand only a patois or creolized language. Their first day of school is also their first contact with white people. Furthermore, the differences between the progessive-minded individuals and those who oppose the acculturation process has reached the point where there is little communication between the two groups. The younger people are noticeably indifferent to improvement in their educational level or their living and social conditions. This lack of interest and motivation can be attributed in great part to the failure of the Christian missionary societies and churches who, over the long period of reservation life, shirked their educational responsibilities at

Fort Hall, however ruthless and in opposition to the right of self-determination their methods may have been.[130]

NOTES CHAPTER XIII
SCHOOLS AND THE OLD WAYS

1. W. H. Danilson to Floyd-Jones, Aug. 16, 1896, *Idaho Superintendency*, Microcopy 832, Roll 2; *C.I.A. Annual Report, 1869*, 730.
2. Ibid., *1870*, 651–653.
3. Ibid., *1871*, 959–960; J. N. High to C.I.A., Jan. 12, 1872, *Idaho Superintendency*, Roll 339.
4. M. P. Berry to C.I.A., Aug. 10, 1871, ibid.; M. P. Berry to C.I.A., Oct. 31, 1871, *Fort Hall Letter Book*, 403; M. P. Berry to C.I.A., Feb. 20, 1872, *Idaho Superintendency*, Roll 340.
5. *C.I.A. Annual Report, 1872*, 657; M. P. Berry to C.I.A., Jan. 1, 1872, *Fort Hall Letter Book*, 101.
6. *C.I.A. Annual Report, 1873*, 616.
7. Ibid., *1874*, 592.
8. James Wright to C.I.A., Nov. 21, 1874, *Idaho Superintendency*, Roll 342.
9. James Wright to C.I.A., Dec. 28, 1874, *Fort Hall Letter Book*, 205–206.
10. *C.I.A. Annual Report, 1873*, 432–433.
11. James Wright to C.I.A., Jan. 21, 1875, *Idaho Superintendency*, Roll 343; James Wright to C.I.A., Jan. 30, 1875, ibid.; James Wright to C.I.A., Feb. 6, 1875, ibid.; James Wright to C.I.A., Feb. 6, 1875, *Fort Hall Letter Book*, 235; James Wright to C.I.A., March 13, 1875, ibid.; James Wright to C.I.A., June 1, 1875, ibid., 278; see Ch. V, footnotes 4 and 10.
12. James Wright to C.I.A., April 19, 1875, *Idaho Superintendency*, Roll 343; James Wright to C.I.A., April 20, 1875, ibid.; James Wright to C.I.A., June 2, 1875, ibid.; W. H. Danilson to C.I.A., Sept. 10, 1875, ibid.
13. James Wright to C.I.A., April 19, 1875, ibid.
14. J. M. Fisher to C.I.A., July 1, 1875, ibid.
15. W. H. Danilson to C.I.A., Dec. 13, 1875, *Idaho Superintendency*, Roll 344. Mrs. S. E. Danilson may very well have been a relative of the agent. In his letter to the commissioner, Agent Danilson noted that he had not placed her name on 'the regular list of employees" because her salary was being paid from fees collected for pasturing cattle.
16. James Wright to C.I.A., Jan. 28, 1875, *Idaho Superintendency*, Roll 343; H. W. Reed to C.I.A., Feb. 20, 1875, ibid.; *C.I.A. Annual Report, 1875*, 761.
17. Ibid., *1876*, 447.
18. W. H. Danilson to C.I.A., June 16, Aug. 9, 1876, *Idaho Superintendency*, Roll 345; *C.I.A. Annual Report, 1877*, 474–475.
19. *C.I.A. Annual Report, 1878*, 546; W. H. Danilson to C.I.A., Jan. 28, 1878, *Idaho Superintendency*, Roll 347.
20. W. H. Danilson to C.I.A., Dec. 16, 1878, ibid.; *C.I.A. Annual Report, 1879*, 158–159.
21. John A. Wright to C.I.A., Sept. 27, 1879, *Idaho Superintendency*, Roll 351.
22. J. M. Haworth to C.I.A., Oct. 17, 1879, *Idaho Superintendency*, Roll 350; J. M. Haworth to C.I.A., Oct. 23, 1879, ibid.
23. J. M. Haworth to C.I.A., Nov. 11, 1879, ibid.; J. M. Haworth to C.I.A., Dec. 15, 1879, ibid.
24. Ibid.
25. W. N. Fisher to W. H. Danilson, Feb. 27, 1879, *Idaho Superintendency*, Roll 351.
26. *C.I.A. Annual Report, 1880*, 184; John A. Wright to C.I.A., April 9, 1880, *Idaho Superintendency*, Roll 353.
27. John A. Wright to C.I.A., June 2, 1880, ibid.
28. John A. Wright to C.I.A., July 5, 1880, ibid.
29. *C.I.A. Annual Report, 1881*, 121.
30. Ibid., *1882*, 110.
31. Idib., *1881*, 121.
32. Ibid., *1882*, 110; Cyrus Beede to C.I.A., March 13, 1884, U. S. National Archives, *Records, Office of Indian Affairs*.
33. Arden R. Smith to C.I.A., Nov. 30, 1882, ibid.
34. Jim to Annie, Nov. 23, 1884, Idaho State University Archives, Ms. 650.
35. *C.I.A. Annual Report, 1883*, 112.
36. Ibid., *1884*, 108.
37. Ibid., *1885*, 291.
38. Shoshonee Jim to the President, July 9, 1884, U. S. National Archives, *Records, Office of Indian Affairs*.
39. Cyrus Beede to C.I.A., March 13, 1884, ibid.
40. *C.I.A. Annual Report, 1885*, 75.
41. J. M. Haworth to Sec. of Interior, Sept. 25, 1883, *Report of the Superintendent of Indian Schools*.
42. *C.I.A. Annual Report, 1886*, 325; P. Gallagher to C.I.A., Dec. 2, 1886, U.S. National Archives, *Record Group No. 75*.
43. *C.I.A. Annual Report, 1887*, 150–151; William Parsons to C.I.A., April 16, 1887, U.S. National Archives, *Record Group No. 75*; Geo. B. Parsons to C.I.A., Jan. 1, 1887, U.S. National Archives, *Record Group No. 48*.
44. John B. Riley to A. B. Upshaw, April 27, 1887, *Record Group No. 75*.
45. J. D. Everest to C.I.A., May 7, 1887, ibid.
46. *C.I.A. Annual Report, 1888*, 81.
47. Ibid., *1889*, 3.
48. Ibid., 176–177.
49. *Report on Indians Taxed and Indians Not Taxed in the United States, Eleventh Census; 1890*, Department of Interior (Wash., 1894), 237.
50. *C.I.A. Annual Report, 1891*, 559–561.
51. Ibid., *1890*, 76–77; S. G. Fisher to C.I.A., April 11, 1890, U.S. National Archives, *Record Group No. 75*.
52. *C.I.A. Annual Report, 1891*, 559.

53. Ibid., *1892*, 233.
54. Ibid., 150.
55. Ibid., 151–152.
56. Sec. of Interior to C.I.A., June 21, 1892, U.S. National Archives, *Record Group No. 75.*
57. Daniel Dorchester to C.I.A., Dec. 16, 1892, ibid.
58. C.I.A. to Agents and School Superintendents, Aug. 17, 1892, U.S. National Archives, *Records, Office of Indian Affairs.*
59. *C.I.A. Annual Report, 1893,* 415.
60. John Lane to C.I.A., August 23, 1893, U.S. National Archives, *Record Group No. 75.*
61. J. T. Van Orsdale to C.I.A., Jan. 10, 1894, ibid.; *C.I.A. Annual Report, 1894,* 131.
62. J. T. Van Orsdale to C.I.A., March 21, 1894, U.S. National Archives, *Record Group No. 75.*
63. *Pocatello Advance,* June 27, 1895.
64. *C.I.A. Annual Report, 1895,* 142–143; Sec. of Interior to C.I.A., June 19, 1895, U.S. National Archives, *Record Group No. 75.*
65. *Idaho Herald,* April 12, 1895.
66. Isaac M. Yandell to C.I.A., Sept. 11, 1895, U.S. National Archives, *Record Group No. 75;* A. H. Heinemann to Superintendent of Indian Schools, Oct. 26, 31, 1895, ibid.; *Idaho Herald,* see Ch. VIII, footnotes 89-108.
67. *Blackfoot News,* Dec. 21, 1895.
68. Thomas B. Teter to Superintendent of Indian Schools, Jan. 18, 1896, U.S. National Archives, *Record Group No. 75;* School Statistics Accompanying Annual Report, July 15, 1896, ibid.
69. *Pocatello Tribune,* Sept. 29, 1897, Jan. 8, 1898; *C.I.A. Annual Report, 1898,* 144.
70. Charles D. Rakestraw to Superintendent of Indian Schools, Jan. 13, 1898, U.S. National Archives, *Record Group No. 75.*
71. *C.I.A. Annual Report, 1897,* 129; F. G. Irwin to C.I.A., Feb. 10, 1898, U.S. National Archives, *Record Group No. 75;* see this chapter, footnote 62.
72. W. J. McConnell to Sec. of Interior, April 12, 1898, ibid.
73. *Pocatello Tribune,* Jan. 19, 1898.
74. Ibid., Dec. 1, 1897.
75. Ibid., Aug. 28, 1897.
76. Governor Heber W. Wells to C.I.A., June 20, 1896, U.S. National Archives *Record Group No. 75.*
77. *Pocatello Tribune,* Oct. 3, 10, 1896.
78. Ibid., May 2, 1901.
79. Ibid., Aug. 31, 1901.
80. Ibid., Feb. 2, 1901.
81. Ibid., Feb. 23, March 2, 1901.
82. *C.I.A. Annual Report, 1899,* 181–183; ibid., *1900,* 216; ibid., *1901,* 209.
83. Ibid., 207.
84. *Pocatello Tribune,* Nov. 12, 1901.
85. *C.I.A. Annual Report, 1901,* 207.
86. *Pocatello Tribune,* Aug. 8, 1900.
87. *C.I.A. Annual Report, 1902,* 182.
88. Ibid., *1903,* 155.
89. Ibid., *1905,* 196.
90. Ibid., *1904,* 177.
91. *Pocatello Tribune,* Feb. 7, April 8, Dec. 24, 1907.
92. Ibid., May 28, 1903.
93. Ibid., Aug. 25, 1902.
94. Ibid., Sept. 4, 1903.
95. *C.I.A. Annual Report, 1904,* 175.

96. Ibid., *1902,* 13–16.
97. *Pocatello Tribune,* June 26, 27, July 2, 5, 1906.
98. Ibid., Dec. 1, 1907.
99. *C.I.A. Annual Report, 1908,* 129.
100. Charles L. Davis to C.I.A., May 13, 1908, U.S. National Archives, *Record Group No. 75,* 74, 78.
101. Ibid., 1, 2.
102. Ibid., 85–87.
103. *Pocatello Tribune,* Oct. 1, 1910.
104. C.I.A. to H. H. Miller, Feb. 21, 1918, U.S. National Archives, *Record Group No. 75.*
105. James H. McGregor to C.I.A., Nov. 17, 1921, ibid.
106. William Donner to C.I.A., Sept. 5, 9, 1922, ibid.
107. Six Indian Leaders to William Donner, Feb. 6, 1923, ibid.
108. William Donner to C.I.A., April 6, 1923, ibid.; *Second Deficiency Appropriation Bill,* Hearing before Sub-Committee of House Committee on Appropriations, U.S. Congress 68th Cong., 1st Sess. (Wash., 1924).
109. Charles L. Davis to C.I.A., May 13, 1908, U.S. National Archives, *Record Group No. 75.*
110. C.I.A. to H. H. Miller, Feb. 21, 1918, ibid.
111. Charles E. Burke to W. J. Burns, March 19, 1924, ibid.
112. Charles L. Davis to C.I.A., May 13, 1908, ibid.; C.I.A. to H. H. Miller, Feb. 21, 1918, ibid.; see Ch. XIV, 54–58.
113. *Pocatello Tribune,* June 27, July 8, 1912.
114. Ibid., Jan. 13, July 23, 1910.
115. William Donner to C.I.A., Sept. 9, 1922, U.S. National Archives, *Record Group No. 75.*
116. H. M. Gillman to C.I.A., July 26, 1928, ibid.
117. F. A. Gross to A. C. Cooley, Sept. 6, 1930, *Fort Hall Agency Records.*
118. *Survey of Conditions of the Indians in the United States,* U.S. Congress, Senate, 72d Cong., 1st Sess., Part 27, Wyoming, Idaho and Utah, Sept. 12, 13 and 14, 1932 (Wash., D.C., 1934), 14638.
119. "J. E. White Report on Social and Economic Information for the Shoshone-Bannock Tribes, Sept. 24, 1938," U.S. National Archives, *Record Group No. 75.*
120. Supt. Indian Schools at Large to F. A. Gross, Nov. 8, 1938, *Fort Hall Agency Records;* Carl Stevens to Paul L. Fickinger, Oct. 1, 1941, ibid.; Nybroten, *Economy and Conditions of the Fort Hall Indian Reservation,* 116; Carl W. Beck to C.I.A., June 10, 1946, *Fort Hall Agency Records.*
121. Nybroten, *Economy and Conditions . . . ,* 116.
122. "Report of Education Field Agents, Nov. 30, 1945," *Fort Hall Agency Records.*
123. F. A. Gross to Henry Dworshak, Dec. 12, 1939, ibid.; Carl Stevens to Paul L. Fickinger, Oct. 1, 1941, ibid.; Liljeblad, "Some Observations on the Fort Hall Indian Reservation," *The Indian Historian,* Fall 1974, Vol. 7, No. 4, 12.
124. *Pocatello Tribune,* March 12, 1949.
125. B. W. Davis to Henry Dworshak, July 15, 1949, *Fort Hall Agency Records.*
126. Bertha A. Ellinger to Willard W. Beatty, April 21, 1944, ibid.
127. Nybroten, *Economy and Conditions . . . ,* 119–120.
128. Fry, "An Investigation of the Relationships between Descriptive Data about Trainees and Past Training Employment in an M.D.T.A. Project Held between 1968-1970 at Fort Hall, Idaho," M.A. thesis, Idaho State University, 1973, 4.
129. Liljeblad, "Some Observations on the Fort Hall Indian Reservation," 9–13.
130. Ibid.

CHAPTER XIV

MEDICINE MEN: OLD AND NEW

Dearth of Missionary Effort

The establishment of a reservation at Fort Hall meant that for the first time there was a settled place where a mission station could be built to minister to the religious needs of the wandering Shoshoni and Bannock. Under the policy of the Office of Indian Affairs of assigning each Indian reserve to a particular church organization, the Fort Hall Reservation was placed under the care of the Methodist Episcopal Church. For some reason, perhaps the uninviting windswept Snake River Plains or the purported unsavory reputation of the "Snake" and Bannock tribes, the nearest Methodist Episcopal headquarters at Salt Lake City failed to send a missionary to Fort Hall during the first two years of reservation activity. In 1871 Agent High requested appropriations of $2,500 for a residence for a missionary and $3,500 for a mission building. When no funds were earmarked for these purposes, apparently the church again responded with dedicated apathy.[1]

1861

At least some of the Shoshoni and Bannock might not have cared about the lack of a Christian religion at Fort Hall and would have agreed with their Idaho neighbor to the north, Chief Joseph of the Nez Perce, who, in a famous interview in 1873, indicated he wanted no churches working with his people. "They will teach us to quarrel about God, as the Catholics and Protestants do on the Nez Perce Reservation and at other places. . . . We may quarrel with men sometimes about things on this earth, but we never quarrel about God. We do not want to learn that."[2] Besides, the Indians had their own "primitive" religion, which worked well for them [3]

The religious vacuum at Fort Hall soon attracted the attention of Father Touissant Mesplie of the Roman Catholic faith. He wrote the commissioner of Indian Affairs that, prior to a visit to Fort Hall, he had expected to find the Shoshoni and Bannock "degraded beyond redemption." To his surprise he had found them "as well disposed and as apt of cultivation as any other Indians east of the Cascade mountains. . . ." He asked that the reservation be assigned to the Catholics so that he might name the agent and begin missionary work among a people which, he claimed, already included 450 members of the Catholic faith.[4] The

secretary of the Interior responded two weeks later by transferring the Fort Hall Agency from the Methodist Episcopal Church to the Roman Catholic.[5] Father Mesplie had M. P. Berry appointed agent and was at the reservation on August 8, 1871, ready to begin his missionary work.[6]

As indicated in another chapter, Mesplie soon left his station because there were no buildings in which to conduct a school or religious services and no funds to pay his salary. By November 1871 he was at Silver City, Idaho, announcing to the press that he still had hopes of returning to Fort Hall to work with Agent Berry in looking after the spiritual welfare of the Fort Hall Indians.[7] His hopes were doomed when no funds were advanced, and Berry was replaced by Johnson N. High who reported, "There are neither schools nor missions here." High said the Indians were anxious for both. Through no fault of theirs the government had failed to live up to the third and tenth articles of the Fort Bridger Treaty.[8]

1872

With the failure to support Father Mesplie, and with his departure from the agency to become chaplain at Fort Boise, the Office of Indian Affairs now returned the religious assignment for Fort Hall to the Methodist Episcopal Church. An army officer acquainted with affairs on the reservation deprecated the change, claiming that the new agent, High, as a Methodist, was administering the agency and preaching sermons but was not promoting the material progress of the Indians. Captain H. A. Finney, although not a Catholic himself, believed that only "Catholics have had success in Christianizing them."[9] The *Idaho Statesman* poked fun at the government's practice of parcelling out Indians to the various churches "for salvation, just as a father would divide up a basket of apples among his children."[10] The Catholic Church did seem to have a stronger hold on the souls of the Shoshoni and Bannock — as revealed when fifty of them traveled to Fort Boise to have five of their children baptized by Father Mesplie.[11]

1873

1874

Methodist Episcopal authorities finally became active in 1875 with the appointment of an Indian teacher, P. O. Mathews, who organized a church society of six members, held services each Sunday, and established a Sabbath school. Also the Reverend J. M. Jameson was assigned from Salt Lake City to serve as a missionary and govern-

1875

ment teacher at Fort Hall.[12] By the following year, however, things had returned to normal; Agent Danilson noted that the Reverend Jameson was holding religious meetings in addition to his duties as a teacher but "not at the expense of the church. There seems to be an indifference to its obligation and responsibility in this work." The burst of activity during 1875 may have been the result of the Mormon "scare" at Corinne, already discussed, which had attracted Fort Hall Indians to lower Bear River.[13]

In fact, religious activity at Fort Hall during the entire 1870s seemed to ebb and flow as the result of Mormon proselyting efforts in northern Utah. Not only had the Reverend G. W. Dodge, special agent for the Northwestern Shoshoni, stirred up anxieties about Mormon "meddling" with the Shoshoni and Bannock as early as 1872,[14] but the 1875 troubles and then the Bannock War of 1878 aroused further apprehensions of a combined Mormon-Shoshoni and Bannock attack on all whites. It was at this time that the U.S. Attorney General's Office investigated charges that the Mormon cooperative stores were selling guns and ammunition to the Indians.[15] The *Idaho Statesman* explained that Mormon teachings which held that the Indians would become "a white and delight-some people," were designed solely to intimidate all non-Mormons from settling in the bountiful valleys of the Great Basin and adjacent regions.[16] The Nez Perce and Bannock wars only sharpened this paranoia toward the Utah Saints.

Occasionally Fort Hall agents complained of Mormon proselytizing among the Shoshoni and Bannock; in 1883 A. L. Cook warned that Mormon missionaries were persisting in holding meetings at the agency, claiming to have baptized three hundred converts. He particularly objected to their instructions "in polygamy and other vicious doctrines" which made the Indians discontented.[17]

Except for the Mormon "annoyance" in 1883, nothing of importance disturbed the desert of religious tranquility at the reservation. The agents monotonously reported the inactivity of the Methodist Episcopal Church,[18] the crudity of the Indians' ideas about revealed religion,[19] but their interest in Bible history.[20] They appealed for missionaries to work "among these poor red men" who were "religiously inclined" and needed to be "Christianized as much as the people of foreign lands."[21] Peter Gallagher spoke for all agents when he discovered upon taking over the agency in 1886, that as far as missionary work was concerned

nothing has ever been done in this direction. Why it is that the Methodist Episcopal Church, in whose care and keeping this work was placed, have never established a mission among them, is for them to explain. Surely it can not be said that this is not an "inviting field" and an "open door" to the "soldier of

the Cross," having a self-sacrificing disposition and love for souls, and an ardent and burning desire to bring up poor fallen humanity to a higher plane.[22]

In most instances during these years the agents made no mention at all of religion at Fort Hall.

Then, after eighteen years of religious neglect by the Methodist Episcopal organization, help came from the Connecticut Indian Association, an auxiliary of the Women's National Indian Association. Amelia S. Quinton of the parent organization wrote the commissioner that she was prepared to send "two highly recommended and suitable missionaries" to Fort Hall if they could be furnished supplies from the government stores on the same basis as the employees, if a mission cottage could be erected for them, and if three or four acres of land could be provided.[23] In July 1887 Miss Amelia J. Frost of Albion, New York, arrived at Fort Hall, followed in October by Miss Ella J. Stiles. Agent Gallagher thought the missionaries deserved "richly much sympathy and prayer" in their "labor of love and self-sacrifice."[24]

The forthright action of the Women's National Indian Association must have prodded their male counterparts out of the Rip Van Winkle sleep into which they had fallen. It is true that two years earlier Catholic Father E. W. Nattini had inquired about the possibility of getting five or six acres of land near Pocatello for construction of a chapel, but nothing had come of the request.[25] Now, in December 1887, the Right Reverend A. J. Glorieux, vicar apostolic of Idaho, decided to go all out; he asked for a grant of 160 acres of land for missionary and school purposes.[26] The Reverend F. A. Riggin, superintendent of the Montana Mission of the Methodist Episcopal Church, had already asked for 200 square feet of land adjacent to Pocatello for a chapel and a parsonage. This was in May 1878.[27] The Indian Office granted Methodist Episcopal authorities the right to erect a tent for religious services while awaiting word that Congress had approved the cession of the additional acres for the Utah and Northern Railroad at Pocatello.[28] The request of the Catholic Church was not granted.

While others applied for land and wrote letters, the Misses Frost and Stiles were hard at work. They received extravagant praise from Agents Gallagher and Fisher, who commended them for "raising up poor degraded humanity" with their "untiring" good work.[29] The Connecticut Indian Association, pleased with the success of the mission, asked and was allowed to occupy 160 acres of land on which the organization planned to build cottages — for the two missionaries and for a missionary farmer which the association expected to send to teach the Indians better methods of agriculture.[30]

Idaho State Historical Society

Hubert Tetoby (left), Pat Tyhee (right), and Charles Peterson cooperated in the Nez Perce missionary effort at Fort Hall.

1890

As the decade of the 1890s dawned, a reporter for the official United States census described the life-style of the Fort Hall Indians, including a superficial statement of their beliefs concerning life beyond the grave:

> The Bannock and Shoshone Indians' belief in the future life is simply that the braves, those who have taken scalps from an enemy or are successful horse thieves, will go to a land ruled by a big Indian god who will be most gorgeously decorated with beautiful feathers and wear the full robes of a great chief, and, riding a very fast horse, will lead them all in the buffalo chase. Game and fish of all kinds will be in abundance and easily captured. The quiet, honest fellows may possibly be admitted, but will not be allowed to take part in any of the royal sports. They believe they will have their horses in heaven. . . .[31]

This simplistic evaluation came just at the beginning of the so-called "messiah craze" which was sweeping through the western reservations and which led the Idaho governor, as well as the commissioner of Indian Affairs, to write Agent Fisher at Fort Hall inquiring about the attitude of the Indians and about the possibility of an outbreak as a result of the new religious movement.[32] The agent thought the Indians were "sullen" and decided to proceed cautiously to try to discover their true feelings.

The prophet of the new Indian religion was a northern Paiute called Wovoka from Walker Lake, Nevada. He preached that the earth was getting old and worn out and was to be renewed. The Indian dead were to be resurrected and the old ones still alive would be rejuvenated so that no one would be more than forty years old. Indians and whites were to cease fighting and become one people, and the resurrected Indians would drive back with them immense herds of buffalo and elegant wild horses. The white man would no longer be able to make gunpowder, and the supply now on hand would be so weak that it could not project a bullet through the skin of an Indian. There were other variations of the theme as the doctrine spread from tribe to tribe and subordinate prophets took up the call.[33]

The Ghost Dance religion was just the latest version of the attempt on the part of frustrated and disheartened North American tribes to try to recreate the kind of existence they had known before the coming of Europeans. It was a cry of despair, a last supplication before succumbing to the tidal wave of white "progress" which was engulfing them.

The Shoshoni and Bannock of Fort Hall were deeply involved in the new gospel. Their long acquaintance with Mormon theology (from the time of Latter-day Saint penetration of the Great Basin in 1847 to the troubles at Corinne in the 1870s and the missionary efforts of Mormon Elders at Fort Hall in the 1880s) had given them hope that at some future time their brothers, the "ten lost tribes," would come down from the frozen north and rejoin them. They remembered hearing that "by being baptized and going to church the old men would all become young, the young men would never be sick, that the Lord had a work for them to do, and that they were the chosen people of God to establish his kingdom upon the earth." Spurred on by these beliefs the Shoshoni and Bannock had received hopes of a better life from the Mormon missionaries and may even have been the originators of the "ghost shirt," an invulnerable sacred garment of the Ghost Dance religion, which probably came from the "endowment robe" that many of the Indians received upon joining the Utah church. James Mooney, an investigator of the Ghost Dance movement, was of the opinion that "the Mormons took an active interest in the religious ferment then existing among the neighboring tribes and helped to give shape to the doctrine which crystallized some years later in the Ghost Dance."[34]

The Indians at Fort Hall were among the first to take up the new religion in early 1889, chiefly because of the easy communication with Wovoka and his people. The Bannock, being of Northern Paiute stock, understood the doctrines and passed them on to their Shoshoni neighbors at Fort Hall who, in turn, visited the Wind River area where the Eastern Shoshoni transferred the ideas to the Arapaho who gave them to the Cheyenne and the Sioux. Fort Hall, therefore, became one of the distribution centers of the new religion to the Indians of the northern plains.[35]

1889

The location of Fort Hall at the junction of a north-south railroad from Utah to Montana and an east-west transcontinental line made it the stopping place for Indians travelling to and from Walker Lake. The Shoshoni and the Bannock, therefore, became principal disseminators of the new religion. When the Mighty Porcupine, the Cheyenne medicine man, traveled to the Walker River Reservation in November 1889 to get the truth directly from the lips of the prophet himself, he stopped off at Fort Hall for food, information, and directions.[36] The Shoshoni and Bannock never threatened any military action as a result of the Ghost Dance religion, but there were many comings and goings and much religious excitement at Fort Hall during the "messiah craze." Agent Fisher was happy to see the Ghost Dance disappear but feared it might be revived at any time by some "weak-brained individual or medicine men."[37]

1891

Except for the above attempt at creating an Indian church, the only other religious ferment at Fort Hall continued to be the activities sponsored by Miss Amelia J. Frost of the Connecticut Indian Association. Miss Stiles had left, but Fred Peck had arrived to take over as the farming missionary and, incidentally, to grow food for the mis-

Idaho State Historical Society

Original Presbyterian Mission building at Fort Hall.

sion. From 1891 on, for the next ten years, the various agents praised the efforts of Miss Frost, who not only taught seven or eight girl students each year but also comforted "the sick and needy." She was liked and respected by both Indians and whites.

Each agent, as he took over the reservation, expressed surprise at the lack of religious activity. 1899 As C. A. Warner put it in 1899, "Strange to say, no active missionary work has ever been carried on upon this reservation" with the exception, of course, of the indefatigable and always-enduring Miss Frost.[38] Occasionally other church groups evinced a passing interest in the salvation of the 1894 Shoshoni and Bannock. In 1894 Catholic Bishop A. J. Glorieux of Idaho requested permission to establish a Catholic cemetery on forty acres of reservation land donated to the church by an Indian, Mrs. Thomas Lavatta. It was to be used by "White and Red Catholics" and indicated the persistence of communicants in that faith at Fort Hall despite the long absence of any missionary 1896 activity.[39] Also, starting in 1896, a band of Nez Perce missionaries visited the reservation every summer but had no success until three years later when a young Shoshoni who had spent some time at the Nez Perce Reservation joined the mission- 1900 ary effort. By 1900 the Reverend Mr. Hayes of the group announced a congregation of twenty as the result of his spiritual labors.[40]

The inauguration of a new century seemed to usher in a period of repentance and rededication on the part of the Episcopal Church — which after forty years of abstinence took over the property of the Connecticut Indian Association and, upon application, received enough land to provide a mission of 160 acres.[41] Bishop J. B. Funsten assigned Miss Susan C. Garrett to head the missionary work and began to improve the property.[42] At the same time the faithful Miss Frost accepted the sponsorship of the Presbyterian Church, which was granted 160 acres of ground about eight miles north of the agency. A new church building and living quarters were completed by August 1901, and Miss Frost re- 1901 ported seven baptisms by that time. Her fellow servant in Christ, Miss Garrett, also had the pleasure of witnessing eight baptisms at her station.[43] After many years of un-Christianlike neglect, apparently the Shoshoni and Bannock were to have the opportunity of selecting from among at least three denominations the type of religious instruction they preferred.

The Episcopal and Presbyterian missions were very active. Both Miss Frost and Mrs. Susan Gar- 1902 rett Nelson devoted much time and attention to the girls under their charge, as well as ministering to the needs of various Indian families. Bishop J. B. Funsten also spent a lot of his time on the reservation and played an active role in support of Episcopal missionary work.[44]

By 1908 the Episcopal Church apparently con- 1908 sidered its position so solidly based at Fort Hall that Bishop Funsten requested a patent in fee for

Idaho State Historical Society

Amelia Frost (center) at the Fort Hall Agency building.

Idaho State Historical Society

Girls at the Fort Hall Presbyterian Mission School.

the 160 acres which had been provisionally by the Indians. Funsten indicated that his denomination had invested $40,000 at the agency,[45] and authorization was asked from Congress to approve the grant of land.[46] The order was approved without getting the consent of the Indians, who very much opposed the change. Indian Supervisor Charles L. Davis reported that, while there were twelve small children enrolled at the mission, there were only three communicants and no resident minister; and Mrs. Nelson indicated the Episcopal Church would probably have to abandon its school work. The Indians complained that the church was "too much inclined to grasp valuable land rights" and noted that the Presbyterian mission under Miss Frost had been at Fort Hall much longer, "has accomplished far more in way of spiritual success, and have not asked for anything further than both churches have enjoyed for several years, namely, an executive order setting aside the lands in use by each." Davis thought the action of the Episcopal Church in getting the patent would retard their work "which is now at low ebb."[47]

1926   Nevertheless, Episcopal authorities continued their small mission school, which by 1926 had twenty-six girls enrolled in the boarding school and a "waiting list of students such as private
1930   schools of distinction will have."[48] By 1930 Superintendent F. A. Gross of the agency reported three denominations active at Fort Hall, although he noted that "The missionary work in the

field as conducted by these churches is limited." Of the three denominations, he thought the Episcopal boarding school was excellent; he commented that the Presbyterian Church (located eight miles north of the agency and headed by an Indian missionary) was working with the Indian families in their homes; and he noted that the Roman Catholics were again showing some interest in trying to establish a chapel, although very few Indians on the reservation were of the Catholic faith.[49]

Except for the tiny Episcopal mission school and the work of the lone Indian Presbyterian missionary, little was being done by the late 1920s in the way of promoting Christian worship among the Shoshoni and Bannock. The Presbyterian buildings were unused except for an hour or two on Sunday. Inspector Flora Seymour summarized her feelings, "If there was ever a place where good field work of a missionary and social service nature is needed, it is on this reservation." She quoted a Nez Perce Presbyterian missionary who had spent some time at Fort Hall trying to preach the faith which had helped raise the standards of "life and character" among his people: "These Bannocks and Shoshones are a strange people, a hard people to reach." Mrs. Seymour believed that the Fort Hall Indians had become too sophisticated for their old "animistic worship" but nothing was being offered to fill the vacuum. They were not sending out any "Macedonian cry for help . . . but these empty mission buildings

Idaho State Historical Society

Dedication of First Presbyterian Church at Fort Hall.

1964

certainly speak of the failure of our race to grasp an opportunity or to fulfill a duty."[50]

By 1964 the Episcopal mission was still active, ministering to the spiritual needs of the Indians but also engaged in a number of social service activities — distributing clothing and offering shower and laundry facilities, a kindergarten, a library, a crafts room, and a recreation program.[51] Throughout the years the Shoshoni and Bannock had neither forgotten nor forgiven the issuance of a patent fee deeding the 160-acre mission area to the Episcopal Church, whose officials finally capitulated in 1967 and returned all but twenty acres to the tribes "hoping to avoid any more disputes and such" over the question of their land ownership.[52]

The Sun Dance and Native Religion

Not only had the Christian missionaries failed in their efforts with the Shoshoni and Bannock, but the old religious ceremonies and dances continued to be as vital as ever, despite the determined program of the Office of Indian Affairs to eradicate them in the interests of "civilizing" the Fort Hall residents. Especially did the tribes persist in maintaining their dances, holding a drum dance, for example, at Christmastime in connec-

tion with a "red Santa Claus" giving out presents; observing funeral or death dances; and staging their Sun Dance each summer.[53]

The Indian Department and the Shoshoni and Bannock finally met head-on about continuance of the Sun Dance. In 1911 the commissioner issued an order banning any further ceremonies of the kind. The following year the tribes ignored the order; they were allowed to continue because the dance was already underway. In 1913 taking the advice of some white friends in Pocatello, the Indians set up the dance on the Tendoy farm at Inkom, south of Pocatello. This was off the reservation where, supposedly, the commissioner's orders did not reach, but the agent at once sent his Indian police to break up the dance. The Indians were angry and were supported by a number of local Mormons, who "are just now great belivers in religious liberty." The tribesmen finally accepted the order, but white neighbors split over the issue. Some wanted the annual dance to continue as a sight-seeing spectacle, others as an outlet for "religious liberty." A few supported it as a means of exterminating the Indians by allowing them to dance themselves to death. Certainly the ordeal of dancing for three days and nights without eating, drinking, or sleeping was a trying test of physical endurance and religious orthodoxy.[54]

1911

1913

In 1916 the Indians again gathered for the Sun Dance. The Indian police tore down the structure erected for the dance, cut up the poles, and lodged seven of the leaders in jail to serve ten-day sentences. Again the Shoshoni and Bannock were angry and bitter over the action of the Indian Department, one of whose motives was to try to reduce the "promiscuous intercourse" believed to take place during the ceremony. The special agent in charge at Fort Hall was positive the Indians would attempt to hold the dance again the following year, perhaps under the guise of another more innocuous type of dance.[55]

The Office of Indian Affairs finally surrendered, although the retreat was gradual. In 1918 the commissioner criticized the reigning agent for having permitted "at least three Sun Dances" the past summer but very carefully explained that the government did not intend to interfere with religious dances as long as "vicious elements do not enter."[56] After four or five years, during which the Sun Dance was not allowed at all, permission

was granted in 1926 for a revival of the dance. It was true that some of the self-torture aspects had been eliminated, with the result being a kind of medicine dance, but it was held for the traditional three days. Mrs. Seymour considered "the whole thing as a gesture of defiance rather than of faith."[57] A 1937 report announced that the outstanding annual event for the Fort Hall Indians was the Sun Dance because of its "special religious significance."[58] Today, the inhabitants of Fort Hall hold an Annual Shoshone-Bannock Indian Festival, a week-long event which lacks some of the traditional Sun Dance elements but is cogent proof that traditions die hard.

The Office of Indian Affairs also had to deal with a newfound religion which was based on the use of peyote. The drug was introduced at Fort Hall in 1920, and soon agency officials were struggling with the legal problem of how to contain the spread of the habit when there were no state or federal laws dealing with the drug. The commissioner suggested the promulgation of a local reservation order which the Indian judges could announce as being in effect. The only trouble here was that one of the judges, Tom Edmo, along with seventeen other leaders, had signed a petition requesting the Indian Office to recognize the use of peyote as part of their religious practices. According to the resolution the drug had

Idaho State Historical Society

Shoshoni dancers ready for Drum Dance.

Idaho State Historical Society

Tom Edmo, son of Arimo.

been successful in curing a number of sick people. The petition ended with the plea, "We claim the peyote is next to God Our Father and Jesus Christ, and we worship it. . . . The white people worship God through the Bible and we worship through peyote."[59] The agent continued to try to suppress the use of the drug despite the plea for 1930 religious toleration, but by 1930 he reported that its use was increasing.[60]

A more recent event in the religious history at Fort Hall was the opening of an Indian branch by 1966 the Mormon Church in 1966. Apparently religion at the reservation had come full circle from a century ago, when the Latter-day Saints were under attack for proselytizing among the Shoshoni and Bannock.[61]

Today over half the people at Fort Hall identify themselves with a Christian church, while a rather large number claim membership in the Native American Church, incorporated by the State of 1925 Idaho on April 1, 1925. The latter seems to be of growing importance because of the healing powers attributed to the religion and also because of its attraction as a symbol of Indian culture.[62] To the Shoshoni and Bannock, religious belief has been and is the very private concern of each indi-

vidual, to be regarded with respect and consideration.

One Medical Doctor per Tribe

The care of the soul and a regard for the physical body have been parallel concerns of government officers who have had the responsibility of watching over the Indian residents of Fort Hall. Because physical illness and distress are more readily observable, the Office of Indian Affairs has paid more attention to, and certainly expended more money for, medical services throughout the long history of the reservation.

As soon as the first Indians were settled at Fort Hall in October 1869, Superintendent Floyd- 1869 Jones requested and was granted the money to hire a physician for the Indian and white employees at the agency.[63] Agent Danilson constructed a story-and-a-half cottage, twenty by thirty feet, as a residence for the prospective physician, who was hired in the spring of 1870. 1870 Floyd-Jones recommended that Dr. J. Reagles, Jr., also be given the task of acting as agency clerk, a task which was "usually performed by the Supdt of Teaching," until such time as a clerk could be employed.[64]

A new medical doctor, Milton Shoemaker, took over the physician's duties in August 1873. In a 1873 special report written at the same time the agent had some pertinent recommendations about the type of physician who should be hired to serve the Indians: "He should be a man of good, practical, common sense, as well as Physician . . . a man who sympathizes with Indians & is not unkind in feeling or habit, or remarks." Agent Reed also advised that the doctor's salary was $1,500 per year and the cost of medicines amounted to $550; that about one-third of the Indians relied upon their own medicine men rather than the agency physician; that the most prevalent diseases were venereal, scrofulous, rheumatic and lung disorders; and that most fatalities resulted from venereal, rheumatic, and lung diseases.[65]

Early in 1875 Dr. George H. Fuller was ap- 1875 pointed as physician at Fort Hall and joined with Agent Wright in asking for a hospital building.[66] Wright requested $4,000 to pay a labor force which could construct a carpenter shop, a shoe shop, and a hospital — in that order.[67] At that time Dr. Fuller was using his kitchen as a dispensary.[68] When no money was appropriated for a building, Fuller then asked for funds to purchase an army hospital tent, writing that "without some hospital accomodations many of them [Indians] suffer from neglect." The doctor argued that the tent could be moved easily if sanitary reasons demanded and that the structure would "more nearly resemble the dwellings to which these people are accustomed."[69] The secretary of the Interior thought the U.S. government might be able to afford the required $55.08.[70] After six years of reservation life the Shoshoni and Bannock finally received a tent hospital to care for their ill and afflicted.

1878 W. H. Danilson, practical and go-ahead as ever, was not content with a hospital built of canvas. In December 1878 he proposed to erect a small wooden structure "without any additional expense to the government" if Washington would agree only to furnish enough money to hire an Indian nurse to cook for the patients and minister to their needs.[71] Apparently the structure was never built.

While the agents wrote and hired and built, the Indians suffered through periods of good health and bad, as usual, with the additional help a medical practitioner could offer to the most serious 1869 cases. The first spring at Fort Hall was particularly hard on the Boise and Bruneau Shoshoni, who suffered from "chills and fevers."[72] During 1874 the next few years health conditions seemed to improve somewhat and were better than "would be expected considering their exposures."[73] The winter of 1874 was particularly hard, with much sickness and a number of deaths — some due to 1875 an epidemic of measles which struck the camps.[74] Agent Wright, in asking for some unusual medical instruments and books, explained that their great distance from other medical personnel and libraries made the items necessary.[75]

1877 The 1877 annual report of the commissioner of Indian Affairs listed 378 cases receiving medical assistance during the previous year, with an al-1879 most equal ratio of births to deaths — 55 to 57.[76] Special Agent Haworth introduced evidence which became too common at Fort Hall; this was the psychological trauma of acculturation which the Shoshoni and Bannock were beginning to suffer. He reported two suicides. One was a young man who said he wished to carry "to that Other Country" the news of how his people were getting along. The other was a young man who wished to prove that a small pistol he owned was not large enough to kill a man. His demonstration sent him to the "Other Country" involuntarily.[77]

1870 Agency physicians faced a continuing challenge with the Shoshoni and Bannock when they tried to vaccinate them for smallpox. The first doctor, J. Reagles, Jr., was able to persuade 150 to endure 1875 the ordeal.[78] By 1875 Dr. Fuller was estimating that not more than one-fourth of the Indians would consent to vaccination.[79] Five months later Fuller had revised his estimate down to nothing. He thought that no Indian would submit to the operation unless an epidemic struck the reservation.[80]

1882 When Dr. Fuller gave up his position at Fort Hall he was succeeded by Dr. Jesse K. Dubois, the brother of Fred T. Dubois. The Dubois appoint-

ment started a series of difficulties at the agency, including some ill-chosen physicians who failed to provide competent medical care for the Shoshoni and Bannock. As indicated in a previous chapter, Dr. Dubois and Agent A. L. Cook did not get along, each preferring charges against the other. Brother Fred advised Dr. Jesse that Cook was a "miserable curr" and to be "calm and use duplicity" to try to get rid of the agent.[81] Cook replied with affidavits from Chiefs Gibson Jack, Captain Jim, and Tyhee that Dr. Dubois was given to drunkenness and failed to take care of the needs of the Indians.[82] Cook stayed, and Jesse Dubois lost out in the political struggle which ensued.

1884 Dubois was replaced by Dr. W. D. Monnet, who was characterized in March 1884 as unfit for the service — being a habitual user of opium and having been gone from his post for three and a half months during the six months prior to an inspection by Special Agent Cyrus Beede. The inspector reported that the Indians were very much diseased, "full of syphilis," and requiring constant attention. But the physician was never around; he prescribed for his patients by taking the statement of an Indian messenger who brought news of the sick person; he did not take the trouble to visit the patient. Monnet was forced out and was succeeded by Dr. W. R. Maddox on March 30, 1884.[83]

1887 Dr. Maddox soon came under criticism for "living the life of a hermit." Agent Gallagher defended the doctor, explaining that Maddox was very efficient, well-liked by the Indians, and always "ready to obey a call." He said the reservation was very large, with the Indians quite scattered, which explained why the doctor's visits "could not be called frequent."[84]

Dr. J. M. Masenia soon took over and was there only long enough to be charged with being so much under the influence of opium that he was 1889 incapable of taking care of patients.[85] Dr. Maddox came back to relieve him. By 1889 Dr. M. A. Miller was in charge of medical affairs at Fort Hall.[86]

By the late 1880s the annual report of the commissioner of Indian Affairs began to include tables containing vital statistics for the various reservations, but some of the figures apparently did not reflect careful record keeping. For example the 1883 report stated that 680 Indians had 1883 received medical treatment during the year, while the 1884 report listed 356. There may have been an epidemic in 1883, but, if so, little notice was given to it.[87]

1890 The census report for 1890 included an interesting description of the difficulties encountered by the agency doctor at Fort Hall:

For instance, he may visit a person in his lodge or shanty, sometimes 10 or more miles from the Agency headquarters. He finds his patient lying on the ground, with scarcely any bedding, and with no interpreter at hand it is impossible for them to understand each other. There being no glass or spoon about the place, he may be obliged to give the sick person his doses from an old oyster or tomato can. He can only tell him how often to take the medicine by motions, and points at the relative place of the sun for the time when the dose should be taken.[88]

The report added that it would do no good to build a hospital because the first death would end its use by any other Indians, who traditionally burned all lodges where deaths occurred.

Medicine Men Also Practice

The one constant in the picture of medical care at Fort Hall was the concern over the incidence of veneral disease among the Indians, especially the "roving and dissolute" Bannock. Whole families of children died very young due to hereditary syphillis; some families never had a child who lived to be a year old. By the late 1880s some improvement was being noted, as more and more of the older Indians began to turn to the white doctor for treatment instead of relying on the cures of the tribal medicine men.[89]

These tribal doctors rarely prescribed medicines to be taken internally but used the tried-and-true sweathouse or applied poultices made of crushed roots and leaves for flesh wounds or swellings. More and more the medicine men themselves began to consult the agency physician about broken bones. Sometimes they used the visit for an excuse to get a little 1886 sugar or coffee. In 1886 some of the old prejudices were dissipated when the doctor was able to make a successful amputation of a "diseased 1889 limb." Dr. Miller reported in 1889 that he had even been called upon to treat the wife of one of the medicine men, who more and more were losing their practices — especially when their cures failed with the patients, who at once turned to the white doctor for relief. Miller thought that if a modern hospital could be constructed the medicine men "would become a thing of the past."[90]

Occasional epidemics swept through the reservation, many of them starting at the boarding school. Scarlet fever was introduced at the school 1890 in November 1890 by a boy who had been living in Pocatello. Soon nearly all the students were infected. The agency physician was away in Montana. The patients were nearly all delirious, which exhausted those caring for them, and eventually sixty-eight students out of one hundred and five caught the disease. Together with an epidemic of measles, which also started at the school, the vital statistics for the year showed a loss of ninety in the population count, with thirty-four more deaths than births. Thirty-eight children died of scarlet fever. The medicine men took satisfaction in saying, "I told you so," as some of the parents

considered keeping their remaining children out of school.[91]

Although the medicine men still had a follow- 1892 ing, Dr. M. A. Miller reported with some satisfaction that more and more Indians were calling him to their camps and many were now willing to take medicine internally.[92] In fact, a number of the medicine men had given up their practice and were turning their full attention to their farms.[93] In August of 1898 Dr. G. M. Bridges reported he 1898 was sure the medicine men were on the wane and that they nearly always discontinued their practice when he requested them to do so.[94] But within another two years, Bridges thought the influence 1900 of the Indian doctors was increasing. He was particularly incensed toward them because if a school child became ill the parents often would take the child home and turn to a medicine man for help, believing the school and the white doctor to be at fault for the illness. The prescribed treatment was to place the sick child in a sweathouse which, Bridges charged usually caused the death of the child.[95] Six former students died in this way dur- 1901 ing 1901.[96]

Agent Caldwell took direct action by ordering the arrest of the medicine men who insisted on 1902 practicing their old "healing" rites.[97] Still, sick children taken from the school were being referred to local medicine men — although in other respects the influence of the tribal doctors seemed to be decreasing.[98]

The agency had trouble with its white doctors, too. Special Agent John Lane noted in 1893 that 1893 Dr. M. A. Miller had once been dismissed from the service and had then been reinstated. It was Lane's opinion that he probably should be discharged permanently. Lane appended affidavits to his report which alleged that the physician gambled so heavily at faro that he was reduced to pawning his watch and borrowing money from Pocatello saloonkeepers.[99]

Miller soon left Fort Hall and was replaced by 1895 Dr. Howard L. Dumble, who quickly was denounced by Agent Teter. When Dumble was transferred to another post, he became "loud in his remarks," refused to visit sick Indians patients, and told them he "did not care a damn, if they all died."[100]

With the increase in school enrollment a second 1899 physician was hired in 1899 to care for the students. The new doctor, W. L. Shawk, proudly reported that, although there were sixty ill children during the year, he did not lose a single case.[101] The position of physician at the school was 1903 abolished in January 1903; reponsibility for the care of the school children, as well as the almost fourteen hundred other Indians, was returned to the lone agency doctor.[102]

During the 1890s the prevailing diseases were syphilis, rheumatism, conjunctivitis, eczema, scabies, and pneumonia. The "lax ideas of the marriage relation" and the refusal of many of the Indians to undergo treatment made syphilis one of the constant debilitating diseases on the reservation.[103] Yet Dr. Dumble did not consider veneral disease to be as rampant at Fort Hall "as is usual among the Indians."[104] Dr. Bridges was of the opinion that many of the lung-associated ailments came as a result of the close confinement in school dormitories and in the new frame houses being furnished Indians families. During one year he carefully inspected forty-three Indian houses and found two were perfect, twenty-one good, eleven poor, and ten in bad condition. The lack of proper ventilation was caused chiefly because the Indian builders were each given only one-half a window which was set in a solid frame and could not be raised or lowered. Again the Shoshoni and Bannock were being treated to half rations.[105]

1903   As late as 1903 several cases of typhoid were reported at the boarding school because of contaminated water.[106] The following year Dr. Frank
1904   H. Poole discovered that the school dairy herd was infected with tuberculosis which was being transmitted to the students.[107]

1901   Smallpox had not made its appearance at Fort Hall for several years, although the worry was always there. Agent Caldwell was instructed to take care of the problem of vaccination; he did so by announcing that no Indian resident of the reservation would receive his or her $34.50 share of $10,000 due the Indians unless the individual submitted to vaccination. Immediately there was a great hullabaloo; each Indian child yelled "like a young fiend fresh from the pit," to use the purple prose of the *Pocatello Tribune*. Although there was some opposition, the process got underway — until a rumor spread that the doctors "were cutting great chunks out of every arm." Then a real mutiny began, and it was not quelled until Jim Ballard was called and counselled submission. All were vaccinated except Snook Smoshaw. Caldwell threatened to tie him down and administer the vaccine.[108]

By the time of the new century the Office of Indian Affairs had learned the new art of statistical quantification and soon began to drown in its own reports. This was especially true of medical data. Vital statistics, however, were hard to come by, due to the superstitions of the Indians about
1892   reporting births and deaths. The 1892 annual report for Fort Hall listed fifteen deaths, but the figure was incomplete. There were 722 males and 358 females treated for disease during that
1898   year.[109] Dr. G. M. Bridges was especially adept with figures. He reported in 1898 that he had made 132 calls to 109 individuals, had visited the school 65 times, and had traveled 5,295 miles during the year.[110] A year later he reported he had
1899   extracted 122 teeth and "prescribed for 588 trivial

troubles."[111] For 1900 he gave some comparative   1900
figures which indicated that from 1896 to 1900 the number of Indians treated had risen from 178 to 647 and the number visited from 8 to 139.[112] Perhaps of more significance was the population trend, which had decreased from 1,630 Indian residents at Fort Hall in 1881 to 1,403 in 1891 and to 1,351 by 1904.[113]

A Hospital and Nurses

Throughout the entire period from the establishment of the reservation in 1869 to the end of the century, the Shoshoni and Bannock never had access to a hospital at Fort Hall. Most agency officials agreed with Dr. Bridges, who in 1898 wrote   1898
that the Indians were not "sufficiently advanced" to be able to use the services of a hospital.[114] Three years later he reported ten applications for   1901
hospital treatment and recommended that it was now appropriate to construct a building to house Indian patients.[115] Agent Caldwell supported the request, and a hospital and dispensary were built at the school and were ready for occupancy in   1902
August 1902.[116]

Evidently the building was not large enough to accommodate the anticipated increase in business which the Lemhi removal would bring, so the government authorized an expenditure of   1907
$25,000 in 1907 to construct a larger hospital at the agency.[117] By 1923 some of the Indian leaders   1923
were commending the superintendent for obtaining a hospital at the agency, the old structure being used to serve the needs of the school.[118] The new Fort Hall hospital had been built from tribal funds and was being supported from tribal funds. Superintendent William Donner was understandable upset when the commissioner informed him in 1925 that the tribal hospital was to   1925
be closed after only a year and a half of operation: "I am sorry to have the hospital close; there is a great need for it at this agency and it should gradually become more extensive in its mission as the Indians become accustomed to it."[119]

The superintendent's plea to maintain the hospital was heeded, and when Inspector Samuel Blair visited the facility in May 1925 he described the "beautiful new hospital," built at a cost of $12,000, as clean and modern. He foresaw the time "when the Fort Hall Indians will . . . bring their sick and afflicted for treatment."[120] Three   1928
years later another inspection report described the twenty-bed boarding school hospital and the fourteen-bed agency hospital, both under the care of Dr. H. W. Wheeler, the only physician stationed at Fort Hall. There was one small operating room but insufficient personnel to aid Dr. Wheeler in his numerous duties.[121] The inspector pointed out that the hospital did not have the facilities to care for adult tubercular patients.

His report concluded that, because of lack of funds, medical service at Fort Hall was "insufficient. For any white community to have been so meagerly supplied with medical personnel, equipment, and attention would have been considered criminal."[122]

1930   Another medical inspector, Dr. H. J. Warner, recommended in 1930 that the school hospital be closed and the agency hospital be doubled in size to care for the increasing number of Indian

1932 patients.[123] Two years later the commissioner was regretting that there were no funds for enlarging the hospital,[124] although numerous reports recommended closing the inefficient school hospital and building a dormitory so the nursing staff would not have to be housed in the agency hospital.[125]

Even worse than the lack of proper hospital facilities was the obvious dearth of medical personnel. Dr. H. W. Wheeler, who served as agency physician from 1907 until his retirement twenty-five years later in 1932, was conscientious and, of necessity, a hard worker; he did "all one man in his position could do." But with almost two thousand Indians to care for and not enough nurses, he was forced to divide his attention between running the two hospitals, traveling over the reservation to visit patients, and, in between times, completing the multitude of reports demanded by Washington. There were constant appeals for another physician.[126]

With only Wheeler to minister to their sick, it was little wonder that the Shoshoni and Bannock continued to turn to their Indian doctors, who

1931 were still doing a "thriving business" in 1931.[127] Superstition and tradition were very much in control at Fort Hall. For example, a congressional subcommittee investigating the conditions of Indians in the United States found at Fort Hall that the so-called "moon house" could be seen near almost every Indian home on the reservation:

This house is usually very small — about 4 by 6 feet and usually barely high enough to permit a woman to stand up. In this house the Indian woman is forced to spend several days during her monthly period with barely enough fuel and food to sustain herself. The men are to blame for this for they are afraid, superstitious. When an Indian woman gives birth to a child in the home she is obliged to confine herself in this "moon house" for thirty days for the men believe that where a birth enters the regular home a life must leave it. Very often the mothers have so little nourishment and warmth while thus imprisoned that they come forth much weakened and naturally the new-born child is more or less affected.[128]

Sometimes neighboring white doctors at Pocatello had their own problems with the In-

1912 dians and disease on the reservation. In 1912 the city physician examining the baby of Corinne Daylight discovered to his horror that the child did not have a case of poison ivy but smallpox. The doctor immediately sent Mrs. Daylight back to Fort Hall and quarantined the entire reservation,

warning that any Indian leaving the reserve would be placed under arrest. A few days later four other doctors examined the Daylight infant and diagnosed the disease as eczema. The quarantine was lifted. One wonders whether the agency physician could have quarantined the city of Pocatello to protect his Indian wards if smallpox had been discovered in the town.[129]

During the early twentieth century the principal diseases among the Indians continued to be trachoma, prevalent among 50 percent of the population; tuberculosis, about 30 percent; veneral disease; and pneumonia.[130] An epidemic of   1922 the latter hit the boarding school in 1922. Superintendent Donner thought it was caused by the overcrowding and poor ventilation in the dormitories. He noted that among twenty-five boys who slept on screened sleeping porches there was not a single case of the disease.[131] Another headache for the agency doctor was the custom of Indian families to abandon their homes if a member happened to die in the house. To forestall such an eventuality a sick individual was usually moved outside. Superintendent Donner discovered one young woman (dressed in her best clothes, already for her funeral and burial) living outside her home. The doctor saved her from a early grave by offering prompt treatment.[132]

The death rate among the Shoshoni and Bannock continued to be high. In 1928 there were 59   1928 deaths out of a population of 1,770, a ratio of 35 per thousand. At the same time the death rate for the white population in Idaho was only 10 per thousand.[133] The principal diseases by 1932 were   1932 still tuberculosis, 350 cases for the year; trachoma, 350 cases; and veneral disease.[134]

The chief problem during the 1930s was the high incidence of trachoma, which kept many children out of school. The Blackfoot and Pocatello public schools sent the infected children home, and the superintendent did not want them in his day schools either. The affliction was the most virulent type of trachoma. The number with the disease increased from 45 to 1935 to 190 cases   1939 by 1939. Superintendent Gross, as has been indicated earlier, recommended that the old boarding school be converted into a trachoma school, but a   1935 cost of $9,000 a year forced the commissioner to veto the project. Gross kept up his entreaties, finally attempting to get the support of one of Idaho's congressmen. All to no avail.[135] The children had to be treated at small clinics on the reservation; there was no room for them in the small hospital.

By 1934 the "greatly crowded" hospital did not   1934 even have an operating room.[136] Somewhat in desperation the Fort Hall Business Council petitioned the commissioner in 1935 for a larger   1935 hospital with at least fifty beds because "our Indian people are getting used to the idea of proper care of the sick and are more and more anxious to go to the hospital when sick."[137] No funds were appropriated to construct a larger building. By 1941 the Indians were still struggling along with the tiny and outmoded structure. When the physician at the Duck Valley Reservation politely inquired why two of his Western Shoshoni patients could not be admitted for emergency treatment at Fort Hall, the answer was very simple — the hospital "was filled."[138]

General health conditions gradually began to improve. In 1935 the agency physician reported 76 births compared to 73 deaths, 68 percent of the maternity cases hospitalized, 7 percent reported active cases of tuberculosis, 18 percent of the 250 students afflicted with trachoma, and approximately 3 percent affected by gonorrhea and 1 percent by syphilis.[139]

Eight years later, in 1943, the annual report for Fort Hall listed a total of 282 hospital patients, with an average daily patient load of 7.9, and 1,500 dispensary treatments or an average of 4.2 a day. A few years later, after medical care for the Indians had been transferred to the Public Health Service, the statistics for 1957 listed 3,766 authorizations for medical care, including 4,950 days of hospital care. The poor housing on the reservation was a principal cause of the high disease rate. In 1957 only 10 percent of the homes had more than two rooms; 20 percent were two-room frame houses; and 70 percent were one-room log structures. Sanitary facilities were completely absent in one-half the homes.[140]

A report using late 1950 figures showed that five times as many Fort Hall Indians died of tuberculosis as in the United States generally and thirteen times as many as in Idaho. Influenza and pneumonia killed more than four times as many Fort Hall Indians in proportion to the deaths from that disease in Idaho. The death rate among the Shoshoni and Bannock was three times the national average. More than half the Indians still preferred an agency hospital, but the trend was away from reservation facilities and toward the use of other hospitals and other physician care.[141]

By the 1960s, and increasingly today, the Shoshoni and Bannock are getting involved in their own health-care programs. For example, the business council meeting of October 13 and 14, 1942, listed as one item for discussion, "Stamping out syphilis on the Reservation and a List of names presented to Council."[142] The *Fort Hall News* of April 1963 dealt with the statistic of seventy-eight patients being treated each day at the Fort Hall Medical Clinic and a detailed discussion of planning services available for the installation of home sewer and water systems.[143] The 1970 annual report of the Shoshone-Bannock tribes included such diverse items as expenditures for eyeglasses, the serving of diabetic breakfasts,

the appointment of a second community health representative, the announcement of classes on child care, the inauguration of a baby clinic and a report on an All-Indian Conference on Alcoholism.[144] The Indians at Fort Hall were beginning to take control of their own health and medical programs, after a long history of faltering and inadequate service from the Great Father in Washington.

The neglect of the Shoshoni and Bannock at Fort Hall by the Methodist Episcopal Church during the nineteenth century, and the disgruntlement of the Indians toward Mormon efforts at proselyting, left no religious institutions to teach Christianity to the tribes until the early 1900s. As a result, the churches of the white man have not taken deep root at Fort Hall, although the Indian people are basically religious and today tend to be attracted to their own Native American beliefs.

Similarly, medical practice was insufficient and poorly funded at the reservation from the beginning, with too many incompetent physicians and an overworked medical and nursing staff. Superstitions and medicine men stood in the way of a successful program of health and medical care, but a more energetic effort on the part of the government would have saved much illness and suffering throughout the hundred years of reservation life.

NOTES CHAPTER XIV
MEDICINE MEN: OLD AND NEW

1. J. N. High to C.I.A., Jan. 12, 1871, U.S. National Archives, *Idaho Superintendency*, Roll 339.
2. Commissioners John P. C. Shanks, T. W. Bennett, Henry W. Reed to C.I.A., Nov. 17, 1873, ibid., Roll 342.
3. *Deseret News*, May 25, 1870.
4. *Idaho Statesman*, March 14, 1871.
5. Sec. of Interior to C.I.A., March 24, 1871, U.S. National Archives, *Idaho Superintendency*, Roll 339.
6. M. P. Berry to C.I.A., Aug. 10, 1871, ibid.
7. *Idaho Statesman*, Nov. 21, 1871; see Ch. XIII, note 3.
8. *C.I.A. Annual Report, 1872*, 657.
9. *Idaho Statesman*, June 21, 1873.
10. Ibid., June 10, 1873.
11. Ibid., Aug. 27, 1874.
12. *C.I.A. Annual Report, 1875*, 761.
13. Ibid., *1876*, 447–448; see Ch. VI, notes 59–83.
14. G. W. Dodge to C.I.A., July 24, Oct. 28, 1872, U.S. National Archives, *Utah Superintendency*, Roll 903.
15. Attorney General to Sec. of Interior, Aug. 1877, ibid., Roll 905; Dave Alexander to Sec. Interior, July 16, 1878, ibid., Roll 906; E. A. Hoyt to John J. Critchlow, August, 1878, ibid.
16. *Idaho Statesman*, Aug. 13, 1878.
17. *C.I.A. Annual Report, 1883*, 112.
18. J. M. Haworth to C.I.A., Dec. 15, 1879, U.S. National Archives, *Idaho Superintendency*, Roll 350.
19. *C.I.A. Annual Report, 1881*, 121.
20. Ibid., *1882*, 110.
21. Ibid., *1884*, 109.
22. Ibid., *1886*, 326.
23. Amelia S. Quinton to C.I.A., April 20, 1887, U.S. National Archives, *Record Group No. 75*.
24. P. Gallagher to C.I.A., Oct. 7, 1887, ibid.; *C.I.A. Annual Report, 1887*, 151.
25. E. W. Nattini to John Hailey, April 4, 1887, U.S. National Archives, *Record Group No. 75*.
26. J. A. Stephan to C.I.A., Dec. 7, 1887, ibid.
27. F. A. Riggin to C.I.A., May 21, 1887, ibid.
28. P. Gallagher to A. B. Upshaw, Oct. 7, 1887, ibid.
29. *C.I.A. Annual Report, 1888*, 82; ibid., *1890*, 78.
30. Ibid.; E. Whittlesey to C.I.A., Oct. 4, 1888, U.S. National Archives, *Record Group No. 75*; General O. O. Howard to S. G. Fisher, Oct. 5, 1889; Idaho State Historical Society, Ms. 106.

31. "Report on Indians Taxed and Indians Not Taxed," Eleventh Census: 1890 (Wash., D.C., 1894), 236.
32. Gov. Geo. L. Shoup to S. G. Fisher, Nov. 20, 1890, Idaho State Historical Society, Ms. 106; S. G. Fisher to C.I.A., Dec. 27, 1890, U.S. National Archives, *Record Group No. 75*.
33. Mooney, *The Ghost-Dance Religion and the Sioux Outbreak of 1890*, 785; *C.I.A. Annual Report, 1891*, 125.
34. Mooney, *The Ghost-Dance Religion . . .* , 703, 704, 790.
35. Ibid., 805–806.
36. Ibid., 817–181; *C.I.A. Annual Report, 1891*, 123.
37. Ibid., 230.
38. Ibid., *1891; 1892; 1893; 1894; 1895; 1896; 1897; 1898; 1899*, 181.
39. A. J. Glorieux to J. T. Van Orsdale, Jan. 17, 1894, U.S. National Archives, *Records, Office of Indian Affairs*.
40. *C.I.A. Annual Report, 1899*, 182; ibid., *1900*, 216.
41. Elisha B. Reynolds to C.I.A., March 20, 1900, U.S. National Archives, *Record Group No. 75*.
42. *C.I.A. Annual Report, 1900*, 216; ibid., *1901*, 207.
43. Ibid.; Elisha B. Reynolds to C.I.A., March 24, 1900, U.S. National Archives, *Record Group No. 75*; "A. F. Caldwell to C.I.A., May 18, 1900," ibid.
44. *C.I.A. Annual Report, 1902*, 182; ibid., *1903*, 155; *Pocatello Tribune*, Sept. 13, 1902.
45. J. B. Funsten to C.I.A., July 22, 1904, U.S. National Archives, *Record Group No. 75*.
46. "Act Authorizing the Secretary of the Interior to Issue Patent in Fee to . . . Protestant Episcopal Church . . . ," U.S. Congress, Senate, 60th Cong., 1st Sess., Report No. 252, Feb. 18, 1908, Report No. 497, April 9, 1908 (Wash., D.C., 1908).
47. Charles L. Davis to C.I.A., May 13, 1908, U.S. National Archives, *Record Group No. 75*.
48. Flora Warren Seymour to Board of Indian Commissioners, Sept. 15, 1926, ibid., 8; *Pocatello Tribune*, July 28, 1909, Oct. 8, 1910.
49. F. A. Gross to A. C. Cooley, Sept. 6, 1930, *Fort Hall Agency Records*, 3–4.
50. Flora Warren Seymour to Board of Indian Commissioners, Sept. 15, 1926, U.S. National Archives, *Record Group No. 75*.
51. Nybroten, *Economy and Conditions . . .* , 110.
52. John L. Pappan to Dale M. Baldwin, April 18, 1967, Bureau of Indian Affairs, Portland Regional Office.
53. *Pocatello Tribune*, Dec. 27, 1902, Jan. 17, 1910.
54. Ibid., July 1, 1913; Evan W. Estep to C.I.A., July e, 1913, U.S. National Archives, *Record Group No. 75*.
55. C. L. Ellis to C.I.A., June 19, 1916, ibid.
56. C.I.A. to H. H. Miller, Feb. 21, 1918, *Fort Hall Agency Records*.
57. Flora Warren Seymour to Board of Indian Commissioners, Sept. 15, 1926, U.S. National Archives, *Record Group No. 75*.
58. J. E. White, "Social and Economic Information for the Shoshone-Bannock Tribes, Sept. 24, 1937," ibid.
59. L. W. Aschemeier to C.I.A., Jan. 15, 1921, ibid.
60. F. A. Gross to A. C. Cooley, Sept. 6, 1930, *Fort Hall Agency Records*.
61. *Journal History*, January 30, 1966, L.D.S. Department of History.
62. Nybroten, *Economy and Conditions . . .* , 110; "Articles of Incorporation, Native American Church," Dept. of State, Idaho.
63. De L. Floyd-Jones to C.I.A., Oct. 5, 1869, U.S. National Archives, *Idaho Superintendency*, Microcopy 832, Roll 3; C.I.A. to Floyd-Jones, Oct. 16, 1869, ibid.
64. De L. Floyd-Jones to W. H. Danilson, March 12, 1870, ibid.; *C.I.A. Annual Report, 1870*, 653.
65. "Special Report, July 24, 1873," U.S. National Archives, *Idaho Superintendency*, Roll 341.
66. James Wright to C.I.A., Dec. 24, 1874, *Fort Hall Letter Book*, 203; James Wright to C.I.A., Jan. 18, 1875, U.S. National Archives, *Idaho Superintendency*, Roll 343.
67. James Wright to C.I.A., Jan. 21, 1875, ibid.
68. James Wright to C.I.A., March 16, 1875, ibid.
69. Geo. H. Fuller to W. H. Danilson, Nov. 20, 1875, ibid.
70. Sec. of Interior to C.I.A., Dec. 16, 1875, ibid.
71. W. H. Danilson to C.I.A., Dec. 16, 1878, U.S. National Archives, *Idaho Superintendency*, Roll 347.
72. Charles F. Powell to D. W. Ballard, May 30, 1869, U.S. National Archives, *Idaho Superintendency*, Microcopy 832, Roll 2.
73. *C.I.A. Annual Report, 1874*, 592.
74. Henry W. Reed to C.I.A., March 1, 1874, *Fort Hall Record Book*, 172.
75. James Wright to C.I.A., March 11, 1875, U.S. National Archives, *Idaho Superintendency*, Roll 343.
76. *C.I.A. Annual Report, 1877*, 689.
77. J. M. Haworth to C.I.A., Jan. 8, 1879, U.S. National Archives, *Idaho Superintendency*, Roll 352.
78. J. Reagles, Jr., to W. H. Danilson, June 18, 1870, ibid., Roll 339.
79. Geo. H. Fuller to Jame Wright, Jan. 22, 1875, ibid., Roll 343.
80. Geo. H. Fuller to James Wright, June 30, 1975, ibid.
81. Fred T. Dubois to Dr. Jesse K. Dubois, March 15, 1882, U.S. National Archives, *Records, Office of Indian Affairs;* Jesse K. Dubois to Sec. of Interior, April 4, 1882, U.S. National Archives, *C.I.A. Annual Report, 75*; see Ch. XIII, notes 17–24.
82. A. L. Cook to C.I.A., April 27, 1882, ibid.; A. L. Cook to C.I.A., Jan. 16, 1883, U.S. National Archives, *Records, Office of Indian Affairs*.

83. Cyrus Beede to C.I.A., March 13, 1884, U.S. National Archives, *Record Group No. 75*.
84. P. Gallagher to C.I.A., June 2, 1887, ibid.
85. J. M. Needham to C.I.A., July 8, 1887, ibid.
86. *C.I.A. Annual Report, 1889*, 180.
87. Ibid., *1883*, 328; ibid., *1884*, 333.
88. "Report on Indians Taxed and Not Taxed," Eleventh Census, 1890 (Wash., D.C., 1894), 235–236.
89. *C.I.A. Annual Report, 1882*, 110; ibid., *1885*, 291; ibid., *1886*, 326.
90. Ibid.; ibid., *1887*, 151, ibid., *1888*, 82; ibid., *1889*, 180; "Report on Indians Taxed and Not Taxed," Eleventh Census, 1890, 236.
91. John Y. Williams to C.I.A., Nov. 17, 18, 22, 1890, U.S. National Archives, *Record Group No. 75*; *C.I.A. Annual Report, 1891*, 229, 559.
92. Ibid., *1892*, 235.
93. Howard L. Dumble to Van Orsdale, July 27, 1894, U.S. National Archives, *Record Group No. 75*.
94. *C.I.A. Annual Report, 1898*, 143.
95. Ibid., *1900*, 217.
96. Ibid., *1901*, 208.
97. Ibid., *1902*, 183.
98. Ibid., *1903*, 154.
99. John Lane to C.I.A., Aug. 23, 1893, U.S. National Archives, *Record Group No. 75*.
100. Thomas B. Teter to C.I.A., July 1, 1895, ibid.
101. *C.I.A. Annual Report, 1899*, 183.
102. Ibid., *1903*, 154.
103. Ibid., *1892*, 235.
104. Howard L. Dumble to Van Orsdale, July 27, 1894, U.S. National Archives, *Record Group No. 75*.
105. *C.I.A. Annual Report, 1900*, 217.
106. Ibid., *1903*, 154; *Pocatello Tribune*, March 18, 1903.
107. *C.I.A. Annual Report, 1904*, 176.
108. *Pocatello Tribune*, Oct. 5, 1901, Sept. 30, 1902.
109. *C.I.A. Annual Report, 1892*, 234–235.
110. Ibid., *1898*, 142.
111. Ibid., *1899*, 182.
112. Ibid., *1900*, 217.
113. "Census of Indians, June 30, 1904," U.S. National Archives, *Records, Office of Indian Affairs*.
114. *C.I.A. Annual Report, 1898*, 142.
115. Ibid., *1901*, 208.
116. *Pocatello Tribune*, April 27, 1901, Aug. 29, 1902.
117. Ibid., Feb. 7, 1907.
118. William Donner to C.I.A., Feb. 22, 1923, U.S. National Archives, *Record Group No. 75*.
119. William Donner to C.I.A., April 20, 1925, ibid.
120. Samuel Blair to C.I.A., May 8, 1925, ibid.
121. D. C. Turnipseed to C.I.A., May 10, 1929, *Fort Hall Agency Records*.
122. D. C. Turnipseed to C.I.A., Jan. 26, 1929, ibid.
123. H. J. Warner to C.I.A., Dec. 5, 1930, ibid.
124. C.I.A. to F. A. Gross, Aug. 3, 1932, ibid.
125. F. A. Gross to C.I.A., Oct. 4, 1932, ibid.; "Survey of Conditions of the Indians in the United States," U.S. Congress 72d Cong., 1st Sess., Hearings, Part 27, Wyoming, Idaho and Utah, Sept. 12, 13, 14 (Wash., D.C., 1934), 14636.
126. William Donner to C.I.A., Feb. 22, 1923, U.S. National Archives, *Record Group No. 75;* Flora Warren Seymour to Board of Indian Commissioners, Sept. 15, 1926, ibid.; H. J. Warner to C.I.A., Dec. 5, 1930, *Fort Hall Agency Records;* Mabel L. Morgan to C.I.A., April 27, 1931; F. A. Gross to C.I.A., March 25, 1932, ibid.
127. Mabel L. Morgan to C.I.A., April 27, 1931, ibid.
128. "Survey of Conditions of the Indians in the United States," Hearings, 14636.
129. *Pocatello Tribune*, Aug. 16, 20, 1912.
130. William Donner to C.I.A., Sept. 2, 1922, U.S. National Archives, *Record Group No. 75*.
131. William Donner to C.I.A., July 28, 1922, ibid.
132. William Donner to C.I.A., Sept. 2, 1922, ibid.
133. O. H. Lipps to C.I.A., Oct. 22, 1928, *Fort Hall Agency Records*.
134. "Survey of Conditions of the Indians of the United States," Hearings, 14636.
135. F. A. Gross to C.I.A., Oct. 24, 1935, *Fort Hall Agency Records;* Special Physician to Polk Richards, Sept. 13, 1936, ibid.; S. E. Johnson to Gross, March 13, 1937, ibid.; J. E. White, "Social and Economic Information for the Shoshone-Bannock Tribes, Sept. 24, 1937," U.S. National Archives, *C.I.A. Annual Report, 75;* Samuel H. Thompson to C.I.A., Nov. 20, 1937, *Fort Hall Agency Records;* F. A. Gross to C.I.A., April 15, 1939, ibid.; F. A. Gross to Henry Dworshak, Dec. 12, 1939, ibid.; see Ch. XIII, note 123.
136. F. A. Gross to C.I.A., Dec. 28, 1934, ibid.
137. F. A. Gross to C.I.A., May 16, 1935, ibid.
138. Ray J. Davis to Ralph B. Snavely, Jan. 30, 1941, ibid.
139. J. E. White, "Social and Economic Information for the Shoshone-Bannock Tribes, Sept. 24, 1937," U.S. National Archives, *Record Group No. 75*.
140. Zimmerman, Jr., *The Fort Hall Story: An Interpretation*, 7.
141. Nybroten, *Economy and Condition . . .* , 184.
142. Fort Hall Business Council Meetings, Oct. 13, 14, 1942, *Fort Hall Agency Records*.
143. *The Fort Hall News*, April, 1936.
144. *Shoshone-Bannock Tribes Annual Report, 1969-70*, 9–10.

CHAPTER XV

WHITE SHERIFFS AND INDIAN POLICE

Defining the Legal Status of the Reservation

The process of education at Fort Hall, whether by the establishment of schools, the introduction of religion, or the administration of medicines, was also aided by the use of force — the imposition of law and order according to the white man's definition. Killing an enemy in mortal combat or stealing a horse from a neighbor tribe were no longer considered sure entries into manhood or leadership positions of the Shoshoni and Bannock nations. All at once, after generations of worshipping at the shrine of the God of War, the young men learned that such activities were now taboo. They could sit around the campfires and listen to the old men recount their exploits as warriors, but the braves could dream only of hitching a team of horses to a plow and growing wheat — quite a comedown for an autonomous people used to riding the plains to glory and adulation. It was little wonder that the young Indians occasionally violated the new laws which frowned on such martial adventures.

At the same time the Indians were quick to perceive that there seemed to be a double standard. 1869 Too often white men could break the law against Indians with impunity. Within a month of settling at Fort Hall Agent Powell was reporting "the first difficulty of any kind" to take place at the new reservation. An employee of the Wells Fargo Stage Lines assaulted an Indian woman. When the husband intervened the white man whipped him "unmercifully." Powell had a difficult time restraining the Indians from killing the white man.[1]

Except for such incidents the early agents were so preoccupied with establishing farms and obtaining rations that little attention was paid to law and order among the tribesmen. They were left to their old methods of maintaining peace and quiet. 1874 Agent Reed expressed that feeling well in his 1874 report: "There may have been two or three Indians killed among themselves, on account of personal difficulty or family feuds. . . ."[2] Otherwise, he was not aware of any killings.

1870 A constant problem from the beginning was the whiskey traffic on or near the reservation. Frustrated in displaying their prowess in the time-honored ways, many of the Indian men undertook to assuage their warrior instincts by imbibing strong drink. An early whiskey seller, Cayuse George, was condemned by Chief Tahgee for selling liquor to the Bannock. He was arrested by the soldiers from the military post and incarcerated in a "potato pit" for five months until he could be sent to Fort Boise.[3]

Except for the post trader, who was not permitted to sell liquor, the nearest retail stores prior to the building of the Utah and Northern were located at Corinne, Utah. This soon became the mecca for many thirsty Fort Hall Indians, as well as for the Northwestern bands who made their home there. The Corinne newspapers carried many editorials condemning the "debased" liquor sellers, demanding their arrest, and critizing Utah officials for not stopping the traffic.[4]

When the railroad approached the reservation 1878 boundary in 1878, Agent Danilson began to fret about unscrupulous whites who might find easy pickings among the Indians, especially in the sale of whiskey. Danilson telegraphed Washington asking what force he could use to prevent the railroad from establishing a terminus town in the center of the reservation, where "whiskey saloons" would act as a "demoralizing" influence on the Shoshoni and Bannock.[5] Although the Utah and Northern was allowed to pause for a short while at Black Rock before proceeding to Blackfoot at the northern edge of the reserve, Danilson was very careful to ensure that the few stores at Black Rock did not carry liquor.[6] Nevertheless, the camel had his nose in the reservation tepee, and the founding of Pocatello station in the heart of the reserve soon introduced a whole century of problems to Indian officials at Fort Hall.

The entry of a railroad into the reservation sharpened the concern of Indians and white officials alike concerning the legal status of the tract of land set aside for the Shoshoni and Bannock. In the case of Hyde v. Harkness in 1874, the Supreme Court of the Territory of Idaho decreed 1874 that the District Court in Oneida County had "jurisdiction over Indian reservations in any organized county of this territory, and its processes may run and be served there, if there be no treaty to the contrary with the Indians there of."[7] Under the decision, therefore, all white citizens residing in the Marsh Creek section of the reservation or any other spot within its boundaries were subject to taxation and enjoyed other rights and benefits of citizens of the territory. Agent Reed expostulated against the decision, arguing that the white families should be taxed not for the betterment of the citizens of Oneida County but for the benefit of the Indians.[8]

1879 The problem of territorial or federal jurisdiction over the Fort Hall Reservation came into sharp focus in early 1879 when an Oneida County Mormon candidate for the Council of the Idaho Legislature challenged the election of Johnson N. High to the post, on the grounds that a number of votes had been cast illegally for High by people living on the reservation. It was true that in at least three elections voters on the Fort Hall reserve had voted in territorial elections at the Ross Fork precinct — 127 out of 842 votes cast in the county in 1874, 82 out of 775 votes in 1876, and 166 out of 1,172 votes in 1878.[9] The Council Committee on Elections held that, because taxes had been collected from the citizens living on the reservation, this was proof positive that they also had the right to vote. High was admitted to his seat.[10]

The editor of the *Idaho Statesman* now made a cause celebre out of the dispute by proving, to his satisfaction, that under the Fort Bridger Treaty of 1868 the Fort Hall Reservation had not been established for the Indians of southern Idaho, that the treaty only "proposed" to establish a reservation somewhere, and that the Fort Hall reserve was therefore a "dead letter" and did not legally exist. Thus Oneida County had full power over any citizen living in the area circumscribed by the nonexistent reservation.[11] It was at this time, as noted earlier, that Governor Mason Brayman began to question the legal existence of the reservation.[12]

1870 Federal officials in Washington paid little attention to the local squabble in Idaho and during the 1870s dealt with law and order problems at Fort Hall by relying on the military post for police assistance. At first the commanding officer at Fort Hall refused to accept the responsibility, telling Agent Danilson in November 1870 that he would assist a U.S. marshal in arresting two white men accused of assaulting some Indian women but would not assume to arrest the two men on his own.[13] Soon the commandant was taking custody of five Bannock accused of murdering a white 1873 man on Wood River[14] and, more seriously, was reporting the killing of four out of seven Indian prisoners who attempted to escape from guard detail.[15]

1875 The procedures were cumbersome, to say the least, as Danilson discovered in 1875 when he asked the military to remove from the reservation a troublesome white man named James Dempsey. The request proceeded quite properly and slowly through all military channels to the desk of the secretary of War, who sent his approval to the secretary of the Interior.[16]

The commissioner of Indian Affairs saw the 1878 futility of this avenue and by 1878 instructed Danilson to establish his own Indian police force. The pay for a group of twenty officers was to be $5 a month for each man, which caused the Indians he approached to "laugh at the idea." The men insisted on at least $15 a month. The agent advised that he was ready to proceed as soon as the higher salaries could be funded and uniforms and equipment furnished.[17] The Bannock War was probably the chief impetus for organization of the police force.

Two years later there were still no Indian police 1880 at Fort Hall. The pay of $5 a month was ridiculous, especially when the military was hiring Indian scouts at $35 a month for man and horse. Agent John A. Wright suggested an ingenious way around the department's rigid adherence to the $5 a month scale — add fifty cents a day for the rental of the policeman's horse, which would raise the base salary to about $20 a month.[18] The suggestion was not accepted. By 1884 the commis- 1884 sioner himself was complaining that in the previous year 128 police throughout the United States had resigned on account of "inadequate salary." He suggested that Congress approve an increased scale of pay to $15 for officers, $12 for sergeants, and $10 for privates.[19]

Agent A. L. Cook was able to organize his 1882 police force in 1882 with eight men, and he proudly announced that during the year "but two Indians have been known to be drunk on the reserve since the police were organized" — a claim which may have been slightly optimistic. He also reported that the Indian police had broken up horse stealing on the reservation.[20] The reports for the next two years were equally affirmative, 1884 with the police working "assiduously" to break up the scalp dances and plural marriages, which were now "relics of the past." Here Cook was definitely a victim of his own conceit. He had been unable to establish a court to handle offenses. No Indian would act as a judge without pay, so the agent served as judge of the court and was able to get the convicted Indians to accept his verdict and the penalties assessed.[21]

The railroad town at Blackfoot introduced a 1880 new problem to the agents; members of the tribes began to frequent the saloons and shops, getting drunk, and causing trouble "even so far as killing each other."[22] The agents appealed for help from Idaho Delegate Ainslie and of course from the commissioner — who authorized the use of a detective dressed in "Indian costume." The Indian plainclothesman soon had enough evidence to arrest James Gilliland, while Mrs. Jane Gordon escaped to Odgen, Utah. Agent Wright expected to have Mrs. Gordon "on hand" in a few days as well 1881 as three other suspects from Blackfoot. One difficulty was the necessity of having to travel to Oxford, Idaho, sixty-five miles away, to get arrest warrants.[23]

1882 An incident which nearly caused a small civil war on the reservation occurred on December 6, 1882. A ten-year-old Bannock boy, idling around the gristmill, got his blanket caught in the cogs of the machinery and was drawn into the gears and crushed to death. The following morning the mill burned to the ground, destroying fifteen hundred bushels of wheat and twelve thousand pounds of flour, nearly every bit of which was the property of Shoshoni farmers. The boy's father, Prociberoo, who had been a Bannock warrior during the war of 1878, was the prime suspect, but he denied being involved in any way. Agent Cook called a council, during which the Bannock denied any knowledge of who might have started the fire. Chief Tyhee asked Cook if Prociberoo "looked ashamed as if he burned the mill." The Shoshoni were angry, the Bannock protested innocence, and, as the agent wrote, "There is not the best of feeling between the Shoshones who are more numerous, and the Bannocks who are more warlike."[24]

The Indian boy was buried with full honors by the agent, an accommodating white minister, and the Bannock tribe, with three ponies being shot near the graveside to provide the dead boy with "ponies when he arrives at the happy hunting ground." The high feeling eventually dissipated, and Cook wrote that he was convinced the fire had started from the furnace in the mill. But while a few of the Bannock were "riding about rapidly" around the dying embers of the mill and flourishing their weapons, there was some tension at Fort Hall. Chief Tyhee finally helped quiet the young men. He asserted that his people were willing to sell enough hay and ponies to finance the construction of a new mill if "Washington" would build it.[25]

1880 While the agents slowly began to establish Indian police and court systems on the reservation, the judiciary and legislature of Idaho Territory still wrestled with the problem of the legal status of the reserve. The U.S. Supreme Court reversed the 1874 decision of the Idaho Supreme Court in the Hyde v. Harkness case, and the Idaho court followed the national ruling by finding in 1880, in the case of Utah and Northern Railroad Company v. Willard Crawford, District Attorney for Oneida County, that Idaho courts had jurisdiction over any matter concerned with individuals living on Indian reservations. To resolve the problem, the Idaho Statesman called for a congressional act to establish law and order for the reserve.[26]

To clarify the situation, the U.S. Supreme Court reversed itself and overturned its decision in Hyde v. Harkness. In Langford v. Monteith the court declared it had erred in the earlier case by supposing that the Fort Bridger Treaty contained a clause excluding the lands of the Indians from territorial or state jurisdiction. This was a mistake, so the new judgment held that Oneida County and the Territory of Idaho did have jurisdiction over the lands held by the Indians on the Fort Hall Reservation — although the Indians themselves were exempt from that jurisdiction. Therefore the railroad and the white citizens on the reserve were subject to taxation by Oneida County and to other regulations which might be imposed by the county. Also, white residents would have the right to vote in county and territorial elections, as they did in November 1884 when they 1884 cast 224 of the 2,071 votes counted that fall for Idaho's delegate to Congress. The sheriff of Oneida County was instructed to serve civil and criminal processes on the reservation from the federal courts. The Idaho Supreme Court affirmed the action of the U.S. Supreme Court in the case of Utah and Northern Railroad Company v. Fisher, County Assessor, on February 16, 1884.[27]

With the civil rights of white residents of the reservation clarified, there was now a question about the civil privileges of the Shoshoni and Bannock. Some attorneys in Idaho held that the Indian was not an American citizen, could not vote, could not dispose of his land, could not "drink whiskey legitimately," and was still a ward of the government. But in 1896 the state attorney 1896 general ruled that Idaho Indian taxpayers were citizens and voters. In response, a number of Idaho Indians who paid taxes began to register and to appear at the polls.[28] There were liabilities as well as benefits to citizenship — as a group of 1897 Fort Hall Indians discovered when they were arrested by a Blackfoot deputy sheriff for gambling on the streets of the town. The Pocatello Tribune noted "general surprise"; nearly every white considered that the local gambling laws did not cover the Indian blanket games, which few white men understood anyway.[29]

Establishing an Indian Police Force

The Indian police at Fort Hall were not as efficient in enforcing either the letter or the spirit of the law. Agent Peter Gallagher would not accept 1888 the "rose-colored" statements of agents at other reservations concerning the efficiency of their police. He wrote off his efforts in establishing an effective force as being a "failure .... My poor Bannack and Shoshone Indians . . . are ignorant, verily." A year later the police were "doing mod- 1889 erately well."[30]

His successor, S. G. Fisher, emphasized the 1890 chief reason for an inefficient constabulary — the pay was so small it taxed his ingenuity to keep any kind of men on the force. By this time there were fifteen policemen — a captain and fourteen privates. Soon one of the privates was advanced to the rank of lieutenant to give the captain a little help in his command duties.[31]

By the late 1890s the various agents seemed much more pleased with their "reasonably efficient" police force. A. F. Caldwell could write in 1900, "The police have cheerfully and promptly executed my order, and in every instance especially when dealing with whites, have exercised good judgment and avoided friction with rare and commendable discernment."[32] He thought they were a valuable aid to him in the reservation work.

1892 Where tribal custom sustained the police, as in the case of murder, robbery and other obvious major crimes, the arrest and incarceration of "bad Indians" were uncomplicated matters. But when white ideas of morality or discipline came into conflict with Indian philosophy the Indian police system broke down. As already noted, forcing unwilling children into school brought the police into collision with distraught and angry parents. Some police refused to serve in these cases and either resigned or were discharged.[33] They also were reluctant to inform on medicine men or ar-
1900 rest them.[34] In 1900 Caldwell issued an order that all police must wear short hair; he soon had a "neat . . . and . . . faithful . . . force" after having to replace several of the men who resigned rather than cut their hair.[35]

The police court went through the same gradual improvement from 1885 to 1900, from a judicial body which "does the best it can" to a court whose decisions were "universally . . .
1890 marked by thoughtfulness and equity."[36] In 1890 Agent Fisher described the operations of the court under its three judges: two Shoshoni, Joe Wheeler and Billy George, and one Bannock, John Mopier. Only one understood English. Their pay was $8 a month. During the year there were about fifty trials. Over half of them concerned disputes about the boundaries of natural hay meadows. Five were for wife-beating, three for stealing other Indians' wives, one for selling government-issue articles, and five for larceny. The court kept no record of its proceedings. It was fairly lenient for first offenses but rather severe with second offenders, who were usually forced to wear "Oregon boots" (a heavy steel band around one or both ankles) for sentences of from ten to sixty days —- or, as Fisher said, "what is still greater punishment, is compelled to work." Witnesses were not sworn, attorneys were not appointed, and witnesses and principals in the cases nearly always told the truth. The court decisions were invariably accepted as final "and as a rule give universal satisfaction." The agent said it was rarely necessary to call witnesses, since the defen-

dent hardly ever denied a crime of which he was guilty.[37] Agent Warner admired the fairness with which the court dispensed justice but thought it was rather severe in its punishments.[38]

From 1887 to 1890, while only 21 Indian criminals were punished by civil courts, the Indian court handled 259 cases, ranging from a low of 3 in 1895 to a high of 53 in 1890. The average was about 24 cases a year.[39] Among about two thousand Shoshoni and Bannock at Fort Hall this was a remarkably light record of crime. As Gallagher said, "Whatever else may be charged to these Indians, it will not be that they are given to petty thieving, stealing, drunkenness, and many of the evils and sins which can be laid at the door of their white friends."[40] In fact, an Indian who had committed a crime and was being pressed by the police often would commit suicide rather than face the opprobrium of his friends and relatives. A good example was an Indian who became crazed after drinking Jamaica ginger and killed two white men. A few hours later, with the police 1891 in pursuit, he killed himself.[41]

Most of the cases which appeared before the three Indian judges were concerned with those of 1892 "no . . . more serious nature than stealing women and horses," both of which seemed to draw rather light sentences. Promiscuous cohabitation, "an evil which it seems impossible to break up," often con- 1895 stituted half the cases on the court docket. Wife beating, usually associated with running off with another man, also seemed to come up frequently for adjudication and punishment.[42] Indian and white concepts of morality and propriety came into conflict in these areas.

The honorable profession of stealing horses especially caused trouble. In one incident in 1886 1886 Agent Gallahger had to deal with the "stealage" of about twenty horses from some Shoshoni at the Wind River Agency. His Indian police were afraid to arrest the two Bannock horse thieves involved, having been threatened by the guilty parties. Gallagher discharged the entire police force and announced he would get along without one. The chiefs and headmen, dismayed by Gallagher's action, proposed a new cadre of police, which was soon organized. The second force was no better than the first, according to the agent. Finally, on his own, he arrested the two horse thieves. Two of the new police then resigned rather than face their fellow Bannock; the remaining Shoshoni police said they were willing to arrest Shoshoni lawbreakers but not Bannock offenders.[43] It would take some time before the "obstreperous" Bannock would accept the Indian court's jurisdiction over the time-honored exploit of stealing a horse.

Although there were occasional lapses in Indian justice for other Indians, it was much more dif- 1889 ficult to secure the punishment of white men who broke the law on the reservation. In one case a white man name Fritz Tyler set fire to the prairie grass near American Falls to clear debris from a area where he proposed to do some placer mining. The fire destroyed an Indian's house, two haystacks, and a hay rake, as well as burning other property belonging to some whites just off the reservation. Tyler paid the claims of the white men but refused to settle with the Indian property owner. Agent Gallagher appealed to the commissioner for help.[44]

1898 In another incident Jim Ballard and Tom Edmo took matters into their own hands in 1898 by ordering fifteen Indian police under Captain Pumpkin to eject a white man, Isaac M. Yandell, from Montana Island in the Snake River. They also proposed to run off all the white men occupying Horse Island, Munn's Island, and Burnt Island. The police entered Yandell's cabin and took the cartridges out of his rfle. They found Yandell at work in his field and ordered him to leave at once. (The Indians claimed the islands as reservation property.) Yandell refused to leave and asked for protection from Pocatello authorities.[45] Apparently the Indians were not supported in their claims against either Tyler or Yandell.

The Whiskey Traffic

A constant problem with some white men in Pocatello and Blackfoot was the lure of easy money by selling whiskey to an eager clientele — a few young Indian men from Fort Hall. Agent Fisher, particularly, did his best to stamp out the 1892 practice. In 1892 he was able to get some stiff sentences meted out to a few whiskey sellers. A good example was Cecil Smith, convicted of selling a bottle of whiskey to Shoshone Jim and sentenced to two years in the penitentiary, with a fine of $100.[46] Agent Fisher noted that a number of those engaged in the whiskey traffic were tramps who easily eluded arrest.[47] Although the penalties were severe, it is doubtful whether many of the white dealers were caught and punished. The statistical tables in the commissioner's annual reports listed only fifteen cases of whiskey sellers 1899 prosecuted during the years 1887 to 1900. A few tried to get around the law by selling lemon extract to the Indians — until a local judge ruled that the flavoring was an intoxicant.[48]

1897 The citizens of Pocatello did their best to help quell the trade in whiskey, showing some apprehension about Indians crazed with drink, who could be a real menace. In one incident four drunken Indians rode their horses around the house of one Pocatello resident "in their demonstrations of war," until the chief of police and a deputy from the city were able to capture two of the invaders.[49] When another drunk Indian fell into 1893 the river and was drowned, the *Pocatello Tribune*

probably spoke for a number of whites; the editor wrote of the whiskey seller arrested for selling liquor to the Indian, "Why didn't he furnish every red on the reservation with a bottle of firewater?"[50] The whiskey traffic, even though it involved only a few Shoshoni and Bannock, did not improve relations with their white neighbors at Pocatello.

1901 Agent Caldwell was convinced in 1901 that the whiskey trade at Pocatello had been "practically broken up,"[51] but ten years later U.S. Commissioner Theodore Turner was quoted as saying, in some frustration and anger,

1912 I hereby serve notice that the practice of giving whiskey to Indians must stop. It has gone on long enough. I do not care what means are employed or measures taken to put a stop to the practice. All I have to say is that it must stop.[52]

An analysis of articles carried in the *Pocatello Tribune* for the years 1900 to 1913 reveals the reason for Turner's exasperation. During that period sixty-five arrests were made for giving or selling liquor to the Fort Hall Indians.[53]

1902 The Indian court on the reservation did its part by sentencing drunken Indians to from three to six weeks at hard labor.[54] The Pocatello courts not only jailed drunk Indians but also followed the practice of the Indian court and cut their hair, 1903 which was an even worse punishment.[55] There was a question whether selling liquor to half-breeds was technically a crime under the law. A Pocatello judge was not sure but advised saloonkeepers to stop the practice until the courts could 1906 determine what the law meant.[56]

The worst aspects of the whiskey traffic were the crimes committed by the Indians while under the influence of liquor. Murders, horse stealings, and beatings were some of the acts committed. Drunken Indians were shot by sheriffs, died of poisoned liquor, or lost their lives through accidents while drunk.[57] The sordid business of dealing in liquor to the Fort Hall Indians continued during the early part of this century and still does.

1903 The Indian police force continued to improve, although Agent Caldwell found it impossible to employ men who would stay on their beats. The police were quite effectual in keeping stock belonging to white men off the reservation and in acting as truant officers to keep children in the boarding school.[58]

The stealing of horses and cattle was perhaps 1908 the most common crime, involving Indians as well as whites. The *Pocatello Tribune* noted especially the case of an Indian, a graduate of Carlisle, who was caught in the act of stealing two horses. The editor thought that the "higher education of Indians is not a brillant success."[59] On the other hand whites seemed to be much more involved in the theft of horses and cattle from the reservation. Superintendent Evan W. Estep asked for 1912 some help from the commissioner in rounding up an organized gang of cattle and horse thieves headed by a "notorious character" by the name of "Six-shooter Sal." This woman gang-leader had been involved in rustling stock from the reservation for ten years and had never been convicted of the offense, according to Estep. The agent estimated that at least one thousand horses and three thousand head of cattle had been stolen from the Indians during the ten-year period. He had found it difficult to get convictions because the "average white jury does not appear to regard it as much of an offense to steal from an Indian."[60]

One other white man did not escape the law so easily. Indian justice finally caught up with Isaac Yandell, who had been able to maintain ownership of his island in Snake River, as well as about six hundred acres of property on the reservation. Superintendent Estep allotted the land to various Indian residents at Fort Hall and ordered Yandell off "under penalty of death." Yandell left and started for Canada; he hoped to get the British government to support his title, which he claimed to have acquired in 1852. As he departed he threatened to have British officials dispatch a warship up Snake River to enforce his rights.[61]

The Indians who were now receiving allotments of land at Fort Hall were affected by a decision of the Idaho Supreme Court in 1912. In the case of State of Idaho vs. Lott and Jabeth the court ruled that Indian people of the state, whether residents of reservations or not, would come under the jurisdiction of Idaho courts "upon all charges of criminal and civil offenses excepting the introduction of intoxicating liquor upon the reservations." Some were of the opinion that the decision now gave the Indians the right to vote in local and state elections.[62]

The white man's system of justice began to change Indian customs in other ways. Agent Caldwell seemed to have a particular concern about Indian marriages — or lack of them. The "consent" arrangement between a man and woman, long considered quite a proper union by the Shoshoni and Bannock, came under attack by Caldwell, as did the divorces granted by the Indian court on what he thought were very "flimsy grounds." Each year he reported quite proudly on the number of "legal" marriages performed either by himself or a local minister. By the time he left 1910 the agency in 1910 he could report "very few cases of illegal cohabitation." His edict that no annuities would be issued and legal ownership of property be recognized outside a licensed marriage no doubt helped in this improvement in the "moral status" of the Shoshoni and Bannocks.[63]

A more serious matter was the custom of "marriage by abduction," which had long been one means of acquiring a wife among the Shoshoni and Bannock — at least before white civilization began to encroach on tribal ways. Under this form of marriage a man summoned help from his male relatives or close friends and obtained a wife by either capture or rape. Under state and federal laws, such attacks came under the statutory rape provision if the girl were under sixteen. Agent Caldwell reported one case in 1901 in which the 1901 man was sentenced to nine months in jail. Three others were sentenced to the penitentiary on a similar charge during the next two years. Caldwell thought the sentences "had quite a good effect,"[64] but it was difficult to eradicate the practice. Three young Indians accused in 1908 were finally freed 1908 when the prosecution was unable to prove the girl was under sixteen.[65]

Of all the challenges to law and order at Fort Hall, the liquor traffic nearly always led the list when offenses were named. Drunkenness on the reservation was punished by sentences from the Indian court, and a special liquor supervision officer was employed during the last years of the Prohibition Era to help track down bootleggers, most of whom were located in Pocatello.[66] The Shoshoni and Bannock tried to get the cooperation of Pocatello authorities to reduce the illegal liquor outlets in the town.[67] Two meetings were held with white officials in 1936 and 1938 to work 1936 out cooperative measures to curtail the whiskey trade. At the first meeting seventeen leading Indians took turns making speeches about how to stop the "stream of this crazy water" from defiling their young men. Superintendent F. A. Gross acknowledged there were not sufficient police officers on the reservation and said he had been unable to hire more because the Indian Department's funds were "exhausted."[68] The second meeting, held in the Indian Buffalo Lodge on Christmas night 1938, brought forth some 1938 simple eloquence from one of the old men:

Whiskey is bad, makes short life, don't live long. The white man since discovering this country in 1492, since then they have something that tastes good, but is intoxicating liquor, hurts stomach, makes Indian go mad and wild. Every year want to make liquor, more liquor, that is all right but do not give Indian any liquor. Indian should not have any whiskey not a drop.[69]

Of eight leading offenses against law and order in 1937 1937, drunkenness again was mentioned first as the most common crime.[70]

Despite all the troubles caused by the availability of liquor, the Shoshoni and Bannock, like Indians everywhere, were humiliated by having to face signs in restaurants which declared, "No beer or wine will be served in booths where Indians are seated." The Fort Hall people answered one question propounded by a congressional investigating committee in 1942 by saying that, while they 1942 wanted the sale or drinking of liquor on reservations prohibited to both Indians and whites, they also wanted the federal law changed so that Indians could buy liquor off the reservations on the same basis as white men.[71]

1940 In one experiment to try to reduce the amount of drinking by Fort Hall Indians, Superintendent Balsam proposed to treat drunkenness as a disease and not as a crime. He told the business council in 1940 that after years of jailing the offenders, a course which had failed, he wished to try "kindness and sympathy," to "make them ashamed of themselves for drinking." The experiment was to run for two months; if it did not succeed, Balsam intended to return to "harsher methods." At least in some cases he was forced to resort to jail sentences again.[72]

As the Indian leadership exerted itself more and more, and as professional help from outside the reservation was brought in, new and more sophisticated methods of dealing with the drinking problem have been introduced at Fort Hall. 1975 The 1974-75 annual report of the Shoshoni-Bannock tribes lists the work done at the tribal rehabilitation center, where meetings on alcoholism are held. Trained personnel are now used to work with problem drinkers and to offer counsel and encouragement.[73]

Indian versus State Authority

The use of enforcement methods to uphold and sustain the law at Fort Hall suffered as the number of Indian police declined from the fifteen employed at the turn of the century to a force of two policemen and two judges by the 1930s.[74] As the superintendent said, the law enforcement staff was entirely inadequate and had to be supported from time to time by using the services of some of the Indian stockmen on the reservation. 1925 Superintendent William Donner thought it was shortsighted of the Indian Department not to support the Indian court with sufficient funds and personnel. He cited the case of one Indian accused of horse stealing who was taken before a justice of the peace in Pocatello. Both sides were forced to hire attorneys ("a lot of petty parasites who live on the amounts that they get out of some poor ignorant fellow"), a dozen Indians were taken from their farm work to appear before the Pocatello court, and the entire cost of the trial came to $300.[75] Donner was of the opinion that the Indian court would have saved the expense and much wasted time. Eventually the depart-1967 ment responded; by 1967 there were four Indian police, one game warden, and eight Bureau of Indian Affairs police at Fort Hall.[76]

1937 Crimes which kept the police busiest in 1937 were drunkenness, nonsupport, theft, adultery, sale of stock without permit, jailbreaking, assault and battery, and contributing to delinquency.[77] 1964 By 1964 it was reported that, compared with rates in 1,789 cities in the country, arrest rates at Fort Hall were higher in every category. On the reservation there were 161 arrests per 1,000 people, compared with 46 per 1,000 in the cities listed. Jail facilities were inadequate, and law enforcement generally was quite costly.[78] The crime statutes for 1974 showed only six federal cases inves-1974 tigated in 1974, compared with forty-seven for 1973. On the other hand the tribal court processed 1,127 offenses, of which 992 dealt with adults and 135 with juveniles. That number was much higher than the previous year's total of 586 offenses.[79]

The adoption of a Law and Order Ordinance by the Shoshone-Bannock tribes on September 27, 1938, not only formalized regulations and 1938 procedures but also helped in educating the Indian people about their responsibilities if they were to have full control over such affairs on the reservation. The five divisions of the document were concerned with the Indian court, civil actions, domestic relations, sentences, and code of Indian tribal offenses. There were thirty-five of the latter, with sentences ranging from five days for simple assault to six months at hard labor or a fine not to exceed $300, or both, for such crimes as theft or misbranding. The list of offenses was a good indicator of the troubles, both minor and major, which presently face law enforcement officials on the reservation.[80]

When away from the reserve the Shoshoni and Bannock continued to face discrimination, both open and subtle. One white citizen of Pocatello protested to the Fort Hall superintendent in 1950 1950 about two white policemen dragging an intoxicated Indian woman up the steps of the county courthouse "by her feet somewhat like the poundmaster would handle a dead dog. . . . Don't you think it might be done in a little less rigid and 'whiter' fashion?"[81] Nine years later the chairman 1959 of the Shoshone-Bannock Business Council was refused service at a Blackfoot restaurant.[82] He later expostulated to the editor of a Pocatello newspaper, "It distresses me very much to see how our good people are being discriminated against in the Police and Justice Courts of the State. If the trend continues it will be impossible for any Indian to endure this society without being hailed into one of the Courts and made a criminal regardless of the merits of any actions of complaint filed against him."[83] The civil rights laws of the 1960s and 1970s have no doubt eliminated the crasser amd more open violations of human decency against the Shoshoni and Bannock, although the more subtle forms remain.

The question of possible state jurisdiction over offenses committed on the Fort Hall Reservation has, in the past and up to now, agitated both Indian and white leaders about the propriety or necessity for such action. In 1939 the commis-1939 sioner of Indian Affairs was forced to point out to a local attorney at Blackfoot that the federal courts had jurisdiction over the ten major crimes, as listed in Section 548, Title 18 of the U.S. Code, but that lesser crimes and misdemeanors committed by Indians on Indian reservations did not come under the jurisdiction of either federal or state courts; the tribal courts handled these matters under the new Indian Reorganization Act.[84]

As for restricted property on the reservation, no action could be taken to dispose of any of it without the approval of the secretary of the Interior. The state courts could have no jurisdiction here.[85]

1942
The Fort Hall Indians replied to the congressional questionnaire of 1942 that they did not want state law to be in force on the reservation. They liked their system of law and order and wanted no interference with it. They recognized, however, that when an Indian lived off the reservation among whites, then state law should apply.[86] To reinforce their determination, seventy-one leading Indians petitioned the Idaho

1950
Legislature in 1950 "to not adopt any resolutions or to pass any legislation making it possible for state enforcement officers to enter upon the Indian Reservation and to make arrests thereon."[87]

1963
Nevertheless, by 1963 the legislature was considering a bill which would allow the state to assume jurisdiction, the system to be paid for by federal monies withdrawn from tribal funds. The Fort Hall Business Council opposed the legislation. In the first place, it was a unilateral action in which they were not consulted. Secondly, in the states of Washington, Nevada, and Nebraska, where the system had been tried, federal monies had been withdrawn and "chaos" had resulted, with no criminal justice process at all.[88] The controversy still continues, and the Shoshoni and Bannock zealously guard against any attempt at state encroachment upon their rights and privileges at Fort Hall.[89]

Hunting and Fishing on the Reservation

Any examination of the history of law and order at Fort Hall would not be complete without including an analysis of the troubles between Pocatello sportsmen and the Shoshoni and Bannock over the privilege of hunting and fishing on the reservation. Unfortunately for the Indians, the best fishing and duck hunting in the Pocatello area can be found along a ten-mile stretch of the Portneuf River where it flows into the Snake. Located there are numerous cold and warm springs, bays and ponds, and meadows which would delight the heart of any angler or hunter. Furthermore, for almost forty years after establishment of the reservation, the white citizens of Pocatello enjoyed the illegal pleasures of fishing and hunting

along the lower Portneuf despite the objections of Indian agents and government officials.
1897

All at once, in April 1897, Agent F. G. Irwin, Jr., posted notices in the *Pocatello Tribune* that all such activities would henceforth be forbidden under Section 2137, Revised Statutes of the U.S. Code, which forbade any form of trespass on the Indian reservation. The *Tribune* thought it strange "that a law forbidding hunting and fishing permits should be discovered after all these years" but did publish the notice.[90] Few citizens paid any attention to the warning. Six weeks later Irwin gathered his police and employees and raided the camps of some weekend fishermen, confiscated their gear, and took them under arms to the agency, where he gave all a stern lecture before releasing them.[91]

Pocatellans were outraged at the agent's concern with the "letter of the law." A local judge challenged Irwin's interpretation of the statute cited. The agent in return fell back on the Fort Bridger Treaty, which the judge reluctantly recognized as being in force. There was talk of a petition to Congress and of retaliation against the "dirty blanket bucks and disreputable looking squaws [who] loafed about the streets of Pocatello, sat among tin cans and manure on vacant lots and played incomprehensible gambling games or begged for biscuits at back doors." After the anger had somewhat subsided, talk of forcing the Indians out of town also ceased.[92] Irwin's successor, 1898 C. A. Warner, continued to warn of arrest and prosecution for any whites caught fishing or hunting on the reservation.[93]

From then on there was a continuing battle between the Indians (and their representatives) and the sports-minded, determined people of Pocatello, who kept up an unflagging effort to pursue their custom of fishing and hunting on the reservation. Various agents pointed out the dangers of allowing camping and fishing parties — who often set fires which destroyed Indian haystacks, introduced liquor onto the reservation, shot cattle and horses belonging to the Indians, and in a few instances wounded some of the Indians. What was almost as bad, they depleted the fish and game on which many Indians depended for food.

When A. F. Caldwell, long-time resident and former postmaster of Pocatello became superintendent in 1901 he announced that a few permits 1901 for fishing on the reservation would be issued to certain people who had purchased state licenses.[94] Having opened the reserve again to whites from Pocatello, Caldwell then found it necessary to post warnings against setting up campfires near haystacks, against bringing liquor onto the reservation, disallowing duck hunting or camping overnight, and restricting the length of the fishing season.[95] It soon was obvious that the few whites

1903 who received permits were close friends of Caldwell, and other disgruntled and empty-handed fisherman began demanding that the Indians not be allowed to hunt or fish on the ceded lands around Pocatello. Caldwell was forced to quote the cession agreement to them.[96]

1908 Finally the Indians began to complain about Caldwell's tactics. An investigation revealed that the superintendent had issued 104 permits to his special friends.[97] The department instructed him to stop issuing any permits, which soon brought from Pocatellans a strong protest in the form of a 1909 petition to U.S. Senators William E. Borah and Weldon B. Heyburn. They passed it on to the secretary of the Interior, who firmly supported the angry Shoshoni and Bannock on the grounds that the fish and game should be reserved to them as a source of food. He thought such action would also remove what had become a source of irritation between the Indians and neighboring whites over the whole problem of trespass on the reservation.[98]

1911 By 1911 the new superintendent, Evan Estep, was warning all whites to stay away from the reservation boundary lines or "the Indian police will get them," with a resultant confiscation of their fishing gear and arms and a possible maximum fine of $200. As far as the citizens of Pocatello were concerned, the source of irritation was in not being allowed to fish the lower Portneuf.[99]

In fact, many of the white sportsmen blatantly continued to fish the streams and ponds and hunt on the reservation. Finally Superintendent Estep 1913 decided to take strong action, and in early 1913 he arrested three citizens of Pocatello who were hunting ducks on the reservation about a thousand feet beyond the boundary line. Estep asked for advice about how to proceed against the hunters. He thought the only way to handle the problem was "make as much trouble for the men as possible." The commissioner advised him to release the white men only after they had signed affidavits that they would never again trespass on the reservation.[100]

Estep further informed Washington that it was useless to take legal action against such trespassers because the U.S. attorney and marshal were convinced it would be impossible to secure convictions. In one recent case a grand jury had refused to return an indictment against some white men who pleaded guilty to having liquor in their possession while on the reservation.[101]

In a council with the Indians Estep noted their strong opposition to allowing whites to hunt and fish on the reservation. Some of the Indians indicated that they lived chiefly on jackrabbits, with whatever fish and other game they could get, and that the whites were taking away from them even this small supply of supplemental meat. The peo-ple of Pocatello seemed unconcerned about the needs of the poor Indians. Estep reported, "They have said they were going to get that privilege if they had to get my official scalp in order to do it." The Idaho state fish hatchery refused to stock any stream that flowed through the reservation "because white men are not allowed to fish on the reservation." In a final blast Estep indicated that, although only ten miles of the hundred-mile-long Portneuf River flowed through the reservation "the fishermen have convinced themselves that nearly all the fish in the country are wise enough to know the location of the reservation lines and stay in that part of the stream flowing through the reservation."[102]

Undaunted by Estep's opposition the citizens of Pocatello enlisted the aid of Senator James H. Brady and Congressman Burton L. French. Both made strong appeals to lift the restrictions against hunting and fishing on the reservation. The commissioner instructed Estep to call a council of the Indians, who reiterated their refusal to permit whites access to the fish and game along the lower Portneuf. The commissioner refused to bow to the congressional delegation, pointing out that the Indians looked upon the Treaty of Fort Bridger with the same reverence as whites regarded the Constitution. He concluded "These reservations were set apart as homes for the Indians and for their sole and unrestricted use and benefit, and it appears wrong and eminently unfair that any white person should covet or make any attempt to procure the advantages thereof," especially when the Indians were unalterably opposed.[103]

The unceasing and aggressive designs of Pocatello sportsmen were finally successful in the 1920s, when the commissioner capitulated and advised Superintendent William Donner to devise some means of allowing whites to fish and hunt on the reservation. Donner produced a hunting and fishing permit, which from 1921 to 1925 1925 raised $6,102.25 in revenue to the Indians, although it did not eliminate all the trespass problems which indifferent and careless whites brought to the reservation.[104]

By 1930 the Fort Hall Business Council had been organized and began to take a more active role in deciding whether to grant permission to whites to fish and hunt on the reservation. In a business meeting of May 14, 1930, the vote was 209 to 2 opposed to granting hunting and fishing rights to whites. An additional reason for the prohibition was the manufacture of moonshine by bootleggers, who would have easier access if hunting and fishing were permitted.[105]

For two years, 1930 and 1932, the business 1930 council declined to approve any white permits, even though the Pocatello Sportmen's Association met with the council several times to attempt to get a change in regulations.[106] In anger and frus-

1932 tration the Pocatello group exercised its influence with local officials to have the state game wardens arrest "any Indian found bringing fish off the reservation."[107] The Shoshoni and Bannock did allow certain of their white friends the privilege of fishing reservation waters — Agency employees, the sheriffs of Bingham and Bannock counties, certain workers in the Pocatello railroad shops, and the potato inspector.[108]

Except for an opening of two days in 1933 "to provide food for the poor,"[109] hunting and fishing on the reservation was closed to whites until 1937 1937, when the business council opened a portion of the reserve to outsiders for a fee of $15 each. Not many permits were sold, which led council members to the conclusion that what Pocatello residents really wanted was hunting and fishing for a small fee or none at all.[110]

1940 By 1940 enough sportsmen indulged in the luxury of a reservation permit at $5 each for hunting and fishing licenses to bring in a yearly 1950 revenue of $2,358.75.[111] Ten years later the fee for a hunting permit alone had been raised to $10.[112] The practice of selling the permits continued and was given legal support by the Regional Solicitor's Office in 1963, which ruled that 1963 the council was within Fort Bridger Treaty rights to sell outside hunting and fishing permits.[113] During the 1960s the Shoshoni and Bannock sold from 400 to 1,000 permits each year for both hunting and fishing "depending on the fees charged and quality of the fishing."[114]

The Indian council cooperated with the Idaho Fish and Wildlife Service in stocking reservation 1945 streams with fish. In one transaction in 1945 the state agency delivered 75,000 black-spotted trout and 50,000 rainbow trout to the reservation.[115]

To keep pace with the increased interest on the part of white sportsmen in fishing and hunting at Fort Hall, the Indian council adopted a series of regulations to control the activities of those involved. Idaho game laws established the season and bag limits, unless specifically changed by the council. The council was rather lenient at first toward Indians who were nonmembers of the Shoshoni and Bannock tribes, toward enrolled members of the tribes who had moved off the reservation, and toward white spouses of Fort Hall Indians. Later it became more and more restrictive in its rules. Today only "enrolled members of the Shoshone-Bannock Tribes, who reside within the exterior boundaries" of the Fort Hall Reservation have hunting, fishing, and trapping privileges according to the Fort Bridger Treaty.[116]

Furthermore, the rules governing Indian hunters and fishermen also became quite strict. The 1952 tribal game seasons were set with specific periods for various game: beaver trapping, December 1 to May 1; doe deer, September 1 to January 1; buck deer, all year around; elk, moose, and antelope,

both male and female, September 1 to January 1; sage hen, September 1 to December 1; rabbits and rockchuck, all year; and fishing open the entire year. Other regulations sought to reduce stream pollution and to prohibit unsportsmanlike methods of obtaining fish and game.[117] The modern Shoshoni and Bannock were under obligation to conserve the little wildlife still left on the reservation.

When the American Falls Reservoir site was established, white people in the area at once assumed they had the right to hunt and fish on what they thought was now public property. The Bureau of Indian Affairs had a difficult time with errant sportsmen until sufficient arrests and confiscation of arms and fishing gear convinced them otherwise.[118] In another attempt to encroach on reservation streams, certain legal-minded whites claimed the privilege of fishing the south bank of 1930 the Blackfoot River and the east bank of the Snake River, until Indian officials established that reservation boundary lines went down the middle of both streams.[119]

The chronic disregard by neighboring whites of Shoshoni and Bannock hunting and fishing regulations on the reservation still occupies much time on the part of the tribal council in endeavoring to control the situation. Sometimes drastic measures were taken; in November 1935 the Indian police 1935 confiscated thirty guns, "and the parties whose guns were taken were up in arms."[120] Thirteen 1948 years later the council found that such procedures were no longer in force and decreed they should be reinstated, but white trespassers continued to destroy the boundary markers and to fish illegally, even on centrally located Ross Fork Creek.[121] One white gentlemen who was adopted as a member of the tribe and given the name "Queen 1946 'y Toash . . . at appropriate ceremonies" was informed that his adoption did not include hunting or fishing rights at Fort Hall.[122]

The legality of Indian police arresting non-Indians came into question late in the 1950s. 1958 When little support for the control of white hunters and fishermen came from the Bureau of Indian Affairs, the tribes turned to U.S. Senator Henry Dworshak for help in stopping the "wanton trespass" at Fort Hall.[123] Three years later In- 1961 dian council members protested their inability to stop the "many, many hunters" who continually crossed Snake River to hunt in the bottoms. The tribal game wardens were not commissioned and could not arrest whites, and any information they secured about trespass was ignored by federal authorities. The council acknowledged that non-Indian hunting and fishing on the reservation was not a crime under the law but was certainly a civil trespass which the Bureau of Indian Affairs should help to eradicate.[124]

As late as the annual report of 1974-1975 the 1975

Shoshoni and Bannock were complaining about the activities of Idaho Fish and Game Commission employees who announced they were going to enter the reservation to band geese, even though they had no authorization from the Fort Hall Business Council. The report ended, "The present council does not believe in allowing Idaho Fish and Game to come on the reservation and take over. NOT AT ALL." The last three words, in capital letters, perhaps best expressed the anger and frustration of a century of exploitation by whites of the very little wild game and fish still left on the Fort Hall Reservation.[125]

1959

Perhaps a 45-page brochure issued by the Pocatello Chamber of Commerce in 1959 to attract industry to the city best expressed the chief concerns of neighboring whites toward the Fort Hall Indians and their home. There were only two references to the reservation. One indicated that Fort Hall provided sport fishing for trout and whitefish, facilities for camping, but no motels. The second mentioned that the "undeveloped farm land between Pocatello and Blackfoot, while it may not be bought, may be leased from the Indians."[126] From the Indian point of view all that the whites ever wanted from the Shoshoni and Bannock were the fish and game, which provided the Indians with food, and their land, which gave them a home. What else was there for the white man to covet?

NOTES CHAPTER XV
WHITE SHERIFFS AND INDIAN POLICE

1. Charles F. Powell to D. W. Ballard, May 30, 1869, U.S. National Archives, *Idaho Superintendency*, Microcopy 832, Roll 2.
2. *C I A. Annual Report, 1874*, 592.
3. *Idaho Statesman*, November 19, 1870.
4. *Corinne Reporter*, July 1, 1871, April 4, 1873; *Corinne Mail*, Sept. 28, Oct. 1, 2, 5, 1874, Jan. 8, July 26, 1875.
5. Danilson to C.I.A., Sept. 22, 1878, U.S. National Archives, *Idaho Superintendency*, Roll 347.
6. W. H. Danilson to C.I.A., Nov. 13, 1878, ibid.
7. Prickett, *Reports of Cases Argued and Determined in the Supreme Court of Idaho Territory, Jan. 1866 to Sept. 1880*.
8. Henry W. Reed to C.I.A., May 14, 1874, U.S. National Archives, *Idaho Superintendency*, Roll 342.
9. *Abstract of Votes in Oneida County at General Elections, Nov. 3, 1874; Nov. 5, 1878*, Idaho State Historical Society, Drawer 4.
10. *Idaho Statesman*, Jan. 28, 1879.
11. Ibid., Jan. 21, 28, 30, Feb. 4, 8, 13, 1879.
12. "Report of the Governor of Idaho," U.S. Congress, 46th Cong. 2d Sess., House, Exec. Doc. Vol. 10 (Wash., D.C., 1880), 422.
13. George Wilson to W. H. Danilson, Nov. 30, 1870, U.S. National Archives, Military Records, Fort Hall, *Record Group No. 393*.
14. Commander, Fort Hall Military Post to Dept. of California, March 26, 1873, ibid.
15. Henry W. Reed to C.I.A., July 10, 1873, U.S. National Archives, *Idaho Superintendency*, Roll 341; Henry W. Reed to C.I.A., July 28, 1873, *Fort Hall Record Book*, 159–160.
16. Sec. of War to Sec. of Interior, Dec. 2, 1875, U.S. National Archives, *Idaho Superintendency*, Roll 343.
17. W. H. Danilson to C.I.A., Nov. 18, 1878, ibid., Roll 347.
18. John A. Wright to C.I.A., Aug. 20, 1880, ibid., Roll 353.
19. *C I A. Annual Report, 1884*, 13.
20. Ibid., 110.
21. Ibid., *1885*, 290–291.
22. Roberts to C.I.A., March 24, 1880, U.S. National Archives, *Idaho Superintendency*, Roll 352; John A. Wright to C.I.A., July 3, 1880, ibid., Roll 353; W. Shilling to Delegate Ainslie, April 12, 1880, ibid., Roll 352.

23. John A. Wright to C.I.A., Jan. 20, 1881, U.S. National Archives, *Record Group No. 75*.
24. Arden S. Smith to C.I.A., Dec. 6, 1882, ibid.; A. L. Cook to C.I.A., Dec. 8, 1882, ibid.; S. Baker to Dept. of the Platte, Dec. 8, 1882, U.S. National Archives, Military Records, Fort Hall, *Record Group No. 393; C I A. Annual Report, 1883*, 111–112.
25. Ibid.; *Blackfoot Register*, Dec. 30, 1882; A. L. Cook to C.I.A., Dec. 19, 1882, U.S. National Archives, *Record Group No. 75*; A. L. Cook to C.I.A., Jan. 15, 1883, ibid.
26. *Idaho Statesman*, Feb. 14, 1880; "Utah & Northern Rd Co vs Willard Crawford Dist Atty Brief," Idaho State Historical Society, Drawer 9.
27. "Utah and Northern Railway Company v. Fisher, County Assessor," *Reports of Cases Argued and Determined in the Supreme Court of Territory of Idaho*, Vol. 2 (San Francisco, 1903), 53–58; *Idaho Statesman*, March 20, 1880; *Blackfoot Register*, Oct. 29, 1881; "Utah & Northern Ry Co v. Wm F. Fisher, Assessor Motions etc.," Idaho State Historical Society, Drawer 9; "Official Returns of Idaho Terr., Nov. 4, 1884," ibid., File 13, Drawer 4.
28. *Pocatello Tribune*, Oct. 10, 1896.
29. Ibid., Aug. 28, 1897.
30. *C I A. Annual Report, 1887*, 151; ibid., *1888*, 82; ibid., *1889*, 178.
31. Ibid., *1890*, 77; ibid., *1898*, 142.
32. Ibid., *1897*, 128; ibid., *1898*, 142; ibid., *1899*, 182; ibid., *1900*, 216.
33. Ibid., *1892*, 234; ibid., *1895*, 142.
34. Ibid., *1892*, 234; see Ch. XIII, notes 51–71.
35. Ibid., *1900*, 216.
36. Ibid., *1888*, 82; ibid., *1900*, 216.
37. Ibid., *1890*, 77.
38. Ibid., *1897*, 142.
39. Ibid., *1887 to 1900*, statistical tables.
40. Ibid., *1888*, 83.
41. Ibid., *1891*, 230.
42. Ibid., *1892*, 234; ibid., *1895*, 142.
43. P. Gallagher to C.I.A., Dec. 4, 1886, U.S. National Archives, *Record Group No. 75*.
44. W. P. Ramsey to Fritz Tyler, Mar. 19, 1889, U.S. National Archives, *Records of Office of Indian Affairs*; P. Gallagher to C.I.A., June 3, 1889, ibid.
45. *Pocatello Tribune*, Nov. 30, 1898.
46. Ibid., Sept. 15, 1897.
47. *C I A. Annual Report, 1891*, 230; ibid., *1892*, 234.
48. *Pocatello Tribune*, Dec. 13, 1899.
49. Ibid., Aug. 14, 1897.
50. Ibid., March 3, 1893.
51. *C I A. Annual Report, 1901*, 207.
52. *Pocatello Tribune*, Feb. 8, 1912.
53. Ibid., numerous articles from 1900 to 1913.
54. *C I A. Annual Report, 1902*, 183.
55. *Pocatello Tribune*, Dec. 3, 1903.
56. Ibid., May 28, 1906.
57. Ibid., many articles during years 1900 to 1913.
58. *C I A. Annual Report, 1903*, 155.
59. *Pocatello Tribune*, Nov. 11, 1908.
60. Evan W. Estep to C.I.A., March 21, 1912, U.S. National Archives, *Records, United States Indian Service*.
61. *Pocatello Tribune*, May 21, 1912.
62. Ibid., April 24, 1912.
63. *C I A. Annual Report, 1901*, 206; ibid., *1902*, 181; ibid., *1903*, 154; ibid., *1904*, 176; ibid., *1905*, 197.
64. Ibid., *1901*, 206; ibid., *1903*, 154.
65. *Pocatello Tribune*, Oct. 6, 8, 10, 1908.
66. "Survey of Conditions of the Indians in the United States," U.S. Congress, 72d Cong., 1st Sess., Senate, Part 27, Wyoming, Idaho, and Utah, Sept. 12, 13 and 14, 1932 (Wash., D.C., 1934), 14636.
67. "Annual Report, 1936. Narrative Section for Fort Hall Indian Agency, Fort Hall, Idaho," *Fort Hall Agency Records*; "F. A. Gross to A. C. Cooley, Sept. 6, 1930," ibid.
68. J. A. Youngren to Balderson and Resalter, Feb. 13, 1936, ibid.
69. Talks to J. A. Youngren, Dec. 25, 1938, ibid.
70. White "Social and Economic Information for the Shoshone-Bannock Tribes, Sept. 24, 1937," U.S. National Archives, *Record Group No. 75*.
71. "Investigate Indian Affairs," U.S. Congress, 78th Cong., 1st Sess., House, Res. 166, "Hearings Before the Committee on Indian Affairs, March 23, 1943" (Wash., D.C., 1943), 1098–1101.
72. Minutes of Fort Hall Business Council, Nov. 12, 13, 1940, *Fort Hall Agency Records*.
73. "Sho-Ban Annual Report, 1974-1975, March, 1975," ibid.
74. C.I.A. to H. H. Miller, Feb. 21, 1918, U.S. National Archives, *Record Group No. 75*; "Annual Report, 1936, Narrative Section for Fort Hall Indian Agency, Fort Hall, Idaho," *Fort Hall Agency Records*; Minutes, Fort Hall Business Council, June 8, 1948, 4, ibid.
75. William Donner to C.I.A., April 23, 1925, U.S. National Archives, *Record Group No. 75*, 8.
76. "Fourth Annual Idaho State Indian Conference, Boise, Idaho, March 29-30, 1967," *Fort Hall Agency Records*.
77. White, "Social and Economic Information for the Shoshone-Bannock Tribes, Sept. 24, 1937," U.S. National Archives, *Record Group No. 75*, 33.
78. Nybroten, *Economy and Conditions . . .* , 186.
79. "Sho-Ban Annual Report, 1974-1975," *Fort Hall Agency Records*.
80. "Law and Order Ordinance of the Shoshone-Bannock Tribes of the Fort Hall Reservation, Idaho," ibid.
81. A Citizen & White of Pocatello to Indian Agency, Fort Hall, March 30, 1950, ibid.
82. Zimmerman, *The Fort Hall Story*, 19.
83. Edward Boyer to Pocatello Newspaper, 1958(?), *Fort Hall Agency Records*.

84. F. A. Gross to Congressman Henry Dworshak, Dec. 12, 1939, U.S. National Archives, *Record Group No. 75*, C.I.A. to Donald R. Good, July 18, 1939, ibid.
85. Ibid.
86. "Investigate Indian Affairs," U.S. Congress, 78th Cong., 1st Sess., House, Res. 166, Hearings Before the Committee on Indian Affairs, March 23, 1943 (Wash., D.C., 1943), 1099.
87. Petition to State Legislature of Idaho from Seventy-One Indian Residents at Fort Hall, 1950, *Fort Hall Agency Records*.
88. Edward Boyer to Robert E. Smylie, Feb. 25, 1963, ibid.
89. Nybroten, *Economy and Conditions . . .* , 186.
90. *Pocatello Tribune*, April 18, 1894.
91. Ibid., May 26, 1897.
92. Ibid., June 9, 1897.
93. Ibid., Aug. 27, 1898.
94. Ibid., March 16, 1901.
95. Ibid., Aug. 20, 1901; May 8, 1902; April 2, May 15, Dec. 31, 1903; March 27, Sept. 25, 1907.
96. Ibid., May 16, 1903.
97. Charles L. Davis to C.I.A., May 13, 1908, U.S. National Archives, *Record Group No. 75*, 18–19; C.I.A. to A. F. Caldwell, Feb. 18, 1908, ibid.
98. *Pocatello Tribune*, April 22, June 11, 1909.
99. Ibid., March 4, 1911.
100. Evan W. Estep to C.I.A., Jan. 8, 1913, U.S. National Archives, *Record Group No. 75*; C.I.A. to Evan W. Estep, Feb. 7, 1913, ibid.
101. Evan W. Estep, C.I.A., May 16, 1913, ibid.
102. Ibid.
103. Series of letters, April 8 to Oct. 15, 1913 between James H. Brady Burton L. French and others with C.I.A., ibid.
104. Samuel Blair to C.I.A., May 8, 1925, ibid., 26; C.I.A. to H. H. Miller, Feb. 21, 1918, ibid.
105. Minutes of Fort Hall Business Council, May 14, 17, 1930, *Fort Hall Agency Records*.
106. Minutes of Fort Hall Business Council, May 28, Oct. 3, Dec. 30, 1930, March 4, 1931, April 1, 1932, ibid.
107. Congressman Addison T. Smith to C.I.A., May 5, 1932, U.S. National Archives, *Record Group No. 75*.
108. Minutes of Fort Hall Business Council, April 1, 1932, *Fort Hall Agency Records*.
109. F. A. Gross to C.I.A., Feb. 15, 1934, U.S. National Archives, *Record Group No. 75*.
110. F. A. Gross to C.I.A., Nov. 17, 1937, ibid.
111. F. A. Gross to C.I.A., Aug. 23, 1940, ibid.; "Ordinance Regarding Fishing and Hunting on the Fort Hall Reservation, April 8, 9, 1941," *Fort Hall Agency Records*.
112. Minutes, Fort Hall Business Council, Sept. 19, 1950, ibid.
113. Charles S. Spencer to Edward Boyer, Oct. 7, 1963, ibid.
114. Joseph Thorpe, Jr., to V. W. Cameron, April 11, 1969, ibid.
115. Edward H. Langworthy to Carl W. Beck, Sept. 19, 1945, ibid.
116. "Ordinances Adopted by Fort Hall Business Council, April 8, 9, 1941, October 19, 1945, November 9, 1948, June 12, 1951, September 17, 1951," ibid.; Frell M. Owl to Lucille Hincy, April 8, 1960, ibid.; B. W. Davis to Lucille Hincy, April 12, 1961, ibid.
117. "Tribal Game Seasons as set by the Tribal Council, 1952," ibid.
118. F. A. Gross to C.I.A., April 18, 1933, U.S. National Archives, *Record Group No. 75*; Florence Ingawaneys to Woolridge, March 27, 1953, *Fort Hall Agency Records;* Omar W. Halvorson to B.I.A., Portland, Oregon, April 29, 1963, ibid.
119. C.I.A. to F. A. Gross, Aug. 18, 1930, U.S. National Archives, *Record Group No. 75*.
120. Minutes of the Fort Hall Business Council, Nov. 5, 1935, *Fort Hall Agency Records*.
121. Minutes of the Fort Hall Business Council, June 28, 1948, ibid.; Frank W. Parker to Frell M. Owl, March 30, 1959, ibid.
122. G. L. Becker to Chief of the Bannock & Shoshone Tribe of Indians, Oct. 1, 1946, ibid.; Gwen Briscoe to G. L. Becker, Oct. 3, 1946, ibid.
123. B. W. Davis to Senator Henry Dworshak, April 9, 1958, ibid.
124. Joseph Thorpe, Jr. to Charles S. Spencer, Oct. 5, 1961, ibid.
125. "Sho-Ban Annual Report, 1974-1975," ibid.
126. Zimmerman, *The Fort Hall Story*.

CHAPTER XVI

OUR LITTLE LAND

Allotments in Severalty

Throughout the history of the Shoshoni and Bannock there has been a constant theme — their love for the land. In the beginning they claimed and roamed over a territory extending from the Wind River Mountains, the Yellowstone Park country, and the buffalo plains of Montana on the east to the Weiser-Boise-Bruneau valleys of the west, and from Great Salt Lake and Bear Lake on the south to the Salmon River of the north. The twin hearts of this immense area were Camas Prairie and the Portneuf-Snake River bottoms, the first a summer home and the latter a sheltered haven against winter storms.

The land belonged to all, and the products of the land — the fish and game, the roots and berries, the grass and timber — became "property" only when harvested by a family or the tribes. As an observer has expressed it,

When there were good crops in any locality, they ripened so fast and fell to the ground so quickly that the people who ordinarily lived in the area could not possibly gather them all. When a good harvest was promised, they therefore spread the news abroad, so that people whose crops had failed could come to share their bounty with them.[1]

Any game killed by hunters was usually retained by the families involved (unless starvation dictated a broader distribution), and related families could share in the good fortune. Hunting was a cooperative affair. A planned drive could bring in so much more game that individuals ordinarily were not allowed to hunt alone. Sometimes families or bands would agree to split up, one group going after buffalo while the other would travel west to gather camas and salmon and to trade buffalo hides for Nez Perce horses. The following year they would reverse the annual pilgrimages.

In winter camp on the Snake River bottoms or the plains above, the land was still held in common. Chief Tecumseh, the great Shawnee chieftain, despairing at the rapid advance of the whites, tried to explain to General William Henry Harrison in 1810 this Indian concept of land ownership:

The way, the only way to stop this evil, is for all the red men to unite in claiming a common and equal right in the land, as it was at first, and should be now — for it never was divided, but belongs to all. No tribe has a right to sell, even to each other, much less to strangers, who demand all, and will take no less.

. . . Sell a country! Why not sell the air, the clouds and the great sea, as well as the earth? Did not the Great Spirit make them all for the use of his children?[2]

To Harrison, as to all American whites steeped in the centuries-old European concept of individual ownership of a piece of ground, the Indian reverence for communal holdings was incomprehensible. The two cultures collided, with the most powerful having its way and imposing on the weaker a system which was not understood, was resisted, and is today slowly losing ground at Fort Hall and on other reservations where tribal land holdings are being restored.

The process of forcing a nomadic people, used to wandering over a area of approximately 64 million acres, to settle on a reservation of 1.8 million acres and eventually reduced to about 520 thousand acres, was a difficult and, at first, impossible task for the officials of the Office of Indian Affairs. Determined to "civilize" the Shoshoni and Bannock, the method was clear: Force them to settle on individual farms and give up their roving habits. Agent Peter Gallagher spoke for nearly all progressive white Americans when he wrote in 1887 that the Indian way of life must be transformed

1887

from half-way cultivated patches to decent fields and farms, ownership, "my land, my farm," marked by metes and bounds, lands in severalty if you please, in which delight can be taken in building houses and barns, stables, etc., rather than work in common principle, led to in a great measure by the ownership in common, planting where you please, if at all, this year, and somewhere else next, lacking everything in the way of an incentive to those having some disposition to do.[3]

"Ownership," "my land," "metes and bounds," "incentive." These were the magic words which had made the white man master of the earth, and the Shoshoni and Bannock were to be given the opportunity to emulate that example.

In the year that Agent Gallagher spoke so eloquently for his way of life, the U.S. government announced its grand design for the Indian people as outlined in the Dawes Act: to allot individual farms to each Indian family. The underlying purpose of the law was, of course, much broader. Eventually the allotment of lands in severalty would abolish the reservation system, abrogate the Indian tribal organization, and make Indians citizens equal in every respect to white citizens. The government was to hold individual lands in trust for each Indian family for twenty-five years, after which a patent in fee was to be issued. Supplementary laws in 1891 and 1906 allowed an Indian to lease his allotment and receive his patent in fee much sooner by a declaration of competency. Both programs designed to speed up the process of breaking up the reservation system.[4]

1886   An additional motive for the passage of the Dawes Act was to return all excess and unallotted lands to the public domain, which could then be thrown open for white settlement. At Fort Hall Peter Gallagher explained what this would mean. Under the Fort Bridger Treaty the Shoshoni and Bannock heads of families were promised 320 acres each, and individuals reaching the age of eighteen were to be granted 80 acres each. The Agreement of May 14, 1880, granted each head of family 160 acres of agricultural land and 160 acres of grazing land, while a person reaching the age of eighteen was to receive 80 acres of each type of land. If and when the 1880 agreement was ratified, Gallagher pointed out that about 500 thousand acres would return to the public domain, which would still leave each man, woman and child with 351 acres. Then, if the department followed his advice and cut off the eastern portion of the reservation, each Indian would still have 276 acres, freeing another 150 thousand acres for white settlement.[5] It was little wonder that the local whites looked with eagerness toward the time when the allotment process would be completed at Fort Hall.

1895   Even before the Dawes Act, agents at the reservation had pressed for some form of allotment, complaining about the annual disputes among the Indians which seemed to occur every year over a division of the meadowland on the Snake River bottoms.[6] But they also pointed out, as indicated in some detail in the section of this narrative dealing with irrigation, that without a means of getting water to the land the allotment process could not be completed.[7] A further doubt about the proposed system was voiced by the commissioner
1901   in 1901 — that "the general leasing of allotments instead of benefiting the Indians, as originally intended, only contributed to their demoralization."[8]

1887   From 1887, when Agent Gallagher reported that few of the Indians understood what "land in severalty" and "citizenship" meant and that allotments at that time would "do much more harm
1908   than good,"[9] to 1908, when at least a partial irrigation system would now permit the allotment of lands to proceed, the leading Indians had come to accept the serious intentions of the government to divide up the land, and they became quite anxious about what would happen to their present holdings. A further concern was that the bottomlands would be so reduced there would be none left for grazing their herds. Supervisor Charles L. Davis

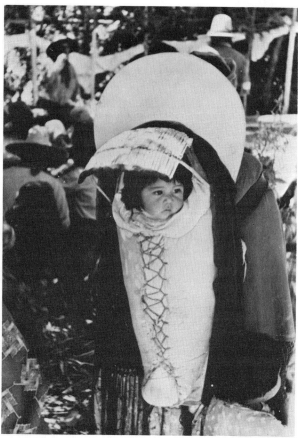

Idaho State Historical Society

Shoshoni baby in cradleboard

recommended in his 1908 report that each head of family of the 1,782 Indians at Fort Hall be granted forty acres of irrigable land and every other member twenty to thirty acres, with the balance being allotted as grazing land. He also concurred with the desire of the Shoshoni and Bannock that the northeast section of the reservation be set aside as a common upland grazing area. Choosing his words very carefully, Davis was of the opinion that as soon as patents could be issued "white farmers will begin to come in gradually, which has so much better effect on the Indian population than to suddenly obliterate the reservation boundaries and leave the Indians to fight out the new conditions under a strange legal status, and among an unsettled and adventurous population." The supervisor supported allotments in severalty but expressed a finely honed word of caution.[10]

With an irrigation system by 1910 that would 1910 supposedly irrigate thirty-six thousand acres of land at Fort Hall, and with the Indians becoming more and more anxious about allotments, U.S. Senator Weldon B. Heyburn introduced an amendment to the Indian appropriation bill in March 1910 providing for allotments to the

Shoshoni and Bannock. The Indians wrote that they had "never seen the man on our reservation," doubted that he understood the conditions at Fort Hall, but were sure the senator represented the citizens of Idaho "and will take care of their interests."[11] After passage of the bill Agent W. B. Sams arrived at the reservation in August 1910; by October an allotment of the lands was underway.[12] Pocatello citizens learned to their disappointment that there would be no land left over after all the Indians had received their grants.[13] The news was announced that the allotted lands could be leased by whites, which would allow the Indians, "proverbially poor farmers," the opportunity to learn by example from the more proficient Anglo-Saxon tillers of the soil.[14]

1911
1912
The allotment process was temporarily suspended in late 1910 while the Office of Indian Affairs procured additional legislation from Congress, but action was finally completed in 1911.[15] The following spring a hearing was held at Fort Hall to investigate any problems which the Indians might wish to present. Pat L. Tyhee took up most of the time complaining that the twenty-acre allotment of irrigable lands to each head of household, plus another twenty acres to the spouse, was not enough to support a family. Tyhee asked for eighty acres, saying, "The Red Man was the first man that was on the continent here in North America; but . . . he ought to have the right to get some part of the land and the best part anyhow of what little land he has left."[16]

1911
Congress finally repealed the provisions of the acts of February 23, 1889, and April 4, 1910, establishing the amount of land to be given to each Indian, and passed the act of March 3, 1911. The new law provided for an allotment of 40 acres of irrigable land and 320 acres of grazing land to each head of a family whose spouse was dead and 20 acres of irrigable land and 160 acres of grazing land to every other Indian having rights on the reservation. The 1,863 allotments granted were approved on October 28, 1914.[17]

1920
For several years after the allotment process had been completed, numerous questions were raised concerning the regulations governing enrollment in the tribes and the possibility of further allotments. The commissioner ruled in 1920 that children born on the reservation after their parents had been allotted were not eligible for any grant of land, the allotments having been closed as of March 17, 1913.[18] Patents in fee could not be issued for the land until the applicants had cleared any indebtedness to the government.[19] In 1925 the superintendent had to deal with Garfield Pocatello who — claiming to be the hereditary chief of the Bannock on the reservation and in typical Bannock fashion — began issuing allotments on his own to Maggie Groundhog, Joe

1925

Barber, and other Northern Shoshoni from Nevada. Superintendent Donner informed Pocatello that he could not defy the Indian Office in this way and suggested that the Bannock "chief" convey the title of some of his own extensive land holdings to the aspirants from Nevada. Garfield Pocatello politely declined the invitation.[20] Finally, Senator William H. King of Utah, of the Senate Committee on the Judiciary, requested an investigation of charges made to him by Jimmie Chicken and Jim Pazegant of Fort Hall that certain white employees on the reservation were circumventing the regulation which barred them from purchasing allotments by having relatives bid for the land and receive title, with the understanding that the property would eventually go to the white employees.[21]

1928

With allotment transactions completed, and looking to the future of the dismembered reservation, the Bureau of Indian Affairs in 1918 requested congressional legislature which would authorize the establishment of a townsite on the reservation at Fort Hall.[22] Four years later the bill was passed, with the qualification that only lots and blocks west of the railroad would be surveyed and offered for sale, leaving the area east of the tracks as property for the agency.[23] A few stores and dwellings were built to offer a shopping service to the Indians and to tourists on the Yellowstone Highway, but after a new freeway was constructed along the hills east of the agency the little settlement dwindled away until today it is not very significant. In fact, as early as 1948 Superintendent Carl W. Beck informed the Bureau of Indian Affairs that the town was moribund and "there seems to be no dire need for additional lands at this time" for the town.[24]

1918
1922
1948

Although there seemed to be little interest among whites to speculate in the Fort Hall townsite lots, there was a great desire to acquire any Indian allotments of land offered for sale. Increasingly, as some Indian owners died and the land became fractionalized among a number of heirs, various superintendents undertook to sell these allotments. Some old people who had no descendants could thus be taken off the ration roll by the sale of their heirship land.[25] In other cases there were so many descendants owning "scarcely more than a shovel full" portion of a tract that they chose to dispose of their tiny shares by selling the whole to a white purchaser.[26] Superintendents were reluctant to sell grazing lands, "as it is the means of permitting cow thieves on our ranges," but were seemingly not averse to helping to "civilize" the Shoshoni and Bannock by selling their property out from under them — at the request, of course, of the Indians themselves.[27] A typical case was the sale in 1921 of twenty acres of the allotment of Ella Evening, a deceased member of the Shoshoni tribe, to a white man for $1,325.

1921

The money went to two descendants — Frank Quagagant, one third, and Charles Evening, two thirds.[28] In the same year the superintendent advertised for sale 63 allotments of about 6,400 acres for an appraised value totaling $117,720.[29]

1925   As already discussed under the topic of irrigation, many of the allotments were leased to whites either because the Indian owner did not wish to farm the land or because operations became so complicated by heirship problems that the multiple owners chose to lease. There was a flurry of discontent and much investigation in 1925 when a number of Indians complained about the practice of the superintendent in leasing allotments to whites without gaining the consent of Indian owners. Inspector Samuel Blair reported that such leasing had been conducted by the various superintendents over a number of years to ensure that the lands would not lie idle and to bring in some financial return so the Indians would not "suffer for the necessities of life." Additionally it was necessary to lease some lands to save certain water rights which would be lost to the land unless put to use.[30]

By 1925 the superintendent reported that 1,916 Indians had received allotments totaling 338,909 acres of land; 553 Indians were listed as having no allotments.[31] A more comprehensive report in 1932 gave the following picture of land ownership at Fort Hall: 1,525 allotments totaling 235,120 acres leased to whites; 416 allotments totaling 70,302 acres leased to Indians; 925 leased allotments in the heirship class; and 170 allotments sold during the previous five years at a average price of $1,650. (Sixty-one of these were sold to provide for the American Falls Reservoir.) The sale of Indian lands came to a halt by the late 1926   1920s; the last general sale was held on December 22, 1926, and the last private sale on July 29, 1929.[32]

The same report listed more disadvantages than advantages for the allotment system particularly with regard to the heirship problem. Agency officials affirmed that the cost of clerical work in keeping a proper accounting of ownership among many heirs was often greater than the income. The superintendent at Fort Hall thought that grazing lands should never be allotted but held in common by the tribe. He also thought that the 850 unallotted Indians could each be granted at least 20 acres from the remaining lands. Most of the property leased to whites was grazing land; very little irrigable land was leased. Certificates of 1932   competency for patents in fee had been issued to only 164 Indians by 1932. The Indians were farming 16,000 acres of irrigable land, with another 23,000 acres of irrigable land "in a raw state." They were thus farming an average of almost ten acres per capita for each man, woman, and child on the reservation, a good average compared to white farmers.[33]

Establishment of a Tribal Organization

As the allotment machine rolled to a gentle stop, a new commissioner of Indian Affairs, John Collier, began encouraging the practice of Indian customs and religion and in other ways indicated that a "new deal" for Indians was on its way.[34] Superintendents like F. A. Gross at Fort Hall had already voiced dissatisfaction with the old forced acculturation program. At a 1931 council meeting 1931 at the reservation a tribal member, Frank Randall, was quoted as saying he was always bragging about Mr. Gross "because he is fair and square with us and he let us wear feathers on our hats, he doesn't make remarks about the paints on some of our Indians and he is doing more good than we expected of him."[35] These early, informal council meetings were usually held in the superintendent's office and were therefore very much under his supervision, nevertheless they demonstrated that a shift in the balance of power toward more Indian control was beginning. Superintendent Gross, furthermore, encouraged 1932 the change. In one meeting he counseled those in attendance "not to have their mouth shut when any confusing problem is put before them to act upon. It is their duties to ask freely all thing concerning about those confusing problem."[36] Later superintendents have found it unnecessary to encourage the Shoshoni and Bannock to speak out.

John Collier's philosophy concerning an Indian-oriented program of help from Washington was enacted into law under the Indian Reorganization Act of June 18, 1934. The basic idea 1934 was to revitalize tribal organizations and community life among the Indians of the United States — specifically, to encourage tribes to form councils to manage community affairs, to help the Indians form business corporations, to create a revolving fund to provide credit, and to end the allotment process.[37] A year earlier Superintendent Gross had requested advice from the commissioner about the usefulness of adopting a formal organization for the council, which had been functioning rather informally for several years.[38] With the concurrence of Commissioner Collier, the Shoshoni and Bannock in early 1934 established a constitution and bylaws, with five voting districts: Gibson District, two council members; Lincoln Creek, one member; Fort Hall District, two members; Ross Fork District, one member; Bannock Creek District, one member.[39] The constitution and bylaws were approved by the secretary of the 1936 Interior on April 30, 1936.[40] On April 17, 1937, 1937 the tribe ratified the Corporate Charter of the Shoshone-Bannock Tribes of the Fort Hall Reservation.[41] Within a few years the various dis-

Idaho State Historical Society

Jacob Browning (left) and Garfield Pocatello.

tricts also began to establish local organizations such as the Constitution and Bylaws for the Tah-yah-ru-kont (Ross Fork Creek) Progressive Farm and Home Organization founded in 1939.[42]

1939

The enactment of a constitution and bylaws soon brought a demand for more precise requirements for membership in the Shoshone-Bannock tribes. By an ordinance passed April 9, 1941, the Fort Hall Business Council decreed that no person would be considered for adoption into the tribes unless he or she was eighteen years of age, was at least one-half degree Indian blood, and had maintained a residence of at least three years within the reservation boundaries.[43] On May 9, 1950, the council ordained that "no future adoption of members will be made by the Shoshone-Bannock Tribes."[44] In another move two years later the council agreed that "no person may be considered for enrollment into the Shoshone-Bannock Tribes" unless the individual was one-half degree or more Shoshone-Bannock blood.[45] In later years much council time has been devoted to "enrollment hearings," during which individuals are approved or disapproved for enrollment. At a typical meeting on December 3, 1970, the council discussed the applications of fifty-nine people ten of whom were approved as members and forty-nine disapproved as members of the tribes.[46]

1941

1950

1952

1970

The Indian Reorganization Act brought new hope to the Shoshoni and Bannock that finally they were being allowed to work out their own destiny with the help of a beneficent government. When the commissioner asked for an expression from the tribes in 1940 about the effectiveness of the act, the tribal council answered that Fort Hall Indians had more voice in administering their own affairs than ever before, that the act had benefited them, and that they wished to continue under the legislation.[47]

1940

The request from Washington was a fire bell in the night to the Fort Hall Indians. Soon a nation-wide movement started to work the Bureau of Indian Affairs out of a job and to place all the tribes in the United States in the position of managing their own affairs with no direct help from an agency in Washington. A 1947 formula placed all tribes in one of three categories: group one to be released immediately from federal supervision, group two to be released in ten years, and group three at an indefinite time in the future. Fort Hall was placed in category three.[48]

1947

Facing the frightening prospect of no more support from Washington, the Shoshoni and Bannock began to prepare (as did other tribes) for the inevitable termination — or "extermination," as the tribal newspaper called it.[49] On April 28, 1953, the chairman of the tribal council addressed the following to all members of the tribes:

1953

The Government must remember that what it owes us cannot be measured in money. It took from us our own Tribal self-government; it undermined and destroyed our faith and confidence in our own leaders; and it brought complete disunity among us. It owes us help and guidance in restoring these things to us which it took many years ago.

The white man must remember that the Indian people are not immigrants. He must remember that the Indian people have had to undergo a complete change in their way of life and have had to accept the white man's way by reason of conquest and not by Indian choice. The white man must also remember that he will never fully understand the Indian feeling for our lands and that it is a feeling which he does not have for his land.[50]

In bitter irony, the tribal newspaper also wrote of the Indians being "liberated" and "emancipated" from their tribal lands.[51]

1955

A questionnaire sent to all Indian officials in 1954 resulted in a second evaluation of the readiness of each tribe to assume control of its own affairs. Fort Hall officers of the bureau placed the Shoshoni and Bannock in the "Yes (if gradual)" category. The frantic responses of some of the tribes began to seep into the consciousness of Washington officialdom as local white friends, some senators and congressmen, and others began to realize the drastic change, after a century and a half, from wardship to a cold-turkey approach for the advancement of the American Indian. An indication of a more moderate diet appeared in 1961, when the Department of the Interior and the Bureau of Indian Affairs changed their official land policies to permit tribes or individual Indians the first opportunity to purchase lands offered for sale by other Indians. As will be shown, this move had a dramatic impact on the land consolidation program at Fort Hall. The shift from "termination" to "self-determination" proposed by President Lyndon B. Johnson and supported later by President Richard M. Nixon relieved the Shoshoni and Bannock of much of their fear about being set adrift in a sea of whites without compass or sails. With the new directions given the Bureau of Indian Affairs to coordinate federal, state, and local resources in behalf of helping the Indians to help themselves, the Fort Hall people today feel more reassured about controlling their own affairs, especially the administration of their "little land" at Fort Hall.[52]

1954

1961

Aboriginal Lands Case

Coincident with the shift in policy at Washington, the Shoshoni and Bannock received long-awaited payment for their aboriginal lands, which had been taken from them for sums which the court called "grossly inadequate and unconscionable."[53] The early history of the case has already been recounted in the discussion of the Northwestern Shoshoni, but the way in which

1967

Bureau of American Ethnology

Jack Edmo with his wife, daughter, and grandchildren.

the Fort Hall and Lemhi Indians became involved needs to be explained.

1936 As early as June 1936 five leading Indians petitioned the commissioner to allow them to file a claim for "Portneuf Valley and Camas Prairie."[54] The Northwestern case had already been underway for several years when a bill was introduced in Congress to include the Northwestern Shoshoni at Fort Hall — numbering about 750, a much larger number than the 200 or so Northwestern Shoshoni at Washakie, Utah.[55] The bill also proposed that the Boise and Bruneau Shoshoni and the Bannock be allowed to assert their claims in the Court of Claims along with the two Northwestern groups.

1937

The law firm of Moyle, Wilkinson, Suydam, & Harlan of Washington, D.C. was granted a contract on May 15, 1936, by the Fort Hall Indians to represent them in the case, and Ernest L. Wilkinson of the firm made the presentation before the court. After a long, historical introduction, Mr. Wilkinson introduced the Governor James Duane Doty map, which had just been discovered in the files of the National Archives. The map proved to be pivotal in persuading the subcommittee that the aboriginal boundaries of the area claimed by the Northwestern Shoshoni were much more extensive than those proposed in the original Washakie case. The subcommittee recommended a bill allowing the Fort Hall Indians to become a party to the suit then pending for the Washakie Northwestern group.[56]

1936

1938

1940 After another two years the Fort Hall Indians asked Idaho Congressman Henry Dworshak to use his influence to have the government also consider the aboriginal land interests of the Weiser and "Brunow" Shoshoni, but expert witnesses later testified that these groups could not claim exclusive use and occupancy because they had shared the areas with the Northern Paiute and probably the Nez Perce. The Indian Claims Commission requires that, in order to establish joint occupancy or joint aboriginal title, the joint users must be in fact a consolidation of tribes; mere friendly joint use is insufficient.[57]

The Treaty of Box Elder of 1863, used by the Northwestern Indians as a basis for their claim to compensation for fifteen million acres of land, now came into question. The Court of Claims reached the conclusion that the treaty was one of peace and amity and did not acknowledge, on the part of the United States, any exclusive right or occupancy right for the Northwestern bands. On March 12, 1945, the U.S. Supreme Court affirmed the findings of the Court of Claims in a five-to-four decision.[58]

1945

1947 Two years after this disappointment Ernest Wilkinson was at Fort Hall explaining the strategy his firm intended to follow in the case. He pointed out that President Harry S. Truman had

created an Indian Claims Commission, which was to start functioning in three months. The attorneys intended to present separate suits for the Northwestern Band and the "Mixed Bands of Shoshones" from north of the Snake River. The tribes unanimously ratified a new contract with the law firm, which was signed in Washington, January 22, 1947.[59]

Fifteen years later, in 1962, the Indian claims commissioner finally rendered a decision. The commission had found that the land claimed was originally in possession of four groups of Shoshoni: The Shoshone Tribe, which included the Northwestern, Fort Hall, and Wind River Shoshoni and the Bannock; the Lemhi; the Gosiute; and the Western Shoshoni. The commission defined the boundaries of each of the four groups and ultimately determined acreage for Gosiute and Western Shoshoni. The Shoshone Tribe claim and the Lemhi claim were settled without trial on the valuation issue. The acreage (determined, of course, by the boundaries drawn by the commission) was agreed upon by the parties. The commission acknowledged original Fort Hall, Wind River, and Northwestern Shoshoni ownership of thirty-eight million acres of land and Lemhi ownership of five million acres. The Washington firm of lawyers at once began to search out experts who could help appraise the land to determine its value at the time the government took possession.[60]

1962

A decision in the several cases resulted in a net judgment of $15.7 million for 38,319,000 acres. There were two types of claims involved in the settlement: (1) The aboriginal claims of the Eastern Shoshoni, the Northwestern Shoshoni, and the mixed bands of Bannock and Shoshoni, which the commission treated as constituting the Shoshone Tribe, and (2) four separate claims of Indians of the Fort Hall Reservation arising from reduction of the Fort Hall Reservation or misuse of Shoshone-Bannock tribal funds. The judgment did not, of course, include all the claims pled in the original Shoshone Nation petition. The land claims of the Lemhi, the Western Bands, and the Gosiute, as well as the accounting claims of these bands and those of Fort Hall, have been or are in process of being separately litigated.

The settlement was presented to the Indians at Fort Hall for their approval in 1967 and met with stern opposition from some of the descendants of the Boise and Bruneau bands, whose aboriginal holdings had not been included in the final judgment. The attorneys present explained that under the concept of "exclusive use and occupancy," they had been unable to persuade the court that no other tribe or band had occupied the two river valleys. Robert W. Barker of the Washington firm promised to write some legislation concerning the two river valleys to present to the Idaho congres-

1967

sional delegation at the next session of Congress. He did so on March 27, 1968, including, in addition to the proposed bill, a statement for the benefit of a sponsoring congressman and a draft of a letter to the Idaho congressman requesting introduction of the bill. It apparently was never introduced. Many of the Shoshoni at Fort Hall still have not accepted the commission's judgment in the case of the Boise and Bruneau bands and do not understand the idea of "exclusive use and occupancy."

As already indicated, the main problem was concerned with evidence presented that Northern Paiute from Nevada and Oregon, as well as Indians from northern Idaho, had occasionally used the valleys for hunting and fishing.[61] The documentation was apparently strong enough to establish the principle of "joint occupancy," for which no claim was allowed because it could not be established that the Boise and Bruneau were in control of their aboriginal areas. The Boise and Bruneau groups, therefore, were eliminated from any consideration for compensation for the lands they once called their homeland.

1971   A general council of the Shoshone-Bannock tribes met January 30, 1971, and by a margin of 207 to 52 approved a final judgment of $4.5 million for the Lemhi tribe for 5,022,000 acres of land taken from them without compensation by the Executive Order of February 12, 1875.[62] The 53 negative votes were cast because those people believe the government had not satisfied them concerning the possibility of minerals on the land which would have increased the value. Later the government was able to establish that there were no minerals of any considerable worth. Some of the Lemhi continued to hold out because they wanted their land back. Indian leaders found it difficult to explain that the Lemhi had lost aboriginal title to most of their lands when they accepted their Executive Order reservation in Lemhi Valley.[63] Again, Indian and white concepts of land holdings came into sharp conflict.

As already indicated in the section concerned with the Northwestern Shoshoni, the Shoshoni and Bannock at Fort Hall also received $8,864,000 as their 50 percent share of the balance of the total amount of $15.7 million plus accrued interest and earnings. They also received a special award of $500,000, of which they proposed to use $125,000 for the construction of a diagnostic and rehabilitation center. The tribal governing body agreed to distribute 75 percent of the award on a per capita basis, and an initial sum of $2,000 was paid to each of 2,754 tribal members. The remaining 25 percent was designated to be used for needed tribal programs at Fort Hall.[64]

Tribal Land Purchase Program

The long court and legislative battle to gain reimbursement for their aboriginal lands heightened the apprehension of the Shoshoni and Bannock about the necessity of retaining the few acres left to them at Fort Hall. As they watched their fellow tribesmen sell precious allotments to white owners, the business council leaders sought a means of returning the lands to tribal ownership. The initial motivation came from observing white 1933 cattlemen engage in "grazing and hunting trespass, wood stealing and water 'hogging' " on adjacent Indians lands.[65] In summarizing the justifications for requesting permission to expend 1937 $50,000 in tribal funds for the purchase of lands from Indians and non-Indians within the confines of the reservation Superintendent Gross stated that the council desired to invest surplus funds in a permanent manner, to recover the acres now tied up in heirship status, to provide farming lands for the young Indians of the reservation, to make use of idle lands held by old and incapacitated individuals, to purchase lands from Indians who had received certificates of competency, and to secure lands from white owners when the acreage was interspersed with Indian lands. In a more explicit explanation of the last reason, Gross argued that white owners got better and more water service; they took "advantage of their so-called superior tactics by dealing in an underhanded way and probably not too squarely with the Indians;" and there was always the very convenient possibility of encroachment. In a final argument the superintendent thought that isolated tracts prohibited proper water conservation.[66] An unspoken motive was a fear, better expressed by a white reporter of the *Pocatello Tribune*, that the white man was not satisfied with placing the American Indian on the "most barren and worth- 1949 less lands" of the continent, but now "we want that land too. And we're out to get it now."[67]

The Bureau of Indian Affairs had aided the Fort Hall Indians in 1935 by purchasing 43,247 acres of submarginal land adjacent to the reservation. By 1937 this consisted of 475,244 acres — 1937 299,432 acres of allotted land, 174,700 acres of tribal land, and 1,111 acres for administrative sites. There were 200,014 acres under Indian operation (including 20,000 irrigated acres and 150,370 acres in grazing areas) and 275,230 acres under white operation — 465 leases of farmland involving 24,168 acres and 23 leases of grazing land for 251,061 acres.[68]

With a larger share of Fort Hall lands being controlled by whites, the Shoshoni and Bannock were appreciative when the New Deal agency, the Resettlement Administration, entered the picture to give them some financial assistance in trying to regain control of their reservation home. In 1936 1936 the Indians were granted $182,318, with which they purchased 11,802 acres.[69] The Indian Reorganization Act also was of some help, appropriating $53,000 for land purchase at Fort Hall in 1936.[70] By late 1937 the commissioner was able to report that more than $200,000 had been expended in the purchase of lands for the Fort Hall Indians.[71] Another $40,000 was set aside by the Indians from their own tribal funds in 1938 for the Fort Hall Scattered Lands Project, as it was now called.[72] Land values were beginning to rise, making the land purchase programs more and more difficult. Nevertheless, since 1938 the Shoshoni and Bannock have expended and are still expending every effort and every dollar available to buy back the lands they lost under the allotment program.

1937

1938

The intensity of their drive to repossess their lands and place them once again under tribal control was revealed in their answers to the questionnaire sent to them in 1943 by the House Committee on Indian Affairs. Out of twelve questions asked, the Fort Hall leaders managed to insert in three of the answers the plea that "assistance is needed in buying back land lost to Indian ownership and bring it under tribal control." They were particularly concerned about wishing to place lands in heirship status under the jurisdiction of the Fort Hall Business Council.[73]

1943

The Land Purchase and Adjustment Enterprise of the tribes was formally approved by the commissioner on April 18, 1947, after which the business council adopted a number of ordinances governing the entire program. On April 19, 1949, the council decided that lands having the most heirs would be purchased first, that any such heir should have the opportunity to purchase the land for his own use, and that after all heirship lands had been purchased, lands belonging to old and indigent Indians would then be bought.[74]

1947

1949

To improve the effective use of Fort Hall lands the tribes also established an "exchange assignment," in which an individual could trade his or her tract for one of equal value owned by the tribes. A "standard assignment" allowed a person without land to receive a tract from the business council as long as he continued to work the land.[75]

The tribes adopted a more detailed plan of operations for purchasing lands during a meeting of April 10, 1951: Only lands which fell within the appraised value would be considered for purchase; all surplus funds were to be invested in lands; the lands were to be leased as soon as the purchase was completed; and a land field agent was to be employed. Priority of purchaser would follow the order of heirship lands in the Michaud area to owners sixty years of age and older; heirship lands of owners sixty years or older whose holdings were located any other place on the

1951

reservation; and, thirdly, tracts having the largest number of heirs, particularly grazing lands, which usually produced a smaller income to the many owners.[76]

Retrieving lands from white ownership was a slow, difficult, and costly process; a survey of 1952 showed that lands under tribal control had reached 193,578 acres — only 18,878 acres more than held in 1937. Other figures dramatized the heirship problem: 925 tracts held by original allottees, 85,080 acres; 755 held by other single owners, 53,025; 1,200 held by a multiple ownership of five or less, 99,948 acres; and 585 held by a multiple ownership of six or more, 54,723 acres — a total of 3,465 tracts and 292,778 acres.[77]

1952

The unscrupulous methods used by some white lessees, and the ridiculously low prices for the leases, led the business council at Fort Hall to raise the fee from $3 an acre, as it had been for several years prior to 1951, to $8 an acre in 1952 and $15 an acre in 1953. The council cited a specific case of one white lessee who had used devious methods to lease 1,000 acres at 15 cents an acre for a ten-year period, when comparable land was renting for $9.25 an acre. He then attempted to sublease part of the land for $6 an acre. Immediately upon notice of the increase of $15 an acre, the agrieved white lessees went on the offensive. They attempted to get some sympathetic agency employees removed from their jobs, wrote letters of complaint to Idaho congressmen about the new high lease prices, hired attorneys to try to block the change in fees, and attempted to use their influence to create dissension among tribal council members to get the new increases annulled. Joseph Thorpe, Jr., one of the Indian leaders, appealed to his people to stand together and announced that "we can not use bow-and-arrow methods in our fight for our rights."[78] The Shoshoni and Bannock won their battle with the help of a petition addressed to President Dwight D. Eisenhower.

1953

Two years later the Indians took a stand against a Bureau of Indian Affairs decision to allow the assignment of individual patents in fee, which the Fort Hall Business Council denounced as a form of land alienation that would destroy the tribal program of attempting to consolidate their grazing and timber lands. Four national Indian organizations protested the action, which seemed to be part of the "termination" program then underway.[79]

1955

In a masterful understatement in 1957 the Shoshoni and Bannock reported to a House of Representatives Special Indian Subcommittee investigating conditions at Fort Hall that "there has been some feeling among our Indian people that there is a concerted effort on the part of non-Indian interests in leasing Indian lands on the reservation dictating the terms of such leases and

1957

the policies established for the administration for such property." The Indians also informed the subcommittee that during the previous four years they had purchased 5,695.79 acres of land at a cost of $251,889.48. They pointed out that if they only had proper capital, credit, and training their people would not lease so much land to whites. Frank W. Parker expressed their feelings, "We here on the Reservation are like a man who stands before a warehouse full of food and starves because he lacks the keys necessary to open the doors; the keys of education and finance."[80]

1956   The tribal council had already in 1956 established a land committee to supervise hay-meadow assignments on the Fort Hall bottoms, standard and exchange assignments, and land purchases. In the precise language of the memorandum of understanding setting up the land purchase enterprise, it was "to consolidate and improve the tenure of the reservation land base in order to eliminate obstacles to proper land use, which have grown out of the alienation of Indian lands and the breaking up of the individual holdings through inheritance, for the immediate and future use and benefit of members of the Shoshone-Bannock Tribes, Inc." When the citizens of Pocatello formed a committee for the purpose of promoting better understanding between Indians and non-Indians, the Fort Hall Business Council requested the committee to study the sale of Indian lands and to "help us in our efforts to preserve our reservation." In a more direct move the council instructed its attorneys to take legal action against four white men who had bid for lands at a supervised land sale. These men were to be arrested for trespass if they attempted to take possession of the lands they had purchased or if they attempted to cross other Indian lands to get to their prospective new property.[81]

Adamantly opposed to the sale of any reservation lands to non-Indians, the Fort Hall tribes continued to struggle with the problem of heirship status. Usually the multiple heirs were unable to agree on use by one of them, which resulted in lease to non-Indians or in allowing the land to be idle, as was the case with 14,000 acres of irrigable

1959   land in 1959. The original 20-acre allotments were too small for efficient farming, and to acquire a 160-acre tract would require the agreement among the owners of eight allotments, ordinarily an impossible task. In 1959 the tribes also faced the possibility that the use of another 17,000 acres of allotted lands on Michaud Flats would soon deteriorate under the heirship system. One solution was for Congress to pass a law providing that all heirship land be sold when the number of heirs exceeded three.[82]

The Bureau of Indian Affairs hindered the solution to the multiple ownership of lands at Fort Hall by forbidding the use of tribal funds to buy fractional interests in such lands, claiming that the process would complicate and increase the clerical work of administration — an excuse which even some of the Indian officials discounted. Secondly, the bureau would not allow the tribes to borrow money with which to purchase lands.[83] As the tribal council said, "Nothing whatever had been done by the Commissioner's office to assist in solving the problem."[84] Nevertheless, the Shoshoni and Bannock persisted in attempting to buy interests in heirship tracts.[85]

The very low income derived from the land (not much more than $1 an acre) led the superin-   1960 tendent at Fort Hall in 1960 to lease about 13,000 acres of idle land. Many Indians opposed this move because non-Indians would become the lessees and also because the ten-year leases would leave many young people landless for several years. The superintendent and the Indian leaders were faced with a dilemma — low income from the land and leases to white farmers.[86]

The land-purchase program has become a fixed and resolute purpose of Indian leadership at Fort Hall, limited only by the lack of funds. In typical transactions the business council, at one meeting on December 8, 1964, purchased a twenty-acre-al-   1964 lotment from Betty T. Wenee for $3,700, another twenty acres from six heirs of the Coby family for $4,050, and twenty acres from Louise Two Eagles for $3,000.[87] During the July 11, 1972, meeting   1972 the council approved the purchase of two 160-tracts for $4,000 and $3,600, respectively.[88]

During 1973 the tribes spent $855,341.31 in land purchases, and in 1974, $621,518.83. There   1974 were by this time 244,653 acres under tribal ownership, 237,018 acres owned individually, and 41,343 acres controlled by the government. The tribe had been able to buy all or parts of the "most highly fractionated allotments" but still had 150,000 acres in heirship status. A new approach, which was helping, included properly prepared wills, gift deeds, and divisions of property.[89]

In recognition of the constant and unchecked commerical development within reservation boundaries, the business council adopted an "interim ordinance on commerical development" in 1974 and spent most of the next annual meeting of April 26, 1975, discussing and approving a   1975 permanent ordinance of land use which would place some controls on commerical intrusions by non-Indians on the reservation. One compelling reason for the move was a radio news release which announced plans to build a large motel complex at the Pocatello Municipal Airport located right in the center of the reservation. There were already many trailer homes located on what was formerly Indian lands. Their location next door to the second largest metropolitan area in Idaho make the Shoshoni and Bannock lands inviting prospects to aggressive and imaginative white businessmen.[90]

The location of an airport in the midst of the reservation has been another difficult fact of life for Fort Hall Indians to accept. The city of Pocatello established its airport early in the air age and in 1936 purchased 18.2 acres of additional land from the allotment of Pansy Coopoowee to enlarge the facility.[91] World War II brought further needs; the federal government, under its war powers, condemned another 2,100 acres of Indian land for airport purposes. The land had been used for grazing, but, with the prospect of the Michaud Project bringing irrigation water to the area, land values had risen.[92] The Bureau of Indian Affairs asked that the condemned acres be appraised as irrigable and sought, unsuccessfully, to get the army to exchange the needed acres for others of equal value.[93] The attorney representing the Indians also tried to get a "commitment for [from] the War Department that if it ever abandons the airport for military purposes that the land would go back to the Tribe." The lawyer did not have much hope of succeeding.[94]

Expert appraisers testified that the land was worth as much as $100 an acre, but the final award was set at $10 an acre. The Shoshoni and Bannock were unhappy with the transaction but were assured by the attorney, in front of other witnesses, that the airport lands would be returned to them after World War II or lands of equal value would be acquired for them. Apparently there was no written document attesting to this promise.[95] After the war the air base was declared surplus; its disposal was handled by the War Assets Administration; and under Public Law 289, Eighty-Sixth Congress, the City of Pocatello acquired the airport.[96] Since then, the city has sold part of the land and leased other tracts — but not to the Indians who so much wanted it returned.[97] From the point of view of the Fort Hall Indians, neither the War Department nor the City of Pocatello seemed concerned with Indian rights and the loss of more valuable acres from their dwindling Reservation.

Reclaiming Lands Taken by Pocatello

Another skeleton in the land closet of the Shoshoni and Bannock came into public view in 1962 when Idaho Congressman Ralph Harding introduced a bill to provide for the sale of thirty-eight lots still remaining from the auction sale of lots in the Pocatello townsite as outlined under the Agreement of 1888.[98] Earlier, in a tribal council meeting of April 19, 1932, Superintendent Gross had informed the Indian leaders about the lots "laying near University of Idaho (Southern Branch). The exact location is not well defined.

. . . The appraised value is insufficient to invite buyers. Therefore it remains unsold."[99] The 1962 congressional action brought a strong remonstrance from the business council. The Indians wished to retain the lots to provide a retail outlet in the city for the Arts and Crafts Division of their Rehabilitation and Adult Education Department, to furnish housing and assistance for Indian students attending the university, and to provide rental income to the tribe.[100]

A judgment from one of the Bureau of Indian Affairs real property officers held in 1968 that the act of June 6, 1900, had extinguished the tribe's interest in the undisposed Pocatello lots.[101] The commissioner explained that the ownership of the lots "remains vested in the United States." [102] The Indians were sure, and have been all along, that the lots still belong to them. Some of the tracts have by now become quite valuable; they are located in the parking lot of Idaho State University's Minidome, in the parking lot to the university gymnasium, in residential areas of the city, and "under a grocery store."[103] At the present time attorneys for the Indians are attempting to get recognition of tribal ownership.[104]

The Pocatello cession came under the scrutiny of the Shoshoni and Bannock in another way in 1960 when the Oregon Short Line Railroad sold ten acres of their old right-of-way through Pocatello to the Church of Jesus Christ of Latter-day Saints. The Indians argued that according to the act of 1901 the land should have reverted back to the tribes if not needed by the railroad. To ensure legality, those interested in the transaction had a bill enacted into law which held that under the act of June 6, 1900, the tribes had ceded their interests in the land for $600,000 and had no further claim on it. Attorney Ben W. Davis wrote, "You will observe that the Tribal rights were completely disregarded and ignored and the proposition of telling us that we can sue in the Court of Claims . . . is of very little benefit to the Tribe. There was simply too many votes on the other side for us to get any consideration." The Indians are still quite bitter today about the loss of the land and feel they should have received the compensation, not the Oregon Short Line Railroad.[105]

Those involved in the transactions and legislation described above were, of course, far removed from conditions at Fort Hall and had never had the experience of *Pocatello Tribune* reporter, Sam Hansen, who wrote of his visit in 1949 to the Bannock Creek area of the reservation:

I saw family after family living in single room log cabins. The average measurement was about 10 by 10 feet. Some had plain board floors. Others were dirt. Some had no chairs. Some had no beds or chairs. One cabin had no chairs or tables. The single article of furniture, except for the stove, was an old, rickety bed.

1936

1943

1970

1962

1968

1960

1949

I saw one family eating its evening meal. Four or five plates were spread on the floor. They ate with their hands. There was no silverware. The menu was a thin soup or broth made from joint bones of some small animal, some kind of a flat, sour-dough bread, and greens made from wild onions. . . .

They can't farm their sagebrush lands. . . . No horses. No tractors. No money to be saved. No loans. Nothing. Just rabbits and squirrels and wild onion. A deer, a fish; a few dollars for groceries. That is all.[106]

With the conditions described by reporter Hansen as late as 1949 one can understand the determination of the Shoshoni and Bannock to "buy back" their reservation. Everything but the land seems to disappear and become lost. Only the land is always there. The Fort Hall bottoms and the upland areas remain to be maintained and tended for their children's sake. Perhaps even tribal customs and traditions can be preserved if only the land remains intact.

NOTES CHAPTER XVI
OUR LITTLE LAND

1. Laidlaw, *Federal Indian Land Policy and The Fort Hall Indians*, 1–4.
2. Josephy, *The Patriot Chiefs*, 155.
3. *C.I.A. Annual Report*, 1887, 150.
4. Tyler, *A History of Indian Policy*, 95–104.
5. Peter Gallagher to C.I.A., Dec. 2, 1886, U.S. National Archives, *Record Group No. 75.*
6. A. L. Cook to C.I.A., Sept. 1, 1884, ibid.
7. *C.I.A. Annual Report*, 1895, 143.
8. Ibid., *1901*, 1.
9. P. Gallagher to C.I.A., March 29, 1887, U.S. National Archives, *Record Group No. 75.*
10. Charles L. Davis to C.I.A., May 13, 1908, ibid.
11. Dixie, Lavatta, and Browning to C.I.A., Feb. 12, 1910, ibid.
12. *Pocatello Tribune*, March 12, 18, April 13, Aug. 6, Sept. 24, 1910.
13. Ibid., Oct. 22, 1910.
14. Ibid., Dec. 21, 1910.
15. "Report of hearing held April 26, 1912, regarding Fort Hall matters," U.S. National Archives, *Records of Office of Indian Affairs.*
16. "Allotments of Land, Fort Hall Indian Reservation, Idaho," U.S. Congress, 61st Cong., 3rd Sess., House, Report No. 2043, Vol. 2 (Wash., D.C., 1911), 1–2.
17. E. B. Merritt to Sec. of Interior, May 10, 1915, *Records, Bureau of Indian Affairs, Portland, Oregon.*
18. C. F. Hauke to L. Wesley Aschemeier, March 4, 1920, U.S. National Archives, *Record Group No. 75.*
19. "To All Superintendents from C.I.A., Aug. 14, 1922," ibid.
20. William Donner to C.I.A., June 20, 1925, *Fort Hall Agency Records.*
21. Senator William H. King to C.I.A., April 28, 1928, U.S. National Archives, *Record Group No. 75.*
22. "Claims of Certain Indian Tribes," U.S. Congress, 65th Cong., 2nd Sess., Senate, Hearings before Committee on Indian Affairs, Bills No. 3663, 3923, 3572; H. Representative 4910, "The Establishment of a Townsite on the Ft. Hall Reservation," Vol. 110, Part 4 (Wash., D.C., 1918), 38.
23. C.I.A. to Sec. of Interior, Sept. 21, 1922, *Records, Bureau of Indian Affairs, Portland, Oregon..*
24. Carl W. Beck to C.I.A., Feb. 20, 1948, *Fort Hall Agency Records.*
25. William Donner to C.I.A., Aug. 25, 1921, U.S. National Archives, *Record Group No. 75.*
26. Laidlaw, *Federal Indian Land Policy*, 21.
27. William Donner to C.I.A., Aug. 25, 1921, U.S. National Archives, *Record Group No. 75.*
28. F. M. Goodwin to Sec. of Interior, Sept. 28, 1921, ibid.
29. C.I.A. to Sec. of Interior, Feb. 26, 1923, ibid.
30. Samuel Blair to C.I.A., May 12, 1925, ibid.; Samuel Blair to C.I.A., May 8, 1925, ibid.; see Ch. XI, notes 23–29.
31. C.I.A. to Addison T. Smith, Dec. 5, 1925, ibid.
32. "Survey of Conditions of the Indians in the United States," U.S. Congress, 72nd Cong., 1st Sess., Senate, Hearings Before a Subcommittee, Part 27, Wyoming, Idaho and Utah, Sept. 12, 13 and 14, 1932 (Wash., D.C., 1934), 14642.
33. Ibid., 14642-14643.
34. Tyler, *A History of Indian Policy*, 125–129.
35. Minutes of Fort Hall Council Meeting, Jan. 30, 1931, *Fort Hall Agency Records.*
36. Minutes of Fort Hall Council Meeting, April 19, 1932, ibid.
37. Tyler, *A History of Indian Policy*, 126–133.
38. C.I.A. to F. A. Gross, Sept. 2, 1933, U.S. National Archives, *Record Group No. 75.*
39. F. A. Gross to C.I.A., May 9, 1935, ibid.
40. "Investigation of the Bureau of Indian Affairs," U.S. Congress, 82nd Cong., 2nd Sess., House, Report No. 2503, Dec. 15, 1952 (Wash., D.C., 1953), 594.
41. "Corporate Charter of the Shoshone-Bannock Tribes of the Fort Hall Reser-
vation, Idaho, Ratified April 17, 1937," U.S. Department of Interior, *Office of Indian Affairs*, (Wash., D.C., 1937), 1–6.
42. Minutes of Meeting of Ross Fork Organization, Jan. 29, 1939, *Fort Hall Agency Records.*
43. Louis Balsam to George P. LaVatta, March 24, 1941, ibid.
44. "Ordinance Revoking Part of Ordinance Covering Membership in the Shoshone-Bannock Tribes of the Fort Hall Indian Reservation, May 9, 1950," ibid.; C.I.A. to Willie George, Aug. 8, 1950, ibid.
45. "Ordinance Covering Membership in the Shoshone Bannock Tribes, Inc., of the Fort Hall Reservation, Nov. 10, 1952," ibid.
46. Fort Hall Business Council Enrollment Hearings, Dec. 3, 1970, ibid.
47. Minutes of Fort Hall Business Council, July 9, 1940, U.S. National Archives, *Record Group No. 75.*
48. Tyler, *A History of Indian Policy*, 161–168.
49. *Ged-za-dump*, August 1955, *Fort Hall Agency Records.*
50. "Report and Alert, July 6, 1953," ibid.
51. *Ged-za-dump*, Aug. 17, 1955, ibid.
52. Tyler, *A History of Indian Policy*, 169–181, 317.
53. "General Services Administration Report, Petitions of Shoshone-Bannock Tribes of the Fort Hall Reservation, May 17, 1967," *Indian Claims Commission Nos. 326-E and 326-F Amended.*
54. Peter Jim and Four Others to C.I.A., July 1, 1936, *Fort Hall Agency Records;* see Ch. VI, notes 115-124.
55. "Shoshone and Bannock Indians, Fort Hall Reservation, Idaho Jurisdictional Act," U.S. Congress, 75th Cong., 1st Sess., Senate, Report No. 1123, Vol. 2 (Wash., D.C., 1937), 1–4.
56. "Fort Hall Indians Jurisdictional Act," U.S. Congress, 75th Cong., 3rd Sess., House, Hearing Before the Sub-Committee, on House Report No. 6559 and Senate Report No. 2253, April 11, 1938 (Wash., D.C., 1938), 1–39.
57. F. A. Gross to Henry Dworshak, Dec. 12, 1939, U.S. National Archives, *Record Group No. 75; Plaintiffs Proposed Findings of Fact,* Shoshone Nation litigation before the Indian Claims Commission, 123–125.
58. "The Northwestern Bands of Shoshone Indians, Opinion of the Supreme Court of the United States, March 12, 1945," U.S. Congress, 79th Cong., 1st Sess., House, Doc. No. 135 (Wash., D.C., 1945), 1–19.
59. Minutes of Annual Tribal Meetings, May 15, 1947, *Fort Hall Agency Records.*
60. Robert W. Barker to Edward Boyer, Dec. 5, 1953, ibid.; Roger C. Coonrod to Edward Boyer, Dec. 24, 1963, ibid. At this point the cases were broken up into four separate claims. The first decision finding that the claim was in the possession of the four groups was handed down October 16, 1962 and is reported in 11 Ind. Cl. Comm. 387. The compromise settlement for the "Shoshone Tribe" was approved by Order of February 13, 1968 and is reported in 19 Ind. Cl. Comm. 3. The Lemhi five-million-acre claim was decided March 8, 1971 in 24 Ind. Cl. Comm. 482. The Western Shoshone claim and the Gosiute claim were each separately valued. The Western Shoshone value was determined on October 11, 1972, 29 Ind. Cl. Comm. 5, but the case is still pending. Gosiute value was determined on August 9, 1973, 31 Ind. Cl. Comm. 225, affirmed by the Court of Claims, March 1975, 202 Ct. Cl. 401. A final award based upon settlement was entered in 1975, 37 Ind. Cl. Comm. 41.
61. "Indian Claims Commission, Dockets No. 326-D-G, 326-H, 366, 367, Shoshone-Bannock Tribes, Fort Hall, Idaho *et al.*, Nov. 9, 1967," (Wash., D.C.),1–159; files of Wilkinson, Cragun & Barker, Wash. D.C.
62. "Indian Claims Commission — Lemhi Tribe, represented by Shoshone-Bannock Tribe, Fort Hall, Docket No. 326-I, March 3, 1971," (Wash., D.C.), 2–14.
63. "Indian Claims Commission, Opinions, Findings of Fact, Orders," Vol. 26, Library of Wilkinson, Cragun & Barker, Wash., D.C., 1–90.
64. "Providing for the Disposition of Funds to Pay a Judgment in Favor of the Shoshone-Bannock Tribes of Indians of the Fort Hall Reservation, Idaho as Representatives of the Lemhi Tribe, in Indian Claims Commission Docket Numbered 326-I, and For Other Purposes," U.S.Congress, 92nd Cong., 2nd Sess., Senate, Calendar No. 947, Report No. 92-10000, July 27, 1972 (Wash., D.C.), 1–6; "Providing for the Apportionment of Funds in Payment of a Judgment in Favor of the Shoshone Tribe in Consolidated Dockets Numbered 326-D, 326-E, 326-F, 326-G, 326-H, 366, and 367 Before the Indian Claims Commission, and For Other Purposes," U.S. Congress, 92nd Cong., 1st Sess., Senate, Calendar No. 392, Report No. 92-393, Oct. 11, 1971 (Wash., D.C.), 1–41; "Providing for Disposition of Portion of Funds to Pay Judgment in Favor of Shoshone-Bannock Tribes of Indians of Fort Hall, Idaho; The Shoshone Tribe of Indians of Wind River Reservation, Wyo.; The Bannock Tribe and the Shoshone Nation or Tribe of Indians in Indian Claims Commission Dockets Nos. 326-D, 326-E, 326-F, 326-G, 326-H, 366 and 367, Consolidated," U.S. Congress, 92nd Cong., 1st Sess., Senate, Calendar No. 139, Report No. 92-143, June 4, 1971 (Wash., D.C.), 1–10; the special award of $500,000 was for claims arising from the negligent or wrongful use of $99,320.80 of irrigation funds, for additional compensation for the cession of 1889 and 1898, and for the failure to provide a reservation for the Bannock as promised in the Treaty of 1868; see Ch. VI, note 124.
65. F. A. Gross to C.I.A., Jan. 10, 1933, *Fort Hall Agency Records;* F. A. Gross to C.I.A., Feb. 10, 1933, U.S. National Archives, *Record Group No. 75.*
66. F. A. Gross to C.I.A., Nov. 17, 1937, ibid.; Fred A. Baker to J. M. Stewart, Nov. 22, 1937, *Fort Hall Agency Records;* Maurice T. Price to Georges M. Weber, May 5, 1938, U.S. National Archives, *Records of Office of Indian Affairs.*
67. *Pocatello Tribune*, April 12, 1949.
68. J. E. White, "Social and Economic Information for the Shoshone-Bannock Tribes, Sept. 24, 1937," U.S. National Archives, *Record Group No. 65.*
69. J. M. Stewart to E. M. Johnston, June 9, 1936, *Fort Hall Agency Records.*
70. C.I.A. to F. A. Gross, Feb. 4, 1937, ibid.
71. C.I.A. to F. A. Gross, Oct. 25, 1937, U.S. National Archives, *Record Group No. 75.*
72. Fred A. Baker to James M. Stewart, Sept. 6, 1938, ibid.
73. "Investigate Indian Affairs," U.S. Congress, 78th Cong., 1st Sess., House, Res. 166, Hearings before the Committee on Indian Affairs, March 23, 1943 (Wash., D.C., 1943), 1098–1100.

74. "Resolution of Fort Hall Business Council of Shoshone-Bannock Tribes, July 12, 1949," *Fort Hall Agency Records.*
75. Minutes of Fort Hall Business Council, May 25, October 13, 1949, ibid.
76. "Revised Resolution No. 95 of the Fort Hall Business Council of the Shoshone-Bannock Tribes, April 10, 1951," ibid.
77. Earl Woolridge to E. Morgan Pryse, Sept. 10, 1952, ibid.
78. "Joseph Thorpe, Jr., Report and Alert, July 6, 1953," ibid.; "Petition to President Dwight D. Eisenhower, Aug. 5, 1953," ibid.
79. *Ged-za-dump,* Aug. 17, 1955, ibid.
80. "Fort Hall Reservation, Idaho," U.S. Congress, 85th Cong., 1st Sess., House, Hearings Before a Subcommittee, Serial No. 18, Oct. 15 and 16, 1957 (Wash., D.C., 1957), 5, 6, 9, 10, 12.
81. "Indian Land Transactions, Dec. 31, 1957," *Fort Hall Agency Records.*
82. Zimmerman, *The Fort Hall Story,* 11–12; "Indian Heirship Land Survey, April 30, 1959," *Fort Hall Agency Records.*
83. Zimmerman, *The Fort Hall Story,* 13.
84. "Petition to the Secretary of the Interior and Commissioner of Indian Affairs, March 10, 1959," *Fort Hall Agency Records.*
85. "Indian Heirship Land Survey, June 24, 1959," ibid.
86. Laidlaw, *Federal Indian Land Policy,* 37–38.
87. Minutes of Fort Hall Business Council, Dec. 8, 1964, *Fort Hall Agency Records.*
88. Minutes of Fort Hall Business Council, July 11, 1972, ibid.
89. "Sho-Ban Annual Report, 1974-1975," ibid.
90. Ibid.
91. F. A. Gross to C.I.A. Jan. 2, 1936, ibid.
92. Geraint Humpherys to C.I.A., May 19, 1943, ibid.
93. C.I.A. to Geraint Humpherys, June 29, 1943, ibid.; Geraint Humpherys to C.I.A., Aug. 26, 1943, ibid.
94. Geraint Humphreys to E. C. Fortier, Oct. 5, 1943, ibid.
95. Evelyn F. Broodhead to Peru Farver, Oct. 27, 1954, ibid.
96. C.I.A. To Senator Frank Church, Aug. 1, 1968, ibid.
97. L. P. Towle to C. C. Thornhill, Aug. 9, 1949, ibid.
98. Shoshone-Bannock Tribes to Wayne N. Aspinall, March 5, 1962 and other letters, March 14, Sept. 7, Sept. 27, 1962, ibid.
99. Minutes of Fort Hall Council Meeting, April 19, 1932, ibid.
100. Edward Boyer to C.I.A., Nov. 8, 1963, ibid.; C.I.A. to Legislative Council, Dec. 9, 1963, ibid.
101. John Vaninetti to W. A. Mehojah, Sr., June 20, 1968, ibid.
102. C.I.A. to Senator Frank Church, Aug. 1, 1968, ibid.
103. C.I.A. to Legislative Council, Dec. 9, 1963, ibid.
104. Frances L. Horn, Memorandum for File, Jan. 13, 1970, Offices of Wilkinson, Cragun and Barker, Washington, D.C.
105. Minutes of Fort Hall Business Council, March 26, 1960, *Fort Hall Agency Records;* Roger Ernst to Wayne N. Aspinall, May 9, 1960, U.S. Congress 86th Cong., 2nd Sess., House, Report No. 2172, Aug. 26, 1960 (Wash., D.C., 1960), 3–4; B. W. Davis to Lucille Hincy, Sept. 12, 1960, *Fort Hall Agency Records.*
106. *Pocatello Tribune,* April 21, 1949

CONCLUSION

The four different groups of Northern Shoshoni who, with the Bannock finally located on the Fort Hall Reservation originally inhabited a wide and diverse region, from the sagebrush deserts of southwestern Idaho to the mountain heights and rocky gorges of the Salmon, Wasatch, Yellowstone Park, and Teton ranges, and beyond to the buffalo plains of Montana and Wyoming. Except for the Lemhi to the north, their homeland lay astride the Oregon, California, and Salt Lake-Montana trails, with Fort Hall being the fulcrum. To the west, the Boise and Bruneau bands watched the white pioneers push through and then settle the river valleys which gave these Indians their name. To the south, in Utah, the Northwestern Shoshoni very early found themselves being evicted from their traditional hunting grounds by aggressive Mormon farmers. And at the confluences of the Blackfoot and Portneuf rivers with Snake River, the Fort Hall Shoshoni and Bannock were soon under harassment from the wagon trains of emigrants moving to the Pacific Coast and later to western Montana.

This accident of geography, combined with the historical vagary of an artificial boundary along the forty-second parallel, also placed the Fort Hall Indians under the tutelage of government officials far away in the Willamette Valley of Oregon and at Puget Sound in Washington, while the officials at nearby Salt Lake City could only wonder with the Northern Shoshoni at the senseless whimsicality which barred any supervision or aid from the much closer City of the Saints. The creation of Idaho Territory in 1863 shortened the distance between native and government official but still placed the latter in Boise, many a long horseback ride or wagon trip from Fort Hall. Not until the establishment of the reservation in 1869 did the Northern Shoshoni have frequent communication and direction from agents of the Indian Service.

Despite the lack of government supervision and the encroachment of emigrant and settler, the Fort Hall Indians remained surprisingly friendly. Only in 1863, when Mormon farmers and Montana miners drove the desperate Northwestern bands to resist at the Massacre of Bear River, and in 1878, when starvation on the reservation and destruction of the camas beds on the Big Prairie precipitated the Bannock War, did the Indians at Fort Hall express their fears and frustrations in hostility.

Government neglect and indifference were probably best demonstrated by the inattention to formulating proper treaties and agreements with the various bands. The Treaty of Box Elder with the Northwestern Shoshoni in 1863 was not honored; the Treaty of Soda Springs with the Fort Hall Shoshoni and Bannock, negotiated the same year, was not ratified because of an unimportant technicality; the treaties of 1864 and 1866 with the Boise and Bruneau bands were ignored as inconsequential; and, in a final demonstration of absurdity, the Treaty of Fort Bridger of 1868, which became the basis for the relationship between the government and the Fort Hall Indians, was predominantly directed to the Eastern Shoshoni under Chief Washakie and originally had little to do with the Fort Hall Shoshoni and Bannock. The Bannock were merely bystanders who gained a vague promise about receiving a reservation somewhere else. Only when the Union Pacific Railroad wanted two rights-of-way through the reservation and later, when the residents of Pocatello wished to free themselves from their isolation in the midst of an Indian reserve, did the well-oiled governmental machinery begin to function smoothly and turn out approved agreements. The abortive Agreement of 1873, which was aimed at helping the Indians curtail trespass on their reservation, was ignored and unratified.

Similarly, once the related Shoshoni groups of southern Idaho and northern Utah were deposited on the barren Snake River sage plains at Fort Hall, the various agents encountered only indifference and apathy in Washington in their efforts to make a decent home for their wards. Especially was this true during the difficult first decade of forced abandonment of traditional hunting and food-gathering activities and the trying adjustment to white men's ways. Insufficient rations and annuities (with resultant starving and freezing times), the lack of farming implements and instructions in agricultural methods, the absence of help to construct an essential irrigation system, the failure to provide a school, the apathy of the Methodist Episcopal Church toward its missionary responsibility at Fort Hall, and the paucity of medical services all contributed to the anger and frustration culminating in the Bannock outbreak near the end of the 1870s. The only segment of reservation life which seemed to be well-supported and adequately financed was the military post on Lincoln Creek.

The twenty-year period from 1880 until the end of the century saw a gradual increase in the supervision and interest which Washington officials directed toward Fort Hall, although the records do not indicate any sustained or energetic effort to improve the lot of the Shoshoni and Bannock. Most of the Northwestern Shoshoni reluctantly gave up their homelands in northern Utah and drifted to Fort Hall because there was no other place to go. Much of each agent's time during this period was concerned with white complaints about wandering Indians from Fort Hall engaged in their age-old habits of root digging and hunting. The United States Supreme Court decision in the Race Horse case raised questions about hunting on the unoccupied lands of the United States. However, in a more recent case [State v. Tinno, 486 P. 2d 1386 (1972)], the Idaho Supreme Court has held that the legal rationale in the Race Horse decision is no longer valid, and thus, hunting rights on the unoccupied lands still remain in effect.

By 1900 the attention of the Shoshoni and Bannock was engaged in cattle raising, expanded farming operations, a developing irrigation system, more attention to the development of mineral resources, and forced acculturation supported by more rigorous schooling and an incipient though small missionary activity. The proximity of Idaho's second largest city, Pocatello, to the reservation influenced developments in all these areas, particularly policies of law and order. As the Indians struggled to improve their lot, covetous white neighbors continually trespassed in search of fish and game and, of more importance, attempted to gain land rights on the reservation.

With the allotment of lands in severalty prior to World War I, the way was opened for whites to buy or lease Indian lands. The history of the Shoshoni and Bannock since that time has increasingly been the story of their attempts to curtail white encroachment on Fort Hall lands. The fragmentation of property ownership, as many heirs divided titles to reservation farms, tended to encourage sales to white owners, and the Indians were slowly losing control of the "little land" remaining from the once rather large reserve.

The Indian Reorganization Act of the 1930s helped start a reversal of this trend, and the adoption of a constitution and bylaws by the tribes in 1936 gave the Indians a legal mechanism to begin to determine their own fate. Gradually the old concept of communal ownership of land began to reassert itself. A land-purchase program was instituted and has gained momentum until today it has become the basic feature of reservation life. A successful claim for proper compensation for aboriginal lands returned several million dollars to the tribes in 1971, part of which was used to further the land-purchase program. A more recent move has been to establish land-use procedures and regulations, placing the Shoshoni and Bannock in an even stronger position to control the operation of their lands.

Today the population at Fort Hall is increasing, an effective business council directs the economic and social development of the reservation, and the rich lava soil of their Snake River homeland is beginning to reward them with productive farms. The Shoshoni and Bannock again are beginning to direct their own affairs and to regain the cultural identity and proud heritage which once made them the independent hunters and warriors who ruled the Snake River Plains.

APPENDIXES

APPENDIX A

SIGNIFICANT DATES IN THE HISTORY OF
THE NORTHERN SHOSHONI

Oct. 23, 1811 — Wilson Price Hunt records first journey of white men through Snake River area.

1818 — First "Snake Expedition" led by Donald McKenzie of British North West Company into Northern Shoshoni area.

1824-1829 — Peter Skene Ogden leads "Snake Expedition" through Shoshoni area.

1824-1840 — American Mountain Men trap eastern sections of Northern Shoshoni territory.

1832 — Nathaniel J. Wyeth travels through Snake River area.

1833 — Captain Benjamin L. E. Bonneville visits Snake River area.

1834 — Nathaniel J. Wyeth builds Fort Hall.

1836 — Missionary Henry H. Spalding traverses Snake River area.

1838 — Hudson's Bay Company occupies Fort Hall.

1840-1869 — Several thousand emigrants travel across Oregon Trail through Northern Shoshoni homeland.

July 24, 1847 — First Mormon pioneers arrive at Great Salt Lake.

March 3, 1849 — Oregon Territory established and assumes control of Northern Shoshoni.

May 24, 1852 — Brigham Young, Utah Supt. of Indian Affairs, meets with Fort Hall Shoshoni.

1853 — Brigham Young meets with Bannock delegation.

June 12, 1855 — Mormon missionaries found Fort Lemhi on branch of Salmon River.

March 1858 — Shoshoni-Bannock hostility forces abandonment of Fort Lemhi.

July 20, 1859 — F. W. Lander distributes presents to Chief Mopeah's band of Bannock near Salt River, Wyoming.

April 1, 1861 — Utah Supt. gives presents to Chief Bear Hunter of Northwestern Shoshoni.

May 1861 — Washington Territory assumes charge of Northern Shoshoni.

Jan. 29, 1863 — Massacre of Bear River; 300-400 Northwestern Shoshoni killed by troops under Gen. Patrick E. Connor.

March 3, 1863 — Idaho Territory organized, with a Supt. of Indian Affairs at Boise.

July 2, 1863 — Treaty with Chief Washakie's Eastern Shoshoni at Fort Bridger.

July 30, 1863 — Treaty of Box Elder with Northwestern Shoshoni.

Oct. 14, 1863 — Treaty of Soda Springs with mixed bands of Bannock and Shoshoni.

Oct. 10, 1864 — Treaty of Fort Boise with Boise Shoshoni.

Sept. 22, 1865 — Sec. of Interior issues order to C.I.A. to provide reservation for "Great Kammas Indians."

April 12, 1866 — Treaty of Bruneau River with Bruneau Shoshoni.

June 14, 1867 — Pres. Executive Order establishes Fort Hall Indian Reservation.

Aug. 21, 1867 — Gov. D. W. Ballard agreement with Chief Tahgee of Bannock to move tribe to a reservation by June 1, 1868.

July 3, 1868 — Treaty of Fort Bridger with Eastern Shoshoni and Bannock.

Feb. 24, 1869 — Treaty of Fort Bridger signed by the President.

April 1869 — Fort Hall Reservation opened by Agent J. W. Powell.

June 12, 1869 — Col. De Lancey Floyd-Jones becomes Idaho Supt. of Indian Affairs.

July 30, 1869 — Pres. Executive Order assigns Bannock to Fort Hall Reservation.

July 30 1869 — William H. Danilson becomes agent at Fort Hall.

April 1870 — Fort Hall military post established on Lincoln Creek.

Dec. 20, 1870 — Agent Johnson N. High replaces W. H. Danilson.

Winter 1871 — Agent Montgomery P. Berry replaces J. N. High.

Dec. 25, 1871 — Agent Johnson N. High replaces M. P. Berry.

Jan.-Dec. 11, 1871 — Special Agent George W. Dodge assigned to Northwestern Shoshoni.

Jan. 7, 1873 — Agent Henry W. Reed replaces J. N. High.

April 1873 — George W. Hill appointed as Mormon missionary to Northwestern Shoshoni.

May-Nov. 1873 — J. W. Powell and G. W. Ingalls report on Northwestern Shoshoni.

Nov. 7, 1873 — Unratified agreement with the Shoshones and Bannocks.

Oct. 24, 1874 — Agent James Wright replaces H. W. Reed.

Sept. 9, 1874 — First day school started with twenty pupils.

July 1, 1875 — Agent W. H. Danilson replaces James Wright.

Aug.-Sept. 1875 — "War Scare" at Corinne, Utah, results in abandonment of Northwestern Shoshoni farm on lower Bear River.

1876 — George W. Hill establishes new Indian farm near Bear River crossing for Northwestern Shoshoni.

March 28, 1876 — First day school closed due to lack of funds.

June 13, 1877 — Nez Perce War begins.

Aug.-Sept. 1877 — Fifty Bannock scouts enlisted to fight Nez Perce.

Aug. 8, 1877 — Two white teamsters shot by Bannock warrior at Fort Hall.

Aug. 1877 — Company of infantry sent to Fort Hall from Camp Douglas, Utah.

Nov. 1877 — Bannock warrior, Tambiago, kills white man, Alex Rhoden.

Dec. 1877 — Additional 100 soldiers sent to Fort Hall.

Jan. 1878 — Three companies of cavalry sent to Fort Hall to disarm Bannock.

April 1878 — Troops returned to Camp Douglas from Fort Hall.

May 30, 1878 — Bannock War begins at Camas Prairie.

June 1878 — Utah and Northern Railroad reaches Arimo Station on reservation.

Sept. 1878 — Judgment against Union Pacific for cutting timber on reservation.

Oct. 23, 1878 — Shoshone-Bannock agree to cede right-of-way to UNRR for 500 cattle.

Jan. 8, 1879 — Second day school opens with eight pupils.

Sept. 3, 1879 — Agent John A. Wright replaces W. H. Danilson.

May-Oct. 1879 — Sheepeater War in Salmon River area.

Feb. 1880 — First boarding school opens with three students.

April 15, 1880 — Mormon Church purchases 1,700-acre farm at Washakie, Utah, for Northwestern Shoshoni.

May 14, 1880 — Agreement with Shoshone-Bannock to cede southern portion of reservation and to accept Lemhi if they agree to move.

May 21, 1881 — Agent E. A. Stone replaces John A. Wright.

July 8, 1881 — Shoshone-Bannock agree to cede right-of-way to Oregon Short Line Railroad.

Nov. 14, 1881 — Shoshone-Bannock ratify agreement of May 14, 1880.

Early 1882 — Agent A. L. Cook replaces E. A. Stone.

1882 — Indian police force of eight men organized at Fort Hall.

July 1883 — Fort Hall military post closed.

Fall 1883 — Industrial boarding school opened in abandoned buildings of Fort Hall military post on Lincoln Creek.

May 1886 — Union Pacific Railroad requests additional 1,600 acres at Pocatello.

May 24, 1886 — Agent Peter Gallagher replaces A. L. Cook.

May 27, 1887 — Shoshone-Bannock agree to sell 1,840 acres at Pocatello to Union Pacific Railroad.

July 1887 — Amelia J. Frost of Connecticut Indian Association opens mission at Fort Hall.

1888 — Tribal police court established.

Sept. 1, 1888 — President approves Agreement of May 27, 1887.

1889 — Foote irrigation survey of Fort Hall Reservation.

Feb. 23, 1889 — Congress approves Agreement of May 14, 1880 ceding southern portion of reservation.

July 29, 1889 — Agent Stanton G. Fisher replaces Peter Gallagher.

1889-1891 — Ghost-Dance religion active at Fort Hall.

July 1, 1893 — Agent J. T. Van Orsdale replaces S. G. Fisher.

April 11, 1895 — Agent Thomas B. Teter replaces J. T. Van Orsdale.

July 17, 1895 — Nine Bannock arrested for killing game in Jackson Hole, Wyoming.

Nov. 21, 1895 — Test case of Race Horse tried before Judge Riner of Wyoming.

Jan. 25, 1896 — Idaho Canal Company contract approved to construct canal on reservation.

May 25, 1896 — U.S. Supreme Court denies right of Bannock to hunt on unoccupied lands of U.S.

Spring 1897 — Agent F. G. Irwin replaces T. B. Teter.

June 28, 1897 — War Scare occurs at Camas Prairie.

Sept. 1897 — Tentative agreement by Shoshone-Bannock to cede 150,000 acres around and south of Pocatello for $600,000.

Feb. 1898 — Shoshone-Bannock agree to cede 418,500 acres of reservation around and south of Pocatello for $600,000.

March 29, 1898 — Idaho Canal Company goes into hands of a receiver.

June 7, 1898 — Agent C. A. Warner replaces F. G. Irwin.

Sept. 1898 — Rocky Mountain Bell Telephone Co. runs line through reservation.

Winter 1899 — Agent E. B. Reynolds replaces C. A. Warner.

1900 — Methodist Church and Presbyterian Church open missions at Fort Hall.

1900 — James H. Brady takes control of Idaho Canal Company.

March 5, 1900 — Agent A. F. Caldwell replaces E. B. Reynolds.

June 6, 1900 — Congress ratifies Pocatello Cession Agreement.

May 7, 1902 — Pres. T. Roosevelt signs proclamation opening ceded portion of reservation.

June 17, 1902 — "Day of the Run" as ceded lands opened for sale.

July 17, 1902 — Five-mile-limit lands opened for sale.

Aug. 1902 — First hospital built on reservation.

Fall 1904 — New school built on reservation at cost of $75,000.

1907 — Government purchases Gray's Lake water for Fort Hall Project.

March 1, 1907 — Congress establishes Fort Hall Irrigation Project.

April 9, 1907 — Government acquires water of Bannock Creek for Shoshone-Bannock.

1908 — Government purchases Idaho Canal Company from James H. Brady.

April 4, 1910 — Act of Congress sets fee of $6 per acre for water rights for whites.

Oct. 1, 1910 — Agent E. W. Estep replaces A. F. Caldwell.

Mar. 3, 1911 — Congressional act provides for allotment of land in severalty at Fort Hall.

1912 — Yellowstone Highway across reservation made a hard-surface road.

March 17, 1913 — Allotments of land in severalty closed at Fort Hall.

Spring 1914 — Agent C. L. Ellis replaces E. W. Estep.

Oct. 28, 1914 — Total of 1,863 allotments approved at Fort Hall.

March 4, 1921 — Act to establish Minidoka Project and construction of American Falls Reservoir.

1922 — Organization of Fort Hall Indian Stockmen's Association.

1922 — Act establishing town of Fort Hall, Idaho.

May 24, 1922 — Act to rehabilitate Fort Hall Project at cost of $760,000.

May 9, 1924 — Act to purchase bottomlands of reservation for American Falls reservoir at price of $700,000.

April 1, 1925 — Native American Church organized at Fort Hall.

1928 — Bannock Creek Stockmen's Association organized.

March 23, 1928 — House Committee on Indian Affairs recommends Court of Claims be granted jurisdiction on claim of compensation for aboriginal lands of Northwestern Shoshoni.

1930 — Organization of Fort Hall Business Council.

Feb. 4, 1931 — Act to develop 30,000 acres of irrigated farmland at Michaud Flats.

April 18, 1932 — Announcement to Shoshone-Bannock that thirty-eight lots in Pocatello are still owned by the tribes.

1934 — Hearings held at Ogden, Salt Lake City, and Pocatello on land claims of Northwestern Shoshoni.

1934 — Shoshone-Bannock adopt a constitution and bylaws.

June 18, 1934 — Indian Reorganization Act.

May 15, 1936 — Moyle, Wilkinson, Suydam & Harlan law firm contract to represent Shoshone-Bannock in land claims case.

June 1936 — Shoshone-Bannock petition Commissioner of Indian Affairs to file claim for "Portneuf Valley and Camas Prairie."

April 17, 1937 — Corporate charter of Shoshone-Bannock Tribes ratified by Indians of Fort Hall.

Sept. 27, 1938 — Shoshone-Bannock adopt a Law and Order Ordinance.

Fall 1938 — Boarding school closed and day schools opened at Ross Fork, Lincoln Creek, and Bannock Creek.

Jan. 1939 — Moroni Timbimboo of Washakie, Utah, ordained as first Indian bishop in L.D.S. Church.

Dec. 29, 1939 — Northwestern Shoshoni file 'Request for Findings of Fact and Brief' in land claims case.

1944 — Ross Fork and Lincoln Creek day schools closed and students placed in public schools of counties.

March 12, 1945 — U.S. Supreme Court ruled (five to four) that Treaty of Box Elder did not acknowledge land occupancy right of Northwestern Shoshoni.

1947 — Contract with Simplot Fertilizer Company to mine phosphates at Gay Mine on reservation.

1947 — Shoshone-Bannock at Fort Hall placed in group 3 of termination program.

Jan. 22, 1947 — New contract with law firm of Wilkinson *et. al.* to pursue land claims case under new Indian Claims Commission.

April 18, 1947 — Commissioner of Indian Affairs approves Land Purchase and Adjustment Enterprise of Shoshone-Bannock.

1960 — Contract with Food Machinery & Chemcial Corporation to mine phosphates on reservation.

Jan. 1966 — Washakie Mormon Indian Ward "discontinued."

Jan. 30, 1971 — Council of Shoshoni-Bannock tribes approves judgment of $4,500,000 to Lemhi.

1971-1972 — Shoshone-Bannock receive $8,864,000 as settlement of claims for aboriginal lands, plus special award of $500,000.

April 26, 1975 — Land-use ordinance adopted by Shoshone-Bannock for Fort Hall Reservation lands.

APPENDIX B

LIST OF AGENTS AT FORT HALL — 1869-1914

Chas. F. Powell (Special) .... April 18, 1867
Lt. William H. Danilson (Special) .... June 11, 1869
Johnson N. High (Special) .... November 8, 1870
Montgomery P. Berry (Special) .... March 25, 1871
Johnson N. High (Special) .... December 25, 1871
Henry W. Reed .... November 15, 1872
James Wright .... October 24, 1874
W. H. Danilson .... May 21, 1875
John A. Wright .... September 3, 1870
James M. Haworth .... October 9, 1870
John A. Wright .... January 19, 1880
E. A. Stone .... May 21, 1881

A. L. Cook .... Early 1882
Peter Gallagher .... May 24, 1886
Stanton G. Fisher .... July 29, 1889
J. T. Van Orsdale .... June 23, 1893
T. B. Teter .... April 11, 1895
F. G. Irwin .... Spring 1897
C. A. Warner .... June 7, 1899
E. B. Reynolds (Special) .... Winter, 1899
A. F. Caldwell .... March 5, 1900
E. W. Estep .... October 1, 1910
C. L. Ellis (Special) .... Spring 1914

APPENDIX C

TREATY WITH THE EASTERN BAND SHOSHONI AND BANNOCK, JULY 3, 1868

Articles of a treaty made and concluded at Fort Bridger, Utah Territory, on the third day of July, in the year of our Lord one thousand eight hundred and sixty-eight, by and between the undersigned commissioners on the part of the United States, and the undersigned chiefs and head-men of and representing the Shoshonee (eastern band) and Bannack tribes of Indians, they being duly authorized to act in the premises:

Article 1. From this day forward peace between the parties to this treaty shall forever continue. The Government of the United States desires peace, and its honor is hereby pledged to keep it. The Indians desire peace, and they hereby pledge their honor to maintain it.

If bad men among the whites, or among other people subject to the authority of the United States, shall commit any wrong upon the person or property of the Indians, the United States will, upon proof made to the agent and forwarded to the Commissioner of Indian Affairs, at Washington City, proceed at once to cause the offender to be arrested and punished according to the laws of the United States, and also re-imburse the injured person for the loss sustained.

If bad men among the Indians shall commit a wrong or depredation upon the person or property of any one, white, black, or Indian, subject to the authority of the United States, and at peace therewith, the Indians herein named solemnly agree that they will, on proof made to their agent and notice by him, deliver up the wrong-doer to the United States, to be tried and punished according to the laws; and in case they wilfully refuse so to do, the person injured shall be re-imbursed

for his loss from the annuities or other moneys due or to become due to them under this or other treaties made with the United States. And the President, on advising with the Commissioner of Indian Affairs, shall prescribe such rules and regulations for ascertaining damages under the provisions of this article as in his judgment may be proper. But no such damages shall be adjusted and paid until thoroughly examined and passed upon by the Commissioner of Indian Affairs, and no one sustaining loss while violating or because of his violating the provisions of this treaty or the laws of the United States, shall be reimbursed therefor.

Article 2. It is agreed that whenever the Bannacks desire a reservation to be set apart for their use, or whenever the President of the United States shall deem it advisable for them to be put upon a reservation, he shall cause a suitable one to be selected for them in their present country, which shall embrace reasonable portions of the "Port Neuf" and "Kansas Prarie" countries, and that, when the reservation is declared, the United States will secure to the Bannacks the same rights and privileges therein, and make the same and like expenditures therein for their benefit, except the agency-house and residence of agent, in proportion to their numbers, as herein provided from the Shoshonee reservation. The United States further agrees that the following district of country, to wit: Commencing at the mouth of Owl Creek and running due south to the crest of the divide between the Sweetwater and Papo Agie Rivers; thence along the crest of said divide and the summit of Wind River Mountains to the longitude of North

Fork of Wind River; thence due north to mouth of said North Fork and up its channel to a point twenty miles above its mouth; thence in a straight line to head-waters of Owl Creek and along middle of channel of Owl Creek to place of beginning, shall be and the same is set apart for the absolute and undisturbed use and occupation of the Shoshonee Indians herein named, and for such other friendly tribes or individual Indians as from time to time they may be willing, with the consent of the United States, to admit amongst them; and the United States now solemnly agrees that no person except those herein designated and authorized to do so, and except such officers, agents, and employees of the Government in discharge of duties enjoined by law, shall ever be permitted to pass over, settle upon, or reside in the territory described in this article for the use of said Indians, and henceforth they will and do hereby relinquish all title, claims, or rights in and to any portion of the territory of the United States, except such as is embraced within the limits aforesaid.

Article 3. The United States agrees, at its own proper expense, to construct at a suitable point of the Shoshonee reservation a warehouse or storeroom for the use of the agent in storing goods belonging to the Indians, to cost not exceeding two thousand dollars; an agency building for the residence for the physician, to cost not more than two thousand dollars; and five other buildings, for a carpenter, farmer, blacksmith, miller, and engineer, each to cost not exceeding two thousand dollars; also a school-house or mission building so soon as a sufficient number of children can be induced by the agent to attend school, which shall not cost exceeding twenty-five hundred dollars.

Article 4. The Indians herein named agree, when the agency house and other buildings shall be constructed on their reservations named, they will make said reservations their permanent home, and they will make no permanent settlement elsewhere; but they shall have the right to hunt on the unoccupied lands of the United States so long as game may be found thereon, and so long as peace subsists among the whites and Indians on the borders of the hunting districts.

Article 5. The United States agrees that the agent for said Indians shall in the future make his home at the agency building on the Shoshonee reservation, but shall direct and supervise affairs on the Bannack reservation; and shall keep an office open at all times for the purpose of prompt and diligent inquiry into such matters of complaint by and against the Indians as may be presented for investigation under the provisions of their treaty stipulations, as also for the faithful discharge of other duties enjoined by law. In all cases of depredation on person or property he shall cause the evidence to be taken in writing and forwarded, together with his finding, to the Commissioner of Indian Affairs, whose decision shall be binding on the parties to this treaty.

Article 6. If any individual belonging to said tribes of Indians, or legally incorporated with them, being the head of a family, shall desire to commence farming, he shall have the privilege to select, in the presence and with the assistance of the agent then in charge, a tract of land within the reservation of his tribe, not exceeding three hundred and twenty acres in extent, which tract so selected, certified, and recorded in the "land-book," as herein directed, shall cease to be held in common, but the same may be occupied and held in the exclusive possession of the person selecting it, and of his family, so long as he or they may continue to cultivate it.

Any person over eighteen years of age, not being the head of a family, may in like manner select and cause to be certified to him or her, for purposes of cultivation, a quantity of land not exceeding eighty acres in extent, and thereupon be entitled to the exclusive possession of the same as above described. For each tract of land so selected a certificate, containing a description thereof, and the name of the person selecting it,

with a certificate indorsed thereon that the same has been recorded, shall be delivered to the party entitled to it by the agent, after the same shall have been recorded by him in a book to be kept in his office subject to inspection, which said book shall be known as the "Shoshone (eastern band) and Bannack land-book."

The President may at any time order a survey of these reservations, and when so surveyed Congress shall provide for protecting the rights of the Indian settlers in these improvements, and may fix the character of the title held by each. The United States may pass such laws on the subject of alienation and descent of property as between Indians, and on all subjects connected with the government of the Indians on said reservations, and the internal police thereof, as may be thought proper.

Article 7. In order to insure the civilization of the tribes entering into this treaty, the necessity of education is admitted, especially of such of them as are or may be settled on said agricultural reservations, and they therefore pledge themselves to compel their children, male and female, between the ages of six and sixteen years, to attend school; and it is hereby made the duty of the agent for said Indians to see that this stipulation is strictly complied with; and the United States agrees that for every thirty children between said ages who can be induced or compelled to attend school, a house shall be provided and a teacher competent to teach the elementary branches of an English education shall be furnished, who will reside among said Indians and faithfully discharge his or her duties as a teacher. The provisions of this article to continue for twenty years.

Article 8. When the head of a family or lodge shall have selected lands and received his certificate as above directed and the agent shall be satisfied that he intends in good faith to commence cultivating the soil for a living, he shall be entitled to receive seeds and agricultural implements for the first year, in value one hundred dollars and for each succeeding year he shall continue to farm, for a period of three years more, he shall be entitled to receive seeds and implements as aforesaid in value twenty-five dollars per annum.

And it is further stipulated that such persons as commence farming shall receive instructions from the farmers herein provided for, and whenever more than one hundred persons on either reservations shall enter upon the cultivation of the soil, a second blacksmith shall be provided, with such iron, steel, and other material or other annuities provided.

Article 9. In lieu of all sums of money or other annuities provided to be paid to the Indians herein named, under any and all treaties heretofore made with them, the United States agrees to deliver at the agency house on the reservation herein provided for, on the first day of September of each year, for thirty years, the following articles, to wit:

For each male person over fourteen years of age, a suit of good substantial woollen clothing, consisting of coat, hat, pantaloons, flannel shirt, and a pair of woollen socks; for each female over twelve years of age, a flannel skirt, or the goods necessary to make it, a pair of woollen hose, twelve yards of calico; and twelve yards of cotton domestics.

For the boys and girls under the ages named, such flannel and cotton goods as may be needed to make each a suit as aforesaid, together with a pair of woollen hose for each.

And in order that the Commissioner of Indian Affairs may be able to estimate properly for the articles herein named, it shall be the duty of the agent each year to forward to him a full and exact census of the Indians, on which the estimate from year to year can be based; and in addition to the clothing herein named, the sum of ten dollars shall be annually appropriated for each Indian roaming and twenty dollars for each Indian engaged in agriculture, for a period of ten years, to be used by the Secretary of the Interior in the purchase of such articles as from time to time the condition and necessities of the Indians may indicate to be proper. And if at any time within the ten years it shall appear that the amount of money needed for clothing under this article can be appropriated to better uses for the tribes herein named, Congress may by law change the appropriation to other purposes; but in no event shall the amount of this appropriation be withdrawn or discontinued for the period named. And the President shall annually detail an officer of the Army to be present and attest the delivery of all the goods herein named to the Indians, and he shall inspect and report on the quantity and quality of the goods and the manner of their delivery.

Article 10. The United States hereby agrees to furnish annually to the Indians the physician, teachers, carpenter, miller, engineer, farmer, and blacksmith, as herein contemplated, and that such appropriations shall be made from time to time, on the estimates of the Secretary of the Interior, as will be sufficient to employ such persons.

Article 11. No treaty for the cession of any portion of the reservations herein described which may be held in common shall be of any force or validity as against the said Indians, unless executed and signed by at least a majority of all the adult male Indians ocupying or interested in the same; and no cession by the tribe shall be understood or construed in such manner as to deprive without his consent, any individual member of the tribe of his right to any tract of land selected by him, as provided in Article 6 of this survey.

Article 12. It is agreed that the sum of five hundred dollars annually, for three years from the date when they commence to cultivate a farm, shall be expended in presents to the ten persons of said tribe who, in the judgment of the agent, may grow the most valuable crops for the respective year.

Article 13. It is further agreed that until such time as the agency-buildings are established on the Shoshonee reservation, their agent shall reside at Fort Bridger, U.T., and their annuities shall be delivered to them at the same place in June of each year.

N. G. Taylor, [seal]
W. T. Sherman,
   Lieutenant-General, [seal]
Wm. S. Harney, [seal]
John B. Sanborn, [seal]
S. F. Tappan, [seal]
C. C. Augur,
   Brevet Major-General,
   U.S. Army,
   Commissioners. [seal]
Alfred H. Terry,
   Brigadier-General and
   Brevet Major-General,
   U.S. Army. [seal]

Attest:

  A. S. H. White, Secretary

    Shoshones:

Wash-a-kie,	his x mark.
Wau-ny-pitz,	his x mark.
Toop-se-po-wot,	his x mark.
Nar-kok,	his x mark.
Taboonshe-ya,	his x mark.
Bazeel,	his x mark.
Pan-to-she-ga,	his x mark.
Ninny-Bitse,	his x mark.

    Bannacks:

Taggee,	his x mark.
Tay-to-ba,	his x mark.
We-rat-se-won-a-gen,	his x mark.
Coo-sha-gan,	his x mark.
Pan-sook-a-motse,	his x mark.
A-wite-etse,	his x mark.

Witnesses:

  Henry A. Morrow, Lieutenant-Colonel Thirty-sixth Infantry and Brevet Colonel U.S. Army, Commanding Fort Bridger,
  Luther Manpa, United States Indian Agent,
  W. A. Carter,
  J. Van Allen Carter, Interpreter.

APPENDIX D

Fort Hall	Acres Tillable	Acres Cultivated by Indians	Acres Cultivated by Government	Allotments — Families	Acres Fenced	Wheat — Bushels	Families Farming / Worked agency farm	Barley — Bushels	Oats — Bushels	Corn — Bushels	Vegetables — Bushels	Potatoes — Bushels	Turnips — Bushels	Onions — Bushels	Beans — Bushels	Hay — Tons	Horses	Cattle	Sheep	Swine	Goats	Mules	Domestic Fowl	Butter — Pounds Made	New Acres Broken	Acres in Pasture
1871		2	81			250		450				4,100	50			100	3	156								
1872		3	250			2,500		30	500			4,300	1,500	200		100	4	180							58	
1873	10,000	0	285			2,500		150	300			2,300	800			280	10	142							48	
1874	3,000	28	292			3,100	32		650		240	1,800	500			300	1,200	6		61		2			20	
1875		42	235		30	285	5		20		210	210				200				100						100,000
1876	5,000	120	100			1,000	25		—75—		3,034	500/				160	3,000	21		1						
1877	10,000	240	35			600	70		—100—		4,500	2,500				25	2,500	50								
1878	10,000	400	17			6,000	125		—100—		5,060	4,500	50			20	3,500	50		20					50	
1879	10,000	530	20	150		6,200		45			9,385	5,000	500	10		50	3,800	100		20					130	
1880	10,000	460	14	150		5,750		1,025	260		3,500	8,100				180	2,400	600	4	6					46	1,300,000
1881	10,000	496	22			3,816			—3,380—		3,120	2,430				600	3,228	821				2	100		100	
1882	10,000	609	20		960	4,725			—4,965—		3,519		1,000			900	3,180	800							123	
1883	10,000	686	24		1,400	4,200			—5,100—		4,000	5,000				800	2,950	590					300		105	
1884	10,000	593	33		1,400	3,000		650	8,000		7,500	6,000	2,000			1,000	2,800	580					500		210	
1885	7,000	873	33		2,000	5,600		400	16,000		8,300	10,950	2,000			1,200	2,400						500		240	
1886	9,000	798	40		2,000	17,390	161	450	4,500	900	13,313					700	4,500	500		40		2	450		110	
1887	9,000	1,007	40		3,200	8,523	380		7,395		9,790	5,634	600			2,100	5,000	1,000		50		2	450	400	341	
1888	325,000	1,100	30		4,500	4,500			—9,000—		2,000	1,490	400			2,500	6,000	1,000		45		2	350	500	275	
1889	325,000	1,070	30		4,500		100		—4,450—							1,800	6,140	400		50			400	100	110	
1890		500	10		1,000		125			125						3,000	3,000			40			200		50	
1891		600	10		1,500	9,000	130		—7,000—							2,000	3,000	450		20			250		100	
1892																										
1893		800			6,000	4,000			—9,100—	20	2,320					2,000	3,506	400		33			500	100	40	
1894		1,000			8,000	7,000			—7,000—	20	3,320					3,000	3,400	500	5	40			500	100	200	
1895		925			9,150	8,398			—10,680—	270	5,390					1,650	4,000	3,500	5	100			700	2,000	182	
1896		975			1,000	9,000			—12,000—		5,800					2,000	5,000	4,000	2	125		2	800	2,200	50	
1897		1,527			7,500	7,000			—9,000—	200	5,150					3,250	7,012	3,000		80		2	1,000	2,000	275	
1898		1,800			8,200	7,800			—10,040—		8,200					3,400	7,003	3,500		100			1,000	1,000	180	
1899		1,822			9,500	7,550			—5,475—	125	4,920					3,250	7,003	2,300		50			60	700	172	
1900		2,050			10,250	7,000			—5,000—	200	4,265					3,500	7,503	2,350		25			450	200	110	
1901		2,400			11,000	8,000			—4,000—	250	4,980					5,000	5,003	2,600					675	300	175	
1902		2,500		33	11,500	7,000			—3,000—	100	3,125					4,000	4,000	3,800		20			700	200	100	
1903		2,950		33	12,700	4,000			—3,300—	50	3,775					6,000	6,120	4,300					1,000	800	450	
1904		3,000		33		4,500			—3,500—	65	3,500					8,000	6,000	4,500					1,215	450	50	
1905		3,250																		50				100	250	
1906																								250		

BIBLIOGRAPHY

Manuscripts

Berkeley, California. Bancroft Library. Utah Early Records MSS.

Boise, Idaho. Idaho State Historical Society. MSS.

Daughters of Utah Pioneers. Testimony of Daniel B. Richards Taken from Hill Family Record.

Fort Hall, Idaho. Fort Hall Letter Book, Copies of Letters Sent, 1869-1875.

Helena, Montana. Montana State Historical Society. *George Crook, Letters, 1875-1888, No. 4.*

Pocatello, Idaho. Idaho State University Archives. MSS 106 to 468.

Portland, Oregon. Area Office of Bureau of Indian Affairs. Fort Hall Allotment Schedule 14A, Original Book of Names and Areas.

Salt Lake City, Utah. Colin H. Sweeten, "Washakie," 1973 (unpublished article in author's files).

Salt Lake City, Utah. L.D.S. Department of History. Brigham Young, Indian Affairs, Indian Correspondence.

Salt Lake City, Utah. L.D.S. Department of History. Brigham Young, Indian Affairs, J. H. Holeman Correspondence.

Salt Lake City, Utah. L.D.S. Department of History. Brigham Young, Indian Affairs, Miscellaneous Correspondence.

Salt Lake City, Utah. L.D.S. Department of History. Brigham Young, Indian Affairs, Stephen B. Rose Correspondence.

Salt Lake City, Utah. L.D.S. Department of History. Brigham Young, Indian Affairs, Miscellaneous Licenses, Permits, etc.

Salt Lake City, Utah. L.D.S. Department of History. Brigham Young Manuscript History.

Salt Lake City, Utah. L.D.S. Department of History. Brigham Young, Utah Superintendency Files (field records), Misc. 1862-3-4.

Salt Lake City, Utah. L.D.S. Department of History. Journal History.

Salt Lake City, Utah. University of Utah. Gilmer & Salisbury, Letterbook, April 6, 1881-May 5, 1882.

Salt Lake City, Utah. Utah State Historical Society. Military Records. MSS.

Virginia City, Montana. (Fairweather Hotel). *Letter Book.* Charles Bovey Papers.

Washington, D.C. Indian Claims Commission, Opinions, Findings of Fact, Orders. Library of Law Office of Wilkinson, Cragun & Barker, Vol. 26.

Washington, D.C. Memorandum for File, Jan. 13, May 26, 1970, by Frances L. Horn. Law Office of Wilkinson, Cragun & Barker.

U.S. Government Documents

Annual Reports of the Commissioner of Indian Affairs.

Commissioner of Indian Affairs. *Letter Books.* Vol. 70. U.S. National Archives.

U.S. Congress. House. *Allotments of Land, Fort Hall Indian Reservation, Idaho.* Report No. 2043, Vol. 2, 61st Cong., 3rd Sess., 1911.

U.S. Congress. House. *Bannock and Other Indians in Southern Idaho.* Ex. Doc. No. 129, Vol. 10, Serial No. 1608, 43d Cong., 1st Sess., 1874.

U.S. Congress. Boise. *C.I.A. to Sec. of Interior, Feb. 23, 1888.*

Report No. 2754, Serial No. 2605, 50th Cong., 1st Sess., 1888.

U.S. Congress. House. *Court of Claims to Hear Claim of Northwestern Band of Shoshoni Indians.* Report No. 1030, Vol. 2, Report No. 1579, Vol. 4, 70th Cong., 1st Sess., 1928.

U.S. Congress. House. *Fort Hall Indians Jurisdictional Act.* "Hearing Before the Subcommittee." House Report No. 6559, 75th Cong., 3d Sess., 1938.

U.S. Congress. House. *Fort Hall Reservation, Idaho.* "Hearings Before a Special Indian Subcommittee of the Committee on Interior and Insular Affairs." Held at Fort Hall, Idaho, Oct. 15 and 16, 1957. Serial No. 18, 85th Cong., 1st Sess., 1957.

U.S. Congress. House. *Indians of Skull Valley and Deep Creek, Utah.* Doc. No. 389, Vol. 139, 62d Cong., 2d Sess., 1912.

U.S. Congress. House. *Investigate Indian Affairs.* "Hearings Before the Committee on Indian Affairs, March 23, 1943." House Res. 166, 78th Cong., 1st Sess., 1943.

U.S. Congress. House. *Investigation of the Bureau of Indian Affairs.* Report No. 2503, Dec. 15, 1952, 82d Cong., 2d Sess., 1953.

U.S. Congress. House. *Minidoka Irrigation Project, Idaho, March 6, 1924.* "Hearing Before a Subcommittee of the Committee on Indian Affairs." Report No. 6864, Vol. 342, Part 1, March 6-13, 1924, 68th Cong., 1st Sess., 1924.

U.S. Congress. House. *Providing for the Apportionment of Funds in Payment of a Judgment in Favor of the Shoshoni Tribe in Consolidated Dockets Numbered 326-D, 326-E, 326-F, 326-G, 326-H, 366, and 367.* Report No. 92-701, 92d Cong., 1st Sess., Dec. 1, 1972.

U.S. Congress. House. *Ratification of Agreement with Indians of Fort Hall Reservation,* June 4, 1898. Report No. 1507, Vol. 6, 55th Cong., 2d Sess., 1898.

U.S. Congress. House. *Report of Brig. Gen. J. J. Coppinger, Aug. 28, 1895.* Doc. No. 2, Vol. 1, 54th Cong., 1st Sess., 1895.

U.S. Congress. House. *Report of Brig. Gen. J. J. Coppinger, Aug. 31, 1896.* Doc. No. 2, Vol. 1, 54th Cong., 2d Sess., 1896.

U.S. Congress. House. *Report of the Governor of Idaho.* Exec. Doc., Vol. 10, 46th Cong., 2d Sess., 1880.

U.S. Congress. House. *Report of the Secretary of the Interior on Pacific Wagon Roads.* Ex. Doc. 108, 35th Cong., 2d Sess., Serial No. 1008, 1859.

U.S. Congress. House. *Report of the Secretary of War.* Vol. I, Exec. Doc. 1, Part 2, 44th Cong., 2d Sess., Serial No. 1748, 1876.

U.S. Congress. House. *Second Deficiency Appropriation Bill,* "Hearing Before Subcommittee of House Committee on Appropriations." 68th Cong., 1st Sess., 1924.

U.S. Congress. House. *Sec. of Interior to President, Feb. 4, 1888.* Ex. Doc. No. 140, Serial No. 2558, 50th Cong., 1st Sess., 1889.

U.S. Congress. House. *Statement of Major J. W. Powell.* Misc. Doc. No. 86, 43rd Cong., 1st Sess., 1874.

U.S. Congress. House. *The Establishment of a Townsite at the Fort Hall Indian Reservation.* Bill No. 49010, Vol. 110, Part 4, 65th Cong., 2d Sess., 1918.

U.S. Congress. House. *The Northwestern Bands of Shoshone Indians, Opinion of the Supreme Court of the United States, March 12, 1945.* Doc. No. 135, 79th Cong., 1st Sess., 1945.

U.S. Congress. Senate. *Agreement with Crow, Flathead, and Other*

Indians, etc., March 3, 1898. Misc. Doc. No. 169, Vol. 11, 55th Cong., 2d Sess., 1899.

U.S. Congress. Senate. *Ceded Lands on Fort Hall Indian Reservation.* Report No. 2213, Vol. 1, 57th Cong., 2d Sess., 1903.

U.S. Congress. Senate. *Claims of Certain Indian Tribes.* "Hearings Before Committee on Indian Affairs." Bills No. 3663, 3923, 3572, 65th Cong., 2d Sess., 1918.

U.S. Congress. Senate. *Fort Hall Indians Jurisdictional Act.* "Hearing Before the Subcommittee." Report No. 2253, 75th Cong., 3d Sess., 1938.

U.S. Congress. Senate. *Message from President of U.S.* Ex. Doc., 48th Cong., 1st Sess., 1884.

U.S. Congress. Senate. *Military and Indian Affairs in Oregon.* Ex. Doc. I, No. IV, no. 11, 32d Cong., 1st Sess., Serial No. 611, 1851.

U.S. Congress. Senate. *Providing for the Apportionment of Funds in Payment of a Judgment in Favor of the Shoshone Tribe in Consolidated Dockets Numbered 326-D, 326-E, 326-F, 326-G, 326-H, 366 and 367 Before the Indian Claims Commission, and For Other Purposes.* Calendar No. 392, Report No. 92-393, Oct. 11, 1971, 92d Cong., 1st Sess., 1971.

U.S. Congress. Senate. *Providing for the Disposition of Portion of Funds to Pay Judgment in Favor of Shoshone-Bannock Tribes of Indians of Fort Hall, Idaho: The Shoshone Tribe of Indians of Wind River Reservation, Wyo.: The Bannock Tribe and the Shoshone Nation or Tribe of Indians in Indian Claims Commission Dockets Nos. 326-D, 326-E, 326-F, 326-G, 326-H, 366 and 367, Consolidated.* Calendar No. 139, Report No. 92-143, June 4, 1971, 92d Cong., 1st Sess., 1971.

U.S. Congress. Senate. *Providing for the Disposition of Funds to Pay a Judgment in Favor of the Shoshone-Bannock Tribes of Indians of the Fort Hall Reservation, Idaho, as Representatives of the Lemhi Tribe, in Indian Claims Commission Docket Numbered 326-I and For Other Purposes.* Calendar No. 947, Report No. 92-1000, July 27, 1972, 92d Cong., 2d Sess., 1972.

U.S. Congress. Senate. *Shoshone and Bannock Indians, Fort Hall Reservation, Idaho, Jurisdictional Act.* Report No. 1123, Vol. 2, 75th Cong., 1st Sess., 1937.

U.S. Congress. Senate. *Survey of conditions of the Indians in the United States.* "Hearing Before a Subcommittee of the Committee on Indian Affairs." Pursuant to Senate Resolution 79 and Senate Resolution 308, Part 6, 71st Cong., 2d Sess., January 21, 1930.

U.S. Congress. Senate. *Survey of Conditions of the Indians in the United States.* Part 27, Wyoming, Idaho and Utah, Sept. 12, 13, 14, 1932, 72d Cong., 1st Sess., 1934.

U.S. Congress. Senate. *Utah and Northern Railroad.* Ex. Doc. No. 20, Vol. 1, Serial No. 2333, 49th Cong., 1st Sess., 1886.

U.S. Court of Claims. *The Northwestern Band or Tribe of Shoshoni Indians and the Individual Members Thereof v. The United States, Plaintiff, Indians' Request for Findings of Fact, and Brief, No. M-107.* Filed December 29, 1939. Batavia, N.Y.: 1939.

U.S. Department of Interior. Bureau of Indian Affairs. *Corporate Charter of the Shoshone-Bannock Tribes of the Fort Hall Reservation, Idaho, Ratified, April 17, 1937.*

U.S. Department of Interior. Bureau of Indian Affairs. *Fort Hall Agency Records.* Fort Hall, Idaho: 1921-1975.

U.S. Department of Interior. Bureau of Indian Affairs. *Planning Project for Michaud Unit of Fort Hall Project, Dec. 1955,* by Paul F. Henderson. Portland, Oregon: 1955.

U.S. Department of Interior. Bureau of Indian Affairs. *Records, Portland, Oregon, Area Office.*

U.S. Department of Interior. Bureau of the Census. *Report on Indians Taxed and Indians Not Taxed in the United States, Eleventh Census: 1890.* Washington, D.C.: Government Printing Office, 1894.

U.S. Department of Interior. Interior Department Territorial Papers. *Idaho: 1864-90. M191.* U.S. National Archives: Microfilm Rolls, 1 to 3.

U.S. Department of Interior. *Letters Received, Utah, 1868.* U.S. National Archives.

U.S. Department of Interior. Records of the Bureau of Indian Affairs. Record Group 75. *Indian Census Rolls, 1888-1940. M595: Fort Hall (Shoshoni and Bannock Indians).* U.S. National Archives: Microfilm Rolls, 138 to 144.

U.S. Department of Interior. Records of the Bureau of Indian Affairs. Record Group 75. *Letters Received. 1824-1881. M234: Idaho Superintendency, 1863-80.* U.S. National Archives, Microfilm Rolls 337 to 353.

U.S. Department of Interior. Records of the Bureau of Indian Affairs. Record Group 75. *Letters Received. 1824-1881. M234: Idaho Superintendency, 1864-1875.* U.S. National Archives, Microfilm Rolls 488 to 501.

U.S. Department of Interior. Records of the Bureau of Indian Affairs. Record Group 75. *Letters Received. 1824-1881. M234: Oregon Superintendency, 1842-1859.* U.S. National Archives: Microfilm Rolls 607 to 611.

U.S. Department of Interior. Records of the Bureau of Indian Affairs. Record Group 75. *Letters Received. 1824-1881. M234: Utah Superintendency, 1849-1880.* U.S. National Archives: Microfilm Rolls 897 to 906.

U.S. Department of Interior. Records of the Bureau of Indian Affairs. Record Group 75. *Letters Received. 1824-1881. M234: Washington Superintendency, 1853-1864.* U.S. National Archives: Microfilm Rolls 907 to 908.

U.S. Department of Interior. Records of the Bureau of Indian Affairs. Record Group 75. *Letters Received. 1824-1881. M234: Wyoming Superintendency, 1869-1877.* U.S. National Archives: Microfilm Rolls 953 to 1955.

U.S. Department of Interior. Records of the Bureau of Indian Affairs. Record Group 75. *Records of the Superintendencies and Agencies of the Office of Indian Affairs, Idaho, M832.* U.S. National Archives: Microfilm Rolls 1 to 3.

U.S. Department of Interior. Records of the Bureau of Indian Affairs. Record Group 75. *Records of the Superintendencies and Agencies of the Office of Indian Affairs, Montana. M833.* U.S. National Archives: Microfilm Roll 2.

U.S. Department of Interior. U.S. Geological Survey. *Geography, Geology, and Mineral Resources of the Fort Hall Indian Reservation, Idaho,* by G. R. Mansfield. U.S.G.S. Bulletin 713. Washington, D.C.: Government Printing Office, 1920.

U.S. Government Records. *The War of the Rebellion; A Compilation of the Official Records of the Union and Confederate Armies.* Series I, Vol. L, Part I. Washington, D.C., 1897.

U.S. Indian Claims Commission. *Dockets No. 326-D-G, 326-H, 366, 367.* Washington, D.C., Nov. 9, 1967.

U.S. Indian Claims Commission. *Dockets No. 326-D-G, 326-H, 366, and 367, Shoshone Bannock Tribes, Fort Hall, Idaho et al., Nov. 9, 1967.*

U.S. Indian Claims Commission. *Idaho Superintendency, Field Papers.* Exhibit No. 214, Docket No. 326, 366, 367.

U.S. Indian Claims Commission. *Lemhi Tribe, Represented by Shoshone-Bannock Tribe, Fort Hall, Docket No. 326-I, March 3, 1971.*

U.S. National Archives. Bureau of Indian Affairs. *Case No. 72.*

U.S. National Archives. Bureau of Indian Affairs. *Case No. 99.*

U.S. National Archives. Bureau of Indian Affairs. *Idaho, Letters Received.*

U.S. National Archives. Bureau of Indian Affairs. *Idaho Superintendency, Field Papers.*

U.S. National Archives. Bureau of Indian Affairs. *Irregular-sized Papers.*

U.S. National Archives. Bureau of Indian Affairs. *Nevada, Letters Received.*

U.S. National Archives. Bureau of Indian Affairs. *Record Group No. 75.*

U.S. National Archives. *Records, Office of Indian Affairs.*

U.S. National Archives. Bureau of Indian Affairs. *Utah, Letters Received.*

U.S. National Archives. Record Group 393. U.S. Army Continental Commands. *Post Records, Fort Hall, Idaho.*

U.S. National Archives. *Map Collection.*

United States Statutes at Large.

State and Local Government Documents

Utah. *Brigham Young, Message to the Legislative Assembly of the Territory of Utah, Fillmore City, Utah Terr., Dec. 11, 1855.* Utah State Historical Society,

Idaho. Bureau of Land Management, Boise. *Field Notes of the Survey of the Exterior Boundaries of Ft. Hall Indian Reservation in the Territory of Idaho,* by John B. David, April, 1873.

Idaho. *Reports of Cases Argued and Determined in the Supreme Court of Territory of Idaho* (Bancroft-Whitney Company, 1903).

Books and Pamphlets

Beal, Merrill D. *Intermountain Railroads: Standard and Narrow Gauge.* Caldwell, Idaho: The Caxton Printers, Ltd., 1962.

Beal, Merrill D., and Wells, Merle W. *History of Idaho.* New York: Lewis Historical Publishing Company, Inc., 1959.

Brimlow, George F. *The Bannock Indian War of 1878.* Caldwell, Idaho: The Caxton Printers, Ltd., 1938.

Codman, John. *The Round Trip: By Way of Panama, Through California, Oregon, Nevada, Utah, Idaho, and Colorado.* New York: G. P. Putman's Sons, 1879.

Daughter of Utah Pioneers. Box Elder County Chapter. *History of Box Elder County.*

Elliott, Wallace W. & Co. *History of Idaho Territory.* San Francisco: Wallace W. Elliott & Co., 1884.

Frederick, James V. *Ben Holladay, The Stagecoach King.* Glendale, California: Arthur H. Clark Co., 1950.

Fuller, George W. *A History of the Pacific Northwest.* New York: Alfred A. Knopf, 1938.

Hasbrouck, Sol. *Reports of Cases Argued and Determined in the Supreme Court of Territory of Idaho.* San Francisco: Bancroft-Whitney Co., 1903.

Heggie, Andrew. *Story of the Shoshoni Indians in Clarkston.* Daughters of Utah Pioneers.

Hull, William. *Autobiography.* Daughters of the Utah Pioneers.

Hultkrantz, Ake. *The Shoshones in the Rocky Mountain Area.* New York: Garland Publishing, Inc., 1974.

Irving, Washington. *The Adventures of Captain Bonneville, U.S.A., in the Rocky Mountains and the Far West.* New York: G. P. Putman's Sons, 1898.

Josephy, Alvin M., Jr. *The Patriot Chiefs.* New York: The Viking Press, 1961.

Kappler, Charles J. *Indian Affairs, Laws and Treaties.* Washington, D.C.: Vol. II, 1904.

Laidlaw, Sally Jean. *Federal Indian Land Policy and the Fort Hall Indians.* Pocatello, Idaho: Occasional Papers of the Idaho State College Museum, Number 3, 1960.

Liljeblad, Sven. *The Idaho Indians in Transition, 1805-1960.* Pocatello, Idaho: Idaho State University Museum, 1972.

Lowie, Robert H. *The Northern Shoshoni.* Anthropological Papers, Vol. 2: American Museum of Natural History, 1909.

Madsen, Brigham D. *The Bannock of Idaho.* Caldwell, Idaho: The Caxton Printers, Ltd., 1958.

Mooney, James. *The Ghost-Dance Religion and the Sioux Outbreak of 1890.* Fourteenth Annual Report of the Bureau of Ethnology, Part 2. Washington, D.C.: Government Printing Office, 1896. New edition: Glorieta, New Mexico: The Rio Grande Press, Inc.

Nybroten, Norman. *Economy and Conditions of the Fort Hall Indian Reservation.* Moscow, Idaho: University of Idaho, 1964.

Peterson, Jack G. *Futures: A Comprehensive Plan for the Shoshone-Bannock Tribes, Fort Hall Indian Reservation, June 28, 1974.* Fort Hall, Idaho: Fort Hall Agency Records.

Prickett, H. E. *Reports of Cases Argued and Determined in the Supreme Court of Idaho Territory, Jan. 1866 to Sept. 1880,* Vol. I. San Francisco: Bancroft Whitney Co., 1904.

Rogers, Fred B. *Soldiers of the Overland.* San Francisco: Grabhorn Press, 1938.

Stansbury, Howard. *Exploration and Survey of the Valley of the Great Salt Lake of Utah.* Lippincott, Grambo & Co., 1852.

Steward, Julian H. *Basin-Plateau Aboriginal Sociopolitical Groups.* Washington, D.C.: United States Government Printing Office, 1938.

Stewart, George R. *The California Trail.* New York: McGraw-Hill Book Company, Inc., 1962.

Tullidge, Edward W. *History of Salt Lake City,* Salt Lake City: The Author, 1886.

Tyler, S. Lyman. *A History of Indian Policy.* Washington, D.C.: Government Printing Office, 1973.

Walker, Deward E., Jr. *American Indians of Idaho.* Moscow, Idaho: University of Idaho, 1973.

Wells, Merle W. *Caleb Lyon's Bruneau Treaty, 12 April 1866.* Boise, Idaho: Idaho Historical Society, No. 369, August, 1968.

Williams, Glyndwr, ed. *Peter Skene Ogden's Snake Country Journals, 1827-28 and 1828-29.* London: The Hudson's Bay Record Society, 1971.

Union Pacific Railroad. *The Direct Route to Colo., Ida., Utah., Mont., Nev., and Calif.* Chicago: Horan & Leonard, 1868.

Zimmerman, William, Jr. *The Fort Hall Story: An Interpretation.* Philadelphia: Indian Rights Association, 1959.

Periodicals

Baker, Ray S. "The Day of the Run." *The Century Magazine,* Vol. LXVI (Sept. 1903): 644–646.

Dibble, Charles E. "The Mormon Mission to the Shoshoni Indians." *Utah Humanities Review* (July 1947): 284–287.

Henderson, W. W., ed. "Extracts from Journal of L. W. Shurtliff." *Utah Historical Quarterly,* V (January 1932): 517–530.

Liljeblad, Sven. "Some Observations on the Fort Hall Indian Reservation." *The Indian Historian,* Vol. 7, No. 4 (Fall 1974); 12.

Madsen, Brigham D. "Shoshoni-Bannock Marauders on the Oregon Trail, 1859-1863." *Utah Historical Quarterly,* Vol. 35, No. 1 (Winter 1967): 3–30.

Wells, Merle W. "Caleb Lyon's Indian Policy." *Pacific Northwest Quarterly,* (October 1970): 193–200.

Wells, Donald N., and Wells, Merle W. "The Oneida Toll Road Controversy, 1864-1880." *Oregon Historical Quarterly,* LVIII (June 1957): 113–116.

Theses and Dissertations

Barta, Edward J. "Battle Creek: The Battle of Bear River." M.A. thesis. Idaho State College, 1962.

Coates, Laurence G. "A History of Indian Education by the Mormons, 1830-1900." Ph.D. dissertation. Ball State University, 1969.

Fry, Ralph H. "An Investigation of the Relationships Between Descriptive Data About Trainees and Past Training Employment in an M.D.T.A. Project Held Between 1968-1970 at Fort Hall, Idaho." M.A. thesis, Idaho State University, 1973.

Grant, Louis Seymour. "Fort Hall on the Oregon Trail." M.A. thesis, University of British Columbia, 1938.

Newspapers

Blackfoot News, Idaho, Dec. 21, 1895.
Blackfoot Register, Idaho (1881-1884).
Corinne Mail, Utah (1874-1875).
Corinne Reporter, Utah (1870-1873).
Deseret News, Salt Lake City, Utah (1850-1974).
Ged-za-dump, Fort Hall, Idaho, August 1955.
Helena Herald, Montana (1870-1880).
Helena Independent, Montana, May 31, 1878.
Idaho Herald, Pocatello, Jan. 26, Feb. 9, 16, 1894, April 12, 1895, Jan. 1896.
Idaho Journal, Pocatello, April 12, 1896.
Idaho Statesman, Boise (1865-1900).
New Northwest, Deer Lodge, Montana (1874-1879).
Ogden Freeman, Utah, Aug. 30, Sept. 3, 1878.
Ogden Junction, Utah (1875-1878).
Ogden Standard-Examiner, Utah, June 28, 29, 30, July 1, 2, 1931.

Owyhee Avalanche, Idaho, Jan. 20, 1866.
Pocatello Advance, Idaho, June 27, 1895.
Pocatello Tribune, Idaho, (1893-1974).
Salt Lake Herald, Utah, July 3, 1870, March 14, 1883.
Salt Lake Tribune, Utah (1871-1931).
The Fort Hall News, Idaho, April 1963.

Union Vedette, Salt Lake City, Utah, March 15, 22, April 25, 1864.
Utah Reporter, Corinne (1869-1870).
Wood River News-Miner, Idaho, May 4, July 11, 1883.
Wood River Times, Idaho, Sept. 10, 1883.

INDEX

Bear Hunter, Chief, 33, 36, 239
Bear Lake, 25, 51, 223
Bear Lake Shoshoni, 26
Bear Lake Valley, 30, 33, 34, 48, 90, 99
Bear River, 24, 28, 34, 36, 49, 90, 92, 94, 95, 96, 97, 98, 99, 105, 107, 196, 239
Bear River City, Utah, 102
Bear River Crossing, 93, 98
Bear River High School, 102
Bear River Indians, 98
Bear River Massacre, see Battle of Bear River
Bear River Valley, 91, 92
Beaver Canyon (Idaho), 132
Beaver, Utah, 97
Beaverhead (Montana), 37
Beck, Carl W., 225
Bedell, E. A., 31
Bee-ah, See Mrs. Mary Wise Fisher
Beede, Cyrus, 130, 131, 146, 182, 183, 205
Belle Marsh Creek (Fort Hall Reservation), 173
Bennett, Governor Thomas, W., 67, 69, 70, 71, 72, 95, 107, 144
Benson, Ezra T., 36
Bering Strait, 17
Berry, Judge C. H., 116
Berry, Montgomery P., 64, 65, 66, 67, 68, 92, 93, 94, 144, 155, 172, 180, 195, 239, 241
Big Camas Prairie, see Camas Prairie
"Big Chief Spit-in-his-Mit," 192
Big Dipper, 21
Big Foot, 48
Big Hole River, 18
Big Joe, 114
Big Lost River, 133
Big Medicine Dance, 190
Bingham County, 156, 220
Birch Creek (Idaho), 17, 143
Bistline, F. M., 175
Biting Bear, Chief, 45
Bitterroot Culture, 17, 18
Bitterroot Valley, 33
Black Beard, Chief, 38
Blackfeet Indians, 18, 22, 24, 25, 26, 27, 43, 65, 128
Blackfoot Dam, 165
Blackfoot, Idaho, 121, 124, 125, 129, 130, 132, 138, 143, 147, 167, 172, 175, 177, 182, 184, 186, 192, 193, 211, 212, 213; legal problems with Indians, 215; discrimination, 217, 218; 221
Blackfoot Land Office, 124
Blackfoot Marsh, 162
Blackfoot News, 136, 147
Blackfoot Public School, 192, 193
Blackfoot Register, 111, 128, 129, 172
Blackfoot Reservoir, 162, 163, 165
Blackfoot River, 23, 49, 107, 109, 145, 155, 156, 157, 158, 159, 160, 163, 164, 165, 166, 169, 175, 177, 220, 237
Blackfoot School District, 208
Black Hawk, Chief, 107
Black Rock, Idaho, 109, 110, 211
Blair, Samuel, 207, 226
Bliss, Idaho, 138
Blue Mountains, 28, 29
Boise, Idaho, 40, 43, 46, 47, 48, 51, 52,

53, 55, 56, 58, 59, 60, 62, 63, 67; militia unit organized, 69; 72, 78; Indians visit, 79; council with Idaho Governor, 80; 109, 117, 133, 169, 172, 178, 192, 237, 239
Boise Jim, 60
"Boise Pets," see Boise Shoshoni
Boise River, 19, 23, 24, 37, 43, 45, 47, 48, 54, 60, 68, 69
Boise Shoshoni, 13, 19; Chief Peiem, 20; 23, 24, 25, 26; commit Ward Massacre, 28; 43, 45; in starving condition, 46; 47, 48, 51, 52; moved to Fort Hall, 53; 54, 55, 56; early attempts at farming, 59; 60, 64; Captain Jim, 80; 91; illness of, 205; land claims case, 230, 231, 237, 239
Boise Valley, 18, 19, 24, 44, 223
Bonneville, Captain B. L. E., 25, 239
Boonack, See Bannock Indians
Boone & Crockett Club (New York City), 133
Borah, Senator William E., 177, 219
Botany Bay, 87
Bourdon, Michel, 24
Boyd, Robert, 81
Box Elder County, Utah, 33, 37, 38, 40, 70, 91, 101, 104
Box Elder School District, 101, 102
Brady, James H., 161, 162, 163, 219, 240
Brayman, Governor Mason, 79, 80, 83, 84, 86, 87, 212
Bridges, Dr. G. M., 206, 207
Brigham City, Utah, 40, 90, 91, 92, 95, 96, 104, 105, 109, 171, 192
British, 216
Brady, John, 54
Brancho Jim, 81, 91
Browne, J. Ross, 29
Browning, D. M., 160
Browning, Jacob, 227
Bruneau Jim, 54, 91
Bruneau River, 45, 47, 48, 54, 69, 72, 239
Bruneau Shoshoni, 13, 19, 26, 45; in starving condition, 46; 47, 48, 51, 52; moved to Fort Hall, 53; 54, 55, 56; early attempts at farming, 59, 60; illness of, 205; land claims case, 230, 231; 237, 239
Bruneau Valley, 45, 46, 128, 130, 223
Brunow Shoshoni, see Bruneau Shoshoni
Buck, Norman, 171
Buffalo Horn, Chief, 80, 81, 83, 84, 88
Bulletin 713 of the United States Geological Survey, 74
Burnt Island, 215
Buterbaugh, George, 144
Butte, Montana, 134

— C —

Caleb of Dale, see Governor Caleb Lyon
California, 21, 23, 25, 27, 32, 35, 46, 49, 60, 69, 172
California Trail, 27, 33, 34, 35, 40, 49, 111, 237
California Volunteers, 35, 36, 37
Camas Prairie (Idaho), 19, 23, 47, 49,

51, 52, 53, 56; not part of Treaty of Fort Bridger, 58; 59, 60, 62; hogs destroying camas roots, 65; 66, 67, 68, 70, 71; Indians sent to hunt at, 75; 76, 79, 80, 82; shootings at, 83; outbreak of war, 84; 86; Indians withdraw from, 87; 88, 93, 107, 130, 138, 223; aboriginal land claims case, 230; 237, 239, 240, 241
Camas Prairie War, see Bannock War of 1878
Cameahwait, 20
Camp Bidwell (California), 60
Camp Brown (Wyoming), 62
Camp Connor (Idaho), 36, 44, 49
Camp Douglas, 36, 38, 81, 82, 83, 93, 239
Camp Floyd, (Utah), 35
Campbell, James S., 132, 133
Campbell & Walker Company, 132
Canada, 28, 216
Canby, General Edward, 65, 69
Captain Jack (Modoc), 69
Captain Jack (Shoshoni), 138
Captain Jim Collins, Shoshoni Chief, 64, 71, 79, 80, 85, 91, 110, 113, 115, 169, 205
Captain Joe, 113
Captain John, 91
Captain Sam, Chief, 130
Cariboo, Idaho, 134
Cariboo Mountains, 134
Carlin Farms, Nevada, 102
Carlisle Industrial School, 182, 186, 215
Carpenter's Stage Station, 144
Carr, Captain, C. C. C., 129
Carson Valley, 32
Cartee, La Fayette, 63, 107, 108
Carter, J. Van Allen, 243
Carter, M. A., 44
Carter, W. A., 243
Cascade Mountains, 29, 195
Cascades (Columbia River), 23
Cash [Cache] Valley Tom, 71
Catherine Creek (Idaho), 47, 55
Catholic Church, 64, 195, 196, 200, 201
Catholic Mission (Idaho), 69
Cayuse George, 211
Cayuse Indians, 23, 28
Central Pacific Railroad, 70, 90, 129
Challis, Idaho, 18
Chandler, James J., 99
Chesterfield, Idaho, 149
Cheyenne Indians, 23, 29, 32, 62, 65, 93, 198
Chicago, Illinois, 59, 160
Chicken, Jimmie, 225
Chickering, Charles A., 122
"Chief Work-the-Corners," 192
China Hat Dike, 165
Chinese, 53
Chinese Vermillion, 182
Church of Jesus Christ of Latter-day Saints, 234, 240
City Creek (Cache County, Utah), 40
City Rocks (Idaho), 34
Civil War, 35, 83, 139, 174
Clark, Barzilla, 163
Clark, Joseph A., 157
Clark's Cut, 165
Clark's Ferry, Snake River, 56
Clarkston, Utah, 40

Liljeblad, Dr. Sven, 14, 27
Lincoln Creek, 60, 145, 146, 155, 166, 183, 238, 239
Lincoln Creek Boarding School, 182, 183
Lincoln Creek Day School, 192, 240
Lincoln Creek Industrial School, 183, 184, 185, 186, 187, 240
Lincoln Creek Trail, 149
Lincoln Creek Voting District, 226
Little Camas Prairie, 49, 130
Little Indian Unit, 163, 166, 169
Little Lost River, 24
Little Soldier, Chief, 34, 35, 37
Little Wolf, 134
Locke, Hosea, 188
Logan, Thomas E., 79, 80
Logan, Utah, 93, 99
Long Tom Creek (Idaho), 52
Lord's Battle Axes, The, 96
Lost Horse Claim, 174
Lower Snakes, 24
Lynde, Major Isaac, 34
Lyon, Governor Caleb, 43, 44, 45, 46, 48, 49, 51, 56
Lyons, Reverend A. H., 136

— M —

MacDonald, Finan, 24
Mackenzie, Donald, 22, 24, 25
Maddox, Dr. W. R., 205
Major Bannock Jim, see Bannock Jim
Major George, Chief, 80, 130
Major Jim, see Bannock Jim
Malad City, Idaho, 51, 55, 69, 81, 82, 83, 143, 144, 146
Malad Divide, 143
Malad River, 45, 49, 96, 98
Malad River (Alturas County), 83
Malad River Shoshoni, 24
Malad Valley, 13, 30, 33, 34, 99
Malheur County, Oregon, 134
Malheur River, 69
Manasseh, 93
Mandan Indians, 23
Mann, Luther, Jr., 32, 35, 37, 46, 48, 49, 53
Manning, Constable William, 137, 138
Manpa, Luther, 243
Mansfield, G. R., 174, 175
Map No. 747, U. S. National Archives, 107
Marley, Gwenllian Mrs. 125
Marsh Creek, 107, 110, 111, 112, 113, 114, 116, 118, 125, 143, 211
Marsh Valley, 27, 38, 69, 82, 107, 109, 110, 112, 113, 116, 126, 144, 146, 171
Marshall, Major L. H., 45
Martin, Henry, 32, 35
Martin, Mary, 186
Marysvale, Wyoming, 136, 138
Masenia, Dr. J. M., 205
Mason, Walter, 55
Massacre of Bear River, see Battle of Bear River
Matigund, Chief, 37
Mathews, Peter O., 180, 181, 195
Maughan, Peter, 35, 92
Mayhugh, John S., 130
Medicine Men, 183, 184, 198, 206, 208

Merrill, John F., 171
Mesplie, Father Touissant, 64, 69, 180, 195
Messiah Craze, 185, 198
Messlin Brothers, 146
Methodist Episcopal Church, 64, 182, 193, 195, 196, 200, 201, 202, 209, 237, 240
Mexican Cession, 30, 37, 38
Michaud Flats, 156, 166, 167, 232, 233, 240
Michaud Project, 166, 167, 234
Michaud Trail, 149
Mighty Porcupine, 198
Miles, General Nelson A., 80
"Milk Pan Drill," 186
Miller, C. H., 29
Miller, Dr. M. A. 205, 206
Mills, F. J., 159
Minidoka Project, 167, 240
Missouri, 97
Missouri River, 18, 23, 26
Mitchell, Mr., 160
Mixed Bands of Bannock and Shoshoni, 230
Modiss, 149
Modoc Indians, 94
Modoc War, 69
Moe, Stephen, 129
Monnet, Doctor W. D., 129, 205
Montana Island, 215
Montana Mission of Methodist Episcopal Church, 196
Montana Plains, 68
Montana Stage Road, 80
Montana, State, 13, 14, 100, 132, 176
Montana Territory, 13, 19, 23, 27, 35, 36, 37, 38, 40, 43, 49, 59, 60; Bannock War, 84; 109, 112, 143, 144, 172, 174, 198, 206, 223, 237
Montana Trail, 27, 35, 49, 81, 111, 143, 145, 237
Montpelier Republic, 118
Montreal, Canada, 24
Mooney, James, 198
Moose, Dave, 128
Mopeah, 31, 239
Mopier, John, 214
Moore's Creek (Idaho), 44
Mormon Church, 13, 95, 96, 98, 99, 100, 101, 102, 104, 105, 204, 240
Mormon Elders, 99, 198
Mormon Indian Branch, 204
Mormons, 28, 29, 30, 31, 33, 34, 35, 36, 38, 40, 49, 90, 91, 92, 93, 94, 95, 96, 97, 98, 99, 100, 102, 105, 106, 112, 129, 143, 146, 182, 196, 198, 202, 209, 212, 237, 239, 241
Mormon Temple, Logan, Utah, 99
Morrow, Colonel Henry A., 93, 94, 243
Mountain Meadows Massacre, 97
Mountain Shoshoni, 20, 26
Mountain Snakes, also known as Sheepeaters, 19, 28, 29
Mower, Mr., 158, 159
Moyle, Wilkinson, Suydom & Harlan, 230, 240
Mt. Putnam, 150, 152, 175
Munn's Island, 215
Murphy, Frank, 159
Murphy, J. A., 159
Murphy, William, 143
Musselshell River, 19

McBeth, Ravenel, 136, 138
McCammon, Idaho, 107, 121, 124, 125, 143, 177
McCammon, Joseph K., 111
McCandless, E. S., 47
McConnell, Governor William J., 135, 139, 187
McCormick, Province, 137, 159, 160
McDermitt, Nevada, 104
McGuffey Readers, 180
McKenzie, Donald, 239
McNeil, John, 87

— N —

Nar-kok, 243
National Defense Program, 177
National Industrial Recovery Act, 104
Native American Church, 204, 209, 240
Nattini, Father E. W., 196
Navajo Indians, 30
Neaman, Jim John, 100
Nebraska, 218
Nelson, Mrs. Susan C. Garrett, 200, 201
Nesmith, James W., 28, 44
Nevada, 13, 17, 19, 23, 35, 37, 45, 70, 80, 93, 95, 102, 104, 129, 172, 218, 225, 231
Nevada Indians, 36
Nevada Shoshoni, 31, 130
New Mexico, 18, 23
New Northwest, 82
New York City, New York, 133
Nez Perce Indian Agency, 72, 195, 200
Nez Perce Indians, 19, 21, 22, 23, 24, 25, 27, 43, 79, 80, 81, 121, 195, 197, 200, 201, 223, 230, 239
Nez Perce War, 79, 80, 86, 87, 88, 196, 239
Nichols, Alvin, 95
Ninny-Betse, 243
Nixon, President Richard M., 228
North America, 17, 18
North Canal, 162
North Dakota, 23
Northern Bannock, see Lemhi
Northern Paiute Indians, 13, 19, 22, 23, 80, 84, 129, 198, 230, 231
Northern Shoshoni, 13, 14; archaeological evidence of early culture, 17; 18, 19, 20; Circle dance, 22; land occupation and golden age, 23; exposure to fur traders, 24; 25, 26, 27; grazing lands exploited, 28; Mormon instigations, 29; 30, 31, 32, 33, 34, 36; Treaty of Soda Springs, 37; 38, 40; Band along Payette River, 46; 47; reservation, 52; Treaty of Fort Bridger, 53; 54, 55, 56; assigned to Fort Hall Reservation, 58; 59; a starving time, 60; 61; budget problems at Fort Hall, 62; more hunting than farming, 64; 65; farming, 66; war scare on Camas Prairie, 67; 69; Agreement of 1873, 70; Agent Reed fired, 71; 72, 73, 75, 76; Nez Perce War, 79; visited by Nez Perce, 80; friendly during 1878 troubles, 81; alarmed by Bannock outbreak, 82; 83; importance of

United States Bureau of Reclamation, 166

United States Code, 218

United States Court of Claims, 102, 105

United States Department of the Interior, 98, 114, 118, 133, 145, 172, 173, 175, 176, 178, 228

United States Department of Justice, 137

United States District Attorney, 98, 171, 219

United States Eighty-Sixth Congress, 234

United States Forest Service, 148, 150, 152

United States Forty-First Congress, 60

United States General Land Office, 37, 51, 107, 123

United States Geological Survey, 160, 174, 175

United States House of Representatives, 44, 121, 122, 176

United States House of Representatives, Committee on Indian Affairs, 102, 104, 155, 232, 240

United States Justice Department, 116, 171

United States Marshal for Idaho, 128

United States National Archives, 14, 230

United States Post Office Department, 144

United States Secretary of the Interior, 40, 44, 51, 64, 70, 79, 86, 112, 113, 123, 144, 148, 156, 158, 159, 160, 162, 167, 171, 172, 185, 195, 205, 212, 219, 226, 239, 243

United States Secretary of War, 80, 212

United States Senate, 37, 38, 43, 45, 48, 79, 82, 121, 192

United States Senate Committee on Indian Affairs, 152, 164

United States Senate Judiciary Committee, 225

United States Supreme Court, 104, 137, 138, 140, 163, 213, 230, 238, 240

United States Tenth Circuit Court of Appeals, 104

United States Treasury Department, 114, 147

United States War Department, 60, 109, 130, 234

University of Idaho (Southern Branch), 234

University of Utah, 14

Unoccupied Lands of the United States, 120, 132, 134, 136, 137, 240

Utah and Northern Railroad, 27, 85, 94, 109, 111, 112, 114, 116, 143, 156, 171, 176, 177, 196, 211, 239, 240

Utah and Northern Railroad Company v. Willard Crawford, 110, 213

Utah and Northern Railway Company v. Fisher, 112, 213

Utah Central Railroad, 109

Utah Chief Justice, 36

Utah Indian Superintendency, 13, 14, 29, 30, 31, 32, 35, 36, 38, 40, 43, 46, 53, 55, 90, 91, 92, 93, 94, 97, 239

Utah Journal, 99

Utah Legislature, 30, 31

Utah Northern Railroad, see Utah and Northern Railroad

Utah Power and Light Company, 177

Utah Saints, see Mormons

Utah Shoshoni, 30, 92

Utah, State, 14, 17, 104, 105, 187, 225

Utah Supreme Court, 35

Utah Territory, 13, 23, 28, 30, 31, 32, 33, 34, 35, 36, 37, 40, 43, 48, 53; Gosiute Indians, 70; troops from Camp Douglas, 82; 90, 91; Shoshoni in, 92; 93, 95; Corinne Indian Scare, 96; 97; U.S. District Attorney, 98; 99, 143, 144; timber exploitation, 171; 196, 198, 211, 237, 238, 241, 243

Utah War, 30, 31, 34

Ute Indians, 22, 30, 32, 33, 35, 91, 104, 181

— V —

Van Orsdale, J. T., 118, 134, 158, 173, 185, 240, 241

Vaughan, Governor Vernon H., 90

Virginia, 36

Virginia City, Montana, 49, 53, 79

Virginia City, Nevada, 93

"Visions of the War," 186

Viven, Captain John L., 75

— W —

Wagner, Dr. C., 48

Walker & Willis Company, 146

Walker, Captain J. H., 44

Walker Lake, Nevada, 198

Walker River Indian Reservation, 198

Walla Walla Indians, 23

Wallace, Governor William H., 43, 48

Walters, James, 128

War Assets Administration, 234

Ward, George M., 100

Ward Massacre, 28

Ward, Moroni, 99, 100

Warner, C. A., 139, 177, 200, 214, 218, 240, 241

Warner, Dr. H. J., 208

Warren, Idaho, 69

Wasakee Reservation, see Wind River Reservation

Wasatch Mountains, 237

Washakie, Chief, 28, 30, 32, 33, 37, 38, 40, 46, 48, 51, 53, 55, 65, 99, 128, 237, 239, 243

Washakie Day School, 102

Washakie Indians (Utah), 13, 99, 100, 101, 102, 104

Washakie Indian Reservation (Utah), 103, 107

Washakie Indian Subagency, 105

Washakie Shoshoni (Utah), 104, 105

Washakie, Utah, 13, 14, 99, 100, 101, 104, 105, 230, 240

Washakie Ward (L.D.S.), 99, 101, 241

Washington, D.C., 29, 31, 35, 36, 43, 45, 47, 48, 51, 52, 54, 58, 59, 60, 64, 71, 72, 73, 75, 78, 79, 81, 84, 87, 88, 93, 94, 100, 101, 104, 105, 107, 109, 110, 111, 112, 113, 114, 118, 120, 121, 126, 129, 130, 132, 134, 136, 138, 140, 144, 145, 158, 172, 173, 174, 175, 177, 181, 182, 185, 188, 190, 205, 208, 209, 211, 212, 213, 219, 226, 228, 230, 237, 238, 241

Washington Indian Superintendency, 13, 28, 29, 31

Washington, State, 218

Washington Territory, 28, 29, 237, 239

Was-pitch, 99

Wastawana, 69

Wau-ny-pitz, 243

Weber Canyon, see Weber Valley

Weber Ute Indians, 37

Weber Valley, 30, 104

Weerahsoop, Chief, 37

Weiser River, 23, 48, 54, 55, 67, 69, 70, 72

Weiser Shoshoni, 55, 72, 78, 138, 230

Weiser Valley, 54, 80, 223

Wells, Governor Heber W., 187

Wells-Fargo Stage Lines, 211

Wells, Merle W., 13, 17

Wenee, Betty T., 233

We-rat-se-won-a-gen, 243

Western Saloon, 116

Western Shoshoni, archaeological evidence of early culture, 17; 19; starving condition, 31; Treaty of Ruby Valley, 37; encouraged to move to Fort Hall, 70; George W. Dodge as Agent, 92; Powell-Ingalls Commission, 94; land claims case, 102; 104; wish to settle at Fort Hall, 129; 130, 134, 209, 230, 233

Western Snakes, see Snake River Shoshoni

Westvaco Corporation, 176

Wham J. W., 62

Wheeler, Dr. H. W., 207, 208

Wheeler, Joe, 214

White, A. S. H., 243

White, B. F., 51, 144

White Bird Canyon, battle of, 79

White, J. E., 104

"Whites Have Married My Girls," see Shinek

Whitman, Dr. Marcus, 28

Wilkinson, Ernest L., 230, 241

Willamette Valley, 237

Williams, John Y. 184

Wind River, 80, 92, 198, 242

Wind River Indian Agency, 96, 214

Wind River Indian Reservation, 53, 56, 65, 66, 68, 80, 95, 96; land claims case, 104, 106, 128, 129, 131, 134, 187, 242, 243

Wind River Mountains, 37, 53, 55, 223, 241

Wind River Shoshoni, 31, 33, 105, 230

Winnemucca, Chief, 70, 79

Winnemucca, John, 70

Winter, George, 159

Winters Case, 163, 164

Winters Doctrine, 167, 169

Wisconsin, 183

Wolf Mountain, 80

Women's National Indian Association, 196

Wood River, 49, 55, 67, 212

Wood River News-Miner, 130

Woonsook, Henry, 100

World War I, 238

World War II, 101, 102, 192, 234

Wovoka, 198